Post-Colonial Theory and English Literature

POST-COLONIAL THEORY AND ENGLISH LITERATURE

A READER

Edited and with an introduction by
Peter Childs

EDINBURGH UNIVERSITY PRESS

To Edith Mary Bowery and Robert William Childs

Edinburgh University Press
22 George Square, Edinburgh

Typeset in Gill Sans and Sabon
by Bibliocraft Ltd, Dundee, and
printed and bound in Great Britain
by the Cromwell Press, Trowbridge

A CIP record for this book is available
from the British Library

ISBN 0 7486 10693 (hardback)
ISBN 0 7486 10685 (paperback)

CONTENTS

ACKNOWLEDGEMENTS

For suggesting that I embark on this project, I would like to thank Jackie Jones at Edinburgh University Press. For assistance and advice, I would like to thank Ross Dawson, Patrick Williams and Gerry Smyth.

INTRODUCTION:
Colonial History, National Identity and 'English' Literature

Peter Childs

> Basic truth about the colonies, Heaslop. Any time there's trouble, you can put it down to books.—The Resident, in Shashi Tharoor's *The Great Indian Novel*

I

One of the chief difficulties of Edward Said's seminal study of *Orientalism*, which marks the Western academy's late entry into an awareness of post-colonial theorising in 1978, is the fact that it does not adequately break up or stratify its subject. Orientalist discourse begins for Said – with all the attendant problems of beginnings – with Homer, Euripides and Aeschylus, and continues into the present. To say, as Said does, that Europe's imaginative geography has 'essential motifs' which persist from antiquity is insufficient and unsatisfactory in terms of geographical and historical particularities.[1] An introduction to post-colonial theory and 'English' literature has similar attendant problems, and it is one of the advantages of an assembly of essays such as this that, by concentrating on eight texts, it can retain many of the specificities of different colonial contact zones, in terms of literature, history and textual analysis, even though the focus on so few books limits the identification of crosstextual discourses. In this introduction, I do not propose to survey British Imperialism, 'English' literature or post-colonial theory, but to review aspects to the narrative of colonialism from 1600 to the present day, by examining some literary discourses of national and cultural identity in relation to the British Empire and particularly India – a genealogy of colonial attitudes that have consistently sought to fix Englishness as much as other identities. Sometimes these constructions of identity are in competition and tension, but always they expose what Homi Bhabha would consider threats or menaces to authority in their revelation of colonial anxiety and anti-colonial resistance.[2]

II

British Imperialism and 'English' literature have at least one theoretical tradition in common: the belief that they both happened by chance. According to one previously very strong but now largely discredited opinion, the British unwittingly stumbled upon most of their Empire, but especially India, about which it was said that the steady decline of the Mughal Empire and the ferocity of French aggression in the first half of the eighteenth century had necessitated a strong military presence to protect British interests and re-establish order.[3] Historians from Macaulay onwards have argued that it was also only the ambition or luck of one individual or another, such as Robert Clive, that turned the British from traders to rulers. In *The New Machiavelli*, H. G. Wells also maintained that English rule in India was an extraordinary historical accident. Even Nehru argued that the British 'won a great empire and enormous wealth' through little effort and fortuitous circumstances, and that a small change in events would have stopped them from ruling India after the collapse of Mughal power. James Morris's *Pax Britannica*, published in 1968, states that 'the various pieces of the Empire had accrued so gradually, often so imperceptibly, like layers of molluscs clinging to a rock in the ebb and flow of the tide, that the process seemed altogether motiveless.'[4] In this version of history, the 'process' was natural, like the movement of the oceans.

With respect to literature, Q. D. Leavis argues that 'the English novel', which for her is a national tradition and a distinct brand of fiction, was formed by two forces: accident and history. Unlike the novel in other countries, it did not grow from a deliberate effort to achieve a national identity.[5] Accident supplied the individual writers that she believes form the backbone of the English novel while English art and history provided them with models and themes: from narrative painting, autobiography, Elizabethan drama and the Victorian popular theatre, to the early unification of the country, social mobility and, most importantly, an essentially Protestant culture. An early but distinct national literature begins with Chaucer.

In her survey, Leavis gives many examples of comparison from other European countries (Balzac, Cervantes, Carlo Levi, Moore and Tolstoy) but says nothing of literatures or events outside Europe (the implication is that the English novel was only influenced by forces outside England in the sense that novelists took note of continental examples like *Don Quixote*). Yet her parabolic development of the English novel uncannily charts English Imperialism's rise and fall.[6] It has its first seeds in Shakespeare's plots, germinates in the eighteenth century (indeed 'it started, apparently quite suddenly, in the middle of the eighteenth century', at the time of the Battle of Plassey), blossoms in the nineteenth century, continues to flower up to the pre-war modernists, stagnates with Bloomsbury and the later modernists, withers after the Second World War and is in 1980 in such decay that its imminent death is not to be mourned. Leavis concludes:

> The England that bore the classical English novel has gone forever, and we can't expect a country of high-rise flat-dwellers, office workers and factory robots and unassimilated multi-racial minorities, with a suburbanized countryside, factory farming, sexual emancipation without responsibility, rising crime and violence, and the Trade Union mentality, to give rise to a literature comparable with its novel tradition of a so different past.[7]

Leavis alludes to Britain's imperial past and post-colonial present in her reference to 'multi-racial minorities', but there is no sense in her essay of Britain's expansion and world position playing any kind of role in the condition of fiction. The Englishness of the English novel is distinguished by domestic social considerations different from and unrelated to foreign or international events. Englishness, like the English novel, is a self-defining, solitary and largely accidental phenomenon.

Alternatively, Gayatri Spivak begins one of her essays, 'Three Women's Texts and a Critique of Imperialism', by asserting that imperialism played a key role in the cultural representation of national European identities in the nineteenth century and that literature inevitably contributes to cultural representation. She says that 'If these "facts" were remembered, not only in the study of British literature but in the study of the literatures of the European colonizing cultures of the great age of Imperialism, we would produce a narrative, in literary history, of the "worlding" of what is now called "the Third World."'[8] That literature should play a part in the organisation of Empire is in no sense a new idea – indeed the institutionalised study of English literature for purposes of moral instruction began in colonial India. Gauri Viswanathan has argued that English culture, and particularly literature, was promoted by the British in India in the early nineteenth century to cover their material exploitation.[9] Famously, in the 1830s Macaulay's educational policies advocated 'a class of persons, Indian in blood and colour, but English in taste, in opinions, in morals, and in intellect'.[10] It would be true to say that at this time English literature played a far greater role in colonialism than colonialism seemed to play in literature. One contemporary supporter of Macaulay's policies, George Trevelyan, wrote:

> The natives of India have, with marvellous eagerness and unanimity, abandoned the dead or effete learning of the East for the living and vigorous literature of England . . . A young Hindoo who has made the most of his time at college will write by the hour a somewhat florid and stilted English with perfect ease and accuracy; and will read, enjoy, and criticize any of our authors from Chaucer down to Robert Browning and Carlyle.[11]

In terms of its civilising mission, in which literature replaced religion as the key ingredient, the British Empire liked to compare itself to classical civilisation.

Colonial administrators saw themselves as Plato's guardians from *The Republic*[12] and historians have often sought to draw parallels between the Roman and British Empires.[13] To give one example from the writers Trevelyan notes above, Carlyle affirmed that:

> The stream of World-History has altered its complexion; Romans are dead out, English are come in. The red broad mark of Romanhood, stamped ineffacably on that Cart of Time, has disappeared from the present, and belongs only to the past. England plays its part; England too has a mark to leave, and we will hope none of the least significant.[14]

The most famous of such comparisons in literature comes at the start of Conrad's *Heart of Darkness*, but, more recently, in Tom Stoppard's *In the Native State*, an Englishwoman in the 1990s still insists on reaffirming 'we were your Romans' to a visiting Indian.[15] The commonalities between the Roman and British Empires are explored and largely rejected in E. T. Salmon's *The Nemesis of Empire*, where he argues the Empires were radically different in terms of government, ideology, trade and finance. But why did the British so like to see themselves as heirs to the Romans? Salmon places it in terms of growing egalitarianism in France and liberalism in Britain after the loss of the American colonies in the 1770s:

> The British nation sought to rationalise its behaviour and to ask itself whether what it was doing was either morally right or materially worthwhile. And it was in that age of missionary zeal that there emerged a view of the purpose of empire that was often compared at the time to that of Rome. The British Empire, it was thought, would bring a new era of peace in which unity and good government would spread over the world as in the best years of the Pax Romana.[16]

The seal on this peace was again to be education in British culture – a stance considered vital to Englishness centuries earlier, when Milton had declaimed in 'The Doctrine and Discipline of Divorce' in 1643: 'let not England forget her precedence of teaching nations how to live'.[17] Nearly two hundred years later, Charles Trevelyan's 1838 pamphlet on *The Education of the People of India* predicted a permanent alliance between England and a free India if the former could lead the latter to improvement without violence: 'Trained by us to happiness and independence, and endowed with our learning and political institutions, India will remain the proudest monument of British benevolence.'[18] Fifty years on again, reviewing the importance of such interventions in the 1830s, J. R. Seeley declared in *The Expansion of England* that

> The decision to which Macaulay's Minute led remains the great landmark in the history of our Empire, considered as an institute of civilisation. It marks the moment when we deliberately recognised that a function had devolved on us in Asia similar to that which Rome fulfilled in Europe, the

> greatest function which any Government can ever be called upon to discharge.[19]

Alongside English literature, the other cornerstone of the policy of anglicisation was language. After the eighteenth-century Orientalists had asserted that the British should learn India's languages, the response to Macaulay's Minute ensured that English would from then on be the language in which the administrators conversed with the class of 'mimic men' acting as a buffer between the colonisers and the Indian people. More generally, Carlyle, like many others, saw a commercial bond created by the English language and wanted an Emigration Service to create 'new Colonies of Englishmen in all quarters of the Globe': '"Hostile Tariffs" will arise, to shut us out; and then again will fall, to let us in: but the sons of England, speakers of the English language were it nothing more, will in all times have the ineradicable predisposition to trade with England.'[20] From another perspective, language is seen as the basis of a common ancestry, of a shared 'race'. For example, Hugh MacDougall explains:

> Initially the term 'Aryan' (Sanskrit *arya*, noble) was the adjective applied to the division or family of languages which included Sanskrit, Zend, Persian, Greek, Latin, Celtic, Teutonic and Slavonic with their modern derivatives. In time 'Aryan' was restricted to 'Indo-European' (a term first used by Thomas Young, an English physicist, in an article in *The Quarterly Review*, in 1813). Gradually, the term 'Indo-Germanic' worked its way into the English language and for a time was more popular than either Aryan or Indo-European. Its appeal to Anglo-Saxon enthusiasts is obvious.
>
> The work of philologists attracted the attention of cultural nationalists. They were quick to identify those who spoke languages with Aryan roots as people who also possessed a common biological origin. Language became a test of race.[21]

While other forces were at work to insist upon radical differences between English and Indian identities, there persisted a trend towards partial assimilation through anglicisation and through the identification of linguistic and cultural links. So, R. Campbell argued in the *Fortnightly Review* in 1884 that studies showed: 'that the language and mythology, and the types of village organization which belong to the more advanced races of India have a common origin with those of Europe'.[22]

What emerges from such examples is a story in which connections, between language, literature, history, commerce and empire, are used to underpin distinct narratives of kinship, loyalty, civilisation and morality that run alongside more familiar assertions of Manichean aesthetics in colonial discourse.[23] Having briefly considered some of the ways in which culture played a role in colonialism, I want now to discuss the role of the Empire in general, and India in particular, in the plotting of history and literature.

III

Linguistic history can be construed in ways which appear to separate or to join cultures. The divisions of political geography, however, split and arrange the globe into factions which outline and define each other. There is no Occident without Orient.[24] The East has always already existed as the opposite of the West, and, in terms of surviving texts, Said locates this binary construction as early as Aeschylus's *The Persians*.[25] Yet, from its early establishment up to the time of colonisation, Europe saw a vague Other and not a precise one: 'the Indies' was less a place than the general term for everything that was not Europe to the south or the east, as drawn on medieval maps.[26] To Columbus, the Indies were simply known as *otro mundo*, the taken-for-granted imagined alternative world.[27]

Of those still in existence, the first reports of India in the West were made by a Greek officer in the sixth century BC. He stated that the Indians' gold came from anthills and that their feet were so large they could be used as umbrellas. Up to the time of Alexander, Indians were cannibals for some, while for others they were satyrs; but above all, they were a 'monstrous race'. In medieval times, the Bible was the principal source of knowledge of the world, and the Indus, like all other major rivers, was deemed to have its source in Eden, while Indian people were reported to be horned pygmies.[28] Such beliefs were not prevalent when merchants started to establish trading posts in India, but the English had not moved on significantly in terms of alternative knowledge: the categories of difference authorised by the Bible and the Church were still those through which they understood alterity.

Direct interaction between England and India began in the sixteenth century, following the first incursions of European traders. Up to 1600, when for a century the Portuguese had had a virtual monopoly on Eastern trade, India was primarily associated with wealth. As Marlowe has it in *Doctor Faustus*: 'I'll have them fly to India for gold, / Ransack the ocean for orient pearl' (i, 81–2) or Shakespeare in *Othello*: 'Like the base Indian, threw a pearl away, / Richer than all his tribe' (V, ii, 348–9).[29] The much later denigration of Africa for its lack of appreciation of its own mineral wealth and of the value placed on jewels, in *King Solomon's Mines* for instance, was a component in the English representation of the Orient centuries earlier. However, in addition to their fondness for Eastern wealth, the Elizabethans had an attraction and aversion to black skins, and there are occasional signs in Elizabethan England of the kind of fascination and anxieties expressed later at the height of the Imperial project, as when Bassanio in *The Merchant of Venice* draws a comparison which is prophetic of Frantz Fanon's discussion of the threat of the veil: 'ornament is but the guiled shore / To a most dangerous sea: the beauteous scarf / Veiling an Indian beauty; in a word, / The seeming truth which cunning times put on / To entrap the wisest' (III, ii, 97–101).[30] It should also be remembered that 'India' is often used to refer to the 'East and West Indies' and therefore it lacks specificity and is often simply used as a part of a figurative phrase: so, in *Twelfth Night*, Maria is complimented as 'the metal of India', gold.[31] By contrast, England is not a country of jewels, but

Shakespeare's 'precious stone set in a silver sea'. As Martin Green has noted, England itself is made into a treasure, 'something that needs defending from predators and barbarians.'[32]

Before the seventeenth century, pronouncements on English differences from Indians were nearly all second-hand. The first Englishman definitely known to have visited India did so in 1579. He was a Jesuit called Thomas Stevens who served as a missionary in India for forty years. Stevens's description of the Indians he meets in Goa uses two bases of comparison:

> The people be tawny, but not disfigured in their lips and noses, as the Moors and Cafres of Ethiopia. They that be not of reputation – or, at least, the more part – go naked, saving an apron of a span long and as much in breadth before them, and a lace two fingers broad before them girded above with a string, and no more. And thus they think themselves as well as we with all our trimming.[33]

Typically, the differences outlined here emphasise physical externalities: appearance and clothing. However, this initial restriction to cataloguing visual distinctions was soon deepened by observations of cultural difference.

Four years after Stevens, Ralph Fitch, a London merchant, described his encounters in terms that were to characterise the kinds of fascination the English were to have with Indians for the next three centuries:

> They have a strange order among them – they worship a cow and esteem much of the cow's dung to paint the walls of their houses. They will kill nothing, not so much as a louse, for they hold it a sin to kill anything. They eat no flesh, but live by roots and rice and milk. And when the husband dieth his wife is burned with him, if she be alive; if she will not her head is shaven.[34]

He goes on:

> Here be many beggars in these countries which go naked, and the people make great account of them; they call them *Schesche*. Here I saw one which was a monster among the rest. He would have nothing upon him, his beard was very long, and with the hair of his head he covered his privities. The nails of some of his fingers were two inches long, for he would cut nothing upon him, neither would he speak. He was accompanied with eight or ten and they spake for him. When any man spake to him he would lay his hand upon his breast and bow himself, but would not speak.[35]

Indians' elevation and denigration in the English imagination as a spiritual and at the same time hypocritical and lazy people starts here:

> In Patenaw I saw a dissembling prophet, which sat upon an horse in the market-place and made as though he slept; and many of the people came

> and touched his feet with their hands and then kissed their hands. They took him for a great man, but sure he was a lazy lubber. I left him there sleeping. The peoples of these countries be much given to such prating and dissembling hypocrites.[36]

Such merchants' and travellers' tales were all that informed reports and representations until after 1615, when James I sent out Sir Thomas Roe, funded by the East India Company, to initiate official Anglo-Indian diplomatic relations (on 31 December 1600, Queen Elizabeth had granted the year-old East India Company its first royal charter to trade – a monopoly that was not broken until 1813). Roe's accounts were to stimulate some change in European perceptions of India, enlarging it from a land of 'wealth and spices', the language of traders and adventurers, to a place whose systems of law and government were a basis for comparison: 'the Gouerment so vncertayne, without written law, without Policye, the Customes mingled with barbarisme, religions infinite'.[37] However, such reconsiderations of India, in terms of culture, rule and administration, did not supersede so much as add to earlier views. Macaulay was later to write that even in the early eighteenth century

> The most absurd notions were entertained in England respecting the wealth of India. Palaces of porphyry, hung with the richest brocade, heaps of pearls and diamonds, vaults from which pagodas and gold mohurs were measured out by the bushel, filled the imagination even of men of business.[38]

However, in the seventeenth and eighteenth centuries, up to Edmund Burke's writings in the 1780s, English and Indian ethnicities (unlike their religions) were rarely explicitly compared in plays, novels, poems or papers. Throughout this time, the assumption (which resurfaced in the early to mid-twentieth century) was that Englishness existed in terms of its 'island race', its nobility, the English countryside, and a cultural separation from other European nationalities, or non-Germanic races, along a north/south axis that was only later to be shifted to west/east.[39] India remained a source of fascination for travellers and traders but as Marshall and Williams argue, up to Edmund Burke's intervention, 'it is doubtful whether more than one or two British political figures found it necessary to acquire anything more than the most superficial knowledge of India'.[40] (Records of the reigns of Akbar, Jahangir and later rulers show that their relationship with the English attracted little attention in Moghul India either, beyond the two countries' relative military achievements.) This was because in the middle of the eighteenth century India still played a small part in overseas markets as a whole even though Britain had become the largest European country trading with the subcontinent, having eclipsed the Dutch and the French (at this time the East India Company shipped goods worth about a million pounds from Asia each year). Bombay, Calcutta, and Madras, the three Company 'Presidencies' set up in the seventeenth century with their own governors and councils, were well-established cities by the mid-century. While Clive's exploits at Plassey in 1759 drew great attention, as did his extraction of the financial administration or *diwani* of Bengal and Bihar in 1765 through the treaty of Allahabad, for many years after 1775 foreign policy, at least in the public eye, was dominated by the American War of Independence and only the Mysore wars involving Tipu Sultan diverted attention to India again at the end of the century (the wars were later to become the subject of the opening to Wilkie Collins's 1868 novel *The Moonstone*).

However, while colonial affairs concentrated on Europe and the settler-invader countries (e.g. the United States wrestled free from British rule in 1776, the first convicts were transported to Australia in 1788, the Canada Act was passed in 1791 and Britain embarked on over twenty years of imperial war with France in 1792, during which the Irish rebelled in 1798), British rule in India had changed. Warren Hastings had been appointed Governor General by the Regulating Act in 1773 – the first time Parliament had taken a hand in the Company's affairs, and it was through Hastings's seven-year state trial for misgovernment, beginning in 1788, that Edmund Burke made India a live issue in England again. Hastings (unlike his followers, from Cornwallis on) was an Indianist and favoured the study and continuation of indigenous art, languages and religion. This interest in another culture, in addition to his central role in running an overseas administration, placed him on a different footing from almost every other influential politician at the time. Burke felt that Hastings had misunderstood the basics of government and, against the spirit of the time, was trying to govern India as though it were England. For Burke this was not just a decision about India, however: 'It is not only the interest of India, now the most considerable part of the British Empire, which is concerned, but the credit and honour of the British nation itself will be decided by this decision.'[41] In the year when the American Declaration of Independence was signed, losing the previous 'most considerable part of the British Empire', Adam Smith, like many after him up to the twentieth century, argued in *Wealth of Nations* that 'under the present system of management Great Britain derives nothing but loss from the dominion which she assumes over her colonies.'[47] Jeremy Bentham urged the French to *Emancipate Your Colonies* in 1793 and James Mill argued in the year he published his *History of British India* that colonies produced wars but no real benefits to their possessors.[43]

By the close of the century, however, through the studies of Sanskrit published in 1786 (the year Lord Cornwallis became Governor General) by Hastings's close friend, the lawyer and Persian scholar William Jones, the English had come to one important conclusion about India's civilisation: that it was far older than Europe's. For many commentators, this moment marks the inauguration of Indology, and Jones is the pioneering 'Orientalist' of India – the first of those who, through the study of Eastern languages, constructed the West's celebratory versions of Indian culture to vie with the denigratory views of the Anglicists for dominance in England and for hegemony, as far as the West reached, in India.[44]

The Orientalists endeavoured to safeguard Indian traditions but the policies they advocated were later represented for alternative purposes of conservative non-interference. This later standpoint can be found in the policy of 'benign neglect' promoted by Whitehall and voiced in such places as this statement on governmental incorporation by the soon-to-be Governor of Bombay, John Malcolm, in 1826, only a few years before Macaulay's Minute:

> The most important lesson we can derive from past experience is to be slow and cautious in every procedure which has a tendency to collision with the habits and prejudices of our native subjects. We may be compelled by the character of our government to frame some institutions, different from those we found established, but we should adopt all we can of the latter into our system.'[45]

However, the perspective and recommendations of Jones (who died in 1794) in many ways lost out to those of James Mill, the influential 'Anglicist' who in his 1817 *History of British India* responded to Jones's Orientalist position and argued that understanding of Indian culture only revealed its inferiority and the necessity for its replacement by Western knowledge and systems. Nigel Leask speaks of a straightforward 'decline of British orientalism in the years after 1820', in some ways most noticeable in the deterioration of Jones's pioneering Fort William College in Calcutta.[46] Jones, Thomas Munro, Hastings, and Malcolm lost out to the views of the Anglicists because the latter took the appropriate high ground on the issues that mattered to the English: efficiency, profitability, propriety, religion, education and morality. The abolitionist William Wilberforce pleaded in 1813:

> Let us endeavour to strike our roots into the soil by the gradual introduction and establishment of our own principles and opinions; of our laws, institutions, and manners; above all, as the source of every other improvement, of our religion, and consequently of our morals.[47]

Such appeals to a confidence in the superiority of English culture made the introduction of anglicisation a matter of national responsibility as well as pride. The stage was set for Macaulay's assertion that leading India to its self-government along European principles would culminate in 'the proudest day in English history'.[48]

The years of Lord Bentinck's rule, from 1828–35 were those in which the reconstruction of Indian society was undertaken, partly with the aim of eradicating such practices as *sati* and groups such as the *thuggees* (these were also the areas of Indian culture of most fascination to the Europeans, evidenced by the success of the first best-selling novel by a Briton in India, *Confessions of a Thug* (1839) by Philip Meadows Taylor[49]). The education of women was promoted, as was the remarriage of widows, while caste-marks were not allowed among sepoys and mission schools were subsidised; economic changes were also introduced, allowing such European concepts as individual land ownership and fixed money rents (new systems which led to debt, bankruptcy and the confiscation of land). Since Burke's speeches against Hastings, India had figured as the terrain on which England could demonstrate what it had done, or would have liked to have done, with its own past. India was England's in trust and so civilising reforms were a duty and an obligation.

Which is to say that Anglicists like Mill were 'criticising British society as much as Indian, [at a time when] two intellectual traditions, radical and Tory at home, Anglicist and Orientalist in India, struggled to define each other.'[50] Mill eschewed the Romantic attitude towards India, disliked the effect of Imperial rule on home government, and thought India held few material benefits for Britain – instead he favoured education and bourgeois reform, the values he wished to promote in Britain, by attacking the British system in India. Mill's multi-volume account of (the British in) modern India was to remain the dominant text on the subject until the Great War even though William Jones and others had shown, as G.O. Trevelyan later wrote, that Indian civilisation had been formed 'when the ancestors of English dukes still paddled about in wicker canoes'.[51] The debate then became one of not ancestry or antiquity but progress.

IV

Few still-read literary works which deal with India at any length were published before 1800.[52] For the Romantic writers, India was both inferior and superior to Britain – their attitude was one of ambivalence, in terms of an awareness of differences they desired as well as ones they denigrated.[53] John Drew suggests that some of the Romantics took India as an ideal: a sublime culture of imagination and contemplation to which the West could aspire.[54] For example, Thomas De Qunicey wrote in 1818 that 'No man can pretend that the wild, barbarous, and capricious superstitions of Africa, or of savage tribes elsewhere, affect him in the way that he is affected by the ancient, monumental, cruel, and elaborate religions of Hindostan.'[55]

Both Africa and India were now the sites of a struggle over perceptions of human nature, development and civilisation. Following Rousseau (1712–78), for many of the Romantic writers in the early nineteenth century, Africa was a place of innocence, a possibly Edenic, paradisiacal garden. This was just one of the factors that culminated in the British abolition of slavery in 1833. However, for the Victorians who followed after the 1830s, with their disquiet over sexuality, the body and the uncivilized other, Africa became a site of sin and cannibalism, a 'Dark Continent' of licence and barbarity, not innocence and simplicity. Consequently, Africa at this point, because of a change in Europe, became a place of fascination onto which the West projected repressed desires. At the very end of the Victorian period, Conrad says in *Heart of Darkness* that the difference between Europe and Africa is that the former has butchers and police officers to prevent Westerners from acting on their most fundamental drives and desires.

As Darwinism, ethnology and anthropology developed as disciplines in the 1860s, these new sciences lent their weight to the idea of there being a gulf between African and European, fuelled by the search for a missing link between humans and anthropoid apes. India, like Africa in imperialist writing, was often also deemed to have remained fixed in a pre-European state. The difference was that Africans were considered arrested in the infancy of the species while Hindus, in Mill's recasting of the work of the Orientalists, were thought to have taken steps on the path of progress, but none of them recent: 'in beholding the Hindus of the present day, we are beholding the Hindus of many ages past; and are carried back, as it were, into the deepest recesses of antiquity.'[56] European material progress was the measure of civilisation and civilisation the gauge of a 'race'. Prior to the incursions of European reforms, Hindu society was generally deemed priest-ridden, like that of the Irish to the English: despotic, superstitious, pre-feudal and enslaving (Ireland itself was of course newly joined to Britain by the 1800 Act of Union but remained a site of extreme poverty, degradation and gross mistreatment on a par with colonial exploitation elsewhere – but drew few English sympathies even at the time of the 1840s famine).

If we turn at this point directly to literature, in terms of realist fiction the British Empire moves very gradually from the boundaries of canonical novels towards their centre throughout the nineteenth century. Several critics have shown how Jane Austen's novels keep the colonies at the margins of their narrative, while colonialism remains central to the material and moral substance of a household such as the Bertrams' in *Mansfield Park* (1814) – most specifically because Sir Thomas Bertram spends much of the temporal span of the novel at his lucrative sugar plantations in Antigua.[57]

To understand this particular historical context to the Bertrams' lives, we need to remember that at the time Austen was writing the British Caribbean was a single-crop slave economy producing sugar for export with no attention given to local needs. Tobacco, cotton, ginger, cocoa and coffee were also grown but the 'white gold', as sugar was known, became the primary export after the middle of the seventeenth century. It has been estimated that money from this trade brought at the start of the eighteenth century the greatest increase in British wealth in modern times. For this economy, credit was needed – and provided by English bankers – and so was labour. There was little local labour – the indigenous peoples, the Caribs and the Arawaks, having been wiped out – and so the transatlantic slave market developed. On the gold coast in West Africa, English products such as textiles, cutlery, and brass and copper goods were exchanged for human beings who were then taken to the Americas and sold for money that was returned to London, creating a triangular slave trade. Over 500 ships were sent by the Royal African Company in the late seventeenth century on this three-cornered journey. In all, these 500 ships transported about 125,000 Africans of whom only 100,000 completed the voyage. Slaves were shipped out at the rate of about 5,000 a year and it is estimated that Africa lost forty to fifty million people to the slave trade. Up to the 1830s, Britain made about 450 million pounds from its triangular trade and about 150 million from the West Indian sugar trade. Over half of Britain's exports were by this time sold in its

Empire. Throughout the majority of the 1700s, the slave trade was frequently described as the cornerstone of the British economy. Several groups and influential individuals argued for better treatment of the Africans but few spoke against slavery as such. Slaves were regarded as simply machines for labour. Up to ten per cent of the slave population, most of whom were under thirty, would die annually – and one in three was severely punished each year.[58]

Slavery was legally abolished on 1 August 1834 at a time when Britain had control of Jamaica, Barbados, Trinidad, Tobago, the Leeward and Windward Islands, the Bahamas, the Turks and Caicos islands, Honduras and Guyana. In many history books this legislation is portrayed as first and foremost a great humanitarian move on the part of the British, in contrast with the rest of Europe. Certainly, the campaigning of Wilberforce and the radical working-class movement gained a high profile but there were other, arguably more significant factors. Economic dictates and rebellion were the two most important. From their first enslavement, Africans damaged tools, refused to work and made repeated escape attempts. These were construed as various kinds of laziness and ingratitude attributed to a racial weakness. All slave ships had to travel with extensive armouries because of slave unrest and the constant threat of 'mutiny'. There were no fewer than seventy-five slave rebellions in the West Indies between 1638 and 1837. The Jamaican uprising of 1831–2 was perhaps decisive at a time when widespread unrest across the Caribbean was feared. The number of runaway slaves, known as maroons, had also greatly increased in the 1820s. Britain's half-a-million slaves were made free, slowly, but their ex-owners were compensated to the tune of twenty million pounds. The process was especially slow because freed people were required to work forty-five hours a week without pay for four years after their emancipation; this was called an apprenticeship. Ex-slaves turned to small-scale farming, skilled labour and local trading. This was the time when indentured or low-paid contract labour began – a kind of serfdom on three- to five-year contracts that were irrevocable. Half a million Indians were encouraged to migrate to the West Indies, to find conditions of which they could have no conception in advance. Known as 'coolies', these indentured workers were not allowed to leave the estates they worked on without a permit, could be sentenced to up to two months' hard labour for neglecting their work, and could be flogged for what was called 'malingering', or put in the stocks for other offences.

In Dominica, one of the settings for Jean Rhys's response to *Jane Eyre*, *Wide Sargasso Sea*, maroon resistance had a long, almost unbroken history back to the beginning of British rule in 1761. Escaped slaves campaigned for the right to work for themselves and in 1802, 600 black troops mutinied. The Second Maroon War, as it is known, took place from 1809 to 1814, when 800 ex-slaves engaged the English in continuous fighting. The guerrila war came to an end only because two successive hurricanes destroyed the maroons' encampments in the mountains. In a way the most significant rebellion was in the French colonies and the most successful revolt in Haiti. This happened in 1791, the time of the

French Revolution, from which the maroons took much of their ideological strength in the theory of liberty, equality and fraternity. Wordsworth even wrote a sonnet to the leader of the revolt, 'Toussaint L'Ouverture'.

It is such details that fill the gaps, in terms of both time of publication and history, between *Mansfield Park* in 1814 and *Jane Eyre* in 1847, which share West Indian 'offstage' settings and have their English country house families rely upon money from the Caribbean. Brontë's novel, written after 1834, is full of references to enslavement, revolt, bondage, forced labour and emancipation – even though none of this is in relation to Africans and one of the novel's key characters is a creole heiress.

Also linking the colonies to themes of freedom and profit, when Dickens uses the Empire, it is usually as a means of escape or a spur to changes in fortune. In terms of textual space, little is devoted to overseas territories, but in terms of narrative, these are crucial. For example, Grandfather Trent's brother can rescue little Nell with the money he has made in the colonies, Magwitch and Micawber can become rich in Australia (in 1841 alone 33,000 British had emigrated there), Pip can end *Great Expectations* (1860–1) in the Eastern Branch of Clarriker and Co., and Tom Gradgrind can scarper abroad to elude English law in *Hard Times* (1854). The East India Company is mentioned in *David Copperfield* (1849–50) and *Pickwick Papers* (1836–7), but only in *Dombey and Son* (1846–8) do we get Dickens's Imperial vision of the subcontinent when India House is described as 'teeming with suggestions of precious stuffs and stones, tigers, elephants, howdahs, hookahs, umbrellas, palm trees, palanquins, and gorgeous princes of a brown complexion sitting on carpets, with their slippers very much turned up at their toes'.[59] Dickens's attitude to the colonies is most uncharitably revealed through Mrs Jellyby's philanthropy in *Bleak House* (1852–3): her care is directed to Africa and Dickens condemns her for it because Africa should be far less important than her domestic duties with her children and the London poor.[60]

At the same time, Thackeray's use of India is as a place of rest and recreation: *Vanity Fair*'s (1848) backdrop of the Napoleonic Wars means that the Empire can be seen as a place of respite, an English playground. Thackeray famously describes the English in India in generic terms: 'Those who know the English colonies abroad know that we carry with us our pride, pills, prejudices, Harvey-sauces, cayenne-peppers, and other Lares, making a little Britain wherever we settle down.'[61] The entrenched insularity of the islanders abroad means that Thackeray need say very little about India or a military career there: India has been made into a little Britain.[62] Also around mid-century, the Empire is envisioned as the place of a resolution to class conflict for Gaskell's emigrants from industrial Manchester at the end of *Mary Barton* (1848), to take just one example, while India becomes the place where at the end of *Jane Eyre* 'the high master-spirit' St John Rivers can 'labour for his race' (*Jane Eyre* in fact has all of the three typical nineteenth-century fictional endings, with a marriage, death, and colonial emigration).[63]

Representations of India specifically shift again towards images of exotic barbarity after the 1857 rebellion or 'Mutiny', although writers had previously used the country as a place of wild tales but cruel conditions, as Gaskell does in 1853 in *Cranford*.[64] After the rebellion, Indians themselves become inscrutable, threatening figures, and, as in Wilkie Collins's opening chapter to *The Moonstone* in 1868, India features up to the Great War as the romantic and melodramatic terrain of numerous adventure novels just as Africa does in more famous examples from *King Solomon's Mines* (1885) to *Tarzan of the Apes* (1914). The missionary's intermediary role is then taken over by the explorer or the empiricist. For example, in Conan Doyle's 'The Sign of Four' India is the uncivilised and irrational other that can be mastered by Sherlock Holmes's logic in the drawing-room of 221B Baker Street – the story stretches from London to the Andaman Islands, but Holmes, with a treasure-house of Orientalist writing at his disposal, can encompass the Empire without leaving the English capital. Such hubris is most evident in the science fiction romances that began to appear in the second half of the nineteenth century, in which almost every conceivable space is colonised by European explorers, not just the territorial regions encircled in, for example, Jules Verne's *Around the World in 80 Days* (1873). The English also claim the moon for Queen Victoria in *The First Man in the Moon* (1901); Captain Nemo dominates the underwater world in *20,000 Leagues Under the Sea* (1870); and the very core of the planet is sought out in *A Voyage to the Centre of the Earth* (1864).

By the turn of the century, the imperial other is present in two kinds of narrative which I might ally to Edward Said's manifest and latent Orientalism.[65] Manifest Orientalist narrative is found in the many canonical novels on the threshold of the twentieth century that, for the first time, are, like the previous adventure novels, wholly set in colonial locations: Kipling's *Kim* (1901) and Conrad's *Nostromo* (1904) would be famous early examples.[66] Narratives with a latent Orientalist content are evident in the rash of fantasy novels in the 1890s. In these texts the colonised are allegorised as an uncivilised, threatening other: in *Dracula*, *Dr Jekyll and Mr Hyde*, *The Picture of Dorian Gray* and even Wells's *The Time Machine*, in which the classical Grecian Eloi live above but are prey for the ape-like, cannibalistic Morlocks: such stories invoke the colonies by allegory, by implication and by casual observation.[67] These novels do not inform manifest Imperial texts in the way that travel writing, phrenology and eugenics served as buttresses for manifest Orientalism, but their designation of split worlds lends weight to the Manichean readings of self and other on which the justifications for imperial rule rested. They convey an unassailable belief in two kinds of humanity: a civilised, humane, conscious, bourgeois and Western rational self in danger from an other that is in almost every respect its antithesis.

Much of this is to do with national identity. As Raymond Williams writes, around the turn of the century 'the vision of Englishness itself changes: whereas earlier it is really internal to England, in the 1880–1920 period it is far more defined in terms of an external imperial role ... It was defined ... within increasingly standardised and masculine institutions'.[68] That role changes however after the Great War, when, Martin Green writes, 'everyone assumed the British empire was dying, and everyone in serious literature was openly hostile to it.'[69] After 1918 paternalism and liberalism were no longer key ideologies – in Europe or in the British Empire. In India, the First Non-Cooperation Movement of 1920–1 fully established Gandhi's nationalist struggle and inaugurated the first full-blooded repudiation of the Raj. In the year of the Amritsar massacre, 1919, there were 'race riots' in Liverpool, Cardiff, London and elsewhere in Britain. These attacks by whites on blacks were indicative of the shift occasioned by the First World War and other events. In brief, there was a move away from a dominant view of Englishness as a quality that found its reflection in the Empire to one that tried to expunge the colonies from its self-representation. Causes for this shift are too numerous to discuss in detail, but a short list would include: disillusionment with empire after the Great War between the imperial powers; British Imperial unrest (Afrikaner uprising of 1914; Irish Rebellion of 1916; Australian and French Canadian rejection of conscription); an increased concern with domestic issues during the postwar crisis of the twenties and the poverty of the thirties; the move away from discussions of liberalism and conservatism (and their debate over imperialism) to the relatively new (in England) creeds of communism and fascism; Indian resistance after Amritsar (which caused an opposite but similarly momentous shift in perceptions of India to the 'Mutiny'); a change in world view occasioned by the aeroplane and increased travel; and, lastly, the increasing realisation that trade with a Commonwealth could perhaps be more lucrative than gains from a continued hold on an expensive Empire (and Britain had large war debts).

By the interwar years, Britain's possession of an empire was a cause of regret to most literary writers, yet their response was not protest but a passive boycott. Despite increases in overseas travel and news reporting, India became a minor subject within high culture on the left. Orwell's view is characteristically damning:

> In a prosperous country, above all in an imperialist country, left-wing politics is always partly humbug. There can be no real reconstruction that would not lead to at least a temporary drop in the English standard of life . . . What we always forget is that the overwhelming bulk of the British proletariat does not live in Britain, but in Asia and Africa.[70]

With this domestic and Imperial working class, the one dependent on the other for its material comfort, the Labour Party attempted to formulate an anti-colonial policy but was always stymied by the need to maintain employment and the standard of living that British subjects derived from the Empire.[71] Stephen Howe comments on the interwar years: 'Most of the party's leaders, most of the trade unionists who formed the bulk of Labour's parliamentary strength, and most of the Fabians who so dominated its political thinking, were primarily if not exclusively concerned with domestic problems.'[72] (The most insistent political force for Independence in Britain was the India League which, after V. K. Krishna Menon joined, became by 1930 the chief mouthpiece of Indian nationalism.) The outcome for British literary discussion of India was mostly silence, but when the Empire was discussed the focus was kept firmly on its familiar areas, such as Anglo-India, the section of the Imperial map that was most English.

One of Paul Scott's characters in *The Raj Quartet* describes in this way the difference between the nineteenth-century view of India's importance and that prevailing after 1918:

> For at least a hundred years India has formed part of England's idea about herself and for the same period India has been forced into a position of being a reflection of that idea. Up to say 1900 the part India played in our idea about ourselves was the part played by anything we possessed which we believed it was right to possess . . . Since 1900, certainly since 1918, the reverse has obtained. The part played since then by India in the English idea of Englishness has been that of something we feel it does us no credit to have. Our idea about ourselves will now not accommodate any idea about India except the idea of returning it to the Indians in order to prove that we are English.[73]

Getting rid of India, politically but also textually, became from a literary or high cultural perspective proof of Englishness even though imperialism was still a mainstay of mass culture where the Empire Marketing Board, British and US movies, and popular fiction kept a belief in Britain's Imperial preeminence firmly in the public's mind. Even here, however, by the time of the Second World War, Orwell in 'England Your England' could maintain that English hypocrisy took the form in the working class of not knowing that the Empire existed.[74]

So, during the interwar years, according to a writer such as Scott, Britain became a country disillusioned with its Imperial status, especially because aspects of imperialism seemed to bear comparison to totalitarianism. That is to say, territorial occupation, expansionism and enforced rule were not English traits, whereas their nineteenth-century synonyms, moral leadership and the civilising mission, had been.[75] Scott's point would suggest that, after the burgeoning of the Imperial adventure novel, there was an almost inverse relationship between the role that the Empire played in an idea of Englishness and the centrality of the Empire in English fiction. In the first half of the twentieth century the Empire featured as a common setting but played a diminishing part in the literary construction of Englishness. Even knowledge of the East, which was so valuable and sought-after in the nineteenth century, is denied or disavowed in the twentieth: J. R. Ackerley prefaces his 1932 journal *Hindoo Holiday* with an 'Explanation' in which he says

> this isn't a history of India. About all that I knew of that country when I sailed for it was what I was able to recollect from my schooldays – that

> there had been a mutiny there, for instance, and that it looked rather like an inverted Matterhorn on the map, pink because we governed it.[76]

This vagueness about India in the minds of interwar writers is coupled with a willed ignorance that covers everything beyond the embarrassing fact of ownership. Partly in consequence, it is the English in India who are substituted for, and cover over the silence about, the subcontinent. Sir John Marriott's account *The English in India: A Problem of Politics*, published in the same year, also begins its preface with the words: 'I wish to make it clear to all readers, critical or casual, of this book that it is not a history of India'.[77] For an example from fiction, in Edward Thompson's *An Indian Day*, first published in 1927, the narrator describes how

> Those who were great when in India, sometimes incredibly great and influential, rulers of provinces and heads of huge departments, when they retired to England became stagnant pastures of fat contentment ... So India sank in England's estimation, envisaged as the paradise and playground of the second-rate.[78]

This contrasts sharply with the experiences of the eighteenth-century Nabobs or with Maud Diver's pre-war view that, in the face of European 'degeneration', true Englishness was to be found in the 'unconsidered corners' of Empire.[79]

In interwar fiction, the colonised also represent an inauthentic Englishness. This is a period in which the mimic Indian and the mimic African appear often, from Forster's Dr Aziz in *A Passage to India* and Orwell's Dr Veraswami in *Burmese Days* to Cary's *Mister Johnson* and Waugh's Seth in *Black Mischief*. (Of interest here is Frantz Fanon's important psychological study of the ways in which Africans were encouraged to see themselves in terms of white culture, *Black Skin, White Masks* (1953). Fanon argues that white skin was associated with power, status and wealth – and therefore seen as desirable itself. Films promoted white heroes: Fanon talks of the Tarzan movies shown in Martinique which encouraged audiences to side with the Lord of the Apes against the Zulus. In Martinique French religion, language and culture were seen as targets of attainment, and the French policy of assimilation suggested the possibility of social advancement while all the people with power had white skin.) These characters are situated as a part of the embarrassment of Empire, as a discredited Englishness is projected onto the anglicised colonised and an authentic English identity is located primarily in England, away from these part-familiar, part-threatening 'caricatures'. Anything colonial is associated with a subordinate English identity while the paradise and playground of the first-rate becomes Europe and the West, not the perceived margins of the Empire. For example, in *British Writers of the Thirties* Valentine Cunningham provides a long list of the places to which British authors travelled during the decade; India does not receive a mention.[80] Similarly, Robin Skelton's anthology of *Poetry of the Thirties* has no entry for the Empire and no poem that focuses on India at all.

Edward Said poses the difference between pre-war and interwar Orientalism in this way:

> No longer did it go without much controversy that Europe's domination over the Orient was almost a fact of nature; nor was it assumed that the Orient was in need of Western enlightenment. What mattered during the interwar years was a cultural self-definition that transcended the provincial and the xenophobic.[81]

I would argue that this cultural self-definition resulted not in a significantly different view of India but in a silence over the Empire and colonialism. In English writing on India in the interwar years, the focus remains on England, the exiles' distant home which is still central to a vision – whether of H. V. Morton's village communities, Auden's industrial landscapes, or Greene's seedy metropolitan life.[82] The way in which these writers transcended the provincial was, for Morton, by going in search of other European countries, for Auden, by looking to northern England, Germany and Spain, and for Greene, by incorporating the exotic into his potboilers; *Stamboul Train* is the most obvious example, a text that journeys across Europe to end at the threshold of the East in Constantinople.

By the 1930s, the north of England and developments in Europe almost entirely replaced the Empire in literature as subjects of pseudo-ethnographical investigation and political fascination. The tropes that had previously been associated with India – travel, anthropology, cultural differences, sickness, poverty and wealth – had come to be associated with a north/south divide; by which time Morton had gone *In Search of England* (1927), Priestley on his *English Journey* (1934) and Orwell on *The Road to Wigan Pier* (1937), all of which could be seen to culminate in Herbert Read's exemplary collection, *The English Vision* (1939). The Empire, though not an uncommon setting for pointedly anti-colonial fiction, had sunk back to the same level it held in Jane Austen's novels: materially central but deemed peripheral. Virginia Woolf's *Mrs Dalloway* in 1925 provides a good early example. Peter Walsh, 'back from the East', experiences a moment of epiphany outside the greatest material storehouse of any empire, the British Museum.[83] He is moved by what he calls the 'triumphs of civilization' and the order of London, just as he is moved by other vestiges of Empire: 'Boys in uniform, . . . on their faces an expression like the letters of a legend written round the base of a statue praising duty, gratitude, fidelity, love of England.'[84] This love of England is contrasted with Walsh's antipathy to India:

> Coming as he did from a respectable Anglo-Indian family which for at least three generations had administered the affairs of a continent (it's strange, he thought, what a sentiment I have about that, disliking India, and empire, and army as he did) there were moments when civilization . . . seemed dear to him as a personal possession; moments of pride in England.[85]

Peter Walsh's English feeling is, as he recognises, strange. It rests on a sense of personal pride in civilised London, the hub of Imperial England, combined with a dislike not only of the idea of empire but of India. The interwar English vision rejects its imperialism, but in doing so rejects not England but its dominions and colonies. A similar attitude is expressed in Lawrence's 'England, My England': '[Egbert] had no conception of Imperial England and Rule Britannia was just a joke to him. He was a pure-blooded Englishman, perfect in his race . . .'[86] By a shift in understanding of 'true' national identity, the Empire is unrelated to Lawrence's pure-blooded Englishman just as in the Victorian period its ownership was the exact reverse: the dominant symbol of Englishness. Returning to Woolf's novel, we still find that for Clarissa Dalloway it is this quintessential Englishness that Indians are supposed to look up to: 'it was character, she thought something inborn in the race; what Indians respected.[87]

Another interwar writer who focuses on London to convey a sense of Englishness is Graham Greene. In his 1934 Conradian novel *It's a Battlefield* the Assistant Commissioner walks down Northumberland Avenue 'eyes on the pavement, safe in London, safe in the capital city of the Empire, safe at the heart of civilization'.[88] He is however, being stalked by a man with a gun who intends to kill him: Conrad Drover is an ironic embodiment of the threat in *Heart of Darkness* that it is only 'the policeman' who keeps the European from murder. Greene positions the Assistant Commissioner's knowledge of swift justice and police work 'out East' in contrast with the in-fighting, party politics and factionalism found in London. Though frequently referred to, the Empire remains in the novel no more than 'out East': a place of huts and jungles in the Assistant Commissioner's memory where the European's id is less conspicuously policed. Discussing Greene's later *Journey Without Maps* (1936), Patrick Brantlinger notes that in the interwar years: 'Africa, India, and the other dark places of the earth become a terrain upon which the political unconscious of imperialism maps its own desires, its own fantastic longitudes and latitudes.'[89] A hideous example of this would be Beverley Nichols's *Verdict on India*, a pre-Independence tirade against everything Indian that even manages to draw many parallels between Gandhi and Hitler in a chapter entitled 'Heil Hindu!'.[90] Another somewhat different text that illustrates the fantasy of India in one way is Malcolm Lowry's *Under the Volcano*, written in the interwar period but revised and finally published in 1947. The novel ends with the ex-consul Geoffrey Firmin's phantasmagoric visions of hell and paradise as he plunges to his Faustian death in a Mexican barranca. His mind in a drunken haze, he imagines that he is not falling but setting out to climb the Himalayas. Lowry's Consul at this point projects his desire across two continents and maps it onto a conflation of his boyhood vision of meadows and violets in Kashmir and the mytheme of Yudhistira climbing the Himalayas to heaven at the close of the Mahabhrata. The violence of Mexico and of the Spanish Civil War are bypassed by the Consul's regressive fixation on a colonial *space* that represents for him a *time* both before his own father and wife had deserted him and before Europe was polarised by fascism and communism.

In short, it is the English disavowal of Empire in the interwar years that I think bears out Said's remarks on the very end of *A Passage to India* that 'We are left with a sense of the pathetic distance still separating "us" from an Orient destined to bear its foreignness as a mark of its permanent estrangement from the West.'[91] Said uses the word 'still', but there has been a change: the distance and foreignness are no longer those of the exotic, mysterious East; they have become those between the English at home and the English in exile, of whom the colonised are an extension or caricature. India, as such, has been removed from most discussions of the Empire and a British literary rejection of Imperial values results in not a protest but a silence or boycott on Empire even in texts set there. Consequently, Englishness is not denigrated for its imperialism, but relocated away from Empire – closer to home in the English countryside. An embarrassing possession, the Empire is hidden away and its most-disliked representative is the Kiplingesque paternalist who, still locked in the glory of pre-war Edwardian summers, is distanced less by space than by the temporal fracture in experience represented by the war of the imperial powers in Europe – a situation that would not change until the second such war ended in 1945.

V

In 1940 Churchill contemplated defeat in his famous Dunkirk speech. His insistence on solidarity ended thus: 'we shall never surrender, and even if, which I do not for a moment believe, this island or a large part of it were subjugated and starving, then our Empire beyond the seas, armed and guarded by the British Fleet, would carry on the struggle'.[92] Great Britain is a small, single island but its command of Greater British loyalties, strengthened by the navy lines, stretches around the globe. The most important country in this Empire was, for Churchill, and many others, India. Somewhat against the spirit of Churchill's rhetoric, two years later in 1942 Gandhi's 'Quit India' campaign, as it came to be known, resulted in mass demonstrations, the banning of the Indian National Congress, reprisals by the colonial authorities that left thousands of Indians dead, declarations of independence in some parts of British India, widespread rioting and the setting up of an anti-government radio station. Most of these incidents are touched upon in R. K. Narayan's love story *Waiting for the Mahatma* and also form the backdrop to Paul Scott's *The Jewel in the Crown*. Far from being times of solidarity, these were the moments that most clearly sowed the final seeds that were to grow into Indian freedom in August 1947.

The 1945 Labour election manifesto *Let Us Face the Future* contained no details of Indian Independence. Stephen Howe writes that

> For many members of the new Cabinet and Parliamentary Labour Party [the Empire] was evidently a peripheral subject. Thus after 1945, as in the 1920s, Labour policy would develop less as the expression of a coherent and consistent philosophy of colonial affairs than in a fragmented, complex, often *ad hoc* fashion.[93]

And the Imperial forgetting would continue. Having rid itself of an Empire, Britain would not often return its attention there for another twenty years – when Enoch Powell pointed out what Rushdie calls 'the new Empire within Britain'. Rightly, therefore, Stuart Hall argues that prior to Powellism, Britain underwent in terms of Empire what he calls 'a kind of historical amnesia, a decisive mental repression'.[94] But in English literature this amnesia had started to set in not with the process of Imperial secession, but in the 1920s.

Powell, a soldier and minor poet who returned from the army the year before Independence, forged his ideas on British colonialism while in India. His influential meditations culminated in this pronouncement in 1968, a year in which he became famous for a different speech: 'the psychoanalysis through which lies the cure for Britain's sickness has to be twofold: first, we must identify and overcome the mythology of the late Victorian empire; then, we must penetrate to deeper levels and eradicate the fixation with India from our subconscious.'[95] Powell in fact evinced a fixation with India greater than that of any leading postwar politician in the UK. He saw England's connection with the subcontinent as the spur to all its other Imperial efforts. Take away India, and the Empire, the idea of which Powell considered the greatest impediment to England's self-regeneration, goes with it. 'The British Empire, as we know it in political mythology,' he says, 'was an invention.'[96] Powell goes as far as to claim that, to its great cost, Britain had for a century and a half before 1947 been two nations, by which he means the British Isles on the one hand and British India on the other.[97] Powell's stress on the importance of India to Britain's Imperial image is also suggested by various kinds of ignorance after Independence. On the one hand, in 1951 nearly sixty per cent of the UK population were unable to name a single British colony.[98] On the other hand, R. K. Narayan recorded that on *his* visit to the UK in the fifties 'Most people in England, especially those living outside London, were unaware that India was no longer a colony.'[99] And this at a time when Powell was actually planning India's reconquest.[100]

Since the 1960s, one of the most notable changes in 'English' literature has been the steady rise of Indian fiction. A significant proportion of this writing counters the persistence of colonial conceptions of national identities – through revisions of representations of India but also through a corpus of statements about what Rushdie calls 'The Trouble With the English'.[101] One approach places Englishness in an unfamiliar accusative case: positioned as an object in relation to an*other* subject. The reversal of assumptions and stereotypes often also echoes English accounts of India. There is, for example, the description of Haroon's arrival in London in Hanif Kureishi's *The Buddha of Suburbia*:

> Dad was amazed and heartened by the sight of the British in England ... He'd never seen the English in poverty, as roadsweepers, dustmen, shopkeepers and barmen. He'd never seen an Englishman stuffing bread into his mouth with his fingers, and no one had told him that the English didn't wash regularly ... [or] that not every Englishman could read.[102]

The details in such a description, which might be found in many postwar British social novels, seem carefully chosen to echo various kinds of English expectation of India. They are more significant in Kureishi's novel because they are placed in the context not of internal society but of national difference. Amit Chaudhuri attempts a similar effect in *Afternoon Raag* when he describes the aboriginal island life of the English he finds in parts of Oxford: people eating cheap, unhealthy food, begging in the street, and speaking an odd English with queer proverbs and turns. Chaudhuri explicitly draws a distincton between a familiar, varsity Oxford which still symbolises the ideals of the Raj and these local people who had 'scarcely heard of Empire': 'Not for them history, old buildings, literature, but an England of small comforts and marriages, happy or unhappy.'[103]

Since Independence, not least because far more Indian novels in English have been written after 1947 than before, the idea of Indian identity has also figured more prominently in narratives of Englishness as the troubled margins of the nation have increasingly been located not just at its geo-cultural edges but internally. In Indian English writing, Englishness becomes a subject for explicit discussion, review and satire in terms of imperialism (as in Gita Mehta's *Raj* or Shashi Tharoor's *The Great Indian Novel*) or in terms of the aftermath of imperialism (as in Ruth Prawer Jhabvala's novels or parts of Naipaul's *An Area of Darkness*). Accompanying this is the redefinition of anglicised or Westernised Indian identity post Independence (in several of Anita Desai's novels, Upamanyu Chatterjee's *English, August*, Vikram Seth's *A Suitable Boy*, Arundhati Roy's *The God of Small Things*, or Rukun Advani's *Beethoven Among the Cows*). In British writing there is the growing English self-analysis of events from 1857 (*The Siege of Krishnapur*) through to Partition (*The Raj Quartet*). Many novels of national crisis chart the shift more forcibly in terms of a post-Imperial malaise, as also do a number of plays which feature characters left over from the Raj, such as John Osborne's *Look Back in Anger* and David Edgar's *Destiny*. But, nearly all postwar British novels about India are retrospective: Farrell, Scott, Masters, Kaye and others write historical fiction. This is not true of Indian novels in English. Such differences are noticeable elsewhere. There are scores of British novels about the 'Mutiny' but only one Indian one: Manohar Malgonkar's *The Devil's Wind*. By contrast, far more Indian than English novels have been written about Partition.[104] More importantly there is the welter of texts that articulate or examine new Indian English or migrant ethnicities in the UK (by Rushdie, Chaudhuri, Amitav Ghosh, Sunetra Gupta, Kureishi, Meera Syal and others).

The discussion above has not generally sought to analyse more subtle discursive distinctions than national ones, which are themselves perpetual sites of contestation open to question ('English' literature and 'Indian' fiction in English also cannot be straightforward categories). Several critics have additionally pointed out that analyses which assume a change in all cultural forms at the moment of colonial Independence and national emergence are at best unduly simplistic.[105] Aleid Fokkema writes critically that

> Indianness is constructed as a counterpart of Englishness. It is peripheral, rural, and young, searching for an identity; it is mysterious, timeless, and feminine. Indianness pertains to all Indians, whether from the Punjab or Mysore, Hindu, Buddhist, or Moslem, man or woman, prince or servant. Such ideas not only reigned before Independence, they continued to inform the British reception of Indian writing. Even in the Eighties, it determined most of the criticism of Salman Rushdie.[106]

Colonialism fosters such homogenisations, which is why Paul Scott once observed that 'in India the English stop being unconsciously English and become consciously English'.[107] Similarly but conversely Rushdie argues that in a sense there are only 'Indians' outside of India, in places like England. While there are stratifications of class, gender, religion and so on, 'There are no Indians in India'.[108] Again, Hanif Kureishi says of his first visit to Karachi, 'In Pakistan, England just wouldn't go away.'[109]

After the dismantling of the colonies and the diasporic culture that has flourished since, Indians and Euroamericans have continued to try to find their identities in and against each other. On the one hand, in the sixties India developed an important role as the West's immaterial opposite. From the legacy of Huxley, Hesse and Isherwood, the British, from the Beatles to Iris Murdoch (e.g., *Bruno's Dream* [1969]), like the Americans, sought enlightenment in India just as their ancestors claimed to export it there. Ruth Jhabvala's novels provide good examples. On the other hand, disavowal of connections with India, along the lines of Fanon's observations of cultural (dis)identification in Martinique, are acknowledged in Indian writing, as in Meera Syal's *Anita and Me*:

> Before Nanima arrived, this urge to reinvent myself, I could now see, was driven purely by shame, the shame I felt when we 'did' India at school, and would leaf through tatty textbooks where the map of the world was an expanse of pink, where erect Victorian soldiers posed in grainy photographs, their feet astride flattened tigers, whilst men who looked like any one of my uncles, remained in the background holding trays or bending under the weight of impossible bundles, their posture servile, their eyes glowing like coals. There would be more photographs of teeming unruly mobs, howling like animals for the blood of the brave besieged British, the Black Hole of Calcutta was a popular image, angelic women and children choking on their own fear whilst yet more of my uncles and aunties in period clothes danced an evil jig of victory outside.[110]

National and post-colonial identifications thus become complicated by diaspora, historiography, popular culture, the urge to belong and the desire to embrace or deny hybridity. An example occurs in *The Satanic Verses*, when one of Rushdie's minor characters is described thus:

> [Changez] would be English, even if his classmates giggled at his voice and excluded him from their secrets, because these exclusions only increased

> his determination, and that was when he began to act, to find masks that these fellows would recognize, paleface masks, clown-masks, until he fooled them into thinking he was *okay*, he was *people-like-us*.[111]

In post-Independence Indian writing in English, acting in general is a frequent metaphor for shifting, metamorphosing identities, used in Dhondy's *Bombay Duck* and Desani's *All About H. Hatterr* as well as *The Buddha of Suburbia*, and *The Satanic Verses*. The transcultural experience of adopting masks, of playing a role, of changing between characters is most easily demonstrated in an actor's world of assumed but confined identities. Similarly, the common fantasy mode in narrative, which Rushdie argues is the only form suitable to the modern world, is as often employed to convey the unreality of cultural miscegenation, as when instances of reincarnation stand in for transmigration or independence. Most importantly, identities continue to be understood and worked through in terms of national differences inscribed under imperialism.

To return to an issue touched upon at the start of this essay, the last thing I can note here is the change in the 'English' language that has been wrought by post-colonial writing. Rushdie, though not single-handedly and with an acknowledged large debt to G. V. Desani, has made Indian English a literary style. This is in opposition to a long colonialist tradition which argued that the spread of English was likely to lead to 'infection' (languages are often discussed in similar ways to 'races', in terms of purity, beauty and contamination), as in the views of *The Society for Pure English*, founded in 1913:

> Wherever our countrymen are settled abroad there are alongside of them communities of other-speaking races, who, maintaining amongst themselves their native speech, learn yet enough of ours to imitate it, and establishing among themselves all kinds of blundering corruptions, through habitual intercourse infect therewith the neighbouring English.[112]

Such prejudices persist despite the success of a novelist such as Rushdie, and, writing in the 1990s, Farrukh Dhondy argues that still 'publishers want completely conventional grammar or some grammar that someone has made up. They are not willing to accept the kind of English that has really evolved in a place like India.'[113] Dhondy points out the idiosyncratic hybridity of Indian culture in Britain, in terms of language and food:

> There's no such thing as 'onion bajee'. What they hand out under that name is onion pakodas, or onion bhajias as they are known in Bombay.
>
> Popadom is a corruption of the south Indian word. In the rest of India, the crisp, brittle biscuit is called 'paapudd'.
>
> Bombay Duck is not a duck at all. In fact it should be spelt Bombay Dak. What it is, is dried fish (known in Bombay as Bombil) and when the British introduced the railway system to western India under their Raj, it started going in waggonloads to the interior from Bombay. The crates stank of dried fish, like stale penises. They were marked 'Bombay Dak' literally

> 'Bombay Mail'. At the time the railway was run by whiteys. The English may call a spade a spade, but they don't call 'stinking fish' by that name. They referred to it euphemistically as 'Bombay Dak', the Bombay Mail.[114]

'English' literature remains a colonised area of culture in which language, history and identity are fought over in terms of Imperial and national categories. While this book focuses on canonical literary writing, the struggle over the legacy of colonialism is conducted as much in other texts, from arthouse films to popular fiction. Post-colonial discourses and subjectivities also exist as much in the writing of Angela Carter and Martin Amis as Anita Desai and Chinua Achebe. The essays that follow serve as a reminder of the breadth of approaches taken by critics who have influenced and been influenced by post-colonial studies over the last twenty years, and each underlines the significance of both theoretical awareness and historical specificity in analysing familiar texts which are still frequently studied with insufficient attention to their colonial roots.

NOTES

1. Edward Said, *Orientalism*, [1978] Harmondsworth: Penguin, 1991, p. 56.
2. For example, Henry Dundas, president of the Board of Control, voiced what many feared when he informed the House of Commons in 1793 that if Europeans settled in India, it would result in the annihilation of respect for the British, the eradication of the feeling that Europeans were of a superior character and the ruin of the Empire (cited in Kenneth Ballhatchet, *Race, Sex and Class Under the Raj*, London: Weidenfeld and Nicolson, 1980, p. 96).
3. The expression 'we seem, as it were, to have conquered and peopled half the world in a fit of absence of mind' is J. R. Seeley's, from the opening of *The Expansion of England*, [1883], London: Macmillan, 1897.
4. James Morris, *Pax Britannica*, London: Faber and Faber, 1968, p. 61.
5. Q. D. Leavis, 'The Englishness of the English Novel', in G. Singh (ed.), *Collected Essays*, I, Cambridge: Cambridge University Press, 1983, p. 305.
6. There is no need to rehearse this argument further here. Interested readers should see Edward Said, *Culture and Imperialism*, London: Chatto and Windus, 1993 and Firdous Azim, *The Colonial Rise of the Novel*, London: Routledge, 1993.
7. Leavis, 'The Englishness of the English Novel', p. 325.
8. G. C. Spivak, 'Three Women's Texts and a Critique of Imperialism' in Henry Louis Gates jnr. (ed.), *'Race', Writing, and Difference*, Chicago: University of Chicago Press, 1986, p. 262.
9. John MacKenzie responds to Viswanathan's indictment of the Orientalists that 'neither administrators nor missionaries and educators, in this period at any rate, would have made any distinction between their economic and their spiritual and cultural missions'. John M. MacKenzie, *Orientalism: History, Theory and the Arts*, Manchester: Manchester University Press, 1995, p. 33.
10. Thomas Macaulay, 'Minute on Indian Education', reprinted in Bill Ashcroft, Gareth Griffiths and Helen Tiffin (eds), *The Post-Colonial Studies Reader*, London: Routledge, 1995, p. 430.
11. G. O. Trevelyan, *The Competition Wallah*, London: Macmillan, 1864, pp. 424–5.
12. The English also tried to inspire similar kinds of synchronous love and awe. For example, Macaulay said of Hastings:

    > Even now, after the lapse of more than fifty years, the natives of India still talk of him as the greatest of the English; and nurses sing children to sleep with a

jingling ballad about the fleet horses and richly caparisoned elephants of Sahib Warren Hostein. Thomas Macaulay, (*Warren Hastings*, London: Macmillan, 1893, p. 89).

13. For examples, see the lecture entitled 'Mutual Influence of England and India' in Seeley, *The Expansion of England.*
14. Thomas Carlyle, *Chartism*, Book 8.
15. Tom Stoppard, *In the Native State*, London: Faber, 1991, p. 9.
16. E. T. Salmon, *The Nemesis of Empire*. Oxford: Oxford University Press, 1974, p. 26.
17. D. M. Wolfe et al., *The Complete Prose Works of John Milton*, 8 vols. vol. 2, 1643–9, New Haven and London: Yale University Press and Oxford University Press, 1959, pp. 231–2.
18. C. E. Trevelyan, *The Education of the People of India*, [1838], pp. 192–5, quoted in Eric Stokes, *The English Utilitarians and India*, Oxford: Oxford University Press, 1959, p. 47.
19. Seeley, *The Expansion of England*, p. 293.
20. Thomas Carlyle, 'The One Institution', *Past and Present*, [1843], London: Chapman and Hall, 1904, p. 225.
21. Hugh A. MacDougall, *Racial Myth in English History*, New England: Harvest House, 1982, p. 119.
22. Quoted in Christine Bolt, *Victorian Attitudes to Race*, London: Routledge and Kegan Paul, 1971, p. 187.
23. See Abdul R. JanMohamed, 'The Economy of Manichean Allegory: The Function of Racial Difference in Colonialist Literature', in Gates jnr., *'Race' Writing, and Difference*.
24. This is not just to assert that meaning is constructed through difference, not identity, but also to emphasise the importance to national/tribal self-constructions of distinctions. For example, when discussing Englishness, Simon During writes about the late eighteenth century: 'With the birth of the new French nation, other European nationalisms shudder and change. Each state acquires a national identity which covers *all* its activities in imitation of, and differentiation from, the French contraction into national unity', 'Literature – Nationalism's Other?', in Homi Bhabha (ed.), *Nation and Narration*, London: Routledge, 1990, p. 145.
25. Said, *Orientalism*, p. 21.
26. Zia Sardar, Ashis Nandy and Merryl Wyn Davies, *Barbaric Others: A Manifesto on Western Racism*, London: Pluto Press, 1993, p. 46.
27. Ibid, p. 43.
28. Ibid, pp. 29 and 35.
29. There are similar references in, for example, *Tamburlaine the Great*, *Henry VIII*, and Spenser's *The Faerie Queene*.
30. Fanon's discussion of the threat of the veil is in 'Algeria Unveiled', in *Studies in a Dying Colonialism*, trans. Haakon Chevalier, London: Earthscan Publications, 1989.
31. For more information on this representation, see the Arden edition of *Twelfth Night*, J. M. Lothian and T. W. Craik (eds), London: Methuen, 1975, p. 63. To the Elizabethans, India is both East and West (India and the West Indies) – the former the India of spice, the latter that of gold.
32. Martin Green, *Dreams of Adventure, Deeds of Empire*, London: Routledge and Kegan Paul, 1980, p. 47.
33. Thomas Stevens, letter to his father, 1579, in *The First Englishmen in India*, London: Routledge, 1930, p. 30.
34. Ralph Fitch, ibid., p. 77.
35. Ralph Fitch, ibid, p. 106.
36. Ralph Fitch, ibid, p. 113.

37. Sir Thomas Roe, quoted in M. E. Chamberlain, *Britain and India*, London: David and Charles, 1974, p. 26.
38. Macaulay, *Warren Hastings*, p. 20.
39. This is the case at both ends of the spectrum from Richard Hawkins's celebratory *A Discourse of the National Excellencies of England* (1658) to Defoe's ironic but denigratory *The True-born Englishman* (1701) which, after William of Orange's accession, considers the heterogeneous English to be composed of the 'auxiliaries' and 'dregs' of Europe.
40. P. J. Marshall and Glyndwr Williams, *The Great Map of Mankind*, London: Dent, 1982, p. 78.
41. 'Speech in Opening the Impeachment of Warren Hastings', in B. W. Hill (ed.), *Edmund Burke: On Government, Politics, and Society*, London: Fontana, 1975, p. 266.
42. Adam Smith, *Wealth of Nations*, 1776, Book 4, ch. 7, pt. 3.
43. See C. A. Bodelsen, *Studies in Victorian Imperialism*, [1924], London: Heinemann, 1960, pp. 14–15.
44. For example, Ronald Inden writes that Jones

> Was responsible for founding the first Indological institution, the Asiatic Society of Bengal, in 1784. If any one person can be named as the founder of Indology, if any one man can be called the 'knowing subject' of the East India Company within the rising Anglo-French imperial formation, it is certainly he. (Ronald Inden, *Imagining India*, London: Blackwell, 1990, p. 44)

45. Quoted in Stokes, *The English Utilitarians and India*, p. 23.
46. Nigel Leask, 'Towards an Anglo-Indian Poetry?: The Colonial Muse in the Writings of John Leyden, Thomas Medwin and Charles D'Oyly' in Bart Moore-Gilbert (ed.), *Writing India 1757–1990*, Manchester: Manchester University Press, 1996, p. 72.
47. Stokes, *The English Utilitarians and India*, p. 35.
48. Ibid., p. 45.
49. For discussions of the novel, see Patrick Brantlinger, *Rule of Darkness: British Literature and Imperialism, 1830–1914*, Ithaca: Cornell University Press, 1988, pp. 86–90 and Javed Majeed, 'Meadows Taylor's *Confessions of a Thug*: the Anglo-Indian Novel as a Genre in the Making', in Moore-Gilbert, *Writing India 1757– 1990*.
50. MacKenzie, *Orientalism: History, Theory and the Arts*, p. 27.
51. G. O. Trevelyan, *The Competition Wallah*, London: Macmillan, 1864, p. 254.
52. For discussion of the period 1600–1800, see Kate Teltscher, *India Inscribed*, Delhi: Oxford University Press, 1997.
53. See Nigel Leask, *British Romantic Writers and the East: anxieties of Empire*, Cambridge: Cambridge University Press, 1992.
54. John Drew, *India and the Romantic Imagination*, Delhi: Oxford University Press, 1987.
55. Thomas De Quincey, *The Confessions of an English Opium-Eater*, [1821], rev. 1856], ed. G. Lindop, London: Folio, 1948, p. 203.
56. James Mill, *The History of British India* [1817] Chicago: Chicago University Press, 1975, p. 248.
57. The most well known of such analyses is Edward Said's in *Culture and Imperialism*, pp. 100–16. However, Said was by no means the first critic to outline the importance of these connections. For example, Ann Dummett in *A Portrait of English Racism* (Harmondsworth: Penguin, 1973) devotes a short chapter to fiction in which she gives fine miniature critiques of colonialism in *Mansfield Park* as well as *The Moonstone*, *Robinson Crusoe*, *Vanity Fair* and others.

58. For more information, readers are directed to Peter Fryer, *Black People in the British Empire*, London: Pluto, 1988, to which this section is indebted.
59. Charles Dickens, *Dombey and Son*, 1848, ch. 4.
60. A full discussion of this, and the various critical stands that have been taken over Dickens's attitude to telescopic philanthropy, can be found in Bruce Robbins, 'Telescopic Philanthropy: professionalism and responsibility in *Bleak House*', in Homi Bhabha (ed.), *Nation and Narration*, London: Routledge, 1990.
61. W. M. Thackeray, *Vanity Fair*, 1848, ch. 64.
62. For further discussion, see Brantlinger, *Rule of Darkness*.
63. Charlotte Brontë, *Jane Eyre*, Harmondsworth: Penguin, 1966, p. 477.
64. While Mr Peter's 'wonderful stories' are doubted, Mrs Brown remembers saying: 'I will save, and I will hoard, and I will beg, – and I will die, to get a passage home to England, where our baby may live!' (Elizabeth Gaskell, *Cranford*, Oxford: Oxford University Press, 1972, pp. 108–9).
65. Said speaks of latent Orientalism as an attitudinal discourse naturalised by the vision of the pioneering Orientalists:

> There were two principal methods by which Orientalism delivered the Orient to the West in the early twentieth century. One was by means of the disseminative capacities of modern learning, its diffusive apparatus in the learned professions, the universities, the professional societies, the explorational and geographical organizations, the publishing industry. All these ... built upon the prestigious authority of the pioneering scholars, travelers and poets, whose cumulative vision had shaped a quintessential Orient; the doctrinal – or doxological – manifestation of such an Orient is what I have been calling here latent Orientalism. (Said, *Orientalism*, p. 221)

These covert and overt levels to colonialism are fruitfully discussed by Abdul R. JanMohamed in terms of Lacan's categories of the 'imaginary' and the 'symbolic' in his article 'The Economy of Manichean Allegory: The Function of Racial Difference in Colonialist Literature'.

66. Novels had of course been set in the colonies before but few had been considered of high literary merit; one of the first English novels set in India was the anonymous *Hartly House, Calcutta* (1789) while the first Indian novel in English was Bankim Chandra Chatterjee's *Rajmohan's Wife* (1864).
67. An example of casual comment occurs in H. G. Wells's late Victorian scientific romance *The Time Machine*, whose narrative otherwise functions chiefly as an allegory of class or 'race' divisions:

> Conceive the tale of London which a negro, fresh from Central Africa, would take back to his tribe! What would he know of railway companies, of social movements, of telephone and telegraph wires, of the Parcels Delivery Company, and postal orders and the like? Yet we, at least, should be willing enough to explain these things to him! And even of what he knew, how much could he make his untravelled friend either apprehend or believe? Then, think how narrow the gap between a negro and a white man of our own times, and how wide the interval between myself and those of the Golden Age! (H. G. Wells, *The Time Machine*, London: Everyman, 1985, p. 42)

68. Raymond Williams, *Politics and Letters*, London: New Left Books, 1979, p. 263.
69. Green, *Dreams of Adventure, Deeds of Empire*, p. 264.
70. George Orwell, 'Not Counting Niggers' (1939), in *Collected Essays, Journalism and Letters*, vol. 1, Harmondsworth: Penguin, 1976, pp. 434–7.
71. Anticolonialism in the Labour Party and within the trade union movement was more successful in the 1950s and 1960s. For a discussion of this period, see

Stephen Howe, *Anticolonialism in British Politics: The Left and the End of Empire 1918–1964*, Oxford: Clarendon Press, 1993.
72. Ibid., p. 45.
73. Paul Scott, *A Division of the Spoils*, London: Panther, 1977, p. 105.
74. George Orwell, 'England Your England,' in *Inside the Whale and Other Essays*, [1941], Harmondsworth: Penguin, 1962, p. 69.
75. Orwell outlines this purblind attitude to the Empire in 1941 in 'England Your England':

> English anti-militarism disgusts foreign observers [because] it ignores the existence of the British Empire. It looks like sheer hypocrisy. After all, the English have absorbed a quarter of the earth and held on to it by means of a huge navy. How dare they turn round and say that war is wicked? (Ibid., p. 69).

E. M. Forster makes a similar point in *A Passage to India* when he says that the Westerner's demon is 'hypocrisy' (Harmondsworth: Penguin, 1985, p. 251).
76. From the 'Explanation' at the start of J. R. Ackerley, *Hindoo Holiday: An Indian Journal*, [1932], Harmondsworth: Penquin, 1983.
77. Sir John A. R. Marriott, *The English in India: A Problem of Politics*, Oxford: Clarendon Press, 1932.
78. Edward Thompson, *An Indian Day*, [1927] London: Macmillan, 1933, p. 208.
79. Maud Diver, *The Great Amulet*, Edinburgh and London: A. P. Watt, 1908, p. 211.
80. Valentine Cunningham, *British Writers of the Thirties*, Oxford: Oxford University Press, 1988, p. 345. Cunningham later mentions Ackerley in another long list, along with Orwell's Indian writings, but not in the context of Empire, just of 'places in titles' (pp. 350–1).
81. Said, *Orientalism*, p. 257. Said argues that the interwar years are marked by a cultural self-consciousness in the West. In *A Passage to India*, this self-consciousness is evident in Mrs Moore's experience of the Marabar caves. This involves her in the 'twilight of the double vision' in which the nullity of the universe and her own smallness within it are visible simultaneously (p. 193). After this, Mrs Moore sinks into a lethargy.
82. This is very different from the image of India which is propagated at the cinema. Films such as *Gunga Din* and *Kim* continue the idea of India as land of adventure and the White Man's Burden. See Jeffrey Richards's essay in J. M. MacKenzie (ed.), *Imperialism and Popular Culture*, Manchester: Manchester University Press, 1986.
83. *Mrs Dalloway*, [1925], London: Grafton, 1976, p. 134. For a discussion of the British Museum in relation to the Empire, see Thomas Richards, *The Imperial Archive: Knowledge and the Fantasy of Empire*, London: Verso, 1993.
84. Ibid., pp. 46–7.
85. Ibid., p. 50.
86. D. H. Lawrence, 'England, My England', in D. H. Lawrence, *England, My England and Other Stories*, Bruce Steele (ed.), Cambridge Edition of the Works of D. H. Lawrence, Cambridge: Cambridge University Press, 1990, p. 27.
87. Virginia Woolf, 'Mrs Dalloway in Bond Street', in Susan Dick (ed.), *Complete Shorter Fiction*, London: Grafton, 1991, p. 153.
88. Graham Greene, *It's A Battlefield*, Harmondsworth: Penguin, 1940, p. 161.
89. Brantlinger, *Rule of Darkness*, p. 246.
90. Beverley Nichols, *Verdict on India*, London: Jonathan Cape, 1944.
91. Said, *Orientalism*, p. 244.
92. From *Into Battle: War Speeches by Right Hon. Winston S. Churchill*, compiled by Randolph S. Churchill, 1941, extracted in Judy Giles and Tim Middleton (eds.), *Writing Englishness*, London: Routledge, 1995, pp. 131–2.
93. Howe, *Anticolonialism in British Politics: The Left and the End of Empire 1918–1964*, p. 143.

94. Stuart Hall, 'Racism and Reaction', *Five Views of Multi-Racial Britain*, London: Commission for Racial Equality, 1978, p. 25.
95. Enoch Powell, review of Colin Cross, *The Fall of the British Empire*, in *The Spectator*, 13 September 1968, quoted in Patrick Cosgrave, *The Lives of Enoch Powell*, London: Bodley Head, 1989, p. 91.
96. See Powell's important essay 'Myth and Reality' in J. Enoch Powell, *Freedom and Reality*, John Wood (ed.), London: Batsford, 1969, p. 248.
97. Powell, 'Myth and Reality', p. 244.
98. See Errol Lawrence, 'Just plain common sense: the "roots" of racism', in *The Empire Strikes Back*, CCCS, London: Routledge, 1983, pp. 69–70.
99. R. K. Narayan, 'After the Raj', in *A Story-Teller's World*, New Delhi: Penguin, 1990, p. 32.
100. See Tom Nairn, *The Break-up of Britain*, 2nd edn, London: Verso, 1981, p. 265.
101. Salman Rushdie, *The Satanic Verses*, London: Viking, 1988, p. 343. Rushdie's phrase echoes Heaney's view in 'Englands of the Mind' that 'English poets are being forced to explore not just the matter of England but what is the matter with England' (*Preoccupations: Selected Prose 1968–1978*, London: Faber, 1980, p. 169).
102. Hanif Kureishi, *The Buddha of Suburbia*, London: Faber, 1990, p. 25.
103. Amit Chaudhuri, *Afternoon Raag*, London: Minerva, 1994, p. 92.
104. For discussions of the wide range of texts see R. K. Dhawan (ed.), *Modern Indo-English Fiction*, New Delhi: Bahri, 1982 (especially Saros Coswajee's essay on 'The Partition in Indo-English Fiction') and Viney Kirpal (ed.), *The New Indian Novel in English*, New Delhi: Allied, 1990.
105. For example, see Sara Suleri's introduction to *The Rhetoric of English India*, Chicago: Chicago University Press, 1992.
106. Aleid Fokkema, 'English Ideas of Indianness: The Reception of Salman Rushdie', in Geoffrey Davis and Hena Maes-Jelinek (eds), *Crisis and Creativity in the New Literatures in English*, Amsterdam: Rodopi, 1990, p. 363.
107. Paul Scott, *The Day of the Scorpion*, in *The Raj Quartet*, London: Heinemann, 1976, p. 245.
108. Quoted in Malise Ruthven, *A Satanic Affair*, London: Chatto and Windus, 1990, p. 20.
109. Hanif Kureishi, 'The Rainbow Sign', in *My Beautiful Laundrette and The Rainbow Sign*, London: Faber 1986, p. 27.
110. Meera Syal, *Anita and Me*, London: Flamingo, 1996, pp. 211–12.
111. Rushdie, *The Satanic Verses*, p. 43.
112. Society for Pure English, Tract XXI, quoted in Philip Dodd, 'Englishness and the English Character', in Robert Colls and Philip Dodd (eds), *Englishness: Politics and Culture: 1880–1920*, Kent: Croom Helm, 1986, p. 15.
113. Farrukh Dhondy, *Bombay Duck*, London: Picador, 1991, p. 212.
114. Ibid., p. 241.

PART 1
WILLIAM SHAKESPEARE:
THE TEMPEST

INTRODUCTION

The first two essays in this section provide historical contexts to both performances and interpretations of *The Tempest*. As such they are intended to serve as models of certain kinds of post-colonial approach which will not often be found in the textual readings that comprise the rest of this book: the first is exemplary because it considers in terms of colonialism the critical heritage to the play and its political appropriations; the second because it charts the ways in which English literature has been used to 'answer back' to the colonial centre.[1] Trevor R. Griffiths's essay, '"This Island's Mine": Caliban and Colonialism', sketches the genealogy of Caliban's theatrical and critical representations since the start of the nineteenth century. Surveying productions up to the 1980s, Griffiths discusses the play's invocation in, for example, the Republican cause, the anti-slavery lobby, the Boer War and debates over Darwinism. The essay serves as an excellent contextual prologue to the following three analyses which are more consciously concerned with 'post-colonial' readings.

As Rob Nixon himself notes, his essay complements Griffiths's by shifting from past 'British' performances to recent 'colonial' reworkings of the play by African and Caribbean writers such as Lamming, Césaire, and Mannoni.[2] To mention just one of these, Mannoni, anticipating later theorists such as Homi Bhabha, developed a contentious psychological theory of colonialism through his analysis of the post-Second World War Madagascan revolt. His theory hinged on a reading of the dynamics of Shakespeare's play and identified two complexes: the Prospero complex, in which Europeans with inferiority feelings display a need to find themselves highly regarded by others, and therefore seek out situations in which they will be able easily to dominate subservient people;

and the Caliban complex, marked by dependency, in which the colonised evince a desire for a comforting authority within the competitive structure of a newly introduced Western society. Mannoni's emphasis on dependency and betrayal, rather than resistance and exploitation, provoked a range of angry responses during the process of decolonization when so many countries were seeking an 'independence' which Mannoni seemed to deny. With this conflict in mind, Nixon considers how the rise of English studies in general, and of Shakespeare criticism in particular, was allied to colonialism, and asks what is at stake when African and Caribbean writers use the play as a post-colonial intertext. A late and slightly different example of these readings included here is Sylvia Wynter's article 'Beyond Miranda's Meanings: Un/silencing the "Demonic Ground" of Caliban's "Woman"'. Wynter takes as her starting point the hierarchical shift brought by colonialism from emphases on a primary male/female anatomical difference to assertions of a more significant white/black physiognomical racial distinction. Wynter therefore reads Miranda's growing emergence from Prospero's control as a corollary to Caliban's reification and enslavement: while they represent the black/white male split, she is the only woman, and the space where Caliban's female mate should be is unoccupied. Therefore, in the play, the 'doubly oppressed' figure of the black woman is once more silenced: not able to speak even in colonial-patriarchal representation.

By contrast, in her important book, *Decolonizing Feminisms*, which analyses 'the ways in which feminism's universalist stance disguises its white, middle-class solipsism', Laura E. Donaldson advances her theory of the 'Miranda complex'.[3] Donaldson here denotes a 'cultural and psychological mis-recognition' that she theorises in terms of Miranda's and Caliban's inability to see that each is engaged in resistance to Prospero. For example, she takes up Spivak's criticism of Anglo-American feminist readings of *Jane Eyre* (see below) that champion a Western heroine at the expense of Bertha Mason. Donaldson does this by arguing that Spivak in turn foists on Jane an imperialist Anglo-European masculinity which is equally one-sided. Instead, in the context of resistance, Donaldson argues that Jane and Bertha can be read as 'oppressed rather than opposed sisters' acting in defiance of Rochester's imperial patriarchy; and Miranda and Caliban might also be seen in terms of their shared resistance to white, male rule.[4]

In recent years there have also been many essays which have upbraided post-colonial critics for their lack of (adequate or precise) attention to history. For example, there is the essay by Ben Ross Schneider, jr., '"Are we Being Historical Yet?": Colonialist Interpretations of Shakespeare's *Tempest*'.[5] Schneider argues that colonial readings in their analyses of 'discourse' have insufficiently taken into account the dominant meanings attached to such key aspects as 'anger' and 'freedom' in Shakespeare's time. Also, William M. Hamlin has argued that studies of *The Tempest* must pay attention to contemporary ethnographical studies if they wish to find links between Shakespeare's play and European encounters with the 'New World'.[6] An example of this kind of intervention included below is Meredith Anne Skura's essay 'Discourse and the Individual: The Case of Colonialism in *The Tempest*'. Skura challenges new historicist and 'colonialist discourse' readings of the play on the grounds of their inattention to Shakespeare's own position and knowledge. In a cautionary argument, which is again useful when considering other texts, she warns against superficial attempts to fit *The Tempest* into preset post-colonial approaches and sketches the problems inherent in considering the play 'colonial' and so participating in a 'discourse' of colonialism.

For those interested in further reading, another important essay is Peter Hulme's 'Prospero and Caliban'.[7] Hulme compares *The Tempest* with various contemporary texts and reads the play through shared discursive tropes. In particular, he looks at the Atlantic/Mediterranean frames of reference and the play's involvement with issues of origins and possession – themes which have a particular importance for post-colonial studies. Readers should also consult the well-known essays by Francis Barker and Peter Hulme, and Paul Brown.[8] The former is an important example of contextual colonial discourse analysis while the latter takes an original angle by looking at *The Tempest* through contemporary events in and discourses on Ireland. Accordingly, Brown reads the play against the grain for some of 'the ideological contradictions of its political unconscious', finding as much significance in its omissions and silences as in its surface detail.[9]

Lastly, while Gesa Mackenthun has written a valuable essay on the figure of Sycorax and monstrosity, Ania Loomba's chapter on *The Tempest* in *Gender, Race, Renaissance Drama* offers an insightful critique of the colonial readings mentioned above, and also assesses the play's limitations for academic practice and for decolonisation, when the text itself resists any parable of post-colonial emancipation in terms of society in general and women in particular.[10]

NOTES

1. There are so many anti-colonial responses to *The Tempest* that I have elected to include Nixon's survey rather than make invidious choices between the large number of important critics. Readers are encouraged to return from Nixon's wide-ranging summaries to the essays and books themselves, which are also more recently reviewed by Thomas Cartelli in his 'After *The Tempest*: Shakespeare, Postcoloniality, and Michelle Cliff's New, New World Miranda', *Contemporary Literature*, 36:1, 1995.
2. For a discussion of post-colonial reworkings on the stage, see Helen Gilbert and Joanne Tompkins, *Post-Colonial Drama*, London: Routledge, 1996.
3. For example, see Albert Memmi, *The Colonizer and the Colonized*, New York: Orion Press, 1965 and O. Mannoni, *Prospero and Caliban: the Psychology of Colonization*, New York: Praeger, 1964.
4. Laura Donaldson, *Decolonizing Feminisms*, London: Routledge, 1993, p. 31.
5. Ben Ross Schneider, jr., '"Are we Being Historical Yet?": Colonialist Interpretations of Shakespeare's *Tempest*', in Leeds Barrall (ed.), *Shakespeare Studies*, vol. 23, Associated University Presses, 1995.
6. William M. Hamlin 'Men of Inde: Renaissance Ethnography and *The Tempest*', in Leeds Barrall (ed.), *Shakespeare Studies*, vol. 22, Associated University Presses, 1994.

7. Peter Hulme, 'Prospero and Caliban', in *Colonial Encounters: Europe and the Native Caribbean*, 1492–1797, London: Methuen, 1986, pp. 89–136.
8. Francis Barker and Peter Hulme, 'Nymphs and Reapers Heavily Vanish: The Discursive Con-texts of *The Tempest*', in John Drakakis (ed.), *Alternative Shakespeare*, London: Methuen, 1985. Paul Brown, '"This thing of Darkness I acknowledge mine": *The Tempest* and the discourse of colonialism', in Jonathan Dollimore and Alan Sinfield (eds.), *Political Shakespeare*, Manchester: Manchester University Press, 1985.
9. The continuing symbolic importance of *The Tempest* to issues of language, representation and history in post-colonial studies is also evident in Homi Bhabha's recent essay '"Caliban Speaks to Prospero": Cultural Identity and the Crisis of Representation', in Phil Mariani (ed.), *Critical Fictions*, Seattle: Bay Press, 1991.
10. Gesa Mackenthun, 'A monstrous race for possession. Discourses of monstrosity in *The Tempest* and early British America', in Tim Youngs (ed.), *Writing and Race*, Essex: Longman, 1997, pp. 52–79 and 'Seizing the book', Ania Loomba, *Gender, Race, Renaissance Drama*, Delhi: Oxford University Press, 1992, pp. 142–58.

1.1

FROM '"THIS ISLAND'S MINE": CALIBAN AND COLONIALISM'

Trevor R. Griffiths

The political and colonial themes of *The Tempest* excited a considerable degree of theatrical interest in Britain, both in the later part of the nineteenth century, at a time when Social Darwinian ideas and Imperialistic doctrines were making a major impact on the British public, and in the 1970s, when the retreat from Empire permitted a very different view of the relationship between Prospero and Caliban. In this paper I propose to trace such politico-colonial interpretations of *The Tempest*, and critics' responses to them from their beginnings in the nineteenth century to the present day. In so doing, I do not wish to suggest that a theatrical or critical interpretation of *The Tempest* which gives prominence to the play's specifically colonial elements has more or less intrinsic worth than one that does not. Nor will I confine myself rigidly to what might be seen as the purely colonial aspects of the Prospero–Caliban relationship since, as we shall see, these aspects are often both treated as part of a continuum of ideas involving domestic as well as colonial attitudes and also discussed in language which has been applied virtually interchangeably to matters of class and race. Rather, I am concerned with a cluster of ideas, associated with Caliban in particular, which have been applied to or directly influenced a considerable number of interpretations of *The Tempest* over the past 150 years.

Prior to the nineteenth century, critical responses to Caliban were dominated by the interest in 'preternatural beings' which exercised most notably Dryden,

In G. K. Hunter and C. J. Rawson (eds), *The Yearbook of English Studies*, vol. 13, London: MHRA, 1983, pp. 159–80. Extract: pp. 159–67, 169–73 and 175–80.

Rowe, Warton, Johnson, and Mrs Montagu. In the theatre the supremacy of Dryden–Davenant based alterations of *The Tempest* over Shakespeare's original meant that Caliban was characterized as a comic wodwo, albeit one whose strong rebellious streak was a medium for the adapters' anti-democratic sentiments. With critical and theatrical interest directed elsewhere, little attention was paid in the eighteenth century to the colonial elements in Shakespeare's *Tempest*.

The play, however, written at the time of England's first major overseas expansion and under the very direct influence of accounts of the wreck of the *Sea Adventure*, is thoroughly imbued with elements which have encouraged actors and reviewers in the nineteenth and twentieth centuries to approach it through its responses to colonial topics.[1] The main focus of such attention has been, naturally enough, the relationship between Prospero and Caliban, the colonizer and the colonized, the ruler and the ruled, the white and the black, the aristocrat and the democrat. In the nineteenth-century theatre, interpretations of Caliban gradually came to reflect broadly colonial and republican themes with Caliban appearing as, variously, an 'underdeveloped native', a 'red Republican', a Darwinian missing link, and latterly, to some sensitive critics, an oppressed minority.

Although 1838, the year of Macready's successful restoration of Shakespeare's text as the basis for *Tempest* productions, was also, coincidentally, the year of the final abolition of slavery in the British Empire, the anti-slavery campaigners appear not to have used Caliban as a vehicle for propaganda. Perhaps the misshapen creature was too double-edged a weapon to be readily adopted in such a cause, even if George Bennett's subtle and sympathetic interpretation of the role for Macready encouraged at least one member of the audience to develop an analysis of Caliban along colonial lines. Although P. MacDonnell was exceptional in developing his response in this way, and at pamphlet length, he was not alone in recognizing the importance of Bennett's interpretation. This recognition was manifested in two main ways: through engagements to repeat the part for Phelps in 1847 and 1849 and at the Surrey in 1853, and through universal praise, well encapsulated in the *Era*'s response to the Surrey revival: 'Even Caliban, with all his grossness and hideous deformity, is a poetical character, and Mr George Bennett . . . gave to it great breadth and vigour, without a particle of vulgarity' (9 October). Part of Bennett's success presumably stemmed from his close attention to the text, which is exemplified in his adopting long nails and high foreheads in response to Caliban's offer to dig for pignuts with his long nails and his fear of being turned into a low-browed ape. None of the productions Bennett appeared in aimed at making specifically colonial points, indeed only the single 'Indian Landscape' in the Surrey playbill's scenery synopsis could be construed as having direct colonial connotations.

Nevertheless, Bennett's attention to detail and presentation of much of Caliban's complexity was enough to move MacDonnell to declare that his performance was an example, like Macklin's Shylock, of how 'some of the characters drawn by Shakspere, were never altogether understood, till the excellence of the histrionic art developed them' and to express a truly Romantic 'degree of pity for the poor, abject, and degraded slave'. He believed that Prospero was partly to blame for Caliban's behaviour, since he imprudently placed 'this wild and untutored creature' in a position which made his rape attempt more feasible. Furthermore he argued that Caliban 'amidst the rudeness of his nature and possessing an exterior ugly and misshapen ... stimulated to revenge, by the severity he suffers ... has withal, qualities of a redeeming nature'. From this perception it was but a small step for MacDonnell to make a link with a moral obligation to civilize the natives: Bennett delineated 'the rude and uncultivated savage in a style which arouses our sympathies in behalf of those, whose destiny, it has never been, to enjoy the advantages of civilisation'.[2] Here, then, we have, in MacDonnell's response to Bennett's subtlety, the germ of an idea which was to grow in importance under the stimulus of the popularity of Darwinian and Imperialist theories.

Although the readoption of Shakespeare's text and Bennett's sensitivity to Caliban's complexity led the way for a gradual displacement of the traditional comic wild man associated with the Dryden–Davenant versions progress was by no means regular, and there were many simplistic interpretations after Bennett's breakthrough. His immediate successor James Bland for example, who played the part for Charles Kemble in 1842, was 'wholly appetite', 'grossly corporeal', and, appearing like the 'grotesque ready to change into the clown of a pantomime', succeeded only in 'giving a very broad burlesque of the part'.[3]

Burlesque as a form was, in fact, responsible for the next development in approaches to Caliban since William and Robert Broughs' *The Enchanted Isle* offered the first overtly republican Caliban.[4] The play, written and first performed in 1848, is full of satirical allusions to the social upheavals of that year, many of them made through Caliban, who is described in the cast list as 'an hereditary bondsman who, in his determination to be free takes the most fearful liberties' (p. 164). Although contemporary illustrations give no indication that the Broughs' Caliban 'blacked up', he is certainly identified textually with anti-slavery campaigns. When Miranda calls him a slave he replies 'Slave! Come, drop that sort of bother; / Just let me ax, "Ain't I a man and a brother?"', and he also appeals to the 'Sons of freedom' (the audience) to 'Pity and protect the slave' (pp. 179, 180). The anti-slavery slogan was later to prove its versatility by being applied to an ape in a *Punch* cartoon about evolution, thus illustrating the close popular interlinking of ideas about evolution and slavery which was to include Caliban's assumption of increasingly ape-like characteristics. The Broughs' Caliban, as well as appropriating anti-slavery slogans, turned revolutionary, entering to the Marseillaise, '*with a Cap of Liberty on his head*' and '*a red flag in one hand*' (p. 186). When the revolution fails he capitulates to Prospero with considerable insouciance:

Governor, we surrender at discretion,
And to your government send in adhesion;
We own that this a just and fair defeat is,
So take these chains off, and let's sign some treaties.

(p. 197)

The Broughs appear to have been aware of the implicit contradictions between their use of language which elicited sympathy for the slave and their deploring the revolutionary, since they give the final plea for applause to Caliban in these terms:

[*Pushing forward and interrupting.*]
Excuse me, pray, my lawless acts completing,
With stirring language I'll inflame this meeting.
[*To audience.*]
Be noisy—and excuse this observation—
Get up a *devil* of a *demon*stration;
But not with *arms*—no, only with the *hand*. [*Indicating clapping.*]
That's all we want and please to understand,
Tho' noise 'mongst you we're wishing to increase—
Here on the stage we wish to *keep the piece*!

(p. 200)

The plea for applause must not be mistaken for an incitement to riot, the audience's enthusiasm must be contained within the theatre, their appreciation of Caliban must be confined to the purely aesthetic dimension. With the success of *The Enchanted Isle*, however, the idea of Caliban as a republican and as a 'native' was established as a strand in nineteenth-century interpretations of the Shakespearian character.[5]

The period between the first performances of *The Enchanted Isle* and the publication of *The Origin of Species* in 1859 offered little development in colonial interpretations of *The Tempest*. At the Marylebone Theatre in 1852, for example, there was a programme redolent with imperial overtones in which a routine *Tempest* production shared the bill with a ballet divertissement called 'Britannia the Gem of the Ocean', in which 'Europe, Asia, Africa and America dance *pas seuls*, while *Britannia* looks on, until the end, when she achieves her triumph and all pay her homage' (*Illustrated London News*, 17 April, p. 310). In Charles Kean's 1857 revival, the major *Tempest* production of the period, archaeology and spectacle so eclipsed the play that there was, as one disenchanted critic remarked, comparatively little room for the acting. Despite this, the production did move Henry Crabb Robinson to the thought 'that Caliban was innocent after all and ill treated but this was a theological impression'.[6] Unlike MacDonnell, Crabb Robinson did not develop his impression into a colonial reading, though one can see how easily such a perception of innocence could lead in that direction.

The promulgation of Darwin's evolutionary theories in *The Origin of Species* and *The Descent of Man* (1871) served to enhance Caliban's status as a representative figure. Although Caliban had been referred to as ape as early as 1770,[7] the widespread impact of Darwin's ideas in the 1860s caused him to be seen as Shakespeare's imaginative precreation of Darwin's 'missing link' as well as an under-developed native and a member of a rebellious proletariat. These categories were by no means discrete and the virtual interchangeability of typifications of class and race in much later nineteenth-century thought makes it particularly difficult to differentiate between Caliban as native, as proletarian, and as missing link.

The anti-slavery slogan, 'Am I not a man and a brother', provides a good example of the way in which concepts like natural selection, slavery, and the proletariat could be associated linguistically. We have already seen that the Broughs' republican Caliban utilized the slogan, thus linking republican and anti-slavery sentiments. On 18 May 1861, *Punch* linked natural selection with the Wedgwood cameo which showed a black with the famous slogan, by printing a cartoon of an ape carrying a placard inscribed 'Am I a man and a brother?'. This was accompanied by a poem in the name of 'Gorilla':

> Am I satyr or man?
> Pray tell me who can,
> And settle my place in the scale.
> A man in ape's shape,
> An anthropoid ape,
> Or monkey deprived of his tail?

Although Caliban is not referred to in the poem, one can see that his combination of bestial and human qualities makes him a potential analogue to 'the missing link', and future theatrical treatments of the character would develop along the lines of 'an anthropoid ape'. They would also take account of the slavery element in Caliban which allowed *Punch* to appropriate him in an anti-American Civil War cartoon on 24 January 1863. In the cartoon a black talks to a Union soldier whilst a Confederate glowers in the background; the caption reads 'CALIBAN (SAMBO). "*YOU* BEAT HIM 'NOUGH, MASSA! BERRY LITTLE TIME, I'LL *BEAT HIM TOO*"—SHAKESPEARE. (*Nigger Translation*)'. Caliban was thus now intellectually available as a (black) slave and as a republican and, although he had, as yet, been presented only incidentally as an ape, *Punch*'s and the Broughs' use of the anti-slavery slogan together illustrate his potential for development as gorilla and missing link. The connexions between Caliban, blacks, evolution, and apes were not, of course, logical but rather a matter of association of ideas and by no means unrelated to what Greta Jones has described as the liberal belief in the 1860s that 'the question of arbitrary government and political and racial equality was indivisible'.[8]

The evolution controversies established Caliban the missing link alongside Caliban the slave and Caliban the republican. In *The Descent of Man* Darwin presented the theory that the races were separated along a graduated evolutionary chain of development. The 'primitive' races were assumed to represent earlier stages in evolution than civilized European man, and psychological faculties such as intelligence and moral sense were also seen as part of a graduated evolution. Thus races 'lower' in the evolutionary scale also had 'inferior' mental development. Caliban as a creature who could learn language but had no developed moral sense could be slotted very neatly into such a scheme, which could also be appropriated to justify European tutelage of 'underdeveloped' (that is, black) natives in colonial territories.

In the light of these developments and the intellectual ferment generated by the evolution controversy, it is not surprising that John Ryder's 1871 production of *The Tempest* boasted in George Rignold the first Caliban since Bennett's to give a complex reading of the character and also a significant innovation in staging which was to bear full pro-Imperial fruit in Herbert Beerbohm Tree's production. The final scenes of nineteenth-century *Tempest* productions had concentrated on Ariel and Prospero, often with spectacular scenes of Ariel's flight and Prospero's departure on the restored ship. In such versions no specific provision was made either for leaving Caliban on the island or taking him away. Ryder, whose production was otherwise very heavily influenced by Kean's, offered the usual departure of Prospero in his ship and release of Ariel, 'who is seen suspended in the air over a glittering expanse of ocean' but added to this 'the abandonment of the island to the sole charge of *Caliban*, who as the curtain descends lies stretched upon the shore basking in the rays of the setting sun'.[9] Clearly this was a Caliban glad to be left behind in charge of his island and, if we are to judge from Richard Dickins's comments on George Rignold's characterization, there was a distinctly 'aboriginal' tinge to Rignold's interpretation:

> He was, I believe, exactly what Shakespeare intended, fierce, strong, hideous, almost all animal, but with glimmerings of human intellect, the undeveloped soul feeling up for the light through the mass of brute instinct in which it is encased. Shakespeare's scheme was admirably conveyed of animal strength and passion (typified in Caliban), and irresponsible, amiable mischief (exemplified by Ariel), controlled by educated developed human intellect.[10]

Dickins's response to Rignold's performance is similar to MacDonnell's reaction to Bennett's. Rignold's sensitivity to Caliban's emotional and intellectual range encourages Dickins to a colonial analysis with Caliban as the 'undeveloped' native who may be controlled by Prospero's 'educated developed' intellect. Rignold re-established Caliban as a character with intellectual as well as brutish aspects, which fitted readily into the climate established by the evolution debates.

The process of claiming Caliban as imaginative evidence for evolution received its greatest boost with the publication of Daniel Wilson's *Caliban: The Missing Link*. In this book, written from Toronto where the author was

Professor of History and English Literature, Wilson argued explicitly the case advanced implicitly by MacDonnell, the Broughs, and Dickins. In Caliban, Shakespeare had anticipated the missing link in the Darwinian evolutionary chain: 'The not wholly irrational brute, the animal approximating in form and attributes as nearly to man as the lower animal may be supposed to do while still remaining a brute, has actually been conceived for us ... in one of the most original creations of the Shakespearean drama. Wilson was, however, something of a degenerationist, arguing that Caliban was a creature not only in whom 'the moral instincts of man have no part; but also in whom the degradation of savage humanity is equally wanting. He is a novel anthropoid of a high type – such as on the hypothesis of evolution must have existed intermediately between the ape and man – in whom some spark of rational intelligence has been enkindled, under the tutorship of one who has already mastered the secrets of nature'. The argument is splendidly double-edged: Caliban is in need of tutoring and development, an argument similarly advanced by Imperialist theorists in defence of the European 'civilising mission', but he is also more advanced than the actual 'underdeveloped' peoples: 'the half-human link between the brute and man' who 'realises, as no degraded Bushman or Australian savage can do, a conceivable intermediate stage of the anthropomorphous existence, as far above the most highly organized ape as it falls short of rational humanity'. Even Caliban's fear of being turned into an ape with a low forehead is grist to the Wilsonian mill since, as he notes, 'Darwin claims for the bonnet-monkey "the forehead which gives to man his noble and intellectual appearance"'.[11]

In the same discussion Wilson also suggests that Caliban's jaws would have been prognathous. Thus Caliban's incidental expression of fear becomes further proof of Shakespeare's prophetic anticipation of Darwin's scientific analysis, and his presumed ability to crack pignuts an indication of his negritude and, by extension in later scientific theorizing, proof of his lack of culture since 'the decrease of the action of jaw muscles is concomitant with rise in culture, that is to increased mental activity'.[12] There is, of course, a certain circularity in such arguments, but we are discussing not rigorous scientific proofs but much looser processes of association in which prejudice and simplification distort popular perceptions of complex scientific analysis.

Whereas Wilson pursued a broadly Darwinian and degenerationist line in his discussion of Caliban, Andrew Lang argued that Caliban and the 'primitive' peoples were exploited innocents whose potential was abused by the colonizers. In an article for *Harper's New Monthly Magazine*, 84 (April 1892), Lang put what was to become a standard defence of Caliban:

> He was introduced to the benefits of civilization. He was instructed. The resources of his island were developed. He was like the red men in America, the blacks in Australia, the tribes of Hispaniola. Then he committed an offence, an unpardonable offence, but one that Caliban was fated to commit. Then he was punished. Do we not 'punish the natives' all over the

> world, all we civilized powers? . . . All this appears to be as inevitable as it is odious, and all this occurred in Caliban's island. My own sympathies have always been with 'the natives', with Caliban. He is innocent and simple; he only asks Stefano [*sic*] not to torment him. He is modest, and addicted to a mistaken but generous hero-worship . . . Poor Caliban, like all these lower peoples, is easily misled by the juice of the grape . . . If Caliban wants to kill Prospero, as he does, can one blame him? Prospero had taken his land, had enslaved him, had punished him cruelly. (p. 660)

Lang's interpretation of Caliban was more liberal than Wilson's but both were to bear some fruit in theatrical productions at the turn of the century.

At the end of the nineteenth century, two major actors played the part of Caliban in ways which made explicit many of the various strands of interpretation we have examined thus far. F. R. Benson and Beerbohm Tree each wielded tremendous influence but in very different contexts: Benson, by reason of his tireless touring for fifty years, left his impression on generations of actors and audiences throughout Britain, whereas Tree captured the fashionable and influential London audience. Benson first played Caliban in the 1890s and, although he was not (as he believed) the first actor 'to bring out his responsive devotion to music, songs and sweet airs that give delight and hurt not', he was the first consciously to play the part 'as a sort of missing link'. Constance Benson, who was not altogether impressed by the performance, records that Benson took his missing-link conception seriously enough to spend 'many hours watching monkeys and baboons in the zoo, in order to get the movements in keeping with his "make-up"'. Attired in a 'curious costume', which his wife all too accurately described as 'half monkey, half coco-nut', the future knight would swarm up trees, hang head down from branches and gibber at Trinculo. His devotion to animal realism extended to carrying a real fish in his mouth, an almost Stanislavskian ploy which caused considerable distress to both Benson and his casts when the property master forgot to change it often enough.[13]

Benson was to admit later that he probably carried his athleticism as Caliban to extremes, and it certainly tended to overshadow the other elements in his performance when he first essayed the part at Stratford in 1891. The *Illustrated Sporting and Dramatic News* (2 May) was moved to contrast Shakespeare's Caliban with Benson's:

> Shakespeare's Caliban is a monster, but human. The product of superstitition and ignorance, he is surly, brutal, cunning, servile, lustful and vindictively cruel. The best use to which he can put the language he has been taught is the uttering of horrible curses against his teacher, whom he at once fears and hates. His chief pleasure is eating, and he is ready to sell his soul for drink to Stephano and be his slave for ever if he will kill Prospero and give him Miranda. Mr Benson's Caliban is a comic and amusing one; it provoked peal after peal of merry laughter. He was a kind of man-monkey performing various acrobatic feats, and passing through a

series of grotesque antics, grimacing and gesticulating, grinning and chattering and making a series of discordant, inarticulate noises expressive of delight, or, when the master showed his whip, of mingling rage and terror, slavishly licking the dust from the footsteps of the drunken butler as he implores him to be his god.

. . .

Tree's *Tempest* was, in fact, organized round his own performance of Caliban and culminated in a pro-Imperial final tableau. Two weeks before the production even opened, the *Era* (27 August) was informing its readers that Tree 'realises that the "savage and deformed slave" is not a comic character and will enact it accordingly' (p. 14). In practice this meant that Tree's customary massive reorderings and massagings of Shakespeare established Caliban as the star of the show, eating fish, cracking oysters, catching flies, and regarding Ferdinand as a rival in his continued aspirations to Miranda.

The Imperial overtones were most marked in the last act. The *Era* (17 September) described the poetic effect of 'the uncanny figure of Caliban seated on a rock and silhouetted against an azure sky watching the departing vessel sailing away from the enchanted shores sped by auspicious gales' (p. 17); but Tree's own published acting arrangement was much more specific, and clearly indicates that Caliban regrets being deprived of the human companions who have 'gladdened and saddened his island home, and taught him to "seek for grace"'. He turns 'sadly' in the direction of the ship, stretches out his arms to it 'in mute despair' and, as night falls, he is left 'on the lonely rock' as 'a king once more'.[14] The implications of all this are quite clear: Caliban is lost without the civilizing influence exerted upon him by Prospero and his companions; the islander needs the Europeans, the slave needs the master as much as the master needed the slave. Although Benson's 'missing-link' Caliban was political in the sense that analogies had been drawn between 'underdeveloped natives' and the missing link in non-theatrical contexts, Tree expanded the political dimensions of his Caliban, who was clearly the ignorant native to whom the colonist Prospero had brought an enlightenment which he had spurned before learning its true value.

The analogy was not lost on the contemporary audience, but it was somewhat controversial. Indeed, W. T. Stead, visiting his first play at the age of fifty-five, was struck by so many analogies that it is impossible to do them all justice.[15] Nevertheless, several of them are particularly relevant to the current discussions. Under the heading, 'What About Rhodesia?' Stead raised some central questions of Imperialism:

> When the man-monster, brutalised by long continued torture, begins, 'This island's mine, by Sycorax my mother, which thou takest from me', we have the whole case of the aboriginal against aggressive civilisation dramatised before us. I confess I felt a sting of conscience—vicariously

> suffered for my Rhodesian friends, notably Dr Jameson—when Caliban proceeded to unfold a similar case to that of the Matebele. It might have been the double of old King Lobengula rehearsing the blandishments which led to his doom: 'When thou camest first/Thou strok'dst me, and mad'st much of me; would'st give me'—all that was promised by the Chartered Company to secure the charter. Who could help sympathising with his outburst after recollecting how he had helped the newcomer? (pp. 364–65)

Under the heading 'The Instinct of Paternity' Stead remarks that Caliban's desire to people the isle with Calibans implies 'more of a craving for paternity than the satisfaction of a brute instinct' and has some sternly eugenic reflections: 'Poor Caliban! Ferdinand and Miranda nowadays would have one child, or perhaps two, leaving the task of perpetuating the race almost entirely to Caliban. It is he who fills the isle with progeny. The cultured, the wealthy and refined shrink from the duty of replenishing the earth.' On the same tack, Caliban's profiting from language only to curse is 'a result that not unseldom follows our educating of the common people even in the twentieth century' (p. 365). Ignoring the Calibanization of the theatre, latter-day parables of the fall, and Stead's worries about the raising of the age of consent after his successful campaign, we come to 'Contemporary History in Parable', 'Trinculo-Rosebery', 'Stephano-Chamberlain', 'Mafeking Night', and 'The Khaki Election of 1900'. Out of Tree's interpretation, Stead wrests one which seems to run counter to the emotional appeal of the final tableau. To Stead, Caliban is 'the representative of the democracy, robbed of its rightful inheritance, punished without end for an attempted crime, endowed with just enough education to curse its master, and abandoned by him to a condition of brutish ignorance and hopeless slavery' (p. 365). Rosebery (Trinculo) shelters from the storm under Caliban's gaberdine and 'there for a time they lie. Trinculo-Rosebery with Caliban-Democracy, head to feet—even as it was'. Stephano is 'the incarnate representative of Jingo Toryism' carrying 'the bark-made flagon—I looked to see if it was labelled the *Daily Mail* or *Daily Telegraph*—full of the heady wine of Jingoism!' (p. 366).

Allegory is now in full spate and Caliban, Lobengula only a page before, is now the British electorate deluded by the politicians into attacking the Boers. Stead appears to be unaware of the inherent contradictions of the two analyses:

> Then we see the pitiful tragedy of the Jingo fever and the South African War. Both political parties combine to pass the bottle to the poor monster, but even while assisting at the process Trinculo, after Lord Rosebery's fashion, cannot resist a sneer at the shallow wits of the half-witted monster who swallows with trusting simplicity the absurd stories and the heady liquor of his 'brave god'. Nevertheless, despite the Roseberian gibes and sneers, the poor, scurvy monster kisses the foot of the Jingo Party, and finally the scene ends with a deliriously drunken dance, in which Caliban-Democracy, supported by Trinculo-Rosebery and Stephano-Chamber-

> lain, howl in maudlin chorus: ''Ban, 'Ban, Ca-Caliban / Has a new master – Get a new man.' As the curtain fell amid the roars of laughter, I remembered I had seen it all before on a much larger scale. It was Mafeking night over again.

From this it is but a short step to the Khaki Election of 1900:

> After Mafeking we have a still further development of the close parallel. Caliban-Demos being now well drunk with Jingo wine takes the lead. Just as Mr Chamberlain himself shrank with reluctance from the policy of farm burning and concentration camps, which was nevertheless pressed on ruthlessly by a populace maddened by its daily drench of Jingo journalism, so Caliban incites his drunken god Stephano to murderous exploits. 'Monster', says the sailor sententiously, 'I will kill this man; his daughter and I will be king and queen'—and in that saying I seemed to hear the decision proclaimed to annex the Boer Republics!
>
> In the next scene, in which the worthy trio appear, we have the true and faithful presentment of the Khaki Election of 1900, in which the drunken Caliban, despite the scoffing of Trinculo, in humbly abject fashion licks the shoe of Stephano. (p. 366)

Stead's was the most fully allegorical reading of Tree's production and he certainly turned some aspects of it on its head, but he was responding to a quite obvious invitation from the production's treatment of Caliban. All Stead's allegorizing was too much for the *Era* (22 October 1904), which took the resolutely pragmatic line one might expect from the theatrical trade-paper, only to prove equally susceptible to the allegorical tendency which characterizes so much *Tempest* criticism of all kinds:

> It would have been just as easy to see an equivalent of Caliban in the Boer nation, and take Prospero as fore-shadowing Lord MILNER, and Ariel as a composite of Lord ROBERTS, Lord KITCHENER, and the British Army. Caliban was undoubtedly in possession of the island when Prospero, the 'medicine man', arrived as an emigrant; so were the Boers. To put it mildly, he was somewhat rude and primitive in his ideas; so, admittedly were the Boers. Prospero tried giving him personal independence, but he behaved so badly that his republican arrangements had to be extinguished; thus it was with the Boers. And Mr STEAD—who, of course, believes that eventually we shall be outnumbered by his friends in the Transvaal, and ejected from South Africa—may complacently complete the parallel by pointing to Prospero's exit from the isle after burning his books and breaking his rod. How explicit a prophet SHAKESPEARE was may be proved by Caliban's straightforwardly expressed intention to 'people the isle with Calibans'—evidently a *clairvoyant* allusion to the extinction of the British from South Africa by the sheer force of multiplication of the Dutch. (p. 21)

In all of the *Era*'s comments there is, of course, no mention of any other inhabitants of South Africa but, having disposed to its own satisfaction of Stead's case, the *Era* was moved, without preliminaries, to declare that 'analysed, Caliban is much nearer to a modern decadent Frenchman than he is to the chimpanzee or the Wild Man of the Woods'. One allegorical reading disposed of and another enemy of the Empire sniped at, the *Era* is safe to demolish any associations of Caliban with 'the common herd'. Such direct political controversy is unusual, but after Benson's and Tree's performances Caliban was established as a barometer of attitudes to imperialism and democracy, if not, *pace* Stead, of attitudes to eugenics or the raising of the age of consent.

During and after the First World War, Caliban continued to be treated along the lines established at the turn of the century. Thus we find Ben Greet's Old Vic programme for 19 November 1917 describing Caliban as 'a solitary savage—a member of an almost prehistoric race with witches as ancestors', neatly encapsulating the Darwinian idea that contemporary 'savage' races exemplified the prehistory of modern civilized man. At the same time there was a swing towards a costuming which, unlike Tree's or Benson's, stressed the fishy side of Caliban. For example, Murray Carrington, a former member of Benson's company, played the role at Stratford in 1919 as 'half-seal, half-man' (*Stage*, 14 August) and George Foss, who directed the play at the Old Vic in 1918, believed that Caliban should be 'slow moving and walrus-like'. Although Foss's production was virtually ruined by war-time difficulties, he was able to develop his analysis of Caliban at some length in his book, *What the Author Meant* (London, 1932). Curiously, his 'walrus-like' description of Caliban's appearance was matched with an analysis of his character which was more generally associated with a missing-link or ape-like appearance:

> The part typifies Demos—just one degree above the beasts, of immense strength but with brutalised, degrading passions that had not been eradicated or refined by education, and with no human sympathies ... On several occasions throughout the ages Caliban has got free for a little time and indulged in a senseless orgy of blood and destruction. He has 'made a hell of earth' until some strong hand has forced him into subjection again. (p. 40)

With these views it is not surprising that Foss suggests that 'Prospero typifies paternal wise government' (p. 41), and once again we can see how closely linked are ideas of democracy, family, and colonial government. As Greta Jones has remarked, the Victorians in describing subordination 'took much of their imagery from an area where subordination was legitimised—that of the family'. They 'talked in terms of dependence, of development, of benevolent and paternal supervision and of the "child" or the childlike qualities of the "primitive" peoples' (p. 144). Similarly, Foss's Prospero was both the head of a family and a governor doing his best to keep an unruly population in check.

. . .

In general, however, despite the relative frequency of comments about Prospero's mistreatment of Caliban, there was no developed approach to the colonial subtext in performance or in criticism during the interwar period. The final large-scale pre-war *Tempest* exemplifies this situation very well. Tyrone Guthrie's 1934 Old Vic *Tempest* was given major press coverage because of the presence in the cast of Charles Laughton as Prospero and Elsa Lanchester as Ariel, but Caliban did not bulk large in the critics' responses to the production, and the more extended discussions of Caliban's 'meaning' are to be found in weekly or monthly journals rather than in daily newspapers.

Roger Livesey's scaly and hairy Caliban, perhaps over-liberally covered in black grease-paint, was generally regarded as bringing out both Caliban's pathos and his monstrosity. Peter Fleming extended this to argue that Livesey's 'distinctly aboriginal make-up underlined the parable of Civilization and the Savage which Shakespeare has here prophetically presented' (*Spectator*, 12 January 1934). Similarly Ivor Brown pursued a line that was to become familiar in his reviews of subsequent productions: 'Caliban should be the oppressed aboriginal as well as the lecherous monster, a case for the radical politician's sympathy as well as for Prospero's punishment' (*Observer*, 14 January). Prince Nicolas Galitzine also developed a political insight from the play, objecting to Livesey's Caliban helping with the comedy instead of interpreting 'the message of humanity's suffering, blindness and progress that is so clearly at the disposal of its sub-human prototype' (*Saturday Review*, 20 January). Livesey appears to have been the first Caliban to have actually blacked up, but this excited virtually no critical comment, except for complaints that the black came off on Trinculo and Stephano. George Warrington's remark that one way of staging the *Tempest* was in 'a pantomime-set for "Robinson Crusoe" complete with Caliban's footprints' (*Country Life*, 20 January) may have been inspired by Livesey's costuming and indicates the possibility, at that time, of an equation of Caliban with a black character from another colonial fiction.[16]

Throughout the thirties and forties the broad pattern of incidental references to simian and missing-link Calibans, occasionally expanded to a couple of lines, remained much the same: James Dale 'touchingly suggested the monstrous reaching up to the human' at Stratford in 1938; Jack Hawkins was 'an unregenerate Darwinian orang-outang' at the Old Vic in 1940; and Baliol Holloway, 'getting uglier' was 'still a child-like savage' at Stratford in 1941 and 1942.[17] Among the critics, Ivor Brown was the most consistent propagator of the colonial Caliban, moving on from his analysis of Livesey's performance to see Holloway as a 'dispossessed aboriginal' at Stratford in 1934, Bernard Miles minimizing 'the appeal to sympathy for an oppressed aboriginal' at the Mermaid in 1951, and Michael Hordern as 'a most human and even poignant representative of the Backward and Underprivileged Peoples' at Stratford in 1952.[18]

There were few productions of *The Tempest* in the fifties and sixties. At Stratford, after productions in 1946–47 and 1951–52, there was a gap until 1957 and further longer gaps between the subsequent productions in 1963, 1970, 1974, and 1978. At the Old Vic, the first postwar production was in 1954, the second in 1962, and the third, by the National Theatre, not until 1974. The majority of such productions as there were yielded little in the way of colonial insight until Jonathan Miller's 1970 Mermaid revival, which offered a full-scale colonial analysis. The status quo before Miller's production is well exemplified by the reaction to Oliver Neville's generally undistinguished 1962 Old Vic revival. Only Roger Gellert commented on Caliban in imperial terms: 'Mr Selway looked genuinely and quite solemnly aboriginal, with the wild dignity that this implies. One was all the more inclined to join him in cursing the White Settler' (*New Statesman*, 8 June). This solitary comment is, perhaps, surprising in that the programme made the point that 'the island does not in fact belong to Prospero, but to the man monster Caliban, both by inheritance and by right, for it is Caliban who "knows the best springs", "how to snare the nimble marmoset", and "where to dig for pig-nuts"'. It appears that the production failed to convey the point with enough vigour to elicit a critical response. In the case of the 1963 production at Stratford the colonial references were again submerged, in this instance beneath the directors' attempts to stress what they saw as the play's deliberate irresolution. This innovatory conception was highly controversial and dominated critical response to the production, so that a programme note which stressed that 'the Elizabethans, like ourselves, had a prickly conscience about the ethics of their colonial enterprise' elicited only the usual incidental use of words like simian or aborigine to describe Roy Dotrice's Caliban, 'black and almost naked, with a forehead as low as that of the Java man' (*The Times*, 3 April 1963).

So, during the great period of British withdrawal from Empire there were few productions of *The Tempest*, and the play's colonial themes were largely uncanvassed. In the early sixties, however, three sociological studies were published in which the Prospero – Caliban relationship was taken as a paradigm of Imperialism. In George Lamming's *The Pleasures of Exile* (1960), Prospero was the colonist and Caliban the West Indian who has an alien language and culture imposed on him. Philip Mason actually took the magician into the title of his analysis, *Prospero's Magic: Some Thoughts on Class and Race* (1962), in which both Ariel and Caliban are seen as black nationalists, with Caliban the more extreme. Mason's book, which is also concerned with the interchangeability of the vocabulary of class and race, was a response to O. Mannoni's *Prospero and Caliban: The Psychology of Colonization* which, however, was not published in English translation until 1964. Mannoni, like Mason and Lamming, used an analogy between Caliban and the natives, and Prospero and the colonists, in his study of the French in Madagascar.

It was partly under the influence of Mannoni's study that Jonathan Miller chose to give serious consideration to the colonial dimension in his 1970 revival of *The Tempest*. Perhaps the new willingness to present the colonial dimension arose from a sense that it was now feasible to approach the colonial elements more dispassionately than had been possible during the retreat from Empire. Miller's production was certainly the most overtly colonial since Tree's, although the analysis of colonialism was far removed from its predecessor's. Apart from Mannoni, Miller's decision to treat the play in terms of colonialism was influenced by his own reading of accounts of the Elizabethan voyages of exploration and a production of Lowell's *The Old Glory*, with its long account of Puritan sailors making Indians drunk. In the programme, which included a lengthy extract from Mannoni, Caliban was without his traditional description as 'a savage and deformed slave' but Ariel was still 'an airy spirit'. In the production, Ariel and Caliban, played for the first time by black actors (Norman Beaton and Rudolph Walker), became examples of two opposing ways in which native black populations responded to the Europeans. Ariel was the accomplished servant who learnt European ways and literally picked up Prospero's broken wand at the end, dressing in European breeches but carrying a Kenyatta flywhisk, whilst Caliban was a detribalized field hand, with faint memories of matrilineal gods, who got drunk with Trinculo and Stephano (whom Miller likened to sergeants getting off the boat at Port Said). The frippery became trade goods and the goddesses were black sopranos.[19]

In general, the critical reaction was extremely favourable to Miller's conception, although the *Financial Times*, 16 June, dismissed the theory on the grounds that 'colonialism, the dominion of one race (as opposed to one nation) over another, is something that Shakespeare had never heard of' and that 'it isn't possible to set any party unequivocally in the position of colonialist or of subject'. Other critics, however, found no difficulty in relating Miller's production specifically to the Bermuda wreck and generally to the subsequent history of colonialism:

> Alonso and his courtiers ... are half-bewildered, half-enraptured by an island which seems to them, as the Bermudas seemed to Shakespeare's contemporaries, 'a most prodigious and enchanted place'; and they are almost immediately discontented. They scarcely listen to the old courtier, Gonzalo's, proposals for founding an ideal commonwealth; no sooner have they grasped the possibilities of this magical new world, than they fall—much as the 'Sea Venture's' company did—to plotting murder.
>
> It will be hard after Mr Miller's production, ever again to see *The Tempest* as the fairytale to which we are accustomed—or indeed to see it in any other terms than as Shakespeare's account, prosaic and prophetic, of the impact of the Old World on the New: a confrontation which, beginning in amazed delight, moves so swiftly to drawn swords and 'bloody thoughts' that the opening storm seems only a prelude in a minor key to the 'tempest of dissension' that sweeps Prospero's island. (Hilary Spurling, *Spectator*, 27 June)

As this response (which was much more typical than the *Financial Times*'s) suggests, it is not necessary for an investigation of the colonizing impulse to set up unequivocal colonists and colonized, each acting in accordance with one fixed approach, and, moreover, it is surely desirable that within a complex dramatic structure different characters should manifest different aspects of a central theme. Indeed one of the strengths of Miller's colonial interpretation lay in the way that it embraced all the characters. Thus the often criticized scenes between Caliban, Stephano, and Trinculo were 'transformed from irrelevant low comedy into another expression of the main theme' (*Plays and Players*, 17 August 1970, p. 29). Miranda fitted into the theme by showing 'a mind awakening to many things new and strange' (*Stage*, 18 June) and the *Observer* discovered 'a terrible new irony' in Miranda's 'welcome to the master race'. Perhaps most significantly, the relationship between Caliban and Ariel gained new associations in Miller's interpretation and, as with the other great colonial interpretation, we find that the last vision is of the island's original inhabitants: 'Ariel you'd say is the Uncle Tom, Caliban the black rebel. In fact as the play reminds you, it's Ariel who insists on his liberty, and gains it, Caliban who demands a master to worship and serve. As the Europeans depart, Caliban picks up Prospero's wand and points it icily at his fellow: *uhuru* has begun' (*Observer*, 21 June). In fact it was Ariel who picked up Prospero's wand, but the difference between Tree's tableau and this picture is truly indicative of the aesthetic and political distance between the two productions.

The success of Miller's *Tempest* ensured that the colonial themes would be accorded a greater significance than they had had in the fifties and sixties. Even in productions which operated on different intellectual premises to Miller's, the colonial elements were inescapable. In John Barton's 1970 Stratford production, for example, Ben Kingsley's Ariel was 'a slow moving, secretive native servant, naked except for a G string and a Sioux hairpiece, suggesting the victims depicted in those ancient prints of the Conquest of the Americas' (*Guardian*, 16 October). Similarly, although the main thrust of Peter Hall's 'emblematic' production for the National Theatre at the Old Vic in 1974 was directed elsewhere, he succeeded in presenting Caliban as a savage, a democrat, and a missing link through an ingenious costume design. Dennis Quilley did full justice to the 'paradoxical dignity' and 'impressive seriousness' of Caliban's 'blunt rhetoric' in a bisected make-up, 'one half the ugly scrofulous monster whom Prospero sees, on the other an image of the noble savage ... striving to break from the first stage into the second. His delivery of the word "freedom" even in the catch ... echoes with more passion and meaning than anything else in the evening'.[20] Quilley's costuming represented a considerable breakthrough in terms of doing full justice to the complexity of Caliban, and would seem to be an entirely appropriate visual representation of the paradoxical elements which make up the character.

Miller's black Ariel and Caliban had been a successful and integral part of the whole conception of his production, but, when Keith Hack used the black actor

Jeffrey Kissoon as Caliban at The Other Place in Stratford in 1974, the result was not so happy. Several critics complained that the actor was far too handsome for Caliban, and the *Coventry Evening Telegraph* (23 October) argued that 'in attempting to illustrate the white man's mental and physical cruelty to the black races' Hack had succeeded 'only in being offensive to them'. In this case it would seem that casting a black actor as Caliban misfired, but there is no doubt that the casting was intended to emphasize the play's colonial elements.

Indeed, some emphasis on colonialism is now expected, and Michael Billington castigated the most recent Stratford *Tempest*, directed by Clifford Williams in 1978, for not going far enough 'in mining the play's political-colonial sub-text', despite the blacked-up David Suchet's 'stunning performance with both the anger and the pathos of the unreasonably exploited' as Caliban (*Guardian*, 4 May). Bernard Levin also praised Suchet's performance in terms of its colonial elements: 'no deformed monster but a Man Friday conscious of his usurped rights, and clutching a voodoo figure to help him curse his enemy' (*Sunday Times*, 7 May). Here, with Caliban once more linked with that other great colonial fiction, the story ends for the moment, but there seems to be little likelihood that the 'political-colonial sub-text' of *The Tempest* will not remain an important part of theatrical productions in the future.

NOTES

1. For a discussion of the Bermuda pamphlets and the influence of the New World on *The Tempest*, see *The Tempest*, edited by F. Kermode (London, 1954), pp. xxv–xxxiv. My quotations from reviews, where page-references are not given, are from clippings in collections held variously at the Shakespeare Centre Library, Stratford-upon-Avon; the Harvard Theatre Collection, Cambridge, Massachusetts; Birmingham Public Libraries; the Library of the Vic-Wells Association; and the Enthoven Collection at the Victoria and Albert Museum.
2. P. MacDonnell, *An Essay on the Play of The Tempest* (London, 1840), pp. 18–19.
3. *John Bull*, 12 November 1842, and *Sunday Times*, partially unidentified clipping in the Enthoven Collection, Victoria and Albert Museum.
4. Page references are to the text reprinted in *English Plays of the Nineteenth Century*, edited by Michael R. Booth, 5 vols (Oxford and London, 1969–76), v, *Pantomimes, Extravaganzas and Burlesques* (1976), 163–201.
5. 'Ariel', F. C. Burnand's *Tempest* burlesque, also illustrates this. In it Caliban sang, 'You *landed* on dryland on this *Is*land which is *my*land | And by night [*sic*?] belongs to me; | O I was so riled and vexed to see it "annexed" | By a foreign authoritee', *Selections from the Songs and Words of the Concerted Pieces in 'Ariel'* London, 1883), p. 10.
6. *The London Theatre, 1811–1866*, edited by Eluned Brown (London, 1966), p. 204.
7. In Thompson's *Trinculo's Trip to the Jubilee*, second edition (London, 1770), Trinculo's song includes the lines 'There was Caliban too, a most monstrous ape, | No beast had before such a whimsical shape' (p. 33).
8. *Social Darwinism and English Thought* (Brighton, 1980), p. 140. My discussions of Darwinism and of typifications of race and class are greatly indebted to this work.
9. Dutton Cook, *Night at the Play* (London, 1883), pp. 123–24.
10. *Forty Years of Shakespeare on the English Stage* (London, [1908]), pp. 13–14.
11. *Caliban: The Missing Link* (London, 1873), pp. 9, 79, 89–90, 78.
12. A. C. Haddon, *The Study of Man* (London, 1898), p. 63, quoted in Jones, p. 106.

13. F. R. Benson, *My Memoirs* (London, 1930), p. 298; Constance Benson, *Mainly Players* (London, 1926), p. 179. For the fish, see J. C. Trewin, *Benson and the Bensonians* (London, 1960), p. 150.
14. *The Tempest, as Arranged for the Stage by H. B. Tree* (London, 1904), p. 63.
15. 'First Impressions of the Theatre', *Review of Reviews*, 30 (October, 1904), 360–67.
16. Malcolm Keen's Caliban in the 1933 Old Vic revival reminded the *Daily Mail* (19 April) of another colonial hero, since his make-up suggested 'a compromise between Tarzan and the Old Man of the Sea'.
17. *Birmingham Mail*, 3 May 1938; *Catholic Herald*, 7 June 1940; Stratford *Herald*, 24 April 1942.
18. *Observer*, 29 April 1934; 23 September 1951; 30 March 1952.
19. Based on notes of a telephone conversation with Dr Jonathan Miller, 22 September 1977.
20. *New Statesman*, 15 March, and *The Times*, 6 March.

1.2

FROM 'CARIBBEAN AND AFRICAN APPROPRIATIONS OF *THE TEMPEST*'

Rob Nixon

Remember
First to possess his books.
—The Tempest

The era from the late fifties to the early seventies was marked in Africa and the Caribbean by a rush of newly articulated anti-colonial sentiment that was associated with the burgeoning of both international black consciousness and more localized nationalist movements. Between 1957 and 1973 the vast majority of African and the larger Caribbean colonies won their independence; the same period witnessed the Cuban and Algerian revolutions, the latter phase of the Kenyan 'Mau Mau' revolt, the Katanga crisis in the Congo, the Trinidadian Black Power uprising and, equally important for the atmosphere of militant defiance, the civil rights movement in the United States, the student revolts of 1968, and the humbling of the United States during the Vietnam War. This period was distinguished, among Caribbean and African intellectuals, by a pervasive mood of optimistic outrage. Frequently graduates of British or French universities, they were the first generation from their regions self-assured and numerous enough to call collectively for a renunciation of Western standards as the political revolts found their cultural counterparts in insurrections against the bequeathed values of the colonial powers.

In the context of such challenges to an increasingly discredited European colonialism, a series of dissenting intellectuals chose to utilize a European text as

Critical Inquiry, 13, Spring 1987, pp. 557–78. Extract: pp. 557–73.

a strategy for (in George Lamming's words) getting 'out from under this ancient mausoleum of [Western] historic achievement.'[1] They seized upon *The Tempest* as a way of amplifying their calls for decolonization within the bounds of the dominant cultures. But at the same time these Caribbeans and Africans adopted the play as a founding text in an oppositional lineage which issued from a geopolitically and historically specific set of cultural ambitions. They perceived that the play could contribute to their self-definition during a period of great flux. So, through repeated, reinforcing, transgressive appropriations of *The Tempest*, a once silenced group generated its own tradition of 'error' which in turn served as one component of the grander counterhegemonic nationalist and black internationalist endeavors of the period. Because that era of Caribbean and African history was marked by such extensive, open contestation of cultural values, the destiny of *The Tempest* at that time throws into uncommonly stark relief the status of value as an unstable social process rather than a static and, in literary terms, merely textual attribute.

Some Caribbean and African intellectuals anticipated that their efforts to unearth from *The Tempest* a suppressed narrative of their historical abuse and to extend that narrative in the direction of liberation would be interpreted as philistine. But Lamming, for one, wryly resisted being intimidated by any dominant consensus: 'I shall reply that my mistake, lived and deeply felt by millions of men like me—proves the positive value of error' (*PE*, p. 13). Lamming's assertion that his unorthodoxy is collectively grounded is crucial: those who defend a text's universal value can easily discount a solitary dissenting voice as uncultured or quirky, but it is more difficult to ignore entirely a cluster of allied counterjudgments, even if the group can still be stigmatized. Either way, the notion of universal value is paradoxically predicated on a limited inclusiveness, on the assumption that certain people will fail to appreciate absolute worth. As Pierre Bourdieu, Barbara Herrnstein Smith, and Tony Bennett have all shown, a dominant class or culture's power to declare certain objects or activities self-evidently valuable is an essential measure for reproducing social differentiation.[2] But resistance to the hegemony of such hierarchies is still possible. In this context, Lamming's statement exudes the fresh confidence of the high era of decolonization, in which a 'philistinism' arose that was sufficiently powerful and broadly based to generate an alternative orthodoxy responsive to indigenous interests and needs.

For Frantz Fanon, decolonization was the period when the peoples of the oppressed regions, force-fed for so long on foreign values, could stomach them no longer: 'In the colonial context the settler only ends his work of breaking in the native when the latter admits loudly and intelligibly the supremacy of the white man's values. In the period of decolonization, the colonized masses mock at these very values, insult them, and vomit them up.'[3] From the late fifties onward, there was a growing resistance in African and Caribbean colonies to remote-controlled anything, from administrative structures to school curricula, and the phase of 'nauseating mimicry' (in Fanon's phrase) gave way to a phase in which colonized cultures sought to define their own cultures reactively and aggressively from within.[4] In short, decolonization was the period when 'the machine [went] into reverse.'[5] This about-face entailed that indigenous cultural forms be substituted for alien ones—inevitably a hybrid process of retrieving suppressed traditions and inventing new ones. Both approaches were present in the newfound preoccupation with *The Tempest*: hints of New World culture and history were dragged to the surface, while at other moments the play was unabashedly refashioned to meet contemporary political and cultural needs.[6]

Given the forcefulness of the reaction against the values of the colonial powers, it may appear incongruous that Caribbean and African intellectuals should have integrated a canonical European text like *The Tempest* into their struggle; it made for, in Roberto Fernández Retamar's words, 'an alien elaboration.'[7] And this response may seem doubly incongruous given Shakespeare's distinctive position as a measure of the relative achievements of European and non-European civilizations. In discussions of value, Shakespeare is, of course, invariably treated as a special case, having come to serve as something like the gold standard of literature. For the English he is as much an institution and an industry as a corpus of texts: a touchstone of national identity, a lure for tourists, an exportable commodity, and one of the securest forms of cultural capital around. But the weight of Shakespeare's ascribed authority was felt differently in the colonies. What for the English and, more generally, Europeans, could be a source of pride and a confirmation of their civilization, for colonial subjects often became a chastening yardstick of their 'backwardness.' The exhortation to master Shakespeare was instrumental in showing up non-European 'inferiority,' for theirs would be the flawed mastery of those culturally remote from Shakespeare's stock. A schooled resemblance could become the basis for a more precise discrimination, for, to recall Homi Bhabha's analysis of mimicry in colonial discourse, 'to be Anglicized is *emphatically* not to be English.'[8] And so, in colonial circumstances, the bard could become symptomatic and symbolic of the education of Africans and Caribbeans into a passive, subservient relationship to dominant colonial culture.

One aspect of this passive orientation toward Europe is touched on by Lamming, the Barbadian novelist who was to appropriate *The Tempest* so actively for his own ends. Discussing his schooling during the early 1940s, Lamming recalls how the teacher 'followed the curriculum as it was. He did what he had to do: Jane Austen, some Shakespeare, Wells's novel *Kipps*, and so on. What happened was that they were teaching exactly whatever the Cambridge Syndicate demanded. That was the point of it. These things were directly connected. Papers were set in Cambridge and our answers were sent back there to be corrected. We had to wait three to four months. Nobody knew what was happening till they were returned.'[9] Given the resistance during decolonization to this kind of cultural dependency, those writers who took up *The Tempest* from the standpoint of the colonial subject did so in a manner that was fraught with complexity. On the one hand, they hailed Caliban and identified themselves with him; on the other, they were intolerant of received colonial definitions of Shakespeare's value. They found the European play compelling but insisted on engaging with it on their own terms.

The newfound interest in *The Tempest* during decolonization was, in terms of the play's history, unprecedentedly sudden and concentrated. However, in the late nineteenth and early twentieth century, *The Tempest*'s value had been augmented by a prevalent perception of it as a likely vehicle first for Social Darwinian and later for imperial ideas. This tendency, which Trevor Griffiths has thoroughly documented, was evident in both performances and critical responses to the play.[10] A notable instance was *Caliban: The Missing Link* (1873), wherein Daniel Wilson contended that Shakespeare had preempted some of Darwin's best insights by creating 'a novel anthropoid of a high type.'[11] Amassing evidence from the play, Wilson deduced that Caliban would have been black, had prognathous jaws, and manifested a low stage of cultural advancement. Wilson's text shuttles between *The Tempest*, Darwin, and Linnaeus and is interlarded with detailed brain measurements of gibbons, baboons, chimpanzees, and a range of ethnic groupings.

Ironically, it was Beerbohm Tree's unabashedly jingoistic production of *The Tempest* in 1904 that elicited the first recorded response to the play in anti-imperial terms, as one member of the audience assimilated the action to events surrounding the Matabele uprising in Rhodesia:

> When the man-monster, brutalised by long continued torture, begins, 'This island's mine, by Sycorax my mother, which thou takest from me', we have the whole case of the aboriginal against aggressive civilisation dramatised before us. I confess I felt a sting of conscience—vicariously suffered for my Rhodesian friends, notably Dr Jameson—when Caliban proceeded to unfold a similar case to that of the Matebele. It might have been the double of old King Lobengula rehearsing the blandishments which led to his doom: 'When thou camest first / Thou strok'dst me, and mad'st much of me; would'st give me'—all that was promised by the Chartered Company to secure the charter.[12]

Just as the Matabele uprising was a distant, premonitory sign of the anti-colonial struggles to come, so, too, W. T. Stead's unorthodox response to *The Tempest* anticipated a time when the play would be widely mobilized and esteemed as an expression of 'the whole case of the "aboriginal" against aggressive civilisation.'

But it was another forty-four years before any text provided a sustained reassessment of *The Tempest* in light of the immediate circumstances leading up to decolonization. That text was *Psychologie de la colonisation*, written by the French social scientist, Octave Mannoni. However much Third World intellectuals have subsequently quarreled with his manner of mobilizing the play, Mannoni's inaugural gesture helped to shape the trajectory of those associated appropriations which lay ahead and, concomitantly, to bring about the reestimation of *The Tempest* in Africa and the Caribbean. Mannoni's novel response enabled him to evolve a theory of colonialism with Prospero and Caliban as prototypes; conversely, his hypotheses about colonial relations, arising from his experiences in Madagascar, made it possible for him to rethink the play. This reciprocal process was not gratuitous but prompted by an early stirring of African nationalism: Mannoni is insistent that his theory only fell into place through his exposure to one of the twilight moments of French colonialism—the Madagascan uprising of 1947–48 in which sixty thousand Madagascans, one thousand colonial soldiers, and several hundred settlers were killed. In 1947 his ideas began to take shape, and, by the time the revolt had been suppressed a year later, the manuscript was complete. The occasional character of *Psychologie de la colonisation* is foregrounded in the introduction, which Mannoni closes by marking the coincidence of his ideas with 'a certain moment in history, a crisis in the evolution of politics, when many things that had been hidden were brought into the light of day; but it was only a moment, and time will soon have passed it by.'[13] The pressing horrors of the Madagascan crisis prompted Mannoni to find a new significance for *The Tempest*, encouraging him to weave a reading of Shakespeare's poetic drama through his reading of the incipient drama of decolonization.

Mannoni's account of the psychological climate of colonialism is advanced through an opposition between the Prospero (or inferiority) complex and the Caliban (or dependence) complex. On this view, Europeans in Madagascar typically displayed the need, common among people from a competitive society, to feel highly regarded by others. However, the Prospero-type is not just any white man, but specifically the sort whose 'grave lack of sociability combined with a pathological urge to dominate' drives him to seek out uncompetitive situations where, among a subservient people, his power is amplified and his least skills assume the aspect of superior magic (*PC*, p. 102). Whether a French settler in Africa or Shakespeare's duke, he is loath to depart his adopted island, knowing full well that back home his standing will shrink to mundane dimensions. Mannoni found the Madagascans, on the other hand, to be marked by a Caliban complex, a dependence on authority purportedly characteristic of a people forced out of a secure 'tribal' society and into the less stable, competitively edged hierarchies of a semi-Westernized existence. According to this theory, colonialism introduced a situation where the Madagascan was exposed for the first time to the notion and possibility of abandonment. Crucially, the colonist failed to comprehend the Madagascan's capacity to feel 'neither inferior nor superior but yet wholly dependent,' an unthinkable state of mind for someone from a competitive society (*PC*, p. 157). So, in Mannoni's terms, the Madagascan revolt was fueled less by a desire to sunder an oppressive master-servant bond than by the people's resentment of the colonizers' failure to uphold that bond more rigorously and provide them with the security they craved. What the colonial subjects sought was the paradoxical freedom of secure dependence rather than any autonomous, self-determining freedom. This assumption clearly shaped Mannoni's skepticism about the Madagascans' desire, let alone their capacity, to achieve national independence.

Mannoni values *The Tempest* most highly for what he takes to be Shakespeare's dramatization of two cultures' mutual sense of a trust betrayed: Prospero is a fickle dissembler, Caliban an ingrate. The nodal lines here, and those that draw Mannoni's densest commentary, are spoken by Caliban in the play's second scene. They should be quoted at length for they are taken up repeatedly by subsequent Caribbean and African appropriators of *The Tempest*.

> When thou cam'st first,
> Thou strok'st me, and made much of me, wouldst give me
> Water with berries in't, and teach me how
> To name the bigger light, and how the less,
> That burn by day and night, and then I lov'd thee
> And show'd thee all the qualities o' th' isle,
> The fresh springs, brine-pits, barren place and fertile:
> Curs'd be I that did so! All the charms
> Of Sycorax, toads, beetles, bats, light on you!
> For I am all the subjects that you have,
> Which first was mine own king; and here you sty me
> In this hard rock, whiles you do keep from me
> The rest o' th' island.[14]

To Mannoni, it appears evident that 'Caliban does not complain of being exploited; he complains of being betrayed.' He 'has fallen prey to the resentment which succeeds the breakdown of dependence' (*PC*, p. 106). This view is buttressed by an analogous interpretation of Caliban's revolt in league with Trinculo as an action launched 'not to win his freedom, for he could not support freedom, but to have a new master whose "foot-licker" he can become. He is delighted at the prospect. It would be hard to find a better example of the dependence complex in its pure state' (*PC*, pp. 106–7).

Such statements rankled badly with Caribbean and African intellectuals who, in the fifties, for the first time sensed the imminence of large-scale decolonization in their regions. In such circumstances, the insinuation that Caliban was incapable of surviving on his own and did not even aspire to such independence in the first place caused considerable affront and helped spur Third Worlders to mount adversarial interpretations of the play which rehabilitated Caliban into a heroic figure, inspired by noble rage to oust the interloping Prospero from his island. Fanon and Aimé Césaire, two of Mannoni's most vehement critics, found the 'ethno-psychologist's' disregard for economic exploitation especially jarring and accused him of reducing colonialism to an encounter between two psychological types with complementary predispositions who, for a time at least, find their needs dovetailing tidily.[15] *Psychologie de la colonisation*, these critics charged, made Caliban out to be an eager partner in his own colonization. Mannoni, in a statement like 'wherever Europeans have founded colonies of the type we are considering, it can safely be said that their coming was unconsciously expected—even desired—by the future subject peoples,' seemed to discount any possibility of Europe being culpable for the exploitation of the colonies (*PC*, p. 86). Mannoni's critics foresaw, moreover, just how readily his paradigm could be harnessed by Europeans seeking to thwart the efforts for self-determination that were gathering impetus in the fifties.

Fanon and Césaire's fears about the implications of Mannoni's thesis were vindicated by the appearance in 1962 of *Prospero's Magic: Some Thoughts on Class and Race* by Philip Mason, an English colonial who sought to give credence to Mannoni's ideas by using them to rationalize resistance to colonialism in Kenya ('Mau Mau'), India, and Southern Rhodesia. The upshot of this effort was Mason's conclusion that 'a colonial rebellion may be a protest not against repression but against progress, not against the firm hand but against its withdrawal' and that (for such is every 'tribal' society's craving for firm authority) 'countries newly released from colonialism ... [will experience] a reduction of personal freedom.'[16]

Prospero's Magic is an intensely autobiographical and occasional work. Its author, in siding with Mannoni, was also seeking to counteract the first fully fledged Caribbean appropriation of *The Tempest*, Lamming's recently published *Pleasures of Exile* (1960). The lectures comprising *Prospero's Magic* were delivered at the University College of the West Indies on the eve of Jamaica's independence and are based on Mason's more than twenty years as a colonial employee in India, Nigeria, and Rhodesia, where he witnessed the death throes —or as he terms it, the fulfillment—of British imperialism. Rereading *The Tempest* in the political atmosphere of 1962, he was discomfited by his recognition of the Prospero in himself. Circumstances had altered: 'While many of us today find we dislike in Prospero things we dislike in ourselves, our fathers admired him without question and so indeed did my generation until lately' (*PM*, p. 92).[17] Mason tried to square his awareness that colonialism was becoming increasingly discredited with his personal need to salvage some value and self-respect from his decades of colonial 'service.' So he was at once a member of the first generation to acknowledge distaste for Prospero and personally taken aback by his own sudden redundancy: 'With what deep reluctance does the true Prospero put aside his book and staff, the magic of power and office, and go to live in Cheltenham!' (*PM*, p. 96). Mason, for one, conceived of himself as writing at the very moment when the colonial master was called upon to break and bury his staff.

By the time Caribbeans and Africans took up *The Tempest*, that is, from 1959 onward, widespread national liberation seemed not only feasible but imminent, and the play was mobilized in defense of Caliban's right to the land and to cultural autonomy. 'This island's mine by Sycorax my mother / Which thou tak'st from me' (1.2.333–34) are the lines that underlie much of the work that was produced by African and Caribbean intellectuals in the 1960s and early 1970s.[18] Those same two lines introduce Caliban's extended complaint (quoted at length above), the nodal speech Mannoni had cited as evidence that

Shakespeare was dramatizing a relation of dependence, not one of exploitation. But, significantly, and in keeping with his very different motives for engaging with the play, Mannoni had lopped off those two lines when working the passage into his argument. On this score, Third World responses consistently broke with Mannoni: Caliban, the decolonizer, was enraged not at being orphaned by colonial paternalism but at being insufficiently abandoned by it.

The first Caribbean writer to champion Caliban was Lamming. His nonfictional *Pleasures of Exile* can be read as an effort to redeem from the past, as well as to stimulate, an indigenous Antillean line of creativity to rival the European traditions which seemed bent on arrogating to themselves all notions of culture. Lamming's melange of a text—part essay on the cultural politics of relations between colonizer and colonized, part autobiography, and part textual criticism of, in particular, *The Tempest* and C. L. R. James' *The Black Jacobins* (1938)—was sparked by two events, one personal, the other more broadly historical.[19] Lamming began his text in 1959, shortly after disembarking in Southampton as part of the great wave of West Indian immigrants settling in Britain in the fifties. But his circumstances differed from those of most of his compatriots, for he was immigrating as an aspirant writer. As such he was keenly aware of taking up residence in the headquarters of the English language and culture and, concomitantly, of being only ambiguously party to that language and culture, even though a dialect of English was his native tongue and even though—for such was his colonial schooling—he was more intimate with Shakespeare and the English Revolution than with the writings and history of his own region.

Lamming's reflections on the personal circumstances which occasioned *The Pleasures of Exile* are suffused with his sense of the book's historical moment. Writing on the brink of the sixties, he was highly conscious that colonial Africa and the Caribbean were entering a new phase. The political mood of the book is expectant ('Caliban's history ... belongs entirely to the future' [*PE*, p. 107]), most evidently in his account of an envious visit to Ghana, the first of the newly independent African states. That trip sharpened his anguished sense of the British West Indies' failure as yet to achieve comparable autonomy. He recalls the intensity of that feeling in his introduction to the 1984 edition: 'There were no independent countries in the English-speaking Caribbean when I started to write *The Pleasures of Exile* in 1959. With the old exceptions of Ethiopia and Liberia, there was only one in Black Africa, and that was Ghana. Twenty years later almost every rock and pebble in the Caribbean had acquired this status' (*PE*, p. 7). While looking ahead to Caribbean self-determination, Lamming was also writing self-consciously in the aftermath of an action one year back that had quickened nationalist ambitions throughout the area: 'Fidel Castro and the Cuban revolution reordered our history. ... The Cuban revolution was a Caribbean response to that imperial menace which Prospero conceived as a civilising mission' (*PE*, p. 7).

Lamming's relationship to decolonization is markedly distinct from Mannoni's. The Frenchman was in Madagascar as a social scientist observing and systematizing the psychological impulses behind an incipient struggle for national autonomy, while the Barbadian's reflections on decolonization are less distanced and more personal, as he declares himself to be Caliban's heir. Lamming's and Mannoni's different tacks are most conspicuous in their treatment of Caliban's pronouncement: 'You taught me language; and my profit on't / Is, I know how to curse' (1.2.363–64). From that quotation Mannoni launches an analysis of the role in 1947–48 of the westernized Malagasies, some of whom had become so acculturated during study abroad that they could no longer engage with their countryfellows. The cross-cultural status of yet others who were less thoroughly assimilated but had become fluent in acrimony facilitated their rise to positions of leadership in the national resistance. Lamming, by contrast, takes up Caliban's remarks on language as one who is himself a substantially Europeanized Third Worlder, a West Indian nationalist living in England, and someone reluctant to segregate his theoretical from his autobiographical insights.[20] Much of the personal urgency of Lamming's text stems from his assimilation of Caliban's linguistic predicament to his own. As a writer by vocation, he is especially alert to the way colonialism has generated linguistic discrimination, to how, as a West Indian born into English, he is branded a second-class speaker of his first language.

Though Lamming addresses the question of the unlanded Caliban who declares 'This island's mine,' he dwells most obsessively on the educational inheritance which he finds enunciated in the speech 'You taught me language.' While the nationalist struggle provides a shaping context for *The Pleasures of Exile*, Lamming's Caliban is not just any colonial subject but specifically the colonized writer-intellectual, the marginal person of letters. Lamming's root frustration is the ostensible lack of parity between the possibilities for political and for cultural freedom. Come formal independence, the people may establish their own laws and governments, but won't Caribbean writers still lag behind, permanently shackled to the colonizer's language—whether English, French, or Spanish – since it is the only one they have? 'Prospero lives in the absolute certainty that Language which is his gift to Caliban is the very prison in which Caliban's achievements will be realised and restricted. Caliban can never reach perfection, not even the perfection implicit in Miranda's privileged ignorance' (*PE*, p. 110).[21] That is, as long as Caliban is still bound to his former master's language, he is still partly condemned to live the life of a servant.

What holds for language holds equally for culture in general. If Caliban's accent sounds sour and deformed to the British ear, so too his knowledge of British traditions—no matter how relentlessly they have been drummed into him in Barbados—will be shown up as flawed and fragmentary. Yet on this score Lamming is unevenly pessimistic, for his very appropriation of *The Tempest* testifies to his faith in the Caribbean intellectual's capacity to scale the conventional heights of British culture. Instead of deferring slavishly to a British norm, Lamming manages—with Caliban's lines at the ready—to treat that norm as a pretext for and object of abuse. To write about Shakespeare is a strategy for commanding a hearing in the West, but he values this audibility primarily because it enables him to draw attention to his ostracism. He is only too aware of the implications of quoting Shakespeare to legitimate his 'illegitimate' treatment of that same hallowed author:

> It is my intention to make use of *The Tempest* as a way of presenting a certain state of feeling which is the heritage of the exiled and colonial writer from the British Caribbean.
>
> Naturally, I anticipate from various quarters the obvious charge of blasphemy; yet there are occasions when blasphemy must be seen as one privilege of the excluded Caliban. [*PE*, p. 9]

Lamming seizes the outcast's prerogative to impiety in part to shake the insiders' monopoly of a text that draws and bears on Caribbean history. But this destructive impulse feeds a more positive one: the desire to mount an indigenous countertradition, with a reinterpreted Caliban from 1611 and the contemporary, about-to-be-liberated Antillean of 1959 flanking that tradition. So for all its dense, original analogies between *The Tempest* and the Caribbean of the late fifties, what is at stake in *The Pleasures of Exile* is something larger than the immediate, local value of a Shakespearean play: it is the very possibility of decolonizing the area's cultural history by replacing an imposed with an endemic line of thought and action. Within the context of this grand design, the initial gesture of annexing Shakespeare was pivotal, as it generated a Caliban who could stand as a prototype for successive Caribbean figures in whom cultural and political activism were to cohere. Lamming's reconstructed tradition runs through Toussaint Louverture, C. L. R. James, and Fidel Castro to the author himself who, like many of his generation of West Indian writers, immigrated to England to embark on a literary career but while there also pressed for his region's independence. That these particular figures should have been selected to brace the countertradition points to Lamming's conviction that —linguistic dilemmas notwithstanding—Caribbean culture and politics had been and should ideally continue to be allies in each other's decolonization.

In spirit, Lamming's dissident reassessment of one of the high texts of European culture had been matched by the Trinidadian James' reverse angle in *The Black Jacobins* on one of the most celebrated periods of European history, the French Revolution. *The Pleasures of Exile* is designed to make these two unorthodox gestures seem of a piece, through remarks such as '[there] C. L. R. James shows us Caliban as Prospero had never known him' (*PE*, p. 119). James' Caliban is Toussaint Louverture, leader of the first successful Caribbean struggle for independence, the Haitian slave revolt of 1791–1803. As the title of his book might suggest, James was concerned to dredge up a counternarrative, from a Caribbean perspective, of events which had been submerged beneath the freight of Eurocentric history. For Lamming, James' action and others like it were essential to the establishment of a Calibanic lineage; but once established, that lineage had still to be sustained, which would require one salvaging operation after another. This apprehension was borne out when, at the time of writing *The Pleasures of Exile*, Lamming discovered that James' book, out of print for twenty years, was in danger of sinking into neglect. So he set himself the task of doing in turn for James what James had done for Louverture: keeping afloat a vital, remedial tradition that was threatening to disappear.

During the era of decolonization, negritude proved to be one of the strongest components of this remedial tradition, and it was the negritudist from Martinique, Césaire, who came to renovate *The Tempest* theatrically for black cultural ends in a manner indebted to Lamming if fiercer in its defiance. These two writers' approaches coincided most explicitly in their determination to unearth an endemic lineage of cultural-cum-political activists; it is telling that within the space of two years, each man published a book resuscitating Toussaint Louverture and celebrating his example.[22]

Césaire's *Une Tempête* (1969) exemplifies the porous boundaries between European and Afro-Caribbean cultures even within the anticolonial endeavors of the period. As an influence on Césaire's response to Shakespeare, Lamming keeps company with Mannoni and the German critic, Janheinz Jahn. Mannoni had experience of French island colonies in both Africa and the Caribbean for, prior to his stint in Madagascar, he had served as an instructor in a Martinican school where Césaire had been his precocious student. More than twenty years later, in *Discours sur le colonialisme*, Césaire upbraided his former schoolmaster for not thinking through the implications of his colonial paradigm. And Césaire's subsequent, inevitably reactive adaptation of Shakespeare further demonstrated just how far he had diverged from Mannoni's motives for valuing *The Tempest*. More in keeping with the spirit of *Une Tempête* was Jahn's *Geschichte der neo-afrakanischen Literatur*, which appeared a few years before Césaire wrote his play. Jahn's pioneering study gave prominence to the Calibanesque in Mannoni and Lamming and, by designating the negritude writers (Césaire, Leopold Senghor, and Ousmane Diop) black cultural liberators à la Caliban, hinted at ideas that Césaire was to develop more amply. Notable among these was Jahn's attempt to counteract Lamming's dejected pronouncements about the confining character of Prospero's language by exhorting Caliban to free himself through cultural bilingualism—by recovering long-lost African strains and using them to offset the derivative, European components of his cultural identity. Jahn urged further that suitable elements of European culture be transformed into vehicles for black cultural values. Along these lines, negritude could be defined as 'the successful revolt in which Caliban broke out of the prison of Prospero's language, by converting that language to his own needs of self-expression.'[23]

Césaire has been quite explicit about his motives for reworking *The Tempest*:

> I was trying to de-mythify the tale. To me Prospero was a complete totalitarian. I am always surprised when others consider him the wise man who 'forgives'. What is most obvious, even in Shakespeare's version, is the man's absolute will to power. Prospero is the man of cold reason, the man

> of methodical conquest—in other words, a portrait of the 'enlightened' European. And I see the whole play in such terms: the 'civilized' European world coming face to face for the first time with the world of primitivism and magic. Let's not hide the fact that in Europe the world of reason has inevitably led to various kinds of totalitarianism ... Caliban is the man who is still close to his beginnings, whose link with the natural world has not yet been broken. Caliban can still *participate* in a world of marvels, whereas his master can merely 'create' them through his acquired knowledge. At the same time, Caliban is also a rebel—the positive hero, in a Hegelian sense. The slave is always more important than his master—for it is the slave who makes history.[24]

Césaire's perception of Prospero as 'the man of methodical conquest' and his insistence on the slave as the preeminent historical agent become the touchstones for his radically polarized adaptation of Shakespeare. Forgiveness and reconciliation give way to irreconcilable differences; the roles of Ferdinand and Miranda are whittled down to a minimum; and the play's colonial dimensions are writ large. Antonio and Alonso vie with Prospero for control over newly charted lands abroad, and Shakespeare's rightful Duke of Milan is delivered to the island not by the providence of a 'happy storm' but through a confederacy rooted in imperial ambitions. Prospero is demythologized and rendered contemporary by making him altogether less white magical and a master of the technology of oppression; his far from inscrutable power is embodied in antiriot control gear and an arsenal. Violating rather than communing with life on the island, he is, in Caliban's phrase, the '*anti-Natur*.'

Une Tempête self-consciously counterpoises the materialist Prospero with an animistic slave empowered by a culture that coexists empathetically with nature. Indeed, Caliban's culture of resistance is his sole weaponry, but it is more formidable than the shallow culture Shakespeare permits him, as Césaire plumbs the depths of the slave's African past to make him a more equal adversary.[25] Caliban's defiance is expressed most strongly through the celebration of the Yoruba gods Shango and Eshu; two of his four songs of liberation fete Shango, an African figure who has survived in Caribbean voodoo and Brazilian macumba. And in a critical irruption, Eshu scatters Prospero's carefully ordered classical masque, making the imported divinities seem precious, effete, and incongruous.

Césaire's Caliban also goes beyond Shakespeare's in his refusal to subscribe to the etiquette of subjugation:

> CALIBAN: Uhuru!
> PROSPERO: Qu'est-ce que tu dis?
> CALIBAN: Je dis Uhuru!
> PROSPERO: Encore une remontée de ton langage barbare. Je t'ai déjà dit que n'arrive pas ça. D'ailleurs, tu pourrais être poli, un bonjour ne te tuerait pas![26]

This opening exchange between Caliban and his colonial overlord sets the stage for Césaire's conviction that the culture of slaves need not be an enslaved culture. Here he is more optimistic than Lamming, who saw Caribbean cultures of resistance as ineluctably circumscribed by the colonizer's language; one thinks particularly of Lamming in Ghana, casting an envious eye over children chatting in their indigenous tongue, a language that 'owed Prospero no debt of vocabulary' (*PE*, p. 162). Even if Césaire's Caliban cannot throw off European influences entirely, his recuperation of a residual past is sufficient to secure his relative cultural autonomy. Crucially, his first utterance is 'Uhuru', the Swahili term for freedom which gained international currency through the struggles for decolonization in the late fifties and sixties. And Caliban retorts to Prospero's demand for a *bonjour* by charging that he has only been instructed in the colonial tongue so he can submit to the magisterial imperatives, and by declaring that he will no longer respond to the name Caliban, a colonial invention bound anagramatically to the degrading 'cannibal.' Instead, the island's captive king christens himself '*X*' in a Black Muslim gesture that commemorates his lost name, buried beneath layers of colonial culture. The play supposes, in sum, that Caribbean colonial subjects can best fortify their revolt by reviving, wherever possible, cultural forms dating back to before that wracking sea-change which was the Middle Passage.

Césaire's remark that the slave, as maker of history, 'is always more important than his master' has both a retrospective and an anticipatory force, pointing back to Louverture, Haiti, and the only triumphant slave revolt, and forward through the present to colonialism's demise. Césaire steeps his play most explicitly in the contemporary Afro-Caribbean struggles for self-determination when he stages, via Ariel and Caliban, the debate, ubiquitous in the late fifties and sixties, between the rival strategies for liberation advanced by proponents of evolutionary and revolutionary change. The mulatto Ariel shuns violence and holds that, faced with Prospero's stockpiled arsenal, they are more likely to win freedom through conciliation than refractoriness. But from Caliban's perspective Ariel is a colonial collaborator, a political and cultural sellout who, aspiring both to rid himself nonviolently of Prospero and to emulate his values, is reduced to negotiating for liberty from a position of powerlessness. The success of Caliban's uncompromising strategies is imminent at the end of the drama. When the other Europeans return to Italy, Prospero is unable to accompany them, for he is in the thrall of a psychological battle with his slave (shades of Mannoni here), shouting 'Je défendrai la civilisation!' but intuiting that 'le climat a changé.' At the close, Caliban is chanting ecstatically, 'La Liberté Ohé, La Liberté,' and defying the orders of a master whose authority and sanity are teetering.[27]

Césaire, then, radically reassessed *The Tempest* in terms of the circumstances of his region, taking the action to the brink of colonialism's demise. He valued the play because he saw its potential as a vehicle for dramatizing the evolution of colonialism in his region and for sharpening the contemporary ideological alternatives open to would-be-liberated Antilleans. Césaire sought, from an openly interested standpoint, to amend the political acoustics of Shakespeare's play, to make the action resonate with the dangers of supine cultural assimilation, a concern since his student days that was accentuated during the high period of decolonization. This renovation of the play for black cultural ends was doubly impertinent: besides treating a classic sacrilegiously, it implicitly lampooned the educational practice, so pervasive in the colonies, of distributing only bowdlerized versions of Shakespeare, of watering him down 'for the natives.' *Une Tempête* can thus be read as parodying this habit by indicating how the bard might have looked were he indeed made fit reading for a subject people.

Césaire's play was published in 1969. The years 1968 through 1971 saw the cresting of Caribbean and African interest in *The Tempest* as a succession of essayists, novelists, poets, and dramatists sought to integrate the play into the cultural forces pitted against colonialism. During those four years, *The Tempest* was appropriated among the Caribbeans by Césaire, Fernández Retamar (twice), Lamming (in a novelistic reworking of some of the ideas first formulated in *The Pleasures of Exile*), and the Barbadian poet Edward Brathwaite. In Africa, the play was taken up during the same period by John Pepper Clark in Nigeria, Ngugi wa Thiong'o in Kenya, and David Wallace in Zambia.[28] Among these, Brathwaite and Fernández Retamar followed Lamming's lead, finding a topical, regional urgency for the play through articulating the Cuban revolution to Caliban's revolt. Brathwaite's poem, 'Caliban,' salutes the Cuban revolution against a backdrop of lamentation over the wrecked state of the Caribbean. The body of the poem, with its clipped calypso phrasing, knits together allusions to Caliban's song, ''Ban, 'Ban, Ca-Caliban,' Ferdinand's speech, 'Where should this music be?' and Ariel's response, 'Full fadom five.' But it is Caliban the slave, not the royal Alonso, who suffers a sea-change, falling 'through the water's / cries / down / down / down / where the music hides / him / down / down / down / where the si- / lence lies.' And he is revived not by Ariel's ethereal strains and, behind them, Prospero's white magic, but by the earthy music of the carnival and the intercession of black gods.[29]

But it was Fernández Retamar, a prominent figure in the cultural renovation of postrevolutionary Cuba, whose interest in the play was most specifically sparked by that nation's experience of decolonization. He first brought *The Tempest* glancingly to bear on the circumstances of his region in 'Cuba Hasta Fidel' (1969); two years later he elaborated more fully on this correspondence. The second essay, 'Caliban: Notes Towards a Discussion of Culture in Our America,' at once passionately chronicles the accumulative symbolic significance of Caliban and commemorates those whose deeds and utterances bodied forth the author's conception of the Calibanesque. This sixty-five-page exhortative history draws together many of the issues deliberated by earlier writers:

> Our symbol then is not Ariel . . . but rather Caliban. This is something that we, the *mestizo* inhabitants of these same isles where Caliban lived, see with particular clarity: Prospero invaded the islands, killed our ancestors,

> enslaved Caliban, and taught him his language to make himself understood. What else can Caliban do but use that same language – today he has no other – to curse him, to wish that the 'red plague' would fall on him? I know no other metaphor more expressive of our cultural situation, of our reality. ['C,' p. 24]

Fernández Retamar proceeds to list thirty-five exemplary Calibans, among them Louverture, Castro, Césaire, and Fanon. And just as Lamming had singled out Louverture for special treatment, here José Martí, the late nineteenth-century Cuban intellectual and political activist who died in the struggle for Cuban independence, is commended at length for his fidelity to the spirit of Caliban.[30]

Fernández Retamar, as flagrantly as Lamming, makes it apparent how little interest he has in affecting any 'scholarly distance' from *The Tempest*. Far from striving to efface his personality, affiliations, and the circumstances of his reading of *The Tempest*, he steeps his essay in occasion and function and speaks consistently in the first-person plural, a voice that inflects his words with a sense of collective autobiography. His interest is in the advantage to be derived from the play by a community who, from a European perspective, could possess at best an ancillary understanding of Shakespeare and, at worst, would be likely perpetrators of barbarous error.[31] Yet that very exclusion conferred on them a coherent identity: 'For it is the coloniser who brings us together, who reveals the profound similarities existing above and beyond our secondary differences' ('C,' p. 14). Oppositional appropriations of *The Tempest* could be enabling because 'to assume our condition as Caliban implies rethinking our history from the *other* side, from the viewpoint of the *other* protagonist' ('C,' p. 28). Put differently, having the nerve to push the play against the Western critical grain, marginalized Caribbeans were relieved of the struggle, unwinnable in Western terms, to gain admission to the *right* side. Their brazen unorthodoxy thus became instrumental in redefining the *wrong* as the *other* side, in opening up a space for themselves where their own cultural values need no longer be derided as savage and deformed.

NOTES

1. George Lamming, *The Pleasures of Exile* (New York, 1984), p. 27; all further references to this work, abbreviated PE, will be included in the text.
2. See Pierre Bourdieu and Jean-Claude Passeron, *La Reproduction: Eléments pour une théorie du système d'enseignement* (Paris, 1970), and Bourdieu, *La Distinction: Critique sociale du jugement* (Paris, 1979); Barbara Herrnstein Smith, 'Contingencies of Value,' *Critical Inquiry* 10 (Sept. 1983): 1–35; Tony Bennett, *Formalism and Marxism* (London, 1979), '*Formalism and Marxism* Revisited,' *Southern Review* 16 (1982): 3–21, and 'Really Useless "Knowledge": A Political Critique of Aesthetics,' *Thesis 11* 12 (1985): 28–52.
3. Frantz Fanon, *The Wretched of the Earth*, trans. Constance Farrington (New York, 1968), p. 43.
4. Jean-Paul Sartre, preface, ibid., p. 9.
5. Ibid., p. 16.
6. Shakespeare's debt to the Bermuda pamphlets and other Elizabethan accounts of the

New World has been extensively analyzed, often in relation to the evolution of British colonial discourse in the seventeenth century. See especially Frank Kermode, introduction to *The Tempest* (New York, 1954), pp. xxv–xxxiv; Stephen J. Greenblatt, 'Learning to Curse: Aspects of Linguistic Colonialism in the Sixteenth Century,' in *First Images of America: The Impact of the New World on the Old*, ed. Fredi Chiappelli, 2 vols. (Berkeley and Los Angeles, 1976), 2:561–80; Leslie A. Fiedler, 'The New World Savage as Stranger: Or, "'Tis new to thee,"' *The Stranger in Shakespeare* (New York, 1972), pp. 199–253; Peter Hulme, 'Hurricanes in the Caribbees: The Constitution of the Discourse of English Colonialism,' in *1642: Literature and Power in the Seventeenth Century: Proceedings of the Essex Conference on the Sociology of Literature, July 1980*, ed. Francis Barker et al. (Colchester, 1981), pp. 55–83; Barker and Hulme, 'Nymphs and Reapers Heavily Vanish: The Discursive Con-texts of *The Tempest*,' in *Alternative Shakespeares*, ed. John Drakakis (London, 1985), pp. 191–205; and Paul Brown, '"This thing of darkness I acknowledge mine". *The Tempest* and the Discourse of Colonialism,' in *Political Shakespeare: New Essays in Cultural Materialism*, ed. Jonathan Dollimore and Alan Sinfield (Ithaca, N.Y., 1985), pp. 48–71.

7. Roberto Fernández Retamar, 'Caliban: Notes Toward a Discussion of Culture in Our America,' trans. Lynn Garafola, David Arthur McMurray, and Robert Marquez, *Massachusetts Review* 15 (Winter/Spring 1974): 27; all further references to this work, abbreviated 'C,' will be included in the text.
8. Homi Bhabha, 'Of Mimicry and Man: The Ambivalence of Colonial Discourse,' *October*, 28 (Spring 1984): 128.
9. Ian Munro and Reinhard Sander, eds., *Kas-Kas: Interviews with Three Caribbean Writers in Texas: George Lamming, C. L. R. James, Wilson Harris* (Austin, Tex., 1972), p. 6. For kindred treatments of the way British-centered curricula generated mimicry and cultural dependency in the former British West Indies, see Austin Clarke, *Growing Up Stupid Under the Union Jack: A Memoir* (Toronto, 1980), and Chris Searle, *The Forsaken Lover: White Words and Black People* (London, 1972).
10. Trevor R. Griffiths, '"This Island's Mine": Caliban and Colonialism,' *Yearbook of English Studies* 13 (1983): 159–80. Although Griffiths does not tackle the question of value directly, his essay complements mine insofar as it focuses on how *The Tempest* was appropriated not in the colonies but in Britain. Griffiths' analysis treats both the heyday of imperialism and the subsequent retreat from empire. For discussion of how *The Tempest* was taken up from the seventeenth century onward, see Ruby Cohn, *Modern Shakespeare Offshoots* (Princeton, N.J., 1976), pp. 267–309. Cohn's account of the two adaptations of the play by the nineteenth-century French historian and philosopher Ernest Renan is especially comprehensive.
11. Daniel Wilson, *Caliban: The Missing Link* (London, 1873), p. 79.
12. W. T. Stead, 'First Impressions of the Theatre,' *Review of Reviews* 30 (Oct. 1904); quoted in Griffiths, '"This Island's Mine,"' p. 170.
13. [Dominique] O. Mannoni, *Prospero and Caliban: The Psychology of Colonization*, trans. Pamela Powesland (New York, 1964), p. 34; all further references to this work, abbreviated PC, will be included in the text. The centrality of *The Tempest* to Mannoni's theory was given added emphasis by the extended title of the English translation.
14. William Shakespeare, *The Tempest*, act 1, sc. 2, II. 332–44; all further references to the play will be included in the text.
15. See Fanon, *Peau noire, masques blancs* (Paris, 1952), and Aimé Césaire, *Discours sur le colonialisme*, 3d ed. (Paris, 1955). See also the section, 'Caliban on the Couch,' in O. Onoge, 'Revolutionary Imperatives in African Sociology,' in *African Social Studies: A Radical Reader*, ed. Peter C. W. Gutkind and Peter Waterman (New York, 1977), pp. 32–45.
16. Philip Mason, *Prospero's Magic: Some Thoughts on Class and Race* (London,

1962), p. 80; all further references to this work, abbreviated *PM*, will be included in the text.

17. Though it is underscored by a different politics, Sartre makes a related remark in his preface to *The Wretched of the Earth*: 'We in Europe too are being decolonized: that is to say that the settler which is in every one of us is being savagely rooted out' (Sartre, preface, p. 8).
18. For a thematic rather than a historical survey of the figure of Caliban in Third World writing, see Charlotte H. Bruner, 'The Meaning of Caliban in Black Literature Today,' *Comparative Literature Studies* 13 (Sept. 1976): 240–53.
19. See C. L. R. James, *The Black Jacobins: Toussaint Louverture and the San Domingo Revolution* (New York, 1963).
20. Given the antipathy between Trinidadian-born V. S. Naipaul and the more radical Lamming, and given Lamming's identification with Caliban, it is probable that Naipaul had the Barbadian in mind in his fictional *A Flag on the Island*, where the narrator parodies Caribbean celebrations of Caliban by citing a local autobiography, *I Hate You: One Man's Search for Identity*, which opens: '"I am a man without identity. Hate has consumed my identity. My personality has been distorted by hate. My hymns have not been hymns of praise, but of hate. How terrible to be Caliban, you say. But I say, how tremendous. Tremendousness is therefore my unlikely subject"' (Naipaul, *A Flag on the Island* [London, 1967], p. 154).
21. Cf. the remark by Chris Searle, another writer who reads Caribbean culture through the Prospero – Caliban dichotomy: 'The ex-master's language . . . is still the currency of communication which buys out the identity of the child as soon as he begins to acquire it' (Searle, *The Forsaken Lover*, p. 29).
22. See Lamming, *The Pleasures of Exile*, and Césaire, *Toussaint Louverture: la révolution française et le probléme colonial* (Paris, 1961).
23. Janheinz Jahn, *Neo-African Literature: A History of Black Writing*, trans. Oliver Coburn and Ursula Lehrburger (New York, 1969), p. 242.
24. Césaire, quoted in S. Belhassen, 'Aimé Césaire's *A Tempest*,' in *Radical Perspectives in the Arts*, ed. Lee Baxandall (Harmondsworth, 1972), p. 176.
25. For the fullest discussion concerning Césaire's Africanizing of Shakespeare, see Thomas A. Hale, 'Aimé Césaire: His Literary and Political Writings with a Bio-bibliography' (Ph.D. diss., University of Rochester, 1974), and 'Sur *Une tempête* d'Aimé Césaire,' *Etudes Littéraires* 6 (1973) 21–34.
26. Césaire, *Une Tempête: D'aprés 'la Tempête' de Shakespeare – Adaptation pour un théâtre négre* (Paris, 1969), p. 24.
27. Ibid., p. 92.
28. See Fernández Retamar, 'Cuba Hasta Fidel,' *Bohemia* 61 (19 September 1969): 84–97, and 'Caliban: Notes Toward a Discussion of Culture in Our America'; Lamming, *Water with Berries* (London, 1971); Edward Brathwaite, *Islands* (London, 1969), pp. 34–38; John Pepper Clark, 'The Legacy of Caliban,' *Black Orpheus* 2 (Feb. 1968): 16–39; Ngugi Wa Thiong'o, 'Towards a National Culture,' *Homecoming: Essays on African and Caribbean Literature, Culture, and Politics* (Westport, Conn., 1983); David Wallace, *Do You Love Me Master?* (Lusaka, 1977). In Lamming's allegorical novel, Caliban resurfaces in the form of three West Indian artists who reside in London and collectively play out the dilemmas of colonizer – colonized entanglements during the era of decolonization. Clark's reflections turn on the relation between 'the colonial flag and a cosmopolitan language.' Clark both follows and reroutes Lamming's insights on this subject as, unlike his Caribbean predecessor, he approaches English from an African perspective, that is, as a second language. Ngugi's essay, published in 1972, was originally delivered at a conference in 1969. In it he assails Prospero for first dismantling Caliban's heritage and then denying that such a culture ever existed. Ngugi proceeds to sketch strategies for reaffirming the value of that damaged inheritance, notably by decolonizing language and education. Wallace's play was first performed in 1971. Regional

nuances aside, *Do You Love Me Master?* is much of a piece with trends already discussed: aided by rioting prisoners, Caliban, a cursing Zambian 'houseboy,' drives the 'bossman,' Prospero, out of the country. In the final scene Prospero's stick, more truncheon than wand, is broken, and the crowd encircles the master shouting 'Out, out!' and waves banners proclaiming freedom. The play incorporates songs in three African languages.

29. Brathwaite, 'Caliban,' *Islands*, p. 36.
30. The strong historical presence of Martí in the essay is redoubled by Fernández Retamar's invocation, from the same era, of José Enrique Rodó's *Ariel*. Published in 1900, this Uruguayan novel was written in direct response to the 1898 American intervention in Cuba. Rodó identifies Latin America with Ariel, not Caliban.
31. The European suspicion that colonized people would treat Shakespeare with, to invoke Fernández Retamar's phrase, 'presumed barbarism' was starkly evident when the Parisian critics dismissed Césaire's *Une Tempête* as a 'betrayal' of the bard. See Hale, 'Sur *Une Tempête* d'Aimé Césaire,' p. 21.

1.3

FROM 'DISCOURSE AND THE INDIVIDUAL: THE CASE OF COLONIALISM IN *THE TEMPEST*'

Meredith Anne Skura

For many years idealist readings of *The Tempest* presented Prospero as an exemplar of timeless human values. They emphasized the way in which his hard-earned 'magical' powers enable him to re-educate the shipwrecked Italians, to heal their civil war—and, even more important, to triumph over his own vengefulness by forgiving his enemies; they emphasized the way he achieves, if not a wholly 'brave,' at least a harmoniously reconciled new world. Within the last few years, however, numbers of critics have offered remarkably similar critiques of this reading. There is an essay on *The Tempest* in each of three recent anthologies of alternative, political, and reproduced Shakespeare criticism, and another in the volume on estranging Renaissance criticism; *The Tempest* was a focus for the 1988 SAA session on 'Shakespeare and Colonialism' and was one of the masthead plays in the Folger Institute's 1988 seminar on new directions in Shakespeare studies.[1] Together, the revisionists call for a move to counteract some 'deeply ahistorical readings' of *The Tempest*,[2] a play that is now seen to be not simply an allegory about 'timeless'[3] or universal experience but rather a cultural phenomenon that has its origin in and effect on 'historical' events, specifically in English colonialism. 'New historicist' criticism in general, of which much recent work on *The Tempest* is a part, has itself begun to come under scrutiny, but the numerous historical reinterpretations of *The Tempest* deserve closer attention in their own right,[4] and they will be the subject of the rest of this essay.

Shakespeare Quarterly, 40:1, Spring 1989, pp. 42–69. Extract: pp. 42–57.

In assessing the 'new' historicist version of the play, it is important to realize that here, even more than in other new historical criticism, an historical emphasis in itself is not new. Since the early nineteenth century *The Tempest* has been seen in the historical context of the New World, and Frank Kermode, citing the early scholars, argued in the fifties that reports of a particular episode in British efforts to colonize North America had precipitated the play's major themes.[5] In 1609 nine ships had left England to settle the colony in Jamestown, Virginia, and the *Sea Venture*, carrying all of the colonial officers, had disappeared. But its passengers reappeared in Virginia one year later, miraculously saved; they had wrecked off the Bermudas, until then believed demonically dangerous but now found to be providentially mild and fruitful. These events, much in the news in the year just preceding *The Tempest*, have long been seen as a relevant context for the play by all but a very few critics.[6] These earlier historical interpretations generally placed the play and its immediate source in the context of voyaging discourse in general, which stressed the romance and exoticism of discoveries in the Old as well as the New World. Even the 'factual' reports in this discourse, as Charles Frey notes, were themselves colored by the romance of the situation, for better and for worse; and the traditional view was that *The Tempest*'s stylized allegory abstracts the romance core of all voyagers' experience.[7]

Nor had traditional criticism entirely ignored either Prospero's flaws[8] or their relation to the dark side of Europe's confrontation with the Other. Kermode had identified Caliban as the 'core' or 'ground' of the play, insofar as confrontation with this strange representative of 'uncivilized' man prompts the play's reexamination of 'civilized' human nature. Harry Levin, Leslie Fiedler, Leo Marx, and others had suggested that in trying to understand the New World representatives of 'uncivilized' human nature, Prospero, like other Europeans, had imposed Old (and New) World stereotypes of innocence and monstrosity on the Native Americans, distorting perception with hope and fear.[9] Fiedler's landmark book had indeed placed *The Tempest* suggestively in the context of a series of plays about the Other (or, as he called it in 1972, the 'Stranger') in Shakespeare, showing Caliban's resemblance to the demonized women, Moors, and Jews in the canon. O. Mannoni had added that, in this process, Prospero displayed the psychology of colonials who projected their disowned traits onto New World natives.[10]

Why, then, so many recent articles? In part they are simply shifting the emphasis. Revisionists claim that the New World material is not just present but is right at the center of the play, and that it demands far more attention than critics have been willing to grant it. They argue that the civil war in Milan that had ousted Prospero should be recognized as merely an episode in a minor dispute between Italian dynasties, of little import compared to the transatlantic action;[11] they show how the love story can be seen as a political maneuver by Prospero to ensure his return to power in Milan,[12] and how even Caliban's attempted rape of Miranda can be seen as an expression not merely of sexual but also of territorial lust, understandable in its context.[13]

These recent critics are not simply repeating the older ones, however; they are making important distinctions. First and most explicitly, they are not calling attention to history in general but rather to one aspect of history: to power relations and to the ideology in which power relations are encoded.[14] The revisionists look not at the New World material in the play but to the play's effect on power relations in the New World. What matters is not just the particular Bermuda pamphlets actually echoed in the play but rather the whole 'ensemble of fictional and lived practices' known as 'English colonialism,' which, it is now being claimed, provides the 'dominant discursive con-texts'[15] for the play. (Though the term 'colonialism' may allude to the entire spectrum of New World activity, in these articles it most often refers specifically to the use of power, to the Europeans' exploitative and self-justifying treatment of the New World and its inhabitants—and I shall use it in that sense.) If Caliban is the center of the play, it is not because of his role in the play's self-contained structure, and not even because of what he reveals about man's timeless tendency to demonize 'strangers,' but because Europeans were at that time exploiting the real Calibans of the world, and *The Tempest* was part of the process. It is no longer enough to suggest that Europeans were trying to make sense of the Indian; rather, the emphasis is now on the way Europeans subdued the Indian to 'make sense/order/money—not of him, so much as out of him.'[16] Revisionists argue that when the English talked about these New World inhabitants, they did not just innocently apply stereotypes or project their own fears: they did so to a particular effect, whether wittingly or unwittingly. The various distortions were discursive strategies that served the political purpose of making the New World fit into a schema justifying colonialism.[17] Revisionists therefore emphasize the discursive strategies that the play shares with all colonial discourse, and the ways in which *The Tempest* itself not only displays prejudice but fosters and even 'enacts' colonialism by mystifying or justifying Prospero's power over Caliban.[18] The new point is that *The Tempest* is a political act.

Second, this shift in our attitude toward the object of interpretation entails a less explicit but extremely important move away from the psychological interpretation that had previously seemed appropriate for the play (even to its detractors) largely because of its central figure who, so like Shakespeare, runs the show. Where earlier criticism of Prospero talked about his 'prejudice,' the more recent revisionists talk about 'power' and 'euphemisation.' Thus, a critic writing in 1980 argued that *The Tempest*'s allegorical and Neoplatonic overlay masks some of the most damaging prejudices of Western civilization'[19] but by 1987 the formulation had changed: '*The Tempest* is ... fully implicated in the process of "euphemisation", the effacement of power,' in 'operations [that] encode struggle and contradiction even as they, or *because* they, strive to insist on the legitimacy of colonialist narrative.'[20]

Psychological criticism of the play is seen as distracting at best; one recent critic, for example, opens his argument by claiming that we need to conceive *The*

Tempest in an historical context that is not 'hamstrung by specious speculations concerning "Shakespeare's mind"'.[21] Even in less polemical examples the 'political unconscious' often replaces, rather than supplements, any other unconscious; attention to culture and politics is associated with an implicit questioning of individuality and of subjective experience. Such a stance extends beyond an objection to wholesale projections of twentieth-century assumptions onto sixteenth-century subjects, or to psychological interpretations that totally ignore the cultural context in which psyches exist. As Fredric Jameson argued in a work that lies behind many of these specific studies, it derives from the desire to transcend personal psychology altogether, because Freud's psychology remains 'locked into the category of the individual subject.'[22] The emphasis now is on psychology as a product of culture, itself a political structure; the very concept of a psyche is seen to be a product of the cultural nexus evolved during the Renaissance, and indeed, psychoanalysis itself, rather than being a way of understanding the Renaissance psyche, is a marginal and belated creation of this same nexus.[23] Thus the revisionists, with Jameson, may look for a 'political unconscious' and make use of Freud's insights into the 'logic of dreams'[24]—the concepts of displacement, condensation, the management of desire[25]—but they do not accept Freud's assumptions about the mind—or the subject—creating that logic.[26] The agent who displaces or manages is not the individual but the 'collective or associative' mind; at times it seems to be the text itself, seen as a 'libidinal apparatus' or 'desiring machine'[27] independent of any individual creator.

The revisionist impulse has been one of the most salutary in recent years in correcting New Critical 'blindness' to history and ideology. In particular it has revealed the ways in which the play has been 'reproduced' and drafted into the service of colonialist politics from the nineteenth century through G. Wilson Knight's twentieth-century celebration of Prospero as representative of England's 'colonizing, especially her will to raise savage peoples from superstition and blood-sacrifice, taboos and witchcraft and the attendant fears and slaveries, to a more enlightened existence.'[28] But here, as critics have been suggesting about new historicism in general, it is now in danger of fostering blindness of its own. Granted that something was wrong with a commentary that focused on *The Tempest* as a self-contained project of a self-contained individual and that ignored the political situation in 1611. But something seems wrong now also, something more than the rhetorical excesses characteristic of any innovative critical movement. The recent criticism not only flattens the text into the mold of colonialist discourse and eliminates what is characteristically 'Shakespearean' in order to foreground what is 'colonialist,' but it is also—paradoxically—in danger of taking the play further from the particular historical situation in England in 1611 even as it brings it closer to what we mean by 'colonialism' today.

It is difficult to extrapolate back from G. Wilson Knight's colonialist discourse to seventeenth-century colonialist discourse without knowing more about the particulars of that earlier discourse. What is missing from the recent articles is the connection between the new insights about cultural phenomena like 'power' and 'fields of discourse' and the traditional insights about the text, its immediate sources, its individual author—and his individual psychology. There is little sense of how discourse is related to the individual who was creating, even as he was participating in, that discourse. The following discussion will suggest how such a relation might be conceived. Sections *I* and *II* briefly elaborate on *The Tempest*'s versions of problems raised by new historicist treatment of the text and its relation to the historical context; sections *III* and *IV* go on to suggest that the recognition of the individuality of the play, and of Shakespeare, does not counter but rather enriches the understanding of that context. Perhaps by testing individual cases, we can avoid the circularity of a definition that assumes that 'colonialism' was present in a given group of texts, and so 'discovers' it there.

I

How do we know that *The Tempest* 'enacts' colonialism rather than merely alluding to the New World? How do we know that Caliban is part of the 'discourse of colonialism'? To ask such a question may seem perversely naive, but the play is notoriously slippery. There have been, for example, any number of interpretations of Caliban,[29] including not only contemporary post-colonial versions in which Caliban is a Virginian Indian but also others in which Caliban is played as a black slave or as 'missing link' (in a costume 'half monkey, half coco-nut'[30]), with the interpretation drawing on the issues that were being debated at the time—on the discursive contexts that were culturally operative—and articulated according to 'changing Anglo-American attitudes toward primitive man.'[31] Most recently one teacher has suggested that *The Tempest* is a good play to teach in junior colleges because students can identify with Caliban.

Interpretation is made even more problematic here because, despite the claims about the play's intervention in English colonialism,[32] we have no *external* evidence that seventeenth-century audiences thought the play referred to the New World. In an age when real voyages were read allegorically, the status of allegorical voyages like Prospero's can be doubly ambiguous, especially in a play like *The Tempest*, which provides an encyclopedic context for Prospero's experience, presenting it in terms of an extraordinary range of classical, biblical, and romantic exiles, discoveries, and confrontations.[33] Evidence for the play's original reception is of course extraordinarily difficult to find, but in the two nearly contemporary responses to Caliban that we do know about, the evidence for a colonialist response is at best ambiguous. In *Bartholomew Fair* (1614) Jonson refers scornfully to a 'servant-monster,' and the Folio identifies Caliban as a 'salvage and deformed slave'[34] in the cast list. Both 'monster' and 'salvage' are firmly rooted in the discourse of Old World wild men, though the latter was of course also applied to the New World natives. In other words, these two seventeenth-century responses tend to invoke the universal and not the particular implications of Caliban's condition. A recent study of the play's history suggests that 'if Shakespeare, however obliquely, meant Caliban to personify America's natives, his intention apparently miscarried almost completely.'[35]

Despite this lack of contemporary testimony, the obvious reason for our feeling that the play 'is' colonialist—more so than *The Winter's Tale* or *Henry VIII*, for example, which were written at roughly the same time—is, of course, the literal resemblance between its plot and certain events and attitudes in English colonial history: Europeans arrive in the New World and assume they can appropriate what properly belongs to the New World Other, who is then 'erased.' The similarities are clear and compelling—more so than in many cases of new historical readings; the problem, however, is that while there are also many literal differences between *The Tempest* and colonialist fictions and practice, the similarities are taken to be so compelling that the differences are ignored. Thus Caliban is taken to 'be' a Native American despite the fact that a multitude of details differentiate Caliban from the Indian as he appeared in the travelers' reports from the New World.[36] Yet it does seem significant that, despite his closeness to nature, his naiveté, his devil worship, his susceptibility to European liquor, and, above all, his 'treachery'—characteristics associated in writings of the time with the Indians – he nonetheless lacks almost all of the defining external traits in the many reports from the New World—no superhuman physique, no nakedness or animal skin (indeed, an English 'gaberdine' instead), no decorative feathers,[37] no arrows, no pipe, no tobacco, no body paint, and—as Shakespeare takes pains to emphasize—no love of trinkets and trash. No one could mistake him for the stereotyped 'Indian with a great tool,' mentioned in passing in *Henry VIII*. Caliban in fact is more like the devils Strachey expected to find on the Bermuda island (but didn't) than like the Indians whom adventurers did find in Virginia, though he is not wholly a monster from the explorers' wild tales either.[38]

In other ways, too, it is assumed that the similarities matter but the differences do not: thus Prospero's magic occupies 'the space *really inhabited in colonial history* by gunpowder'[39] (emphasis mine); or, when Prospero has Caliban pinched by the spirits, he shows a 'similar sadism' to that of the Haitian masters who 'roasted slaves or buried them alive';[40] or, when Prospero and Ariel hunt Caliban with spirit dogs, they are equated to the Spaniards who hunted Native Americans with dogs.[41] So long as there is a core of resemblance, the differences are irrelevant. The differences, in fact, are themselves taken to be evidence of the colonialist ideology at work, rationalizing and euphemizing power—or else inadvertent slips. Thus the case for colonialism becomes stronger insofar as Prospero *is* good and insofar as Caliban *is* in some ways bad—he did try to rape Miranda—or is *himself* now caught trying to falsify the past by occluding the rape and presenting himself as an innocent victim of Prospero's tyranny. Prospero's goodness and Caliban's badness are called rationalizations, justifications for Prospero's tyranny. Nor does it matter that the play seems *anti*-colonialist to the degree that it qualifies Prospero's scorn by showing Caliban's virtues, or that Prospero seems to achieve some kind of transcendence over his own colonialism when at the end of the play he says, 'This thing of darkness I acknowledge mine.'[42] Prospero's acknowledgement of Caliban is considered a mistake, a moment of inadvertent sympathy or truth, too brief to counter Prospero's underlying colonialism: in spite of the deceptively resonant poetry of his acknowledgement, Prospero actually does nothing to live up to the meaning which that poetry suggests;[43] it has even been argued that Prospero, in calling Caliban 'mine,' is simply claiming possession of him: 'It is as though, after a public disturbance, a slaveowner said, "Those two men are yours; this darkie's mine."'[44]

Nonetheless, in addition to these differences that have been seen as rationalizations, there are many other differences as well that collectively raise questions about what counts as 'colonialist discourse' and about what, if anything, might count as a relevant 'difference.' Thus, for example, any attempt to cast Prospero and Caliban as actors in the typical colonial narrative (in which a European exploits a previously free—indeed a reigning—native of an unspoiled world) is complicated by two other characters, Sycorax and Ariel. Sycorax, Caliban's mother, through whom he claims possession of the island, was not only a witch and a criminal, but she came from the Old World herself, or at least from eastern-hemisphere Argier.[45] She is a reminder that Caliban is only half-native, that his claim to the island is less like the claim of the Native American than the claim of the second generation Spaniard in the New World.[46] Moreover, Caliban was not alone when Prospero arrived. Ariel either came to the island with Sycorax or was already living on the island – its true reigning lord[47]—when Sycorax arrived and promptly enslaved him, thus herself becoming the first colonialist, the one who established the habits of dominance and erasure before Prospero ever set foot on the island. Nearly all revisionists note some of these differences before disregarding them, though they are not agreed on their significance—on whether they are 'symptoms' of ideological conflict in the discourse, for example, or whether Shakespeare's 'insights exceeded his sympathies.'[48] But however they are explained, the differences *are* discarded. For the critic interested only in counteracting earlier blindness to potentially racist and ideological elements in the play, such ignoring of differences is understandable; for his or her purposes, it *is* enough to point out that *The Tempest* has a 'political unconscious' and is connected in *some* way to colonialist discourse without specifying further.

But if the object is, rather, to understand colonialism, instead of simply identifying it or condemning it, it is important to specify, to notice how the colonial elements are rationalized or integrated into the play's vision of the world. Otherwise, extracting the play's political unconscious leads to the same problems Freud faced at the beginning of his career when he treated the personal unconscious as an independent entity that should be almost surgically extracted from conscious discourse by hypnotizing away the 'defenses.' But, as is well known, Freud found that the conscious 'defenses' were as essential—and problematic—as the supposedly prior unconscious 'wish,' and that they served purposes other than containment.[49] Indeed, in most psychoanalytic practice since Freud, the unconscious—or, rather, unconscious mentation—is assumed to exist in texts rather than existing as a reified 'id,' and interpretation must always return to the text.

As in the case of the personal unconscious, the political unconscious exists only in texts, whose 'defenses' or rationalizations must be taken into account. Otherwise interpretation not only destroys the text—here *The Tempest*—as a unique work of art and flattens it into one more example of the master plot—or master ploy—in colonialist discourse; it also destroys the evidence of the play as a unique cultural artifact, a unique voice in that discourse. Colonialist discourse was varied enough to escape any simple formulation, even in a group of texts with apparent thematic links. It ranged from the lived Spanish colonialist practice of hunting New World natives with dogs to Bartholomew Las Casas's 'factual' account lamenting and exposing the viciousness of that hunt,[50] to Shakespeare's possible allusion to it in *The Tempest*, when Prospero and Ariel set spirit dogs on Caliban, to a still earlier Shakespearean allusion—or possible allusion—in the otherwise non-colonialist *A Midsummer Night's Dream*, when Puck (who has come from India himself) chases Greek rude mechanicals with illusory animals in a scene evoking an entirely English conflict. The same 'colonialist' hunt informs radically different fictions and practices, some of which enact colonialism, some of which subvert it, and some of which require other categories entirely to characterize its effect.

It is not easy to categorize the several links between *The Tempest* and colonialist discourse. Take the deceptively simple example of Caliban's name. Revisionists rightly emphasize the implications of the cannibal stereotype as automatic mark of Other in Western ethnocentric colonialist discourse,[51] and, since Shakespeare's name for 'Caliban' is widely accepted as an anagram of 'cannibal,' many read the play as if he *were* a cannibal, with all that the term implies. But an anagram is not a cannibal, and Shakespeare's use of the stereotype is hardly automatic.[52] Caliban is no cannibal—he barely touches meat, confining himself more delicately to roots, berries, and an occasional fish; indeed, his symbiotic harmony with the island's natural food resources is one of his most attractive traits. His name seems more like a mockery of stereotypes than a mark of monstrosity, and in our haste to confirm the link between 'cannibal' and 'Indian' outside the text, we lose track of the way in which Caliban severs the link *within* the text.[53] While no one would deny *some* relation between Caliban and the New World natives to whom such terms as 'cannibal' were applied, what that relation is remains unclear.

To enumerate differences between *The Tempest* and 'colonialist discourse' is not to reduce discussion of the play to a counting contest, pitting similarities against differences. Rather, it is to suggest that inherent in any analysis of the play as colonialist discourse is a particular assumption about the relation between text and discourse – between one man's fiction and a collective fiction – or, perhaps, between one man's fiction and what we take for 'reality.' This relation matters not only to New Critics trying to isolate texts from contexts but to new historicists (or just plain historicists) trying to put them back together. The relation is also vital to lived practices like censorship and inquisitions – and there are differences of opinion about what counts in these cases. Such differences need to be acknowledged and examined, and the method for reading them needs to be made more explicit before the implications of *The Tempest* as colonialist discourse can be fully understood.

II

Similar problems beset the definition of the 'discourse' itself, the means of identifying the fictional—and the 'lived'—practices constituting 'English colonialism' in 1611. Given the impact of English colonialism over the last 350 years, it may again seem perversely naive to ask what colonialist discourse was like in 1611, as opposed to colonialism in 1911 or even in 1625, the year when Samuel Purchas asked, alluding to the 'treachery' of the Virginian Indians, 'Can a Leopard change his spots? Can a Savage remayning a Savage be civill?' Purchas added this comment when he published the 1610 document that Shakespeare had used as his source for *The Tempest*, and Purchas has been cited as an example of 'colonialist discourse.'[54] Purchas does indeed display the particular combination of exploitative motives and self-justifying rhetoric—the 'effacement of power'[55]—that revisionists identify as colonialist and which they find in *The Tempest*. But, one might reasonably ask, was the discursive context in 1611, when Shakespeare was writing, the same as it would be fourteen years later, when Purchas added his marginal comment?[56]

There seems, rather, to have been in 1611 a variety of what we might call 'New World discourses' with multiple points of view, motives, and effects, among which such comments as Purchas's are not as common as the revisionist emphasis implies. These are 'colonialist' only in the most general sense in which all ethnocentric cultures are always 'colonialist': narcissistically pursuing their own ends, oblivious to the desires, needs, and even the existence of the Other. That is, if this New World discourse is colonialist, it is so primarily in that it *ignores* Indians, betraying its Eurocentric assumptions about the irrelevance of any people other than white, male, upper-class Europeans, preferably from England. It thus expresses not an historically specific but a *timeless* and universal attitude toward the 'stranger,' which Fiedler described in so many of Shakespeare's plays. We might see this discourse as a precondition[57] for colonialism proper, which was to follow with the literal rather than the figurative colonizing of New World natives. But to assume that colonialism was already encoded in the anomalous situation in 1611 is to undermine the revisionist effort to understand the historical specificity of the moment when Shakespeare wrote *The Tempest*.

It is not easy to characterize the situation in 1611. On the one hand, Spain had long been engaged in the sort of 'colonialist discourse' that revisionists find in *The Tempest*; and even in England at the time there were examples of colonialist discourse (in the rhetoric, if not yet often in the lived practices) produced by those directly involved in the colonialist project and expecting to profit from it. The official advertisements in the first rush of enthusiasm about Virginia, as well as the stream of defenses when the Virginia project began to fail, often have a euphemistic ring and often do suggest a fundamental greed and implicit racism beneath claims to be securing the earthly and spiritual well-being of the Virginia natives.[58] ('[We] doe buy of them the pearles of earth, and sell to them the pearles of heauen.'[59]) These documents efface not only power but most practical problems as well, and they were supplemented by sermons romanticizing hardships as divine tribulation.[60] Scattered throughout this discourse are righteous defenses of taking land from the Indians, much in the spirit—and tone—of Rabbi Zeal-of-the-Land Busy defending his need to eat pig. (This was also the tone familiar from the anti-theatrical critics—and, indeed, occasional colonialist sermons included snipes at the 'Plaiers,' along with the Devil and the papists, as particular enemies of the Virginia venture.[61])

On the other hand, even in these documents not only is the emphasis elsewhere but often there are important contradictory movements. For example, 'A True Declaration,' the official record of the Bermuda wreck, refers once to the Indians as 'humane beasts' and devotes one paragraph of its twenty-four pages to the 'greedy Vulture' Powhattan and his ambush. It notes elsewhere, however, that some of the English settlers themselves had 'created the *Indians* our implacable enemies by some violence they had offered,' and it actually spends far more time attacking the lazy 'scum of men' among the settlers, who had undermined the colony from within, than demonizing the less relevant Indians.[62]

And on the whole, the exploitative and self-justifying rhetoric is only one element in a complex New World discourse. For much of the time, in fact, the main conflict in the New World was not between whites and Native Americans but between Spain and England. Voyages like Drake's (1577–80) were motivated by this international conflict, as well as by the romance of discovery and the lure of treasure—but not by colonizing.[63] Even when Raleigh received the first patent to settle and trade with the New World (1584), necessitating more extended contact with Native Americans, the temporary settlements he started in the 1580s were largely tokens in his play for fame and wealth rather than attempts to take over sizable portions of land from the natives.[64]

Only when the war with Spain was over (1604) and ships were free again did colonization really begin; and then 'America and Virginia were on everyone's lips.'[65] But this New World discourse still reflects little interest in its inhabitants. Other issues are much more widely discussed. For example, what would the New World government be like? Would James try to extend his authoritarianism to America? *Could* he? This was the issue, for example, most energizing

Henry Wriothesley, Shakespeare's Southampton, who led the 'Patriot' faction on the London Virginia Council, pushing for more American independence.[66] (As for James's own 'colonial discourse,' it seems to have been devoted to worries about how it would all affect his relations with Spain,[67] and to requests for flying squirrels and other New World 'toyes.'[68]) Of more immediate interest, perhaps, to the mass of real or armchair adventurers were the reports of New World wealth that at first made Virginia known as a haven for bankrupts and spendthrifts, as well as for wild dreamers—followed by the accounts of starvation, rebellion, and hardship brought back by those who had escaped from the reality of colonial existence. Now the issue became 'Is it worth it?' The official propaganda, optimistic about future profits, was soon countered by a backlash from less optimistic scoffers challenging the value of the entire project, one which sent money, men, and ships to frequent destruction and brought back almost no profit.[69]

Even the settlers actually living with the natives in the New World itself were – for entirely non-altruistic reasons—not yet fully engaged in 'colonialist' discourse as defined by revisionists. In 1611 they had not managed to establish enough power to euphemize; they had little to be defensive about. They were too busy fighting mutiny, disease, and the stupidities of the London Council to have much energy left over for Indians. It is true that no writer ever treated Native Americans as equals—any more than he treated Moors, Jews, Catholics, peasants, women, Irishmen, or even Frenchmen as equals; travellers complacently recorded kidnapping natives to exhibit in England, as if the natives had no rights at all.[70] And it is true that some of their descriptions are distorted by Old World stereotypes of wild men or cannibals—though these descriptions are often confined to earlier *pre*-colonial explorers' reports.[71] Or, far more insidiously, the descriptions were distorted by stereotypes of unfallen innocent noble savages—stereotypes that inevitably led to disillusionment when the settlers had to realize that the Indians, like the land itself, were not going to fulfill their dreams of a golden world made expressly to nurture Englishmen. The 'noble savage' stereotype thus fueled the recurring accusation of Indian treachery, a response to betrayal of settlers' fantasies as well as to any real Indian betrayal,[72] and one to which I will return in discussing *The Tempest*.

But, given the universality of racial prejudice towards New World natives along with all 'Others,' in this early period the movement was to loosen, not to consolidate, the prejudices brought from the Old World. The descriptions of these extended face-to-face encounters with Native Americans were perhaps even more varied than contemporary responses to Moors and Jews, who were usually encountered on the white man's own territory, where exposure could be limited and controlled. The very terms imported from the Old World to name the natives—'savages' or 'naturals'—began to lose their original connotations as the differing descriptions multiplied and even contradicted themselves. The reports range from Harriot's widely republished attempt at scientific, objective reporting (1588), which viewed natives with great respect, to Smith's less reliable adventure stories (1608–31), disputed even in his own time by Purchas. And although these do not by any means live up to our standards for non-colonialist discourse, their typical attitude is a wary, often patronizing, but live-and-let-live curiosity, rather than the exploitative erasure which would later become the mark of colonialist discourse. So long as the conflicts remained minimal, Native Americans were seen as beings like the writers;[73] further, tribes were distinguished from one another, and recognition was granted to their different forms of government, class structure, dress codes, religion, and language.[74] And when conflict did trigger the recurring accusation of 'treachery,' the writers never presented the Indians as laughable Calibans, but rather as capable, indeed formidable, enemies whose skill and intelligence challenged that of the settlers.

Horrors had already been perpetrated by the Spanish in the name of colonialism; not learning from these—or perhaps learning all too well—the English would soon begin perpetrating their own. But that lay in the future. When *The Tempest* was written, what the New World seems to have meant for the majority of Englishmen was a sense of possibility and a set of conflicting fantasies about the wonders to be found there; these were perhaps the preconditions for colonialism—as for much else—but not yet the thing itself.[75]

To place colonialist discourse as precisely as possible within a given moment (like stressing the differences between *The Tempest* and colonialist discourse) is not to reduce the discussion to a numbers game. What is at stake here is not a quibble about chronology but an assumption about what we mean by the 'relevant discursive context,' about how we agree to determine it, and about how we decide to limit it. Here too there are differences of opinion about what counts, and these differences need to be acknowledged, examined, and accounted for.

NOTES

1. Two of the earliest of these critiques were actually written, although not published, by 1960: George Lamming, 'A monster, a child, a slave' (1960) in *The Pleasures of Exile* (London: Allison and Busby, 1984); James Smith, 'The Tempest' (1954) in *Shakespearian and Other Essays*, ed. E. M. Wilson (Cambridge: Cambridge Univ. Press, 1974), pp. 159–261. Two more articles, less politicized, followed in the sixties: Philip Brockbank, '*The Tempest*: Conventions of Art and Empire' in *Later Shakespeare*, eds. J. R. Brown and B. Harris (London: Edward Arnold, 1966), pp. 183–201; and D. G. James, 'The New World' in *The Dream of Prospero* (Oxford: Clarendon Press, 1967), pp. 72–123.

   The recent group, returning to the political perspective of the first two, includes: Stephen Greenblatt, 'Learning to Curse: Aspects of Linguistic Colonialism in the Sixteenth Century' in *First Images of America*, ed. Fredi Chiappelli, 2 vols. (Los Angeles: Univ. of California Press, 1976), Vol. 2, 561–80; Bruce Erlich, 'Shakespeare's Colonial Metaphor: On the Social Function of Theatre in *The Tempest*,' *Science and Society*, 41 (1977), 43–65; Lorie Leininger, 'Cracking the Code of *The Tempest*,' *Bucknell Review*, 25 (1980), 121–31; Peter Hulme, 'Hurricanes in the Caribbees: The Constitution of the Discourse of English Colonialism' in *1642: Literature and Power in the Seventeenth Century*, Proceedings of the Essex conference on the Sociology of Literature, eds. Francis Barker et al.

(Colchester: Univ. of Essex, 1981), pp. 55–83; Paul N. Siegel, 'Historical Ironies in *The Tempest*', *Shakespeare Jahrbuch*, 119 (Weimar: 1983), 104–11; Francis Barker and Peter Hulme, 'Nymphs and reapers heavily vanish: the discursive con-texts of *The Tempest*' in *Alternative Shakespeares*, ed. John Drakakis (London and New York: Methuen, 1985), pp. 191–205; Terence Hawkes, 'Swisser-Swatter: making a man of English letters' in *Alternative Shakespeares*, pp. 26–46; Paul Brown, '"This thing of darkness I acknowledge mine": *The Tempest* and the discourse of colonialism' in *Political Shakespeare: New essays in cultural materialism* (Ithaca, N.Y., and London: Cornell Univ. Press, 1985), pp. 48–71; Peter Hulme, *Colonial Encounters: Europe and the native Caribbean, 1492–1797* (London and New York: Methuen, 1986), pp. 89–134; Thomas Cartelli, 'Prospero in Africa: *The Tempest* as colonialist text and pretext' in *Shakespeare Reproduced: The text in history and ideology*, eds. Jean Howard and Marion O'Conner (New York: Methuen, 1987), pp. 99–115; I would include two essays by Stephen Orgel somewhat different in their focus but nonetheless related: 'Prospero's Wife' in *Rewriting the Renaissance*, eds. Margaret Ferguson et al. (Chicago: Univ. of Chicago Press, 1986), pp. 50–64, and 'Shakespeare and the Cannibals' in *Cannibals, Witches, and Divorce: Estranging the Renaissance*, ed. Marjorie Garber (Baltimore and London: Johns Hopkins Univ. Press, 1987), pp. 40–66.

2. Hulme, *Colonial Encounters*, p. 94.
3. See, for example, Paul Brown, 'This thing of darkness,' p. 48.
4. In fact Edward Pechter, in one of the earliest of such scrutinies, cited several of the recent *Tempest* articles as especially problematic. See 'The New Historicism and Its Discontents: Politicizing Renaissance Drama,' *PMLA*, 102 (1987) 292–303. See also Howard Felperin, 'Making it "neo": The new historicism and Renaissance literature,' *Textual Practice*, 1 (1987), 262–77; Jean Howard, 'The New Historicism in Renaissance Studies,' *English Literary Renaissance*, 16 (1986), 13–43; and Anthony B. Dawson, '*Measure for Measure*, New Historicism, and Theatrical Power,' *Shakespeare Quarterly*, 39 (1988), 328–41.
5. *The Tempest*, The Arden Shakespeare, ed. Frank Kermode (London: Methuen, 1954), p. xxv. For an account of the work of earlier scholars exploring the connection between the play and these documents, see Kermode, pp. xxv–xxxiv, and Charles Frey, '*The Tempest* and the New World,' *SQ*, 30 (1979), 29–41.
6. E. E. Stoll and Northrop Frye are the only exceptions I have seen cited.
7. Recently there has been a renewed emphasis on the romance elements. See Gary Schmidgall, '*The Tempest* and *Primaleon*: A New Source,' *SQ*. 37 (1986), 423–39, esp. p. 436; and Robert Wiltenberg, 'The "*Aeneid*" in "*The Tempest*,"' *Shakespeare Survey*, 39 (1987), 159–68.
8. See, for example, Harry Berger's important essay, 'Miraculous Harp: A Reading of Shakespeare's *Tempest*,' *Shakespeare Studies*, 5 (1969), 253–83.
9. Harry Levin, *The Myth of the Golden Age in the Renaissance* (Bloomington: Indiana Univ. Press, 1969); Leslie A. Fiedler, *The Stranger in Shakespeare* (New York: Stein and Day, 1972); Leo Marx, 'Shakespeare's American Fable,' *The Machine in the Garden* (London and New York: Oxford Univ. Press, 1964), pp. 34–72.
10. O. Mannoni, *Prospero and Caliban: The Psychology of Colonization*, trans. Pamela Powesland (1950; rpt. New York: Praeger, 1964).
11. Hulme, *Colonial Encounters*, p. 133.
12. Hulme, *Colonial Encounters*, p. 115; Barker and Hulme, p. 201; Orgel, 'Prospero's Wife,' pp. 62–63.
13. Orgel, 'Shakespeare and the Cannibals,' p. 55.
14. As Paul Werstine wrote in the brochure announcing the NEH Humanities Institute on 'New Directions in Shakespeare Criticism' (The Folger Shakespeare Library, 1988), 'To appreciate *The Tempest* ... today ... we must understand discourses of colonialism, power, legitimation.'

15. Barker and Hulme, p. 198.
16. Hawkes, 'Swisser-Swatter,' p. 28.
17. Thus stereotypes, for example, served as part of a 'discursive strategy ... to locate or "fix" a colonial other in a position of inferiority ...' (Paul Brown, modifying Edward Said on orientalism, p. 58).
18. Actually, this point too is a matter of emphasis. R. R. Cawley ('Shakspere's Use of the Voyagers in *The Tempest*,' PMLA, 41 [1926], 688–726) and Kermode, among others, had noted in passing some similarities between the play's view of Caliban and the distortions of colonialist self-serving rhetorical purposes; but revisionists take this to be the important point, not to be passed over.
19. Leininger, 'Cracking the Code of *The Tempest*,' p. 122.
20. Paul Brown, pp. 64, 66. Brown also contends that *The Tempest* 'exemplifies ... a moment of *historical* crisis. This crisis is the struggle to produce a coherent discourse adequate to the complex requirements of British colonialism in its initial phase' (p. 48).
21. Hulme, *Colonial Encounters*, p. 93. Later he does grant a little ground to the psychological critics in allowing that their 'totally spurious' identification of Prospero with Shakespeare yet 'half grasps the crucial point that Prospero ... is a dramatist and creator of theatrical effects' (p. 115).
22. 'From the point of view of a political hermeneutic, measured against the requirements of a 'political unconscious,' we must conclude that the conception of wish-fulfillment remains locked in a problematic of the individual subject ... which is only indirectly useful to us.' The objection to wish-fulfillment is that it is 'always outside of time, outside of narrative' and history; 'what is more damaging, from the present perspective, is that desire ... remains locked into the category of the individual subject, even if the form taken by the individual in it is no longer the ego or the self, but the individual body ... *the need to transcend individualistic categories and modes of interpretation is in many ways the fundamental issue for any doctrine of the political unconscious*' (*The Political Unconscious: Narrative as a Socially symbolic Act* [Ithaca, N.Y.: Cornell Univ. Press, 1981], pp. 66, 68, italics added).
23. Stephen Greenblatt, 'Psychoanalysis and Renaissance Culture,' *Literary Theory/ Renaissance Texts*, eds. Patricia Parker and David Quint (Baltimore: Johns Hopkins Univ. Press, 1986), 210–24.
24. Jameson, p. 12. So, too, Freud's 'hermeneutic manual' can be of use to the political critic (p. 65).
25. 'Norman Holland's suggestive term,' Jameson, p. 49.
26. Jameson, p. 67. Cf. Paul Brown, 'My use of Freudian terms does not mean that I endorse its ahistorical, Europocentric and sexist models of psychical development. However, a materialist criticism deprived of such concepts as displacement and condensation would be seriously impoverished ...' (p. 71, n. 35).
27. Jameson discussing Althusser (p. 30) and Greimas (p. 48).
28. *The Crown of Life* (1947; rpt. New York: Barnes & Noble, 1966), p. 255.
29. See Trevor R. Griffiths, '"This Island's mine": Caliban and Colonialism,' *Yearbook of English Studies*, 13 (1983), 159–80.
30. Griffiths, p. 166.
31. Virginia Mason Vaughan, '"Something Rich and Strange": Caliban's Theatrical Metamorphoses,' *SQ*, 36 (1985), 390–405, esp. p. 390.
32. Erlich, 'Shakespeare's Colonial Metaphor,' p. 49; Paul Brown, p. 48.
33. Even St. Paul in his travels (echoed in the play) met natives who – like Caliban – thought him a god.
34. Hulme produces as evidence against Shakespeare these four words from the cast list, which Shakespeare may or may not have written ('Hurricanes in the Caribbees,' p. 72).
35. Alden T. Vaughan, 'Shakespeare's Indian: The Americanization of Caliban,' SQ, 39

(1988), 137–53. He argues that the intention miscarried not only at the time but also for the three centuries following. He adds, 'Rather, from the Restoration until the late 1890s, Caliban appeared on stage and in critical literature as almost everything but an Indian' (p. 138).

36. Hulme, while noting Caliban's 'anomalous nature,' sees the anomaly as yet another colonialist strategy: 'In ideological terms [Caliban is] a compromise formation and one achieved, like all such formations, only at the expense of distortion elsewhere' ('Hurricanes in the Caribbees,' pp. 71, 72). This begs the question: Caliban can only be a 'distortion' if he is intended to represent someone. But that is precisely the question – *is* he meant to represent a Native American? Sidney Lee noted that Caliban's method of building dams for fish reproduces the Indians'; though he is often cited by later writers as an authority on the resemblance, the rest of his evidence is not convincing ('The Call of the West: America and Elizabethan England,' *Elizabethan and Other Essays*, ed. Frederick S. Boas [Oxford: Clarendon Press, 1929], pp. 263–301). G. Wilson Knight has an impressionistic essay about the relationship between Caliban and Indians ('Caliban as Red Man' [1977] in *Shakespeare's Styles*, eds. Philip Edwards, Inga-Stina Ewbank, and G. K. Hunter [London: Cambridge Univ. Press, 1980]). Hulme lists Caliban's resemblances to Caribs ('Hurricanes in the Caribbees'), and Kermode cites details taken from natives visited during both the Old and the New World voyages.
37. The Indians who would appear in Chapman's 1613 masque would be fully equipped with feathers. See R. R. Cawley, *The Voyagers and Elizabethan Drama* (Boston: D. C. Heath; London: Oxford Univ. Press, 1938), p. 359, and Orgel, 'Shakespeare and the Cannibals,' pp. 44, 47.
38. Shakespeare had apparently read up on his monsters (R. R. Cawley, 'Shakspere's Use of the Voyagers,' p. 723, and Frey, passim), but he picked up the stereotypes only to play with them ostentatiously (in Stephano's and Trinculo's many discredited guesses about Caliban's identity) or to leave them hanging (in Prospero's identification of Caliban as 'devil').
39. Hulme, 'Hurricanes in the Caribbees,' p. 74.
40. Lamming (n. 1, above), pp. 98–99.
41. Lamming, p. 97; Erlich, p. 49.
42. The play also seems anti-colonialist because it includes the comic sections with Stephano and Trinculo, which show colonialism to be 'nakedly avaricious, profiteering, perhaps even pointless'; but this too can be seen as a rationalization: 'This low version of colonialism serves to displace possibly damaging charges ... against properly-constituted civil authority on to the already excremental products of civility, the masterless' (Paul Brown, p. 65).
43. Greenblatt, 'Learning to Curse,' pp. 570–71; Leininger (n. 1, above), pp. 126–27.
44. Leininger, p. 127.
45. As Fiedler's book implies (n. 9, above), she is less like anything American than like the Frenchwoman Joan of Arc, who also tried to save herself from the law by claiming she was pregnant with a bastard; Joan simply wasn't as successful (see pp. 43–81, esp. p. 77).
46. See Brockbank, p. 193. Even these details can be discounted as rationalizations, of course. Paul Brown, for example, explains Sycorax's presence as a rationalization: by degrading her black magic, he argues, Shakespeare makes Prospero seem better than he is (pp. 60–61). Hulme notes that Sycorax may be Prospero's invention, pointing out that we never see any direct evidence that she was present (*Colonial Encounters*, p. 115). Orgel links Caliban's claims of legitimacy by birth to James I's claims ('Prospero's Wife,' pp. 58–59).
47. See Fiedler, p. 205.
48. Erlich, 'Shakespeare's Colonial Metaphor,' p. 63.
49. The trend, moreover, is to move away from anthropomorphic terms like 'repression' or 'censorship,' themselves inherited from the political terminology on which Freud

drew for his own. Like the vocabulary of 'scientific' hydraulics on which Freud also drew for his notions of libido flowing and damming up, the older terms are being replaced by contemporary terminologies more appropriate to describing a conflict among meanings or interpretations, rather than between anthropomorphized forces engaged in a simple struggle 'for' and 'against.'

50. Spaniards, he writes, 'taught their Hounds, fierce Dogs, to teare [the Indians] in peeces' (*A briefe Narration of the destruction of the Indies by the Spaniards* [1542 (?)], Samuel Purchas, *Purchas His Pilgrimes*, 20 vols. [Glasgow: Maclehose and Sons, 1905–1907], Vol. XVIII, 91). This was apparently a common topos, found also in Eden's translation of Peter Martyr's *Decades of the Newe Worlde* (1555), included in Eden's *Historie of Trauaile* (1577), which Shakespeare read for *The Tempest*. It was also used by Greene and Deloney (Cawley, *Voyagers and Elizabethan Drama*, pp. 383–84).
51. Hulme, 'Hurricanes in the Caribbees,' pp. 63–66; see also Orgel on this 'New World topos' in 'Shakespeare and the Cannibals,' pp. 41–44.
52. Neither was Montaigne's in the essay that has been taken as a source for the play. Scholars are still debating about Montaigne's attitude toward cannibals, though all agree that his critical attitude toward *Europeans* was clear in the essay.
53. This blend of Old and New World characteristics, earlier seen as characteristic of New World discourse, is acknowledged in many of the revisionist studies but is seen as one of the rhetorical strategies used to control Indians.
54. William Strach[e]y, 'A true reportorie . . .,' *Purchas*, Vol. XIX, p. 62. For the citation of Purchas as colonialist, see Hulme, 'Hurricanes in the Caribbees,' p. 78, n. 21.
55. Paul Brown, p. 64.
56. This is an entirely separate question from another that one might ask: How comparable were Purchas's remarks, taken from the collection of travelers' tales which he edited, censored, and used to support his colonialist ideal, on the one hand, and a play, on the other? In *Purchas*, Richard Marienstras argues, 'the multiplicity of interpretations modulates and reinforces a single ideological system. The same can certainly not be said of ... *The Tempest*' (*New perspectives on the Shakespearean world*, trans. Janet Lloyd [Cambridge: Cambridge Univ. Press, 1985], p. 169). This entire book, which devotes a chapter to *The Tempest*, is an excellent study of 'certain aspects of Elizabethan ideology and . . . the way these are used in Shakespeare' (p. 1).
57. See Pechter (n. 4, above). This kind of 'condition,' he argues, is really a precondition in the sense that it is assumed to be logically (if not chronologically) prior. It is assumed to have the kind of explanatory power that 'the Elizabethan world view' was once accorded (p. 297).
58. See, for example, the following contemporary tracts reprinted in *Tracts and Other Papers Relating Principally to the Origin, Settlement, and Progress of . . . North America*, ed. Peter Force, 4 vols. (1836–47; rpt. New York: Peter Smith, 1947): R. I., '*Nova Britania*: OFFERING MOST Excellent fruites by Planting IN VIRGINIA. Exciting all such as be well affected to further the same' (1609), Vol. 1, No. 6; 'Virginia richly valued' (1609), Vol. 4, No. 1; 'A TRVE DECLARATION of the estate of the Colonie in Virginia, With a confutation of such scandalous reports as haue tended to the disgrace of so worthy an enterprise' (1610), Vol. 3, No. 1; Sil. Jourdan, 'A PLAINE DESCRIPTION OF THE BARMVDAS, NOW CALLED SOMMER ILANDS' (1613), Vol. 3, No. 3.

    In *The Genesis of the United States*, ed. Alexander Brown, 2 vols. (New York: Russell & Russell, 1964), see also: Robert Gray, 'A GOOD SPEED to Virginia' (1609), Vol. 1, 293–302; 'A True and Sincere declaration of the purpose and ends of the *Plantation* begun in *Virginia* of the degrees which it hath received; and meanes by *which it hath beene advanced:* and *the . . . conclusion* of *His Majesties Councel* of that Colony . . . until by the mercies of GOD it shall *retribute a fruitful harvest to the Kingdome of heaven, and this Common-Wealth*' (1609), Vol. 1, 337–53; 'A

Publication by the Counsell of Virginea, touching the Plantation there' (1609), Vol. 1, 354–56; R. Rich, 'NEWES FROM VIRGINIA. THE LOST FLOCKE TRIUMPHANT . . .' (1610), Vol. 1, 420–26.

59. 'A Trve Declaration,' p. 6.
60. Alexander Brown, in *The Genesis of the United States*, reprints extracts from the following pertinent documents: William Symonds, 'VIRGINIA: A SERMON PREACHED AT WHITE CHAPPEL . . .' (1609), Vol. 1, 282–91; Daniel Price, 'SAVLES PROHIBITION STAIDE . . . And to the Inditement of all that persecute Christ with a reproofe of those that traduce the Honourable Plantation of Virginia' (1609), Vol. 1, 312–16; and, most important, William Crashaw's sermon titled 'A New-yeeres Gift to Virginea,' and preached, as the title page announced, before 'Lord La Warre Lord Governour and Captaine Generall of Virginia, and others of [the] Counsell . . . At the said Lord Generall his . . . departure for Virginea . . . Wherein both the lawfulnesses of that action is maintained and the necessity thereof is also demonstrated, not so much out of the grounds of Police, as of Humanity, Equity and Christianity' (1610), Vol. 1, 360–75.
61. In Alexander Brown, see William Crashaw for two of these references (in 'A New-yeeres Gift to Virginea' [1610], and 'Epistle Dedicatory' to Alexander Whitaker's '*Good Newes from Virginia*' [1613], Vol. 2, 611–20); and see Ralphe Hamor in *A True Discourse of the Present Estate of Virginea* (1615), Virginia State Library Publications, No. 3 (Richmond: Virginia State Library, 1957).
62. Pp. 16, 17.
63. For the general history of the period, see David Beers Quinn, *England and the Discovery of America, 1481–1620* (New York: Alfred A. Knopf, 1974); Alexander Brown's *Genesis* identifies similar shifting motives in the history of colonization. Such voyages were made famous by often-reprinted accounts, especially in collections by Richard Eden and Richard Hakluyt, both of whose anthologies Shakespeare would consult for *The Tempest*. In the introductory material in these collections, as in the voyages themselves, the self-interest is obvious but so mixed with excitement and utopian hopes, and so focused on competition with Spain, that the issue of relation to Indians was dwarfed by comparison.
64. If he didn't succeed in establishing a settlement, he would lose his patent. His interest in the patent rather than the colony was shown by his apparent negligence in searching for his lost colony (Quinn, n. 63, above, p. 300). He could hold onto his patent only so long as there was hope that the colonists were still alive; clearly the hope was worth more to Raleigh than the colony.
65. Matthew P. Andrews, *The Soul of a Nation: The Founding of Virginia and the Projection of New England* (New York: Scribner's, 1943), p. 125. An entire popular literature developed, so much so that the Archbishop of York complained that 'of Virginia there be so many tractates, divine, human, historical, political, or call them as you please, as no further intelligence I dare desire' (quoted in Andrews, p. 125).
66. It is this issue rather than colonialism that stimulated an earlier period of political commentary on the New World material in *The Tempest*: Charles M. Gayley, *Shakespeare and the Founders of Liberty in America* (New York: Macmillan, 1917); A. A. Ward, 'Shakespeare and the makers of Virginia,' *Proceedings of the British Academy*, 9 (1919); see also E. P. Kuhl, 'Shakespeare and the founders of America: *The Tempest*,' *Philological Quarterly*, 41 (1962), 123–46.
67. Contributing to the welter of contradictory discourses was the Spanish ambassador's flow of letters to Spain insisting, not irrationally, that the whole purpose of maintaining a profitless colony like Jamestown was to establish a base for pirate raids against Spanish colonies.
68. Letter from Southampton to the Earl of Salisbury, 15 December 1609, in Alexander Brown, Vol. 1, 356–57.
69. The quantity and quality of the objections, which have not on the whole survived, has been judged by the nature of the many defenses thought necessary to answer

them. See notes 58, 60, 61.

70. A practice that Shakespeare did not admire if Stephano and Trinculo are any indication.
71. As are the two monsters cited as possible prototypes for Caliban by Geoffrey Bullough *Narrative and Dramatic Sources of Shakespeare*, 8 vols. [New York: Columbia Univ. Press, 1958], Vol. 8, 240). There were exceptions, of course, as in George Percy's *Observations ... of the Plantation of ... Virginia* (1606), in *Purchas*, Vol. XVIII, 403–19.
72. See Karen Ordahl Kupperman, *Settling With the Indians: The Meeting of English and Indian Cultures in America, 1580–1640* (Totowa, N.J: Rowman and Littlefield, 1980), pp. 127–29. The origins of this nearly universal belief in Indian treachery are of course multiple, ranging from the readiness of the English to project their fears onto any available victim, whether Indians or mariners (who were also regularly accused of treachery in these narratives), to the prevailing stereotypes of the Other, to specific English acts of provocation, to the general tensions inherent in the situation. Without arguing for any one of these, I merely wish to suggest that the notion of 'colonialist discourse' simplifies a complex situation.
73. Even as proto-white men, their skin as tanned rather than naturally black, etc. See Kupperman, and Orgel, 'Shakespeare and the Cannibals.'
74. Greenblatt, in his study of the ways in which white men verbally 'colonialized' Indians, discusses the degree to which whites assumed that the Indians had *no* language. Although he notes that there were exceptions, he makes it sound as if these exceptions were rare and were largely confined to the 'rough, illiterate sea dog, bartering for gold trinkets on a faraway beach,' rather than to the 'captains or lieutenants whose accounts we read' ('Learning to Curse,' pp. 564–65). On the contrary, even the earliest travelers had often included glossaries of Indian terms in their reports (e.g., the Glossary in the introductory material of Eden's translation of Martyr's *Decades* [1555], as well as in various later English reports reprinted in *Purchas His Pilgrimes* [1625]); and in reading through Purchas's helter-skelter collection, one is struck by the number of writers who grant automatic respect to the Indians' language. A possibly figurative rather than literal force for comments on the Indians' 'want of language' is suggested by Gabriel Archer's account of a 1602 voyage. Here it is the English, not the Indians, who are deficient in this respect: they 'spake divers Christian words, and seemed to understand much *more then we, for Want of Language, could comprehend*' ('Relation of Captain Gosnold's voyage,' *Purchas*, Vol. *viii*, 304, italics mine).
75. See R. R. Cawley, *Voyagers and Elizabethan Drama*, passim, and *Unpathed Waters Studies in the Influence of the Voyagers on Elizabethan Literature* (Princeton, N.J.: Princeton Univ. Press, 1940), pp. 234–41. Neither of R. R. Cawley's two books about the voyagers' influence on contemporary English literature cites any pre-1611 passage of more than a few lines. It is true that in the 1580s Marlowe's plays took off from the general sense of vastness and possibility opened up by voyages to the New as well as to the Old World. In addition Drayton wrote an 'Ode to the Virginia Voyage,' perhaps expressly for the settlers leaving for Jamestown in 1606; and one line in Samuel Daniel's 'Musophilis' has a colonialist ring: he speaks of 'vent[ing] the treasure of our tongue ... T' inrich unknowing Nations with our stores.' True, too, that in a quite different spirit Jonson, Marston, and Chapman collaborated in *Eastward Ho* (1605) to make fun of gallants flocking to Virginia with expectations as great as those bringing foolish victims to Face and Subtle's alchemical chimeras. But while Marlowe participates in the spirit of romantic adventure associated with voyaging and treasure-hunting, and *Eastward Ho* satirizes it, neither deals at all with the New World or with the New World natives.

1.4

FROM 'BEYOND MIRANDA'S MEANINGS: UN/SILENCING THE "DEMONIC GROUND" OF CALIBAN'S "WOMAN"'

Sylvia Wynter

The point of departure of this *After/Word* is to explore a central distinction that emerges as the dynamic linking sub-text of this, the first collection of critical essays written by Caribbean women. This distinction is that between Luce Irigaray's purely Western assumption of a universal category, 'woman', whose 'silenced' ground is the condition of what she defines as an equally universally applicable, 'patriarchal discourse', and the dually Western and post-Western editorial position of a projected 'womanist/feminist' critical approach as the unifying definition of the essays that constitute the anthology. The term 'womanist/feminist', with the qualifying attribute 'womanist' borrowed from the Afro-American feminist Alice Walker, reveals the presence of a contradiction, which, whilst central to the situational frame of reference of both Afro-American and Caribbean women writers/critics, is necessarily absent from the situational frame of reference of both Western-European and Euro-american women writers. Thus whilst at the level of the major text these essays are projected within the system of inference-making of the discourse of feminism, at the level of the sub-text which both haunts and calls in question the presuppositions of the major text, the very attempt to redefine the term *feminist* with the qualifier 'womanist', expresses the paradoxical relation of Sameness and Difference which the writers of these essays, as members of the Caribbean women intelligentsia, bear to their Western European and Euro-american peers . . .

In Carole Boyce Davies and Elaine Savory Fido (eds), *Out of the Kumbla*, Trenton, New Jersey: Africa World Press, 1990, pp. 355–65.

The central point I want to make in this *After/Word* is that the contradiction inserted into the consolidated field of meanings of the ostensibly 'universal' theory of feminism by the variable *'race'*, and explicitly expressed by the qualifiers of 'womanist' and 'cross-roads situation', of these essays points toward the emergent 'downfall' of our present 'school like mode of thought' and its system of 'positive knowledge' inherited from the nineteenth century and from the Industrial epoch of which it was the enabling mode of rationality and participatory epistemology[1]; and that it does this in the same way as feminist theory itself had earlier inserted the contradiction of the variable *gender* into the ostensibly 'universal' theories of Liberal Humanism and Marxism–Leninism[2] . . .

For with Western Europe's post-medieval expansion into the New World (and earlier into Africa), and with its epochal shift out of primarily *religious* systems of legitimation, and behaviour – regulation, her peoples' expropriation of the land/living space of the New World peoples was to be based on the secular concept of the 'non-rational' inferior, *'nature'* of the peoples to be expropriated and governed; that is, of an ostensible difference in 'natural' substance which, for the first time in history was no longer *primarily* encoded in the male/female gender division as it has been hitherto in the symbolic template of all traditional and religiously based human orders, but now in the cultural-physiognomic variations between the dominant expanding European civilization and the non-Western peoples that, encountering, it would now stigmatize as 'natives'. In other words, with the shift to the secular, the primary code of difference now became that between 'men' and 'natives', with the traditional 'male' and 'female' distinctions now coming to play a secondary – if none the less powerful – reinforcing role within the system of symbolic representations, Lévi-Strauss's totemic schemas,[3] by means of which, as governing charters of meaning, all human orders are 'altruistically' integrated.[4]

Nowhere is this mutational shift from the primacy of the *anatomical* model of sexual difference as the referential model of *mimetic* ordering, to that of the *physiognomic* model of racial/*cultural* difference, more powerfully enacted than in Shakespeare's play *The Tempest*, one of the foundational endowing[5] texts both of Western Europe's dazzling rise to global hegemony, and at the level of human 'life' in general, of the mutation from primarily religiously defined modes of human being to the first, partly secularizing ones. Whilst on the other hand, both mutations, each as the condition of the other, are nowhere more clearly put into play than in the relations between Miranda the daughter of Prospero, and Caliban, the once original owner of the island now enslaved by Prospero as a function of the latter's expropriation of the island. That is, in the relations of enforced dominance and subordination between Miranda, though 'female', and Caliban, though 'male'; relations in which *sex-gender attributes* are no longer the primary index of 'deferent' difference,[6] and in which the discourse that erects itself is no longer primarily 'patriarchal', but rather 'monarchical' in its Western-European, essentially post-Christian, post-religious definition. Therefore, in whose context of behaviour-regulatory inferential system of meanings, as the essential condition of the mutation to the secular, Caliban, as an incarnation of a new category of the human, that of the subordinated 'irrational' and 'savage'[7] *native* is now constituted as the lack of the 'rational' Prospero, and the now capable-of-rationality Miranda, by the Otherness of his/its *physiognomic* 'monster' difference, a difference which now takes the *coding* role of sexual-anatomical difference, with the latter now made into a mimetic parallel effect of the former, and as such a member of the *set* of differences of which the former has now become the primary 'totemic-operator'[8] ...

And here, we begin to pose in this context a new question ... This question is that of the most significant absence of all, that of Caliban's Woman, of Caliban's physiognomically complementary mate. For nowhere in Shakespeare's play, and in its system of image-making, one which would be foundational to the emergence of the first form of a secular world system, our present Western world system, does Caliban's mate appear as an alternative sexual-erotic model of desire; as an alternative source of an alternative system of meanings. Rather there, on the New World island, as the only woman, Miranda and her mode of physiognomic being, defined by the philogenically 'idealized' features of straight hair and thin lips is canonized as the 'rational' object of desire; as the potential genitrix of a superior mode of human 'life', that of 'good natures' as contrasted with the ontologically absent potential genitrix – Caliban's mate ...

To put it in more directly political terms, the absence of Caliban's woman, is an absence which is functional to the new secularizing schema by which the peoples of Western Europe legitimated their global expansion as well as their expropriation and their marginalization of all the other population-groups of the globe, including, partially, some of their own national groupings such as, for example, the Irish[9] ...

In consequence if, before the sixteenth century, what Irigaray terms as '*patriarchal discourse*' had erected itself on the 'silenced ground' of women, from then on, the new primarily silenced ground (which at the same time now enables the partial liberation of Miranda's hitherto stifled speech), would be that of the majority population-groups of the globe – all signified now as the 'natives' (Caliban's) to the 'men' of Prospero and Fernando, with Miranda becoming both a co-participant, if to a lesser *derived* extent, in the power and privileges generated by the empirical supremacy of her own population; and as well, the beneficiary of a mode of privilege unique to her, that of being the metaphysically invested and 'idealized' object of desire for all classes (Stephano and Trinculo) and all population-groups (Caliban).[10]

This therefore is the dimension of the contradictory relation of Sameness and Difference, of orthodoxy and heresy which these Caribbean critical essays must necessarily, if still only partially, inscribe, and inscribe with respect to the theory/discourse of feminism, (as the latest and last variant of the Prospero/Miranda ostensibly 'universally' applicable meaning and discourse-complex); the relation of *sameness* and *difference* which is expressed in the diacritical term '*womanist*'. And if we are to understand the necessity for such an *other* term (projected both from the perspective of Black American women (U.S.) and from that of the 'native' women intelligentsia of the newly independent Caribbean ex-slave polities) as a term which, whilst developing a fully articulated theoretical/interpretative reading model of its own, nevertheless, serves, diacritically to draw attention to the insufficiency of all existing theoretical interpretative models, both to 'voice' the hitherto silenced ground of the experience of 'native' Caribbean women and Black American women as the ground of Caliban's woman, and to de-code the system of meanings of that other discourse, beyond Irigaray's patriarchal one, which has imposed this mode of silence for some five centuries, as well as to make thinkable the possibility of a new 'model' projected from a new 'native' standpoint, we shall need to translate the variable 'race', which now functions as the intra-feminist marker of difference, impelling the dually 'gender/beyond gender' readings of these essays, out of the epistemic 'vrai'[11] of our present order of 'positive knowledge',[12] its consolidated field of meanings and order-replicating hermeneutics. Correspondingly, this order/field is transformative, generated from our present purely secular definition of the human on the model of a natural organism, with, in consequence this organism's 'ends' therefore being ostensibly set extra-humanly, by 'nature' . . . we shall need to move beyond this founding definition, not merely to *another* alternative one, non-consciously put in place as our present definition, but rather to a frame of reference which parallels the 'demonic models' posited by physicists who seek to conceive of a vantage point outside the space-time orientation of the humuncular observer . . . The possibility of such a vantage point, we argue, towards which the diacritical term 'womanist' (i.e. these readings as both gender, and not-gender readings, as both Caribbean/Black nationalist and not-Caribbean/Black nationalist, Marxian and not-Marxian readings)[13] point can only be projected from a 'demonic model' generated, parallely to the vantage point/demonic model with which the laity intelligentsia of Western Europe effected the first rupture of humans with their/our supernaturally guaranteed narrative schemas of origin,[14] from the situational 'ground' or slot of Caliban's woman, and therefore of her systemic behaviour regulatory role or function as the ontological 'native/nigger', within the motivational apparatus by means of which our present model of being/definition-of-the-human is given dynamic 'material' existence, rather than from merely the vantage point of her/our gender, racial, class or cultural being.[15] In other words, if the laity intelligentsia of Western Europe effected a mutation by calling in question its own role as the ontological Other of 'natural fallen flesh' to the theologically idealized, post-baptismal Spirit (and as such incapable of attaining to any knowledge of, and mastery over, either the physical processes of nature or its own social reality, except such knowledge was mediated by the then hegemonic Scholastic *theological* interpretative model), and by calling this role in question so as to clear the ground for its own self-assertion which would express itself both in the political reasons-of-state humanism (enacted in *The Tempest*), as well as in the putting in place of the *Studia Humanitatis* (i.e. as the self-study of 'natural man'), and in the laying of the basis for the rise of the natural sciences,[16] it is by a parallel calling in question of our 'native', and most ultimately, nigger women's role as the embodiment to varying degrees of an ostensible 'primal' human nature. As well, challenging our role as a new 'lay' intelligentsia ostensibly unable to know and therefore to master our present sociosystemic reality, (including the reality of our 'existential weightlessness' as an always 'intellectually indentured'[17] intelligentsia), except as mediated by the theoretical models generated from the vantage point of the 'normal' intelligentsia, clears the ground for a new self-assertion ... In effect, rather than only voicing the 'native' woman's hitherto silenced voice[18] we shall ask: What is the systemic function of her own silencing, both as women and, more totally, as 'native' women? Of what mode of speech is that absence of speech both as women (masculinist discourse) and as 'native' women (feminist discourse) an imperative function? ...

NOTES

1. For the concept of 'participatory epistemology' see Francisco Varela, *Principles of Biological Autonomy* (New York, North Holland Series in General Systems Research, 1979).
2. At the theoretical level 'feminist' theory developed on the basis of its rupture with the purely economic and class-based theory of Marxism, thereby calling into question both the 'universalisms' of Marxian Proletarian identity and of the Liberal humanist 'figure of man'.
3. See C. Lévi-Strauss, *Totémism* (Harmondsworth: Penguin, 1969).
4. See J. F. Danielli, 'Altruism: The Opium of the People', *Journal of Social and Biological Structures* 3, no. 2 (April 1980): 87–94.
5. See D. Halliburton, 'Endowment, Enablement, Entitlement: Toward A Theory of Constitution' in *Literature and the Question of Philosophy*, ed. A. J. Cascari (Baltimore: Johns Hopkins University Press, 1986) where he develops this concept of 'endowment'.
6. A play on the Derridean concept of 'difference' where the temporal dimension is replaced by the stratifying/status dimension, making use of the concept of 'deferent' behaviour which functions to inscribe difference, and to constitute 'higher' and 'lower' ranking.
7. See in this respect, the book by Jacob Pandian, *Anthropology and the Western Tradition: Towards an Authentic Anthropology*. (Prospect Heights, Illinois: Waveland Press, Inc., 1985).
8. See for an excellent analysis of this concept, the book by Claude Jenkins, *The Social Theory of Claude Lévi-Strauss*, (London: The Macmillan Press Ltd, 1979).
9. Recent work by political scientists has begun to focus on the parallels between the discourses by means of which the New World Indians were expropriated and those by which the Cromwellian conquest and partial occupation of Ireland were also legitimated i.e. by the projection of a 'by nature difference' between the dominant and the subordinated population groups.
10. The sailors' dream too, is to be king on the island and to marry Miranda.
11. The term is used by Foucault in his talk, 'The Order of Discourse' given in December 1970 and published as an Appendix of the *Archaeology of Knowledge* (New York: Harper and Row, tr. A. M. Sheridan-Smith, 1972). Here Foucault notes that Mendel's findings about genetic heredity were not hearable at first because they were not within the 'vrai' of the discipline at the time.
12. In *The Order of Things*, Foucault points out that because 'Man' is an object of 'positive knowledge' in Western Culture, he cannot be an 'object of science'.

13. The force of the term *womanist* lies in its revelation of a perspective which can only be *partially* defined by any of the definitions of our present hegemonic theoretical models.
14. With respect to the functioning of the narrative of origins in human orders, including the 'evolutionary' narrative of origin of our own which also functions as 'replacement material for genesis', see Glyn Isaacs, 'Aspects of Human Evolution' in D. S. Bendall, ed., *Evolution from Molecules to Men* (Cambridge University Press, New York, 1983), pp. 509–43.
15. The contradiction here is between 'cultural nationalism' i.e. the imperative to revalue one's gender, class, culture and to constitute one's literary counter-canon, and the scientific question. What is the function of the 'obliteration' of these multiple perspectives? What role does this play in the stable bringing into being of our present human order?
16. See Walter Ullman, op. cit. and Hans Blumenberg, op. cit. as well as Kurt Hubner, *The Critique of Scientific Reason* (Chicago: University of Chicago Press, 1983), for the linkage of the rise of the natural sciences to the overall secularizing movement of humanism.
17. The term is Henry Louis Gates's, and is central to the range of his work. See for example, his use of a variant of this term ('interpretative indenture') in his essay, 'Authority (White) Power and the (Black) Critic' in *Cultural Critique*, Fall 1987, no. 7. pp. 19–46.
18. In a paper given as a panel presentation at the 1988 March West Coast Political Science Conference, Kathy Ferguson of the University of Hawaii pointed to the contradiction, for feminist deconstructionists, between the imperative of a fixed gender identity able to facilitate a unifying identity from which to 'voice' their presence, and the deconstructionist program to deconstruct gender's oppositional categories.

PART 2
DANIEL DEFOE:
ROBINSON CRUSOE

INTRODUCTION

Like the dynamic between Prospero and Caliban, the relationship between Crusoe and Friday is a touchstone for critiques of the cultural representation of colonialism. In his essay 'On Not Being Milton' David Dabydeen remarks that 'European literature is littered with blacks like Man Friday, who falls to earth to worship Crusoe's magical gun'.[1] Like Shakespeare's play, Defoe's novel was repeatedly reinterpreted and rewritten by the Victorians,[2] and has also been reworked from post-colonial perspectives, most notably in Michel Tournier's *Friday*, in which Crusoe metamorphoses from capitalist individualist to egalitarian communalist, and J. M. Coetzee's *Foe*, a text obsessed with writing and representation, narrative and silence, mostly presented from the perspective of *Roxana*'s Susan Barton, a castaway with Crusoe fascinated by the mute Friday who will not communicate. As Spivak writes, 'Coetzee as white creole translates *Robinson Crusoe* by representing Friday as the agent of a withholding.'[3] Other recastings are Sam Selvon's *Moses Ascending* (1975), a satire on British racism, and Derek Walcott's *Pantomime* (1978), which situates the novel on Tobago and reworks it in a different genre, drama.

One of the definitive readings of *Robinson Crusoe* is Ian Watt's chapter on individualism and the novel in his 1957 study of realism and capitalism, *The Rise of the Novel*. Watt reads Crusoe as a paragon of economic individualism, leading his life in terms of profit and loss, money, time, and the Protestant belief in the morality and dignity of labour. In contrast, Peter Hulme discusses the novel as a colonial romance, rather than realism, in his essay 'Robinson Crusoe and Friday' in *Colonial Encounters: Europe and the Native Caribbean,*

1492–1797. The first extract included below from Hulme's book considers the verisimilitude of *Robinson Crusoe* in its Caribbean section, and the tension between the novel's well-documented realism and its mythologizing of the colonial encounter. The second extract analyses the passage in the novel Hulme at one point calls the climax of the kind of colonial discourse he is analysing: the encounter Crusoe and Friday have with the twenty-one cannibals.

Martin Green's influential *Dreams of Adventure, Deeds of Empire* (1980) also sees *Robinson Crusoe* as a romance – though one transformed to suit the modern world – following the three key stages of journey, struggle and exaltation: '*Robinson Crusoe* is a central mythic expression of the modern system, of its call to young men to go out to expand the empire; and the more you know about the latter, the richer the meanings you find in the former.'[4] Indeed, it has since been argued that all Defoe's works are advertisements for colonisation.[5]

In a more theoretical account of the book's spatial relationships, Richard Phillips in 'The Geography of *Robinson Crusoe*', from *Mapping Men and Empire: A Geography of Adventure*, considers British self-representations caught between geographical fantasy and colonial myth, in the divisions between home and away, the known and the unmapped. Roxann Wheeler's essay '"My Savage", "My Man": Racial Multiplicity in *Robinson Crusoe*' weighs up the relative significances of Christianity, cannibalism and savagery in the novel. Wheeler contends that 'race as we understand it today did not anchor European difference and cannot analyze colonial relations adequately.' This is the point made by Ruth Benedict in *Race and Racism* several decades ago, but it is here helpfully applied to the explication of a literary text, reminding the reader that religion, not race, was at least initially the foremost token of difference in British Imperial discourse.

David Dabydeen's 'Daniel Defoe's *Robinson Crusoe* (1719)', in his and Nana Wilson-Tagoe's *A Reader's Guide to West Indian and Black British Literature*, is a reading in terms of the rise of the bourgeoisie and the merchant classes which complements the pioneering work of both Ian Watt and Pierre Macherey (in *A Theory of Literary Production*) but is inflected by a discussion of the relation between capitalism and colonialism.

Lastly, the volume *Robinson Crusoe: Myths and Metamorphoses*, edited by Lieve Spaas and Brian Stimpson, contains several essays that examine Defoe's novel from post-colonial perspectives, particularly Jean-Jacques Hamm's 'Caliban, Friday and their Masters', which traces the master-slave dialectic in *The Tempest* and *Robinson Crusoe*, and Markman Ellis's 'Crusoe, Cannibalism and Empire'.[6] Ellis's essay is a general discussion of contemporary accounts of cannibalism (which is read as a method of othering rather than as a literal accusation) in relation to *Robinson Crusoe*, which evolves into an examination of both the accounts and the novel alongside records and reports of Captain Cook's voyages.

NOTES

1. David Dabydeen, 'On Not Being Milton', in Christopher Ricks and Leonard Michaels (eds), *The State of the Language*, 2nd edn, London: Faber, 1990, p. 4.
2. See Richard Phillips's analysis of Robinsonades in *Mapping Men and Empire*, London: Routledge, 1997, pp. 35–44.
3. Gayatri Spivak, 'The Politics of Translation', in *Outside in the Teaching Machine*, London: Routledge, 1992, p. 195. See also Spivak, 'Theory in the Margin: Coetzee's *Foe* reading Defoe's *Crusoe/Roxana*', in Jonathan Arac and Barbara Johnson (eds), *Consequences of Theory*, Baltimore: Johns Hopkins University Press, 1991. For a discussion of the three texts by Defoe, Tournier and Coetzee in relation to intertextuality, see Brenda K. Marshall, *Teaching the Postmodern: Fiction and Theory*, London: Routledge, 1992, ch. 4.
4. Martin Green, *Dreams of Adventure, Deeds of Empire*, London: Routledge and Kegan Paul, 1980, p. 83.
5. J. A. Downie, 'Defoe, Imperialism, and the Travel Books Reconsidered', in G. K. Hunter and C. J. Rawson (eds), *The Yearbook of English Studies*, vol. 13, London: MHRA, 1983, pp. 66–83.
6. Lieve Spaas and Brian Stimpson (eds), *Robinson Crusoe: Myths and Metamorphoses*, London: Macmillan, 1996, pp. 110–24 (Hamm) and pp. 45–61 (Ellis).

2.1

FROM 'DANIEL DEFOE'S *ROBINSON CRUSOE* (1719)'

David Dabydeen

'Industry' was a key term in the eighteenth century, frequently evoked by pamphleteers and poets alike in their exhortations to the nation. In his poem *The Castle of Indolence*, James Thomson urges people to be sobre and diligent:

> Toil and be glad! Let Industry inspire
> Into your quickened limbs her buoyant breath!
> Better the toiling swain, oh happier far!
> Perhaps the happiest of the sons of men!
> Who vigorous plies the plough, the team, or car,
> Who houghs the field, or ditches in the glen,
> Delves in his garden, or secures his pen:
> The tooth of avarice poisons not his peace;
> He tosses not in sloth's abhorred den.

John Dyer, in his poem *The Fleece*, urges the workers to be cheerful in their tasks – Blithe over your toil with wonted song proceed'. Industry, Dyer claimed, 'lifts the swain / And the straw cottage to a palace turns', a sentiment that echoes Thomson's view that through industry 'the poor man's lot with milk and honey flows'.

Much of the literature on Industry was of course grotesque propaganda since the reality of peasant and labouring class life was a reality of poverty, food shortages and economic exploitation. There was opulence at one end of society, grinding poverty at the other:

In David Dabydeen and Nana Wilson-Tagoe, *A Reader's Guide to West Indian and Black British Literature*, London: Hansib, 1988, pp. 98–103.

> Here, whilst the proud their long-drawn pomps display
> There, the black gibbet glooms beside the way
> (Oliver Goldsmith, 'Deserted Village')

Celebration of the work-ethic in the writings of Thomson, Dyer and others, was bound up with celebration of Britain's commercial strengths and achievements. Commerce is lauded as the catalyst of social, cultural and economic progress. As T. K. Meier put it:

> Literary men of the seventeenth and eighteenth centuries, including Dryden, Pope, Steele, Thomson, most of the georgic poets, and a number of lesser dramatists, essayists, and poets did heap high praise upon both the concept of capitalistic business enterprise and upon businessmen who practiced it . . . Commerce and industry had caught the literary imagination of the period and represented for a time at least, the progressive hope of the future.

But it was by the forced labour of Africans that much of the commercial development of Britain occurred. Blacks were crucial to the business of commerce and civilization. They were, in seventeenth and eighteenth century opinion, 'the strength and sinews of this western world' and 'the mainspring of the machine which sets every wheel in motion'.

Robinson Crusoe can be read as a celebration of the work-ethic. Comparison with previous 'island fictions' reveals how eighteenth-century the novel is. In Shakespeare's *The Tempest* (c. 1611) for instance, the island is a place of magic and poetic strangeness. The dream island is the location for romance and reconciliation. Passions are becalmed, enmities healed. Later in the century we have another 'island fiction', a short novel by Henry Neville called *The Isle of Pines* (1688). The island in the novel is a place where, far from the scrutiny of Europe, Europeans can indulge in all kinds of sexual dreams and fantasies. The story is about a man who is shipwrecked upon an island, together with his master's daughter, his master's black servant woman, and two other women. The man soon takes the opportunity of making love to all of them, and they all bear him dozens of children, who then mate with each other, so that the whole island is soon populated. The shipwrecked islanders lose their European manners and modesty, and walk about stark naked. The island story is a male white dream or fantasy about indulging in sexual pleasures which *breach* the moral, religious and social codes of European society. By mating with his master's daughter for example, the man is breaching the class code; by mating with the black woman, he is breaching certain codes about good taste; by fathering several children by four mothers, he is breaching religious and moral codes about monogamy and fidelity.

By the time we come to *Robinson Crusoe*, the island fiction has nothing of the dream-magic of Shakespeare or the dream-fantasy of Neville. Defoe's dreams are totally dry. The island is a place where European skills can be applied to plant, cultivate and develop. Defoe's dreams are about the Protestant work-ethic.

The novel is an allegory on industry and development. Crusoe progresses from hunting (he goes out and shoots or traps animals) to farming (he plants maize), to manufacturing (he constructs a kiln to make pots and glassware). In this process of evolution from a primitive to a scientific condition, everything is submitted to economic judgement; the economic takes precedence over all aspects of human experience. Take the attitude to Nature – Crusoe's attitude to Nature is this: if it moves, eat it. There is nothing romantic or spiritual about Crusoe's response to nature. He is hard-headed, practical: trees exist to be cut down and hacked into boats, animals exist to be eaten or skinned, and the skins are commodities of trade. Or else animals exist to be domesticated and bred. It is always the economic that matters, not the spiritual. Everything is subject to calculation and accountancy: at one point, Crusoe, feeling sorry for himself in his loneliness, decides to weigh up his good experiences against his bad ones –

> I began to comfort my self as well as I could, and to set the good against the evil, that I might have something to distinguish my case from worse, and I stated it very impartially, like debtor and creditor, the comforts I enjoyed against the miseries I suffered, thus:

Evil	Good
I am cast upon a horrible desolate island, void of all hope of recovery.	But I am alive, and not drowned as all my ship's company was.
I am singled out and separated, as it were, from all the world to be miserable.	But I am singled out too from all the ship's crew to be spared from death; and He that miraculously saved me from death, can deliver me from this condition.
I am divided from mankind, a solitaire, one banished from humane society.	But I am not starved and perishing on a barren place, affording no sustenance.
I have not clothes to cover me.	But I am in a hot climate, where if I had clothes I could hardly wear them.

He sets one against the other as in a ledger book. This ledger book mentality is absurdly manifested when Crusoe saves Friday by killing the Indian savages out to eat him. After the combat, Crusoe, true to form, counts the dead –

3 killed at our first shot from the tree.
2 killed at the next shot.
2 killed by Friday in the boat.
2 killed by ditto, of those at first wounded.
1 killed by ditto, in the wood.
3 killed by the Spaniard.
4 killed, being found dropped here and there of their wounds, or killed by Friday in his chase of them.
4 escaped in the boat, whereof one wounded if not dead.

21 in all.

All this may seem rather charming in its oddity and eccentricity, but when Crusoe's ledger book philosophy is applied to blacks it is deeply dangerous. Crusoe for instance sells Xury, the black boy who had helped him escape from slavery, even though Xury was his devoted friend. Later, when Crusoe needs help in working his plantation, he misses not having Xury around – 'I wanted help, and now I found more than before, I had done wrong in parting with my boy Xury'. But by 'wrong', Crusoe does not mean moral wrong, but economic mistake. 'Wrong' is defined economically, not morally. Crusoe has no moral qualms about buying black slaves, and breeding them like goats, to work on his Brazilian plantation. What matters is the productiveness and profitability of the plantation, not the moral aspect of slavery. Indeed his shipwreck resulted from a slaving voyage to Guinea – he leaves his plantation to trade in slaves, so as to increase his revenue. Looking back on this move Crusoe calls it 'evil', but by 'evil' he does not mean the moral evil of enslaving blacks but the 'evil' of economic miscalculation – leaving his prosperous plantation to gamble on making more money by slave merchandise. Again, it is the ledger book philosophy in which ethics give way to economics.

As to the relationship between Crusoe and Friday, it is a paradigm of the master-slave relationship, in which the slave is depicted as being grateful to his master for saving his life. One of the excuses for slavery was that it was benevolent. John Dunton argued that the Slave Trade saved Africans from the bloody tyranny of their own countrymen, and saved them from being eaten by their fellow cannibals. Crusoe saving Friday is a re-enactment of the myth of salvation. Friday is devoted, he is glad to learn, glad to serve and happy in his servitude. He is dazzled by the skills and the science of the white man. Crusoe also saves his soul by turning him into a Protestant, and this missionary benevolence justifies the master-slave relationship.

2.2

FROM 'ROBINSON CRUSOE AND FRIDAY'

Peter Hulme

Crusoe's concern with accounting is legendary, so the details of his financial career can be easily mapped.[1] Under the direction of the 'honest and plain-dealing' captain (p. 39) he spends his 40 on trinkets and toys which he exchanges for 300 of gold dust. 200 is left with the captain's widow and the rest, converted again into trading goods, lost when the ship is captured by Turkish pirates. Due to the 'generous treatment' of the Portuguese captain who eventually rescues him (p. 55), Crusoe ends up in Bahia – at the southernmost point of the extended Caribbean (and not far from the gold-bearing area of Minas Gerais) – with 220 pieces of eight, payment for his 'possessions', all of them – boat, guns, slave – stolen from his master in Sallee. He learns sugar planting, buys land and sends for half of his English capital, which arrives in useful goods which he sells to great advantage in order to buy a negro slave and a European servant (p. 58). After thirty years of careful management by others in Robinson Crusoe's absence, Crusoe finds himself, as well as owner of a Caribbean island, 'master . . . of above 5,000 *l.* sterling in money, and . . . an estate . . . in the Brasils, of above a thousand pounds a year' (p. 280), plus, if he has not already included it, the money he brings off the island from the wrecks: 36 from his ship (p. 75), 1100 pieces of eight, six doubloons of gold, and some small bars of gold from the Spanish ship (p. 197).

But there is a danger here of not seeing the historical wood for the economic trees. Too great an emphasis on the financial detail of Crusoe's career can obscure the important way in which, however sketchily, the early chapters of the book

From *Colonial Encounters: Europe and the Native Caribbean, 1492–1797*, London: Methuen, 1986, pp. 184–9 and 200–8.

recapitulate the European 'history of discovery': the first tentative voyages down the West African coast, the entanglement with Islam, the crossing of the Atlantic, even the movement of Brazilian expertise to the Caribbean which was essential to the early economies of the English and French islands, This certainly does not mean that Crusoe is in any unproblematic sense an 'embodiment' of European colonialism – that would only make the book another kind of mimetic allegory. It points, if anything, in the opposite direction. Crusoe's colonial career can in fact be divided between the rather bathetically secondary, dependent on the goodwill of a series of benevolent Portuguese, and the heroically, but rather ridiculously, primary. Five days south of Sallee he is speaking of the wild animals never having heard a gun before (p. 47); and twelve days further south, near the point Crusoe is heading for precisely because it is the crossroads of the colonial trade routes ('I know that all the ships from Europe, which sailed either to the coast or Guiney, or to Brasil, or to the East-Indies, made this cape or those islands' (p. 50)), he shoots a leopard to the 'astonishment' and 'admiration' of the 'poor' negroes, who are properly grateful for this manifestation of European technology (pp. 51–2), a rehearsal for Crusoe's more important demonstration of fire-power in front of an equally 'amazed' Friday (p. 213). But Crusoe is most strikingly primary in his island interlude, reliving one of the original Caribbean adventures – Somers and Gates on the Bermudas perhaps, or even Columbus himself on Hispaniola, but in any case a European in a part of the world that has supposedly never seen a white man. Appropriately enough its introduction is to hear what Crusoe believes 'the first gun that had been fired there since the creation of the world' (p. 72).[2]

Those who take Defoe's 'realism' for granted do not often get as far as the Caribbean, so the relevant historical points need making firmly. The only uninhabited islands in the (extended) Caribbean were the unapproachable Bermudas – and they became a favourite reference point for that very reason. John Parry has written that the only uninhabited land in America tended to be uninhabitable:[3] the Amerindians would certainly not have ignored Crusoe's remarkably fertile island unless they had been driven off by the European competition for Caribbean land which was in full swing by 1659. But in *Robinson Crusoe* the Caribs use the island only for periodic picnics, and other Europeans make only a belated appearance, leaving Crusoe to live out alone his repetition of colonial beginnings.

This is said not to indict *Robinson Crusoe* for not being realistic enough, or for not fulfilling its realist promise, but rather to suggest that the realistic *detail* of the text obscures elements of the narrative that, if the above description is accurate, would have to be called mythic, in the sense that they have demonstrably less to do with the historic world of the mid-seventeenth-century Caribbean than they do with the primary stuff of colonialist ideology – the European hero's lonely first steps into the void of savagery, 'those uninhabited lands', in the unforgettable words of Lattimore's doubtless apocryphal parson, 'where only the heathens dwell'.[4]

The island episode of *Robinson Crusoe* is mythic in the same way as *The*

Tempest: it provides a simplifying crucible in which complexities can be reduced to their essential components. Such a formulation would probably gain assent, but the simplification of the episode needs careful, if seemingly paradoxical, glossing. It has of course been seen as simplifying in the sense of being the reduction to a logical starting-point through the resolutive method pioneered by Galileo and applied to political societies by Hobbes and, in a rather different way, by Locke and Rousseau; a method which enables the analyst to recompose the initial complexity of lived experience through a process of imaginative recombination of the relevant simples.[5] This view has Robinson Crusoe on the island, according to two of its variants, as the initial unit of a market economy interacting, when need arises, with similar producers; and as natural man, existing in a pre-social world before combining with others to form a 'society'. Neither of these analyses of the simplification of the island episode has proved convincing. The reasons have been spelled out by Marx and Watt amongst others,[6] but amount basically to two points: the lack of interest shown by the text in the compositive leg of the analysis which, for political and economic analysts, takes methodological precedence; and the 'impurity' of Robinson Crusoe as a simple, so graphically illustrated by the various trips to the wreck, but equally importantly represented by what Christopher Hill calls Crusoe's 'mental furniture',[7] the ideological and cultural presuppositions he inevitably carries with him to the island.

A further reason for rejecting such facile versions of the relationship between the fictional and the politico-economic discourses of the eighteenth century is the latter's indifference, as scientific fables, to the topographical and historical contexts whose very importance to *Robinson Crusoe* this chapter is trying to demonstrate. But two caveats need immediately adding to this statement. Despite the purely hypothetical status of the fables of origin in Hobbes, Locke and Rousseau, it should be remembered that they all in fact seek empirical support for their hypotheses in the contemporary state of America and, in Rousseau's case, refer specifically to the Caribs.[8] Conversely, despite the importance of *Robinson Crusoe*'s topography, there is a sense in which the island episode is, so to speak, a retreat from chronology and from geography into a moment that can in certain respects be called 'Utopian', though again some precision needs adding to this term.

The episode certainly has the mythic qualities of an original encounter between civilization and savagery, and is Utopian therefore in the sense that the specific characteristics of the historical Caribbean in the middle of the seventeenth century are stripped away to highlight the purity of the experience. And the island setting, as in many Utopias, facilitates the isolation necessary for such paradigmatic fables to develop. Then again, Crusoe's island shares some of the paradisaical elements of certain Utopias, especially that tradition of what might be called 'colonial Utopias', those which stand outside the mainstream of the Utopian tradition both by being primarily a sought ideal and only secondarily discursive, and by being constantly anti-authoritarian in impetus.

The model for this tradition comes from the *Odyssey*: the Lotus-Eaters of Book IX whose food makes Odysseus's sailors lose the desire to return home. The first Caribbean example is probably the community established by Roldán in the south of Hispaniola in flagrant challenge to Columbus's authority; the most relevant that outlined by Stephen Hopkins in challenge to Somers after the shipwreck of the *Sea-Venture*, and imperfectly practised by those who remained behind on the Bermudas; the two most resonant, the famous pirate commonwealth of Madagascar and, right at the end of the period covered by this book, that established, or at least held up as a potent ideal, by Fletcher Christian, in revolt from Captain Bligh's attempt to solve the problem of what to feed the Caribbean slaves.[9] *Robinson Crusoe*'s relationship with this tradition is by no means straightforward. More's pun on eutopia is especially problematic given Crusoe's anxiety and despair, but it should not be forgotten that Crusoe's island has the kind of tropical fertility that rewards labour, even if it does not make it unnecessary. In addition, the social dimension of the colonial Utopias is, strangely enough, present: both in Crusoe's benevolent despotism – which, amongst other things, is an insistence that the social relations proper to Europe will not apply on *his* island; and in the language he uses to talk about his property.

But the primary dimension of the narrative's parabolic simplicity is found in Crusoe's solitude on the island, and it is here, surely, in its analysis of the novel's 'radical individualism' that Watt's account stands uncontradicted. The particular significance of the use of the autobiographical memoir as an assertion of the primacy of individual experience by both Descartes and Defoe offers a comparison worth pursuing. The *Discourse on Method* tells a story similar in many respects to *Robinson Crusoe*: a story of travel and adventure cast in autobiographical form which culminates in a period of absolute solitude in which the protagonist is completely isolated from the world in which he lives. This is Descartes' account:

> it is exactly eight years since this wish made me decide to leave all those places where I had acquaintances, and to withdraw here to a country where the long duration of the war has established such discipline that the armies maintained there seem to serve only to ensure that the fruits of peace are enjoyed with the maximum of security; and where, in the midst of a great crowd of busy people, more concerned with their own business than curious about that of others, without lacking any of the conveniences offered by the most populous cities, I have been able to live as solitary and withdrawn as I would in the most remote of deserts.[10]

Descartes' solitude is very much an act of will, Crusoe's seemingly an involuntary exile from the world – although the island episode could also be seen as the logical culmination to a process of voluntary isolation that began with Crusoe's rejection of his father at the very beginning of the book, a denial of the past every bit as symbolic as Descartes' abandonment of the study of letters.[11] Their spheres are clearly different, consciously at least, but Crusoe and Descartes both set out to become very precisely self-made men: involved in a long quest for the composition of the self.

The differences may still seem striking. After all, Descartes arrives through a rigorous process of courageous self-examination at the certainty of a subjectivity that can ground knowledge; Crusoe tries, for the most part unsuccessfully, to compose himself in the face of dreadful anxieties. At best, surely, Descartes is the pure theorist of the self, operating in a world untrammelled by practical considerations; Crusoe an embodiment of the practical man of the world who operates entirely in a realm of trial and error. The differences should not be minimalized, but it has at least to be clear that behind the bland assurance of Descartes' prose lies a maelstrom of narrative and syntactical complexities that severely compromise the purity of that 'I'; and that, despite the 'pure' philosophical tradition stemming from his work, Descartes' own concern was to establish:

> a practical philosophy . . . by which, knowing the power and the effects of fire, water, air, the stars, the heavens and all the other bodies which surround us . . . we might put them in the same way to all the uses for which they are appropriate, and thereby make ourselves, as it were, masters and possessors of nature;[12]

– an enterprise entirely congruent with Crusoe's career and outlook.

. . .

The long-awaited arrival of the cannibals some two-thirds of the way through *Robinson Crusoe* heralds the climactic moments of the book; indeed the description of the battle between, on the one side, Crusoe and Friday, and on the other, twenty-one cannibals, is in many ways the climax of the particular discourse of colonialism being investigated here.

The moment is important for a number of reasons. It marks the second stage of 'beginning', the true colonial encounter when the complex matter of the European/native relationship must be negotiated. It is the moment when the parable of the self comes somewhere near resolution. And, more mundanely but no less important, it is the moment when *Robinson Crusoe* comes into its own as an adventure story in the now conventional sense of the word. Most crucially, these three things are simultaneous, constituting a moment of intense narrative excitement which, without the need for excursus, inscribes matters both colonial and metaphysical.

At the level of adventure a quite straightfoward account of the episode could point to the increase in tension which begins with Crusoe's discovery of the footprint and builds up through his various schemes for dealing with the cannibals, along with his doubts about the morality of killing them, to the moment of greatest excitement when Crusoe rescues Friday; the culmination coming with the final massacre undertaken to rescue the European prisoner and a native who turns out to be Friday's father.

This adventure story is interwoven with the metaphysical level in some obvious ways. The time between the discovery of the footprint and the arrival of the cannibals is the period of greatest anxiety for Crusoe, the period in which, one might say, his notion of self is most under threat; the period which turns to almost unbearable intensity the screw of the paradox that what makes solitude so frightening is that you might not be alone, until, in the firing of the gun, you reach that other paradox that the fear of being eaten is dependent on the *absence* of the cannibals. Their presence dispels Crusoe's anxiety and ends the parable of the self: he has composed his self, as the best adventurers always do, under pressure. The parabolic nature of the whole episode, it could in any case be argued, is signalled right from the beginning in the determinedly unrealistic presence of the single, isolated footprint in the middle of the beach, more like a pure trace of the idea of otherness than the actual track of another human being.

In some respects the colonial aspect of this part of the story is identical with the adventure aspect. On this reading Crusoe's acquisition of Friday is, quite literally, 'peradventure' – the chance result of his confrontation with the dreaded cannibals, and Friday's gratitude towards Crusoe for saving his life is altogether proper. Generically this is the realist reading, inadequate but ideologically useful because it obscures the crux of the colonial question.

The appearance of Friday is obviously important for readings of *Robinson Crusoe* such as Stephen Hymer's, which can see in the Crusoe/Friday relationship an adumbration of capital and labour and, more particularly, a parallel to the 'actual procedures of colonization used in the last two hundred years.'[13] There is a lot to be said in favour of this reading, which traces the stages from Crusoe's naming of Friday, through his teaching Friday English, placing him – in a small-scale version of plantation architecture – in the intermediate position between outer and inner stockade, teaching him Christianity, and finally initiating him into the use of firearms.[14] But the problem remains the same as before: mimetic readings such as this simply reduce the text to another kind of allegory. A more productive contextualization would come from pursuing the comparison with *The Tempest*. As a cannibal, Friday's initial connections would seem to be with his anagrammatic cousin Caliban, but the circumstances of his enrolment into Crusoe's service are remarkably similar to those surrounding Prospero's recruitment of Ariel: crucially, both are dependent on the spontaneous gratitude which results from the liberation of the captive party. The differences between Ariel and Friday are also instructive. Friday, though phenomenally quick about the house and woods, does not have Ariel's supernatural powers; but that may on balance be an advantage for Crusoe. After all, Ariel, freed from imprisonment, is clearly reluctant, after a suitable period of showing his gratitude, to exchange one captivity for another, and Prospero has to depend on a rather volatile mixture of threats and promises to keep him up to the mark. It is not entirely clear whether Prospero's magic would have been sufficient to bring Ariel back from, for example, the 'still-vex'd Bermoothes', had he decided to stay put. A thoroughly socialized Friday has the advantage of being a good deal more dependable.

A closer reading of the episode itself is also revealing. To begin with, Crusoe's actions were not as peradventure as they might have seemed. He presents himself, it is true, in the classic pose of the improvisatory adventurer – 'so I resolved to put my self upon the watch, to see them when they came on shore, and leave the rest to the event, taking such measures as the opportunity should present, let be what would be' (p. 203) – but the appropriate plan has already been revealed to Crusoe by, of all things, a dream that he had had some eighteen months previously:

> I dreamed that as I was going out in the morning as usual from my castle, I saw upon the shore two canoes and eleven savages coming to land, and that they brought with them another savage, who they were going to kill, in order to eat him; when on a sudden, the savage that they were going to kill, jumpt away, and ran for his life; and I thought, in my sleep, that he came running into my little thick grove before my fortification, to hide himself; and that I seeing him alone, and not perceiving that the other sought him that way, showed my self to him, and smiling upon him, encouraged him; and that he kneeled down to me, seeming to pray me to assist him; upon which I shewed my ladder, made him go up, and carry'd him into my cave, and he became my servant; and that as soon as I had gotten this man, I said to my self, 'Now I may certainly venture to the main land; for this fellow will serve me as a pilot, and will tell me what to do, and whether to go for provisions; and whether not to go for fear of being devoured, what places to venture into, and what to escape.' (p. 202)

There are several odd features to this dream, but nothing is so odd as its occurrence in the text in the first place. Crusoe's earlier dream (pp. 102–3) had been suitably religious, dense with the symbolism of storm, cloud, fire and spears. He had read it as a providential threat; we could take it physiologically as a result of his ague, psychologically as an indication of his general depression, and even psychoanalytically as a manifestation of his repressed guilt over disobeying his father. In other words the first dream occupies a perfectly comprehensible place in the narrative. But whereas this earlier dream follows with some logic from Crusoe's antecedent state of mind, the second dream, although the result of a similar agitation, is marked by Crusoe himself as disjunctive from its context. The immediate cause of Crusoe's agitation is his reflection on how he had been 'so near the obtaining what I so earnestly longed for, viz. some-body to speak to, and learn some knowledge from of the place where I was' (p. 202), a reflection brought about by the solitary corpse he finds washed onshore from the wreck of the Spanish ship. The dream is then introduced in this way:

> When this had agitated my thoughts for two hours or more, with such violence, that it set my very blood into a ferment, and my pulse beat as high as if I had been in a feaver, meerly with the extraordinary fervour of my mind about it; nature, as if I had been fatigued and exhausted with the very thought of it, threw me into a sound sleep; one would have thought I should have dreamed of it, but I did not, nor of anything relating to it; but I dreamed that . . . (p. 202)

Crusoe wakes to the dejection of finding that his escape was only a dream and, almost as an afterthought, he takes from the dream the lesson that capturing a savage would be the best way to escape. He makes no attempt to incorporate the dream into the surrounding fabric of his narrative by, for example, reading it as a providential prophecy.

There is no doubt that the presence of the dream, eighteen months but no more than a couple of pages before the arrival of the cannibal party, does strange things to the texture of the fictional 'realism'. As Watt pointed out, classical plots are alien to formal realism because they are not new: 'the impression of fidelity to human experience'[15] can only come from 'the novel' – a novelty which *Robinson Crusoe* announces on its title page: 'The Life and *Surprizing* Adventures'. Readers can hardly be totally surprised by Crusoe's adventure with the cannibals when they have just read a rehearsal for it in Crusoe's dream. To complicate matters, the dream also brings to an end a long section in which Crusoe is recounting how, like a drowning man, he 'run over the whole history of my life in miniature, or by abridgement, as I may call it' (p. 200): in other words another of those complex moments of replication – like the episode of the start of the journal – where the narrative seems to fold over on to itself in a way disturbingly unlike any realistic transcription of the empirically real.[16] In one sense, then, the dream acts, rather like the solitary footprint, as an outcrop against the grain of any straightforwardly mimetic reading of the cannibal episode. But what other kind of reading *could* make sense of it?

It was noted earlier, in discussing Hymer's analysis of the way the Crusoe/Friday relationship parallels the 'actual procedures of colonization', that the last stage in those procedures is Crusoe's initiation of Friday into the use of firearms, a lesson that repays its investment when Crusoe and Friday stand shoulder to shoulder shooting and killing the cannibal hordes. This initiation, though, is a final step that, historically, was never taken, the reason being – and this completes the unravelling of the mimetic reading of the episode – that slavery was never founded on the gratitude of the slave. Friday of course is never *called* a slave; but that absence is merely a symptom of the constant process of denial and renegotiation by which the text attempts to redraw the colonial encounter.

The Caribbean Amerindians were enslaved – though not often by the English – but it is not difficult to see in Crusoe's relationship with Friday a veiled and disavowed reference to the more pressing issue of black slavery. Crusoe's description of Friday is an almost classic case of negation: 'His hair was long and black, not curled like wool ... The colour of his skin was not quite black ... his nose small, not flat like the negroes' (pp. 208–9).

Friday is certainly a slave inasmuch as he has no will of his own; and Crusoe, unwilling as he may be ever to call Friday 'slave' has no qualms about adopting the other half of the dialectic – 'I likewise taught him to say Master, and then let him know, that was to be my name' (p. 209). Yet within the fiction the term 'slave' can be avoided because Friday's servitude is voluntary, not forced:

> At last he lays his head flat upon the ground, close to my foot, and sets my other foot upon his head, as he had done before; and after this, made all the signs to me of subjection, servitude, and submission imaginable, to let me know how he would serve me as long as he lived. (p. 209)

The problem with slavery is that slaves are dangerous because forced to labour against their will; the danger is removed if their 'enslavement' is voluntary and therefore not slavery at all. Defoe, it could be said, has gone one better than Locke's thesis that a person who forfeits his own life through an act that deserves death may justly have that death delayed and be required to give service to whom he has forfeited his life, and be done no injury by it.[17] However, forfeiture, just or not, is no guarantee that the slavery will not need enforcing by violence and therefore the master protecting from the threat of reciprocal violence; while the same paragraph of the *Second Treatise* denies the possibility of 'voluntary enslavement' on the classic liberal grounds that you cannot sign away your own fundamental rights. The circumstances of Friday's recruitment are a brilliant negotiation of these twin difficulties. His life is forfeited through Crusoe's intervention to save him, in keeping with Locke's justification of enslavement. But then – in a novel move – Defoe has Friday offer lifelong subjection, or so at least Crusoe imagines in his confident interpretation of the semiotics of Carib gesture. In Lockeian terms this move is theoretically invalid since Friday has no life to give, but its practical effects are incalculably beneficial to Crusoe since Friday's 'subjection' – his self-interpellation as a subject with no will – removes any need for force. By way of consolidation Crusoe, in a subtle move, avoids what might otherwise have seemed the obvious first step at the beginning of any normal social encounter – asking the name of the escaped prisoner. Instead, by naming him Friday – and remember the importance of Pocahontas's baptism as Rebecca – Crusoe underlines to him that his previous life has been forfeited, providing a weekly mnemonic to remind him who was responsible for giving him that second life.

Crusoe has dreamt a dream of wish-fulfilment. He thinks it is a dream of escape and is disappointed:

> I waked with this thought, and was under such inexpressible impressions of joy at the prospect of my escape in my dream, that the disappointments which I felt upon coming to my self and finding it was no more than a

> dream, were equally extravagant the other way, and threw me into a very great dejection of spirit. (pp. 202–3)

But the dream comes true and the escape that he himself, rather than the dream narrative, had built in ('I said to myself, "Now I may certainly venture . . ."') does not materialize as a direct result: Friday fulfils none of the six roles imagined by Crusoe in his dream. This is because – it might be said – the dream was not the fulfilment of Crusoe's wish to escape, but rather the fulfilment of Europe's wish to secure its Caliban colonies against the danger of rebellion. Friday's gratitude was the fulfilment of that dream. But it was only a dream.

Friday's gratitude proves, however, to be the breakthrough in Crusoe's establishment of social relationships. The Spaniard saved from the barbecue 'let me know by all the signs he could possibly make, how much he was in my debt for his deliverance' (p. 235); and Friday's father likewise 'looked up in my face with all the tokens of gratitude and thankfulness that could appear in any countenance' (p. 239). This is just what Crusoe wants to see. He proves, though, to be no sentimentalist. Addressing the Spaniard:

> I told him with freedom, I feared mostly their treachery and ill usage of me, if I put my life in their hands; for that gratitude was no inherent virtue in the nature of man; nor did men always square their dealings by the obligations they had received, so much as they did by the advantages they expected (p. 243)

– a resolutely Hobbesian view that contrasts starkly with the constant benevolence with which Crusoe is treated by others. The Spaniard, like Friday, has to convert the unguaranteed coin of his gratitude into the ringing currency of an unconditional sworn fealty – backed with a written contract (p. 244). Crusoe is determined to be an absolute sovereign, which is to be in society but not of it.[18]

The final incident in the transitional period of Crusoe's socialization emphasizes his dependence on the gratitude of others. When the English party arrive in the longboat – three prisoners and eight armed men – Crusoe never gives a moment's thought as to who the respective groups might be; whether, for example, the three prisoners might be murderers about to be cast away or executed on the captain's orders. He says with absolute assurance:

> I fitted my self up for a battle, as before; though with more caution, knowing I had to do with another kind of enemy than I had at first. (pp. 251–2)

Poised to attack those whom he unhesitatingly identifies as the 'villains' Crusoe takes time to ascertain from the prisoner he aims to free that the ship 'should be wholly directed and commanded by me in every thing; and if the ship was not recovered, he would live and dye with me in what part of the world soever I would send him' (p. 253), and to lay down his own numbered conditions. Only as absolute despot will Crusoe's composed self enter the social world.

NOTES

1. All page references to *The Life and Adventures of Robinson Crusoe* (1719) are included in the text and are to Angus Ross's 1965 Harmondsworth edition.
2. In his *History of the Principal Discoveries* part of Defoe's defence of his proposed South American colony is that Sir John Narborough landed on that part of the coast (now southern Argentina)

   > and in order to obviate the Pretences of any other Nation, as far as those Pretences may be grounded upon Possession, took a formal Possession of this very Country in the Name of King *Charles* the Second, his then reigning Sovereign; declar'd he found the same uninhabited by any *European* Nation, and fixing up a Cross of Wood, with an Inscription cut in Brass fixt upon it, he proclaim'd King *Charles* Sovereign of the Country: This I mention (not that I think any Body has a Right to dispossess the Natives of a Country) to intimate, that at *least* the *English* have as good a Title to it as any other *Nation* whatsoever. (p. 298)

   Crusoe is a literal cross (*Kreutz*nauer).
3. John H. Parry, 'A Secular Sense of Responsibility', in *First Images of the New World: The Impact of the New World on the Old*, ed. F. Chiappelli, 2 vols, Berkeley, 1976, I, p. 289. Cf.:

   > For supposing a Man, or Family, in the state they were, at first peopling of the World by the Children of *Adam*, or *Noah*; let him plant in some in-land, vacant places of *America*, we shall find that the *Possessions* he could make himself upon the *measures* we have given, would not be very large, nor, even to this day, prejudice the rest of Mankind, or give them reason to complain, or think themselves injured by this Man's Incroachment, though the Race of Men have now spread themselves to all corners of the World and do infinitely exceed the small number [which] was at the beginning. (John Locke, *Two Treatises of Government*, ed. Peter Laslett, New York, 1965, p. 335 (II, 37))

   For Locke America was uncultivated and therefore not possessed. See pp. 157–8.
4. Owen Lattimore, *Studies in Frontier History*, London, 1962, p. 27. And cf. John McVeagh's analogous point that '*Robinson Crusoe* is only seemingly a realistic novel, more truly an abstraction, the myth of western development cast into story form' (*Tradeful Merchants: The Portrayal of the Capitalist in Literature*, London, 1981, pp. 59–60).
5. A good account of this method is given by C. B. MacPherson in his introduction to Hobbes, *Leviathan*, Harmondsworth, 1968, pp. 25–9. Contrast Marx's account of his method in the *Grundrisse: Foundations of the Critique of Political Economy (Rough Draft)* trans. Martin Nicklaus, Harmondsworth, 1973, pp. 100–8.
6. *Capital Volume 1*, trans. Ben Fowkes, Harmondsworth, 1976, pp. 169–77; Watt, '*Robinson Crusoe* as a myth', *Essays in Criticism*, I, 1951, pp. 111–19. Cf. Michael White, 'The production of an economic *Robinson Crusoe*', *Southern Review*, XVI, 1982, pp. 115–41; and John J. Richetti, *Defoe's Narratives*, Oxford; 1975, pp. 15–16.
7. Christopher Hill, 'Robinson Crusoe', *History Workshop*, 10, 1980, p. 12.
8. Hobbes, *Leviathan*, p. 187 (chapter 13); Locke, *Two Treatises*, p. 336 (II, 37), p. 338 (II, 41), p. 343 (II, 49); Jean-Jacques Rousseau, 'Discourse on the origin and basis of inequality', in *The Essential Rousseau*, trans. Lowell Bair, New York, 1974, p. 168.
9. For Roldán, see Carl Sauer, *The Early Spanish Main*, Berkeley, 1966, p. 93; for Stephen Hopkins and Bermuda, see pp. 103–4: Defoe knew this story, possibly from John Smith's *Generall Historie of Virginia*, and repeats it in the text of his *Atlas*

Maritimus & Commercialis, pp. 307–9 (Novak, *Economics*, p. 164, n. 6, suggests that it provided Defoe with the main source for the development of Crusoe's colony in *The Farther Adventures*); on Madagascar, see Defoe's *A General History of the Pyrates* (1724–8), London, 1972; on Christian and the fate of his Utopian ideal, see Richard Hough, *Captain Bligh and Mr. Christian: The Men and the History*, London, 1972. More's narrator in *Utopia*, Hythloday, supposedly travelled with Vespucci to the Caribbean.

10. René Descartes, *Discourse on Method*, trans. F. E. Sutcliffe, Harmondsworth, 1968, pp. 51–2. Cf. 'Everything revolves in our minds by innumerable circular motions, all centering in ourselves . . . Hence man may be properly said to be alone in the midst of crowds and the hurry of men and business' (Daniel Defoe, *Serious Reflections of Robinson Crusoe*, London, 1720, p. 2).

    Descartes' autobiography is of course 'real' as opposed to Crusoe's fictional life story but this makes little difference to the narrative strategies involved. On the rhetoric of the *Discourse* see: Jean-Luc Nancy's two articles, 'Larvatus pro Deo', *Glyph*, 2, 1977, pp. 14–36, and 'Mundus est fabula', MLN, 93, 1978, pp. 635–53; David Simpson, 'Putting one's house in order', *New Literary History*, IX, 1977–8, pp. 83–101; and Bernstein, *The Philosophy of the Novel*, chapter 5. Descartes' realization of his intellectual task was heralded by a dream: see Jacques Maritain, *The Dream of Descartes*, London, 1946. On solitude as a recurrent image in much of Defoe's fiction, see Homer Brown, 'The displaced self in the novels of Daniel Defoe', *English Literary History*, XXXVIII, 1971, pp. 562–90.

11. Descartes, *Discourse on Method*, pp. 33–4.
12. Descartes, p. 78. As Gilson points out, this is 'l'idéal baconien de la science' (René Descartes, *Discours de la méthode: Texte et commentaire*, ed. Etienne Gilson, Paris, 1976, p. 446).
13. Stephen Hymer, 'Robinson Crusoe and the secret of primitive accumulation', *Monthly Review*, XXIII, no. 4, 1971–2, p. 26.
14. Hymer, pp. 27–9.
15. Ian Watt, *The Rise of the Novel*, Harmondsworth: Penguin, 1963 p. 14.
16. Dewey Ganzel suggests that the whole episode is a late interpolation ('Chronology in *Robinson Crusoe*', *Philological Quarterly*, XL, 1961, pp. 495–512). This would be striking evidence of textual disturbance. The arguments are complex, based on five chronological references to a 28 + year cycle (rather than the predominant 27 + cycle); but there are also two anticipatory remarks of Crusoe's – to a meeting with cannibals in his twenty-fourth year on the island, and to the usefulness of his fortifications – that apply only to the dream events.
17. This follows closely Locke's phrasing in paragraph 23 of the Second Treatise (*Two Treatises*, p. 325).
18. In this very precise sense Crusoe is in a 'state of nature' according to Hobbesian theory. The motif of 'rescue' continues from the previous chapters. The Algonquian response operates in terms of 'gift'; Europeans (*viz* Prospero and Crusoe) in terms of forced labour; between Europeans there must be a written contract. Hobbes specifically contrasts 'gift' with 'contract' (*I*, 14 (p. 193)).

2.3

FROM 'THE GEOGRAPHY OF *ROBINSON CRUSOE*'

Richard Phillips

Robinson Crusoe illustrates the general outlines of the geography of modern adventure, the dialectical geography of home and away, in which adventures are set away from home, in unknown space that is disconnected, simplified, liminal and broadly realistic.

The geography and the narrative of *Robinson Crusoe* is divided between home and away. Little is said about Robinson Crusoe's home, but everything that happens to Crusoe, everything he does and everywhere he goes, is a comment on his home – his family home and his home country – as it is and as it might be. Crusoe leaves his family home in York, against his father's wishes. Like all adventurers, he travels 'beyond the veil of the known into the unknown', as Joseph Campbell puts it (Campbell 1949: 82). The unknown space is defined in relation to the known, the unmapped in relation to the mapped. The journey begins in domestic, civilised, mapped space. But since the setting of his adventure is unmapped, it is not possible to map a course that will lead there. Crusoe must simply head for the edges of his known world and abandon himself to chance. Robinson Crusoe's first adventure begins almost the moment he leaves Britain, as 'the wind began to blow, and the sea to rise in a most terrible manner', the beginning of a terrible storm indeed (Anon. undated a: 3). It is not until later, on another sea voyage, that Defoe's adventurer encounters the storm that blows his ship 'out of our knowledge', away from 'all human commerce' and onto a sand bank near an unknown land in the Caribbean or South Atlantic (somewhere near the Spanish dominions – in the vicinity of the Orinoco – he thinks) (Anon. undated a: 21). Robinson Crusoe, along with other passengers of the stricken

In *Mapping Men and Empire: A Geography of Adventure*, London: Routledge, 1997, pp. 29–35.

vessel, is attempting to row ashore when 'a wave mountain high, came rolling astern of us and took us with such fury' (Anon. undated a: 22). The wave plucks the passengers from their boat, scattering them. Like the other men, Crusoe is almost completely passive against the forces of Nature, as he admits.

> I saw the sea coming after me, as high as a great hill, and as furious as an enemy, which I had no means of strength to contend with: my business was to hold my breath, and raise myself upon the water, if I could. (Anon. undated a: 23)

Finally, the waves deposit Crusoe on an unknown shore. The setting of his adventure is completely disconnected from his home, and is completely unknown to him, and, as far as he is concerned, unnamed. The disorienting, life-threatening passage defines the island as a space that is fundamentally disconnected from the world Crusoe has known before, a space that is not on his map. The adventurer surfaces in the setting of his (principal) adventure, in space which is at first blank, unknown. 'Looking round I saw no prospect' – no prospect for himself other than 'perishing', and no visual prospect of the island (Anon. undated a: 24).

The space of Crusoe's island is a simplified, uncomplicated space, malleable in the hands of the author and his fictional adventurer. Washed up on an unknown shore, Crusoe immediately pulls himself together, and begins to explore where he is and, at the same time, who he is, what he can be. Almost immediately, he begins to look around him, seeking a 'place where I might fix my dwelling' and taking a survey of the island as a whole (Anon. undated a: 29). The island Crusoe discovers is whatever he wants it to be, and it is a vehicle for social, political and moral reflection. In the seemingly uncomplicated, simplified geography and economy of the island, Crusoe's Christian, *petit bourgeois* social outlook seems more convincing than it might have done in a more textured setting, with other people, commodity markets and landlords, for example. Ironically, perhaps, Crusoe's social development is helped rather than hindered by his isolation.

The geography of *Robinson Crusoe* is broadly realistic, plausible to nineteenth-century readers. Defoe's geographic imagery, like his hero and narrative, is suffused with the appearance of reality; it is a 'just History' without 'any Appearance of Fiction' (Defoe 1719a: ii). The original frontispiece, among the most enduring elements of Defoe's original since it is reproduced with relatively slight variation in most Crusoes, including the Darton edition, presents an image of Crusoe that reflects and reinforces the realism of the written text.[1] The image follows Defoe's detailed descriptions, omitting only the goat-skin umbrella, saw and hatchet, which have found their way into some later illustrations of the adventurer. Like the text, which reinforces its circumstantial realism through frequent repetition, the picture of Crusoe repeats information supplied in writing, and functions as a visual equivalent of the text (Barr 1986: 14). Meticulous attention to detail, in this engraving, assures the reader that artistic licence is surrendered in the interest of faithful attention to 'fact'. In the nineteenth-century abridgement, repetition is surrendered in the interests of brevity, although the clean, factual style is maintained, preserving the sense of reality, if simplifying it to fit the shorter, juvenile format.

Crusoe's island is literally liminal, as a marginal zone in which the hero experiences a rite of passage.[2] The island inverts but does not, in the nineteenth-century context, ultimately subvert the social order of the adventurer's home country, since the adventure narrative confirms that social order. Although 'strange' and 'surprizing', as the original title puts it, the island adventures of Robinson Crusoe map a conservative vision of Britain and empire, identity and geography.

MAPPING CRUSOE

Robinson Crusoe could be read, in the nineteenth century, as a metaphorical map of Britain. British identities are mapped, through the figurative imagery of the hero, in the geography of his adventure. Crusoe, symbolically reborn as he enters the island, starts out as a man with almost no identity, and is constructed as the story proceeds. Robinson Crusoe devotes a single sentence to introducing himself and his family (quoted above). He gets straight on with his story. The brevity of this introduction is partly due to a (sometimes) spare, eighteenth-century writing style, mediated by close editing and ruthless abridgement, but it is also characteristic of adventure more generally. Since the adventurer is defined primarily by his actions, it is not possible to introduce him in much detail before the action part of his story really begins (Zweig 1974). Like all quest adventurers, Crusoe's 'perilous journey' leads to 'crucial struggle' and finally to 'the exaltation of the hero' (Frye 1990: 186–188; Green 1979). Unlike the ageless classical adventurers who endured and struggled endlessly, Crusoe ages and invents himself on the island. His identity as a white, middle-class, Christian, British man is mapped and affirmed through the course of the story.

But mapping Crusoe is not a matter of inventing identities from scratch. More conservatively, it involves recasting and reasserting existing identities. Crusoe is not washed up naked, and he clings to his cold, wet clothes, the trappings and symbols of his civilisation. Later, despite the hot sun, he is 'unwilling to be quite naked' (Anon. undated a: 44). Of 'good family', the middle-class castaway also finds himself with a shipwreck full of useful capital (tools, provisions and other useful things) and an island to himself. He is still a man, rather than a 'universal' human being. And he also has a Bible (three, in fact), which he reads and learns to understand and value. Robinson Crusoe takes these elements of Britain, of his British social self, and transplants them to the island, where he amplifies them, in himself and in his engagements with the island. Thus, when Crusoe was removed from society, society was not removed from him.

The island and its native inhabitants are vehicles in the mapping of Crusoe. The adventurer's spiritual transformation illustrates this point. Crusoe's act of rebellion against his father symbolises his original sin (Pearlman 1976). He sets out 'without letting [his] father know the rash and disobedient step [he] had taken', driven only by his 'roving disposition', guided by nothing but his sinful nature (Anon. undated a: 5). What he does, first in his 'wicked' years of adventurous wanderings, and then in the twenty-eight years of mostly solitary island life, defines who he is, and what he becomes. Crusoe's survival, after the storm and shipwreck, symbolises his forgiveness and Christian rebirth. Seeing the stranded vessel so far off shore, the morning after he is washed ashore, Crusoe 'began to thank God' for his 'happy deliverance' (Anon. undated a: 24). The waves, which have consumed the other crew-members, and are soon to consume the ship itself, leave Crusoe 'half *dead* with the water [he] took in' (Anon. undated a: 22, my emphasis). This, the adventurer's twenty-sixth birthday, is also the moment of his symbolic rebirth, so that following twenty-six years of 'wickedness' his solitary life begins (Anon. undated a: 6). Crusoe's life on the island, initially solitary, leads him to Christian knowledge. Opening the Bible, the first words that meet his eye are these: 'Call upon me in the time of trouble, and I will deliver thee' (Anon. undated a: 35–37). Alone, on the island, Crusoe kneels down and prays his first prayer, that God would deliver him in time of trouble. Crusoe's 'troubles' include adventures on and around the island. Some of his first adventures take place as he explores. For example, while exploring the island's circumference in a sailing boat he made himself, Crusoe sails into a current and is 'carried along with such violence' that 'I now began to give myself over for lost' (Anon. undated a: 45). Eventually, though, he manages to return to the island, where, 'When I was on shore, I fell on my knees and gave God thanks for my deliverance' (Anon. undated a: 47). Thus the island and the surrounding waters are vehicles of Crusoe's spiritual transformation. So are the native inhabitants, cannibals, who visit the island years after Crusoe's arrival. Crusoe rescues a 'poor creature' who is about to be eaten by the 'savage wretches' (Anon. undated a: 59, 52). He later converts the man, whom he calls Friday, to Christianity, and teaches him to wear clothes and to eat goat rather than human flesh. Friday's conversion is a measure of Crusoe's Christian zeal and spiritual maturity. The other cannibals are also affected by Crusoe's religious fervour. After resolving not to judge their seemingly 'savage' practices, Crusoe decides to save a white 'christian' who is about to become their next meal. Aiming his musket, and having Friday do the same – telling him 'do as you see me do' – he kills and scatters the cannibals (Anon. undated a: 68). At first only two drop, while the others 'ran about screaming and bleeding'; eventually seventeen are killed (Anon. undated a: 70). The cannibals, like Friday and the island, are seen from Crusoe's perspective as vehicles of his own spiritual growth, people and places encountered on his spiritual journey.

MAPPING THE ISLAND

Robinson Crusoe maps nineteenth-century colonial geography, the British Empire in particular. Crusoe's island and its native inhabitants are vehicles for the adventurer's personal growth, for his spiritual, moral and social reflections, but they also represent, map and imaginatively colonise real places and peoples, real colonial geographies. Defoe wrote *Robinson Crusoe* with a particular colonial project in mind – British colonisation in Spanish America – which is why he located the island near the mouth of the Orinoco River. The British never colonised Spanish America quite as Defoe wanted them to, although Britain's sphere of imperial influence did extend throughout much of the region in the nineteenth century (Hyam 1993), but *Robinson Crusoe* did influence the course of British colonialism in a more general way. Although originally set specifically in the Caribbean, Crusoe's island came to be regarded a more generic, colonial space (Hulme 1992). *Robinson Crusoe* was a map of British imperial geography and a myth of British Imperialism.

Transforming the island, Crusoe maps a specifically nineteenth-century brand of colonialism associated with emigration and settlement. Suddenly cut off from his past and thrust into a terrifying new existence, the storm-tossed and shipwrecked Crusoe presents an image of modern, colonial experience. The storm, an image of disorienting modernity (Landow 1982), of powerful forces that Crusoe can neither control nor understand, sweeps him from all that is familiar. He is thrown into a new world, or rather a space in which to invent a new world. In the uncomplicated, unknown and initially unpopulated island, he is cast ashore with a little capital – the contents of the wrecked ship – and given the opportunity to make a new world, a place in which to live. He begins by exploring, imaginatively mapping the island, filling its blank spaces with names. When Crusoe saves a native islander, he also names him (Friday), identifying him with nature (which the God of Genesis created before Adam and Eve, on Saturday) and imaginatively colonising him too.[3] To Crusoe, names bring the island and its native inhabitant into existence, simultaneously colonising them and sketching 'the shadowy outline of a place'.[4] The island and Friday become terms in Crusoe's world view, settings and characters in a colonial encounter, defined from the perspective of the colonist (Brydon and Tiffin 1993). Crusoe also physically colonises the island, building a shelter for himself, building an enclosure for goats, clearing and farming land. Crusoe, a practical colonist, makes everything he needs – and a few things he doesn't, the folly of which is quickly apparent. A cedar boat, for example, is described as a 'preposterous enterprise' (Anon, undated a: 43) from the start, and when complete it is too large to launch. For the most part, Defoe concentrates his practical energies on the sober enterprise of making a place in which to live.

Crusoe, with his initial capital and his own island, is a capitalist, his colonial adventure thoroughly *petit bourgeois*, and acceptable within a broadly *petit bourgeois* value system.[5] Robinson Crusoe was not always a colonist; earlier in life he was a merchant adventurer and a plantation capitalist, and he was shipwrecked while on a slave-trading mission (to procure slaves for his Brazilian plantation). But the adventurer's days as a trader, an investor and a slave trader are relegated to his 'wicked' youth (Anon. undated a: 6), while only his later life, as a colonist, is endorsed. Abridgements of *Robinson Crusoe*, focusing on the island adventure, give little mention to Crusoe's imperial career, prior to his arrival on the island. *Robinson Crusoe*, particularly in abridged form, is not a myth of all imperialisms, but more specifically of practical *petit bourgeois* colonialism (Nerlich 1987). In the words of James Joyce, who as an Irishman saw British colonialism from the perspective of the colonised,

> The true symbol of the British [colonial] conquest is Robinson Crusoe, who, cast away on a desert island, in his pocket a knife and a pipe, becomes an architect, a carpenter, a knife grinder, an astronomer, a baker, a shipwright, a potter, a saddler, a farmer, a tailor, an umbrella-maker, and a clergyman. He is the true prototype of the British colonist, as Friday (the trusty savage, who arrives on an unlucky day) is the symbol of the subject races. The whole Anglo-Saxon spirit is in Crusoe: the manly independence; the unconscious cruelty; the persistence; the slow yet efficient intelligence; the sexual apathy; the practical, well-balanced religiousness; the calculating taciturnity. (Joyce 1909, translated 1964: 25)

In the early eighteenth century, *Robinson Crusoe* was, as James Joyce put it, a 'prophecy of empire', but in the nineteenth century it became a myth, promoting popular colonialism, representing and legitimating the British Empire to the British people.

Crusoe's colonial adventure displays, and diachronically resolves, some of the contradictions of colonialism. Crusoe's adventure, like that of all colonists, is pervaded by a tension between a wandering inclination (which leads to new lands) and a settled condition (in which the adventurous spirit is abandoned and settlement ensues). Crusoe changes from an enthusiastic to a reluctant adventurer, from a wanderer to a settler. Transformed principally by his Christian conversion, he renounces his restless, rebellious ways and rediscovers the domestic virtues (Zweig 1974). Ultimately he fashions a world in which adventure is no longer necessary. His island adventure lasts only as long as it takes him to transform the unknown, to possess it as a known, domesticated, enclosed, home-like space. Nature, in all its forms, is domesticated. At first Crusoe tames one corner of the island, making a secure place for himself, where he finds refuge from the wilderness and possible dangers without. Gradually adventure becomes superfluous, as the island is known, the possible dangers unmasked (the footprint, for example) and the 'savages' killed or converted. Except for the adventures that arise in the course of his practical Christian colonisation, Robinson Crusoe's life is a quiet one, centred around his residence, which is designed for 'security from being surprised by any man or ravenous beast' (Anon. undated a: 29). After an exploring expedition, he reflects, 'I cannot express what a satisfaction it was now, to come into my own hut, and lie down in my hammock bed' (Anon. undated a: 40). The contradiction of Robinson Crusoe, 'the unadventurous hero' (Zweig 1974), was mirrored in British colonies, where colonialism was associated with adventure, perhaps inspired by adventure, but was also at odds with adventure, since settled colonialism was about transforming the unknown into the known, erasing and transforming the spaces of adventure. By the end of *Robinson Crusoe*, adventure had run its course.

Through its narrative of colonisation and transformation on and of an island, *Robinson Crusoe* represents, promotes and legitimates a form of colonialism. When, after twenty-eight years, Crusoe finally leaves the island (on a British merchant ship he has helped save from mutineers), he leaves behind him an idealised British colony, which he hands over to the group of mutineers, whose merciful punishment it is to be left there. Before leaving, he 'talked to the men, told them my story, and how I managed all my household business' (Anon. undated a: 79). Crusoe gives the men his story, the story of how he colonised an island. He intends the story to guide the new colonists, inspiring their practical acts and imaginatively framing their colonial encounters. Crusoe gave his story not only to the mutineers, but also to British readers. Some readers were surely inspired to go off to sea, to seek adventure in distant lands, perhaps to settle in Canada or Australia, and ultimately help to build an empire. 'To many [readers, *Robinson Crusoe*] has given the decided turn of their lives, by sending them to sea', wrote one Scottish observer in 1834 (Ballantyne 1834, cited by Shinagel 1975: 266–267). In the middle of the nineteenth century, another prominent British observer called *Robinson Crusoe*

> a book, moreover, to which, from the hardy deeds which it narrates; and the spirit of strange and romantic enterprise which it tends to awaken, England owes many of her astonishing discoveries both by sea and land, and no inconsiderable part of her naval glory. (Borrow 1851: 1.39)

But while *Robinson Crusoe* inspired many colonial acts, its influence was not limited to the minority of Britons who were directly engaged in such acts. To the majority of Britons who stayed at home, *Robinson Crusoe* was a powerful geographical fantasy but also a colonial myth, a myth that represented British colonialism to the British people, as well as to the colonised peoples (Brydon and Tiffin 1993). Crusoe's island was a Christian utopia, a middle-class utopia, a colonial utopia. The island and the adventurer represented Britain and British colonialism – including colonial land grabs and colonial violence – in the best possible light, conservatively legitimating, powerfully mapping. To the reader in nineteenth-century Britain, Crusoe's island became an image of Britain and the British Empire, not as they had been when Defoe wrote, but as they had become by the nineteenth century.

NOTES

1. On the illustration of *Robinson Crusoe*, see Wackermann (1976).
2. But there are also differences between *Robinson Crusoe* and the tribesmen and women described by anthropologist Arnold van Gennep, who inhabited the most literally liminal space (Turner 1969). In particular, the former is a fictional character while the latter are real people.
3. The story of Crusoe's spiritual rebirth, emerging from the dark waters into an unnamed land, a garden of Eden where he is the sole, Adam-like occupant, is

reminiscent of the Biblical creation story. In Genesis, land creatures including Adam and Eve were created on the sixth day, once the natural environment was in place (night and day; sky; land and vegetation; sun, moon and stars; sea creatures and birds). In other words, Adam appeared on Saturday while (most of) nature appeared by or on Friday.

4. I borrow this phrase from Paul Carter (1987: 17), who traces the emergence of 'the shadowy outline of a place' in Australian exploration literature in *The Road to Botany Bay*.
5. Crusoe takes his capitalist enterprise as far as circumstances permit. Due to his isolation, he is unable to participate in a market economy, and is therefore forced into a more self-sufficient, superficially Jeffersonian form of colonialism.
6. Defoe criticised the brutality of some slave traders, and condemned the more plunderous forms of imperialism, although he was not opposed to slavery or imperialism *per se* (Rogers 1979; Seidel 1991). The 'wickedness' of slavery, identified in *Robinson Crusoe*, was associated less with the suffering of slaves than with the moral effects on white colonists, who might gamble capital and live fast rather than sober lives.

BIBLIOGRAPHY

Anon. (undated a) *The Wonderful Life and Surprising Adventures of Robinson Crusoe*, London: William Darton.

Ballantyne, R. (1834) *The Prose Works of Sir Walter Scott*, Edinburgh.

Barr, J. (1986) *Illustrated Children's Books*, London: British Library.

Borrow, G. (1851) *Lavengro: the Scholar – the Gypsy – the Priest* (3 volumes), London: J. Murray.

Brydon, D. and Tiffin, H. (1993) *Decolonising Fictions*, Sydney: Dangaroo Press.

Campbell, J. (1949) *The Hero with a Thousand Faces*, New York: Bollingen/Pantheon.

Carter, P. (1987) *The Road to Botany Bay: an Exploration of Landscape and History*, New York: Alfred Knopf.

Defoe, D. (1719a) *The Life and Strange and Surprizing Adventures of Robinson Crusoe, of York, Mariner: who lived eight and twenty years, all alone in an uninhabited island on the coast of America, near the mouth of the great river of Oroonoque; having been cast on shore by shipwreck, whereon all the men perished but himself. With an account of how he was at last as strangely deliver'd by pyrates. Written by himself*, London: W. Taylor.

Frye, N. (1990) *Anatomy of Criticism*, Harmondsworth: Penguin Books.

Green, M. (1979) *Dreams of Adventure, Deeds of Empire*, New York: Basic Books.

Hulme, P. (1912) *Colonial Encounters: Europe and the Native Caribbean 1492–1797*, London: Routledge.

Hyam, R. (1993) *Britain's Imperial Century, 1815–1914*, Basingstoke: Macmillan.

Joyce, J. (1964) 'Daniel Defoe', trans. J. Prescott, *Buffalo Studies* I, 1.

Landow, G. (1982) *Images of Crisis: Literary Iconology, 1750 to the Present*, London: Routledge and Kegan Paul.

Nerlich, M. (1987) *Ideology of Adventure, Studies in Modern Consciousness, 1150–1750* (in two volumes), Minneapolis: University of Minnesota Press.

Pearlman, E. (1976) '*Robinson Crusoe* and the cannibals', *Mosaic* 10, 1: 39–55.

Rogers, P. (1979) *Robinson Crusoe*, London: George Allen and Unwin.

Seidel, M. (1991) *Robinson Crusoe: Island Myths and the Novel*, Boston: Twayne.

Shinagel, M. (1975) *Robinson Crusoe*, New York: Norton.

Turner, V. (1969) *The Ritual Process*, Chicago: Aldine.

Wackermann, E. (1976) 'Robinson and Robinsonaden: buch illustration aus drei jahrhunderten', *Illustration*, 63.

Zweig, P. (1974) *The Adventurer*, London: Dent.

2.4

FROM '"MY SAVAGE", "MY MAN": RACIAL MULTIPLICITY IN *ROBINSON CRUSOE*'

Roxann Wheeler

II

Even a simple rehearsal of *Robinson Crusoe*'s plot and its geography supports the customary critical emphasis on the production of differences. Peter Hulme's *Colonial Encounters: Europe and the Native Caribbean 1492–1797* has been instrumental in framing *Robinson Crusoe* as a study of colonial discourse and in making visible the significance of cannibalism to constructions of European identity. Critics, including Hulme, have tended to regard the novel primarily in its construction of difference, and certainly such an emphasis seems warranted given that, overall, power relations in the Atlantic benefited Europeans. My analysis, while also featuring the Caribbean, differs significantly. I link the Caribbean to other aspects of colonialism in the early eighteenth century, especially attending to the way that the novel produces both racial difference and racial multiplicity. Before incorporating racial multiplicity into the analysis, I establish a foundation of racialized differences that shape the colonial narrative. These differences have been addressed predominately in the context of the island segment.[1] Several colonial factors, I argue, give impetus to the plot: Crusoe's desire to improve his station in Britain and in the colonies; his fear of bodily harm from the Caribs: the necessity of eradicating the cannibals; and the desire to domesticate Friday.

Initially, Crusoe's desires for advancement beyond the station allotted to him propel the plot forward. Although Crusoe reiterates that his desire to travel and for wealth is inexplicable, we might explain these goals as results of the unprecedented capital accumulation made possible through global trade and

English Literary History, no. 62, 1995, pp. 821–61. Extract: pp. 825–38

colonization in the late seventeenth and eighteenth centuries. Expanded trade routes and new colonies stripped parts of what was called the 'uncivilized' world of their natural and human resources and permanently altered those economies and ways of life to satisfy spiraling British consumer desire – including a desire for adventure and travel.[2] Crusoe's wish for advancement materializes when he joins a trading expedition to Guinea: 'That evil influence which carryed me first away from my father's house, that hurried me into the wild and indigested notion of raising my fortune ... whatever it was, presented the most unfortunate of all enterprises to my view; and I went on board a vessel bound to the coast of Africa' (38–39).[3] Crusoe notes that 'this voyage made me both a sailor and a merchant'; the gold dust he brought back yielded him 300: 'this filled me with those aspiring thoughts which have since so compleated my ruin' (40). The even greater desire to increase this wealth leads to another African voyage, but Moorish pirates take him prisoner and he is enslaved in Morocco.

Upon Crusoe's escape from the Moors, a generous captain of a Portuguese slave ship allows Crusoe to sell and barter his stolen property, including his companion Xury, for a considerable sum of money. After staying with a man who owns a Brazilian sugar plantation, Crusoe observes: 'seeing how well the planters lived, and how they grew rich suddenly, I resolved, if I could get licence to settle there' (55). By setting up as a planter in Brazil, Crusoe hopes to increase his fortune even more, and he follows the pattern of European settlement in the Americas first by buying land, working it with his own labor, and eking out an existence. Noting that his neighbor is in the same circumstance, Crusoe comments about the difficulty of producing profit: 'we rather planted for food than any thing else, for about two years ... [in] the third year we planted some tobacco, and made each of us a large piece of ground ready for planting canes in the year to come; but we both wanted help' (55). He complains that all the work is by the labor of his own hands and that his standard of living is lower than it was in Britain. To improve his profits, he purchases European and African labor. His excessive desire for advancing more rapidly than he otherwise would leads him to act as a slave trader on behalf of other planters (58–59). Obeying 'blindly the dictates of my fancy rather than my reason' (60), Crusoe sets out on a third voyage to Africa. A shipwreck arrests his trip to the slave coast, and he arrives on the island.

A similar pattern repeats itself on the island as it had on the mainland: he acquires land, improves it with his own labor, and then acquires Friday as additional labor power. Before this point, when Crusoe is convinced he will remain on the island alone, he notes that his desires have dissipated because there are no competitors: by the fourth year 'I had nothing to covet; for I had all that I was now capable of enjoying; I was lord of the whole manor; or if I pleased, I might call my self king or emperor over the whole country which I had possession of. There were no rivals; I had no competitor' (139). There is neither surplus nor a circuit of exchange. This fulfillment should end a novel driven by

Crusoe's desire for economic gain, but another motivating factor takes over the colonial plot. It is no longer Moors or other Africans but Caribs who form the significant point of contrast to Crusoe.

At the point of apparent stasis in the plot when his pecuniary desires have subsided, Crusoe sees a footprint, and the fear of cannibals, rather than a desire for advancement, takes over as the driving force of the plot (162–67, 171). The fear of cannibals renews his desire to escape, but the desire to domesticate Friday soon substitutes for a desire to escape. The novel ends with Crusoe's return to Europe as a wealthy planter and with a synopsis of his island colony's violent fate from internal dissension among the Europeans and from external aggression resulting from a conflict with the neighboring Caribs.

In terms of plot and content, *Robinson Crusoe* is best understood as a colonial narrative. The novel establishes Crusoe's method of rising in the world as possible because of a developed colonial labor force and of the demands of trade: African trade, particularly in slaves, provides Crusoe's capital and labor base for his profitable sugar production in Brazil. *Robinson Crusoe* also rehearses the early stages of European colonial contact in the Atlantic twice, once in Brazil and then on the Caribbean island, and depicts the shift from subsistence planting to a profit-oriented economy. Lastly, the difference between the Englishman Crusoe and the others with whom he comes in contact seems clear cut in terms of establishing the superiority of enslaver to enslaved: the Africans he trades in, the Maresco Xury whom he sells as a slave, and the Carib Friday whom he relegates to perpetual servitude.

Despite the emphasis on differences between Europeans and non-Europeans, *Robinson Crusoe* corresponds to a particular period of colonialism, a stage when the representation of differences was not as concrete as it became later in the eighteenth century. Multiplicity, not simply difference, is produced in relation to the Englishman Crusoe, the Maresco Xury, and the Carib Friday especially. Focusing on difference *and* multiplicity analyzes the complexity of colonial power relations and racial oppression at the same time it acknowledges that difference is not as fixed as we might imagine by reading backward from the present. Emphasizing difference and multiplicity also means that we can read *Robinson Crusoe* as a vindication of the European, specifically the British, colonial spirit and yet that such a method reveals its fissures: emergent categories of race enable both of these emphases.

By examining categories of the savage (especially the cannibal), Carib, Christian, and slave/servant, I contend that race as we understand it today did not anchor European difference and cannot analyze colonial relations adequately. In fact, the novel demonstrates that only some differences could justify European domination, and they did not include skin color or status by themselves. Neither complexion nor a category such as 'slave' explains the power relations represented in *Robinson Crusoe* adequately (though they both emerge as more significant representational issues later), but a focus on 'savage' and 'Christian' is much more applicable. Unless we bring these categories to bear on

Robinson Crusoe, there will be little to say about race, colonialism, or colonial narratives.

The savage and the Christian are the most important racialized categories between Europeans and others that help produce and maintain a sense of European superiority in North and West Africa, South America, and in the Caribbean. In section three, I analyze racial multiplicity also in terms of the several categories pertinent to early eighteenth-century ideas of race and the way that these categories do not maintain difference uniformly.

III

The first part of *Robinson Crusoe* locates the main character in Britain, Africa, and then Brazil; his significant relations are with the Moors, Africans on the west coast farther south, the Spanish Moor Xury, and other Europeans, specifically the Portuguese. The most important racialized categories that the novel produces in this context are the savage, the Christian, and the slave; analyzing these boundaries shows that both difference and multiplicity are relevant to reading *Robinson Crusoe* as a colonial narrative. By focusing on Xury and Crusoe, I demonstrate the similarities of this relationship to Crusoe's subsequent relationship to Friday. Such a focus is instructive because in both cases, the novel depicts Crusoe's association with a younger, non-European man who does not fall easily into categories of difference. Different aspects of colonialism structure such a relation in which the Englishman Crusoe acquires a non-European man as a (naturalized) servant. In Africa, piracy fills the narrative function that the hurricane does in the Caribbean, 'accidentally' situating Crusoe in the realm of an historical power struggle for European hegemony first on the coast of Africa and then in the Americas. The Moors serve a similar narrative function to the Caribs later—as impediments to Crusoe's success as a slave trader. For both Xury and Friday, the issue of their status in relation to Crusoe hinges on (the conversion to) Christianity. Lastly, the relation between Xury and Crusoe (and then between Crusoe and Friday) alters in relation to the presence of other Europeans. These narrative functions are not simply structural similarities but also ideological ones about the importance of race to establishing British power relations.

Difference and multiplicity cannot be separated conceptually, and the depiction of Crusoe's enslavement in Morocco by a Turkish pirate begins to emphasize this issue. What might seem the most significant alteration in Crusoe's status receives little narrative or critical attention. At the level of plot, it is in Morocco, strangely enough, that Crusoe's status is most compromised and his body suspended from its self-mastery in slavery. At the height of Corsair activity in the mid-seventeenth century, thousands of Europeans were enslaved by the Moors, and some were released for ransom money or became wealthy renegades by converting to Islam. Crusoe becomes a prisoner to a pirate and then his household slave; Crusoe's change of fortune results in a temporary change of status from a merchant to a slave, a change that apparently has nothing to do with his national or personal essence (as it does in the case of the Amerindians).[4] Indeed, one of Defoe's contemporaries asked about the comparison between a European in Barbary and an African in the West Indies: 'Doth he [the European] thereupon become a Brute? If not, why should an *African*, (suppose of that, or any other remote part) suffer a greater alteration than one of us?'[5] The juxtaposition of Crusoe, his patron the Moor, and Xury another slave, who is a Maresco or Spanish Moor, becomes a collection of national identities thrown together by the fortunes of international power differences. The novel offers Crusoe's ingenuity in escaping as a significant difference between Crusoe and other slaves.

Multiplicity is produced in terms of the category of slave because Crusoe is a European Christian; the enslavement of European Christians is a little remembered historical phenomenon, particularly for European men.[6] Despite the novel's highlighting his status as a captured slave, the section on Crusoe in Sallee suggests that he was treated more as a household servant than a slave and certainly not subject to reculturation like Xury by the Portuguese Captain or Friday by Crusoe. Although Crusoe's status may give rise to questions, the novel seems quite clear about the difference between Moors and West Africans: Moors are neither savage, naked, nor unfamiliar.[7] But their representation fails to match Crusoe's 'real' peril: the Moors who enslave Crusoe are represented as frightening (rather than inferior or savage); I attribute such a depiction to their centuries of maritime and financial power, which was historically more threatening and much better known to eighteenth-century Europe than either the history or civilization of the Amerindians or West Africans. Thus, it is neither the nature nor the customs of the Moors that define their difference (as it is in regard to the Amerindians), but their power.[8] In such a context, slavery does not appear to be a particularly clear boundary of permanent difference between people since it can happen to any one in spite of religion, national origin, or skin color. In the novel, slaves are Marescos and European Christians as well as Africans and Amerindians. *Robinson Crusoe* constructs black African savagery as the most significant difference to Europeans rather than European slavery in Morocco or the Muslim religion.

Savagery rather than slavery constitutes the dominant contrast to Europeans in the first part of the novel. Crusoe and Xury sail southward from Morocco 'to the truly Barbarian coast, where whole nations of negroes were sure to surround us with their canoes, and destroy us; where we could ne'er once go on shoar but we should be devoured by savage beasts, or more merciless savages of humane kind' (45).[9] Even though Crusoe fears human savages in Africa, the text offers savage animals instead. Crusoe laments 'the horrible noises, and hideous cryes and howlings' on the African shore (47). Finally, Crusoe and Xury sail far enough south to spot people. The West Africans' skin color and nakedness most clearly separate them from the Englishman Crusoe and the Maresco Xury. Although these features seem to constitute signs of the Africans' alleged savagery, they are not sufficient to account for Crusoe's conviction that they are cannibals. Crusoe's first observations of the inhabitants note their outstanding attributes: 'we saw people stand upon the shoar to look at us; we could also perceive they were quite black and stark-naked. I was once inclined to ha'gone on shoar to them; but Xury was my better councellor, and said to me, "no go"' (50). Such a specific identification of African difference does not compare to the unspecified savage cannibalism of the Caribs.

It must be said that Crusoe's fear of African cannibals is completely unfounded in terms of the novel. As opposed to his violent and anonymous encounter with the Caribs later, Crusoe meets and communicates with West Coast Africans who offer not to eat him but to aid him. The people bring him food and water: 'I was now furnished with roots and corn, such as it was, and water, and leaving my friendly negroes, I made forward' (52). The novel quickly reveals that these 'savages' simply eat wild beasts, not men. The scene in which Crusoe gratifies the Africans by shooting 'a most curious leopard' for their culinary delight confirms such a crucial difference (52). Crusoe departs with provisions and a changed perspective. It is important to note that after his encounter with the West Africans, Crusoe's earlier fear of African savages has been replaced entirely with a fear of savage animals in Africa. The novel does not strictly maintain the savagery of the Africans as it does the Caribs'. The only 'real' cannibals, then, are the Amerindians, whose several feasts punctuate the latter part of Crusoe's island sojourn.

Crusoe's relationship to Xury has been interpreted typically as a relation of master to slave, and certainly Crusoe's selling Xury to the Portuguese captain confirms this idea. Initially, however, in the context of Moroccan slavery, Xury and Crusoe resemble each other more than they are dissimilar; in fact, Crusoe's greater age seems the only difference between the two slaves. The similarity between Xury and Crusoe is further emphasized because of their common difference from the Moors (their common European origin weighs most in this respect).[10] Once out of the context of slavery, a different configuration is formed—first in relation to black Africans and then in relation to Christian Europeans. When they escape, Xury and Crusoe are allied in their fear of the Moors who enslaved them and then in their fear of the 'real' savages, the West Africans. The potential danger of the 'wild mans' and the resulting fear of being eaten lead Crusoe to notice that which most clearly separates Xury and himself from the West Africans: their skin color and nakedness.

While Xury's status is neither as powerful as Crusoe's nor as abject as the Africans' on the west coast, his position in the novel is not as clear as it might be. A household slave like Crusoe, he is also a European—but not a Christian. In most cases, the Marescos had been violently segregated from the Christian population in Spain since the sixteenth century, and they often worked on behalf of the African Moors, especially the pirates. Although Marescos often assisted Moorish pirates, they were also subject to slavery in Africa. Marescos therefore occupied a complex position, considered neither fully European nor fully Moor. Upon escape from Sallee, Xury's 'worth' as a person is compromised from the beginning because it is construed only in terms of his usefulness to Crusoe. For example, Crusoe observes of a non-slave and the kinsman of his patron: 'I could ha' been content to ha' taken this Moor with me, and ha' drowned the boy [Xury], but there was no venturing to trust him. . . . I turned to the boy, who they called Xury, and said to him, "Xury, if you will be faithful to me I'll make you a great man"' (45). Crusoe's age and initiative position Xury as a particular kind of subordinate—a servant: Crusoe orders him to perform menial tasks. Yet Xury also advises Crusoe and they hunt together in Africa (47). Theirs is not a relation of equals but roles that can be assumed by a trusty servant in relation to a master: Friday and Crusoe repeat such a pattern later.

The arrival of the Portuguese slave ship alters Xury's status vis-á-vis Crusoe even further. If the least difference between Xury and Crusoe occurs when they are slaves to the Moors, the greatest difference occurs when they are in the presence of other Europeans. In this context, Crusoe assumes the position of the owner of the stolen goods and boat from Morocco (54). In this episode, the Catholic Portuguese captain treats Crusoe as an equal, even though he possesses only the stolen boat—and Xury. Crusoe explains: 'I immediately offered all I had to the captain of the ship, ... but he generously told me he would take nothing from me' (53–54). Indeed, the captain identifies with Crusoe's plight: '"I have saved your life on no other terms than I would be glad to be saved my self"' (54). Instead, the captain offers to purchase Crusoe's goods. Xury's status seems to slip from servant and occasional partner to a slave because he is considered a legitimate object of exchange by both the captain and Crusoe. Xury's position as an object of exchange between the two European men becomes a sign of their friendship and equality. Crusoe's reluctance to part with Xury prompts the captain to mitigate Xury's permanent servitude to a temporary term. Although the eventual terms of Xury's sale are more akin to indentured servitude (of 10 years contingent on conversion to Christianity) than to permanent enslavement, Xury's status is as a slave not a servant precisely because he is understood to belong to Crusoe who has no contractual rights to his labor or person.

Xury's economic mobility and ability to be a 'free' subject are silenced by the European's ostensible concern for his spiritual welfare. The importance of Christianity as a significant bond between Europeans overrides even historical differences between Protestants and Catholics by representing the greater difference as that between Christians and Muslims. It is clearly not Xury's nation that locates him as a slave but his religion: he is a Spanish Moor.[11] Christianity represents the most significant category of difference that excuses European domination and establishes the conditions for enslavement. Xury, however, is not the 'permanent' savage or slave the Africans and Caribs are; he is linked to Europeans by his shared fear of being eaten by the 'wild mans' on the west coast of Africa (47). In comparison to West Africans, Xury is reassuringly similar to Crusoe.

To account for the changeability of Xury's position, it is necessary to bring the categories 'European,' 'Christian,' and 'Muslim' to bear on the juxtaposition of the Englishman Crusoe and the Maresco Xury to the Moors, West Africans, and Portuguese. Clearly it is important to identify the nuances between Xury's national origins, which separate him from west coast Africans (and from Friday), and Xury's Islamic associations, a religious category that compromises the similarity to Crusoe.

Just as Crusoe made his first fortune in England by trading 'trifles' on the African coast for slaves and gold, so the sale of Xury and other goods stolen from the Moor establishes him in Brazil as a land-rich plantation owner. Twice in the novel, Crusoe regrets parting with Xury, not out of loneliness or ethical regret, but because he wishes to command his labor power. Specifically, once Crusoe's plantation begins to be profit-oriented rather than subsistence-based, he desires Xury's presence. On the one hand, the narrative validates Crusoe's prosperity in the colonies; on the other, it reveals the manipulations, expropriations, and betrayals his newfound status requires to attain power.

The ownership of property—land and especially slaves—permits the apparent equality of different nationals of European descent on the Portuguese ship and in Brazil. Thus, the status of European men in a colonial economy depends on the labor supply they command to determine their rank (in South America the labor supply was overwhelmingly either native Amerindian or African).[12] An important explanation for the absence of strife either between countrymen or other European nationals involves shared economic benefits in the Atlantic empire. From the mid-seventeenth century onward, successive travelers noted the undiluted friendliness among planters especially in the Caribbean: important political and religious differences particularly in Britain (and to a lesser extent between European nationals) were often suppressed to pursue common economic goals.[13]

Even though the most significant categories of difference in Africa are the savage, Christian, and slave, 'Christian' is the only one that is not substantially questioned in terms of its 'naturalized' explanatory power. Europeans of various national origins are connected by their common Christian heritage and desire for economic advancement in exploiting African labor and natural resources. Neither savagery nor slavery adequately maintains differences between Europeans and others. The hospitality of the Africans replaces their savagery, though their complexion and lack of clothing still visibly distinguish them from Europeans and from Xury. Human commodities do not initially characterize Crusoe's trading from Britain to Guinea, and, while the difference between enslaver and enslaved is crucial, the novel also shows Moors as slave traders. The category of the slave is not exclusively reserved for Africans, nor is it represented as a permanent state for either Crusoe or Xury.

For the Maresco Xury to be positioned as the naturalized slave rather than a West African speaks volumes about the significance of his religious status in comparison to other racialized categories at this time. For example, in *A Collection of the Dresses of Different Nations, Antient and Modern* (1757), there are several pictures of people from Egypt and Barbary, including an African woman, a noble lady of Alexandria, a woman of Fez, an Ethiopian, and a Morisco slave (illustrations were commonly copied from seventeenth- and early eighteenth-century travel narratives).[14] Of all these people, the features of the Morisco slave are the most stereotypically African. The signification of 'slave' as black African seems fairly stable in this instance. Moreover, some critics have been confused about Xury's color and national origins. Stephen Hymer, who identifies Xury as 'a black Man,' explains Xury's commodity status as a function of his nation (incorrectly identified in his text): 'An African is an African, and only under certain conditions does he become a slave.' Despite the way that Xury has been associated with black Africans, the first illustration of Xury in *Robinson Crusoe* depicts him as a boyish replica of Crusoe, including the same clothing and coloring as well as the possession of a gun.[16] While the novel helps produce European difference from Moors and West Africans, this interest is never as great as Crusoe's difference from the Caribs.

IV

The remainder of *Robinson Crusoe* locates the main character in the Caribbean on an uninhabited island and then briefly in Europe. Unlike the frequent encounters with other populations in Africa and Brazil, Crusoe spends much of this part of the novel alone. His significant relations are with the largely absent Caribs, Friday, and other Europeans, especially the Spaniard and the English captain. Section four examines the same categories that were relevant in an African context: the savage, especially the cannibal, the Christian, the slave, and the indentured servant. Unlike Africa, in the Caribbean, it is not black but white skin color that has the most meaning, and the emphasis on the absence of clothing is more fully developed in relation to the Caribs than it was to the Africans. Multiplicity disrupts the establishment of boundaries. There are three related issues that I explain by this focus on difference and multiplicity: 1) the construction of Friday as neither a savage nor an African in the novel, 2) the depiction of Friday and the Caribs as Africans on the 1720 frontispiece to *Serious Reflections on the Life and Surprizing Adventures of Robinson Crusoe*, and, 3) the changeability of Friday's status as a savage, servant, or a slave. While Friday displays a lingering penchant for human flesh and is reluctant to give up his belief in Benamuckee, the novel distinguishes Friday from other savages in remarkable ways.

The key terms of cannibal, Christian, and slave share a long history in signifying European superiority. In general, the novel sets up a binary of the savage versus the Christian European and stages this distinction in Africa and the Caribbean. As several interpretive works on the eighteenth century suggest, the savage was linked to ideologies of European empire and race at this time.[17] The Amerindians, in general, constituted one if not the most significant population of savages. This system producing the savage and the European operates through its attendant visible racialized categories—especially the absence or presence of clothing and skin color. Savagery comprises, most importantly, cannibalism, paganism, and nakedness. The novel establishes a cluster of boundaries for differences between populations centered on attributes of savagery, and the most casual assumption is just what a 'savage' might be; the word litters the text and is the primary label of difference.[18]

The outstanding characteristic of the savage was cannibalism, and this practice stands in for religious practice. For example, until the eighteenth century, Caribs signified 'the most extreme form of savagery. Truculent by nature and eating human flesh by inclination, they stood opposed to all the tenets of Christian and civilized behaviour.'[19] Richard Blackmore, Defoe's contemporary, identified Indians as 'a middle Species ... a humane salvage Beast.'[20] Not surprisingly, then, in Africa and the Caribbean, cannibalism is the motivating fear most constitutive of Crusoe's subjectivity and his ideas about the inhabitants. In the Caribbean, Crusoe's fear is subsequently 'justified' in narrative terms by his repeated witnessing of the primal scene of cannibalism.[21] Initially, the unsubstantiated fear of cannibals results in Crusoe's altering his mode of production from a subsistence-based to a surplus economy (164); then the first visual verification of cannibalism leads Crusoe to vomit at the scene of frenzied ingestion. Immediately he thanks God 'that had cast my first lot in a part of the world where I was distinguished from such dreadful creatures as these' (172). Crusoe's security in his difference from cannibals participates in a larger cultural phenomenon; in *The Man-Eating Myth*, W. Arens demonstrates that 'anthropology has a clear-cut vested interest in maintaining some crucial cultural boundaries—of which the cannibalistic boundary is one—and [in] constantly reinforcing subjective conclusions about the opposition between the civilized and savage.'[22] This same desire to maintain the boundary between the civilized and the savage may be found in most European travel literature and fiction located in the Atlantic, of which *Robinson Crusoe* is an outstanding instance.

Since the early sixteenth century, Carib savagery, signified most strongly by cannibalism, had been a justification for their enslavement; Europeans had long distinguished between Amerindians and cannibals—at least in theory. Amerindians were members of sovereign nations; cannibals had foreclosed the question of rights by virtue of their threatening behavior. This combination of cannibalism and enslavement constituted a major racialized boundary. In *The Problem of Slavery in Western Culture*, David Brion Davis sketches the shifts in policies and attitudes about Amerindians as slaves.[23] From time to time in North and South America, enslavement of the Amerindians were forbidden.[24] For example, in 1537, the Pope declared that the Indians were rational beings capable of Christianity and therefore could not be deprived of their natural liberty; the resistance of the European colonists undermined this policy a year later, and they continued to force Amerindians into slavery.[25] In contrast, twenty-six years before the Papal policy of forbidding Amerindian enslavement, a Spanish royal edict 'defined as Caribs any Indians who were hostile to Europeans, behaved violently, or consumed human flesh. Caribs, the edict concluded, were without souls, and so were suitable subjects for the slave trade.'[26] Thus, while enslaving inhabitants of the islands was prohibited since the Pope considered their spiritual welfare paramount over the economic interests of the colonialists, cannibals, on the other hand, were legitimate candidates for slavery.[27] Interestingly, *The Farther Adventures of Robinson Crusoe* revises its identification of Friday and his nation as Caribees, thereby eroding a 'valid' reason for their massacre and enslavement on the island.

Historically, one way that Europeans had made Caribs and cannibals equivalent connected their threatening behavior to their alleged monstrous appearance. From Columbus's third voyage onward, there was a close association between cannibals and hideous appearance. Europeans did not have to witness acts of cannibalism to confirm that a certain group of people were cannibals and hence 'legitimate' candidates for servitude or eradication: they could tell by looking at the Caribs.[28] Furthermore, Columbus's text reveals the use of cannibalism as a theme once the possibility and profitability of a slave trade seemed likely to materialize. This increasingly naturalized cluster of terms should alert us that where Europeans 'find' cannibals, their enslavement often ensues, and *Robinson Crusoe* repeats such a pattern. Arens further argues that by the sixteenth century, 'resistance and cannibalism became synonymous and also legitimized the barbaric Spanish reaction.'[29] Europeans thereby developed an imaginary visual referent for the failure to comply with their terms. There were, however, other histories of more favorable Amerindian representations that challenged this older mode of meaning and that could be applied to Friday.

If cannibalism is the most important practice signifying savagery, then Christianity is the most significant feature constituting European identity in *Robinson Crusoe*.[30] The paganism of savages is threatening in a different way than is their cannibalism; again, the Amerindians rather than the Moors or West Africans are the ideological center of this as secondary: national origin, skin color, mode of governance, and use of Western technology. The most thoughtful and extended musings in *Robinson Crusoe* about differences between people concern religion, those to whom God reveals the light and those from whom God hides the light. Crusoe can account for this difference only in terms of a rough geographic injustice (172), which permits some nations to be Christian and 'forces' others to be sinners and punishes them in their absence from God. The ideological work of such developed speculations about religious difference makes these apparent or visible global inequalities seem to be divinely ordained and sanctioned instead of man-made and temporally convenient to European domination.

In *Robinson Crusoe*, religious difference remains paramount despite the multiple categories it introduces. For example, Crusoe's delight in Friday leads him to question what he had previously believed: that God had taken

> from so great a part of the world of His creatures, the best uses to which their faculties and the powers of their souls are adapted; yet that He has

> bestowed upon them the same powers, the same reason, the same affections, the same sentiments of kindness and obligation, the same passions and resentments of wrongs, the same sense of gratitude, sincerity, fidelity, and all the capacities of doing good and receiving good, that He has given to us; . . . this made me very melancholly sometimes, . . . why it has pleased God to hide the like saving knowledge from so many millions of souls. (212)

It is worth emphasizing that this meditation on savages, with Friday uppermost in his thoughts, leads Crusoe to enumerate all of the similarities between the Carib savages and European Christians. The single greatest difference is not located in appearance, mental prowess, or in technological sophistication but in God's inexplicable will. Crusoe finds this 'arbitrary disposition of things' worrying, and it makes him momentarily disbelieve. He notes, however, 'But I shut it up,' and he concludes in a stunning *non sequitur* that 'if these creatures were all sentenced to absence from Himself, it was on account of sinning against that light' (212). Note the shift here from an arbitrary to a just God. These disruptive questions lead not to permanent doubt but to a comforting reinsertion of polarization.

NOTES

1. Strangely, the concentration on the island segment has not also meant that colonialism was considered the most relevant context until recently. The traditional focus on religious and economic aspects of the novel has allowed the novel to remain primarily a national text in the narrow sense of its geographic borders – the island often becoming a miniature England.
2. Several studies of *Robinson Crusoe* have connected the plot's impetus to desire, colonialism, and fear. See chapter two of John Richetti, *Defoe's Narratives: Situations and Structures* (Oxford: Clarendon Press, 1975); Maximillian Novak, *Defoe and the Nature of Man* (Oxford: Oxford Univ. Press, 1963), 25–26, 34, and 37–64; and Maximillian Novak, *Economics and the Fiction of Daniel Defoe* (1962; rpt. New York: Russell & Russell, 1976), especially chapter two.
3. All references are to Daniel Defoe, *The Life and Adventures of Robinson Crusoe*, ed. Angus Ross (Harmondsworth: Penguin, 1965).
4. John Wolf, *The Barbary Coast: Algiers Under the Turks, 1500–1800* (New York: Norton, 1979) shows that despite the fact that 'Cromwell was the first to use naval power effectively for both the protection of commerce and the ransom of prisoners' that 'Slaves not yet sold could be freed, but slaves purchased by individuals had become "private property," and both the English and the French kings respected "private property" even though it happened to be an Englishman or a Frenchman' (159). Thus, as *Robinson Crusoe* confirms, all bodies can be property; for some it is an accident of fate, for others it is their fate. In 1720, Commodore Stewart, on orders from George I, ransomed 296 British subjects from North Africa, a fraction of the captive British population. See Stephen Clissold, *The Barbary Slaves* (New Jersey: Rowman and Littlefield, 1977), chapters 8 and 9.
5. Morgan Godwyn, *The Negro's & Indians Advocate, Suing for their Admission into the Church: or a Persuasive to the Instructing and Baptizing of the Negro's and Indians in our Plantations* (London: J. D., 1680), 28.
6. Today, our recollection of European slavery in Algiers, Morocco, or Turkey is

usually associated with European women in the harems. Novelists such as Eliza Haywood in *Philodore and Placentia* (1727) and Penelope Aubin in *The Noble Slaves* (1722) wrote about European slaves of both sexes.

7. In *Robinson Crusoe*, 'Moors' signify Muslim inhabitants of northwest Africa, particularly Morocco. The OED indicates that people from Algeria and Mauritania, who were of mixed Berber and Arab ancestry, were also called Moors. While Europeans popularly considered Moors very swarthy or, indeed, black until well into the seventeenth century (OED), there were other factors that acknowledge this European 'myth' and that 'Moor' was an unstable category. There was a common distinction between tawny Moors and white Moors which recognized that not all Moors were black; and the simultaneous usage of Moor as a popular synonym for Negro, or black African suggested, on the other hand, that Moor was equivalent to black African. In British literature through the eighteenth century there was a tradition of the Moorish quality ennobling black Africans; Wylie Sypher, *Guinea's Captive Kings: British Anti-Slavery Literature of the XVIIIth Century* (1942; rpt. New York: Octagon, 1969), 234 and 237 discusses this literary phenomenon. In *Robinson Crusoe*, 'Africans' means black Africans farther south on the west coast (near present day Senegal, opposite the Cape Verde islands where the Portuguese ship finds Crusoe and Xury). Commonly, I refer to the black Africans as West Coast Africans in this essay.
8. Anthony Barthelemy, *Black Face, Maligned Race: The Representation of Blacks in English Drama from Shakespeare to Southerne.* (Baton Rouge: Louisiana State Univ. Press, 1987) features an excellent history of the evolution and complexities of the term 'Moor,' especially in chapter one. He makes several crucial arguments: 'Moor' (similar to Turk and Indian) is a difficult term to define but shares with these others the connotation of alien or foreigner (6); in Spain, the earliest form of 'Moor' distinguished Christian from non-Christian (10); Moor could refer to people of different colors and religions; the only certainty is that a Moor is not a European Christian (7); two separate histories of 'Moor' as black and as sinner converged and came to describe all black people, an association that did not change until the seventeenth century (12).
9. The novel implicitly compares Crusoe's fear of African cannibals, the scenes of cannibalism in the Caribbean, and the final eating frenzy of the novel on the border between France and Spain to show that in Europe, one may be eaten by wild beasts, not wild men. The strangely gruesome interlude crossing from Spain into France with the wolves, bestial counterparts to human savages, establishes the other form of eating feared by Crusoe. In all three cases, weapon technology secures Crusoe's superiority.
10. A comprehensive historical analysis of the Moriscos' changing position relative to Western Europe and to the Islamic East, based on the Moriscos' own Aljamiado literature, is found in Anwar Chejne, *Islam and the West: The Moriscos. A Cultural and Social History* (Albany: State Univ. of New York Press, 1983). For a skeleton history of the Moriscos' outsider status, especially in relation to Spain and in Spanish Literature, see Israel Burshatin, 'The Moor in the Text: Metaphor, Emblem, and Silence,' in *"Race," Writing and Difference* (Chicago: Univ. of Chicago Press, 1985), especially 117–18 and 132.
11. The critical treatment of Xury, while not as extensive as the interest in Friday, produces similar results as the confusion about Friday's color and national origins that section four addresses. For example, Stephen Hymer identifies Xury as an African in 'Robinson Crusoe and the Secret of Primitive Accumulation,' *Monthly Review* 23 (1971): 11–36, and Lennard Davis in 'The Fact of Events and The Event of Facts: New World Explorers and the Early Novel,' *The Eighteenth Century* 32 (1991): 240–55, claims that Xury is not easy to classify in terms of national origins: 'Xury, whose exact racial origin is unclear, although he is clearly "Other", is the prototype of the friendly native' (242). In the following sentence, Davis does try to

distinguish Xury from West Africans: Xury 'is somewhat moorish and in this case the natives are "Negroes"' (243).

12. Stuart Schwartz demonstrates the historical transformations of status display in colonial Brazil (in which *Robinson Crusoe* seems to participate): 'Social distinctions of noble and commoner were transferred from Portugal, but in the colony, especially on the frontiers, these tended to be leveled and replaced by a hierarchy based on race and European culture, in which the Indian and later the African provided the basepoint against which status was judged' ('The Formation of a Colonial Identity in Brazil,' in *Colonial Identity in the Atlantic World, 1500–1800*, ed. Nicholas Canny and Anthony Pagden [Princeton: Princeton Univ. Press, 1987], 15–50, 27). He continues: 'Lacking these external proofs of gentility [titles and other marks of European nobility], the colonists sought to demonstrate their nobility by a seigneurial life style, including a landed estate, numerous slaves and retainers, liberality, patriarchal attitudes, and personal justice' (29). This observation describes the style of Crusoe's governance on the island and his own understanding of his desires.
13. Hilary Beckles, *White Servitude and Black Slavery in Barbadoes, 1627–1715* (Knoxville: Univ. of Tennessee Press, 1989), 22.
14. *A Collection of the Dresses of Different Nations, Antient and Modern*, 4 vols. (London: Thomas Jeffreys, 1757), volume 1.
15. Stephen Hymer (note 11), 14–15.
16. Maximillian Novak reprints 'Robinson Crusoe & his boy Xury on the Coast of Guinny Shooting a Lyon' in his *Realism, Myth, and History in Defoe's Fiction* (Lincoln: Univ. of Nebraska Press, 1983), 38. This illustration was one of six plates added to the sixth edition of 1722.
17. *The Wild Man Within: An Image in Western Thought from the Renaissance to Romanticism*, ed. Maximillian Novak and Edward Dudley (Pittsburgh: Univ. of Pittsburgh Press, 1972); Ronald Meek, *Social Science and the Ignoble Savage* (Cambridge: Cambridge Univ. Press, 1976); and Benjamin Bissel, *The American Indian in English Literature of the Eighteenth Century* (New Haven: Yale Univ. Press, 1925) are useful general introductions to issues of savagery in the eighteenth century. Maximillan Novak, *Defoe and the Nature of Man* (note 2), 37–50 usefully situates Defoe in relation to his contemporaries' views of savages. Peter Hulme's two works remain the most significant current interpretations of the way that savagery and British colonial narratives intersect: *Colonial Encounters* (London: Methuen 1986) and *Wild Majesty: Encounters with Caribs from Columbus to the Present Day*, An Anthology, ed. Peter Hulme and Neil Whitehead (Oxford: Clarendon Press, 1992). Phillip P. Boucher, *Cannibal Encounters: Europeans and Island Caribs, 1492–1763* (Baltimore: Johns Hopkins Univ. Press, 1992) focuses on the political, religious, and discursive dynamics of French and British contact with Island Caribs; in doing so, he adds considerably to an understanding of differences between European colonialisms.
18. Savagery is a traditional discourse of absolute difference traceable to Herodotus. For a helpful historical analysis of cannibalism and savagery, see Peter Hulme, *Colonial Encounters*. Stuart Schwartz (note 12), demonstrates the way in which cannibalism and sodomy were most commonly the points of difference Europeans constructed between themselves and Amerindians; both practices were considered crimes against nature and thus justification for enslavement (26).
19. *Wild Majesty* (note 17), 4.
20. Maximillian Novak in *Defoe and the Nature of Man* (note 2) quotes Blackmore's construction of Amerindians as a degenerate race, 43.
21. Replacing copulation with dismemberment as the site of trauma interests me as a failure to negate cannibalism completely from the colonial construction of subjectivity; Europeans' aggression is thus disavowed and transferred to fantasies of their own bodily destruction.

22. Arens, *The Man-Eating Myth: Anthropology & Anthropophagy* (New York: Oxford Univ. Press, 1979), 170–71.
23. David Brion Davis, *The Problem of Slavery in Western Culture* (New York: Oxford Univ. Press, 1966), 167.
24. The need for such a law tends to indicate that in practice Amerindians were regarded as 'legitimate' slaves at this time, even if ideologically there were reasons not to regard them as natural(ized) slaves. See Bernard Sheehan, *Savagism and Civility: Indians and Englishmen in Colonial Virginia* (Cambridge: Cambridge Univ. Press, 1980), 180–81 for a representative account (though specific to Virginia in 1670–90). Also consult Winthrop Jordan, *White Over Black: American Attitudes Toward the Negro, 1550–1812* (Chapel Hill: Univ. of North Carolina Press, 1968), 89–95 for a discussion of why 'Indian slavery never became an important institution in the [North American] colonies' (89).
25. Davis (note 23), 170.
26. Dave Davis, 'Rumor of Cannibals,' *Archaeology* 45 (1992), 49.
27. In the novel, Xury not Friday is promised his eventual liberty by conversion.
28. Friday, of course, does not fit into such a visible economy, and this shows part of his significant difference from his national group. Arens (note 22) points out Columbus's expertise in recognizing cannibals at a glance by his third voyage (48).
29. Arens, 48, 49.
30. Winthrop Jordan (note 24) provides a historical interpretation of the importance of Christianity versus skin color to European colonial identity in the late seventeenth- and early eighteenth-century colonies. In North America, complexion became a determining racialized category earlier than elsewhere. In Africa, black African difference initially signified savagery; in North America, 'the specific religious difference [of Africans] was initially of greater importance than color' (97–98). Carol Barash, 'The Character of Difference: the Creole Woman as Cultural Mediator in Narratives about Jamaica,' *Eighteenth-Century Studies*, Special Issue: 'The Politics of Difference,' 23 (1990): 407–28, argues that the centrality of religious difference gave way to constructions of African sexual difference later in the century in British narratives about Jamaica, a shift that was a understood as a more fixed cultural difference onto which race was mapped.

PART 3
CHARLOTTE BRONTË:
JANE EYRE

INTRODUCTION

Many recent post-colonial readings of *Jane Eyre* have demonstrated what previous analyses seem to have overlooked: that the book is littered with overt and covert references to other cultures and to binary oppositions of civilised and savage.[1] For example, Helen chastises Jane for wanting to 'strike back' because 'Heathens and savage tribes hold that doctrine; but Christians and civilised nations disown it.'[2] When Helen passes Jane by: 'It was as if a martyr, a hero, had passed a slave or victim, and imparted strength in the transit' (99). Blanche has an 'oriental eye', as does Rochester, who, when dressed as a 'gypsy' is 'A shockingly ugly old creature . . . as black as a crock' (221). But most criticism has focused on the figure of Bertha Mason, Rochester's first wife, a creole:

> In the deep shade, at the farther end of the room, a figure ran backwards and forwards. What it was, whether beast or human being, one could not, at first sight tell: it grovelled, seemingly, on all fours; it snatched and growled like some strange wild animal: but it was covered with clothing, and a quantity of dark, grizzled hair, wild as a mane, hid its head and face (321).

As repeated feminist readings have shown, Bertha (described by Jane above) occupies the position in the text of the denied and repressed Other who is necessary for the emergence of the central and coherent unified female subject, Jane. It is, however, a decision over the nature of this repression that conditions the discourse used to read the novel. It is either Jane's psychic and sexual repression, Brontë's repression of female anger in the face of patriarchy, or the West's repression of all that it fears within itself and displaces onto the East.

A second recurring area of debate is slavery, which constitutes one of the novel's key historical contexts. The end of the African slave trade came for Britain in 1807 and the Emancipation Act followed in 1834. In between there were slave uprisings in Jamaica in 1808 and 1831, in Barbados in 1816, in Demerara in 1823. It has been argued that in her depiction of the figure of Jane, Brontë drew on the moral language of the abolitionists, as had many campaigners for the causes of women and the working class (figured in terms of a 'white slavery'), which had the effect of stripping slavery of its racial significance.

A third important aspect to the novel is the issue of missionary work and its project to 'release the heathen from bondage' (from a spiritual 'slavery'). The novel ends with St John Rivers in India:

> Firm, faithful, and devoted, full of energy, and zeal, and truth, he labours for his race; he clears their painful way to improvement; he hews down like a giant the prejudices of creed and caste that encumber it ... His is the sternness of the warrior Greatheart, who guards his pilgrim convoy from the onslaught of Apollyon ... His is the ambition of the high master-spirit[s] ... who stand without fault before the throne of God; who share the last mighty victories of the Lamb; who are called, and chosen, and faithful. (477)

Brontë pictures Rivers as Greatheart, the Christian warrior from Bunyan's *Pilgrim's Progress*, and there is at the novel's close a shift from Jane's personal labour with Rochester to the allegorised work of Rivers's conversion of all India to a Western system of values, 'ending the prejudices of creed and caste'. This is the closing 'signature' to the novel – the last word that underlines Jane's story. Rivers's colonial mission authorises Jane's domestic one in England. Rochester, in the time Jane has spent with Rivers, has grown 'savage', and when she returns, she tells him that someone needs to rehumanise him. Of course, a significant omission in *Jane Eyre* as in much British writing on colonialism is the absence of a curiosity about what the colonised think of a European Other. One traveller in India soon after the publication of Brontë's novel, G. O. Trevelyan, was a rare exception, and his moment of self-reflection is worth quoting at length:

> Imagine the horror with which a punctilious and devout Brahmin cannot but regard a people who eat the flesh of cow and pig, and drink various sorts of strong liquors from morning till night ... The peculiar qualities which mark the Englishman are singularly distasteful to the Oriental, and are sure to be strangely distorted when seen from his point of view. Our energy and earnestness appear oppressive and importunate to the languid voluptuous aristocracy of the East. Our very honesty seems ostentatious and contemptible to the wily and tortuous Hindoo mind. That magnificent disregard of *les convenances*, which has rendered our countrymen so justly beloved by all the continental nations, is inexplicable and hateful to a race who consider external pomp and reticent solemnity to be the necessary

> accompaniments of rank, worth, or power . . . We should not be far wrong if we were content to allow that we are regarded by our Eastern subjects as a species of quaint and somewhat objectionable demons, with a rare aptitude for fighting and administration; foul and degraded in our habits, though with reference to those habits not to be judged by the same standard as ordinary men; not malevolent . . . but entirely wayward and unaccountable; a race of demi-devils: neither quite human, nor quite supernatural; not wholly bad, yet far from perfectly beneficent; who have been settled down in the country by the will of fate, and seem very much inclined to stay there by our own. If this is not the idea entertained of us by an average Bengalee rustic, it is something very near it.[3]

A fourth issue, that of the Hindu practice of *suttee* or widow-burning, is most widely known to have been raised by Gayatri Spivak's often anthologised essay 'Three Women's Texts and a Critique of Imperialism'.[4] *Suttee*, abolished in 1829 by the British, is seen as a possibility for Jane, who considers 'dying' with her husband a 'pagan' idea. Arguably her refusal to be a dutiful Hindu wife through *suttee* (one reading of Bertha Mason's fate) is taken as the possibility of Jane's ultimate denial of Rochester's 'mastery'. Jane later refuses to be 'grilled alive in Calcutta' and declines to go with Rivers because, she tells him: 'you would kill me. You are killing me now.' Earlier she says that it would be like 'committing suicide' to go with him. Spivak argues that it is in Bertha's act of *suttee* that 'the native female' is most clearly excluded from any share in the emerging norm of women's emancipation, such that the articulation of feminist identity repeats the quintessential gesture of colonialism: blindness to the epistemic violence that effaces the colonial subject and requires her to occupy the space of the imperialists' self-consolidating Other. Laura Donaldson, however, says that Spivak's point that Bertha's *suttee* (as good wife sacrificing herself) allows Jane to become full, free femininst subject is too restricting. Bertha's action is also an aggressive, assertive, debilitating attack on Rochester – one that avers her hatred for her husband.[5] Again, Spivak's reading is reductive in the name of Bertha as victim in response to other readings of Bertha as Jane's Other, when Bertha's death is a gesture of defiance and refusal.

An ex-pupil of Spivak's, Jenny Sharpe, in her *Allegories of Empire*, argues that the emergence of a 'female voice' that many critics have detected in the novel is achieved by the clearing of a colonial space: the voice-agency of Jane Eyre is predicated upon a national and racial splitting of femininity. More specifically she also discusses metaphorial aspects to the novel which feature in Jane's narrative, such as slavery, rebellion and *suttee*, which can be read in terms of solidarity or appropriation as they are drawn from contemporary colonial experience, but of the colonised not the coloniser.[6] Another essay, included below, which takes issue with Spivak, is Susan L. Meyer's 'Colonialism and the Figurative Strategy of *Jane Eyre*'. This is a reading of the novel in terms of its sympathetic parallels between class, gender and race. Meyer argues that Brontë denigrates imperialism throughout the text, which is full of cultural metaphors for 'cleaning' away oppression – even if the end of the novel leaves the tensions between the positions of black and white women unresolved.

Inderpal Grewal's short discussion of *Jane Eyre* in *Home and Harem: Nation, Gender, Empire and the Cultures of Travel* also takes up Spivak's argument and discusses her theory of 'worlding', which enables Jane to constitute a new subjectivity through colonial othering.[7] Grewal focuses on the tensions between gender and race that emerge as India figures as a space in which Jane can assert a sexual equality with Englishmen, a superiority to colonised men, and an emancipatory role towards Indian women within the heterosexual, masculine Imperial project.

Lastly, Joyce Zonana's 'The Sultan and the Slave: Feminist Orientalism and the Structure of *Jane Eyre*', considers the harem the central image of gender oppression in the novel and analyses its significance in terms of the novel's understanding of cultural differences between East and West. A key point here is that Jane dislikes 'Eastern allusions' to harems in connection with her and says she will 'Go preach liberty to them that are enslaved'. In this, critics have argued that, typical of other aspects to the novel, Jane positions herself as a missionary woman who will save the women of the harem (she only agrees to go with Rivers when he says she would work with Hindu women). Therefore, Jane's 'human sympathy' arguably only serves to promote her above the harem women in order to save them.

NOTES

1. For example, S. Perera's *Reaches of Empire* (New York: Columbia University Press, 1991) has a chapter on Oriental misogyny and *Jane Eyre*, while Alan Bewell's 'Jane Eyre and Victorian Medical Geography' (*English Literary History*, 63, 1996, pp. 773–808) considers issues such as phrenology and colonial physical stereotypes, and Elsie Michie's 'From Simianized Irish to Oriental Despots: Heathcliff, Rochester and Racial Difference' (*Novel*, 25:2, Winter 1992, pp. 124–40) examines the phobias and fantasies that the Brontë novels exhibit in relation to Ireland (and their own Irish ancestry) and 'Oriental despotism'. The book's position in the development of bourgeois Imperial fiction has also been analysed in Firdous Azim's *The Colonial Rise of the Novel* (London: Routledge, 1993), which fairly straightforwardly reviews feminist positions on *Jane Eyre*, catalogues the references to the colonies in the novel, and ends by considering Bertha Mason in terms of colonial failure and ambivalence.
2. Charlotte Brontë, *Jane Eyre*, Harmondsworth: Penguin, 1985, p. 90. All further references are to this edition.
3. G. O. Trevelyan, *The Competition Wallah*, London: Macmillan, 1864, pp. 442–4.
4. The article most recently reappeared in Bart Moore-Gilbert, Gareth Stanton and Willy Maley (eds), *Postcolonial Criticism*, Essex: Longman, 1997, pp. 145–65. It originally appeared in *Critical Inquiry*, 21:1, Autumn 1985, pp. 243–61.
5. Laura E. Donaldson, *Decolonizing Feminisms*, London: Routledge, 1993.
6. Jenny Sharpe, *Allegories of Empire*, Minneapolis: University of Minnesota Press, 1993.
7. On 'worlding', see, again, G. C. Spivak, 'Three Women's Texts and a Critique of Imperialism', which is additionally available in Henry Louis Gates jnr. (ed.), *'Race', Writing, and Difference*, Chicago: University of Chicago Press, 1986, p. 262.

3.1

FROM 'COLONIALISM AND THE FIGURATIVE STRATEGY OF *JANE EYRE*'

Susan L. Meyer

I

The figurative use of race is so important to *Jane Eyre* that, much as it begins to be in *Emma*, the figure is enacted on the level of character. In representing an actual Jamaican black woman, Brontë finds herself confronting the non-figurative reality of British race relations. And Brontë's figurative use of blackness in part arises from the history of British colonialism: the function of racial 'otherness' in the novel is to signify a generalized oppression. But Brontë makes class and gender oppression the overt significance of racial 'otherness,' displacing the historical reasons why colonized races would suggest oppression, at some level of consciousness, to nineteenth-century British readers. What begins then as an implicit critique of British domination and an identification with the oppressed collapses into merely an appropriation of the metaphor of 'slavery.' But the novel's closure fails, in interesting ways, to screen out entirely the history of British colonial oppression.

This complex figurative use of race explains much of the difficulty of understanding the politics of *Jane Eyre*. In an important reading of the significance of colonialism in this novel, Gayatri Chakravorty Spivak argues that 'the unquestioned ideology of imperialist axiomatics' informs Brontë's narrative and enables the individualistic social progress of the character Jane which has been celebrated by 'U.S. mainstream feminists.' Her reading describes Bertha as a 'white Jamaican Creole' who can nonetheless be seen in the novel as a 'native "subject,"' indeterminately placed between human and animal and consequently excluded from the individualistic humanity which the novel's

Victorian Studies, 33:2, Winter 1990, pp. 247–68. Extract: pp. 250–6 and 259–68.

feminism claims for Jane.[1] While I agree with Spivak's broad critique of an individualistic strain of feminism, I find her reading problematic in its analysis of the workings of imperialist ideology and its relation to feminism, both in general and in *Jane Eyre*.

Spivak describes Bertha as at once a white woman and a colonized 'native,' that is, as what she terms, with little definition, a 'native "subject."' She is thus able to designate Bertha as either native or white in order to criticize both Brontë's *Jane Eyre* and Jean Rhys's *Wide Sargasso Sea* as manifestations of exclusive feminist individualism. *Jane Eyre*, she argues, gives the white Jane individuality at the expense of the 'native' Bertha; *Wide Sargasso Sea*, on the other hand, she contends, retells the story of *Jane Eyre* from Bertha's perspective and thus merely 'rewrites a canonical English text within the European novelistic tradition in the interest of the white Creole rather than the native' (p. 253). Bertha is either native or not native in the interests of Spivak's critique. Thus it is by sleight of hand that Spivak shows feminism to be inevitably complicitous with imperialism.

My own proposition is that the historical alliance between the ideology of male domination and the ideology of colonial domination which informs the metaphors of so many texts of the European colonial period in fact resulted in a very different relation between imperialism and the developing resistance of nineteenth-century British women to the gender hierarchy. *Jane Eyre* was written in response to the same ideological context which led Anthony Trollope, in his short story 'Miss Sarah Jack of Spanish Town, Jamaica,' to describe the fiancée of a post-emancipation West Indian planter with this resonant analogy: 'Poor Maurice had often been nearly broken-hearted in his endeavours to manage his freed black labourers, but even that was easier than managing such as Marian Leslie.'[2] In *Jane Eyre*, Brontë responds to the seemingly inevitable analogy in nineteenth-century British texts that compares white women with blacks in order to degrade both groups and assert the need for white male control. Brontë uses the analogy in *Jane Eyre* for her own purposes, to signify not shared inferiority but shared oppression. This figurative strategy induces some sympathy with blacks as those who are also oppressed, but does not preclude racism. Yet while for the most part the novel suppresses the damning history of slavery and racist oppression, its ending betrays an anxiety that colonialism and the oppression of other races constitute a 'stain' upon English history and that the novel's own appropriation of the racial 'other' for figurative ends bears a disturbing resemblance to that history. Thus while the perspective the novel finally takes toward imperialism is Eurocentric and conservative, I find in *Jane Eyre* not Spivak's 'unquestioned ideology' of imperialism, but an ideology of imperialism which is questioned – and then reaffirmed – in interesting and illuminating ways.

An interpretation of the significance of the British empire in *Jane Eyre* must begin by making sense of Bertha Mason Rochester, the mad, drunken West Indian wife whom Rochester keeps locked up on the third floor of his ancestral mansion. Bertha functions in the novel as the central locus of Brontë's anxieties about oppression, anxieties that motivate the plot and drive it to its conclusion. The conclusion then settles these anxieties partly by eliminating the character who seems to embody them. Yet Bertha only comes into the novel after about a third of its action has taken place. As she emerges, anxieties which have been located elsewhere, notably in the character of Jane herself, become absorbed and centralized in the figure of Bertha, thus preparing the way for her final annihilation.

I read Bertha's odd ambiguity of race – ambiguity which is marked within the text itself, rather than one which needs to be mapped onto it – as directly related to her function as a representative of dangers which threaten the world of the novel. She is the heiress to a West Indian fortune, the daughter of a father who is a West Indian planter and merchant, and the sister of the yellow-skinned yet socially white Mr Mason. She is also a woman whom the younger son of an aristocratic British family would consider marrying, and so she is clearly imagined as white – or as passing as white – in the novel's retrospective narrative. And critics of the novel have consistently assumed that Bertha is a white woman, basing the assumption on this part of the narrative, although Bertha has often been described as a 'swarthy' or 'dark' white woman.[3] But when she actually emerges in the course of the action, the narrative associates her with blacks, particularly with the black Jamaican antislavery rebels, the Maroons. In the form in which she becomes visible in the novel, Bertha has *become* black as she is constructed by the narrative, much as Matilda Fitzgibbon becomes black in *Emma*.

Even in Rochester's account of the time before their marriage, when Bertha Mason was 'a fine woman, in the style of Blanche Ingram: tall, dark, and majestic,' there are hints, as there are in the early descriptions of Matilda Fitzgibbon, of the ambiguity of her race. Immediately after Rochester describes Bertha as 'tall, dark, and majestic,' he continues: 'her family wished to secure me because I was of a good race' (p. 322). In the context of a colony where blacks outnumbered whites by twelve to one, where it was a routine and accepted practice for white planters to force female slaves to become their 'concubines,' and where whites were consequently uneasily aware of the large population of mulattoes, Rochester's phrase accrues a significance beyond its immediate reference to his old family name. In this context the phrase suggests that Bertha herself may not be of as 'good' a race as he.[4] Bertha is the daughter, as Richard Mason oddly and apparently unnecessarily declares in his official attestation to her marriage with Rochester, 'of Jonas Mason, merchant, and of Antoinetta Mason, his wife, a Creole' (p. 318).

The ambiguity of Bertha's race is marked by this designation of her mother as a 'Creole.' The word 'creole' was used in the nineteenth century to refer to both blacks and whites born in the West Indies, a usage which caused some confusion: for instance, in its definition of the word the OED cites a nineteenth-century history of the U.S. in which the author writes: 'There are creole whites, creole negroes, creole horses, &c.; and creole whites, are, of all persons, the most anxious to be deemed of pure white blood.'[5] When Rochester exclaims of Bertha that 'she came of a mad family; idiots and maniacs through three generations! Her mother, the Creole, was both a madwoman and a drunkard!' he locates both madness and drunkenness in his wife's maternal line, which is again emphatically and ambiguously labelled 'Creole.' By doing so, he associates that line with two of the most common stereotypes associated with blacks in the nineteenth century.[6]

As Bertha emerges as a character in the novel, her blackness is made more explicit, despite Rochester's wish to convince Jane, and perhaps temporarily himself, that 'the swelled black face' and 'exaggerated stature' of the woman she has seen are 'figments of imagination, results of nightmare' (p. 313). But when Jane describes to Rochester the face she has seen reflected in the mirror, the *topoi* of racial 'otherness' are very evident: she tells him that the face was

> 'Fearful and ghastly to me—oh sir, I never saw a face like it! It was a discoloured face—it was a savage face. I wish I could forget the roll of the red eyes and the fearful blackened inflation of the lineaments!'
>
> 'Ghosts are usually pale, Jane.'
>
> 'This, sir, was purple: the lips were swelled and dark; the brows furrowed: the black eyebrows widely raised over bloodshot eyes.'
>
> (p. 311).

The emphasis on Bertha's coloring in this passage—she is emphatically not 'pale' but 'discoloured,' 'purple,' 'blackened'—the reference to rolling eyes and to 'swelled,' 'dark' lips all insistently and stereotypically mark Bertha as non-white. Jane's use of the word 'savage' underlines the implication of her description of Bertha's features, and the redness which she sees in Bertha's rolling eyes suggests the drunkenness which, following the common racist convention, Brontë has associated with blacks since her childhood. As Bertha's 'lurid visage flame[s] over Jane' while she lies in bed, causing her to lose consciousness, the ambiguously dark blood Bertha has inherited from her maternal line becomes fully evident in a way that recalls a passage from Brontë's African juvenilia. In this passage in her *Roe Head Journal* the revolutionary Quashia has triumphed in an uprising against the white British colonists, and having occupied the palace built by the colonists, revels drunkenly, in symbolic violation, on the 'silken couch' of the white queen.[7] Like the rebellious Quashia, the Jamaican Bertha-become-black is the novel's incarnation of the desire for revenge on the part of the colonized races, and Brontë's fiction suggests that such a desire for revenge is not unwarranted. The association of Bertha with fire recalls Jane's earlier question to herself: 'What crime was this, that lived incarnate in this sequestered mansion, and could neither be expelled nor subdued by the owner?—what mystery, that broke out, now in fire and now in blood, at the deadest hours of the night?' (p. 239). The language of this passage strongly evokes that used to describe slave uprisings in the British West Indies, where slaves used fires both to destroy property and to signal to each other that an uprising was taking place. White colonists of course responded to slave insurrections with great anxiety, like that expressed by one writer for *Blackwood's* in October 1823, in response to the news of the Demerara slave uprising: 'Give them [the abolitionists] an opportunity of making a few grand flowery speeches about liberty, and they will read, without one shudder, the narrative of a whole colony bathed in blood and fire, over their chocolate the next morning.'[8]

Brontë finished writing *Jane Eyre* in 1846, eight years after the full emancipation of the British West Indian slaves in 1838. But the novel itself is definitely set before emancipation. Q. D. Leavis has shown that it may not be possible to pinpoint the closing moment of the novel further than within a range of twenty-seven years, between 1819 and 1846.[9] When Jane says, at the end of her autobiography, 'I have now been married ten years,' the date is at the latest 1846 when Brontë finished writing the novel; thus Jane's marriage with Rochester probably takes place in 1836 at the latest. The year before their marriage, Rochester tells Jane that he has kept Bertha locked for ten years in his third-story room ('she has now for ten years made [it] a wild beast's den—a goblin's cell,' as he puts it [p. 336]). At the latest, then, Rochester first locked Bertha in that room in 1825, and since he lived with her before that for four years, they were probably married in 1821. Brontë doubtless meant to leave the precise date of the novel ambiguous—she marks the year of Rochester's and Bertha's wedding with a dash in Richard Mason's attestation to their marriage—but it is clear that even at the latest possible dates, events in the novel occur well before emancipation, which was declared in 1834 but only fulfilled in 1838. Brontë may have meant for the events of the novel to occur in the 1820s and '30s, as I have suggested above, during the years in which, due to the economic decline of the British sugar colonies in the West Indies, planters imposed increasing hardship on the slaves and increasingly feared their revolt. When Bertha escapes from her ten years' imprisonment to attempt periodically to stab and burn her oppressors, and as Rochester says, to hang her 'black and scarlet visage over the nest of my dove' (p. 337), she is symbolically enacting precisely the sort of revolt feared by the British colonists in Jamaica.

But why would Brontë write a novel suggesting the possibility of a slave uprising in 1846, after the emancipation of the British (though not the U.S. or French) slaves had already taken place? Indeed, in 1846 it was evident that the British West Indian colonies were failing rapidly, and the focus of British colonial attention was shifting to India. While the novel's use of colonialism is most overtly figurative, nonetheless it in part does engage colonialism on a non-figurative level. The story of Bertha, however finally unsympathetic to her as a human being, nonetheless does indict British colonialism in the West Indies and the 'stained' wealth that came from its oppressive rule. When Jane wonders 'what crime . . . live[s] incarnate' in Rochester's luxurious mansion 'which [can] neither be expelled nor subdued by the owner' (p. 239), the novel suggests that the black-visaged Bertha, imprisoned out of sight in a luxurious British mansion, does indeed 'incarnate' a historical crime. Rochester himself describes Thornfield as a 'tent of Achan' (p. 328), alluding to Joshua 7, in which Achan takes spoils wrongfully from another people and buries it under his tent, thus bringing down a curse upon all the children of Israel. The third floor of the mansion, where Bertha is imprisoned, Jane thinks, is 'a shrine of memory' to which 'furniture once appropriated to the lower apartments had from time to time been removed . . . as fashions changed' (p. 137). The symbolically resonant language Brontë uses as Jane tours the house suggests that Thornfield, and particularly its third floor, incarnates the history of the English ruling class as represented by the Rochesters, whom Mrs Fairfax, acting simultaneously as family historian and guide to the house—that is, guide to the 'house' of Rochester in both senses—acknowledges to have been 'rather a violent than a quiet race in their time.' The atmosphere of the third floor of this 'house' is heavy with the repressed history of crimes committed by a 'violent race,' crimes which have been removed from sight as fashions changed. History keeps erupting into the language of this passage, as it does a few sentences later when Jane, climbing out onto the roof of the hall, finds herself on a level with the black rooks who live there, just above Bertha's head, and who are here referred to, with an eerie—and racist—resonance, as 'the crow colony' (p. 137). Jane's response to this place dense with history—she is intrigued but 'by no means covet[s] a night's repose on one of those wide and heavy beds' (p. 137)—suggests her awareness of the oppressive atmosphere of colonial history and her uneasiness lest she, by lying in the bed of the Rochesters, should get caught up in it.

. . .

III

Jane Eyre associates dark-skinned peoples with oppression by drawing parallels between the black slaves, in particular, and those oppressed by the hierarchies of social class and gender in Britain. So far the narrative function of the dark-featured Bertha and of the novel's allusions to colonialism and slavery has a certain fidelity to history, although as the association between blacks and apes reveals (to take only one example), these analogies are not free from racism. In addition, this use of the slave as a metaphor focuses attention not so much on the oppression of blacks as on the situation of oppressed whites in Britain. Nonetheless, the analogies at least implicitly acknowledge the oppressive situation of the non-white races subjected to the British empire. But oddly, the allusions to dark skin and to empire arise in precisely the opposite context in the novel as well, most strikingly in the description of Blanche Ingram.

The haughty Blanche, with her 'dark and imperious' eye (p. 214), whose behavior makes Jane so painfully aware of her own social inferiority, seems mainly to illustrate class oppression. Yet when Mrs. Fairfax describes Blanche to Jane, she emphasizes her darkness: 'she was dressed in pure white,' Mrs Fairfax relates, she had an 'olive complexion, dark and clear,' 'hair raven-black . . . and in front the longest, the glossiest curls I ever saw' (p. 189). When Jane first sees Blanche, she too emphasizes her darkness—'Miss Ingram was dark as a Spaniard,' Jane notes—adding that Blanche has the 'low brow' which, like dark skin, was a mark of racial inferiority according to nineteenth-century race-science. Rochester directly associates Blanche with Africa: he might be speaking of Bertha when he tells Jane, with unnecessary nastiness, that his apparent fiancée is 'a real strapper ... big, brown, and buxom; with hair just such as the ladies of Carthage must have had' (p. 248).

These references to Blanche's darkness, and to her other similarities to 'inferior,' dark races, only make sense in the context of the odd phrase, 'dark and imperious.' The use of the word 'imperious' to describe Blanche's ruling-class sense of superiority evokes the contact between the British and their dark-skinned imperial subjects. In that contact, it was not the dark people who were 'imperious,' that is, in the position of haughty imperial power, but the British themselves. By associating the qualities of darkness and imperiousness in Blanche, Brontë suggests that imperialism brings out both these undesirable qualities in Europeans—that the British have been sullied, 'darkened,' and made 'imperious' or oppressive by contact with the racial 'other,' and that such contact makes them arrogant oppressors both abroad, and, like Blanche, at home in England.[10] Blanche's white dresses, her mother's pet name for her ('my lily-flower,' p. 207), and the meaning of her name all emphasize the ironic incongruity between what she tries to be and what she is: rather than embodying ideal white European femininity, this aristocratic Englishwoman is besmirched by the contagious darkness and oppressiveness of British colonialism.

The association of the class oppressor with 'dark races' is hinted at in the descriptions of the Reeds as well as the Ingrams. John Reed reviles his mother for 'her dark skin, similar to his own' (p. 47), and Jane compares John to a Roman emperor. John grows into a young man with 'such thick lips' (p. 122), while Mrs. Reed's face in her last illness becomes, like Bertha's, 'disfigured and discoloured' (p. 270). Lady Ingram, who derides governesses in front of Jane, and who within Jane's hearing announces that she sees in Jane's physiognomy 'all the faults of her class' (p. 206) also has features like Bertha's: her face is 'inflated and darkened'—with pride (p. 201). Like John Reed, Lady Ingram has 'Roman features,' and she too is associated with the British empire. She has, Jane says, 'a shawl turban of some gold-wrought Indian fabric [which] invested her (I suppose she thought) with a truly imperial dignity' (p. 201). The novel draws unflattering parallels between the British empire, evoked by Lady Ingram's Indian shawl, and the Roman empire, whose emperors, the young Jane has said, are murderers and slave drivers. Both the class oppressiveness of these wealthy Britons and their dark features arise, in the novel's symbolic framework, from their association with empire.

With this odd twist, racial 'otherness' becomes also the signifier of the oppressor. By using dark-skinned peoples to signify not only the oppressed but also the oppressor, Brontë dramatically empties the signifier of dark skin in her novel of any of its meaning in historical reality and makes it merely expressive of 'otherness.' By assigning these two contradictory meanings to the signifier 'non-white,' the novel follows this logic: oppression in any of its manifestations is 'other' to the English world of the novel, thus racial 'otherness' signifies oppression. This is the most fundamentally dishonest move in the novel's figurative strategy, the one that reveals the greatest indifference to the humanity of those subject to British colonialism. The passages that associate English oppressors with 'dark races' are the most evasive about British participation in slavery and empire. The novel's anti-colonial politics, it becomes clear, are conservative. The opposition to colonialism arises not out of concern for the well-being of the 'dark races' subject to British colonization—the African slaves in the West Indian colonies, the Indians whose economy was being destroyed under British rule—but primarily out of concern for the British who were, as the novel's figurative structure represents it, being contaminated by their contact with the intrinsic despotism and oppressiveness of dark-skinned people.

The novel also associates the gender oppressor with darkness, primarily through Rochester. Rochester's darkness and the symbolic reason for it emerge in the central charade passage. The first two scenes Rochester enacts are thinly disguised episodes from his own life. In the first, which enacts the word 'bride,' Rochester weds a tall, 'strapping,' dark woman. The second scene enacts the word 'well' by representing the meeting of Eliezer with his intended bride, whom, as is the case with Rochester, Eliezer has been directed to wed by his father. The final scene, enacting the word 'Bridewell,' both suggests the imprisonment attendant upon making such a marriage and symbolizes the effects of Rochester's contact with dark-skinned people in search of fortune. In this scene Rochester is himself fettered like a slave and his face is 'begrimed' by a darkness that has rubbed off onto him. That his contact with the colonies is the source of his situation is suggested both by the preceding scenes and by the description of his coat which looks 'as if it had been almost torn from his back in a scuffle' (p. 213) like the one he has with Bertha not long afterward.

Rochester's darkness is emphasized when his 'begriming' past is alluded to and when he asserts the potentially oppressive power of his position in the gender hierarchy. During the period of Rochester's and Jane's betrothal, Brontë continues to use the imagery of slavery to represent Jane's lesser power in the relationship. But she veers away from making a direct parallel with the British enslavement of Africans by associating Rochester's dominating masculine power over Jane with that not of a British but of an Eastern slave master. This part of the novel is rich in images of Turkish and Persian despots, sultans who reward their favorite slaves with jewels, Indian wives forced to die in 'suttee,' and women enslaved in Eastern harems. The reality of British participation in slavery arises at one point in this part of the narrative—Rochester echoes the abolitionists' slogan when he tells Jane that she is too restrained with 'a man and a brother' (p. 169)—but the novel persistently displaces the blame for slavery onto the 'dark races' themselves, only alluding to slavery directly as a practice of dark-skinned people. At one point, for example, the novel uses strong and shocking imagery of slavery to describe the position of wives, but despite references to such aspects of British slavery as slave markets, fetters, and mutiny, the scenario invoked represents not British colonial domination but the despotic, oppressive customs of non-whites. Rochester has just compared himself to 'the Grand Turk,' declaring that he prefers his 'one little English girl' to the Turk's 'whole seraglio' (p. 297), to which Jane responds with spirit:

> 'I'll not stand you an inch in the stead of a seraglio. . . . If you have a fancy for anything in that line, away with you, sir, to the bazaars of Stanboul, without delay, and lay out in extensive slave-purchases some of that spare cash you seem so at a loss to spend satisfactorily here.'
>
> 'And what will you do, Janet, while I am bargaining for so many tons of flesh and such an assortment of black eyes?'
>
> 'I'll be preparing myself to go out as a missionary to preach liberty to them that are enslaved—your harem inmates amongst the rest. . . . I'll stir up mutiny; and you, three-tailed bashaw as you are, sir, shall in a trice find yourself fettered amongst our hands: nor will I, for one, cut your bonds till you have signed a charter, the most liberal that despot ever yet conferred.' (pp. 297–298).

By associating Rochester's position at the top of the oppressive gender hierarchy, like Jane's position at the bottom, with dark-skinned peoples, the novel represses the history of British colonial oppression and, in particular, British enslavement of Africans, by marking all aspects of oppression 'other'—non-British, non-white, the result of a besmirching contact with 'dark races.' Even when Rochester directly asserts his power over Jane, speaking of 'attach[ing her] to a chain' (p. 299), the novel compares him to a sultan, rather than to a white-skinned British slave master. All aspects of oppression in this conservative twist in the novel's figurative strategy become something the British are in danger of being sullied by, something foreign and 'other' to them.

In opposition to this danger—the danger of becoming 'begrimed' by the oppression which the novel associates with the dark-skinned—Brontë poses an alternative directly out of middle-class domestic ideology: keeping a clean house.[11] Clean and unclean, healthy and unhealthy environments form a central symbolic structure in the novel. In *Shirley*, Caroline's illness is anticipated by a passage about the arrival of 'the yellow taint of pestilence, covering white Western isles with the poisoned exhalations of the East, dimming the lattices of English homes with the breath of Indian plague' (p. 421). Similarly, in *Jane Eyre* Brontë consistently associates unhealthy, contagious environments with racial 'otherness' and with oppression, that 'poisoned exhalation of the East.' When Rochester decides to leave Jamaica where he has taken a dark wife as a 'slave,' participated in slavery, and become 'blackened,' the novel poses the opposition between oppressive Jamaica and pure England in terms of atmosphere. As Rochester recounts it:

> 'it was a fiery West Indian night; one of the description that frequently precede the hurricanes of those climates. Being unable to sleep in bed, I got up and opened the window. The air was like sulphur streams—I could find no refreshment anywhere. Mosquitoes came buzzing in and hummed sullenly around the room. ... the moon was setting in the waves, broad and red, like a hot cannon-ball—she threw her last bloody glance over a world quivering with the ferment of tempest. I was physically influenced by the atmosphere. ... I meant to shoot myself. ...
>
> 'A wind fresh from Europe blew over the ocean and rushed through the open casement: the storm broke, streamed, thundered, blazed, and the air grew pure. I then framed and fixed a resolution.'
>
> (p. 335).

Under the influence of 'the sweet wind from Europe,' Rochester resolves to return to England, to 'be clean' in his own sight (p. 334) by leaving the site of colonial oppression.

In a very similar passage Jane associates oppression and freedom with healthy and unhealthy environments. After she has fled Thornfield and settled at Morton, she reprimands herself for repining: 'Whether it is better,' Jane asks, 'to be a slave in a fool's paradise at Marseilles—fevered with delusive bliss one hour—suffocated with the bitterest tears of remorse and shame the next—or to be a village schoolmistress, free and honest, in a breezy mountain nook in the healthy heart of England?' (p. 386). Jane here imagines the gender and class slavery she would endure as Rochester's mistress as a feverish, suffocating, southern atmosphere.[12]

The damp pestilential fog of Lowood School is one of the novel's most drastically unhealthy environments; the atmosphere at this orphan institution where Jane thinks of herself as 'a slave or victim' is the direct result of class oppression. After so many students die of the typhus fever fostered by the unhealthy environment, 'several wealthy and benevolent individuals in the county' transform it into a less oppressive institution by the act of cleaning: a new building is erected in a healthier location, and 'brackish fetid water' (p. 115) is no longer used in preparation of the children's food.

Creating a clean, healthy, middle-class environment stands as the novel's symbolic alternative to an involvement in oppression. As Rochester is engaging in his most manipulative attempt to assure himself of Jane's love, by bringing home an apparent rival, he also orders that his house be cleaned. A great fuss is made over cleaning the house Jane had innocently thought to be already 'beautifully clean and well arranged' (p. 193). But what Rochester most needs to have cleaned out of his house as he is trying to attain an Englishwoman's love is the black-faced wife in his attic who represents his sullying colonial past, his 'marriage' to the colonies. So despite all the cleaning—'such scrubbing,' Jane says, 'such brushing, such washing of paint and beating of carpets, such taking down and putting up of pictures, such polishing of mirrors and lustres, such lighting of fires in bedrooms, such airing of sheets and feather-beds on hearths, I never beheld, either before or since' (p. 193)—the presence remains in Thornfield that makes Rochester call it 'a great plague-house' (p. 173). All that he can do with the 'plague' in his house is to hire a woman to 'clean' her away into a remote locked room. And as a reminder of this 'plague,' Grace Poole periodically emerges, amidst all the cleaning, from the third story, 'damping' Jane's cheerfulness and causing her 'dark' conjectures, in order, as both the most expert cleaner and as the signifier of the great 'stain' in the house, to give advice to the other servants: 'just to say a word, perhaps ... about the proper way to polish a grate, or clean a marble mantlepiece, or take stains from papered walls' (p. 194).

The other great cleaning activity in the novel occurs as Jane decides to 'clean down' Moor House (p. 416), and it marks a more successful attempt at washing away oppression than the one at Thornfield. Jane cleans the house to celebrate the egalitarian distribution of her newly acquired legacy, which will enable her to live there happily with her new-found family. Brontë writes of Jane's 'equal' division of her fortune, using the rhetoric of a revolution against class oppression, although symbolically it represents a redistribution of wealth in favor of only a limited group of people, the lower-middle class. When St John Rivers tells Jane that he, Diana, and Mary will be her brother and sisters without this sacrifice of her 'just rights,' she responds, in a tone of passionate conviction Brontë obviously endorses: '"Brother? Yes; at the distance of a thousand leagues! Sisters? Yes; slaving amongst strangers! I wealthy—gorged with gold I never earned and do not merit! You, penniless! Famous equality and fraternization! Close union! Intimate attachment!"' (p. 413). This sort of redistribution of wealth, Brontë suggests, giving Jane the language of the French revolution—'*Liberté! Egalité! Fraternité!*'—will right the wrongs of the lower-middle class, and clean from it the mark of blackness which represents oppression. Its women will no longer have to 'slave' among strangers like blacks; its men will no longer have to venture into the distant, dangerous environment of the 'dark races' in the colonies. With Jane, Brontë redefines the claims of 'brotherhood,' as her plot redistributes wealth: truly acknowledged 'fraternity,' the novel suggests, requires distributing wealth equally, not letting a brother or sister remain a penniless 'slave.'

But to only a limited group among those who might ask 'Am I not a man and a brother?' does the novel answer 'Yes.' The plot of *Jane Eyre* works toward a redistribution of power and wealth, equalization and an end to oppression just as Jane herself does, but its utopia remains partial; its 'revolution' improves only the lot of the middle class, closing out both the working class and those from whom the figure of 'slavery' has been appropriated in the first place. As Jane phrases her 'revolution,' it is one which specifically depends on erasing the mark of racial 'otherness.'

To signify her utopian end to economic injustice, Jane creates a clean, healthy environment, free of plague: her aim, she tells St John, is 'to *clean down* (do you comprehend the full force of the expression?) to *clean down* Moor House from chamber to cellar' (p. 416). Jane works literally to 'set her own house in order,' creating a clean, healthy, egalitarian, middle-class, domestic environment as the alternative to oppression. This environment is not, however, to the taste of St John, who wants to force Jane into an inegalitarian marriage and to take her to the unhealthy atmosphere of British India (both of which she says would kill her), to help him preach his rather different values of hierarchy and domination to dark-skinned people. Jane recognizes this difference in mentality and their incompatibility when St John fails to appreciate her house-cleaning: 'this parlour is not his sphere,' she realizes, 'the Himalayan ridge, or Caffre bush, even the plague-cursed Guinea Coast swamp, would suit him better' (p. 419).

Instead of deciding that it is her vocation to enter this new environment of plague, 'dark races,' and hierarchical oppression, Jane feels 'called' to return to a house which, being larger and more stained by oppression, will be more difficult to 'clean down'—Rochester's Thornfield. But of course when she gets there she finds that this 'plague-house' has already been 'cleaned down.' Brontë's plot participates in the same activity as Jane—cleaning, purifying, trying to create a world free of oppression. And the plot works precisely in the terms of the rhetoric of Jane's 'revolution.' It redistributes wealth and equalizes gender power, and it does so by cleaning away Bertha, the staining dark woman who has represented oppression.

In the ending of the novel, Brontë creates the world she can imagine free of the forms of oppression the novel most passionately protests against: gender oppression and the economic oppression of the lower-middle class. In the novel's utopian closure lies much of the revolutionary energy that made its contemporary readers anxious: the novel enacts Brontë's conception of a gender and middle-class revolution. The mutilation of Rochester (which interestingly has made critics of the novel far more uneasy than the killing of Bertha) and the loss of his property in Thornfield redistributes power between him and the newly-propertied Jane. Jane tells her former 'master' emphatically that she is now both independent and rich: 'I am,' she says, 'my own mistress' (p. 459). And in the last chapter Jane explicitly describes their marriage as egalitarian, unlike most: 'I hold myself supremely blest beyond what language can express; because I am my husband's life as fully as he is mine' (p. 475). The closure of the novel also severely punishes Rochester for his acquisition of colonial wealth. Fulfilling Rochester's own allusion to the accursed wealth wrongfully stolen by Achan, Brontë's ending enacts a purification like that of Achan, who is 'stoned with stones and burned with fire' (Joshua 7: 25) for bringing the 'accursed thing' into the camp of Israel. Unlike Achan, Rochester survives, but his 'tent of Achan'—his luxurious, oppressive, 'plague-house'—is destroyed and his mis-begotten wealth exorcised from the novel.

But this revolution against gender oppression and the economic oppression of the middle class, and even this purifying away of ill-gotten colonial wealth, is made possible by another sort of oppression and suppression. The revolution behind Jane's revolution is that of the black woman who signifies both the oppressed and the oppressor. Bertha institutes the great act of cleaning in the novel, which burns away Rochester's oppressive colonial wealth and diminishes the power of his gender, but then she herself is cleaned away by it—burned and as it were purified from the novel. Brontë creates the racial 'other' as the incarnate signifier of oppression, and then makes this sign, by the explosive instability of the situation it embodies, destroy itself.

Jane Eyre ends with a glimpse of the purified, more egalitarian world created by this figurative sacrifice of the racial 'other,' Brontë's complex working-out of culturally available metaphors. But the novel does not end as peacefully as we might expect after this holocaust of the sign of racial 'otherness' and oppression. The ending betrays Brontë's uneasiness about her own figurative tactics, about the way in which her use of racial difference as a signifier involves a brutal silencing, an erasing of the humanity of the actual people inside the bodies marked 'other.'

This uneasiness becomes evident in the way the spectre of the racial 'other' remains to haunt the ending of the novel, although evaporated into the form of the 'insalubrious' mist which hovers over Ferndean, where Jane and Rochester settle after the 'cleaning down' of Thornfield (p. 455). The dank and unhealthy atmosphere of Ferndean disrupts the utopian elements of the ending, indicating that the world of the novel is still not fully purified of oppression. And the oppression which that mist must signify, now that it no longer refers to class or gender oppression, is that original oppression which on one level the novel has tried so hard to displace and repress: the oppression of various dark-skinned peoples by the British.

The atmosphere of Ferndean recalls the fact that, even if Rochester's tainted colonial wealth has been burned away, the wealth Jane is able to bring him, enabling her to meet him on equal terms—and the wealth she earlier distributes in such a scrupulously egalitarian and 'revolutionary' spirit—has a colonial source. It comes from her uncle in Madeira, who is an agent for a Jamaican wine manufacturer, Bertha's brother. And the location of Jane's uncle John in Madeira, off Morocco, on the East Africa coast, where Richard Mason stops on his way home from England, also evokes, through Mason's itinerary, the triangular route of the British slave traders, and suggests that John Eyre's wealth is implicated in the slave trade. The details of the scene in which Brontë has Jane acquire her fortune mark Jane's economic and literary complicity in colonialism as well. St John announces Jane's accession to fortune by pulling the letter out of a 'morocco pocket-book' (p. 404), and he is able to identify Jane as the heiress because she has written her name, on a white sheet of paper, in 'Indian ink' (p. 407).

In this way the novel connects the act of writing with colonialism. Specifically writing 'Jane Eyre,' creating one's own triumphant identity as a woman no longer oppressed by class or gender—or writing *Jane Eyre*, the fiction of a redistribution of wealth and power between men and women—depends on a colonial 'ink.' Whether advertently or not, Brontë acknowledges that dependence in the conclusion of *Jane Eyre*. Like colonial exploitation itself, bringing home the spoils of other countries to become commodities, such as Indian ink,[13] the use of the racial 'other' as a metaphor for class and gender struggles in England commodifies colonial subjects as they exist in historical actuality and transforms them into East or West 'Indian ink,' ink with which to write a novel about ending oppression in England.

The eruption of the words 'Indian ink' into the novel suggests, at some level, Brontë's uneasiness about the East Indian colonialism to which England was turning in 1848, as well as about the West Indian colonies which were by then clearly becoming unprofitable after the abolition of slavery. St John, the East Indian missionary who is given the last words in the novel, writes them as he is dying—killed off by the 'insalubrious' atmosphere of oppression in British India, as Rochester just misses dying when his West Indian plague-house collapses on him. Brontë's anxiety about British colonialism is everywhere apparent in the ending of *Jane Eyre*. The novel is finally unable to rest easily in its figurative strategy and its conservative anti-colonial politics: its opposition to a 'contaminating' and self-destructive contact with the colonies, and its advocacy of a middle-class domesticity freed from some of the most blatant forms of gender and class oppression. *Jane Eyre* is thus a fascinating example of the associations—and dissociations—between a resistance to the ideology of male domination and a resistance to the ideology of colonial domination.

The critique of colonialism which the novel promises to make through its analogy between forms of oppression finally collapses into a mere uneasiness about the effects of empire on domestic social relations in England. That disquietude is the only remnant of Brontë's potentially radical revision of the analogy between white women and colonized races, and it is the only incomplete element in the ideological closure of the novel. The insalubrious mist which suggests British colonial contact with the racial 'other,' diffused throughout the ending of the novel, betrays Brontë's lingering anxiety about British colonialism and about her own literary treatment of the racial 'other,' about the way in which, through oppressive figurative tactics, she has tried to make the world of her novel 'clean.'

NOTES

1. Gayatri Chakravorty Spivak, 'Three Women's Texts and a Critique of Imperialism,' *Critical Inquiry* 12 (1985), 243–261. Two other critics have made brief allusions to the significance of race in *Jane Eyre*. In 'Rochester as Slave: An Allusion in *Jane Eyre*,' *Notes and Queries*, 31 (March 1984), R. J. Dingley notes that Rochester uses the phrase 'a man and a brother' in speaking to Jane, Charlotte Brontë, *Jane Eyre*, 1847; rpt. New York: Penguin Books, 1984, p. 66). Dingley interprets the phrase as Rochester's impulsively premature declaration that the intensity of his passion makes him Jane's 'slave.' Patricia Beer frames the chapter on Charlotte Brontë in her *Reader, I Married Him: A Study of the Women Characters of Jane Austen, Charlotte Brontë, Elizabeth Gaskell and George Eliot* (New York: Barnes and Noble, 1974),

by suggesting that the novel draws an analogy between women and slaves and noting that Brontë, unlike Jane Austen, made 'serious ... comment' on this form of the 'slave trade' (p. 84), but she goes no further in exploring the analogy.

2. Anthony Trollope, 'Miss Sarah Jack of Spanish Town, Jamaica,' in his *Tourists and Colonials*, ed. Betty Jane Slemp Breyer (Fort Worth, Texas: Texas Christian University Press, 1981), p. 8.
3. See, for example, Adrienne Rich's reference to Bertha's 'dark sensual beauty,' 'Jane Eyre: The Temptations of a Motherless Woman' (1973), reprinted in her *On Lies, Secrets, and Silence: Selected Prose 1966–1978* (New York: Norton, 1979), p. 99, or Sandra Gilbert and Susan Gubar's description of Bertha as 'a Creole—swarthy, "livid," etc.' (*The Madwoman in the Attic* [New Haven: Yale University Press, 1979], p. 680n).
4. For discussions of the practices of and attitudes toward interracial sex and manumission in the English colonies, see Winthrop Jordan, *The White Man's Burden: Historical Origins of Racism in the United States* (New York: Oxford University Press, 1974), pp. 70–73.
5. M. Ludlow, *History of the United States* (1862), quoted in *The Compact Edition of the Oxford English Dictionary* (New York: Oxford University Press, 1981), I, 601.
6. For the association of the racial 'other' with madness, see Sander Gilman, *Difference and Pathology: Stereotypes of Sexuality, Race, and Madness* (Ithaca: Cornell University Press, 1985), esp. pp. 131–149. A more lengthy discussion of the ambiguity of the word 'Creole' appears in Christopher Miller, *Blank Darkness: Africanist Discourse in French* (Chicago: University of Chicago Press, 1985), pp. 93–107.
7. Only excerpts from this journal entry, which begins 'Well here I am at Roe Head,' have been published. One excerpt appears in Christine Alexander, *The Early Writings of Charlotte Brontë* (Oxford: Blackwell, 1983), p. 148. A different, but partially overlapping, excerpt appears in Fannie Elizabeth Ratchford, *The Brontës' Web of Childhood* (1941; rpt. New York: Russell and Russell, 1964), p. 114.
8. 'The West India Controversy,' *Blackwood's Edinburgh Magazine* 14 (1823), 442.
9. Q. D. Leavis, 'Notes,' in *Jane Eyre*, pp. 487–489.
10. For an excellent discussion of the European fear of 'going native' in the colonies, which includes a discussion of Kurtz in Conrad's *Heart of Darkness*, see Patrick Brantlinger, 'Victorians and Africans: The Genealogy of the Myth of the Dark Continent,' *Critical Inquiry* 12 (1985), 166–203, esp. 193–198. Brantlinger argues that 'the potential for being "defiled"—for "going native" or becoming "tropenkollered"—led Europeans again and again to displace their own "savage" impulses onto Africans' (p. 196).
11. For two very interesting discussions of the Victorian bourgeoisie's equation of dirt with the 'lower orders,' see Leonore Davidoff's analysis of the relationship between the upper-middle-class A. J. Munby and his servant Hannah Cullwick in 'Class and Gender in Victorian England,' in *Sex and Class in Women's History*, ed. Judith L. Newton, Mary P. Ryan, and Judith R. Walkowitz (Boston: Routledge and Kegan Paul, 1983), pp. 17–71, and Peter Stallybrass and Allon White, *The Politics and Poetics of Transgression* (Ithaca: Cornell University Press, 1986), pp. 125–148.
12. Patricia Beer also notes that 'the fresh air and the open countryside remain for [Jane] symbols of personal freedom and independence' which she opposes to the thought of suffocation as Rochester's 'slave' (p. 126).
13. Ironically, the name 'Indian ink' or 'India ink' is a misnomer: the black pigment was actually made in China and Japan. The term entered the English language in the seventeenth century, according to the OED, when the word 'India' was used more broadly for the region of southern Asia to the east of the Indus river, and the British were just beginning to engage in trade with the East.

3.2

FROM 'EMPIRE AND THE MOVEMENT FOR WOMEN'S SUFFRAGE IN BRITAIN'

Inderpal Grewal

JANE EYRE IN THE COLONIES: 'HELPMEET' AND COMRADE

Englishwomen who traveled to the colonies were perceived as intrepid pioneers whose accounts revealed the dangers and discomforts they had to undergo. Their efforts showed them to be able, like Englishmen, to withstand the rigors of life in the supposedly enervating and harmful climates of Asia and Africa. Participating in the project of colonization as travelers, missionaries, teachers, and ethnographers, these Englishwomen broke down the bourgeois ideals of the 'angel in the house' and helped, implicitly and explicitly, in the cause of women's suffrage in Britain. Their narratives showed their attempts to be the equals of bourgeois and upper-class Englishmen and superior to many peoples of the world. By doing so, they also became part of the nationalist discourse of empire.

Charlotte Brontë's *Jane Eyre* reveals this perception of the pioneering Englishwoman and is a text that has caused much discussion in the area of feminism and imperialism in the context of English literary studies. When Jane is asked to join in missionary work with St John Rivers, she believes it to be a life of work and sacrifice. However, she feels she can perform this vocation only as a comrade of Rivers. Missionary work is, to her, an alternative to marriage and family life. Despite the fact that the colonies were seen as places where Englishwomen were to be protected from the rapacious and oversexed 'natives,' imperial needs came to require Englishwomen in order to keep the colonists from cohabiting with 'native' women. Jane, acting within English imperial and racial beliefs but trying to break gender norms, is willing to go as the equal of

In *Home and Harem: Nation, Gender, Empire and the Cultures of Travel*, London: Leicester University Press, 1996, pp. 61–5.

Rivers. Instead, Rivers asks her to accompany him to India as a 'helpmeet and fellow-labourer,' defining this position as that of a wife whom he can 'influence efficiently in life, and retain absolutely till death.'[1] Rivers's needs are those of the colonial state. Realizing Rivers's will to dominate, his 'hardness and despotism,' which recalls the colonial trope of the oriental despot, she refuses to go as his wife. As his comrade, on the other hand, she feels she can endure the life of a missionary, 'cross oceans with him . . . toil under Eastern suns, in Asian deserts,' and even admire him as long as she can remain free and 'still have my unblighted self to turn to.'[2]

Her offer to be his equal, to be his comrade with 'a fellow-soldier's frankness, fidelity, fraternity,' as she describes it, is rejected when Rivers makes her wifely subservience essential to her becoming a missionary.[3] What is made evident in this episode is Jane's strength, which is opposed to Rivers's problematic desire for domination. His recourse to conventional sexual morality is contrasted with her independence and willingness to work in India with him. Male superiority is questioned in the context of missionary work, where it is implied that English-women also possess the capability for such work. More importantly, the Englishwoman's position in the colonies is clearly delineated here. Deemed inferior by Englishmen who see women's subjugation and peripherality as an intrinsic part of the hierarchy of a masculine nation and empire, Englishwomen see the colonies as a space to prove their capabilities and their participation in the work of the nation for civilizing the 'natives.'

It is also important that Brontë's text then goes on to show that, refused her terms by Rivers, Jane becomes instead the wife and comrade of Rochester, who is weakened through his connection with the colonized woman, Bertha Mason. Jane can be comrade to Rochester when the increasing interest in women's concerns and capabilities combined with the Enlightenment ideology of equality turns marriage into companionate marriage.[4] Within such a conceptualization of marriage, Jane and Rochester provide a new bourgeois heterosexual couple, the emerging notion of the nuclear family of the nineteenth century. Furthermore, imperial masculinity, condemned in Rivers's case, is endorsed in Rochester's, when it is not autonomous but is needy. Jane becomes the comrade and wife of the Englishman harmed by a colonized, dark woman. Englishman and Englishwoman support each other to form a new version of the domestic unit in the domestic space. whereas Rivers allows Jane the role of a missionary only when it is combined with that of a wife and mother, in England the strong Englishwoman can be wife and mother and a comrade (though the last occurs only within the ideals of a heterosexual, companionate marriage) in order to nurture and care for a masculinity wounded by the colonial encounter. What is implied is that a strong nation is to be made up of Englishmen and English-women who are comrades; Englishwomen are as central to the formation of empire as the men.

However, the role of 'helpmeet,' despite Jane's implicit superiority, remains a problematic issue, for she does not break out of the domestic space. Few women, even those more involved in struggles for Englishwomen's rights, were able to do so. Yet within the narrative of *Jane Eyre*, Jane's subject constitution becomes central, through opposition and comparison with Bertha and through the battle for her equality with Englishmen who wished to dominate her. Peripheralized herself by a patriarchal culture, Jane's peripheralizing of Bertha Mason enables her entry, however partial, into the colonizer's masculine world and her sharing of Rochester's imperial subjectivity.

The colonies become, therefore, doubly important in showing the capabilities of Englishwomen. As liminal spaces, they can be proving grounds for Englishwomen's attempts at equality with Englishmen, their superiority to colonized men, and their ability to be a part of the project of empire conceived of as a heterosexual and masculinist project. As dangerous spaces, they show the vulnerability of English masculinity and the attempts of Englishwomen to control and share this masculinity that is essential to the English family and nation. Many texts, such as those by Richard Francis Burton, which delineated a colonial space of homosexual masculinity, no doubt compounded this threat. The text thus questions the necessity for the colonial project to be a purely male one, while questioning the subjugation of Englishwomen. However, it does not question the imperial project itself, since it is this very project that enables the subject constitution of the bourgeois Englishwoman.

In her essay, 'Three Women's Texts and a Critique of Imperialism,' Gayatri Spivak suggests that *Jane Eyre* is concerned with the constitution of Jane's subjectivity as 'female individualist' through the Othering of Bertha Mason by the operation of 'imperialist axiomatics.'[5] While, as Jenny Sharpe suggests, the Indian woman remains the shadowy double of Jane, Jane's superior position is not as evident as Spivak suggests.[6] Her subject constitution occurs through comparisons and opposition to the Englishmen in the text as well as through Bertha. It is only because she is deemed inferior by her countrymen, in both her gender and class position, that it becomes essential for Jane to establish herself as a subject. To do this, she claims her class and racial superiority in order to accede to the position of Rochester's comrade by the end of the novel. As comrade, Jane's position supposedly becomes different from St John Rivers's version of a good missionary wife, the subservient 'helpmeet.' However, the 'imperial axiomatics' that allow her to claim her subject position at the same time keep her within the domestic space. Her subject position remains problematic, even at the end of the novel.

The process by which Jane is created as the Other of Bertha in order to constitute herself is called 'worlding' by Spivak. By this term she means the ignored and imperial use of colonized people for the formation of the Western subject.[7] This 'worlding,' as in *Jane Eyre*, was also an intrinsic part of the English movement for women's suffrage, which started around 1860, over a decade after the publication of *Jane Eyre*, in 1847, when women in England fought for their rights with frequent references to the subordination and incarceration of Asian women. At that time a supporter of women's rights such as John Boyd-

Kinnear could ask in an essay published in 1869 on 'The Social Position of Women' whether forbidding women from participating in issues outside the home was not equivalent to placing them in a harem: 'Do we not in truth reduce them to the mere slaves of the harem? Do we not, like those who keep such slaves, deny in fact that they have any souls? What can they do with souls, if nature means them only to be toys of our idle hours, the adornment of our ease and wealth, to be worshipped as idols but never taken as helpmates, permitted at most to gaze from afar at the battles of life . . .'[8]

By contrast with the inhabitants of the harem, Boyd-Kinnear suggests that Englishwomen are not 'idols' or 'toys' or objects for 'adornment,' but must be seen as 'helpmates' who participate in every aspect of an integrated public and private life. His definition of the 'helpmate' is very different from St John Rivers's subservient 'helpmeet,' though both terms reveal that in no case were Englishwomen to lose their roles as nurturers or be the equals of men in the public realm. The woman in the harem is also present in this statement, for it was the 'Eastern' woman who was believed to be the 'toy' of the despotic husband; such women were thought to spend all their time in the harem adorning themselves, indulging in lesbian sexual practices that were deemed unspeakable by the English patriarchy. Englishwomen were to be different.

NOTES

1. Charlotte Brontë, *Jane Eyre*(1847) (London: Penguin Books, 1966), 427, 431.
2. Ibid., 432–33.
3. Ibid.
4. Thanks to Kamala Visweswaran for her useful discussion on this topic.
5. Gayatri Spivak, 'Three Women's Texts and a Critique of Imperialism,' in *'Race,' Writing, and Difference* ed. Henry Louis Gates Jr. (Chicago: University of Chicago Press, 1985).
6. Jenny Sharpe, *Allegories of Empire* (Minneapolis: Minnesota Press, 1993).
7. Spivak, 'Three Women's Texts.'
8. John Boyd-Kinnear, 'The Social Position of Women in the Present Age,' in *Woman's Work and Woman's Culture* ed. Josephine Butler (London: Macmillan and Co., 1869), 355.

3.3

FROM 'THE SULTAN AND THE SLAVE: FEMINIST ORIENTALISM AND THE STRUCTURE OF *JANE EYRE*'

Joyce Zonana

> I proposed to myself to display the folly of those who use authority to bring a woman to reason; and I chose for an example a sultan and his slave, as being two extremes of power and dependence. [Jean François Marmontel]

On the day following Jane Eyre's betrothal to her 'master' Rochester, Jane finds herself 'obliged' to go with him to a silk warehouse at Millcote, where she is 'ordered to choose half a dozen dresses.' Although she makes it clear that she 'hated the business,' Jane cannot free herself from it. All she can manage, 'by dint of entreaties expressed in energetic whispers,' is a reduction in the number of dresses, though 'these . . . [Rochester] vowed he would select himself.' Anxiously, Jane protests and 'with infinite difficulty' secures Rochester's grudging acceptance of her choice: a 'sober black satin and pearl-gray silk.' The ordeal is not over; after the silk warehouse, Rochester takes Jane to a jeweller's, where 'the more he bought me,' she reports, 'the more my cheek burned with a sense of annoyance and degradation' (Brontë [1847] 1985, 296–97).[1]

The shopping trip to Millcote gently figures Rochester as a domestic despot: he commands and Jane is 'obliged' to obey, though she feels degraded by that obedience. At this point in the narrative, Jane is not yet aware that in planning to marry her Rochester is consciously choosing to become a bigamist. Yet the image she uses to portray her experience of his mastery as he tries to dress her 'like a doll' (297) signals that not only despotism but bigamy and the oriental trade in women are on Jane's mind. Riding with Rochester back to Thornfield, she notes: 'He smiled; and I thought his smile was such as a sultan might, in a

Signs, 18:3, Spring 1993. Extract: pp. 592–8 and 605–17.

blissful and fond moment, bestow on a slave his gold and gems had enriched' (297). The image is startling in its extremity: surely Jane seems to overreact to Rochester's desire to see his bride beautifully dressed.

Yet by calling Rochester a 'sultan' and herself a 'slave,' Jane provides herself and the reader with a culturally acceptable simile by which to understand and combat the patriarchal 'despotism' (302) central to Rochester's character. Part of a large system of what I term feminist orientalist discourse that permeates *Jane Eyre*, Charlotte Brontë's sultan/slave simile displaces the source of patriarchal oppression onto an 'Oriental,' 'Mahometan' society, enabling British readers to contemplate local problems without questioning their own self-definition as Westerners and Christians.[2] As I will demonstrate, in developing her simile throughout her narrative, Jane does not so much criticize (in the words of Mary Ellis Gibson) 'domestic arrangements and British Christianity from the point of view of the "pagan" woman' (1987, 2) as define herself as a Western missionary seeking to redeem not the 'enslaved' woman outside the fold of Christianity and Western ideology but the despotic man who has been led astray within it.[3]

Brontë's use of feminist orientalism is both embedded in and brings into focus a long tradition of Western feminist writing. Beginning early in the eighteenth century, when European travelers' tales about visits to the Middle East became a popular genre, images of despotic sultans and desperate slave girls became a central part of an emerging liberal feminist discourse about the condition of women not in the East but in the West. From Mary Wollstonecraft to Elizabeth Barrett Browning to Margaret Fuller and Florence Nightingale, one discovers writer after writer turning to images of oriental life—and specifically the 'Mahometan' or 'Arabian' harem—in order to articulate their critiques of the life of women in the West. Part of the larger orientalism that Edward Said has shown to inform Western self-representation, the function of these images is not primarily to secure Western domination over the East, though certainly they assume and enforce that domination.[4] Rather, by figuring objectionable aspects of life in the West as 'Eastern,' these Western feminist writers rhetorically define their project as the removal of Eastern elements from Western life.

Feminist orientalism is a special case of the literary strategy of using the Orient as a means for what one writer has called Western 'self-redemption': 'transforming the Orient and Oriental Muslims into a vehicle for ... criticism of the West itself' (Al-Bazei 1983, 6).[5] Specifically, feminist orientalism is a rhetorical strategy (and a form of thought) by which a speaker or writer neutralizes the threat inherent in feminist demands and makes them palatable to an audience that wishes to affirm its occidental superiority. If the lives of women in England or France or the United States can be compared to the lives of women in 'Arabia,' then the Western feminist's desire to change the status quo can be represented not as a radical attempt to restructure the West but as a conservative effort to make the West more like itself. Orientalism—the belief that the East is inferior to the West, and the representation of the Orient by means of unexamined, stereotypical images—thus becomes a major premise in the formulation of numerous Western feminist arguments.

The conviction that the harem is an inherently oppressive institution functions as an a priori assumption in the writing I examine here. Even in the twentieth century, such an assumption continues to appear in Western feminist discourse, as Leila Ahmed (1982) and Chandra Mohanty (1988) demonstrate. Actual research on or observation of the conditions of the harem is rare, and what little that has been written tends toward either defensive celebration or violent condemnation. The defences are written with an awareness of the condemnations: their authors must challenge the Western feminist imagination that unquestioningly perceives polygamy as sexual slavery and domestic confinement as imprisonment.[6] The attempt to introduce a genuinely alternate vision is fraught with the difficulties both of documenting the actualities of life in the harem and of achieving a transcultural perspective, though some writers have made the effort.[7]

This article does not claim to demonstrate any truth about the harem that would definitively contradict or even modify the Western views presented here, nor does it systematically engage in the effort to achieve an objective estimate of the harem; rather, it seeks only to show how assumptions about the East have been used to further the Western feminist project instead of either spurring research and theorizing about the actual conditions of harem life or establishing genuine alliances among women of different cultures. For what is most crucial about what I am calling feminist orientalism is that it is directed not toward the understanding or even the reform of the harem itself but toward transformation of Western society—even while preserving basic institutions and ideologies of the West. Coming to recognize the feminist orientalism in *Jane Eyre* and other formative Western feminist texts may help clear the way for a more self-critical, balanced analysis of the multiple forms both of patriarchy and of women's power, and it may also, indirectly, help free global feminism from the charge that it is a Western movement inapplicable to Eastern societies.[8]

That *Jane Eyre*, like so many nineteenth-century British texts, has a diffusely orientalist background has long been recognized and for the most part attributed to the influence of the *Arabian Nights*, a book known to have been a staple of the Brontës' childhood reading.[9] The first simile in the novel, in the fourth paragraph of the first chapter, places Jane, 'cross-legged, like a Turk' (39) in the window seat of the Gateshead breakfast room. Not much later, Jane takes down a book of 'Arabian tales' (70); she reveals that she is fascinated by 'genii' (82); and eventually she makes it plain that the *Arabian Nights* was one of her three favorite childhood books (256). Other characters in the novel also display a loose familiarity and fascination with the Orient: the Dowager Lady Ingram dresses in a 'crimson velvet robe, and a shawl turban' (201); her daughter Blanche admits that she 'dote[s] on Corsairs' (208); Rochester worries when Jane assumes a 'sphinx-like expression' (329).

The specifically feminist quality of *Jane Eyre*'s orientalism, however, has not been recognized, perhaps because feminist orientalism has remained until recently an opaque, underexamined aspect of Western intellectual history. (Ahmed 1982, Spivak 1985, Mohanty 1988, and Perera 1991 are important exceptions.) The feminist orientalism of *Jane Eyre*, furthermore, is only made explicit in the sultan/slave simile, and, although the chords struck in this passage resonate throughout the entire novel, they cannot properly be heard without an understanding of the full eighteenth- and nineteenth-century background that generates them. Before turning to that background, however, it may be helpful briefly to set in relief this key episode in which Jane not only compares Rochester to a sultan but engages with him in an extended discussion of women's rights and uses her comparison of him to a sultan as a means by which to secure more rights for herself.

Among the more interesting features of this passage is the fact that Jane does not tell Rochester that she is mentally comparing him to a sultan. She simply asks him to stop looking at her 'in that way.' Rochester is astute enough to understand Jane's unspoken reference, suggesting that feminist orientalist discourse is so pervasive as to be accessible to the very men it seeks to change: '"Oh, it is rich to see and hear her!" he exclaimed. "Is she original? Is she piquant? I would not exchange this one little English girl for the Grand Turk's whole seraglio—gazelle-eyes, houri forms, and all!"' (297). Rochester suggests that he will take Jane instead of a harem, though Jane bristles at the 'Eastern allusion': '"I'll not stand you an inch in the stead of a seraglio," I said; "so don't consider me an equivalent for one. If you have a fancy for anything in that line, away with you, sir, to the bazaars of Stamboul, without delay, and lay out in extensive slave-purchases some of that spare cash you seem at a loss to spend satisfactorily here"' (297).

When Rochester jokingly asks what Jane will do while he is 'bargaining for so many tons of flesh and such an assortment of black eyes,' Jane is ready with a playful but serious response: 'I'll be preparing myself to go out as a missionary to preach liberty to them that are enslaved—your harem inmates among the rest. I'll get admitted there, and I'll stir up mutiny; and you, three-tailed bashaw as you are, sir, shall in a trice find yourself fettered amongst our hands: nor will I, for one, consent to cut your bonds till you have signed a charter, the most liberal that despot ever yet conferred!' (297–98). Although Jane promises Rochester that she will 'go out as a missionary' to 'Stamboul,' the focus of her remarks is the reform of Rochester himself within England. Her concern is that she herself not be treated as a 'harem inmate,' and her action, immediately following this conversation, succeeds in accomplishing her goal.

It is precisely Jane's experience of degrading dependency, playfully figured here as the relation of rebellious harem slave to despotic Eastern sultan, that leads her to take the step that ultimately reveals Rochester as more like a sultan than Jane had imagined. For it is at this point that Jane makes and executes the decision to write to her Uncle John in Madeira, in the hope that he will settle some money on her. 'If I had ever so small an independency,' she reasons, 'if I had but a prospect of one day bringing Mr Rochester an accession of fortune, I could better endure to be kept by him now' (297). Jane's letter to John Eyre alerts Rochester's brother-in-law, Richard Mason, to Rochester's plans to become a bigamist, and Jane is freed from a marriage that would, in her own terms, have thoroughly enslaved her.

Jane's comparison of Rochester to a sultan proves to be no exaggeration. The narrative makes plain that it is because she sees him in this way that she later is able to free herself from a degrading relationship with a man who has bought women, is willing to become a bigamist, and acts like a despot. The plot thus validates the figurative language, making of it much more than a figure. This Western man is 'Eastern' in his ways, and for Jane to be happy, he must be thoroughly Westernized. To the extent that Brontë has Jane Eyre present hers as a model life—'Reader, I married him'—she suggests that her female readers would also be well advised to identify and eliminate any such Eastern elements in their own spouses and suitors.

More than ten years ago, Peter A. Tasch observed that in having Jane call Rochester a 'three-tailed bashaw,' Brontë 'was echoing the refrain in a song by George Colman the Younger for his extravaganza *Blue Beard*.' Tasch further notes that 'the idea of an English girl in the "grand Turk's" seraglio demanding liberty forms the theme of another stage comedy, [Isaac Bickerstaffe's] *The Sultan; or, A Peep into the Seraglio*' (1982, 232). Tasch may well be correct in identifying these specific sources for Brontë's allusions; yet the image of a harem inmate demanding liberty had by 1847 become so ingrained in Western feminist discourse that Brontë need not have had any specific text in mind; her audience, whether familiar with *Blue Beard* and *The Sultan* or not, would have had a full stock of harem images by which to understand and applaud Jane's sultan/slave simile.

The stage was set for the Western use of the harem as a metaphor for aspects of Western life as early as 1721, in Baron de Montesquieu's *Persian Letters*. The letters in Montesquieu's novel, written primarily by two 'Persian' men traveling in Europe, offer dramatic images of both Eastern and Western ways of structuring domestic and political relations. Usbek and Rica, the travelers who report on the oddities of Western ways, are in constant contact with the women and eunuchs they have left behind in the harem. The Western reader moves between defamiliarized visions of Europe and 'familiar' images of Persia, eventually coming to see, in the words of one modern commentator, that in the seraglio, constructed as the heart of oriental despotism, 'It is myself, and our world, finally, that I rediscover' (Grosrichard 1979, 32–33, translation mine; for further commentary on the self-reflexive function of Western representations of the harem, see Richon 1984 and Alloula 1986).

Montesquieu's work focuses primarily on the nature of political despotism, using images of the Eastern and Western domestic enslavement of women as metaphors for the political enslavement of men. The condition of women is not

Montesquieu's central concern, but because the harem is his functional model of despotism, the novel repeatedly returns to the question of 'whether it is better to deprive women of their liberty or to leave them free' (Montesquieu [1721] 1923, 107) and draws recurrent analogies between the status of women in the East and the West. In its closing pages, *Persian Letters* portrays a full-scale rebellion in the seraglio: in the absence of their masters, the women have taken new lovers and sought to undo the system of surveillance that has kept them imprisoned.

. . .

Examining this narrative structure, one sees that each household in which Jane finds herself is constructed to resemble a harem; each of her oppressors is characterized as a Mahometan despot; and each of her rebellions or escapes bears the accents of Roxanna, the harem inmate declaring her existence as a free soul. At Gateshead, at Lowood, at Thornfield, and at Moor House, one discovers a series of communities of dependent women, all subject to the whim of a single master who rules in his absence as much as his presence and who subjects the imprisoned women to the searching power of his gaze.[10] In each of these households, Jane finds her own power of movement and of vision limited; even when she is most in love with Rochester at Thornfield, she recognizes that he stands in her way, 'as an eclipse intervenes between man and the broad sun' (Brontë [1847] 1985, 302).

The pattern of home as harem is established at Gateshead, where the household consists of John Reed, Mrs Reed, Eliza and Georgiana Reed, Jane, and the two female servants, Bessie and Abbott. There are also a male 'butler and footman' (60), though these are shadowy presences, nameless men inconsequential in the dynamics and management of the household. The 'master' is young John Reed, a boy of fourteen who demands that Jane call him 'Master Reed' (41) and against whose arbitrary rule Jane has no appeal: 'the servants did not like to offend their young master by taking my part against him, and Mrs Reed was blind and deaf on the subject: she never saw him strike or heard him abuse me, though he did both now and then in her very presence' (42).

Like the sultans described by Montesquieu and the eighteenth-century travelers, John considers the privileges of seeing and knowing to be his. What enrages him in the novel's opening scene is that Jane is out of his sight. Hidden behind the curtain of the window seat, reading and looking out the window, she has usurped his role as the 'Turk.' 'Where the dickens is she?' John asks his sisters, and when Eliza finds Jane for him, John castigates his cousin not only for 'getting behind curtains' but also for reading: 'You have no business to take our books' (42). In the course of his tirade, John calls Jane a 'bad animal' (41) and a 'rat' (42); later she will become a 'wild cat' (59). John's descriptions of Jane as beast and his wish to keep her from educating herself through books may recall Wollstonecraft's definition of the 'true style' of Mahometanism: the view of women as 'domestic brutes' ([1792] 1982, 101), 'not as a part of the human species' (80).

The sexuality of the harem is absent from the Reed home, but the indolent, pampered sensuality that so offends Wollstonecraft is not. In the opening scene, Mrs Reed lies 'reclined on a sofa by the fireside . . . with her darlings about her' (39). John is constantly plied with 'cakes and sweetmeats,' even though he 'gorged himself habitually at table, which made him bilious, and gave him a dim and bleared eye with flabby cheeks' (41). John is the effete, attenuated tyrant made weak by his abuse of power, familiar from Wollstonecraft's characterizations of 'bashaws.' The Reed sisters are 'universally indulged' (46) and 'elaborately ringleted' (60); their mother dresses regularly in silks. The luxury of Gateshead, associated as it is with the degeneracy and despotism of the harem, is something Jane learns to abhor, and this abhorrence informs her later attempts to resist Rochester's desire to see her 'glittering like a parterre' (296).

Jane, not unlike Montesquieu's Roxanna, rebels against her imprisonment within Master Reed's 'harem.' Her physical violence is expressed against John, but she reserves her strongest words for Mrs Reed, the adult who has enforced the 'young master's' wishes: 'If anyone asks me how I liked you, and how you treated me, I will say the very thought of you makes me sick, and that you treated me with miserable cruelty . . . You think I have no feelings, and that I can do without one bit of love or kindness; but I cannot live so: and you have no pity' (68). Like Roxanna, Jane exposes the hypocrisy of her keeper, insisting on the freedom of her mind and on her desire for and right to genuine love.

Jane's outburst leads to her departure from Gateshead, though she soon finds herself in another institution that even more closely resembles the harem that haunts the Western feminist imagination. Lowood, 'a large and irregular building' through which on her arrival Jane is led 'from compartment to compartment, from passage to passage' (76), perfectly embodies the confinement of the harem. The building is oppressive, dark, and gloomy, and the garden is no better: 'a wide enclosure,' it is 'surrounded with walls so high as to exclude every glimpse of prospect' (80). These walls not only limit the vision of the institution's 'inmates' but they are 'spike-guarded' (107) to prohibit freedom of movement.

Within the confines of this dwelling, Jane discovers 'a congregation of girls of every age . . . Their number to me appeared countless' (76). Over this community of women rules the redoubtable Mr Brocklehurst, 'the black marble clergyman' (98) whom Jane perceives as a 'black column,' a 'piece of architecture' (94). Like John Reed, Brocklehurst's characteristic gesture is to gaze searchingly upon his assembled dependants. When he makes his first appearance at Lowood, he 'majestically surveyed the whole school' (95); a few moments later he 'scrutinize[s]' the hair of the terrified girls. As with John Reed, Jane seeks to hide from this master's eyes: 'I had sat well back on the form, and while seeming to be busy with my sum, had held my slate in such a manner as to conceal my face' (97). Jane does not escape Brocklehurst's look, however, and is forced to suffer the humiliation of his description of her as a liar. Jane is freed by the good offices of Miss Temple, and later, when the scandal of Brocklehurst's despotic rule is revealed (significantly, it takes the death of a number of the inmates to cause this revelation) he is stripped of some of his power. Lowood becomes a fairly happy home for Jane, though a 'prison-ground' nonetheless (117).

It may be objected that the ascetic aspects of Lowood accord ill with the suggestion that it is figured as a harem. Certainly Lowood harbors neither the sensuality nor the overt sexuality associated with the harem. Yet its structure, with one man controlling an indefinite number of dependent women, mimics that of the seraglio. Further, Brocklehurst's wish to strip the girls of all adornment, of all possibilities of sensual gratification, has its parallel in the sultan's wish to keep the women of the harem restrained from any sexuality not under his control. That Brocklehurst is figured in plainly phallic terms only underscores his identification as a sultan whose perverse pleasure here consists in denying pleasure to the women he rules. For his wife and daughters, however—women over whom presumably he can exert even greater control—Brocklehurst allows a greatest sensuality: these women are 'splendidly attired in velvet, silk, and furs' (97).

When Jane leaves Lowood for her 'new servitude' at Thornfield (117), she happily anticipates entering the domain of Mrs Fairfax, an 'elderly lady' (120) whom she believes to be the mistress of a 'safe haven' (129), a 'snug' and secure realm of feminine 'domestic comfort' (127). To her initial dismay, Jane discovers that this new household of women also has a 'master' the absent yet omnipotent Mr Rochester. Jane first meets Rochester on the moonlit lane connecting Thornfield to the town of Hay, unaware he is her master. She perceives this stranger to have a 'dark face, with stern features and a heavy brow' (145); later she will call his skin 'swarthy,' his features 'Paynim' (212). The man has fallen from his horse, and Jane offers to assist him. Before accepting her help, however, he subjects her to intense 'scrutiny' in order to determine her identity (146).

Jane reveals that she is the governess at Thornfield; Rochester offers no information about himself, except to say, when Jane fails in her effort to lead his horse to him: 'I see ... the mountain will never be brought to Mahomet, so all you can do is to aid Mahomet to go to the mountain' (146). Though uttered in jest, these words do not bode well for Jane's relationship with her master. Rochester gives himself the one name that, to a nineteenth-century audience, would unambiguously identify him as a polygamous, blasphemous despot—a sultan. After such an introduction, it comes as no surprise when Rochester chooses to dress 'in shawls, with a turban on his head' for a game of charades, nor that Jane should see him as 'the very model of an Eastern emir' (212).

The most striking identification of Rochester as an oriental despot—again a characterization that comes from his own lips—occurs when he begins to contemplate marriage with Jane. The intimacy between master and dependent has begun to develop, and in the course of guardedly discussing his past with the governess, Rochester admits that he 'degenerated' when wronged by fate (167). As Jane and the reader will later learn, he is referring to his marriage with Bertha Mason, and his subsequent indulgence in 'lust for a passion—vice for an occupation' (343). With no knowledge of the details of Rochester's 'degeneration,' Jane nevertheless encourages him to repent, though Rochester insists that only pleasure, 'sweet, fresh pleasure' (167), can help him. Jane suggests that such pleasure 'will taste bitter' (167) and warns Rochester against 'error.' Rochester, apparently referring to his wish to love Jane, replies that the 'notion that flitted across my brain' is not error or temptation but 'inspiration': 'I am laying down good intentions, which I believe durable as flint. Certainly, my associates and pursuits shall be other than they have been ... You seem to doubt me; I don't doubt myself: I know what my aim is, what my motives are; and at this moment I pass a law, unalterable as that of the Medes and Persians, that both are right' (168–69).

Rochester's aim is to find happiness with Jane; his motives are to redeem himself from his association with Bertha; the unalterable law that he makes his own has its antecedent in the one decreed by King Ahasuerus—'written among the laws of the Persians and the Medes, that it not be altered'—when he banishes his Queen Vashti and vows to 'give her royal estate unto another that is better than she' (Esther 1.19). Ahasuerus, to whom Jane will later compare Rochester (in the same chapter in which she compares him to a sultan [Brontë (1847) 1985, 290]), had been angered by Vashti's refusal to come at his command. His counselors point out that the queen's refusal to be commanded might 'come abroad unto all women' (Esther 1.17), and the Persian king passes his law so that 'every man should bear rule in his own house' (Esther 1.22). Rochester's decision to banish Bertha and marry Jane is dangerously like Ahasuerus's replacement of Vashti by Esther; Jane's resistance signals her engagement in both the reform of her master and the liberation of her people.

The conversation between Jane and Rochester about Rochester's 'Persian' law offers readers clear signals about how they should perceive Rochester's relationship to Jane. Expressed as a conflict between Judeo-Christian law and Persian arrogance, the conflict can also be understood as Jane's struggle to retain possession of her soul, to claim her rights as a Western, Christian woman. Thus, when Rochester begins his actual proposal to her, Jane insists, 'I have as much soul as you' (Brontë [1847] 1985, 281). Later, when she resists his wish to take her to a 'whitewashed villa on the shores of the Mediterranean,' where, as his mistress, she would live a 'guarded' life (331), she expresses her triumph in precisely the same terms: 'I still possessed my soul' (344).[11]

It is at Thornfield, of course, that the confinement and sexuality of the seraglio/harem are most fully represented. Rochester has a wife whom he keeps literally caged in a 'wild beast's den' (336), 'a room without a window' (321). In her first explicit view of Bertha Mason, Jane depicts her in the ambiguous, nonhuman terms Wollstonecraft had applied to harem inmates: 'What it was, whether beast or human being, one could not, at first sight tell: it grovelled, seemingly, on all fours; it snatched and growled like some strange wild animal: but it was covered with clothing, and a quantity of dark, grizzled hair, wild as a mane, hid its head and face' (321). Referred to by Jane as a 'clothed hyena' (321),

Bertha incarnates a brute sensuality that apparently justifies her imprisonment. Rochester calls her his 'bad, mad, and embruted partner' (320), whom he married without being 'sure of the existence of one virtue in her nature' (333).

When Rochester takes his first wife, he is himself acting purely on the basis of his own 'excited' senses (332), not seeking a rational companion. He discovers in Bertha a 'nature wholly alien' to his own, a 'cast of mind common, low, narrow, and singularly incapable of being led to anything higher, expanded to anything larger' (333). Bertha is characterized here as a woman without a soul. This Western man has married a figuratively Eastern woman, an 'embruted' creature who, through the marriage bond, becomes a 'part of' him (334). When Rochester, responding to the 'sweet wind from Europe,' decides to leave Jamaica and 'go home to God' (335), his behaviour continues to be governed by the 'most gross, impure, depraved' nature that is permanently 'associated' with his own (334). Instead of remaining faithful to his wife, he roams Europe seeking 'a good and intelligent woman, whom I could love' (337). Of course he finds only the 'unprincipled and violent,' 'mindless,' and faithless mistresses his money buys him (338). Rochester knows that 'hiring a mistress is the next worse thing to buying a slave' (339), yet he persists on this course—even with Jane—because, the narrative suggests, his association with Bertha has deformed him into a polygamous, sensual sultan.

Thus Brontë appears to displace the blame for Rochester's Eastern tendencies on the intrusion of this 'Eastern' woman into his Western life. Though Jane protests in Bertha's behalf—'you are inexorable for that unfortunate lady' (328)—Rochester's account of his first marriage serves as the narrative explanation of his own oriental tendencies. The fact that he does not reform until Bertha dies suggests how powerful her oriental hold on him has been.[12]

Bertha, of course, is West Indian, not 'Mahometan,' and she scarcely resembles the conventional image of an alluring harem inmate—no 'gazelle eyes' or 'houri forms' here. Indeed, as Susan L. Meyer convincingly shows, she is consistently figured as a 'nightmare' vision with 'savage,' 'lurid,' and 'swelled' black features (1989, 253–54) and associated with the oppressed races subject to British colonialism. Yet, as Grosrichard points out, 'The West Indies can end by rejoining, in the imagination, the East Indies' (1979, 32, translation mine). Bertha's characterization in other significant ways recalls the terms used by Wollstonecraft to depict the fate of 'Mahometan' women: she is soulless, regarded as 'not ... a part of the human species,' and her all-too-real imprisonment at Thornfield invokes the root meaning of *seraglio*: a place where wild beasts are kept. One might say that Bertha's characterization as a 'clothed hyena' manifests the Western view of the underlying reality of the harem inmate, the philosophical view of women that underpins both their confinement within the harem and their more conventional adornment.[13]

Thus, to note Bertha's 'blackness' and her birth in Jamaica need not preclude seeing that she is also, simultaneously, figured as an 'Eastern' woman. Indeed, in Bertha's characterization a number of parallel discourses converge: she is the 'black woman who signifies both the oppressed and the oppressor' (Meyer 1989, 266); she is Jane's 'dark double' who enacts both Jane's and Brontë's repressed rage at patriarchal oppression (Gilbert and Gubar 1979, 360); she is the Indian woman consumed in sati (Perera 1991); she is Vashti, King Ahasuerus's uncontrollable queen; and she is a harem inmate whose purported soullessness justifies and enforces her own oppression. Bertha is overdetermined; as the 'central locus of Brontë's anxieties about oppression' (Meyer 1989, 252) and as the spark for the redemptive fire that clears the way for Jane's fulfillment, she serves to focus a number of different systems of figuration that structure the novel.

Indeed, Brontë equivocates still further in her presentation of Bertha, never fully indicating whether she is inherently soulless or only made so by Rochester's treatment of her. In a few significant passages, Brontë allows her narrative to suggest that Bertha, like Jane, is consciously aware of and legitimately enraged by her enslavement. On the eve of the doomed wedding, Bertha enters Jane's room, not to harm her as Rochester fears but to rend the veil, which Rochester in his 'princely extravagance' had insisted upon buying (Brontë [1847] 1985, 308). Jane sees in the veil an image of Rochester's 'pride' (309). When Bertha rends it 'in two parts' and 'trample[s] on them' (311), her action may be explained as emanating from her resentment of and jealousy toward Jane. Or, it may be viewed as a warning to Jane about the 'veiled' existence she would have to lead as Rochester's harem slave.

That Bertha kills herself in her attempt to burn down the house of her master can also be linked to Roxanna's ultimately self-destructive rebellion in *Persian Letters*. Defying the master who has enslaved her, she asserts her freedom only to find death as its inevitable price. As long as the despotic system is in place, no woman can truly be free, yet the suicide of a rebellious woman serves as a powerful condemnation—and potential transformation—of that system.[14] Thus it is no accident that Rochester is blinded in the conflagration caused by Bertha's rebellion. Stripped of his despotic privilege to see, he can no longer function as a sultan. Despite her earlier promises to 'stir up mutiny' in the harem (298), Jane owes her freedom not to her own rebellion but to that of the actual 'harem-inmate,' the 'dark double' who acts as her proxy.

After Bertha's death, Rochester is free to reform, and this reform is significantly figured as a conversion: 'Jane! you think me, I dare say, an irreligious dog: but my heart swells with gratitude to the beneficent God of this earth just now . . . I did wrong . . . Of late, Jane—only—only of late—I began to see and acknowledge the hand of God in my doom. I began to experience remorse, repentance, the wish for reconcilement with my Maker. I began sometimes to pray' (471). The man who had passed a 'Persian' law to justify his own behavior here acknowledges the authority of the Christian God who mandates monogamy and respect for the souls of women. Despite the many critiques of Christian ideology and practice that abound in *Jane Eyre*, Brontë's feminist orientalism here takes priority, as she obscures the patriarchal oppression that is also a part of Christianity.

And by ending her novel with the words of the Christian missionary St John Rivers, himself one of the domestic despots Jane has had to defy, Brontë leaves the reader with an idealized vision of Christianity as the only satisfactory alternative to Eastern, 'Mahometan'—and even Hindu—despotism. While this reversal in the characterization of St John and the expressed attitude toward Christianity has struck many readers as a self-contradictory shift in Brontë's focus, it in fact confirms and seals the pattern begun with Jane's promise to 'go out as a missionary to preach liberty to them that are enslaved' (297).

The novel's concluding paean to St John and to Christian values takes place against the backdrop not of a vaguely conceived Middle East but of the Far East, India. The groundwork establishing India as another locale for gendered oriental despotism had been laid early in the novel, in the same chapter that features the 'sultan/slave' simile. Back at Thornfield after the trip to Millcote, Jane objects to a 'pagan' tendency in Rochester (301). Her master has just sung a song to her in which a woman swears 'to live—to die' with her beloved (301). Jane seizes on the seemingly innocent phrase and asserts that she 'had no intention of dying' with Rochester: 'I had as good a right to die when my time came as he had: but I should bide that time, and not be hurried away in a suttee' (301).

Though this identification of India as another Eastern site for the oppression of women is not in my view extensively developed throughout the text, it returns in the novel's conclusion, as well as in the penultimate section of the novel, when Jane faces the threat of being 'grilled alive in Calcutta' (441) if she chooses to accompany St John to India. For during her stay at Moor House, Jane once again encounters a man with a 'despotic nature' (434) who rules over a household of dependent women and who threatens not only to immure but also to immolate her (430).

At first Jane finds Moor House less oppressive than her earlier homes. Yet when Jane consents to give up her study of German in order to help St John learn Hindustani, she discovers another form of 'servitude' (423) and she experiences the kiss that St John gives her as a 'seal affixed to my fetters' (424). Jane's subjection to St John is in fact stronger than any she has felt before. 'I could not resist him,' she uncharacteristically admits (425). Part of Jane's difficulty in resisting St John's wishes is that they come cloaked in Christian doctrine. Jane recognizes the despotism in St John, knowing that to accede to his wishes would be 'almost equivalent to committing suicide' (439). Yet because St John is a 'sincere Christian' (434), not an 'irreligious dog,' she has a harder time extricating herself from the seductions of his proposal that she marry him and accompany him to India: 'Religion called—Angels beckoned—God commanded' (444).

Brontë here reveals the motive behind feminist orientalism as a mode of cultural analysis as well as a rhetorical strategy. Jane finds it possible to resist Rochester because he calls himself and acts in ways that clearly echo the Western conception of 'Mahomet,' not Christ. But a man who assumes the language and posture of Christ is harder to combat. Jane ultimately does find the strength to resist St John, however, when he unwittingly sets her a challenge that obviously mimics the behaviour of a Western feminist's notion of a sultan.

What St John asks of Jane is that she abandon her already established love for Rochester. With this demand, he manifests what was, to Western feminists, perhaps the most threatening feature of 'Mahometan' practice: interference with a woman's free choice of love object. Indeed, what had motivated Roxanna's rebellion in *Persian Letters* was not her desire to escape confinement nor her position as one of many wives. Rather, it was her desire to be free to love another man, coupled with her abhorrence of her sexual 'master.' In denying Jane her freedom to love (and in promising to impose the forms of sexual love upon her), St John becomes the most brutal (and literal) of her harem masters and thus the one who evokes from her the greatest effort of rebellion.[15]

Yet in the concluding paragraphs of the novel, St John—the archetypal Christian man—is redeemed from the flaw in his own nature. By her resistance to his desire to enslave her, Jane frees him from his own oriental tendencies. If she is not a slave, he cannot be a master. Brontë makes explicit the implication behind Wollestonecraft's assertion that the women of the harem have souls 'just animated enough to give life to the body.' A woman of soul, as Jane has by now firmly established herself to be, has the power not only to resist the harem but to transform it: as Jane had once promised Rochester, 'you, three-tailed bashaw as you are, sir, shall in a trice find yourself fettered amongst our hands' (298).

St John, like Rochester, becomes a true Christian after his encounter with Jane and thus is free to pursue her orientalist project. For St John, as a Christian missionary in India, 'labours for his race' with the same impulses as do Jane and her author: 'Firm, faithful, and devoted, full of energy and zeal, and truth . . . he clears their painful way to improvement; he hews down like a giant the prejudices of creed and caste that encumber it' (477). Jane Eyre ends her story with St John's words—'Amen; even so, come, Lord Jesus!' (477)—because they externalize and make global what has been her own internal and local project all along: the purging of oriental elements from her society, the replacement of 'Mahometan' law by Christian doctrine. In voicing these words, St John is recommitting himself to the specifically Christian project of combating alien religious forms. Thus, although the novel's primary focus is the occidentalization of the Occident, it ends with the vision of the occidentalization of the Orient that simultaneously underlies and expands that focus. Readers, both male and female, are encouraged to follow both St John and Jane in the task of clearing the thicket of oriental 'prejudices' abroad, at home, and within their own souls. It remains for readers in the twentieth century to clear yet another thicket, the tangle of feminist orientalist prejudice that continues to encumber Western feminist discourse.

NOTES

1. Hereafter, unidentified page numbers in text refer to the Penguin edition of *Jane Eyre*.

2. Although the feminist orientalism I discern in the novel is parallel to the 'figurative use of blackness' earlier identified by Susan L. Meyer (1989, 250), it also has significant differences. Whereas Meyer focuses on the opposition 'white/black,' I examine the opposition 'West/East.' The two forms of opposition are related but not identical: the one privileges skin color or 'race,' and the other 'culture,' a phenomenon that may be associated with but that is not necessarily reducible to 'race.' Meyer's essay admirably demonstrates how *Jane Eyre* uses racial oppression as a metaphor for class and gender oppression. However, in systematically linking gender oppression to oriental despotism, *Jane Eyre* focuses on a form of oppression that is, from the first, conceived by Westerners in terms of gender.
3. Gibson, one of the few critics to note how the sultan image pervades *Jane Eyre*, makes the sanguine assumption that Brontë's critique of Eastern despotism 'extends to British imperialist impulses themselves,' leading Gibson, like many critics, to find the novel's conclusion 'strange' (1987, 1, 7). As I shall show, however, Jane's concluding paean to her missionary cousin in India is thoroughly grounded in the novel's figurative structure. Gayatri Spivak, for her part, argues that Brontë's novel reproduces the 'axiomatics of imperialism' (1985, 247) and that its 'imperialist project' remains inaccessible to the 'nascent "feminist" scenario' (249). My argument emphasizes less the acts of political domination that constitute imperialism than how its ideology (and specifically its orientalism) infects the analysis of domestic relations 'at home' and posits that orientalism is in fact put to the service of feminism. See also Suvendrini Perera's discussion of how 'the vocabulary of oriental misogyny' became 'an invisible component in feminist representations' in the nineteenth century (1991, 79). Perera's chapter on *Jane Eyre*, published after the research for this article had been completed, focuses on sati as the text's 'central image' (93), while my reading emphasizes the use of the harem as the central image of gender oppression. Western feminist uses of both sati and the harem function equally, as Perera points out, to objectify the 'colonized or imagined "oriental" female subject' (82).
4. See Said 1979 for the definitive exposition of orientalism as a 'Western style for dominating, restructuring, and having authority over the Orient' (71).
5. Al-Bazei's excellent study does not consider the specifically feminist adaptation of this strategy. Interestingly, however, Al-Bazei identifies Byron's Turkish Tales as a crucial locus for the development of 'self-redemption' as the dominant mode of nineteenth-century literary orientalism. Byron's influence on Brontë has been well documented, and further study might establish a link between his Turkish Tales and Brontë's feminist orientalism.
6. For a recent defense of polygamy in the context of Western Mormonism, see Joseph 1991. Earlier in this century, Demetra Vaka argued that women living in harems were 'healthy and happy,' possessing a 'sublimity of soul . . . lacking in our European civilization' (1909, 29, 127–28). Ahmed 1982 argues that the harem can be construed as an inviolable and empowering 'women's space' that enables Islamic women to have 'frequent and easy access to other women in their community, vertically, across class lines, as well as horizontally' (524).
7. See, e.g., Makhlouf-Obermeyer 1979; Gordon (1865) 1983; Delplato 1988; Croutier 1989; Gendron 1991; Leonowens (1872) 1991.
8. See Ahmed 1982 for a pointed analysis of how fundamentalist Islamic movements 'target' feminism as '"Western" and as particularly repugnant and evil' (533). Similarly, Hatem 1989 shows how in the late nineteenth and early twentieth centuries 'European and Egyptian women were influenced by modern national ideologies and rivalries . . . prevent[ing] them from using each other's experience to push for a more radical critique of their own societies' (183).
9. See, e.g., Conant 1908; Stedman 1965; Ali 1981; Caracciolo 1988; Workman 1988.
10. Grosrichard convincingly demonstrates that, in the Western construction of the seraglio, 'To be the master . . . is to see. In the despotic state, where one always obeys

"blindly," the blind man is the emblematic figure of the subject' (73, translation mine). See also Bellis 1987 for an exploration of the politics of vision in *Jane Eyre*.

11. The other Old Testament reference to a 'law of the Medes and Persians, which altereth not' occurs in chap. 6 of the book of Daniel. Here the Persian king Darius orders that anyone who petitions 'any God or Man' other than the king 'shall be cast into the den of lions' (Dan. 6.7). Daniel prays to the God of the Hebrews; the king casts him in the lion's den; Daniel's miraculous deliverance converts Darius to an acknowledgment of the 'living God' (Dan. 6.26). Jane Eyre names Daniel as one of her favorite books in the Bible early in the novel (Brontë [1847] 1985, 65); Daniel's ordeal, as well as Esther's, serves as a model for her own resistance to her master's desire to strip her of 'soul.' I am indebted to Jimmy Griffin for bringing to my attention the relevant biblical passages.
12. See Meyer 1989 for fuller discussion of how contact with the Other serves to besmirch the Englishman in *Jane Eyre*.
13. The reader may be reminded of Horace Walpole's comment that Mary Wollstonecraft was a 'hyena in petticoats' (Wollstonecraft [1792] 1982, 17).
14. See Donaldson 1988 for a similar argument about the self-assertion implicit in Bertha's suicide; Perera 1991, on the contrary, sees Bertha's death as a denial of her subjectivity.
15. See Leonowens (1872) 1991 for a fuller elaboration of this idea: the greatest horror of the harem, for Leonowens, is not polygamy, not confinement, not enforced sexual submission, but denial of the freedom to love.

BIBLIOGRAPHY

Ahmed, Leila. 1982. 'Western Ethnocentrism and Perceptions of the Harem.' *Feminist Studies* 8(3): 521–34.

Al-Bazei, Saad Abdulrahman. 1983. 'Literary Orientalism in Nineteenth-Century Anglo-American Literature: Its Formation and Continuity.' Ph.D. dissertation, Purdue University.

Ali, Muhsin Jassim. 1981. *Scheherazade in England: A Study of Nineteenth-Century English Criticism of the 'Arabian Nights.'* Washington, D.C.: Three Continents.

Alloula, Malek. 1986. *The Colonial Harem*, trans. Myrna Godzich and Wlad Godzich. Theory and History of Literature, vol. 21. Minneapolis: University of Minnesota Press.

Barrell, John. 1991. 'Death on the Nile: Fantasy and the Literature of Tourism, 1840–1860.' *Essays in Criticism* 41(2): 97–127.

Barrett Browning, Elizabeth. 1897. *The Letters of Elizabeth Barrett Browning*, ed. Frederic G. Kenyon. 2 vols. New York: Macmillan.

Bellis, Peter J. 1987. 'In the Window-Seat: Vision and Power in *Jane Eyre*.' ELH 54(3):639–52.

Besant, Walter. (1897) 1986. *The Queen's Reign*. In *Norton Anthology of English Literature*, ed. M. H. Abrams. 5th ed. New York: Norton.

Brontë, Charlotte. (1847) 1985. *Jane Eyre*. New York: Penguin.

Caracciolo, Peter L., ed. 1988. *'The Arabian Nights' in English Literature: Studies in the Reception of 'The Thousand and One Nights' into British Culture*. New York: St Martin's.

Conant, Martha Pike. 1908. *The Oriental Tale in England in the Eighteenth Century*. New York: Columbia University Press.

Croutier, Alev Lytle. (1989). *Harem: The World behind the Veil*. New York: Abbeville.

Delplato, Joan. (1988). 'An English "Feminist" in the Turkish Harem: A Portrait of Lady Mary Wortley Montagu.' In *Eighteenth-Century Women and the Arts*, ed. Frederick M. Keener and Susan E. Lorsch. Westport, n.y.: Greenwood.

Donaldson, Laura E. (1988). 'The Miranda Complex: Colonialism and the Question of Feminist Reading.' *Diacritics* 18(3): 65–77.

Fuller, Margaret. (1854) (1971). *Woman in the Nineteenth Century*. New York: Norton.
Gaskell, Elizabeth. (1853) (1985). *Ruth*. New York: Oxford.
Gendron, Charisse. (1991). 'Images of Middle-Eastern Women in Victorian Travel Books,' *Victorian Newsletter*, no. 79, 18–23.
Gibson, Mary Ellis. (1987). 'The Seraglio or Suttee: Brontë's *Jane Eyre*.' *Postscript* 4: 1–8.
Gilbert, Sandra, and Susan Gubar. (1979). *The Madwoman in the Attic: The Woman Writer and the Nineteenth-Century Literary Imagination*. New Haven, Conn.: Yale University Press.
Gordon, Lucie Duff. (1865) (1983). *Letters from Egypt*. London: Virago.
Grosrichard, Alain. (1979). *Structure du Serail: La Fiction du Despotisme Asiatique dans L'Occident Classique*. Paris: Editions Seuil.
Hatem, Mervat. (1989). 'Through Each Other's Eyes: Egyptian, Levantine-Egyptian, and European Women's Images of Themselves and of Each Other.' *Women's Studies International Forum* 12(2): 183–98.
Jameson, Anna. (1829) (1890). *Memoirs of the Loves of the Poets: Biographical Sketches of Women Celebrated in Ancient and Modern Poetry*. Boston and New York: Houghton Mifflin.
Johnson, Samuel. (1779) (1975). *Lives of the English Poets: A Selection*, ed. John Wain. London: Everyman.
———. (1759) (1977). *Rasselas*. In *Selected Poetry and Prose*, ed. Frank Brady and W. K. Wimsatt. Berkeley: University of California Press.
Joseph, Elizabeth. (1991). 'My Husband's Nine Wives.' *New York Times*, May 23.
Kra, Pauline. (1979). 'The Role of the Harem in Imitations of Montesquieu's *Letters Persanes*.' *Studies on Voltaire and the Eighteenth Century* 182: 273–283.
Kringas, Connie George. (1992). 'The Women of *Rasselas*: A Journey of Education and Empowerment.' m.a. thesis, University of New Orleans.
Leonowens, Anna. (1872) (1991). *The Romance of the Harem*, ed. Susan Morgan. Charlottesville: University Press of Virginia.
Makhlouf-Obermeyer, Carla. (1979). *Changing Veils: A Study of Women in South Arabia*. Austin: University of Texas Press.
Marmontel, Jean François. (1764). *Moral Tales by M. Marmontel Translated from the French*. 3 vols. London.
Meyer, Susan L. (1989). 'Colonialism and the Figurative Strategy of *Jane Eyre*.' *Victorian Studies* 33(2): 247–68.
Mohanty, Chandra. (1988). 'Under Western Eyes: Feminist Scholarship and Colonial Discourses.' *Feminist Review* 30 (Autumn): 61–88.
Montesquieu, Charles de Secondat Baron de. (1721) 1923. *Persian Letters*, trans. John Davidson. London: Routledge.
Nightingale, Florence. (1852) 1980. *Cassandra*. New York: Feminist Press.
———. (1849–50) 1988. *Letters from Egypt: A Journey on the Nile, 1849–1850*. New York: Widenfeld & Nicolson.
Penzer, N. M. (1936). *The Harem: An Account of the Institution as It Existed in the Palace of the Turkish Sultans with a History of the Grand Seraglio from Its Foundation to Modern Times*. London: Spring Books.
Perera, Suvendrini. (1991). *Reaches of Empire: The English Novel from Edgeworth to Dickens*. New York: Columbia University Press.
Poovey, Mary. (1984). *The Proper Lady and the Woman Writer: Ideology as Style in the Works of Mary Wollstonecraft, Mary Shelley, and Jane Austen*. Chicago: University of Chicago Press.
Richon, Olivier. (1985). 'Representation, the Despot and the Harem: Some Questions around an Academic Orientalist Painting by Lecomte-du-Nouy (1885).' In *Europe and Its Others*, ed. Francis Barker, Peter Hulme, Margaret Iverson, and Diana Loxley. Vol. 1. Colchester: University of Essex.

Said, Edward. (1979). *Orientalism*. New York: Vintage Books.
Shelley, Mary Wollstonecraft. (1818) 1974. *Frankenstein or the Modern Prometheus: The 1818 Text*, ed. James Rieger. New York: Bobbs-Merrill.
Spivak, Gayatri Chakravorty. (1985). 'Three Women's Texts and a Critique of Imperialism.' *Critical Inquiry* 12(1):243–61.
Stedman, Jane W. (1965). 'The Genesis of the Genii.' *Brontë Society Transactions* 14(5):16–19.
Tasch, Peter A. (1982). 'Jane Eyre's "Three-Tailed Bashaw."' *Notes & Queries* 227(June):232.
Trumpener, Katie. (1987). 'Rewriting Roxane: Orientalism and Intertextuality in Montesquieu's *Lettres Persanes* and Defoe's *The Fortunate Mistress*.' *Stanford French Review* 11(2):177–91.
Vaka, Demetra (Mrs Kenneth Brown). (1909). *Haremlik: Some Pages from the Life of Turkish Women*. Boston and New York: Houghton Mifflin.
Wollstonecraft, Mary. (1798) 1975. *Maria or the Wrongs of Woman*. New York: Norton.
———. (1792) 1982. *Vindication of the Rights of Woman*. London: Penguin.
Workman, Nancy V. (1988). 'Scheherazade at Thornfield: Mythic Elements in *Jane Eyre*.' *Essays in Literature* 15(2):177–92.
Zonana, Joyce. (1991). '"They Will Prove the Truth of My Tale": Safie's Letters as the Feminist Core of Mary Shelley's *Frankenstein*.' *Journal of Narrative Technique* 21(2):170–84.

PART 4
JOSEPH CONRAD: *HEART OF DARKNESS*

INTRODUCTION

In his analysis of race and the aesthetics of modernism, Simon Gikandi notes that it used to be argued that the great transformations in Conrad's novella could have been staged almost anywhere, but that 'it is now clear that Africa plays such a specific role in the European imagination, that it is the ideal setting in which the central tenets of Western modes of cognition can be unsettled.'[1] So, the modernist interrogation of established European beliefs concerning subjectivity, temporality and linguistic convention is 'ideally' located in a place such as the Belgian Congo because Africa has been associated in the West with alternative modes of thought, perception and art to those that developed out of the Enlightenment.

The most famous critic who has argued that Conrad uses Africa as nothing more than a 'backdrop' to the disintegration of the Western mind is Chinua Achebe. Achebe's often anthologised article, 'An Image of Africa', summarises Conrad's message thus: 'If Europe, advancing in civilization, could cast a backward glance periodically at Africa trapped in primordial barbarity it could say with faith and feeling: There go I but for the grace of God.' The central point that Achebe makes is not that Conrad was more of a racist than other Europeans at the turn of the century, but that in *Heart of Darkness* there is an implicit assumption throughout the narrative that Europeans and their culture are of more human importance and psychological interest than Africans and theirs.[2] Cedric Watts has written a reply to this argument but he is unable to deny Achebe's fundamental contention. Watts's basic point is that writers such as Conrad were subject to the prejudices of their day, including racism and anti-Semitism in particular, but that their best work 'seems to transcend such prejudices'.[3] Less well known than 'An Image of Africa' is Wilson Harris's refinement of Achebe's position in an article published three years later in the same journal, *Research in African Literatures*.

Heart of Darkness has had numerous reworkings in fiction (e.g., by Harris, Naipaul, Emechta, Salih and others) and has also received more post-colonial rereadings than probably any other text.[4] Edward Said, in his essay 'Two Visions in *Heart of Darkness*', in *Culture and Imperialism*, argues that Conrad's novella is exemplary of contemporary attitudes in the West to the world outside Euroamerica.[5] He develops two arguments from the book: that nineteenth-century imperialism still draws the lines on the world map one hundred years later and that Conrad shows a localised, historically situated and dated imperial 'moment' which will pass. In short, Said concludes that the 'darkness' of the book needs to be read as anti-colonial resistance.

With regard to the other three extracts included here, Patrick Brantlinger's article 'Kurtz's "Darkness" and *Heart of Darkness*', from *Rule of Darkness: British Literature and Imperialism, 1830–1914*, scrutinises Achebe's argument and the debate over the book's pro- and anti-imperialist messages. It also offers a necessary overview of the historical scene in terms of the Belgian Congo and Conrad's sources; Robert Hampson's '*Heart of Darkness* and "The Speech that Cannot be Silenced"' analyses language (verbal, aural and visual) in the novella and then weighs Achebe's views in the balance: on both counts Hampson argues for greater textual and historical diligence; Sally Ledger's 'In Darkest England: The Terror of Degeneration in *Fin-de-Siècle* Britain' discusses the interest in eugenics in Britain in the 1890s and then uses it to read tropes of race and cannibalism in *Heart of Darkness* and to recommend a new post-colonial feminism.

Alongside a reading of Conrad's novella in terms of discourses of degeneration, there are several other historical contexts which ought to be remembered. First is the fact that the main story is not set by Conrad in the British Empire. In 1885 a conference of the European Powers at Berlin recognised the area south of the Congo River in equatorial Africa as the 'Congo Free State', a huge territory in the personal possession of King Leopold (reigned 1865–1909), who had been the principal shareholder of a Belgian company which established trading stations on the Lower Congo between 1879 and 1884. Agitation in Britain and the USA in 1903–4, complaining of the ill-treatment of the Africans in the 'Free State', forced Leopold to hand the territory over to the Belgian government, which administered it as a colony from 1908 up until Independence in 1960. The Belgian Congo was eighty times the size of Belgium. Second, there are the many contemporary explorers' accounts which serve as intertexts for Conrad's story.[6] The narrative models itself partly on Henry Stanley's quest for David Livingstone. Marlow is a Stanley figure travelling through Africa to find 'the great man'. A contemporary reader would see the story in 1899 as a journey into the depths of the continent to find the solitary white man at its centre. By 1871, when Stanley went to find him in East Africa, Livingstone was famous throughout the Western world, but he had been out of contact for five years. He had decided in 1866 to devote his life to preaching against the slave trade and was now an icon of the civilising mission. Stanley's expedition to find him in 1871 was funded by an American newspaper, and was perceived even at the time as a publicity stunt. The famous meeting in the jungle was a coup for the press, a staged encounter of two white men in the jungle. Livingstone died two years later in 1873, and it was then that the cult surrounding him as an individual took off. By the time Conrad was writing, Livingstone was almost a martyr. But this was not the only such encounter, and indeed it is in many ways Stanley who is the key figure. Stanley was arguably the opposite of Livingstone. While Livingstone was a missionary and a power for intended good, like Kurtz when he set out for Africa, Stanley used force and violence, like the later Kurtz. In terms of his attitudes towards Africans, Stanley was more like the Kurtz that Marlow actually finds. After Livingstone's death, Stanley became employed by King Leopold. Leopold in fact sent Stanley to establish a colony in the Congo region, and he founded the city of Leopoldville (now Kinshasa). It was Stanley who established the Congo Free State, as it was called, between 1879 and 1885. This was 'Free' in so much as Leopold owned it independently of the French who possessed the rest of the Congo. Stanley finally retired in 1890 and became a Member of Parliament: this is the year that Conrad made his journey along the Congo, the third important context for the book.

Conrad's story is pitched against the Stanley-Livingstone mythology. But, more than this, it is deliberately narrated as a journey into the self, as a psychological self-discovery. Marlow, the 'civilised' white man, journeys into the heart of the dark continent and confronts there a 'savage' white man, Kurtz – his double. For Conrad, the story was reminding his Victorian readers of a message similar to Freud's at the same time: that at the core of every civilised individual are violent desires – at the dark heart. Many phrases in Conrad's book point us towards this conclusion, such as when we are told that 'The mind of man is capable of anything'.[7] However, for a critic such as Frantz Fanon in *Black Skin, White Masks*, it is the unequal power relations between coloniser and colonised that create the structural relation of mutual degradation. Fanon drew his insights from his work in Algerian psychiatric hospitals, where he found that the colonial situation turned the French into torturers and the Algerians into dehumanised sufferers: a Manichean struggle between light and dark, good and evil, reflected throughout in the very language of Conrad's novella.

NOTES

1. Simon Gikandi, 'Race and the Modernist Aesthetic', in Tim Youngs (ed.), *Writing and Race*, Essex: Longman, 1997, p. 155.
2. Chinua Achebe, 'An Image of Africa: Racism in Conrad's *Heart of Darkness*', in *Hopes and Impediments: Selected Essays 1965–1987*, Heinemann: London, 1988. Originally published in *Research in African Literatures*. The article most recently reappeared in Bart Moore-Gilbert, Gareth Stanton and Willy Maley (eds), *Postcolonial Criticism*, Essex: Longman, 1997, pp. 112–25. Conrad's own position

is complex: Polish by birth, he knew no English before the age of twenty, but became a naturalised British subject and served for sixteen years as a British seaman.

3. C. Watts, '"A Bloody Racist": About Achebe's View of Conrad', in G. K. Hunter and C. J. Rawson (eds), *Yearbook of English Studies*, vol. 13, London: MHRA, 1983, pp. 196–209.
4. As good but varied examples, see Benita Parry, *Conrad and Imperialism*, London: Macmillan, 1983, Joseph Bristow, *Empire Boys*, London: HarperCollins, 1991 and the more recent Andrea White, *Joseph Conrad and the Imperial Subject*, Cambridge: Cambridge University Press, 1993.
5. Edward Said, 'Two Visions in *Heart of Darkness*', in *Culture and Imperialism*, New York: Vintage, 1994, pp. 20–35.
6. This is discussed at length in Tim Youngs, *Travellers in Africa*, Manchester: Manchester University Press, 1994. Youngs suggests that *Heart of Darkness* is in many ways based on a later journey of Stanley's to rescue a governor in the Sudan called Emin Pasha in 1889.
7. Joseph Conrad, *Heart of Darkness*, Harmondsworth: Penguin, 1973, p. 52.

4.1

FROM 'KURTZ'S "DARKNESS" AND *HEART OF DARKNESS*'

Patrick Brantlinger

> Conrad died fifty years ago. In those fifty years his work has penetrated to many corners of the world which he saw as dark. It is a subject for Conradian meditation.—V. S. Naipaul, 'Conrad's Darkness' (1974)

In a 1975 lecture the Nigerian novelist Chinua Achebe attacked *Heart of Darkness* as 'racist.' Joseph Conrad, Achebe says, 'projects the image of Africa as "the other world," the antithesis of Europe and therefore of civilization, a place where man's vaunted intelligence and refinement are finally mocked by triumphant bestiality.'[1] Supposedly the great demystifier, Conrad is instead a 'purveyor of comforting myths' and even 'a bloody racist.' Achebe adds: 'That this simple truth is glossed over in criticisms of his work is due to the fact that white racism against Africa is such a normal way of thinking that its manifestations go completely undetected.' Achebe would therefore strike Conrad's novella from the curriculum, where it has been one of the most frequently taught works of modern fiction in English classes from Chicago to Bombay to Johannesburg.

Achebe's diatribe has provoked vigorous defenses of *Heart of Darkness* which predictably stress Conrad's critical stance toward imperialism and also the wide acceptance of racist language and categories in the late Victorian period. Cedric Watts, for example, asserts that 'really Conrad and Achebe are on the same side'; Achebe simply gets carried away by his understandable aversion to racial stereotyping.[2] 'Far from being a "purveyor of comforting myths,"' Watts declares, 'Conrad most deliberately and incisively debunks such myths.'

In *Rule of Darkness: British Literature and Imperialism, 1830–1914*, Ithaca: Cornell University Press, 1988, pp. 255–64.

Acknowledging that Conrad employed the stereotypic language common in his day, Watts contends that he nevertheless rose above racism:

> Achebe notes with indignation that Conrad (in the 'Author's Note' to *Victory*) speaks of an encounter with a 'buck nigger' in Haiti which gave him an impression of mindless violence. Achebe might as well have noted the reference in *The Nigger of the 'Narcissus'* . . . to a 'tormented and flattened face . . . pathetic and brutal: the tragic, the mysterious, the repulsive mask of a nigger's soul.' He might have noted, also, that Conrad's letters are sprinkled with casual anti-Semitic references. It is the same in the letters of his friend [R. B. Cunninghame] Graham. Both Conrad and Graham were influenced by the climate of prejudice of their times . . . What is interesting is that the best work of both men seems to transcend such prejudice. (208)

Their work transcends prejudice in part, Watts believes, because both attack imperialism. Watts is one of the many critics who interpret *Heart of Darkness* as an exposé of imperialist rapacity and violence. Kurtz's career in deviltry obviously undermines imperialist ideology, and the greed of the 'faithless pilgrims'—the white sub-Kurtzes, so to speak—is perhaps worse. 'The conquest of the earth,' Marlow declares, 'which mostly means the taking it away from those who have a different complexion or slightly flatter noses than ourselves, is not a pretty thing when you look into it too much.'[3] There is nothing equivocal about that remark; Conrad entertained no illusions about imperialist violence. But Marlow distinguishes between British imperialism and that of the other European powers: the red parts of the map are good to see, he says, 'because one knows that some real work is done in there' (10). *Heart of Darkness* is specifically about what Conrad saw in King Leopold's African empire in 1890; it is unclear how far his critique can be generalized to imperialism beyond the Congo.

The politics of Conrad's story is complicated by the story's ambiguous style. I use 'impressionism' as a highly inadequate term to characterize the novella's language and narrative structure, in part because Fredric Jameson uses that term in his diagnosis of the 'schizophrenic' nature of *Lord Jim*.[4] Conrad's impressionism is for some critics his most praiseworthy quality; to others it appears instead a means of obfuscation, allowing him to mask his nihilism or to maintain contradictory values, or both. Interpretations of *Heart of Darkness*, which read it as only racist (and therefore imperialist), or as only anti-imperialist (and therefore antiracist), inevitably founder on its impressionism. To point to only the most obvious difficulty, the narrative frame filters everything that is said not just through Marlow but also through the anonymous primary narrator. At what point is it safe to assume that Conrad/Marlow expresses a single point of view? And even supposing Marlow to speak directly for Conrad, does Conrad/Marlow agree with the values expressed by the primary narrator? Whatever our answers, *Heart of Darkness* offers a powerful critique of at least some manifestations of imperialism and racism as it simultaneously presents that critique in ways that can be characterized only as imperialist and racist. Impressionism is the fragile skein of discourse which expresses—or disguises—this schizophrenic contradiction as an apparently harmonious whole. Analysis of that contradiction helps to reveal the ideological constraints upon a critical understanding of imperialism in literature before World War I. It also suggests how imperialism influenced the often reactionary politics of literary modernism.

I

In *Conrad and Imperialism*, Benita Parry argues that 'by revealing the disjunctions between high-sounding rhetoric and sordid ambitions and indicting the purposes and goals of a civilisation dedicated to global . . . hegemony, Conrad's writings [are] more destructive of imperialism's ideological premises than [are] the polemics of his contemporary opponents of empire.'[5] Perhaps. At least it is certain that Conrad was appalled by the 'high-sounding rhetoric' used to mask the 'sordid ambitions' of King Leopold II of Belgium, Conrad's ultimate employer during his six months in the Congo in 1890. *Heart of Darkness* expresses not only what Conrad saw and partially recorded in his 'Congo Diary' but also the revelations of atrocities which began appearing in the British press as early as 1888 and reached a climax twenty years later, in 1908, when the mounting scandal forced the Belgian government to take control of Leopold's private domain. During that period the population of the Congo was decimated, perhaps halved; as many as six million persons may have been uprooted, tortured, and murdered through the forced labor system used to extract ivory and what reformers called 'red rubber' from 'the heart of darkness.'[6] Conrad was sympathetic toward the Congo Reform Association, established in 1903 partly by Roger Casement, whom he had met in Africa, and Casement got him to write a propaganda letter in which Conrad says: 'It is an extraordinary thing that the conscience of Europe which seventy years ago . . . put down the slave trade on humanitarian grounds tolerates the Congo state today.'[7] There follows some patronizing language contrasting the brutalities visited upon the Congolese with the legal protections given to horses in Europe, but Conrad's intention is clear enough.

There is little to add to Hunt Hawkins's account of Conrad's relations with the Congo Reform Association. The association's leader, Edmund Morel, who quoted Conrad's letter to Casement in *King Leopold's Rule in Africa* (1904), called *Heart of Darkness* the 'most powerful thing ever written on the subject.'[8] But as Hawkins notes, apart from his letter to Casement, Conrad backed away from involvement with the association. Other prominent novelists who had never been to the Congo contributed as much or more to its work. Mark Twain volunteered 'King Leopold's Soliloquy,' and Arthur Conan Doyle wrote a book for the association called *The Crime of the Congo*. Conrad, as Hawkins notes, 'had little faith in agitation for political reform because words were meaningless, human nature unimprovable, and the universe dying'—hardly views to encourage engagement in the cause of the association.[9]

All the same, in at least one other work of fiction Conrad registered his abhorrence of King Leopold's rape of the Congo. This is the minor but highly revealing fantasy that Conrad co-authored with Ford Madox Hueffer, *The Inheritors: An Extravagant Story* (1901), Conrad's role in writing it may have been slight, but he obviously shared the views it expresses. The protagonist meets a beautiful young woman who claims to come from the fourth dimension and to be one of those who 'shall inherit the earth.' The Dimensionists were to come in swarms, to materialise, to devour like locusts ... They were to come like snow in the night: in the morning one would look out and find the world white ... As to methods, we should be treated as we ourselves treat the inferior races.'[10] Far from being meek, the inheritors are modern-day imperialists, satirically depicted as invaders from a spiritualist alternative world. Apart from the young woman and one other character, however, no invaders appear in the novel, although the satire upon imperialism is maintained through the portrayal of the Duc de Mersch and his 'System for the Regeneration of the Arctic Regions' (46). Like King Leopold, 'the foreign financier—they called him the Duc de Mersch—was by way of being a philanthropist on megalomaniac lines.' He proves to be no philanthropist at all, but just the 'gigantic and atrocious fraud' that Conrad believed Leopold to be. Greenland is the codeword in *The Inheritors* for the Congo. The journalist hero helps to expose 'the real horrors of the Système Groënlandais—flogged, butchered, miserable natives, the famines, the vices, diseases, and the crimes' (280). The authors are not even particular about the color of the Eskimo victims: one character says that the Duc 'has the blacks murdered' (246–47).

Hueffer and Conrad write some scorching passages in *The Inheritors* about 'cruelty to the miserable, helpless, and defenceless' (282). But the facts of exploitation in the Congo perhaps distress them less than the lying idealism that disguises it: 'More revolting to see without a mask was that falsehood which had been hiding under the words which for ages had spurred men to noble deeds, to self-sacrifice, to heroism. What was appalling was ... that all the traditional ideals of honour, glory, conscience, had been committed to the upholding of a gigantic and atrocious fraud. The falsehood had spread stealthily, had eaten into the very heart of creeds and convictions that we learn upon our passage between the past and the future. The old order of things had to live or perish with a lie' (282). For Conrad, the worst feature of imperialism may have been not violence but the lying propaganda used to cover its bloody tracks.

Conrad did not base his critique of imperialist exploitation in *Heart of Darkness* solely on what he had seen in the Congo. What he witnessed was miserable enough, and personally he was also made miserable and resentful by disease and the conviction that his Belgian employers were exploiting him. As he assured Casement, however, while in the Congo he had not even heard of 'the alleged custom of cutting off hands among the natives.'[11] The conclusion that Casement drew was that most of the cruelties practiced in the Congo were not traditional but the recent effects of exploitation. The cutting off of hands was a punishment for non-cooperation in Leopold's forced labor system and probably became frequent only after 1890. Moreover, just as Conrad had seen little or no evidence of torture, so he probably saw little or no evidence of cannibalism, despite the stress upon it in his story.[12]

It thus seems likely that much of the horror either depicted or suggested in *Heart of Darkness* represents not what Conrad saw but rather his reading of the literature that exposed Leopold's bloody system between Conrad's return to England and his composition of the novella in 1898–99, along with many of the earlier works that shaped the myth of the Dark Continent. Although Conrad's 'Congo Diary' and every facet of his journey to Stanley Falls and back have been scrutinized by Norman Sherry and others, what Conrad learned about the Congo after his sojourn there has received little attention.[13] The exposé literature undoubtedly confirmed suspicions that Conrad formed in 1890, but the bloodiest period in the history of Leopold's regime began about a year later. According to Edmund Morel: 'From 1890 onwards the records of the Congo State have been literally blood-soaked. Even at that early date, the real complexion of Congo State philanthropy was beginning to appear, but public opinion in Europe was then in its hoodwinked stage.'[14]

The two events that did most to bring Leopold's Congo under public scrutiny were the 1891–94 war between Leopold's forces and the Arab slave-traders and the execution of Charles Stokes, British citizen and renegade missionary, by Belgian officers in 1895. The conflict with the Arabs—'war of extermination,' according to Morel—was incredibly cruel and bloody. 'The first serious collision with the Arabs occurred in October 27, 1891; the second on May 6, 1892. Battle then succeeded battle; Nyangwe, the Arab stronghold, was captured in January, 1893, and with the surrender of Rumaliza in January, 1894, the campaign came to an end.'[15] Conrad undoubtedly read about these events in the press and perhaps also in later accounts, notably Captain Sidney Hinde's *The Fall of the Congo Arabs* (1897). Arthur Hodister, whom Sherry claims as the original of Kurtz, was an early victim of the fighting, having led an expedition to Katanga which was crushed by the Arabs. According to Ian Watt, '*The Times* reported of Hodister and his comrades that "their heads were stuck on poles and their bodies eaten."'[16] This and many similar episodes during the war are probable sources for Conrad's emphasis upon cannibalism in *Heart of Darkness*.

Cannibalism was practiced by both sides, not just the Arabs and their Congolese soldiers. According to Hinde, who must also be counted among possible models for Kurtz, 'the fact that both sides were cannibals, or rather that both sides had cannibals in their train, proved a great element in our success.'[17] Muslims, Hinde points out, believe they will go to heaven only if their bodies are intact. So cannibalism was a weapon of fear and reprisal on both sides, as well as a traditional accompaniment of war among some Congolese societies. Hinde speaks of combatants on both sides as 'human wolves' and describes numerous 'disgusting banquets' (69). A typical passage reads: 'What struck me most in these expeditions was the number of partially cut-up bodies I found in every direction for miles around. Some were minus the hands and feet, and some with steaks cut from the thighs or elsewhere; others had the entrails or the head removed, according to the taste of the individual savage' (131). Hinde's descriptions of such atrocities seem to be those of an impartial, external observer, but in fact he was one of six white officers in charge of some four hundred 'regulars' and about twenty-five thousand 'cannibal' troops. His expressions of horror are what one expects of an Englishman; they are also those of a participant, however, and contradict his evident fascination with every bloodthirsty detail.

It seems likely that Conrad read Hinde's lurid account. He must have known about the war also from earlier accounts, such as those in the *Times*, and from E. J. Glave's documenting of 'cruelty in the Congo Free State' for the *Century Magazine* in 1896–97. According to Glave, 'the state has not suppressed slavery, but established a monopoly by driving out the Arab and Wangwana competitors.' Instead of a noble war to end the slave trade, which is how Leopold and his agents justified their actions against the Arabs, a new system of slavery was installed in place of the old. Glave continues: 'Sometimes the natives are so persecuted that they [take revenge] by killing and eating their tormentors. Recently the state post on the Lomami lost two men killed and eaten by the natives. Arabs were sent to punish the natives; many women and children were taken, and twenty-one heads were brought to [Stanley Falls], and have been used by Captain Rom as a decoration round a flower-bed in front of his house.'[18] Captain Rom, no doubt, must also be counted among Kurtz's forebears. In any event, the practice of seizing Congolese for laborers and chopping off the hands and heads of resisters continued, probably increasing after the defeat of the Arabs, as numerous eyewitnesses testify in the grisly quotations that form the bulk of Morel's exposés. According to a typical account by a Swiss observer: 'If the chief does not bring the stipulated number of baskets [of raw rubber], soldiers are sent out, and the people are killed without mercy. As proof, parts of the body are brought to the factory. How often have I watched heads and hands being carried into the factory.'[19]

II

When Marlow declares that 'the conquest of the earth . . . is not a pretty thing,' he goes on to suggest that imperialism may be 'redeemed' by the 'idea' that lies behind it. In the real world, however, idealism is fragile, and in *Heart of Darkness*, except for the illusions maintained by a few womenfolk back in Brussels, it has almost died out. In going native, Kurtz betrays the civilizing ideals with which supposedly he set out from Europe. Among the 'faithless pilgrims' there are only false ideals and the false religion of self-seeking. 'To tear treasure out of the bowels of the land was their desire,' says Marlow, 'with no more moral purpose at the back of it than there is in burglars breaking into a safe' (31). The true nature of European philanthropy in the Congo is revealed to Marlow by the chain gang and the 'black shadows of disease and starvation,' left to die in the 'greenish gloom,' whom he sees at the Outer Station (16–17). Probably these miserable phantoms accurately depict what Conrad saw in 1890; they may also represent what he later learned about Leopold's forced labor system. In any case, from the moment he sets foot in the Congo, Marlow is clear about the meaning of 'the merry dance of death and trade' (14). It thus makes perfect sense to interpret *Heart of Darkness* as an attack on imperialism, at least as it operated in the Congo.

In the course of this attack, however, *all* ideals transform into idols—something, in Marlow's words, which 'you can set up, and bow down before, and offer a sacrifice to' (7). Conrad universalizes 'darkness' in part by universalizing fetishism. Marxist critics of empire describe the era of the Scramble for Africa—roughly 1880 to 1914—as one when the 'commodity fetishism' of 'late capitalism' was most intense, a thesis that complements Conrad's conservative belief in the decay of heroic adventure, eroded by technology and a dishonorable commercialism.[20] The natives in their darkness set Kurtz up as an idol; the Europeans worship ivory, money, power, reputation. Kurtz joins the natives in their 'unspeakable rites,' worshiping his own unrestrained power and lust. Marlow himself assumes the pose of an idol, sitting on shipdeck with folded legs and palms outward like a Buddha. And Kurtz's Intended is perhaps the greatest fetishist of all, idolizing her image of her fiancé. Marlow's lie leaves Kurtz's Intended shrouded in the protective darkness of her illusions, her idol worship.

One difficulty with this ingenious inversion, through which ideals become idols, is that Conrad portrays the moral bankruptcy of imperialism by showing European motives and actions as no better than African fetishism and savagery. He paints Kurtz and Africa with the same tarbrush. His version of evil—the form taken by Kurtz's Satanic behavior—is going native. Evil, in short, *is* African in Conrad's story; if it is also European, that is because some white men in the heart of darkness behave like Africans. Conrad's stress on cannibalism, his identification of African customs with violence, lust, and madness, his metaphors of bestiality, death, and darkness, his suggestion that traveling in Africa is like traveling backward in time to primeval, infantile, but also hellish stages of existence—these features of the story are drawn from the repertoire of Victorian imperialism and racism that painted an entire continent dark.

Achebe is therefore right to call Conrad's portrayal of Africans racist. One can argue, as does Benita Parry, that Conrad works with the white-and-black, light-and-darkness dichotomies of racist fantasy to subvert them, but she acknowledges that the subversion is incomplete: 'Although the resonances of white are rendered discordant ... black and dark do serve in the text as equivalences for the savage and unredeemed, the corrupt and degraded ... the cruel and atrocious. Imperialism itself is perceived as the dark within Europe. ... Yet despite ... momentous departures from traditional European usage ... the fiction gravitates back to established practice, registering the view of two incompatible orders within a Manichean universe.'[21] The imperialist imagination itself, Parry suggests, works with the Manichean, irreconcilable polarities common to all racist ideology. Achebe states the issue more succinctly: 'Conrad had a problem with niggers.'[22]

Identifying specific sources for Conrad's knowledge of the horrors of Leopold's regime is less important than recognizing that sources were numerous, swelling in number through the 1890s. Conrad reshaped his firsthand experience of the Congo in light of these sources. The emphasis on cannibalism in *Heart of Darkness* probably derives from Conrad's reading about the war between Leopold's agents and the Arabs. Yet he does not mention the war—indeed, Arab rivals of the Belgians are conspicuous in the story only by their absence. The omission has the effect of sharpening the light-and-dark dichotomies, the staple of racism; evil and darkness are parceled out between only two, antithetical sides, European and African, white and black. Furthermore, because of the omission of the Arabs Conrad treats cannibalism not as a result of war but as an everyday custom of the Congolese.

In simplifying his memories and sources, Conrad arrived at the Manichean pattern of the imperialist adventure romance, a pattern radically at odds with any realist, exposé intention. *Heart of Darkness* appears to express two irreconcilable intentions. As Parry says, 'to proffer an interpretation of *Heart of Darkness* as a militant denunciation and a reluctant affirmation of imperialist civilisation, as a fiction that [both] exposes and colludes in imperialism's mystifications, is to recognise its immanent contradictions' (39). However, the notion that Conrad was consciously anti-imperialist but unconsciously or carelessly employed the racist terminology current in his day will not stand up. Conrad was acutely aware of what he was doing. Every white-black and light-dark contrast in the story, whether corroborating or subverting racist assumptions, is precisely calculated for its effects both as a unit in a scheme of imagery and as a focal point in a complex web of contradictory political and moral values.

Conrad knows that his story is ambiguous: he stresses that ambiguity at every opportunity, so that labeling the novella anti-imperialist is as unsatisfactory as condemning it for being racist. The fault-line for all of the contradictions in the text lies between Marlow and Kurtz and, of course, it also lies between Conrad and both of his ambiguous characters (not to mention the anonymous primary narrator). Is Marlow Kurtz's antagonist, critic, and potential redeemer? Or is he Kurtz's pale shadow and admirer, his double, finally one more idolator in a story full of fetishists and devil worship? Conrad poses these questions with great care, but he just as carefully refrains from answering them. That evasion, and the ambiguities it generates, reflect the patterns of reification underlying both commodity fetishism and literary modernism—the deliberate ambiguity and refusal of moral and political judgment at the heart of an impressionism and a will-to-style that seem to be ends in themselves, producing finely crafted artifacts and stories with contours smoothed, polished, like carefully sculpted bits of ivory—art itself as the ultimate commodity, object of a rarefied aesthetic worship and consumption.

NOTES

1. Chinua Achebe, 'An Image of Africa,' *Research in African Literatures* 9 (Spring 1978), 1–15. See also Chinua Achebe, 'Viewpoint,' *Times Literary Supplement*, 1 February 1980, 113.

2. Cedric Watts, '"A Bloody Racist": About Achebe's View of Conrad,' *Yearbook of English Studies* 13 (1983), 196–209. For another defense see Hunt Hawkins, 'The Issue of Racism in *Heart of Darkness*,' *Conradiana* 14:3 (1982), 163–171. Among critics who support Achebe see Susan L. Blake, 'Racism and the Classics: Teaching *Heart of Darkness*,' *College Language Association Journal* 25 (1982), 396–404, and Eugene B. Redmond, 'Racism, or Realism? Literary Apartheid, or Poetic License? Conrad's Burden in *The Nigger of the "Narcissus,"*' in Joseph Conrad, *The Nigger of the 'Narcissus,'* ed. Robert Kimbrough (New York: Norton, 1979), 358–68. Achebe is, however, in a minority even among nonwestern writers; see Peter Nazareth, 'Out of Darkness: Conrad and Other Third World Writers,' *Conradiana* 14:3 (1982), 173–87.
3. Joseph Conrad, *Heart of Darkness*, ed. Robert Kimbrough (New York: Norton, 1963), 7. Page numbers from this edition are given parenthetically in the text.
4. Fredric Jameson, *The Political Unconscious: Narrative as a Socially Symbolic Act* (Ithaca: Cornell University Press, 1981), 206–80. See also Ian Watt's discussions of 'impressionism' and 'symbolism' in *Conrad in the Nineteenth Century* (Berkeley: University of California Press, 1979), 168–200.
5. Benita Parry, *Conrad and Imperialism* (London: Macmillan, 1983), 10.
6. See S. J. Cookey, *Britain and the Congo Question, 1885–1913* (London: Longmans, 1968). Cookey dates the beginning of British humanitarian protest against Leopold's policies as early as 1888 (35). Edmund D. Morel estimated the decline of the population of the Congo over a twenty-five-year period as eight million. See his *History of the Congo Reform Movement*, ed. W. R. Louis and Jean Stengers (Oxford: Clarendon Press, 1968), 7. In the appendix the editors cite the Commission for the Protection of Natives formed by the Belgian government, which in 1919 declared that the population of the Congo may have declined by as much as one half over the same period. Exact figures are, of course, impossible to come by. Roger Casement offered the perhaps conservative estimate that Leopold's exploitation reduced the population by three million. See Colin Legum, *Congo Disaster* (Baltimore: Penguin, 1961), 35.
7. Conrad's letter is quoted in E. D. Morel, *King Leopold's Rule in Africa* (1904; Westport, Conn.: Negro Universities Press, 1970), 351–52.
8. See Hunt Hawkins, 'Joseph Conrad, Roger Casement, and the Congo Reform Movement,' *Journal of Modern Literature* 9 (1981), 65–80; 'Conrad and Congolese Exploitation,' *Conradiana* 13:2 (1981), 94–100; and 'Conrad's Critique of Imperialism in *Heart of Darkness*' PMLA 94:2 (1979), 286–99. The Morel quotation appears in the last article, 293, and originally in Morel, *History of the Congo Reform Movement*, 205n.
9. See Hawkins, 'Conrad's Critique of Imperialism,' 292–93.
10. Joseph Conrad and Ford Madox Hueffer, *The Inheritors: An Extravagant Story*. (New York: McLure, Phillips, 1901), 16. Page numbers are given parenthetically in the text. On the collaboration between Conrad and Hueffer see Thomas C. Moser, *The Life in the Fiction of Ford Madox Ford* (Princeton: Princeton University Press, 1980), 40–47.
11. Conrad to Roger Casement quoted in Morel, *King Leopold's Rule in Africa*, 117.
12. See M. M. Mahood, *The Colonial Encounter: A Reading of Six Novels* (London: Rex Collings, 1977), 12.
13. See Norman Sherry, *Conrad's Western World* (Cambridge: Cambridge University Press, 1971); Gerard Jean-Aubry, *Joseph Conrad in the Congo* (1926; New York: Haskell House, 1973); and Henryk Zins, *Joseph Conrad and Africa* (Nairobi: Kenya Literature Bureau, 1982).
14. Morel, *King Leopold's Rule in Africa*, 103.
15. Ibid., 23.
16. Watt, *Conrad in the Nineteenth Century*, 142.
17. Captain Sidney L. Hinde, *The Fall of the Congo Arabs* (London: Methuen, 1897),

124–125. Molly Mahood makes the case for Hinde's book as one of Conrad's sources, in *Colonial Encounter*, 12.

18. E. J. Glave, 'Cruelty in the Congo Free State,' *Century Magazine* 54 (1897), 706. See also Glave, 'New Conditions in Central Africa, '*Century Magazine* 53 (1896–97), 900–915.
19. E. D. Morel, *Red Rubber: The Story of the Rubber Slave Trade on the Congo* (London: T. F. Unwin, 1906), 77.
20. See Edward W. Said, *Joseph Conrad and the Fiction of Autobiography* (Cambridge: Harvard University Press, 1966), 142–43.
21. Parry, *Conrad and Imperialism*, 23. See also Abdul R. JanMohamed, *Manichean Aesthetics: The Politics of Literature in Colonial Africa* (Amherst: University of Massachusetts Press, 1983).
22. Achebe, 'Image of Africa,' 10.

4.2

'*HEART OF DARKNESS* AND "THE SPEECH THAT CANNOT BE SILENCED"'

Robert Hampson

James Clifford, in an insightful essay on Conrad and Malinowski, at one point observes:

> It would be interesting to analyze systematically how, out of the heteroglot encounters of fieldwork, ethnographers construct texts whose prevailing language comes to override, represent, or translate other languages.[1]

As Clifford notes, behind this observation lies Talal Asad's conception of 'a persistent, structured inequality of languages' within the process of 'cultural translation'. In Asad's own words:

> The anthropological enterprise of cultural translation may be vitiated by the fact that there are asymmetrical tendencies and pressures in the languages of dominated and dominant societies.[2]

Elsewhere in the same essay, Clifford refers, in passing, to 'the many complexities in the staging and valuing of different languages in *Heart of Darkness*'.[3] I would like to take this perception and the observations about the problems of 'cultural translation' as the starting-point for an investigation of racism in *Heart of Darkness*.

I

In *Heart of Darkness*, as in reports of ethnographic fieldwork, heteroglot experience is rendered into a largely monoglot text.[4] As Marlow says:

English, 39:163, Spring 1990, pp. 15–32.

> 'An appeal to me in this fiendish row—is there? Very well; I hear; I admit, but I have a voice, too, and for good or evil mine is the speech that cannot be silenced.'[5]

There are two or three places where this largely monoglot text is broken into by other languages, and these instances are highly instructive. For example, Marlow ends his account of the two women knitting outside the door of the Company offices with the following apostrophe:

> '*Ave!* Old knitter of black wool. *Morituri te salutant!*'
>
> (p. 57)

The Latin tag points to the common culture of Marlow and his audience: a culture grounded in the shared educational background of English public schools.[6] The two other instances occur in the same part of the text, but serve a different function. When Marlow recounts his meeting with the 'great man' who runs the Company, he observes:

> 'He shook hands, I fancy, murmured vaguely, was satisfied with my French. *Bon voyage.*'
>
> (p. 56)

Then, after his medical examination, the Doctor concludes:

> '"Adieu. How do you English say, eh? Good-bye. Ah! Good-bye. Adieu. In the tropics one must before everything keep calm ... *Du calme, du calme. Adieu.*"'
>
> (p. 58)

These passages indicate that, though Marlow's narrative is in English, many of the encounters that he subsequently recounts are to be imagined as originally taking place in French. Yet, apart from these two speeches, no attempt is made to indicate that French is generally the medium of communication, except in so far as explicit references to English dialogue serve this end. Marlow is careful to specify that English was the medium for his conversations with the Swedish captain (who spoke 'English with great precision and considerable bitterness', p. 63); that he made a speech in English 'with gestures' to his African bearers (p. 71); and that English was one of the links between Marlow and Kurtz (he 'could speak English to me' since he 'had been educated partly in England', p. 117). But in what language are we to imagine Marlow and the Russian conversing? The Russian could certainly read English (as his annotated copy of Towson's *Inquiry* shows) and he tells Marlow that he had 'served some time in English ships' (p. 123), but would English or French have been the medium for their conversations?[7] The indeterminacy is itself significant, since it suggests that English and French are granted similar status within the narrative.

By comparison, Russian and African languages are present in the text in ways that suggest they have been assigned a lower position in an implicit hierarchy of languages.[8] Russian is encountered in written form in the annotations to Towson's *Inquiry*:

> '... the notes pencilled in the margin, and plainly referring to the text. I couldn't believe my eyes! They were in cipher! Yes, it looked like cipher!' (p. 99)

The annotations, though not actually decipherable by Marlow, are recognised as potentially meaningful. They have the same status as the Russian's signature on the board found with the firewood:

> 'We came to the bank, and on the stack of firewood found a flat piece of board with some faded pencil-writing on it. When deciphered it said: "Wood for you. Hurry up. Approach cautiously." There was a signature, but it was illegible—not Kurtz—a much longer word.'[9]

The Russian annotations are not decipherable because Marlow cannot read the script. Marlow's failure to even recognise Cyrillic script opens a gap between Marlow and Conrad, and suggests that the text's hierarchy of languages is Marlow's rather than Conrad's.[10] This is particularly important in relation to the representation of African languages in the text.

Where Russian exists in the text as script, as a written code that is potentially meaningful, African languages are present only as sound. They appear as 'a burst of yells' (p. 96); 'angry and warlike yells' (p. 112); 'tumultuous and mournful uproar' (p. 102); 'a tremulous and prolonged wail' (p. 112); 'complaining clamour, modulated in savage discords' (p. 102).[11] They are represented consistently as pre-verbal, pre-syntactic sound—as sound that is the direct expression of emotion, as sound that is pure sound (akin to music), as sound that is utterance without meaning:

> '... they shouted periodically together strings of amazing words that resembled no sounds of human language ... all that wild mob took up the shout in a roaring chorus of articulated, rapid, breathless utterance.' (pp. 145–6)

This representation is in accord with the emphasis, elsewhere in the text, on gesture. I have already mentioned Marlow's speech in English to his African bearers. His account implied that it was not the speech that communicated his meaning but rather the accompanying gestures 'not one of which was lost to the sixty pairs of eyes before me' (p. 71).[12] More significant still is Marlow's account of the first appearance of Kurtz's African mistress:

> 'Suddenly she opened her bared arms and threw them up rigid above her head ...' (p. 136)

Marlow produces this iconic image of the African woman, communicating by dramatic gesture, but it is followed by a very different representation of her in the Russian's brief, inset account of an incident involving her and Kurtz:

> '"She got in one day and kicked up a row about those miserable rags I picked up in the storeroom to mend my clothes with ... At least it must have been that, for she talked like a fury to Kurtz for an hour, pointing at me now and then. I don't understand the dialect of this tribe."'
>
> (p. 137)

Instead of an iconic 'noble savage', the Russian presents a domestic drama; instead of pre-verbal Africans, the Russian presents discursive speech; instead of undifferentiated sound, there is an awareness of language and the ability to discriminate between different African dialects.[13] Marlow reduces Russian script to cipher and African speech to noise, but, for the Russian, both have the status of language. The text's hierarchy of languages is again clearly Marlow's, and is presented as the product of Marlow's specifically English incomprehension.

II

The African drumming and Marlow's use of the ship's steam-whistle can usefully be examined in this context of non-verbal means of communication. Drumming is part of Marlow's account of Africa from his description of his first experience of the jungle during his journey to the Central Station:

> 'A great silence around and above. Perhaps on some quiet night the tremor of far-off drums, sinking, swelling, a tremor vast, faint; a sound weird, appealing, suggestive, and wild—and perhaps with as profound a meaning as the sound of bells in a Christian country.'
>
> (p. 71)

We might compare this with W. Holman Bentley's account of his first journey to Kinshasa in 1881:

> We had heard drums before, but until now had not thought much of them. From this time they became an intolerable nuisance. As we passed along, one town would beat a warning to the next.[14]

Bentley's narrative assigns a reasonable purpose to the drumming: it functions as a method of communication within what is perceived as an organised social system. Marlow's representation of the signal-drums is of a piece with his representation of African spoken language: their communicative function is supplanted by his emotional response to what he does not understand.[15] On the other hand, Marlow plays in this passage with the idea of cultural equivalence.[16] In its context, this is clearly part of a narrative strategy designed to undermine the ethnocentricity of his audience.[17] Generally, the drumming becomes the heart-beat of the 'heart of darkness' and signifies 'forgotten and brutal instincts';

> 'This alone, I was convinced, had driven him out to the edge of the forest, to the bush, towards the gleam of fires, the throb of drums, the drone of weird incantations; this alone had beguiled his unlawful soul beyond the bounds of permitted aspirations.'
>
> (p. 114)[18]

Here Marlow's narrative has clearly moved from notation of reality to projection and the demonisation of the other. Bentley, too, slips easily into representing Africans as devils. For example, as he and his companions approached Kinshasa for the first time, they came under attack from the inhabitants of the area ('men, hideous in war paint, armed with spears, guns, and knives, rushed out'), and Bentley comments: 'Perfect fiends they appeared, howling and yelling'.[19] Later, after describing the punishment of a man and woman at Manzi, he observes:

> Fiendish cruelty and heartlessness have made their home in these dark places.[20]

This casual demonizing of the 'other' suggests the unthinking metaphors of stereotyping. It is facilitated by Bentley's missionary project in Africa and his frame of reference as a Christian. (Bentley, for example, regards both Stanley and Leopold II as agents of Providence.) Where Bentley uses the stereotype unthinkingly, unreflectingly and unreflexively, Marlow makes this devilish stereotype the basis for a phantasmagoria:

> 'We were within thirty yards from the nearest fire. A black figure stood up, strode on long black legs, waving long black arms, across the glow. It had horns—antelope horns, I think—on its head ... It looked fiend-like enough.'
>
> (p. 143)[21]

The metaphor calls attention to itself as the scene takes on the overtones of Faustian pact or Walpurgisnacht. This might be criticised as a more pernicious because more powerful presentation of the stereotype: the stereotype empowered by Conrad's superior literary skills and resources. Alternatively, the passage can be approached in terms of Marlow's deployment of the categories of perception of European culture—as Marlow drawing upon the resources of a literary culture that includes Dante and Goethe in his attempt to represent and comprehend this non-European experience. 'All Europe contributed to the making of Kurtz' (p. 117), and 'all Europe' contributes to Marlow's narrative. Marlow's narrative displays the cultural resources that are part of his bond with Kurtz, and Conrad sets that culture up for analysis through its confrontation with Africa in Marlow's narration. One result of this confrontation is, as Marx had put it,—

> The profound hypocrisy and inherent barbarism of bourgeois civilisation lies unveiled before our eyes, turning from its home, where it assumes respectable forms, to the colonies, where it goes naked.[22]

The ship's steam-whistle could be seen as a European equivalent of the African use of signal-drums as a non-verbal means of communication, but, where the drumming is represented as a language used by the Africans which the Europeans cannot understand, the steam-whistle is used in *Heart of Darkness* only as a signal from the Europeans to the Africans. The Russian advises Marlow on the effectiveness of the steam-whistle as a means of dispersing hostile crowds:

> '"One good screech will do more for you than all your rifles. They are simple people."'
>
> (p. 123)

Marlow's narrative has already supplied a demonstration:

> 'With one hand I felt above my head for the line of the steam whistle, and jerked out screech after screech hurriedly. The tumult of angry and warlike yells was checked instantly . . .'
>
> (p. 112)

The word 'screech' converts the steam-whistle into an animal or bird, just as the 'yells and screams' dehumanise the Africans and reduce them to animals or demons. The immediate response of the Africans to Marlow's use of the steam-whistle reinforces this dehumanisation: the subliminal message is of communication on an animal level, but this message does not reduce the Europeans. On the contrary, it re-affirms the superiority of the Europeans, since Marlow has shown his ability to communicate skilfully even on this level, while the Africans have demonstrated their incomprehension of European technology. Norman Sherry has argued that, although there is ample evidence of the use of steam-whistles to disperse armed Africans, such a tactic would be unlikely to have been effective on the Congo in Conrad's time, since steamers and steam-whistles would have been commonplace.[23] Certainly, to judge by Bentley's account, steamers were far more frequent than Marlow's narrative suggests. Bentley, however, also records an incident similar to the one Marlow describes. Grenfell, on board the steamship *Peace*, was exploring the Congo between Stanley Pool and Stanley Falls. He entered one of its northern affluents, the Lubi river, and at Mosaku the following occurred:

> The chief was very friendly, and made us a small present, venturing on board to do so. He was evidently greatly impressed by the white man's fine canoe; when one of our men, not thinking what the result would be, suddenly opened one of the steam valves, this impression was so profoundly deepened, that his kingship and all his satellites jumped overboard, as well as the occupants of some twenty or thirty canoes alongside, and swam ashore.[24]

The Africans' response to the steam-whistle (in *Heart of Darkness*) accords with the representation of their response to the steamer generally. For example, Marlow gives the following account of the steamer's departure:

'I steamed up a bit, then swung downstream, and two thousand eyes followed the evolutions of the splashing, thumping, fierce river-demon beating the water with its terrible tail and breathing black smoke into the air.'

(p. 145)

Even the African fireman on board the steamer is represented as approaching his work in terms of 'the evil spirit inside the boiler' (p. 98). This emphasis on animistic responses to European technology is in line with stereotypes of 'primitive' behaviour and 'primitive' ways of thinking:

'Primitive' man ... spent his whole life in fear of spirits and mystical beings ... he worshipped animals and trees, tried to control the mystical forces of nature by means of ceremony, ritual, taboos and sacrifices, and explained the wonders of the universe in imaginative but 'unscientific' myths.[25]

Indeed, an animistic representation of the 'primitive' response to European technology is a recurrent trope in Victorian fiction.[26] It would be possible to ascribe these stereotypes to Marlow rather than to Conrad, except that, like the Africans' response to the steam-whistle, they are inscribed as events into the narrative. The departure of the steamer is attended by the display of a fetish (p. 145); the African fireman wears a charm 'made of rags, tied to his arm' (p. 98) to protect him from 'the evil spirit inside the boiler' (p. 98). In these instances, it seems to be Conrad rather than Marlow who is making use of conventional racist and imperialist modes of representation.

III

The most forceful attack on Conrad as a racist has been made by Chinua Achebe.[27] Achebe's force, however, is often at the expense of subtlety: what he attacks is a grossly simplified version of *Heart of Darkness*. To begin with, he elides the gap between Marlow and Conrad: he ignores both the text's dramatisation of a consciousness (Marlow's) and Conrad's strategic use of the distance between himself and his narrators.[28] Conrad is not 'pretending to record scenes', he is not presenting an account of Africa: he is presenting Marlow's experience of Africa and Marlow's attempt to understand and represent that experience. Marlow is a fictional character whose consciousness operates according to contemporary codes and categories. Marlow's perceptions are often racist, because those codes and conventions were racist, but the narrative method (which Achebe dismisses) represents a more radical stance since it problematises Marlow's narrative, his perceptions and representations.

Achebe also misrepresents the way in which antitheses operate in *Heart of Darkness*. He describes the narrative as setting up the Congo as the antithesis of the Thames, but then adds:

> It is not the differentness that worries Conrad but the lurking hint of kinship . . . the Thames too 'has been one of the dark places of the earth'. It conquered its darkness, of course, and is now in daylight and at peace. (p. 252)

As Achebe's first statement partly acknowledges, *Heart of Darkness* does not construct its narrative by means of static oppositions: Conrad destabilises the antithesis of imperialist discourse by tracing connections where there should only be oppositions.[29] It is not just that the Thames 'has been one of the dark places of the earth', but, by the end of Marlow's narration, the anonymous primary narrator has learned from it to revalue the Thames:

> The offing was barred by a black bank of clouds, and the tranquil waterway leading to the uttermost ends of the earth flowed sombre under an overcast sky—seemed to lead into the heart of an immense darkness. (p. 162)

This hardly suggests that the Thames has 'conquered its darkness'.[30] In addition, Achebe ignores the way in which Marlow's remark about 'the dark places of the earth' initiates a challenge to the rhetoric of imperialism. Bentley again provides a point of reference. For him, as for Marlow, the European presence in Africa prompts thoughts of the Roman colonisation of Britain:

> It is more than probable that our forefathers were a wild lot. The Romans found the Britons a tough people to tackle.

But Bentley then draws a very different moral:

> The very grit, go, manliness, energy, and general *noblesse*, which, when properly tempered and directed, has resulted in so great a nation, was the cause of their wildness and violence.[31]

Bentley uses the analogy with the Roman colonisation of Britain to justify European interference in Africa. Since the English are manifestly 'so great a nation' (in terms of 'grit, go, manliness, energy'), they are obviously well-placed to 'temper and direct' the Africans. Marlow, by contrast, alludes to the Roman colonisation of Britain in order to subvert his audience's ethnocentricity:

> 'Sandbanks, marshes, forests, savages,—precious little to eat fit for a civilized man . . .' (p. 49)

Marlow's words destabilise the antithesis of savage/civilized from the outset, and the continuation of his speech shows how the idea of 'savagery' is a product of the colonisers' fear in the face of the 'incomprehensible':

> 'He has to live in the midst of the incomprehensible, which is also detestable. And it has a fascination, too, that goes to work upon him. The fascination of the abomination . . .'
>
> (p. 50)

The opposition between Kurtz's African mistress and 'the Intended' is also not as straightforward as Achebe suggests. He reads her as 'a savage counterpart to the refined European woman'.[32] The passage he quotes suggests that an opposition is constructed in terms of the 'savage' (from 'the night of the first ages') and the European woman with her 'mature capacity for fidelity'—that is, an ideological opposition underwritten by evolutionary theory. But Achebe distorts the passage by leaving out one sentence: 'I noticed she was not very young—I mean not girlish' (p. 157). The word 'mature' compares what she is ('not very young') with what Marlow might have expected her to be ('girlish'): it is not, primarily, part of a contrast between the European and the African woman. Achebe also assumes that Marlow's view of 'the Intended' is not problematical: it is worth noting that Marlow's first impression of her ('She seemed ready to listen without mental reservation, without suspicion, without a thought for herself', p. 155) is not supported by the outcome of the interview. Achebe also ignores the way in which the African woman is associated with life, vitality, passion (p. 136), while the European woman is associated with lifelessness and death:

> 'The tall marble fireplace had a cold and monumental whiteness. A grand piano stood massively in a corner; with dark gleams on the flat surfaces like a sombre and polished sarcophagus ... The room seemed to have grown darker, as if all the sad light of the cloudy evening had taken refuge on her forehead. This fair hair, this pale visage, this pure brow, seemed surrounded by an ashy halo from which the dark eyes looked out at me.'
>
> (pp. 156–7)

The opposition between these two women is further complicated by the presence in the text of a third woman: the 'woman, draped and blindfolded, carrying a lighted torch' (p. 79) in Kurtz's painting. Marlow does not specify whether this woman is white or black, but she is configurated with the other two and she reflects unambiguously upon the 'civilizing mission' of the Europeans.

IV

The nub of Achebe's criticism of Conrad is Conrad's representation of Africa and Africans:

> Can nobody see the preposterous and perverse arrogance in thus reducing Africa to the role of props for the break-up of one petty European mind? But that is not even the point. The real question is the dehumanization of Africa and Africans which this agelong attitude has fostered and continues to foster in the world. And the question is whether a novel which celebrates this dehumanization, which depersonalizes a portion of the human race, can be called a great work of art.[33]

Achebe is right: African culture and history have been denied adequate representation in European writing, and *Heart of Darkness* does nothing to remedy this. Bentley again provides an instructive comparison. He devotes his first two chapters to a history of the Congo from 1484 to 1877, and his narrative generally gives much more sense of social relations and social organisation within and between different peoples in the Congo basin, but his history of the Congo is written from the perspective of European contact with the Congo and his narrative generally is firmly fixed within a racist, imperialist Christian framework.[34] *Heart of Darkness*, however, does not offer a representation of Africa: it offers a representation of representations of Africa. Edward Said has described 'Orientalism' as more 'a sign of European-Atlantic power over the Orient' than 'a veridic discourse about the Orient' and that distinction is also important in this context.[35] Conrad does not present himself as an expert on Africa and Africans: he creates a narrator and a narrative situation; he does not use the pseudo-authoritative first-person report of so many magazine articles of the period.[36] *Heart of Darkness* fixes on the power-relation between Europe and Africa and holds up for analysis the European discourses produced in that context. Said argues that

> The imaginative examination of things Oriental was based more or less exclusively upon a sovereign Western consciousness ... according to a detailed logic governed not simply by empirical reality but by a battery of desires, repressions, investments, and projections.[37]

And it is precisely those 'desires, repressions, investments, and projections' that *Heart of Darkness* exposes in the discourses of imperialism. Africa is not the arbitrarily-selected backdrop for a story about 'the break-up of one petty European mind': Kurtz's 'break-up' is the result of his place in the power-laden engagement of Europe and Africa; Kurtz is a victim of one of the discourses of imperialism; and Kurtz's history shows how damaging that discourse is to both Africans and Europeans.

Achebe also ignores the implied reader of *Heart of Darkness*. As Benita Parry reminds us:

> Conrad in his 'colonial fictions' did not presume to speak for the colonial peoples nor did he address them ... His original constituents were the subscribers to *Blackwood's* and *New Review*, an audience still secure in the conviction that they were members of an invincible imperial power and a superior race.[38]

In the case of *Heart of Darkness*, Conrad knew in advance that his readers would be those of *Blackwood's Magazine*, and he also knew what that implied.[39] Talal Asad notes:

> When anthropologists return to their countries, they must write up 'their people', and they must do so in the conventions of representation already circumscribed . . . by their discipline, institutional life, and wider society.[40]

Conrad shows his understanding of the parameters within which he was writing by mirroring them in Marlow's relations with his audience. Marlow's audience, like the readership of *Blackwood's Magazine*, is made up of males of the colonial service class. Marlow is forced to confront the problem of making his experience intelligible to an audience which readily manifests the limits of its understanding and tolerance: '"Try to be civil, Marlow," growled a voice' (p. 94). Marlow adopts various rhetorical strategies in relation to this particular audience, and Conrad similarly shapes his narrative strategies in *Heart of Darkness* to a specific, known implied reader. But far from purveying 'comforting myths' (as Achebe alleges), the narrative strategies of both Conrad and Marlow work to subvert many of the 'comforting myths' accepted by the implied reader. However, as Achebe registers, one myth *Heart of Darkness* fails to challenge is that of racial superiority.

Parry rightly states that Achebe's 'protest at Conrad's insulting representations of Africa should be listened to by critics for the "truth"' it asserts: Achebe's protest is 'a voice that cannot be silenced'.[41] However, as Parry implies, Achebe's 'truth' needs to be situated in relation to other 'truths'. It might be argued, for example, that *Heart of Darkness* needs to be placed in its historical context: Achebe treats *Heart of Darkness* without reference to the context in which it was written and without consideration of the kinds of awareness to be expected from an English novelist of the 1890s. Achebe seems more concerned with *Heart of Darkness* as a text existing within modern institutional parameters: as 'the most commonly prescribed novel in twentieth-century literature courses in English Departments of American universities'.[42] He provides anecdotal evidence of depoliticised readings of the novel within these institutional parameters, but he does not indicate how widespread this depoliticised reading is or was (as he notes, 'travellers' tales' are not trustworthy evidence); nor does he seek to explore the relationship between the depoliticised reading and the institutionalisation of the text; nor does he seek to relate depoliticised institutional readings of *Heart of Darkness* (if such readings are the norm) to the imperialism of the 'wider society'. Furthermore, if we consider the present institutional status of *Heart of Darkness*, the text is now supplemented (literally, in the case of the Norton edition) by Achebe's exposure of its racist attitudes. In short, if *Heart of Darkness* is seen as a text of the 1890s, then Achebe has not attended sufficiently to that context; on the other hand, if *Heart of Darkness* is the text as institutionalised by modern teaching and publishing, then Achebe has not sufficiently explored the implications of institutionalisation—including his own paradoxical position as supplement to what he describes as 'an offensive and deplorable book'.[43]

Finally, Achebe's implicit demand for an adequate 'picture of the peoples of the Congo', the yardstick by which *Heart of Darkness* is measured, is similarly problematical. Said's exploration of orientalism soon raises the question of 'how one can study other peoples', and it is precisely this question that modern dialogic or reflexive anthropology engages with. As Said observed:

> No production of knowledge in the human sciences can ever ignore or disclaim its author's involvement as a human subject in his own circumstances.[44]

Or, as James Clifford puts it, the ethnographic experience involves 'a state of being in culture while looking at culture.'[45] The narrative method of *Heart of Darkness* can be seen as an exemplary response to this part of the problem: Marlow's 'image of Africa' is scrupulously contextualised by the frame narrative. (In this light, Marlow's racism is less surprising, given his involvement in the imperialist enterprise.) Indeed, for Clifford, Conrad provides a model, not just in this one work, but in the entire body of his work, or rather in the act of writing that body of work:

> It is not surprising to find throughout his work a sense of the simultaneous artifice and necessity of cultural, linguistic conventions. His life of writing, of constantly becoming an English writer, offers a paradigm for ethnographic subjectivity; it enacts a structure of feeling continuously involved in translation among languages, a consciousness deeply aware of the arbitrariness of conventions, a new secular relativism.[46]

Conversely, Achebe's rejection of *Heart of Darkness* might be compared to Gabriel García Márquez's comment on representations of colonised peoples generally:

> The interpretation of our reality through patterns not our own serves only to make us ever more unknown, ever less free, ever more solitary.[47]

For Achebe and other black readers *Heart of Darkness* is clearly offensive and imprisoning (although Ngugi, for example, seems to have found Conrad an enabling influence), but for white European readers coming to terms with an imperialist past (or European/American ethnographers engaged with the problematics of the adequate representation of other cultures) *Heart of Darkness* still has much to offer—though not as an 'image of Africa'.[48]

NOTES

1. James Clifford, 'On Ethnographic Self-Fashioning: Conrad and Malinowski' in *The Predicament of Culture: Twentieth-Century Ethnography, Literature, and Art* (Harvard University Press, 1988), p. 112n.
2. Talal Asad, 'The Concept of Cultural Translation in British Social Anthropology' in James Clifford and George E. Marcus (eds.), *Writing Culture: The Poetics and Politics of Ethnography* (University of California Press, 1986), p. 164.
3. Clifford, p. 100n.
4. During his time in the Congo, when he was (presumably) mainly speaking French, Conrad was writing letters in French and Polish and keeping a diary in English (with occasional African and French words).

5. Joseph Conrad, 'Heart of Darkness' in *Youth* (J. M. Dent and Sons, 1923), p. 97. All references are to the Uniform Edition, which has the same pagination as the Dent Collected Edition (1946) and the World's Classics edition (1984).
6. As every English public-schoolboy would have known, Marlow is alluding to the words addressed by Roman gladiators to the Emperor before they engaged in combat. Since access to Latin and Greek was effectively restricted to public-schoolboys, the use of Latin functions as a sign of gender and class. On the role of public schools in relation to imperialism, see Alan Sandison, *The Wheel of Empire* (Macmillan, 1967), pp. 13–16.
7. Their first exchange is not very helpful: 'I swore shamefully ... "You English?" he asked, all smiles. "Are you?" I shouted from the wheel.' (p. 122). Clearly Marlow swears in English (hence the Russian's question), but is the rest of the dialogue to be imagined as taking place in French or English? The Russian's exclamation 'My faith, your pilot-house wants a clean-up!' (p. 123) suggests either French or English with French interference.
8. It is perhaps significant that, in 'The Crime of Partition' (*Notes on Life and Letters*, J. M. Dent and Sons, 1924), Conrad describes France and Poland as the 'two centres of liberal ideas on the continent of Europe' (p. 117), whereas Russia is described as 'an Asiatic Power' (p. 115).
9. 'Heart of Darkness', p. 98. If we continue to interrogate the text according to the logic of realism, these words would presumably have been in French.
10. The picture is further complicated by the suspicion of eloquence and the awareness of what cannot be spoken that are also present in the text. See Jeremy Hawthorn, 'Heart of Darkness: language and truth' in *Joseph Conrad: Language and Fictional Self-Consciousness* (Edward Arnold, 1979), pp. 7–36.
11. A distinction should be made between the Africans on the banks of the river and the African crewmen. According to Sherry, the crew of the *Roi des Belges* were probably Bangalas: see *Conrad's Western World* (Cambridge University Press, 1971), p. 59; also *Heart of Darkness*, pp. 102–3. It is their Bangala speech which is represented as 'short, grunting phrases' (p. 103). This still seems closer to the animal than the human, but we might note that Marlow also refers to the comments of a member of his audience as 'grunting' (p. 97). At other times, these African crewmen are represented as engaging in verbal communication with the Europeans, but it is difficult to say in what language we are to imagine these communications taking place. It seems unlikely that they would have used English to a French-speaking crew; and Conrad does not represent them as speaking Pidgin ('chop' would be more accurate Pidgin than 'eat' p. 103). According to W. H. Bentley, *Pioneering on the Congo*, 2 vols. (Religious Tract Society, 1900), 'Portuguese was the trade language on the Congo' (I, p. 88), but it is also possible that French *patois* might have been used. The representation of their language in the text is perhaps better seen in the context of Loretto Todd's observation: 'literary insertions of pidgins and creoles were, in the past, based less on actual observation than on a form of literary convention' (*Pidgins and Creoles*, Routledge & Kegan Paul, 1974, p. 77).
12. This reading is supported by the entry in Conrad's 'Congo Diary' recording a similar incident: 'Expect lots or bother with carriers tomorrow. Had them all called and made a speech which they did not understand' (Z. Najder ed., *Joseph Conrad: Congo Diary and other uncollected pieces*, [Doubleday & Company, 1978], p. 14).
13. The Africans at the Inner Station are presumably to be imagined as speaking a particular dialectal form of Bantu with which the Russian was unfamiliar. This is not an instance of that racist reductionism according to which Europeans are represented as having languages, while non-European languages are reduced to the status of 'dialects'. (I am indebted to Robert Fraser, here and elsewhere, for information about West Africa.)
14. Bentley, I. 315. Bentley records his work as a missionary in the Congo from 1879 to 1900. Conrad mentions Bentley in his 'Congo Diary' (p. 12).

15. Indeed, he emphasises the Europeans' incomprehension: 'At night sometimes the roll of drums behind the curtain of trees would run up the river and remain sustained faintly ... Whether it meant war, peace, or prayer we could not tell' (p. 95). The stage image draws attention to the Europeans' sense of alienation from African realities: they experience themselves for this moment as spectators, passive and powerless, waiting for a performance to begin.
16. Marlow might be nearer the truth than he realised. Bentley notes that Ntotela, 'King of Congo', ordered drums to be beaten at San Salvador on Saturday night and Sunday morning to announce the Christian Church Service (I, 136).
17. Compare 'I was loafing about, hindering you fellows in your work and invading your homes, just as though I had got a heavenly mission to civilize you' (pp. 51–2) and 'Well, if a lot of mysterious niggers armed with all kinds of fearful weapons suddenly took to travelling on the road between Deal and Gravesend, catching the yokels right and left to carry heavy loads for them ...' (p. 70).
18. Compare Chinua Achebe's use of the same image in *Things Fall Apart* (Heinemann, 1958; reprint 1988): 'The crowd had surrounded and swallowed up the drummers, whose frantic rhythm was no longer a mere disembodied sound but the very heart-beat of the people' (p. 36). Achebe uses the image to signify a sense of collective identity, which he thereby celebrates; for Marlow, it expresses a kinship which is feared.
19. Bentley, I., 352–3.
20. Bentley, I., 386.
21. Achebe singles out this passage for comment in his essay 'An Image of Africa: Racism in Conrad's *Heart of Darkness*', *The Massachussetts Review*, 18 (1977), 782–94. A revised version of this essay is included in Joseph Conrad, *Heart of Darkness*, ed. Robert Kimbrough (W. W. Norton & Co., 1988), pp. 251–62. Since this is more readily accessible, all references will be to this text. (The essay is also included in Chinua Achebe, *Hopes and Impediments*, Heinemann, 1988.) The blackness which Marlow stresses is not, however, a matter of skin colour: he is describing a figure silhouetted against a fire in a forest at night.
22. Karl Marx, 'Future Results of British Rule in India' quoted by Benita Parry, *Conrad and Imperialism* (Macmillan, 1983), p. 128.
23. Sherry, *Conrad's Western World*, pp. 54–5. For Najder's opposed view, see Z. Najder, *Joseph Conrad: A Chronicle* (Cambridge University Press, 1983), p. 134.
24. Bentley, II. 97. Bentley also records an incident during a journey on the Kwangu, when four men in a canoe tried to levy a toll on the steamship: 'They demanded blackmail, and lay across our bows. The two whistles of the *Peace* shrieked their loudes ... There was an instant collapse in the canoe; guns were dropped and paddles were seized and plied to their utmost' (II, 139). Again, however, the distinction perhaps has to be made between people who lived on the banks of the Congo and those who lived on the banks of its tributaries.
25. Brian V. Street, *The Savage in Literature: Representations of 'primitive' society in English Fiction, 1858–1920* (Routledge & Kegan Paul, 1975), p. 7.
26. See, for example, H. G. Wells's short story 'The Lord of the Dynamos'.
27. Chinua Achebe, 'An Image of Africa: Racism in Conrad's *Heart of Darkness*'. See also Achebe's 'Viewpoint', *T.L.S.* 4010 (1 February 1980) and Hunt Hawkins, 'The Issue of Racism in *Heart of Darkness*', *Conradiana*, XIV 3 (1982), 163–71. More recently, Craig Raine's review of Achebe's *Hopes and Impediments* ('Conrad and Prejudice', *London Review of Books*, 22 June 1989, 16–18), which chose to concentrate on Achebe's criticism of Conrad, provoked a lively correspondence. Patrick Parrinder's contribution ('Conrad and Eliot and Prejudice', *London Review of Books*, 14 September 1989, 4) convincingly engaged with the issue of 'cannibalism'.
28. Achebe observes that 'Conrad appears to go to considerable pains to set up layers of insulation between himself and the moral universe of history' (p. 256). But if Conrad

was 'a thoroughgoing racist' (p. 257), it is not clear why he would feel the need for such insulation. The readers of *Black wood's Magazine* would not have demanded such insulation from racist and imperialist ideas. Achebe's subsequent criticism that Conrad 'neglects to hint however subtly or tentatively at an alternative frame of reference by which we may judge the actions and opinions of his characters' (p. 256) misreads the mode of Conrad's fiction: to borrow Andrew Gibson's terms, Achebe seeks to convert an 'immanent' text into a 'transcendent' one. (See Andrew Gibson, 'Sterne, Beckett, and the Novel'.)

29. For a subtle analysis of H. G. Wells's similar explorative use of destabilised oppositions, see John Huntington, *The Logic of Fantasy: H. G. Wells and Science Fiction* (Columbia University Press, 1982).
30. Indeed, as Eric Woods has shown, 'darkness' was appropriated by the discourse of Victorian social reform for the areas inhabited by the urban poor. See Eric Woods, 'A Darkness Visible: Gissing, Masterman, and the Metaphors of Class, 1880–1914', Unpublished D. Phil. Thesis, University of Sussex, 1989.
31. Bentley, *I.*, 443.
32. Achebe, p. 255.
33. Achebe, p. 257.
34. Bentley might be compared with Achebe's District Commissioner (in *Things Fall Apart*) with his book on *The Pacification of the Primitive Tribes of the Lower Niger*. The paragraph he intends to devote to the character who has been the central figure in Achebe's book stands as an eloquent symbol of the European's depth of understanding of African society and culture.
35. Edward Said, *Orientalism* (Vintage Books, 1979), p. 6.
36. See Robert Hampson, 'Conrad and the Idea of Empire' in Jaques Darras (ed.), *L'Epoque Conradienne* (Limoges, 1990) for an account of *Heart of Darkness* in this context.
37. Said, p. 8.
38. Benita Parry, *Conrad and Imperialism* (Macmillan, 1983), p. 1.
39. In November 1911, Conrad wrote to his agent, J. B. Pinker: 'There isn't a single club and messroom and man-of-war in the British Seas and Dominions which hasn't its copy of *Maga*.'
40. Asad, p. 159.
41. Parry, 138n.
42. Achebe, p. 259.
43. Achebe, p. 259.
44. Said, p. 11.
45. Clifford, p. 93.
46. Clifford, p. 96.
47. Quoted by Rana Kabbani, *Europe's Myths of Orient: Devise and Rule* (Macmillan, 1989) as epigraph.
48. For a discussion of the influence of Conrad on Ngugi, see Peter Nazareth, 'Out of Darkness: Conrad and other Third World Writers', *Conradiana*, XIV, 3, (1982), 173–87, and Jacqueline Bardolphe, 'Ngugi wa Thiong'o's *A Grain of Wheat* and *Petals of Blood* as readings of Conrad's *Under Western Eyes* and *Victory*,' *The Conradian*, 12, 1 (May 1987), 32–49.

4.3

FROM 'IN DARKEST ENGLAND: THE TERROR OF DEGENERATION IN *FIN-DE-SIÈCLE* BRITAIN'

Sally Ledger

The twin spectres of degeneration and apocalypse haunted the final years of the nineteenth century. Whilst traditionally characterized as Britain's 'Age of Empire',[1] a time when Britain ruled the world, the economic boom years of the mid-Victorian age had come to an abrupt end with the slump of the 1880s. Increasing competition from abroad meant that Britain no longer dominated world marketplaces with the ease which had been accomplished earlier in Victoria's reign. Twentieth-century historians of the turn-of-the-century in Britain have generally identified the period as one of instability, of social and economic turbulence. Eric Hobsbawm typically evokes the 'uneasiness ... disorientation ... tension' of these 'years of political breakdown';[2] Gareth Stedman Jones regards the political crisis of the 1880s as more 'deep-rooted and comprehensive' than the crisis provoked by the Reform Bills of the mid-century;[3] and Raymond Williams has remarked on the way in which during this period being 'English', sharing any sense of a national identity, became problematic as increasing numbers of immigrants settled in Britain's cities.[4]

The resurgence of the women's movement towards the end of the nineteenth century has been well documented,[5] and the 1880s also witnessed the formation of the first, tiny Marxist parties in England (the Social Democratic Federation and the Socialist League), with the Independent Labour Party establishing itself in 1900, and the great Dockers' Strike of 1889 leading the unionization of unskilled workers.[6] Just at the moment that feminism and socialism began to grow in strength, Britain's hegemony as a global economic power began to

Literature and History, Series 3, 4:2, 1995, pp. 71–86. Extract: pp. 71–74 and 78–86.

falter, now rivalled by Germany and the United States of America: 'Britain, we may say, was becoming a parasitic rather than a competitive world economy, living off the remains of world monopoly, the underdeveloped world, her past accumulations of wealth and the advance of her rivals.'[7] So that although the *fin de siècle* has often been regarded as the high noon of British imperialism, the weakening of the British economy nonetheless raised the spectre of long term decline.

The fear of imperial and economic decline, the social and political turbulence which characterized the *fin-de-siècle* years very quickly filtered through to the socio-cultural and scientific discursive spheres, so that by 1895 Max Nordau, the *fin de siècle*'s prophet of doom, was presaging a 'Dusk of Nations, in which all suns and all stars are gradually waning, and mankind with all its institutions and creations is persisting in the midst of a dying world'.[8] The avalanche of socio-political and cultural challenges to the norms of an earlier, more self-confident Victorian age led to a proliferation of motifs of degeneration and even apocalypse in textual productions of the period.

Focusing on the ideology of eugenics which permeated the cultural politics of the *fin de siècle*, one of the main objects of this essay is to examine the complex discursive conjunctions around imperialism, social class and gender which emerged at the end of the nineteenth century, and their relationship to the social apocalypse feared by so many commentators. My argument is that the preoccupation with 'Empire' at the *fin de siècle*, and the fear that the influence of British civilization abroad was in decline, were in part a projection onto foreign climes of conflicts and tensions on home soil at a time when both the working classes and women were challenging the socio-political and economic *status quo*.[9] Although Britain's economic position in the world was certainly being challenged at the *fin de siècle*, her cultural and political power remained intact, so that the preoccupation with 'Empire' and the fears for the continuance of the 'race' which manifested themselves in theories of degeneration, were culturally overdetermined: it is this overdetermination which I want to elucidate here.

A secondary aim of the essay is to suggest through my analysis that the concepts and conflicts around issues of 'race', class and gender which inform contemporary cultural criticism emerged at the last *fin de siècle*; the critical 'holy trinity' which takes centre stage in our own post-epochal, postmodern *fin de siècle* had its origins in the cultural politics of the end of the nineteenth and the beginning of the twentieth century. It is for this reason that late-twentieth century cultural criticism has rediscovered the last *fin de siècle* with such enthusiasm, with feminist critics in particular creating a whole new field of study based around the turn-of-the-century years.[10] The third and final aim of the essay is to propose that the narrow focus on gender politics which was the hallmark of a good deal of feminist criticism in the 1970s and 1980s has no place in the postcolonial 1990s. Certain feminist accounts of turn-of-the-century texts have appeared to be blind to the issues concerning 'race' and class which were so central to *fin-de-siècle* culture, and such accounts now seem politically inapposite. It is in the last part of the essay, in my account of Conrad's *Heart of Darkness*, that I stake a claim for a postcolonial and class-inflected feminism appropriate to our own *fin de siècle*.

. . .

Eugenics was one highly influential ideological response to fears of racial degeneration at the *fin de siècle*. Doubts about the continuation of the British Empire often concentrated on the necessity to breed a strong, pure *English* 'race', so that it is not surprising that eugenics discourses became most influential in the early part of the twentieth century after the discovery that the general physical condition of British soldiers called up to fight in the Boer War had been remarkably poor. Discourses on degeneration had been current from the mid nineteenth century in the work of Lombroso amongst others,[11] but, as Alex Warwick has argued, they reached a highly developed stage in the 1890s, providing the precursor to Edwardian legislation designed to protect the national stock.[12] Characterized by its founder, Francis Galton, as 'practical Darwinism', the eugenics project was intent on reversing the process of 'race' degeneration which its supporters believed to be endemic in late-Victorian Britain.

Whilst its relationship to the imperialist project is clear, the class component of the ideology of eugenics is equally significant. Galton was unhappy with the Darwinian theory of natural selection inasmuch as that according to this theory there was only one criterion of the 'fittest'. These were the individuals who left the most progeny, and Galton found it impossible to reconcile this with the fact that in the mid and latter parts of the nineteenth century the poorer classes appeared to be the most fertile. As early as 1873 he reflected that the struggle for existence:

> seems to me to spoil and not improve our breed . . . On the contrary, it is the classes of a coarser organization who seem to be on the whole, the most favoured under this principle of selection, and who survive to become the parents of the next.[13]

Galtonian eugenics unabashedly combined the language of natural selection with highly partial and contentious social judgments on the relative worth of different sections of the population: the political emphasis of eugenic discourses was primarily focused on the preservation and continuation of the English middle classes.

A consistent feature of eugenics was the conviction that a high birthrate among the lower classes was a threat to evolutionary progress (Raymond Williams has convincingly argued that theories of evolution and natural selection in biology had a social component before there was any question of re-applying them to social and political theory). Apropos of the imperialist project, 'race' as a term in the Darwinian sense of 'species' rapidly became ideologically conflated with theories of nationality, with Anglo-Saxons being figured as the vigorous stock, the survivors in the competitive battle.[14] The perceived degeneration of the inhabitants of Britain's cities in turn presented itself as a threat to the vigour and purity of the British 'race'.

Despite its insertion into the ideology of imperialism and into socio-political discourses on class, eugenics as a project nonetheless retained the air of catastrophism which was peculiar to the *fin de siècle*. It was Galton's opinion that civilization had been on the decline since the Greeks: they represented civilization's high point in terms of intellectual accomplishment, and yet their civilization had died out. The fear was that the confident 'civilization' of mid-Victorian Britain, with its ethos of progress and easy domination of the world, would meet the same fate. Eugenic discourses reflected in quasi-scientific language the political upheavals which dominated late-nineteenth century culture: the fears surrounding the perceived decline of the British Empire; the fear of working-class disorder and the rise in their numbers; and the resurgence of the bourgeois women's movement in the last years of the century, which meant that women's role as the mothers and nurturers of the 'race' was felt to be under threat. Britain was perceived to be losing control of its colonial subjects just as it was losing control over its working-class subjects, and its women, at home.

. . .

A fear for the future of the British 'race' and its empire and, at the same time, a fear of the British working class, which, amongst other places, appeared to be starving just yards away from the seat of government in London, are manifested here. Whilst they starved quietly, no one much minded, but the fear was that with the rise of the new socialist parties at the *fin de siècle* Britain's poor might start to protest. The part that degenerate working-class women played in reproducing this 'puny and ill-developed race' is something I will address further on.

Stanley's *In Darkest Africa*, published in 1890, had immediately become a best seller. One of several responses to it was William Booth's *In Darkest England and the Way Out*, published later in the same year. In this analysis of Britain's own 'lost continent' in the depths of the cities, Booth makes direct analogies between (and I quote) the 'pygmies' described by Stanley and the slum dwellers of London's East End. The 'Heart of Darkness', it transpires, was all the time right in England's own backyard:

> It is a terrible picture, [Booth wrote of Stanley's Africa,] and one that has engraven itself deep into the heart of civilization. But while brooding over the awful presentation of life as it exists in the vast African forest, it seemed to me only too vivid a picture of many parts of our own land. As there is a darkest Africa is there not also a darkest England? Civilization, which can breed its own barbarians, does it not also breed its own pygmies? May we not find a parallel at our own doors, and discover within a stone's throw of our cathedrals and palaces similar horrors to those which Stanley has found existing in the great equatorial forest?[15]

The answer was an emphatic 'yes'. George Sims, another social explorer, proposed in 1889 to record the 'result of a journey into a region which lies at our own doors – into a dark continent that is within easy walking distance of the General Post Office'.[16] Social explorers such as Booth and Sims of course had ideological preconceptions about the denizens of London's East End, and what they recorded was filtered through a middle-class lens; nonetheless their records, and others like them, provide historical evidence of both the fear and the fascination with which the British middle classes regarded the working classes at this time.

Booth's analysis of 'Darkest England' draws sympathetic attention to the plight of London's prostituted women. He makes a direct analogy between the African women of the Equatorial forest whom Stanley claimed were raped and abused by the Arab traders, and the women of London's East End who were driven by economic distress into prostitution:

> ... here, beneath our very eyes, [he claimed,] ... the same hideous abuse flourishes unchecked. A young penniless girl, if she be pretty, is often hunted from pillar to post by her employers, confronted always by the alternative: Starve or Sin ... and she is swept ... ever downward, into the bottomless pit of prostitution.[17]

Women figure largely in the fears expressed concerning 'race' degeneration in Britain at the *fin de siècle*, not least because of their reproductive function. As a theory of heredity, eugenics was profoundly concerned with women's function as mothers and nurturers of the 'race', most particularly at a time when the 'empire' was felt to be vulnerable and requiring the very 'best of British' to sustain it. The degeneration of women was therefore regarded with even more concern than the perceived degeneration of men in the slumlands.

Margaret Harkness's 1891 novel, *In Darkest London*, opens with an attempt by a Salvation Army officer to 'rescue' a girl of the streets. Harkness's is one of many slumland novels to appear at the *fin de siècle*: other notable examples include Gissing's *The Nether World* (1889), Arthur Morrison's *Child of the Jago* (1896) and Jack London's *The People of the Abyss* (1903). *In Darkest London* was originally published in 1889 as *Captain Lobe*, but was re-named and re-printed after the publication of Stanley's *In Darkest Africa* and Booth's *In Darkest England*. The 'Darkest London' of the title is immediately introduced as a polyglot, cosmopolitan urban slumland. This is Raymond Williams's city of modernity, with its mish-mash of subordinate cultures which threatened and with hindsight exploded the myth of a uniform English cultural identity, let alone any notion of British 'racial' purity.[18] Of the Whitechapel Road Harkness remarks that 'That road is the most cosmopolitan place in London', and she lists Jews, Algerians, Indians, Italians, Russians, Poles and Germans among its denizens, alongside the East End 'loafer' who is 'looked upon as scum by his own nation'.[19]

Captain Lobe's tour of the East End consists of a series of encounters with barely human mutants: an elderly hag whom he picks up drunk off the street; a dying dwarf who regards himself in Darwinian terms as 'the missing link' and a one-armed man from a freak show; a prostitute who is referred to as a vampire (and this recalls *Dracula*, another *fin-de-siècle* text steeped in motifs of degeneration); and a series of alcoholic mothers who beat their children. There is a distinct emphasis on the degeneracy of the women of the East End, the bearers of London's next generation. Referring to female alcoholism, Harkness remarks that 'The thing that strikes one most about East End Life is its soddenness; ... hunger and drink will in time produce a race of sensationless idiots' (p. 10). A small child recounts to one of the Salvation Army Slum Sisters how his mother 'was dead drunk last night. I can't see out of my right eye this morning from the way she banged me about afore you came up and stopped her. Sometimes I think she'll kill me or the baby when she's had too much' (p. 43). 'The men', reflects one of the Slum Sisters, 'are lambs compared to the women' (p. 45). Where the women are not 'demons' they are utterly defeated, unable to fulfil their maternal function: we are told in the novel of the suicide of a wife of a drunkard, who drowns herself in the Thames with her baby – an action which serves as a general metaphor for the degeneracy of mothers and the ensuing destruction of the 'race'. A watery death in the Thames was the fate of so many of London's prostitutes in the nineteenth century, and Harkness's urban landscape is peopled with the 'fallen women' of the working class. Of the East-End factory girls we are told that 'A more miserable set of girls it would be difficult to find anywhere. They had only just escaped from the Board School; but many of them had faces wise with wickedness, and eyes out of which all traces of maidenhood had vanished' (p. 103). It is these girls who degenerate into the 'vampires' figured elsewhere in the novel, one of whom is described as wearing 'a gaudy skirt, with a string of blue beads about her neck, with a fringe of greasy hair on her forehead' (p. 18). These 'vampires' lure many a 'jolly Jack-tar' into vice in the city, and it is interesting how the figure of the vampire is used as a trope for the dangers of 'woman' in a number of *fin-de-siècle* texts, not least in Bram Stoker's *Dracula*.[20] In Stoker's text, the female vampires are shown to be far more sinister than Count Dracula himself, and it is one of the stalwart young British men of the piece – Jonathan Harker – who is endangered by the alluring female bloodsuckers. The blood-sucking metaphor is clearly related to the draining of energy, of life's blood, from the British 'race', and it is women who are shown to be responsible for this: the social and ideological challenge posed by the late-nineteenth century women's movement was doubtless partly responsible for the representation of 'woman' in this way in numerous texts from the period.[21]

In Harkness's novel the 'vampire' figures are presented as victims as well as being a danger, in eugenic terms, to the 'race': Harkness is quite clear about the socio-economic causes of urban degeneration. She observes a people which has given up all hope of regular employment, and admonishes the reader to 'remember that a million men throughout the United Kingdom are out of work ...' (pp. 57–58). Although eugenic theories are hugely influential in this text, they are at the same time explicitly criticised. An East-End doctor, who daily witnesses the hardships borne by the inhabitants of 'Darkest London', remarks of eugenic theorists who explain degeneration through theories of heredity that 'They talk such rubbish. They cannot, or will not, see that while the environment of these people remains what it is, they will indulge in the only two enjoyments they can command ... I generally feel for them nothing but pity, because they are the victims of a state of barbarism which some people call civilization' (pp. 85–86).

Harkness does not articulate a solution to the 'state of barbarism' she locates in London's East End. Like so many Victorian novels, *In Darkest London* closes with an emigration: having signally failed to make any impact on the economic and moral squalor of London, Captain Lobe accompanies six hundred emigrants on a ship to Australia. Colonisation was also William Booth's preferred solution to the problems of his *Darkest England*, and the imperialist subtext of his essay on poverty weakens it as a radical critique of social and economic deprivation in late-Victorian Britain.

Exporting 'Darkest England' to colonies overseas had as its end point the imperialist horrors of Joseph Conrad's *Heart of Darkness*. Analyses of Conrad's critique of imperialism in this novella from 1902 are by no means thin on the ground, and *Heart of Darkness* can certainly be read, in terms of its 'empire' context, alongside the popular imperialist adventure stories discussed earlier.[22] But the relationship between Conrad's text and the urban slumland fiction of the *fin de siècle* has in general been understated by literary critics. Both *Heart of Darkness* and *In Darkest London* begin in London, and in Conrad's text it is initially implied that *this* is where the real 'darkness' is: the ominously 'brooding' 'mournful gloom' of London in the opening description culminates in Marlow's reflection that 'this also has been one of the dark places of the earth'.[23] And yet as the novel proceeds the 'darkness' and the 'horror' are safely displaced and projected onto a suitably 'foreign' adventure tale. The truth is that Conrad's Congo and Harkness's East End have some rather startling similarities: both are neglected and exploited by a dominant economic class, and both appear to be disease-ridden, degenerating and in numerous individual cases dying.[24]

One of the most striking coincidences between Joseph Conrad's and Margaret Harkness's novels is the suggestion of cannibalism attributed to the indigenous populations both of Whitechapel and of the African Congo. Most chilling of all the freaks that Captain Lobe encounters in the East End is a dying man who confesses to a murder and admits that it was a cannibalistic urge which drove him to it:

> People must eat meat, and some one must kill beasts; but to kill and kill makes a man like a cannibal, it gives him a thirst for blood, and I got to feel at last that nothing would quench my thirst but human blood, human flesh. (p. 208)

This suggestion of cannibalism in the East End is symptomatic of a fear of the racial other: the working classes were often figured in *fin-de-siècle* texts as the lower 'race'. Such a fear is also articulated in *Heart of Darkness*, where cannibalism is attributed to the Africans on Marlow's steamship. W. Arens, in his fascinating book on cannibalism – *The Man-Eating Myth* – claims that the cannibal epithet has at one time or another been applied to almost every human group and that it has been used to excuse enslavement, colonisation, warfare and annihilation.[25] Harkness's novel would seem to suggest, though, that it is the British themselves who are the cannibals and, in a more oblique way, so does Conrad's. Marlow actually reflects on the extraordinary restraint of the half-starved Africans on the steamship:

> Why in the name of all the gnawing devils of hunger they didn't go for us – there were thirty to five – and have a good tuck in for once, amazes me when I think of it. They were big powerful men ... And I saw that something restraining, one of those human secrets that baffle probability, had come into play there. (p. 194)

The white Europeans, by contrast, show little restraint, and an early reference in the text to British cannibalism implies that this lack of restraint knows no bounds. In the opening pages of the novella Marlow's directory of the heroes of the British Empire includes a mention of John Franklin (1786–1847), who commanded an expedition from London in 1845 to discover a north-west passage permitting navigation between the North Atlantic and the North Pacific. Marlow reflects that his ships, the 'Erebus' and 'Terror', never returned from the voyage (they became ice-bound in the Arctic, and all the men perished) (p. 137). What he fails to mention, though, is the exact way in which the explorers died. The full significance of the reference to Franklin, which late-twentieth-century readers can so easily miss, lies in the fact that it was subsequently claimed that the last survivors on the 'Erebus' and 'Terror' had resorted to cannibalism in a desperate but unsuccessful attempt to stay alive.[26] Conrad, when praising the character of John Franklin in his *Last Essays*, described the termination of the expedition as 'the end of the darkest drama perhaps played behind the curtain of Arctic mystery'.[27] The horror of cannibalism derives from the self-destruction of a 'race' which it implies. This is particularly pertinent to the imperialist context of the *fin de siècle* when civil unrest and urban degeneration at home appeared to threaten Britain as a world power, by weakening the country from within.

If *Heart of Darkness* makes sense as a response to the urban problems of 'Darkest London' in the late-nineteenth century, then it is equally implicated in the conflicts and tensions within gender relations which loomed large in the cultural politics of the *fin de siècle*. As a late-twentieth-century feminist response, Sandra Gilbert and Susan Gubar's critique of *Heart of Darkness* makes capital of the cultural politics of gender in the 1890s and constructs Conrad's novel as a journey towards a female other. They comment on the way in which Kurtz 'crawls, like Haggard's Billali, back into the jungle, back toward the African Queen of night into whose power he has fallen'.[28] The problem with their reading is that Africa becomes little more than a trope for woman, and the narrow focus on gender means that they fail to address the imperialist context of the novel. Gilbert and Gubar's feminist literary-critical methodology which had its heyday in the 1970s and 1980s, is, in the postcolonial 1990s, beginning to outlive its shelf-life. What is now required is a feminist critical discourse inflected with the flourishing postcolonialisms of our own *fin de siècle*, and one of the objects of this essay has been to some extent at least to answer that need.

The imperialist context of *Heart of Darkness* which Gilbert and Gubar ignore is partly provided by William Booth's allusion in 1890 to African women raped by Arab Traders; but it is Robert Cunninghame Graham, writing in 1897, who enables us to situate the gender politics of *Heart of Darkness* in relation to its imperialist context most vividly. Cunninghame Graham located the *English* as the prime culprits in the rape and pillage of Africa. In a satirically titled essay from 1897, 'Bloody Niggers', one of the most passionate attacks on imperialism to have been articulated in the 1890s, Cunninghame Graham reflected that:

> Their land is ours, their cattle and their fields, their houses are ours; their arms, their poor utensils, and everything they have; their women, too are ours to use as concubines, to beat, exchange, to barter off for gunpowder or gin, ours to infect with syphilis, leave with child, outrage, torment, and make by contact with the vilest of our vile, more vile than beasts.[29]

By turning a blind eye to the historical context of imperialism out of which *Heart of Darkness* grew, Gilbert and Gubar merely reinforce Marlow's description of Kurtz's African lover as 'savage and superb, wild-eyed and magnificent', like 'the immense wilderness' (pp. 225–226). Cunninghame Graham's account of the imperialist oppression of women has, of course, more in common with Margaret Harkness's and William Booth's descriptions of the lives of the women of London's East End than with Gilbert and Gubar's elusive and alluring 'African Queen'. Gilbert and Gubar's reading produces a vampire, whereas a reading of Cunninghame Graham insists on the introduction of the category of victim into the analysis. Grahame's ability to perceive degeneration – moral as well as physical – as a *product* of the imperialist project, rather than as its other, marks him as a truly radical late-Victorian social and political commentator.

If 'Darkest England' is the absent centre of Conrad's *Heart of Darkness*, then I am aware that Imperial Africa and all its terrible wrongs is to a certain extent the absent centre of this essay, which has concentrated on the fears of degeneration which permeated British cultural politics at the *fin de siècle*. This is quite deliberate, as my intention here has been to resituate the horror of Imperialist Britain back to where it really belonged: in 'Darkest England' itself.

NOTES

1. Eric Hobsbawm, *The Age of Empire* (London, 1987).
2. Eric Hobsbawm, *Industry and Empire* (Harmondsworth, 1969), p. 193.
3. Gareth Stedman Jones, *Outcast London* (Harmondsworth, 1971), p. 281.
4. Raymond Williams, *The English Novel From Dickens to Lawrence* (London, 1973), p. 121. I owe these references to Eileen Sypher's fine new book on the turn-of-the-century British novel, *Wisps of Violence: Producing Public and Private Politics in the Turn-of-the-Century British Novel* (London, 1993).
5. Of the dozens of books written on the nineteenth and early-twentieth century women's movement, I would particularly recommend Patricia Hollis, *Women in Public: The Women's Movement 1850–1900* (London, 1979); Susan Kingsley Kent, *Sex and Suffrage in Britain, 1860–1914* (London, 1987); David Rubinstein, *Before the Suffragettes: Women's Emancipation in the 1890s* (Brighton, 1986); Barbara Taylor, *Eve and the New Jerusalem: Socialism and Feminism in the Nineteenth Century* (New York, 1983); Martha Vicinus, *Independent Women: Work and Community for Single Women, 1850–1920* (Chicago, 1985); and Judith Walkowitz, *Prostitution and Victorian Society: Women, Class and the State* (Cambridge, 1980).
6. For the emergence of socialism at the end of the last century see for example E. P. Thompson, *William Morris: Romantic to Revolutionary* (1955; rpt. New York, 1976); Paul Thompson, *Socialists, Liberal and Labour: the Struggle for London 1885–1914* (London, 1967); and C. Tsuki, *H. M. Hyndman and British Socialism* (Oxford, 1961).
7. Eric Hobsbawm, *Industry and Empire* (Harmondsworth, 1969), p. 192.
8. Max Nordau, *Degeneration* (New York, 1895), p. 1.
9. Patrick Brantlinger, in a comparable way, has discussed how imperialism acted as an 'ideological safety valve' in response to domestic crises. See his *Rule of Darkness: British Literature and Imperialism, 1830–1914* (Ithaca and London, 1988), p. 19.
10. See especially Elaine Showalter, *Sexual Anarchy: Gender and Culture at the Fin de Siècle* (London, 1991), and Sandra Gilbert and Susan Gubar, *No Man's Land*, vol. 1: *The War of the Words* (New Haven, Conn; and London, 1988), and Volume Two: *Sexchanges* (New Haven and London, 1989).
11. Cesare Lombroso. Introduction to Gina Lombroso Ferrero, *Criminal Man According to the Classification of Cesare Lombroso* (New York and London, 1911). Studies of degeneration theory in the nineteenth and early-twentieth centuries include William Greenslade's *Degeneration: Culture and the Novel, 1880–1940* (Cambridge, 1994) and Daniel Pick's *Faces of Degeneration: A European Disorder* (Cambridge, 1986).
12. Alex Warwick, 'Vampires and the Empire: Fears and Fictions of the 1890s', in Sally Ledger and Scott McCracken (eds), *Cultural Politics at the Fin de Siècle* (Cambridge, 1995), p. 202.
13. Francis Galton, 'Hereditary Improvement', *Fraser's Magazine*, n.s. 3 (1873), pp. 117–18.
14. Raymond Williams, 'Social Darwinism', in *Problems in Materialism and Culture* (London, 1980), pp. 92–93.
15. William Booth, *In Darkest England and the Way Out* (1890), in Peter Keating (ed.), *Into Unknown England 1866–1913* (London, 1976), p. 145.
16. George Sims, *How the Poor Live and Horrible London* (1889), in Keating, *Unknown England*, p. 65.
17. Booth, *In Darkest England and the Way Out*, p. 147.
18. Raymond Williams, *The Politics of Modernism: Against the New Conformists* (London, 1989).
19. Margaret Harkness ['John Law'], *In Darkest London* (London, 1891), p. 3. All further page references to this text will appear in the main body of the essay.
20. Bram Stoker, *Dracula* (1897; rpt. Oxford, 1989).

21. Twentieth-century readings of *Dracula* which consider it partly as a response to the late-Victorian women's movement include: Carol A. Senf, '*Dracula*: Stoker's response to the New Woman', *Victorian Studies*, 26 (1982); Judith Weissman, 'Women and Vampires: *Dracula* as a Victorian Novel', *Midwest Quarterly*, 18, 4 (Summer 1977); Judith Halberstam, 'Technologies of Monstrosity: Bram Stoker's *Dracula*' in Sally Ledger and Scott McCracken (eds), *Cultural Politics at the Fin de Siècle* (Cambridge, 1995); and Alex Warwick, 'Vampires and the Empire: Fears and Fictions of the 1890s' in Ledger and McCracken (eds), *Cultural Politics at the Fin de Siècle*.
22. For an account of Conrad's attitude to imperialism in *Heart of Darkness*, see for example M. Green, *Dreams of Adventure, Deeds of Empire* (London, 1980) and, more polemically, Chinua Achebe, 'An Image of Africa: Racism in Conrad's *Heart of Darkness*', *The Massachusetts Review*, 18 (1977), 782–94. Most recently Edward Said's *Culture and Imperialism* (London, 1993) also discusses Conrad's treatment of imperialism in *Heart of Darkness*.
23. Joseph Conrad, *Heart of Darkness* (1902; repr. Oxford, 1990), p. 138.
24. Robert Colls has made a similar comparison between *Heart of Darkness* and Jack London's *The People of the Abyss*. See Robert Colls, 'Englishness and the Political Culture' in R. Colls and P. Dodd (eds), *Englishness: Politics and Culture 1880–1920* (London and Sydney, 1987), pp. 29–61.
25. W. Arens, *The Man-Eating Myth* (Oxford, 1979), p. 13.
26. Cedric Watts's excellent notes to the Oxford University Press edition of *Heart of Darkness and Other Tales* give full details of the Franklin expedition.
27. Joseph Conrad, *Last Essays* (London, 1955), pp. 10–11.
28. Sandra Gilbert and Susan Gubar, *No Man's Land*, Volume 2: *Sexchanges* (New Haven, Conn., and London, 1989), p. 44.
29. Robert Cunninghame Graham, 'Bloody Niggers', *Social Democrat*, 1, (1897), pp. 42–48, p. 44.

4.4

'THE FRONTIER ON WHICH *HEART OF DARKNESS* STANDS'

Wilson Harris

I read Chinua Achebe's article on Joseph Conrad[1] with much interest and some sympathy. My sympathy rests on an appreciation of his uneasiness in the face of biases that continue to reinforce themselves in post-imperial western establishments. Perhaps the west does have the bad conscience Achebe attributes to it and is seeking, therefore, some assuagement of its guilt.

There are certainly writers, novelists, reporters, as he indicates, who seem predisposed to see nothing but bankruptcy in the Third World and one wonders in what unconscious degree perhaps the west may desire such bankruptcy—cultural and political—to become a fact of history, whereby it may justify its imperial past by implying that imperial order, across centuries of colonialism, was the only real support the modern world possessed, the only real governance the Third World respected.

Achebe's essay on 'the dehumanisation of Africa and Africans' by 'bloody racists'[2] is, therefore, in the light of western malaise and postimperial hangover, a persuasive argument, but I am convinced his judgement or dismissal of *Heart of Darkness*—and of Conrad's strange genius—is a profoundly mistaken one. He sees the distortions of imagery and, therefore, of character in the novel as witnessing to horrendous prejudice on Conrad's part in his vision of Africa and Africans.

As I weighed this charge in my own mind, I began to sense a certain incomprehension in Achebe's analysis of the pressures of form that engaged Conrad's imagination to transform biases grounded in homogeneous premises. By form I mean the novel form as a medium of consciousness that has its deepest

Research in African Literatures, 12:1, 1981, pp. 86–93

roots in an intuitive and much, much older self than the historical ego or the historical conditions of ego dignity that bind us to a particular decade or generation or century.

The capacity of the intuitive self to breach the historical ego is the life-giving and terrifying objectivity of imaginative art that makes a painting or a poem or a piece of sculpture or a fiction endure long beyond the artist's short lifetime and gives it the strangest beauty or coherence in depth.

This interaction between sovereign ego and intuitive self is the tormenting reality of changing form, the ecstasy as well of visionary capacity to cleave the prison house of natural bias within a heterogeneous asymmetric context[3] in which the unknowable God—though ceaselessly beyond human patterns—infuses art with unfathomable eternity and grace.

I believe that this complex matter may arouse incomprehension in Africa where, by and large, tradition tends towards homogeneous imperatives. In South America where I was born this is not the case. The crucial hurdle in the path of community, if community is to create a living future, lies in a radical aesthetic in which distortions of sovereign ego may lead into confessions of partiality within sovereign institutions that, therefore, may begin to penetrate and unravel their biases, in some degree, in order to bring into play a complex wholeness inhabited by other confessing parts that may have once masqueraded themselves as monolithic absolutes or monolithic codes of behavior in the old worlds from which they emigrated by choice or by force.

It is in this respect that I find it possible to view *Heart of Darkness* as a frontier novel. By that I mean that it stands upon a threshold of capacity to which Conrad pointed though he never attained that capacity himself. Nevertheless, it was a stroke of genius on his part to visualize an original necessity for distortions in the stases of appearance that seem sacred and that cultures take for granted as models of timeless dignity.

There is a dignity in liberal pretensions until liberalism, whether black or white, unmasks itself to reveal inordinate ambitions for power where one least suspects it to exist.

The novel form Conrad inherited is the novel form in which most writers, black and white, write today. For comedy of manners is the basis of protest fiction, fiction of good guys and bad guys, racist guys and liberal guys. Comedy of manners is the basis of realism that mirrors society to identify refinements of behavior that are social or antisocial, heroic or antiheroic. All this is an oversimplification perhaps, but it may help to complement what is less obvious in this analysis.

The novel form Conrad inherited—if I may restate my theme in a more complex way—was conditioned by a homogeneous cultural logic to promote a governing principle that would sustain all parties, all characterizations, in endeavoring to identify natural justice, natural conscience behind the activity of a culture.

It was with such works of disturbing imagination as Edgar Allan Poe's *Arthur*

Gordon Pym and James Hogg's *Confessions of a Justified Sinner*, both published in the 1830s, Melville's *Benito Cereno*, in the middle of the nineteenth century, and Conrad's *Heart of Darkness*, at the beginning of the twentieth century, that the logic of human-made symmetry or absolute control of diversity, the logic of benign or liberal order, disclosed hideous biases within a context of heterogeneous bodies and pigmentations. For the truth was that the liberal homogeneity of a culture becomes the ready-made cornerstone upon which to construct an order of conquest, and by degrees 'the horror, the horror'[4] was intuitively manifest. Conquest is the greatest evil of soul humanity inflicts upon itself and on nature.

Such an admission—such a discovery that sacred human stasis may come to shelter the greatest evil—is a catastrophe for the liberal ego-fixated mind. In it, nevertheless, lies a profound creation myth that may begin to nourish a capacity for meaningful distortion of images through which to offset or transform the hubris of apparently sacred order and to create, by painful and yet ecstatic degrees, a profound, complex, and searching dialogue between confessing and confessional heterogeneous cultures that are no longer the monolithic or absolute civilizations they once were in Africa, China, Europe, India, or the Americas in the fourteenth century and fifteenth century before the circumnavigation of the globe and the fall of ancient America. Creation myth is a paradox. It is a vision of catastrophe and of coherence in depth *nevertheless* within or beneath the fragmented surfaces of given world orders. It is a vision of mysterious regeneration that apprises us of our limits and in so doing awakens a capacity to dream beyond those limits, a capacity for infinite conception of life and of humility, a capacity for complex risk, creativity, and dialogue with others through and beyond institutions inhibited by, or based on, the brute conquest of nature from which creation has recoiled again and again over long ages to leave us and our antecedents bereft and yet intensely aware of the priceless gift of being that begins all over again in the depths of animate perception.

The most significant distortion of imagery in *Heart of Darkness* bears upon Kurtz's liberal manifesto of imperial good and moral light. In that manifesto or consolidation of virtues the 'extermination of all the [alien] brutes'[5] becomes inevitable. Thus Conrad parodies the notion of moral light that devours all in its path—a parody that cuts to the heart of paternalism with strings attached to each filial puppet. (The invasion of Afghanistan in the year of Machiavellian politics 1980 is a late twentieth century version of paternal Kurtz in which the virtues of the Soviet monolith make no bones about the symmetry of Communist power to encircle the globe.)

At no point in his essay does Achebe touch upon the crucial parody of the proprieties of established order that mask corruption in all societies, black and white, though this is essential, it seems to me, to a perception of catastrophe behind the dignified personae monoliths wear. (And, in this context, one is not speaking only of conquistadorial monoliths but of mankind the hunter whose folklore is death; mankind the ritualist who sacrifices female children to maintain the symmetry of males, or mankind the priest who once plucked the heart from the breast of a living victim to feed the sun.)

These distortions of the human mask (hunter, priest, ritualist) set their teeth upon African characters like an initiation ceremony at the heart of the Bush to bite deep as well into the European conquistador/butcher/businessman Kurtz.

Kurtz's manifesto, liberal manifesto, affected Marlow as follows:

> All Europe contributed to the making of Kurtz; and by and by I learned that, most appropriately, the International Society for the Suppression of Savage Customs had intrusted him with the making of a report, for its future guidance. And he had written it, too. I've seen it, I've read it. . . . Seventeen pages of close writing he had found time for! . . . He began with the argument that we whites, from the point of development we had arrived at, 'must necessarily appear to them (savages) in the nature of supernatural beings—we approach them with the might of a deity,' and so on and on. 'By the simple exercise of our will we can exert a power for good practically unbounded,' etc., etc. From that point he soared and took me with him. . . . It gave me the notion of an exotic Immensity ruled by an august Benevolence. It made me tingle with enthusiasm. . . . It was very simple, and at the end of that moving appeal to every altruistic sentiment it blazed at you, luminous and terrifying, like a flash of lightning in a serene sky: 'Exterminate all the brutes!' The curious part was that he had apparently forgotten all about that valuable postscriptum, because, later on, when he in a sense came to himself, he repeatedly entreated me to take good care of 'my pamphlet'.[5]

In this context of parody it is possible, I think, to register a foreboding about the ultimate essence of *Heart of Darkness* and to sense an exhaustion of spirit that froze Conrad's genius and made it impossible for him to cross the frontier upon which his intuitive imagination had arrived. Achebe does not appear to have given any thought to this matter in his essay. My view is that parody tends to border upon nihilism, a fact all too clear in modern fiction and drama. Parody is the flag of the death of god, the death of faith, and without faith imaginative art tends to freeze and cultivate a loss of soul. Perhaps god has been so conditioned by homogeneous or tribal idols that freedom of spirit seems a chimera. When I speak of the necessity for faith I am not referring therefore to cults of idolatry but to a conviction written into the stars as into one's blood that creation is a priceless gift beyond human formula or calculation of Faustian will.

Conrad's despair is so marked that one is conscious of infinite desolation within the very signals he intuitively erects that bear upon a radical dialectic of form. His parody—like Beckett's parody—remains formidable because it cuts to the bone and heart of liberal complacency. The transition beyond parody that humanity needs neither Beckett nor Conrad fulfills.

I am convinced myself that there is a movement of transition in some complex areas of twentieth century literature beyond parody but such an exploration would require another essay. I shall give, however, two examples that may suggest a groping transition. First of all, Wole Soyinka's masterpiece *The Road* is influenced, I am sure, by Conrad in that the unscrupulous professor is psychically related to Kurtz with the profound distinction that the professor's faith in 'the chrysalis of the Word'[7] prepares him for a descent into the fertility of the African mask, so that he sustains in himself the wound that kills those who exist in the depths of place and time. He is, as it were, the involuntary metaphysic that illumines outcast humanity within the dissolution of the mask or persona conferred by the savage god, Ogun, in contradistinction to Kurtz's totalitarian loss of soul within the rigidity of the mask conferred by the hubris of material bias.

My second example of possible transition through and beyond post-Conradian legacies is a remarkable asymmetric American fiction by the black writer Jean Toomer in his book *Cane*, published in 1923, which comprises a series of half-fictions, half-plays shot through by stream of consciousness and lyrical moments as well as by short interludes or poems.

The characters appear implicitly clothed in property and landscapes they wear like bizarre roots and masks to suggest an unfreedom of personality locked in polarizations. This perception is psychic rather than behavioristic and, therefore, it may begin to undermine the polarizations since it is capable of seeing them not for what they appear to be—forms of strength—but for what they essentially are—fragmentations of a community dangerously divided within itself against itself. Paradoxically this psychic apprehension begins to grope for coherence in depth that needs to be grasped ceaselessly by imagery that points through itself, beyond itself, into a visionary comedy of wholeness that can never be structured absolutely. Indeed, where adamant property binds flesh and blood *Cane* is a revelation of bitterness and conflict since it evokes memories of the auction block on which persons were bought and sold, metaphorically nailed to the cross, as it were, as pieces of property.

I must confess, in bringing this article to a close, that I was rather surprised when Achebe quoted F. R. Leavis in support of his thesis. Leavis of all people! Leavis, as far as I am aware, possessed no sympathy whatever for imaginative literature that fell outside of the closed world of his 'great tradition.'

I would question Leavis's indictment of Conrad for an addiction to the adjective. The fact of the matter is that the intuitive archetypes of sensation and nonsensation by which Conrad was tormented are not *nouns*. They are qualitative and infinite variations of substance clothed in nouns. Nouns may reveal paradoxically, when qualified, that their emphasis on reality and their inner meaning can change as they are inhabited by variable psychic projections born of the mystery of creation. There is a *woodenness* to *wood*, there is also a *gaiety* to *wood* when it is stroked by shadow or light that turns *wood* into a mask worn by variable metaphysical bodies that alter the content within the mask. The livingness of wood is the magic of carven shapes that act in turn upon the perceiving eye and sculpt it into a window of spirit.

Marlow's bewilderment at the heart of the original forest he uneasily penetrated reveals unfinished senses within him and without him, unfinished perceptions that hang upon veils within veils.

> The *living* trees, lashed together by the creepers and every *living* bush of the undergrowth, might have been changed into *stone*, even to the *slenderest* twig, to the *lightest* leaf. It was not sleep—it seemed unnatural, like a state of trance. Not the *faintest* sound of any kind could be heard. You looked on amazed and began to suspect yourself of being *deaf*—then the night came suddenly, and struck you *blind* as well. About three in the morning some large fish leaped, and the *loud* splash made me jump as though a gun had been fired. When the sun rose there was a *white* fog, very warm and clammy, and more *blinding* than the night. . . . A cry, a very loud cry, as of infinite desolation, soared slowly in the *opaque* air. It ceased. A complaining clamor, modulated in savage discord, filled our ears.[8]

At this stage I would like to add to the considerations I have already expressed by touching on the issue of 'music' in imaginative literature.

The loud cry and clamor as of an orchestra at the heart of the Bush that come as a climax in the quotation from *Heart of Darkness* are of interest in the context of the human voice breaking through instruments of stone and wood and other trance formations to which the human animal is subject. Indeed it is as if the stone and wood *sing*, so that in mirroring hard-hearted dread and rigid desolation they suffer at the same time a disruption or transformation of fixed bias within themselves.

I am not suggesting that Conrad extends this notion into a profound discovery of new form or radical aesthetic but it is marginally yet significantly visible in the passage I have quoted.

Caribbean writers and poets have been interested in the ground of music in fiction and poetry. Edward Brathwaite, Derek Walcott, and others have complex approaches to music. I have intuitively explored in novels organic metaphors of music. In a recent article[9] I confessed to some of these intuitive archetypes and in particular to the pre-Columbian bone flute as a trigger of organic capacity to release a diversity of sombre or rock-hard images in alliance or attunement with phenomenal forests, walking trees, butterfly motifs within singing bodies of evolutionary hope in the midst of legacies of conquest and catastrophe.

I am reminded now, as I write this, of Beethoven's late quartets in which he wrestled with 'the intolerable muteness' (as Anton Ehrenzweig puts it) 'of a purely instrumental music; he tries to make the instruments sing in a human way . . . In the end the human voice itself must break in as a symbol of extreme disruption in order to obey a more profound logic.'[10]

NOTES

1. Chinua Achebe, 'An Image of Africa,' *Research in African Literatures*, 9, 1 (1978), 9.

2. Ibid.
3. *Asymmetric context* implies that the unknowable God mediates between all structures. Thus if one were to say 'the sun is a rose' one would visualize—in asymmetric context—an inimitable or unstructured mediation existing between *sun* and *rose*. Both *sun* and *rose*, therefore, are partial signatures of—partial witnesses to—a universal principle of mediation, a universal principle of light beyond capture or structure. That principle of mediation at the heart of all metaphor may only be perceived as an *untameable* force mediating between *sun* and *rose*.
   Symmetric context on the other hand would imply a binding locality or materiality or physicality in which *sun* and *rose* are *tameable* extensions or symmetric inversions of each other.
4. Joseph Conrad, *Heart of Darkness and The Secret Sharer* (New York: Bantam, 1978), p. 118.
5. Ibid., p. 84.
6. Ibid., pp. 84–85.
7. Wole Soyinka, *The Road* (London: Oxford University Press, 1965), p. 45.
8. Conrad, pp. 65–66. Italics in this quotation are mine.
9. Wilson Harris, 'The Enigma of Values,' *New Letters*, 40, 1 (1973), 141–49.
10. Anton Ehrenzweig, *The Hidden Order of Art* (London: Paladin, 1970), p. 219.

PART 5
RUDYARD KIPLING:
KIM

INTRODUCTION

Kim is most commonly viewed as a novel about life on the Great Wheel of Life (for the spiritual lama) and the Grand Trunk Road (for the opportunistic Kim) under the British Raj around 1880. It foregrounds mimicry and hybridity in its winding narrative of an Irish boy who thinks in Hindi, is taken to be a street urchin and a Sahib, and oscillates between British and Indian dress, speech and identity. It is also a text to which critics interested in deploying Edward Said's notion of 'Orientalism' have repeatedly turned.[1]

Kim was published in a year in which the British realised the numerical absurdity of their hold over India. According to the 1901 census, there were only 170,000 Europeans on the subcontinent, including soldiers, and half again as many Eurasians, in comparison with 294 million Indians. *Kim* is also a novel about the methods through which these thousands attempted to comprehend these millions while also resisting the threat of Russian incursions; it is additionally an adventure story about a boy's relation to India and the British Empire. In 'Kipling's Children and the Colour Line', S. P. Mohanty argues that *Kim* has to be read in terms of racial positions and the Imperial project. In particular, the essay focuses on issues of spying, scouting, observing and managing: 'a distinctly political project shaping racial meanings, identities and possibilities.'

Another reading which acknowledges the status of Kipling's novel as both, or at least between, a child's and an adult's narrative, is Sara Suleri's 'The Adolescence of Kim'. Suleri reads Kim's repeated adolescent self-questioning as Imperial questioning in which Kim's colonial education carries within it the seed of his alienation from India. To be part of the government of India, Kim must be distanced from it – must graduate from active participation to fixed colonial knowledge, from be(long)ing to knowing. Suleri understands the book as an expression of Kipling's 'apprehension of the futility of empire', and so concentrates on issues of loss, miscommunication and 'colonial casualty'.

In a very different interpretation of the novel, Ian Adam's essay entitled 'Oral/Literate/Transcendent: The Politics of Language Modes in *Kim*' uses the deconstructive strategies of Jacques Derrida to expose the traces of Western binary thinking in Kipling's novel. A systematic argument that is useful in demonstrating the influence of post-structuralism's critique of notions of purity, essentialism and hierarchy on post-colonial readings, it concentrates on spoken/written signs and the associations between characters and language types.

If we turn to other recent work, Thomas Richards considers the functions of *The Imperial Archive* in Kipling's novel through a discussion which complements and expands upon elements of Mohanty's reading. Overall, Richards, whose book's talisman is the British Museum, describes the enormous growth in knowledge as power throughout the Victorian period. In particular, he is interested in the cataloguing, surveying, collecting and documenting of the Empire – the state apparatus 'worlding' a previously uninscribed India.[2] Richards sees Kipling's novel as a *Bildungsroman* in the service of the leviathan of state knowledge. After the Indian 'Mutiny' of 1857, an understanding of India was thought to be valuable again after a period of pronounced anglicisation. Now, the purpose of knowledge was not to learn about an ancient, multi-layered culture, as Orientalists such as William Jones had believed, but to ensure the retention of British power; to avoid another rebellion and to better facilitate change. Through land surveys, railways, telegraphy, ethnography and the census, all of India was under surveillance. Richards's argument is that 'What *Kim* figures more clearly than any other Victorian text is a world in which colonization through ethnocide, deportation, and slavery . . . has begun to give way to colonization through the mediated instrumentality of information.'[3]

In his later work, Bart Moore-Gilbert has argued that *Kim* is more politically equivocal than most studies suggest. The ending of the book, in which Kim decides to continue in the Great Game, has led critics such as Benita Parry, Zohreh Sullivan, John McClure and Edward Said to conclude that Kipling is more clearly pro-Imperial in his novel than he was in his earlier, frequently subversive short stories.[4] Salman Rushdie, for example, speaks in *The Moor's Last Sigh* of 'Kipling's almost schizophrenic early stories of the Indiannesses and Englishnesses that struggled within him.'[5] By contrast, Moore-Gilbert argues that *Kim* also exhibits considerable colonial anxiety in its delineation of 'a vast and complex underground system of counter-insurgency', its references to the 'Mutiny', and its revelations of inadequacy, such as the head of Counter-Intelligence's admission that he doesn't 'know much about natives'. Taking his cue from Robert Moss, Moore-Gilbert decides that the book's ending is ambivalent, and leaves Kim still fluctuating between the identities he has adopted, inhabited and mimicked throughout the novel.[6] The book is thus seen as a series of crises of (Imperial) identity pivoting on the famous repeated question 'Who is Kim?' This is a theme reworked by Michael Ondaatje in his novel *The English Patient*, which features an Indian bomb-disposal expert called Kip, whose insertion in the book's interrogation of national identities is in some ways as a question mark reminding the reader both of Kim's self-inquiry and of Kipling's split self: of the arbitrariness of the historical identity of the interpellated colonial subject at the intersection of nations and names.

Those interested in further reading should also see the analysis by Gail Ching-Liang Low in *White Skins, Black Masks: Representation and Colonialism*.[7] In its discussion of *Kim*, Low's book scrutinises the relationship between colonial cross-dressing and hybridity: the role of clothes in forming a racial fault line. Low concludes that Kim's 'whiteness' under his colonial mimicry has to be constantly avowed by the narrative; she sees native disguise as part of the narrative pleasure enjoyed by the reader eager to indulge in Imperial fantasy, and the book in general as a presentation of an exotic Oriental world for visual and material consumption. It is also worth looking at the relation between domestic and Imperial organisation explored by Daniel Bivona in his book *Desire and Contradiction*.[8] In a short piece on Kipling and the Great Game,[9] Bivona writes that *Kim* 'reveals a complicity between a discourse on play and an imperial ideology whose objectives are presumably served by attracting young readers to the notion of empire as a privileged field of play.'[10] The whole novel is seen as a series of games which, like competing interpellative narratives, vie for Kim's attention until he recognises the importance of the great Imperial adventure. Lastly, Don Randall's 'Ethnography and the Hybrid Boy in Rudyard Kipling's *Kim*' uses the work of James Clifford to look at the novel as a piece of ethnography and also considers the novel's language as more hybridised than it needs to be – seeing Kim and the narrator as child and adult caught in the compromising complexities of cross-cultural confrontation and negotiation.[11]

In some ways, the one aspect to Kim's identity which is left undeveloped by the novel's own meditations and by many of its commentators, is his Irish ancestry – a national identity which places him simultaneously as both coloniser and colonised. Interestingly, however, the gesture is repeated by Rabindranath Tagore in his novel *Gora*: '"No, I am not a Hindu," continued Gora. "Today I have been told that I was a foundling at the time of the Mutiny – My father was an Irishman!"'[12]

NOTES

1. See, for example, Patrick Williams's essay '*Kim* and Orientalism', in Patrick Williams and Laura Chrisman (eds), *Colonial Discourse and Post-Colonial Theory*, Hemel Hempstead: Harvester Wheatsheaf, 1993 and B. J. Moore-Gilbert's book, *Kipling and 'Orientalism'*, Kent: Croom Helm, 1986.
2. See Gayatri Spivak, 'Three Women's Texts and a Critique of Imperialism', in Henry Louis Gates jnr. (ed.), *'Race', Writing, and Difference*, Chicago: University of Chicago Press, 1986, p. 262.
3. Thomas Richards, *The Imperial Archive*, London: Verso, 1993, p. 23.

4. See Benita Parry, 'The Content and Discontents in Kipling's Imperialism', *New Formations*, 6, Winter 1988, pp. 49–64, Zohreh Sullivan, *Narratives of Empire: The Fictions of Rudyard Kipling*, Cambridge: Cambridge University Press, 1993, John McClure, *Kipling and Conrad: The Colonial Fiction*, London: Harvard University Press, 1981 and Edward Said, 'Introduction' to Rudyard Kipling, *Kim*, Harmondsworth: Penguin, 1987, pp. 7–46.
5. Salman Rushdie, *The Moor's Last Sigh*, London: Jonathan Cape, 1995, p. 39.
6. Robert Moss, *Rudyard Kipling and the Fiction of Adolescence*, London: Macmillan, 1981 and Bart Moore-Gilbert, '"The Bhbhbhal of Tongues": reading Bhabha, reading Kipling', in Bart Moore-Gilbert (ed.), *Writing India 1757–1990*, Manchester: Manchester University Press, 1996, pp. 111–38.
7. Gail Ching-Liang Low, *White Skins, Black Masks: Representation and Colonialism*, London: Routledge, 1996, pp. 200–15.
8. Daniel Bivona, *Desire and Contradiction: Imperial Visions and Domestic Debates in Victorian Literature*, Manchester: Manchester University Press, 1990, pp. 42–50.
9. According to Mark Paffard, the expression 'the Great Game' originated in the First Afghan War of 1839 and became a common description of general British Eastern diplomacy (Mark Paffard, *Kipling's Indian Fiction*, London: Macmillan, 1989, p. 83).
10. Bivona, p. 90.
11. Don Randall's, 'Ethnography and the Hybrid Boy in Rudyard Kipling's *Kim*', *Ariel*, 27:3, July 1996, pp. 79–104.
12. Rabindranath Tagore, *Gora*, London: Macmillan, 1924, p. 405.

5.1

FROM 'KIPLING'S CHILDREN AND THE COLOUR LINE'

S. P. Mohanty

In the context of colonial India, as we shall see in a moment, Kipling's novel seems to embody a general cultural project, imagining and elaborating forms of selfhood that have a particular racial inflection as well as a larger historical resonance. It is, in fact, through the prism of 'race' that we begin to discern some of the essential cultural lineaments of this 'history'.

Kim's marvellous facility in inhabiting India – in being able to navigate its social mores just as easily as the narrow and confusing corridors of its urban bazaars, to score points over a small-town policeman by outdoing him in verbal abuse – is underscored from the beginning. Indeed, we miss the force of the novel if we read in it simply the magic of innocence and childhood. The crucial difference is that Kipling's hero is a white boy who can discard his colour at will or whim. He lives and sleeps and eats in the open social world of colonial India, against a backdrop of an inter-imperial war between Britain and Russia, but his identity is never something that ties him down. He is a political abstraction: cunning and beguiling enough to outdo and fool the natives, yet always implicitly and securely on the side of Empire. The pleasure he takes in India and his adventures can thus never quite be mere pleasure; it seems that something else must also be at stake. Even the initial descriptions seem to be seeking out a certain personal capacity that is more than that of a boy who can play innocently, that is, be a world unto himself:

> His nickname through the wards was 'Little Friend of all the World'; and

Race and Class, 31, 1, 1989, pp. 21–40. Extract: pp. 25–7 and 31–40.

> very often, being lithe and inconspicuous, he executed commissions by night on the crowded housetops for sleek and shiny young men of fashion. It was intrigue, of course . . . but what he loved was the game for its own sake – the stealthy prowl through the dark gullies and lanes, the crawl up a water-pipe, the sights and sounds of the women's world on the flat roofs, and the headlong flight from housetop to housetop under cover of the hot dark.

But where did Kim learn all this, one is tempted to ask – who taught him to prowl without being caught, spy without being seen? In some ways, this is an unfair question. For we know that although his parents were white, he grew up as a street urchin in Lahore, in the care of a half-caste Indian woman. We know how boys learn to survive in a difficult world, and learn, like Huck Finn, to value the hardship of an unsheltered life over the privileges of 'sivilization'. But in one sense the question is appropriate.[1] For when we begin to take Kim's cultural identity seriously and the character becomes real in our imagination, we pay attention to the narrative's elusive and mystifying cultural vision and wonder about the sources of its motivation. The question about Kim's 'education' directs us to parallels in Kipling's earlier fiction, to look in fact at Kim's immediate ancestor, Mowgli – again, a child living with strangers who love and take care of him, and from whom he learns to survive in the harsh world. Mowgli, adopted by wolves and befriended by all the other animals of the jungle, is taught to inhabit the jungle by the natives themselves. Here, too, the child lives a charmed life: the world of the other, potentially the enemy, opens up to him as if by magic. I think it is this unexplained possibility on which is predicated what Angus Wilson calls 'the elusive magic' of childhood. Here is the moment of Mowgli's and Kim's necessary education, an education as strategic as it is miraculously effortless:

> [Mowgli] grew up with the cubs, though they, of course, were grown wolves almost before he was a child, and Father Wolf taught him his business, and the meaning of things in the jungle, till every rustle in the grass, every breath of the warm night air, every note of the owls above his head, every scratch of a bat's claws as it roosted for a while in a tree, and every splash of every little fish jumping in a pool, meant just as much to him as the work of his office means to a business man . . . [W]hen he felt dirty or hot he swam in the forest pools; and when he wanted honey . . . he climbed up for it, and that Bagheera showed him how to do. Bagheera would lie out on a branch and call, 'Come along, Little Brother', and at first Mowgli would cling like the sloth, but afterward he would fling himself through the branches almost as boldly as the grey ape. He took his place at the Council Rock, too, when the Pack met, and there he discovered that if he stared hard at any wolf, the wolf would be forced to drop his eyes, and so he used to stare for fun.

As in the case of Kim, Mowgli belongs without ever leaving any doubt in the reader's mind about his alien status. Mowgli can stare down any wolf, and even though he learns the ways of the jungle from his adopted family, he remains superior in clear-cut ways. In effect, after his education, he is an accomplished insider without having given up any of his privileges as an outsider. Kim's attempts to disguise himself are similarly effortless; he moves in and out of his roles as native and British, black and white, with only as much work as it takes to put on make-up. Much of the pleasure of Kim's narrative derives from this 'intrigue' where the danger remains muted; what could potentially be tense race relations are transformed into the innocent game of play-acting. One may indeed see how the *Jungle Books*, written in the mid 1890s, invite an allegorical reading, with the jungle representing the political stage of colonial India.

. . .

In his fiction about India Kipling creates children who embody values and qualities that are essential for white colonial rulers and their agents if they are to survive in and manage a racially tense social and political world. The danger of their existence is first fantasised away by the narrative, as the children's ability to live and move about in a hostile world is presented as a magical, miraculous gift. But the Mowgli tales, just as much as *Kim*, contain enough of a clear sense of danger for the historically informed reader to know what is at stake, to understand the general context of threat which frames and enriches the significance of the child-like play. Nothing is more vivid in this context than the opening of 'The King's Ankus', when Mowgli and Kaa, the python, are playing together: the fantasy is here not so much of pure freedom as of involvement without any real implication. Kaa could crush Mowgli with the slightest slip; and what Mowgli plays with, in fact, is precisely this. Their inequality reduces to a game. Indeed, as we know from the beginning of the story, Kaa acknowledges the young human boy as the Master of the Jungle, and brings the boy all the news that he hears. Here is that breathtaking description of the game that Kaa and Mowgli play – breathtaking to the very extent that we find ourselves attracted and compelled by the sense of danger that would in real life keep us wary:

> 'I will carry thee', said Mowgli; and he stooped down, laughing, to lift the middle section of Kaa's great body, just where the barrel was thickest. A man might just as well have tried to heave up a two-foot water-main; and Kaa lay still, puffing with quiet amusement. Then their regular evening game began – the Boy in the flush of his great strength, and the Python in his sumptuous new skin, standing up one against the other for a wrestling match – a trial of eye and strength. Of course, Kaa could have crushed Mowgli had he let himself go; but he played carefully, and never loosed one-tenth of his power. Ever since Mowgli was strong enough to endure a little rough handling, Kaa had taught him this game, and it suppled his

> limbs as nothing else could. Sometimes Mowgli would stand lapped almost to his throat in Kaa's shifting coils, striving to get one arm free and catch him by the throat. Then Kaa would give way limply, and Mowgli, with both quick-moving feet, would try to cramp the purchase of that huge tail as it flung backwards feeling for a rock or a stump. They would rock to and fro, head to head, each waiting for his chance, till the beautiful statue-like group melted in a whirl of black and yellow coils and struggling legs and arms . . .

But Mowgli, like Kim, reveals the capacity not only to inhabit the jungle through this wishful allegorical fantasy, but also to chart and track it as well. Central to Kipling's conception of both characters is their ability to read the world around them. Here, too, they are perfectly schooled – often better than most of the natives. Notice, in 'The King's Ankus', for instance, the way Mowgli learns as he participates in the hunt for the thieves. Here is one typical moment: '"Now he runs swiftly", said Mowgli. "The toes are spread apart." They went on over some wet ground. "Now why does he turn aside here?" . . . "It is the foot of a Gond hunter", he said. "Look! Here he dragged his bow on the grass . . ."'

Kim, for his part, knows how to read maps better than the lama, but the native boys he is naturally compared with somehow lack the very faculty that makes 'reading' possible. In Simla, when Lurgan Sahib teaches Kim and the Indian boy how to observe people's faces and reactions, to interpret behaviour and identify motive, and then to disguise themselves as other people – in other words, to assume others' roles, Kim seems to learn it quickly, while his native friend is left mysteriously handicapped. The narrator explains why the Hindu child played the game clumsily: 'That little mind, keen as an icicle where tally of jewels was concerned, could not temper itself to enter another's soul; but a demon in Kim woke up and sang with joy as he put on the changing dresses, and changed speech and gesture therewith.' There is a continuity, then, between learning to observe carefully, to observe without being observed (as Kim often does), to interpret people and situations, to move stealthily and unnoticed, and to assume roles. Both Mowgli and Kim learn through their narratives the value of doing these things – to inhabit perfectly without being tied down to the place of their habitation; like their roles and disguises, they discard these places at will.

To understand this project of self-fashioning, it might be useful to recall that the nineteenth century was the period when colonial rule consolidated itself through a phenomenal increase in its 'scientific' knowledge of the various populations of India as well as the land itself. This was the age when the census was introduced, and a preliminary colonial taxonomy was established and solidified in the process of being 'discovered'; this was also the century when the great land surveys (an operation involving engineers and military and revenue officials) mapped and codified much of the subcontinent not only topographically but also in terms of land 'quality', making possible, in effect, the settling of nomadic populations and the conversion of the 'rough pastoral' countryside into

– taxable – agricultural land; and finally, as is well known, this was the age of the railways and the telegraph lines, and the expansion of the road networks, which facilitated revenue administration as much as military control (see the studies by Bayly and Cohn). In varying degrees, this happened both in the portion of India under direct British control and in the territories called the Princely States, which were ruled indirectly through political agents or 'Residents'. One must consider this context to understand the discourse of control and surveillance which pervaded colonial society and culture, a context in which knowledge and politics, the scientific objectification of a social world and its subsequent manipulation, are intertwined in very specific ways. And the racial discourse I have been tracing here provides a 'cultural' barometer of this specificity.

Kim's instruction in the Great Game of espionage is little more than a continuation of the kind of child's-play which involves observing and interpreting while remaining conveniently invisible oneself. A few years after Kipling's novel was published, another best-selling book, this time a non-fictional work, in fact a manual for young English boys that was to prove immensely influential, cited Kim as the prototypical young hero of the Empire. Baden-Powell's *Scouting for Boys*, published first in 1908, was an explicitly ideological book: it sought to induct children into the cause of Empire. Echoing the pervasive feeling that the Empire was in danger – as much from anti-colonial movements (registered as mutinies or criminal acts) as from the appalling weakness of physical and moral constitution of English working-class boys – Baden-Powell sought to educate the country's boys to be 'Prepared', in body and in mind, to fight for the Empire and to rule. 'We have all got to die some day; a few years more or less of our lives don't matter in the history of the world, but it is a very great matter if by dying a year or two sooner than we should otherwise do from disease we can help to save the flag of our country from going under' (cited from the first edition in Rosenthal). The scout's duty consisted of the following: 'Woodcraft. Observation without being noticed. Deduction. Chivalry. Sense of Duty. Endurance. Kind-heartedness.' But this is no abstract list: *Scouting for Boys* has instructions for scout masters in training boys: this is what they must be told:

> You belong to the Great British Empire, one of the greatest that has ever existed in the world.
> (*Show on the map* [B-P's instruction for the scout instructor]).
> From this little island of Great Britain have sprung colonies all over the world, Australia, New Zealand, South Africa, India, Canada.
> Almost every race, every kind of man, black, white, or yellow, furnished subjects of King Edward VII.
> This vast Empire did not grow of itself out of nothing; it was made by your forefathers by dint of hard work and hard fighting, at the sacrifice of their lives – that is, by their hearty patriotism.

By the turn of the century, when Kipling and Baden-Powell were both writing however, the world itself had changed, so that one needed not simply hardihood but also stealth – a capacity to be invisible, to blend with the surroundings, to watch without being watched – in short, to be a good spy. As Michael Rosenthal argues in his valuable book, *The Character Factory*, scouting remained a kind of preparatory training, as well as a substitute:

> If a boy can't be a spy, Scouting still remains important as a technique in solving the various murders he might tend to come across in his daily activities. Early in *Scouting for Boys* Baden-Powell recounts the tale of the Eldson murder, in which a brutal murderer 'was caught, convicted, and hanged through the scoutcraft of a shepherd boy'. The value of the tale is clarified in a note Baden-Powell appends for the use of the potential Scout instructor: 'The following story, which in the main is true, is a sample of a story that should be given by the instructor illustrating generally the duties of a Boy Scout.'[2]

The scouting tradition relied on tales for their pedagogic effectiveness. And, as we have seen, notions of duty and chivalry were valued less as general human virtues than as specific political ones. It is not really a paradox, then, that the specific politics of imperial conquest and colonial rule enabled only an abstract and decontextualised morality. Indeed, even the processes of perception, understanding and reasoning are reduced to the mere application of formula, to easily transferable practices, and selfhood is rendered purely functional. This reduction is one of the essential elements of the racialisation of culture, the inherent logic of the colour line, then as much as now.

Kipling's project is different from Baden-Powell's in so far as it works out, in fictional terms, a fantasy and a narrative of a kind of sentimental education. *Kim* and *The Jungle Books* are not explicit political tracts like *Scouting for Boys*; but then the latter, we tend to forget, has often been considered a mere manual. My analysis indicates the extent to which children's fiction might function in this context to fashion the imperial self from within, simultaneously shaping and articulating desires, patterning images of self and world not only in terms of value, but of possibility and necessity as well. Kipling's texts work as fiction to the extent that they enact an allegory of desire in which we can participate as readers. This is a desire to be invisible, to belong, to contain the threat of any real encounter, to observe without being observed – in short, to rule colonial India without seeming to do so. In order to do this, the tales also reveal that the ruling subject must learn to be above any kind of specific desire, anything that can be identified as *interest*. For if it was Providence that chose the British to rule the world (as was commonly believed and stated), then that mission was above politics, beyond interest and self-interest. Indeed, it must be made clear that they – as rulers – have *no* interests at stake. Consider the way Mowgli can desire the jewel-studded ankus while being able to rise above his desire, to throw the ankus away at crucial moments in the narrative without a second's hesitation. The text drives the point home by re-enacting the attractiveness and desirability of the ankus for the reader (the description is one of Kipling's most effective):

> [Mowgli] found something really fascinating laid on the front of a howdah half buried in the coins. It was a two-foot ankus, or elephant-goad – something like a small boat hook. The top was one round shining ruby, and eight inches of the handle below it were studded with rough turquoises close together, giving a most satisfactory grip. Below them was a rim of jade with a flower-pattern running around it – only the leaves were emeralds, and the blossoms were rubies sunk in the cool, green stone. The rest of the handle was a shaft of pure ivory, while the point – the spike and hook – was gold inlaid steel with pictures of elephant-catching ...

Mowgli is attracted, the narrative goes on to specify, but it does not lead to a desire that can inhibit him or tie him down. We recognise this as significant to the extent that, as readers, we have responded to Kipling's evocative description, and have been introduced into this elementary economy of desire and scarcity. It is then that we appreciate the fact that unlike those who steal the ankus, and who are punished by Fate for the act, Mowgli can both desire and not desire: in fact, he is the only character in the jungle who possesses this capacity to belong completely and yet remain above it all. A strange allegory of colonial rule as possession without implication, penetration without involvement.

. . .

If these readings I have sketched here suggest anything, it is to indicate the extent to which the separate world of childhood that many have seen as the unique charm of Kipling's fiction is not all that insular after all. If the Indian tales are read with the colonial context in mind, they point to what may be an essential ideological concern and, indeed, a political project. They reveal a subterranean mapping of imperial subjectivity as abstract, unspecifiable in its contexts, floating above desire and ideology. They trace the narrative outlines of a desire not to desire, an insistent desire to remain vaguely defined. Indeed, they reveal a crucial pedagogical project; moulding desire and training the sensibility, they 'map' the ruling subject's selfhood *racially*, that is ultimately in the terms of an inflexibly *general* – and hence distant – relationship with the colonised and their world. Kim's anxieties about his identity – 'I am Kim. I am Kim. And what is Kim?' – resonate with no real cultural situation at all, no identity crisis I can imagine. For his relationship with the lama leaves him essentially unchanged. Contrast this with Huck's encounter with Jim, for instance, and it is possible to see how culturally vacuous Kipling's hero's relationships are. And the lama's own otherworldliness is quite convenient for the narrative: the (moral and religious) Law he follows is left sufficiently undefined by the end of the novel for it to blend into the Great Game, spying in the service of the Empire. Racial difference is constructed here to sublimate the political world, enabling an abstraction of personal definition. It may be suggested that 'fiction' – as it has so often done in crucial historical moments – narrates the conditions of existence, the shifting shapes and the multiple expressions, of this politically necessary 'selfhood'. The line that divides does more than separate in this text and in this context; it creates a distinct racial identity for the British colonial rulers of India. Needless to say, it is an open question whether – and in what ways – these identities and relations inform our present contexts, and we might have much to learn from focused genealogical accounts of our current racial discourses and attitudes.

Edward Said says in *Orientalism* that Kipling and his white man emerged from complex historical circumstances. I have suggested some of the specific ways in which understanding these circumstances can help us trace a distinctly political project shaping racial meanings, identities and possibilities. Fiction, I have argued, might have played a crucial role in this. The other major cultural manifestation of colonial rule that needs to be considered for a more complete historical analysis involves the contradictory desire to fashion the self – the British white self – as a spectacle. As numerous scholars have suggested recently, the ritualisation of colonial culture, the adoption and adaptation of the native North Indian *durbar* or royal display – by colonial British administrators, was an essentially new feature in the late nineteenth century. Bernard Cohn has argued that the *durbar*'s adapted forms can be seen anthropologically as the elaboration of a 'colonial sociology', a creation of new hierarchies and divisions in the Indian social order.[31] Immense value now resided in the new project of rendering the rulers *visible in a certain way*. From dress and physical appearance to the determination of when to be visible, how much, and to whom, colonial culture became obsessively concerned with marking difference with ostentation. At one level, then, we are presented with a contradiction between two images of the ruling self: one tending towards the invisible, the other towards the eminently spectacular. They seem to mark the two extreme forms of an imperial subjectivity at that historical and political moment, both perhaps tracing the outlines of an impossible abstraction.

What can be said about this contradiction in general terms? It seems to me that we cannot – and should not – say too much in a purely *theoretical* way. Recent scholarship, drawing on the resources of both anthropologists and historians, has emphasised the spectacular dimension of all European culture in the latter part of the nineteenth century, and the ways in which specifically imperial themes predominate as images for mass consumption in the last two decades.[4] If my suggestions about the thematic of invisibility are convincing, we will need to look carefully at the cultural levels at which these two competing imperatives operate. They might, in fact, be complementary, with different and geographically distinct audiences in mind. Spectacles – exhibitions, *durbars*, the ritualisation of the monarchy and its public activities – seem to be confined to the cities, both in England and in colonial India, while the concern with invisibility reveals itself in the contact with the colonial countryside, the world of the peasant and the sepoy (often the peasant-sepoy), now insistently unreadable as political constituencies. Both invisibility and spectacularisation seek to comprehend and rule, as I have said, and push the image of the ruling self into forms of necessary abstraction. In what ways these different forms coincide in their political significance is a *historical* question, to be analysed and elaborated in specific contexts.

Pursuing this line of enquiry might show us clearly the ways in which imperial culture refracts and shapes the political world. Indeed, it might begin to suggest the important reasons why an analysis of metropolitan imperial culture – insulated from the developments and changes in the colonies – is bound to be partial and misleading. In the same way, histories of colonialism, to the extent that they ignore these obvious cultural and discursive connections and continuities between imperial Europe and the peoples, territories and societies it ruled and exploited, will necessarily remain much less cogent than they can be. For, as in the case of scouting, events and values, strategies for rule and for conceiving of culture have often emerged in the colonial context and travelled inward. They thus reveal a centripetal movement, from the colonised periphery to the European centre. And this movement points to the need to understand the ways in which the metropolitan ruling classes responded to the threats to their domestic and imperial hegemony. Colonial cultural studies might help us in filling in the outlines of the larger social formation suggested here, including both metropolitan Britain and the colonial 'outposts', in which centre and periphery, inside and outside, can be seen as implicating and potentially redefining one another.[5]

NOTES

1. It is this question that Edward Said does not raise in his excellent recent essay on *Kim*, and that is why Said's interpretation of the young boy misses the pedagogic narrative inherent in the image of childhood. I focus exclusively on *Kim* and *The Jungle Books* here in order to deal in some detail with this connection between the two texts. For a wider-ranging analysis of Kipling and a development of the theoretical issues touched on here, see my 'Drawing the color line' ('Bibliography' below). (I came across Said's essay after I had finished writing the major portion of this article, and would at least like to cite it as the best single introduction to the novel and its political contexts. It suggests the need for more detailed biographical and textual analyses of a writer whose work it should no longer be possible merely to celebrate or dismiss.
2. See Baden-Powell (1983), for this tale. The more 'imperialist' sentiments and passages cited earlier are not in this edition; they were omitted from most of the revisions of the 1908 original.
3. See Bernard Cohn, 'Representing authority in Victorian India', in Hobsbawm and Ranger (1983), pp. 165–209.
4. See the essays by David Cannadine and Eric Hobsbawm in Hobsbawm and Ranger (1983), as well as chapters 3 and 4 of Hobsbawm's recent book, *The Age of Empire, 1875–1914*. Mackenzie (1984) provides a specially useful overview of Britain, in particular.
5. I discuss some of the theoretical and political implications of colonial cultural studies, or more generally Third World cultural studies, especially in our contemporary 'post-structuralist' climate, in 'Us and Them: On the philosophical bases of political criticism' (1989).

BIBLIOGRAPHY

I have cited from the following editions of Kipling: *Kim* (Bantam Books); and *The Jungle Books* (Penguin Classics).

Arnold, David, 'European orphans and vagrants in India in the nineteenth century', *Journal of Imperial and Commonwealth History* (Vol. 7, no. 2, 1979).
Baden-Powell, Robert, *Scouting for Boys*, 34th ed (London, 1983).
Ballhatchet, Kenneth, *Race, Sex and Class under the Raj*. (London, 1980).
Barr, Pat, *The Memsahibs: the women of Victorian India* (London, 1976).
Bayly, C. A., *Indian Society and the Making of the British Empire* (Cambridge, 1988), Vol. 2.i of 'The New Cambridge History of India'.
Chaudhuri, Nupur, 'Memsahibs and motherhood in nineteenth-century colonial India', *Victorian Studies* (Vol. 31, no. 4, Summer 1988).
Cohn, Bernard, 'The census, social structure and objectification in South Asia'. In his *An Anthropologist among the Historians and Other Essays* (Delhi, 1987).
Du Bois, W. E. B., *The Souls of Black Folk* (New York, 1969).
Eliot, T. S., 'Rudyard Kipling', In *A Choice of Kipling's Verse made by T. S. Eliot* (Garden City, NY, 1962).
Gopal, S., *British Policy in India* (Cambridge, 1965).
Hobsbawm, Eric., *The Age of Empire, 1875–1914* (New York, 1987).
—— and Terence Ranger (eds), *The Invention of Tradition* (New York, 1983).
Hutchins, Francis G., *The Illusion of Permanence: British imperialism in India* (Princeton, 1967).
MacKenzie, John M., *Propaganda and Empire: the manipulation of British public opinion 1880–1960* (Manchester, 1984).
Metcalf, Thomas, *The Aftermath of Revolt: India 1857–1870* (Princeton, 1964).
Mohanty, S. P., '*Drawing the color line*', in *The Bounds of Race* H. L. Gates Jr and Dominick La Capra (eds), (Ithaca, forthcoming).
—— 'Us and them: on the philosophical bases of political criticism', *Yale Journal of Criticism* (Vol. 2, no. 2, Spring 1989). Rpt (slightly modified) in *New Formations* [London] No. 8, Summer 1989).
Moore-Gilbert, B. J., *Kipling and 'Orientalism'* (London, 1986).
Pandey, Gyan, 'A view of the observable: a positivist "understanding" of agrarian society and political protest in colonial India', *Journal of Peasant Studies* (Vol. 7, no.3, 1980).
Rosenthal, Michael, *The Character Factory* (New York, 1986).
Said, Edward W., 'Introduction', Rudyard Kipling, *Kim* (New York, Penguin Classics edition, 1987).
Stokes, Eric., *The Peasant and the Raj: studies in agrarian society and peasant rebellion. in colonial India* (Cambridge, 1978).
Wilson, Angus, *The Strange Ride of Rudyard Kipling: his life and works* (New York, 1977).

5.2

FROM 'THE ADOLESCENCE OF KIM'

Sara Suleri

As a study of cultural possession and dispossession, Kim remains one of the most disturbing narrations of nineteenth-century colonial astonishment. Much as its opening pages can make the somewhat unusual claim that 'India is the only democratic land in the world,'[1] so too the text distributes cultural surprise equally between colonizer and colonized. The protagonist embodies both aspects of such surprise, in that his status as a dispossessed colonizer is perpetually mediated by his intimacy with and filiation to the cultures of the colonized. While this mobility allows Kim to know the shocks posed by alterities from every angle of the colonial encounter, it nonetheless implies a facility that is ultimately synonymous with his victimization. Kim is either his own victim or that of the Great Game's; he either possesses the lama or is possessed by him: the ambivalence of the narrative allows for no easy resolutions of such questions, but further suggests that the position of dispossession is more primary than secondary, and that each actor on the colonial stage is complicit in it.

From the outset of a story that bases its plot on the continual exchange of misread messages, the possibility of cultural possession implies the most dangerous misreading. In keeping with an imperial intimacy that has surprise, shock, and a 'wholesome feeling of mistrust' as its inception, *Kim* opens to manifest the illegitimacy of possession. Rather than representing an archaic or an alteritist civilization to Kim, the lama is desirable because of his novelty: 'This man was entirely new to all his experience, and he meant to investigate further: precisely as he would have investigated a new building or a strange festival in Lahore city.

In *The Rhetoric of English India*, University of Chicago Press, 1992, pp. 117–31.

The lama was his trove, and he purposed to take possession' (p. 16). The amateur ethnographer, in other words, plans to own the lama's story and to recast its plot in the image of his own excitement. No mere 'adventure tale' can ensue from such an encounter, the first misread message of which implies that the novelty of difference can logically lead to possession. In the combination of the charming and the tragic that characterizes the narrative of *Kim*, the price of such a will to possess constitutes what—at the end of the text—can possibly remain of Kim.

If the initial desire for possession is transmuted by the bonds of affection and intimacy generated between this unlikely pair of questers, the novelty of this union never changes character: Kim's capacity to surprise the lama, and the lama's to surprise Kim, remain a self-repeating constant from the opening to the closing pages of the text. And the very prematurity of surprise—or its epistemological inability to process information as it is received—lends a troubling vacuity to what has been called the 'wisdom' of the novel. In his generous reading of the 'wisdom and humanity' of *Kim*, Mark Kinkead-Weekes argues for the centrality of both literal and figurative representations of vision: 'Kim also embodies the urge to obtain a deeper kind of vision, the urge not merely to see and to know from the outside, but to *become* the "other." Kim's more-than-chameleon ability to change, not only his clothes, but his voice and mannerisms, his whole identity, represents ... something far more creative and imaginative in Kipling: not merely the observer's sharp eye, but the dramatist's longing to get into the skin of many "others." Kim is an expression of what Keats called "negative capability."'[2] While indeed vision is crucial to the cinematic structure of the narrative, the suggestion of deeper visions of racial and cultural difference perhaps gives colonial history more coherence and depth than it deserves. This is by no means to deny the compassion of the text, but to posit that that colonial compassion may well be predicated on the surprise of its own futility, and that the brilliance of *Kim* lies in its ability to represent cultural multifariousness while at the same time illustrating that its historical context must inevitably lead back to the monolith of the Great Game.

Since surprise and possession are largely both the impetus and the results of the Great Game, the lama's and Kim's complicity in such states of mind causes a shifting in the text's demarcation of the parameters of power. It would be too easy a dualism to read the quest as an enclave of innocence that is somehow detached from, rather than subservient to, the experience of the Game. Whatever ideological commitment Kipling had to the supremacy of the imperial ideal, his apprehension of colonial history is too prescient to allow for such ready distinctions between the 'true' and the 'real.' Here, Edward Said's response to Kinkead-Weekes aptly characterizes the ambivalent historicity of Kipling's narrative: 'Yes, the lama is a kind of antiself, and yes, Kipling can get into the skin of others with some sympathy. But no, Kipling never forgets that Kim is an irrefrangible part of British India: the Great Game does go on with Kim a part of it, no matter how many parables the lama fashions. We are naturally entitled to read *Kim* as a novel belonging to the world's great literature ... Yet by the same token, we must not unilaterally abrogate connections *in it*, and carefully observed by Kipling, to its contemporary actuality.'[3] The historical necessity that forces Kim into the course of the Game must be interpreted; however, the lama's quest needs to be examined in equal detail. What, finally, differentiates his desire from an imperial will to create what Francis Hutchins calls the 'illusion of permanence,' or a teleology as bound to the economy of possession as it ostensibly seeks to be released from it?[4] The shock of Kipling's historicity implies that on the contrary, the lama is as much part of the Game as is Kim. While his complicity in the demands of empire are unknown to him, he functions as does Kim: both unwittingly endorse a colonial intimacy in which refinements of the modes of acquisition hardly modify the greater acquisitiveness that necessarily defines the quest that they pursue.

As has been frequently noted by readers of *Kim*, the infantilism of the lama exceeds that of his boy guide: his ostensible otherworldliness sheathes him from the routine cartography that constitutes colonial life, in which rivers are named, in which wheels have more to do with agriculture than with Buddhist mysticism, and in which the 'Middle Way' most typically represents the petty ineptitudes of colonial administration. The lama's studied blindness to such detail, however, cannot be taken as an equivalent for Kipling's equal repression of the facticity of colonial existence, for the former's very childishness can be read as a reactive strategy to address the situation of colonialism. In an acute interpretation of the infantile in Kipling's Indian narratives, S. P. Mohanty suggests that 'the separate world of childhood registers and refracts crucial political anxieties of imperial Britain';[5] the lama's absence of anxiety must be similarly read as an expression of complicity in a Game that does not signify mere espionage but provides instead a dramatic figure for the imperial enterprise. The childishness of Kim, argues Mohanty, tells 'a distinct and specifiable political story in which adventure is indistinguishable from surveillance, pleasure intertwined with power, and the values of childhood a thin allegory for imperial ideology.'[6] Such an allegory assumes a greater thickness when it becomes evident that the childhood of the lama—furthermore his concomitant understanding of colonial pragmatics—is a fiction of surprise equally balanced with a fraught economy of the Game.

Here it becomes necessary to reread the lama in terms of his interceptions in colonial reality. He subsists in post-1857 India, dimly recalling the year of the Great Rebellion as a 'black year'; he charms the would-be imperialist into a recognition of the seductions represented by a failure to recognize the mapping essential to imperial self-fashioning. While his desire to turn a blind eye to the ways of the 'great and terrible' world may be part of the lama's quaint appeal, it calls to be interpreted as a desire rather than as an actuality. Despite his insistence on the 'Middle Way,' the lama knows how to negotiate within a colonial framework, and further knows that 'acquiring merit' can be synonymous with the expedience of 'buying education.' The scene in which the lama negotiates with Mr. Bennet and Father Victor is consequently crucial to the narrative, in that it dramatically revises the lama's otherworldliness even as it effectively disrupts the texture of the novel. Until chapter 5, *Kim*'s buoyancy promises to unfold into a tale of cross-cultural male bonding: with Kim's captivity and the ensuing barter over his future, however, the narrative shifts radically into a parable of male desire and of male separation.

While it would be unnecessarily reductive to read the desire that obtains between the lama and Kim as a figure for the submerged homoeroticism that attends on colonial encounter, it would be equally injudicious to ignore the passion that describes their connection. The moment of passion, of course, is unleashed by the fact of separation, reminding the reader that for at least two-thirds of the text this connection remains in suspended animation. Once Kim has found the fetish of his father's regimental flag and has immediately toppled from a subaltern world into an imperial world, the immediacy of the lama's grief reveals more than a cursory acquaintance with the cultural and political gulf now opened between them:

> Then the lama raised his head, and looked forth across them into space and emptiness.
>
> 'And I am a follower of the Way,' he said bitterly. 'I made believe to myself . . . that thou wast sent to me to aid in the Search. So my heart went out to thee for thy charity and thy courtesy and the wisdom of thy little years. But those that follow the Way must not permit the fire of any desire or attachment . . . I stepped aside from the Way, my *chela*. It was no fault of thine. I delighted in the sight of life, the new people upon the roads, and in thy joy at seeing these things . . . Now I am sorrowful because thou art taken away and my River is far from me. It is the Law which I have broken!'
>
> 'Powers of Darkness below!' said Father Victor, who, wise in the confessional, heard the pain in every sentence. (Pp. 94–95)

Here, the jaunty quality of the picaresque is recast into confessions of a far more enduring desire, in which the vicariousness of Kim's cultural position will seduce the lama far more than his quest for the River.

The lama's acquiescence in the face of desire, however, is less remarkable than his ability to move from the idiom of mourning into that of negotiation. As is typical of the text as a whole, the transaction must be carried out through a mediating translator, emphasizing the precarious potential of misreading that dictates the transmittal of colonial messages:

> 'Do they give or sell learning among the Sahibs? Ask them,' said the lama, and Kim interpreted . . .
>
> 'And—the more money is paid the better the learning is given?' The lama disregarded Kim's plan for an early flight. 'It is no wrong to pay for learning; to help the ignorant to wisdom is always a merit.' *The rosary clicked furiously as an abacus. Then he turned to face his oppressors.*
>
> 'Ask them for how much money do they give a wise and suitable teaching? and in what city is that teaching given?' (P. 96, emphasis added)

The sale of information and the economy of colonial knowledge, in other words, is by no means beyond the ken of the 'otherworldly' lama. He not only understands the structure of oppression, but furthermore has an intuitive knowledge of the price that very literally accompanies such a reality. While Kipling allows the lama to confess to human desire and to no other sense of cultural vulnerability, this moment of rupture in *Kim* crucially reveals the old man's implication in the transactive dynamic generated by colonial rule. When he learns that he may purchase education for his 'beloved,' and when his rosary clicks as 'furiously as an abacus,' then the simile confirms synechdochically the grim thrust of chapter 5: there are no quests that live a charmed life outside the confines of colonial desire, much as the oppression of amorous loss is inevitably subsumed into the abstract oppressiveness signified by the economy of the Great Game.

That a Tibetan priest can resort to utilitarianism, however, implies the density rather than the limitation of Kipling's colonial vision. On one level, the lama's transgression of his code allows for the child a rite of passage into the adolescence of espionage; on a more disturbing level, it forces upon Kim's cultural mobility the tyrannical status of a Macaulayan 'interpreter.' In the infamous claims made by the 'Minute on Indian Education,' Macaulay justifies an Anglicist education policy for the Indian colony by anticipating the creation of a class of native informants: 'It is impossible for us, with our limited means, to attempt to educate the body of the people. We must at present do our best to form a class who may be interpreters between us and the millions whom we govern; a class of persons, Indian in blood and colour, but English in taste, in opinions, in morals, and in intellect.'[7] While Kim is initially the mirror image of such an interpreter, the pragmatics of his education as a sahib severely unhinge the confidence of his cultural transactions. His race manifests itself as an imprisonment: the lama may believe that he is purchasing the liberation of knowledge, but Kipling clearly indicates that such tutelage is merely preparatory to Kim's participation in the tyranny of the Great Game. He will be taught to interpret according to the monolithic needs of imperial ideology, which substitute the acquisition of information for nuanced readings of culture. Where Kim first looked in order to read, he is now confined to the far more imaginatively stultifying task of locating messages in order to convey them.

It is only after the paternity of race and regiment has been bestowed on Kim that the lama becomes the focus of Kim's desire. The figurative trove that the latter represented is literalized through education, forcing the potential of picaresque bonding into the static actuality of separation. In his status as 'Friend of all the World' Kim is most promiscuously sought after for adoption, which suggests that his desire is hardly for a lost parent. Instead, once Kim has been invisibly slotted into a system of message-bearing, the lama becomes the only focus for Kim's intuitive ability to read: he remains the sole territory, as it were, upon which Kim may exercise the diversity of interpretation. After the bereavement of their parting, the mediated and arduous nature of their desire to exchange information provides a brilliant figure for the repetitive intercessions that delay colonial intimacy. Here, the narrative's reliance on the dissemination of information represented by the official 'letter-writer' deftly interweaves the spoken with the written, the vernaculars with the imperial language, and the space for misreading which necessarily intrudes between them. In Benares, the lama dictates a letter—presumably in Hindi—to a letter writer with the skills to translate the message into English. Father Victor consequently receives a somewhat tangled message, which simultaneously exemplifies the urgency underlying the communication of cross-cultural desire:

> Sitting on wayside in grave meditation, trusting to be favoured with your Honour's applause of present step, which recommend your Honour to execute for God Almighty's sake. Education is greatest blessing if of best sorts. Otherwise no earthly use ... So going to Benares, where will find address and forward rupees for boy who is apple of eye, and for God Almighty's sake execute this education, and your petitioner as in duty bound shall ever awfully pray ... Please note boy is apple of eye, and rupees shall be sent per hoondie three hundred per annum. For God Almighty's sake. (Pp. 105–6)

Even though the text informs us that the plea to 'God Almighty' would have annoyed the lama had 'he known how the bazaar letter-writer had translated his phrase "to acquire merit"' (p. 108), the intrusion of the third voice quickens rather than dulls the immediacy of his desire to be read. If Kim alone can read him, the lama would be freed less of the Wheel than of the burden of cultural description. Both partners in the intimate enterprise, therefore, function as shields against the possibility of each other's misreading within the realities of the colonial framework in which they must operate. Their quest is intimately linked to the exigencies of colonial communication, as the hasty desire of Kim's epistolary response indicates. Again, a letter writer transcribes the space of voice into written discourse: 'To Teshoo Lama, the holy one from Bhotiyal seeking for a River ... in three days I am to go down to Nucklao to the school in Nucklao. The name of the school is Xavier. I do not know where that school is, but it is at Nucklao ... Come to me! Come to me! Come to me!' (pp. 117–18). Much as the letter lacks an accurate map for what will be Kim's actual geographic location, it is equally ignorant of the reasons that impel the urgency of its need. In the case of both the lama's letter to 'his oppressors' and of Kim's to the lama, the message is overwhelmed by its own impetus. And now that a mode of colonial possession no longer dictates their idiom of exchange, separation must characterize the vitality of their desire.

In the extraordinary encounter that follows this exchange of letters, the moment of meeting is indeed redefined as a recognition of loss. The lama keeps vigil for Kim outside the gates of St Xavier's School, but insists that his pilgrimage is motivated by a colonial pragmatic: 'A day and a half have I waited—not because I was led by any affection towards thee—that is no part of the Way—but, as they said at the Tirthanker's Temple, because, money having been paid for learning, that I should oversee the end of the matter . . . I had a fear that, perhaps, I came because I wished to see thee' (p. 123). Rather than function as a guide, in other words, Kim clearly represents to the lama a serious impediment to his desire for the River, or his quest to be desireless. Read as a colonial parable, this necessary denial of intimacy obliquely illustrates Kipling's disturbing vision of the psychic price demanded by a repression of colonial desire. Again, Kim proves to be the better reader of such a cost, in that he will not countenance the lama's fiction of practicality: 'But surely, Holy One, thou hast not forgotten the road and all that did befall on it. Surely it was a little to see me that thou didst come? . . . I am all alone in this land; I know not where I go nor what shall befall me . . . Do not altogether go away' (pp. 123–24). If imperial time has no memory, however, if it can read events only one at a time, then the separation it imposes lacks the luxury of recall, causing the articulation of each loss to be defined by the act of going 'altogether away.'

Cultural reading muddies single-minded motives. Thus, even as the lama assumes he is purchasing an educational space in which Kim can read, his ostensible pragmatism is shaken by the immediacy of Kim's appeal. Initially, their territories of control are very neatly demarcated, with the River being the lama's province; the Road, Kim's. With the intrusion of an imperial education, such cartography begins to lose its clarity, suggesting instead the overdetermination that underlies each will to classify. To the lama, the quest for the River is the ultimate model of classification, one that cannot readily accommodate the unclassifiability of Kim. Their second parting is as a consequence a keen refiguration of an attitude toward both cartography and classification. 'Do not weep,' the lama urges Kim, 'for, look you, all Desire is an illusion and a new binding on the Wheel. Go up to the Gates of Learning. Let me see thee go . . . Dost thou love me? Then go, or my heart cracks . . . I will come again. Surely I will come again' (p. 124). The wheel at hand will come again, for its revolutions are too bound to the functioning of a colonized time to support the lama's myth of autonomy. His need for Kim—and Kim's need for him—suggests an alternative colonial cartography upon which classification cannot occur, for the Road and River can no longer determine those proper distinctions that separate their aims. Instead, land and water meld into a new geography, both more troubling and surprising in their ability to mirror one another.

Kim's youth, of course, is the 'gate of learning' that allows for the following betrayal, and for his alacrity in adopting the glamor of the Great Game as an alternative to loving the lama. Adolescence legitimizes misremembrance: it licenses Kim to take on colonial history as though there were only messages to convey, even when they are messages most killing in their bearing. The Great Game that dictates the latter half of the text, however, knows the paucity of such colonial communication well enough to juxtapose motive, plot, and consequence with the sad desire to pose love—specific, individual love—as an alternative to colonial imbrication. His failure must register as an imperial epiphany, whereby reading is no longer a tool useful to the imperial imagination, and thus in Kipling an ineradicable example of the futility represented by empire.

To stress Kiplings intuitive apprehension of the futility of empire is by no means to imply his segregation from the realities and ideologies of imperialism, but to question instead the strange congruences between futility and belief that characterize Kipling's narrative. Much as Burke remains committed to a critique of a particular colonial practice rather than colonialism itself, similarly Kipling is able to read the details of colonial loss without necessarily proceeding to a larger abnegation of the whole. The predicament of *Kim* is precisely its democratic ability to represent a catalog of loss but to swerve into abrupt inconclusion at the very moment when such a list most evidently demands reading, reassessment, revaluation. Here, of course, the text quickens with a more intimate set of congruences, where the reader is forced to examine the replication of the narrative. Both perform necessary acts of misreading that allow them to continue to function as readers within a colonial world, and both are clairvoyantly aware of the price that remains to be exacted. This redoubling, through which character and narrator function as secret sharers in the chronology of the tale, points less to Kipling's ambivalence toward empire than to the inherent limitations that imperialism necessarily imposes on the narratives that seek to represent its chronology.

In David Bromwich's resonant reading of Kipling, these limitations are refigured into a study of what the idiom of the 'jest' signifies to Kipling's prose and poetry. Like journalism, a jest as genre accrues a certain colloquial power of contemporaneity; it is not required to resolve the conflictual surprise with which it claims closure. Bromwich plots the 'jest' of *Kim* by turning to the concluding third of the text, after Kim has been released from education and made to enter the Great Game: the action is set in the Himalayas, where the lama believes that Kim is merely following his quest for the River, whereas Kim is far more closely involved in the knowledge implied by counterintelligence. The irresolvable jest at hand, according to Bromwich, refers to the futility of any interpretive attempt to determine which belief has precedence: 'A jest (the trick that baffles the [Russian] spies by coaxing their wicked designs into the open) leads to a truth (the lama's discovery of the connection between wickedness, self, and the desire for revenge). On this view the jest that gives the story its final turn is a trial of both of the authorities that have set the plot in motion . . . The result is that both authorities are confirmed. We never learn to which of them Kim owes his first loyalty.'[8]

The jest, in other words, confirms the absence of precedence in the narrative, in ways that are illustrative of Kipling's journalistic ability to incorporate colonial dischronology into his tales. This dischronology, however, suggests its own decorum, or a sequence of immediacy that allows Kipling to claim in an 1888 article: 'You stand on the threshold of new [imperial] experiences—most of which will distress you and a few amuse. You are at the centre of a gigantic *Practical Joke*. Strive to enter the spirit of it and jest temperately.'[9] The temperate jest, or a surprise that recognizes its own mediated nature, allows *Kim* to establish those bonds of love that are not only manifested between the lama and Kim, but are further reduplicated by the peculiar reciprocity between narrative and protagonist. As Bromwich notes on the concluding 'adventure' of the novel, 'By now, the analogy between Kim and his maker ought to be clear. They are the hidden agents of a legitimate authority ... One might variously describe what they achieve by the sum of their inventions. A fair name for it, which Kipling himself was happy with, is empire.'[10] That empire may jest, however, cannot minimize its deranging power to limit the powers of reading, and it is only an acknowledgment of jest's curtailment of history that forces a retracing of Kim's trajectory. At what point does the love affair of *Kim* cease to become a colonial joke? When does a reader learn that the tragic erotics of the story have less to do with the lama and Kim than with imperial narrative and an emblem of cultural mobility? Let us return to the passion that informs the separation of the Road from the River; the young from the venerable: "The Gates of Learning" shut with a clang.'

Kipling assiduously omits to describe the education that the lama buys for Kim, and furthermore draws the reader's attention to his omission. In the quick elision of Kim's experiences within the 'gates of learning,' the narrative makes an unmistakable indication concerning the location of its audience, which by implication is situated far from the 'country-born' quality of India and thus requires cultural description in order to understand the machinery of a colonized culture:

> The country-born and bred boy has his own manners and customs, which do not resemble those of any other land; and his teachers approach him by roads which an English master would not understand. Therefore, you would scarcely be interested in Kim's experiences as a St. Xavier's boy ... His quickness would have delighted an English master, but at St. Xavier's they know the first rush of minds developed by sun and surroundings, as they know *the half-collapse that sets in at twenty-one or twenty-three*. (Pp. 124–26, emphasis added)

Here, Kipling supplies a casual but crucial anticipation of the collapsibility of Kim: in keeping his institutional education a secret from the reader, moreover, the narrative suggests that Kim's real instruction lies in the hands of Colonel Creighton, Mahbub Ali, Lurgan Sahib, and Hurree Babu, who train their 'colt' for the Great Game. The jest at hand, of course, indicates the futility of the lama's intervention, which—far from saving Kim—physically secures him for his role in the Game.

As Kim is inexorably reduced to the sum of his utility, his power as a cultural reader is simultaneously curtailed. The magical quality of his hybridity, of his ability to be one with each disguise that he assumes, is modified by the nature of the disguises that the Game requires he adopt. Much as a Macaulayan interpreter, Kim is trained to gather bureaucratically useful facts: his access to cultural 'wisdom' must necessarily be reduced to the acquisition of pragmatic information. In this context, the lama's commitment to 'acquiring knowledge' assumes the fatigued irony that is Kim's undoing, for within the parameters of the Game of colonialism, all epistemologies reduce to utilitarianism.

While it would certainly be erroneous to imply that *Kim* is intentionally an allegory of imperial education in the subcontinent, the text indeed lends itself to such an analogy. Kim's tutors fall into Orientalist and Anglicist camps, with the Anglicists clearly winning over the Orientalism that the lama represents. The text thus fictionally embodies the questions raised by Gauri Viswanathan's cogent reading of the interconnectedness between literary study and British rule in India, particularly when she observes, 'The fact that English literary study had its beginnings as a strategy of containment raises the question, Why literature? . . . What accounts for the British readiness to turn to a disciplinary branch of knowledge to perform the task of administering their colonial subjects? What was the assurance that a disguised form of authority would be more successful in quelling potential rebellion among the natives than a direct show of force?'[11] *Kim* unwittingly aligns itself to such questions by posing, in the first place, the possibility of disguise as an enchantment of cultural mobility, but then grimly collapsing such youthful fantasy into 'a disguised form of authority.' The longer Kim serves the needs of the Great Game, the more circumscribed are his abilities to interpret.

The figure of education in *Kim* thus becomes synonymous with the tautology of colonial encounter, in which the child who is already culturally fluent must be caught in order that he may learn the far more alienating idiom of cultural description. Where cultural authority was once disparate and as dialogical as Kim's delight in his various disguises, the very excesses of the Game render it localized within a colonizer's bureaucracy. Here, Edward Said's reading of colonel Creighton as the emblem of the dialogue between anthropology and colonial chronology deserves attention: 'Creighton embodies the notion that you cannot govern India unless you know India,' claims Said. 'And to know India means understanding the way it operates . . . To the government personality the main consideration is not whether something is good or evil, and therefore must be changed or kept, but whether something works or not, whether it hinders one in ruling what is in effect an alien entity. Thus Creighton satisfies the Kipling who had imagined an ideal India, unchanging and attractive, as an eternally integral part of the Empire.'[12] The stasis of such a model of cultural epistemology is in complete contrast with the readership embodied in the preeducated manifestation of Kim, and calls for further attention to his ability to transmogrify from adolescent mobility into the inflexibility represented by colonial knowledge.

What, however, of the anthropologist as journalist, of a mind ravished by the immediacy of all that colonial knowledge may signify? Under such a rubric, are the attractions of empire further reduced to an adolescent intransigence toward education, pointing to Kipling's interest in a discourse of cessation that proleptically images the language of partition at the historical moment of the most established colonial strength? Which is the idiom in which adolescence must die before it is allowed to attain the colonial maturity that Burke devoutedly desired? *Kim* suggests that the anthropology undertaken by the narrative requires even closer scrutiny than does the figure of Colonel Creighton, for Kipling in the guise of anthropologist locates highly novel forms for the moment of cultural extinction that it is his business to record. Once Kim has been released from St Xavier's, the narrative assumes an oddly deferential tone toward the child who thus far has supplied the tale with an abundance of energy. Even though Kim continues to play the Game, he is increasingly represented in the third person: in the opening chapters of the book, the reader sees the subcontinent through Kim's eyes, but in the concluding sections of the narrative, the reader is forced to cast an anthropologist's eye upon the figure of Kim.

The crucial crossing of the text consists in its swerve from the mode of journalism into anthropology, allowing for the journalistic present tense to assume a more elegiac recognition of its protagonist's unavoidable extinction. If a submerged homoeroticism impelled the initial love of surprise between the lama and Kim the latter sections of the novel redirect that passion to the relation between narrator and protagonist. As Kim learns to play the Great Game, the narrative forces us to conceive of him as a third person: 'The pallor of hunger suited Kim very well as he stood, tall and slim, in his sad-coloured, sweeping robes, one hand on his rosary and the other in the attitude of benediction, faithfully copied from the lama. An English observer might have said that he looked rather like the young saint of a stained-glass window, whereas he was but a growing lad faint with emptiness' (p. 196).

In such a visual reconfiguration, Kim has become the image of the colonizer, but one that is elegiacally mourned as passing in its prematurity. Even though the final 'adventure' of the novel returns the disciple to the alternative knowledge of his tutelary status with the lama, the passion for Kim is curiously displaced into the narrative's desire to hold him as a nonverbal object that is somewhat exempt from its subjugation to the transmittal of colonial information. After having established Kim as the inevitable victim of imperial education, in other words, Kipling seems drawn to an anthropologist's farewell to the emblem that finally reveals the classifiability of cultural dexterity. The impishness of Kim's ingenuity drops away from the verbal into the visual, so that the reader is continually reminded of his bodily presence. Whereas the preeducated Kim was both a voice and a body that commanded comfort wherever it found itself, the posteducated Kim is suddenly vulnerable to the pains of mind and body. Rather than dictate the energy of the narrative, posteducated Kim becomes the focus of the narrative's futile compassion. It is no surprise, therefore, when the crucial scene that allows the Russian spies to destroy the lama's map is envisioned from perspectives that Kim could not possibly see. 'They came across an aged lama . . . sitting cross-legged above a mysterious chart held down by stones, which he was explaining to a young man, evidently a neophyte, of singular, though unwashen, beauty' (pp. 239–40). Until this moment, Kim's beauty has been manifested by his linguistic range, or his ability to read cultures rapidly and well. His sudden elevation into an aesthetic icon, therefore, dangerously anticipates the third-person silence imposed by the education that signifies the playing of the Great Game.

The loneliness of Kim's adolescent question 'Who is Kim?' is thus transferred to the reader, who must now picture the marvelous boy as an analogy for colonial casualty. Whatever may be the journalistic enthusiasm for the present tense of colonialism, *Kim* darkly illustrates its epistemological ill-proportion. Nothing indicates its astonishing obfuscation more than the conclusion of the text, where an Anglicist narrative and an Orientalist lama collide in vying for the affections of the protagonist. The surprise of *Kim* inheres in such a battle, which the text conducts for the fealty of its protagonist: is Kim loved more by the lama or the narrator, or who more totally frames him in colonial imprisonment? As an allegory of colonial education, the conclusion of *Kim* extracts significance at the very point where it appears to confer imperial meaning.

The narrator knows that Kim must be killed. He hands the deed over to the otherworldly lama, however, with whom he remains in perpetual contestation for Kim's love. In the chilling conclusion of the book, Kim's recuperation is necessarily followed by the lama's claim that he alone constitutes the salvation of the boy: 'I meditated a thousand things, passionless, well aware of the Causes of all Things. Then a voice cried: "What shall become of the boy if thou art dead?" and I was shaken back and forth in myself with pity for thee; and I said: "I will return to my *chela*, lest he miss the way"' (pp. 287–88). Such intervention, however, is hardly passionless. Neither is the concluding sentence of the text, which once again images Kim in a magnificent moment of uncontrol: '[The lama] crossed his hands on his lap and smiled, as a man may who has won Salvation for himself and his beloved' (p. 288). Here, Kim is envisioned as the absent other that indicates the silence of classical Urdu poetry, in which the beloved has no voice at all. But it is colonial education that has silenced his voice, and demonstrated that in its adolescence is its end.

NOTES

1. Rudyard Kipling, *Kim* (London, 1901), p. 8. (Henceforth cited in the text.)
2. Mark Kinkead-Weekes, 'Vision in Kipling's Novels,' in *Kipling's Mind and Art*, ed. Andrew Rutherford (London: Oliver and Boyd, 1964), p. 217.
3. Edward Said, 'Kim: The Pleasures of Imperialism,' *Raritan* 2 (Fall 1987): 41.
4. Francis Hutchins, *The Illusion of Permanence: British Imperialism in India*, (Princeton: Princeton University Press, 1967).
5. S. P. Mohanty, 'Kipling's Children and the Colour Line,' *Race and Class* 31, no. 1 (July/Sept. 1989): 21.
6. Ibid., p. 31.
7. Thomas Babington Macaulay, 'Minute on Indian Education,' *Selected Writings*, ed. John Clive (Chicago: Chicago University Press, 1972), p. 249.
8. David Bromwich, 'Kipling's Jest,' *Grand Street* (Winter 1985): 175.
9. Rudyard Kipling, 'A Free Hand,' *Pioneer* 10 (November 1888). Quoted in Lewis D.

Wurgaft, *The Imperial Imagination: Magic and Myth in Kipling's India* (Middletown, Conn.: Wesleyan University Press, 1983), p. 129.

10. Bromwich, 'Kipling's Jest,' p. 175.
11. Gauri Viswanathan, *Masks of Conquest: Literary Study and British Rule in India*, (New York: Columbia University Press, 1989), p. 11.
12. Said, 'Kim,' p. 53.

5.3

'ORAL/LITERATE/TRANSCENDENT: THE POLITICS OF LANGUAGE MODES IN *KIM*'

Ian Adam

I General

I begin by taking three central concepts from Derrida's *Of Grammatology*,[1] the oral, the literate, and the transcendent. For Derrida their relation is not parallel but complexly asymmetrical: the oral is (mistakenly) associated in Western thought with Nature and hence and by implication also with the transcendent, while the written is (mistakenly) thought of as derivative from and inferior to the oral, a secular to its near-sacred. The truth, however, is that there is no transcendent beyond language and that the oral and the written are both conventional sign systems with no derivative relation.

Kipling's *Kim* both confirms and disconfirms Derrida's generalizations about Western thought.[2] They are confirmed in that the novel can be interpreted as a celebration of the oral in its many cultural manifestations; they are disconfirmed in that it may also be interpreted as similarly celebrating written modes. They are confirmed in that the novel endorses a transcendental principle; they are disconfirmed in that this principle is not Western but Eastern; and they are also probably disconfirmed in that it is seen not as related to Nature but as something outside and even alien to it. When the politics of these modes is considered, however, then the assessments must shift, for however favourably the oral may be regarded, it is still shown to be subject to the inevitable and desirable subsumptive control of the written; and however favourably the written is regarded, it is still reduced, equally with the oral, as part of the *maya* or illusion exposed by the transcendent.

In Andrew Gurr (ed.), *The Yearbook of English Studies*, vol. 27, London: MHRA, 1997, pp. 66–78.

Oral modes are primarily associated with the indigenous cultures of India, written ones with the imposed order of English dominion over these, and the transcendent with the Buddhist doctrine expressed through the lama. The first becomes the mode of relaxation, intimacy, ethnographic colour, expression, superstition, and antiquity; the second that of order, efficiency, enlightenment, thought, civilization, and the modern; and the third functions as an ideal reducing the others to insubstantial shadows. The modes do not exist in water-tight compartments, however; there is room enough in Kipling's sensibility for some conscious awareness of contradictions, crossovers, and problematics, as well as for some other, probably unconscious, expressions of these.

II Open Road; Open Word

The oral is seen in *Kim* as embodying life and freedom and is associated particularly with the improvisations of the open road and the sprawl of space that is the novel's India. The language of the omniscient narrator, who surveys, comments, and impels, maintains oral qualities through a variety of means, including such formal features as direct addresses to the reader, heterodoxies of typography and punctuation, and Anglo-Saxonish compoundings. Orality is reinforced through extensive dialogue, largely given vernacular effect. A very high percentage of this is through the representation of Hindi: a representation attained through such elements as the maintenance of vernacular formations, 'Indianized' English ('te-rain'), the occasional use of Hindi terms, and an abundance of folk-sayings, proverbs, and parables. Kipling here carefully discriminates among the cultural idioms of speakers, differentiating, for example, between the Islamic-rooted expressions of Mahbub Ali and the lama's Buddhist ones. Elsewhere, when English is the mode of communication, it is most frequently a 'native English', used by Kim and even more emphatically by Hurree Babu, and characterized by unidiomatic features as well as such formal departures as the omission of the article. Dialogue in standard English is relatively uncommon.[3]

The oral is also maintained through the content of the dialogue, much of which is divagatory—folkloric, anecdotal, or personal. Though the novel has classic temporal dimensions of adventure and quest in the narratives concerning the espionage against the enemies of British rule, and the lama's search for the River of the Arrow, incidental story-telling and sheer talk divert from these and contribute to its expansive structure. There are waysides *en route*: the novel has such plenitude as may be seen through the schoolboys at St Xavier's, British but also native-born, who tell their tales of adventures, 'mixed with quaint reflections, borrowed unconsciously from native foster-mothers, and turns of speech that showed they had been that instant translated from the vernacular' (p. 172); in numerous recapitulatory narratives, such as Kim's account to Mahbub of his holiday activities (pp. 177–78); or in random, associative talk without such direction, embodied perhaps especially in the widow-woman of Kulu, who speaks pell-mell

> of kinglets she had known in the past; of her own youth and beauty; of the depredations of leopards and the eccentricities of love Asiatic; of the incidence of taxation, rack-renting, funeral ceremonies, her son-in-law (this by allusion, easy to be followed), the care of the young, and the age's lack of decency. (p. 275)

When I suggest that all this represents an oral mode, however, I refer not only to the spoken word but also to elements that may be oral in quality. For the oral in *Kim* is the unequivocal symbolic, the symbolic as straightforward convention; that which is honest, direct, publicly transparent, not only through the word, but also through gestures, dress, and other symbolizations.

III Secret Signs

The novel contrasts with this another system of communication marked by concealment, in which words written and spoken, and other signs, primarily visual, are meant to convey secret messages to a select audience. In this mode what appears to be may not be that which is. I shall call this a written mode. I do so not to suggest that the languages of India had no written forms—that would be absurd—but for several other reasons. Writing is normally distinguished from speech by its capacity for distance communication, its enhanced opportunities for privacy, and its later acquisition as a formally taught skill. In these respects it is a technology privileged over speech. Kim, who formerly had to hire a scribe, recognizes some of this with delight after his third year of school, when he learns to write: he discovers, we hear, 'how men can speak to each other without a third party' (p. 173). Further, writing encourages us to think of language as a code derived from a 'natural' speech, and code in various forms, including other visual symbolizations and some oral ones, is characteristic of this mode. It is largely, though not entirely, the mode of the Secret Service, the 'Great Game' in which the Colonel (under his cover as an ethnographer) plays such an important part, and thus a major means of Imperial supervision, surveillance, and control. In its oral manifestations it approximates to a standard rather than vernacular English form.

IV Ultimate Meaning

A further, and ultimate, contrast is seen in the mode of knowing sought by the lama in his quest for the River of the Arrow, the river that gushed forth where Buddha's arrow fell to earth. In this river, says the lama, sin is washed away and 'one attains freedom from the Wheel of Things' (p. 58). According to Vasant A. Shahane, the lama is attached to the Mahayana rather than the Hinayana system of beliefs about salvation, the former placing primacy on the self, and the latter on helping kindred souls as well as self in seeking deliverance.[4] While such deliverance from suffering through a state of nirvana is ultimately ineffable, language can be a means of arrival. Both written and oral modes are so applied. A major item in this significant textuality, for example, is the lama's chart of the

Wheel of Life illustrating Buddhist doctrines of suffering and rebirth (the lama says he 'writes' its pictures (p. 240); at the time of the chart's defilement it is referred to as the 'Written Word' (p. 291). Others are oral: the lama's allegory of his relation to Kim in the story of the elephant bound by a leg-iron and ultimately freed by an orphan elephant calf he has protected is, for example, the tip of the folkloric iceberg of the *Jataka* (pp. 213–14). But the lama's openness and honesty—he never lies (p. 335)—perhaps links him most closely with the transparency of the oral.[5]

V THE RELATIONS TO IDENTITY

As might be expected, the language modes are associated with particular characters: the oral with the folk of India, the written with the British and their Indian allies, and the transcendent with the lama. However, while those associated with the written mode are shown to be at ease in the oral, the reverse is not true. Almost all, however, seem to have some understanding of the transcendent. The lama is given endearing contacts with both the oral and the written world, but an other-worldly remove of innocence is also stressed. But comprehension is one thing, identification is another. Kim and Hurree Babu move freely and easily in both the oral and the written, but of these two only Kim is granted an internalized representation. His self-consciousness about identity is virtually a refrain in the work (for example, 'I am Kim—Kim—Kim—alone—one person—in the middle of it all' (p. 273), and his oscillations between sahibism and nativism (the latter including his discipleship to the lama), which reach a culmination in his breakdown at the novel's conclusion (pp. 331–36) have often been commented on. His uncertainties are frequently emblematized through the different language modes. The discovery of his European origins encapsulates this: the leather amulet-case hanging around Kim's neck is for him an Indian charm with occult power (p. 50), but its contents, three written documents made up of two from the Masonic lodge and Kim's birth certificate, are for Father Victor and the others the evidence and legitimation of a British identity (p. 133). Kim dreams, apparently, in both English and Hindustani, but only the Hindustani is highlighted (pp. 241, 261); implicitly, it is the less abstract, more authentic mode. His initiations are similarly divided; at Lurgan Sahib's he learns (quickly, and with the assistance of the multiplication tables) to see through the *trompe-l'oeil* illusions of hypnotism as well as the *trompe-l'oreille* illusions of the phonograph, in both cases thinking first in Hindi then (with greater perspicuity) in English (pp. 202, 198–99). However, the Powers of Darkness raised by Huneefa the blind witch to make Kim Son of the Charm undermine the scientific and rational consciousness and bring a shudder to the folklore-observing Hurree Babu and, later, to Kim (pp. 226–28, 230).

VI THE RELATIONS TO DIEGESIS

The major actions of the novel correspond to the threefold language division as well, even though diegeses may become complexly tangled. In the latter section of the novel, for example, Kim the devoted *chela* is also Kim the agent with ulterior motive; this is most notably so at the point where the Russian-French incursion is finally thwarted. And it is impossible to separate the activities of the Game and the Quest from the Indian context in which they are acted out, and which, to a lesser extent, interacts with them (with Kim above, for example, in a continuing role as gamin-vagabond). But though they fuse and interact, the diegeses vary considerably in motivation and purpose, energy expended, and activity of relation to each other. The search for the Way is purposeful, but it is also spiritual, having little to do with the world it seeks to renounce, while the adventures on the road are very much of the world but, unlike the Way, serendipitous and spontaneous—picaresque, to speak generically. Only the Game is both of the world and purposeful; it is initiating and interventionist. Let me deal first, then, with the diegesis of the road.

VII The Picaresque

When Kim leaves school and re-enters the world of India, he leaves a world of relative abstraction for the concrete and varied one of India. He rejoices in his freedom; he loses himself in 'this roaring whirl of India' (p. 166); he enters, indeed, the tangible centre of the novel. As I have noted, the wanderings through India are very much of the voice in the stories they invoke or provoke, or in the talk that fills their space. This orality extends to events which are, like talk, spontaneous, uncalculated, and unplotted: a meeting with a farmer is followed by an encounter with a cobra; Kim and the lama continue on through village after village, past Umballa to the 'mile-wide green of the staple crops' (pp. 90–92) and further encounters. Walter Ong speaks of the oral's association with the body,[6] and this world of sounds, sights, textures, and tastes (food is given lingering attention) is very much of its corporeality. The novel's famous descriptions, of the Grand Trunk Road, of Lahore, Simla, or the Hills, or of the sights in the train, are sensuous, rich, and loving, as are many less well-known ones, such as the trip of the sick lama and *dooli* through the Nilang Pass. Here the processive sweep of clauses iconicizes the movement of the journey, the eye engaged with its changing vistas; we are absorbed into corporeal experience:

> in storm when the driven snow-dust filled every fold of the impassive lama's drapery; between the black horns of Raieng where they heard the whistle of wild goats through the clouds; pitching and strained on the shale below; hard-held between shoulder and clenched jaw when they rounded the hideous curves of the Cut Road under Bhagirati; swinging and creaking to the steady jog-trot of the descent into the Valley of the Waters; pressed along the steamy levels of that locked valley; up; up, and out again, to meet the roaring gusts off Kedarnath; set down of mid-days in the dun gloom of kindly oak forests. (p. 318)

Another way of putting this is to say that the oral is characterized by style: when India panoramic is the subject, language-use is rich, supple, and sensuous.

VIII The Game

I have spoken of the written mode as associated with an 'initiating and interventionist' diegesis. Such terms imply control, and control implies the comprehension of underlying abstract principles expressed in specialized symbolizations. Those of science and technology come to mind as well as that of writing and are prominently embodied in the novel in the creations of European modernity in map, telegraph, train, and ethnographic study. The relatively inaccessible principles behind these are allied with even less accessible ones in duplicitous practices of surveillance, disguise, espionage, and coding used by the Secret Service. These represent, to use Simon During's term, the order of simulacra, 'a third (very early) order of modernity'.[7] That they are in gross contradiction with the open values of the India they are designed to maintain is obvious: India is nature, spontaneous life itself, but it must be preserved as such through contrivances. Kim is shown to be almost instinctually qualified for these activities, not only through his chameleon capacity to be Indian or British, but also when, even prior to any training as a secret agent, he eavesdrops on the Colonel, learns of the military expedition, and amazes his Indian audience with his apparent gift of prophecy in forecasting war (p. 88). Later we hear that Creighton is 'a man after his own heart—a tortuous and indirect person playing a hidden game' (p. 165). Duplicity in identities is embodied in the code of the Game: Mahbub Ali is 251B and Hurree Babu R17;[8] in Chapters 11 and 12 the Mahratta (E23) and Strickland Sahib (unnumbered, as befits legend, perhaps) surface more briefly; the involvement of many others is darkly implied. Communications, like identities, are similarly deceptive: an amulet, a pause between the words 'to—look', the phrase 'Son of the Charm' (pp. 231–32)—such is the covert masked as the innocent. The written mode has, paradoxically, no style: it is removed from the comforts of direct reference; it is a trip-switch to interpretation; interpretation leads to action, event. It is, quite literally, plot.

IX The Quest

The lama tells the Curator that he seeks the River of the Arrow, and soon Kim is to join him in this quest. He seeks to do so on a 'broad and open road' (p. 57): this coincides with the material roads (and rail) by which he and Kim travel, but it also exceeds these in its spiritual dimension. Thus the transcendent, consistent with Derrida's formulation, is in *Kim* closely associated with the oral, but it is not identical with it. In a striking analysis, J. M. S. Tompkins demonstrates how the meeting-point of body and spirit, the concrete and the ineffable, is stylistically signalled in the numinous: 'A vibration spreads from the word, and at times the hard edges of multifarious bright objects quiver.'[9] She cites, for example, the Sahiba's 'jewelled forefinger' snapping out 'little sparks of light between the embroideries' of her palinquin, or the lama's farewell blessing to the hills, 'shadows blessed above all other shadows'. Past the meeting-point we encounter the language of transcendence, an oxymoron which is usually expressed in the work through such polarized abstractions as 'freedom' or the 'Great Soul' versus the 'Great Wheel' or 'illusion'.

X THE POLITICS OF THE MODES

In my opening section I suggested a dual attitude underlying the representation of language modes in *Kim*: the oral is nominally valorized over the written, but it is in fact politically subordinate to it. My analysis thus far has tended to confirm this: though India *is* the major presence in the novel, it is as such a plotless one; it may teem, babble, and even seethe, but it does not initiate. Initiative is rather the prerogative of the controlling power, whose means of control are the technologies of modernism, those secrets abstracted from Nature, including secrets of communication, which I term writerly. It was also suggested in my opening section that the transcendent mode embodied in the lama reduced both the oral and the writerly to insignificance through a cosmic perspective. However, I would now have to add a political interpretation of that perspective, for not only does the lama's spirituality reinforce the quietism of oral India, but its other-worldly counsel, equating both India and the Game as *maya*, erases awareness of the Imperial nature of the relation between them. Thus, in function if not intent, it can be argued, the lama's quest for the transcendent reinforces the politics of control.

XI THE POLITICS OF THE UNCONSCIOUS

It is certainly true that the paradigm of a passive oral India controlled by an active writerly *imperium*, with the unconscious support of a native opiate of the people, conforms to much that is obvious in the politics of the novel. It shows in particular the degree to which Kipling, like others of his contemporaries, and even now many of ours, held a conventional view of the relations between the literate, the oral, and the transcendent: that is, that the first two exist in a binary relation, and that the third is latent in the second. Elsewhere I have given considerable attention to this proposition and to the counter-arguments of Derrida and others against it;[10] suffice it to say here that they suggest a connexion that is relative, not polar, and identities of kinship rather than ones of difference. I want to argue that such a relation is operative in the political unconscious of *Kim*, that the walls the novel apparently erects between the oral and the written are not impermeable and cannot be so.

Postcolonial theory has underlined how the unconscious of canonical works is brought to consciousness in counter-discursive practices initiated by postcolonial writers.[11] *Kim* is unusual in the degree to which it draws attention to its own unconscious, and, as described, it does so most strikingly in the figure of Kim himself, caught between an Indian identity and a British one. As Robert F. Moss points out, 'most critics have found it impossible to discuss the book without focusing on Kim's schizophrenia'.[12] As often noted, Kim has three crises of identity at critical junctures in the work;[13] the diegeses of Game and Quest, implicating him, create another, which is that psychological dimension. In Kim, in other words, we have the troubled meeting-point between the oral and the written made manifest. The history of the criticism of the novel suggests such a troubled encounter not only within Kim but also within the novel overall. Some, such as Mark Kinkead-Weekes or Abdul JanMohamed,[14] sense a subversive or at least authentic liberal element in the work, while those who disagree with such readings, such as Said (pp. 21–22) or Patrick Williams,[15] nevertheless find their position less than self-evident and feel compelled to come to terms with those who differ from them. Zohreh Sullivan, in *Narratives of Empire*, gives a very critical account of Kipling's engagement with imperialism, but even she notes an 'ideological contradiction' in the representation of India: that although 'political conflict may literally be absent in his novel',

> In some scenes natives swear to their reliance on the benevolence of colonial government, and the lama would, it seems, perish without Kim's care. Yet, in other scenes the reverse seems true; the lama pays for Kim's education, gets on splendidly without Kim, and India itself appears to be a land of generous plenty that can take care of itself and of Kim.[16]

There are other meeting-points and permeations, less obvious perhaps, bute-qually marked by contradictions, transvaluations, latencies and contaminations.

XII LATENCIES

I want to deal with several instances of these, and begin with some minor ones. I have mentioned how Kim recites the multiplication tables during his initiation with Lurgan Sahib, and how this Western rational mode preserves him from delusion by way of archaic deceptions. But the *recitation* of the tables is talismanic, oral, just as, conversely, 'oral' hypnotism is a non-archaic product, through Charcot and Freud, of modernity's medical interventions. Kim is, of course, a true threshold figure, representing many worlds: through Chapters 7 and 8, for example, he assumes the identities of low-caste Hindu, Muslim, and Eurasian, and one might therefore ask how this person who delights in disguise can yet be seen as part of the open and oral, especially when such an aptitude is shown to be not a product of British training but innate and presumably native. One might similarly raise an eyebrow at Kipling's implicit suggestion that the Masonic lodge (with all its hocus-pocus) is at one with the modernist project. And though I have argued for passivity as a dominant quality in Kipling's account of Indian society, the novel is empirically faithful to the fact that it has been anything but historically inert. We are seldom far from icons of conflict, passage, and achievement, from the 'green-bronze piece' of the opening paragraph, a reference to the tax imposed by the Muslims in their 1757 conquest of Lahore, to the Sikh wars (p. 101), or to Kabir's fifteenth-century Hindu reform movement (p. 300). Further, such activity is not merely a thing of the past: the Game depends upon its Other in the foreign powers of France and Russia (India's enemy being not imperialism but other imperialisms) but also in disreputable allies, such as thieves, prostitutes, and corrupt maharajahs, drawn from the Indian population. These operate according to the same agendas of secrecy and concealment as have been positively associated with the Secret Service and the written mode, though, of course, they are implicit rather than dramatized, and always finally foiled. Echoing Said and others, Sullivan has suggested political conflict to be literally absent from the novel (see n. 16), but the fact is that it is very much present. What seems to be absent is the case to be made for the opposition. This is particularly notable in the novel's representation of the Great Mutiny of 1857, for here absence becomes dismissal: the Mutiny is characterized, through the words of the old soldier, as 'madness' (p. 100). Said rightly notes the tendentiousness of this reduction (pp. 26–28), but the novel is not entirely consistent on the question of madness (the lama's quest would be madness in the eyes of some, a view expressed by Mahbub (p. 221) and exploited by Kim (p. 97). I want to turn to two examples which, if they do not quite represent madness, do represent related states of disorder in the uncanny, the aberrant, or the unnatural.

XIII CONTAMINATIONS

The first concerns the sequence of events that leads Kim to the discovery of his British identity (or, to be more accurate, parenthood): the events, in other words, that enable the novel. Let me summarize these. Kim, impish, streetwise urchin, makes a chance acquaintance with a wandering lama who seeks the River of the Arrow; the lama sees in him a *chela* to replace one who has fortuitously died and Kim, accepting this role, speaks of his own quest for a Red Bull in a green field in accordance with his father's prophecy (p. 64); they set out for Benares and *en route*, after several adventures, encounter, out of all of India, a military regiment bearing the very emblem of the Red Bull Kim is seeking exercising in a green field. Kim prowls about the camp in the evening and is (uncharacteristically) apprehended; his identity is revealed through the secrets contained in an amulet hanging from his neck. This is the work, says Father Vincent repeatedly, of the 'Powers of Darkness' (pp. 133, 135); and the reader, mindful of Mahbub Ali and the lama as the two men of the prophecy 'making ready the ground for these matters' (p. 50) experiences additional confirmation. Though the novel's order of modernity is such as to frame the 'magical' with rational explanation of the same—consider the treatment of Kim's prophecies of war, which are seen as supernatural by his audiences but which are the result of his eavesdropping on the Colonel (pp. 94–97)—there is no such tempering or ironizing of these events. They show, of course, that God (with the assistance of Freemasonry) is on the British side, but they also show a need for validation and authenticity that is anterior to and unavailable from multiplication tables, codes, and writing. A presence, so to speak, outside the text but latent in the Word; a contamination by the oral or, perhaps, Oral. The 'Powers of Darkness' (the phrase is also used, incidentally, in connection with Huneefa (p. 228)) here represent a border-crossing into a dark transcendent.

My second illustration is not diegetic but local. Hurree Babu has infiltrated the French-Russian camp, posing as agent for 'his Royal Highness, the Rajah of Rampur' and has insinuated himself with great skill into the confidence of the enemies of the state. They speak of him: 'He is like the nightmare of a Viennese courier', says the Frenchman, and the Russian replies: 'He represents in little India in transition—the monstrous hybridism of East and West' (p. 288). Once Indian but now neither Indian nor English, fallen from purity, a contaminated product. If the events leading to Kim's becoming Kimball O'Hara partake of the sacred, Hurree's identity as defined here partakes of corruption. The description is, of course, overtly ironic in context: the enemy agents who patronize him so are in fact being deceived by Hurree, who is playing the part of the eccentric Bengali; but it can also be seen as partly sustained by his representation in the novel. One way of highlighting this would be to examine Hurree in relation to the hybrid who is his *alter ego*: Kim. For Kim, like Hurree, is a master of dissimulation and disguise; like Hurree, he is quick-witted and resourceful; like Hurree, he represents the merging of East and West. He is asymmetrical with Hurree, however, in privilege: in his education at a school from which Indians (though not Anglo-Indians) are excluded, in his blood-line (a necessary condition for the education), and in the opportunities for advancement which these will generate.

All these are signified by one overriding token, that of language. Kim's speech can be equated with Hurree's, but there are differences. Kim's lacks Babu's hypertrophy of expression and, as the novel progresses, is clearly adopted by Kim out of choice rather than necessity; there is every indication that he will accommodate himself comfortably to standard form. But Hurree's English idiom is apparently fixed as a deformed, 'monstrous' departure:

> I do not like the South—too much railway travel; but I drew good travelling allowance. Ha! Ha! I meet our mutual at Delhi on the way back. He lies quiett just now, and says Saddhu-disguise suits him to the ground. Well, there I hear what you have done so well, so quickly, upon the instantaneous spur of the moment. I tell our mutual you take the bally bun, by Jove!' (pp. 268–69)[17]

Graham Tulloch's important article discusses Hurree as an enigma, asking not 'Who is Kim?' but 'Who is Hurree Babu?' In particular, Tulloch notes that Babu's deceptiveness is of such an order that it leaves Kim in awe; there is something, in a word, unaccountable in Hurree. This leaves open a possibility, he suggests, that Hurree really does have command of standard English, though this is never dramatized. But even more significantly, he argues, Hurree is an extreme example of what the novel anticipates generally: an Indian standard English. Kipling 'seems [...] to recognize that British English is not fully adequate to describe India: his own narrative language implies that the development of a special Indian literary variety of English will be necessary' (p. 46). That 'special Indian literary variety of English' is now a matter of debate,[18] but at least one major novel, *All About H. Hatterr* (1945),[19] full of such floridities, has been created in it, and at least one earlier study has noted the novel's connection to Hurree.[20] The politics of contamination may be transvalued to a revolutionary politics.

XIV De-Sacrilization

Tulloch also implicitly raises the issue of simulacra, the basis of the Game. If identity can be assumed and the authentic be in fact the inauthentic, who is to say where the acting will end? To release simulacra as a means of control is to release a contamination into the purity of the indigenous; it is to muddy its limpidity. The written culture is introduced into the oral, and no power can prevent its technologies being turned against their authors.[21] One of the ruses used by Hurree to ingratiate himself with the French and Russian agents is that of an opponent of British rule with 'a most complete hatred of his conquerors' (p. 288):

> He became thickly treasonous, and spoke in terms of sweeping indecency of a Government which had forced on him a white man's education and neglected to supply him with a white man's salary. He babbled tales of oppression and wrong until the tears ran down his cheeks for the miseries of the land. (p. 286)

It is not quite accurate to state (as I have done above) that the novel does not contain a case for the opposition, for there is one here. One has to accept it as ironized (but there is a lingering doubt: does Hurree really believe in salary differentials based on 'race'? The question is unanswerable). The point is, however, that such language in its content has as much revolutionary potential from a political point of view as the style of Hurree's English has from a literary one. For if Hurree's stylistic descendant is the G. V. Desani who brings verbal riot into the contact zone, his political one is T. N. Murari, author of *The Imperial Agent*, who takes Hurree's *Doppelgänger*, Kim, past his irresolute or at least unresolved position at the novel's conclusion, into the cause of Indian independence.[22]

XV The Madness of the Lama

Let me conclude with a further reassessment of the lama. While his world-view is certainly quietistic, it may be a Western bias to see such passivity as politically impotent. It certainly would seem to be so ironically in the light of the non-violent Gandhian contributions to Indian history. Indeed, the lama's cyclical view of history as expressed in the images of the Wheel of Life (suffering humanity engaged in futile pursuit of illusion) does not seem that different *in function* from that expressed by Rao in *Kanthapura* (1938). There, too, the European incursion is relativized as an illusory blip of dominance against a backdrop of Eastern myth.[23] Helen Tiffin has argued for this relativization as a representative post-colonial response to imperial history;[24] viewed in this light the lama's language of transcendence is very arguably a model of non-Western political insight. It may be that in reading *Kim* we have first of all to assess the politics of our own first—and easy—readings.

NOTES

1. Jacques Derrida, *Of Grammatology* (Baltimore, MD: Johns Hopkins University Press, 1976).
2. Rudyard Kipling, *Kim* (1901) ed. with an introduction and notes by Edward W. Said (London: Penguin, 1987). All subsequent references are to this edition.
3. I am indebted to two studies for details in this paragraph: David H. Stewart, 'Orality in Kipling's *Kim*', in *Rudyard Kipling's Kim*, ed. by Harold Bloom (New York: Chelsea House, 1987), pp. 101–12, and Graham Tulloch, 'Voices of the Raj: Linguistic Diversity in *Kim*', in *Raj Nostalgia: Some Literary and Critical Implications*, ed. by Annie Greet, Syd Harrex, and Susan Hosking (Adelaide: Centre for Research in the New Literatures in English, 1992), pp. 35–46.
4. *Rudyard Kipling: Activist and Artist* (Carbondale: Southern Illinois University Press, 1973), p. 66.
5. It is tempting to see political significance in Kipling's selection of a Buddhist lama as representative of India; this, after all, is very much out of keeping with the Hinduism of the majority of Indian people. However, I finally think this would be wrong. It is true, interestingly, that Hinduism is not very prominent in the novel—Islam and Jainism are more so—but, as Kim's encounter with the Hindu Holy Man in Chapter 11 suggests, the lama's quest for a transcendent finds echoes in the quests of Hinduism (the terms 'way' and 'one', used by the Lama, are also used by the Hindu, with similar meaning). And while this identification might understandably be disputed by scholars, Indian peoples of all faiths recognize the lama as holy. Chauduri does a good analysis of possible reasons behind Kipling's choice of a Buddhist and Tibetan rather than a Hindu and Indian mentor for Kim. He notes some Hindu and Christian elements in the presentation of the lama, and seems to suggest Kipling was unaware of such inconsistencies: see Nirad C. Chaudhuri, 'The Finest Story About India: In English', in *Rudyard Kipling: The Man, His Work and His World*, ed. by John Gross (London: Weidenfeld and Nicolson, 1972), pp. 27–36 (pp. 34–35).
6. *Orality and Literacy: the Technologizing of the Word* (London: Methuen, 1982); see particularly pp. 71–74 on 'The Interiority of Sound'.
7. 'Waiting for the Post: Some Relations Between Modernity, Colonization and Writing', in *Past the Last Post: Theorizing Post-Colonialism and Post-Modernism*, ed. by Ian Adam and Helen Tiffin (Brighton: Harvester-Wheatsheaf; Calgary: University of Calgary Press, 1990), pp. 23–45 (p. 37).
8. There is an interesting distinction between Mahbub and Hurree: Mahbub is not what he appears to be, but he is never in actual disguise, while Hurree frequently is: is the Pathan to be coded the more authentically Indian?
9. *The Art of Rudyard Kipling* (London: Methuen, 1959), p. 28.
10. See my 'Oracy and Literacy: A Post-Colonial Dilemma', *Journal of Commonwealth Literature*, 31.1 (1996), 97–109.
11. See Helen Tiffin, 'Post-Colonial Literatures and Counter-Discourse', *Kunapipi*, 9.3 (1987), 17–34; Stephen Slemon, 'Monuments of Empire: Allegory/Counter-Discourse/Post-Colonial Writing', *Kunapipi*, 9.3 (1987), 1–16.
12. 'Kipling's Triumph: The Double Boyhood of Kimball O'Hara', in Bloom, pp. 87–100 (p. 87).
13. On the train with Creighton on his way to the British school at Lucknow (p. 166); just after being made 'Son of the Charm' by Huneefa and about to join the lama again (p. 233) and, after foiling the Russians and French, recuperating from his illness (p. 331). There are other points where questions of identity are raised, though not so intensely.

14. Mark Kinkead-Weekes, 'Vision in Kipling's Novels', in *Kipling's Mind and Art*, ed. by Mark Rutherford (London: Oliver and Boyd, 1964), pp. 197–235; Abdul JanMohamed, 'The Economy of Manichean Allegory: The Function of Racial Difference in Colonialist Literature', *Critical Inquiry*, 12 (1985), 59–87.
15. '*Kim* and Orientalism', in *Kipling Considered*, ed. by Phillip Mallett (New York: St Martin's Press, 1989), pp. 33–55 (pp. 33–35 and passim).
16. Zohreh T. Sullivan, *Narratives of Empire: The Fiction of Rudyard Kipling* (Cambridge: Cambridge University Press, 1993), p. 168.
17. Kipling very nicely distinguishes between Hurree's English and his Hindi, which is 'correct': see, for example, pp. 270–71.
18. Tulloch, pp. 44–46.
19. G. V. Desani, *All About H. Hatterr* (New York: McPherson, 1986).
20. Syd Harrex, 'The Game and the Goal: Kipling, Forster and the Indian English Novel', in Greet, Harrex, and Hosking, pp. 75–93 (pp. 90–91).
21. This line of argument is generally consistent with Homi Bhaba's in 'Signs Taken for Wonders: Questions of Ambivalence and Authority under a Tree Outside Delhi, May 1817', *Critical Inquiry* 12 (1985), 144–65. However, Bhaba does not deal with fictional representations of mimics, much less ones presented by imperialist apologists.
22. T. N. Murari, *The Imperial Agent: The Sequel to Rudyard Kipling's 'Kim'* (New York: St Martin's Press, 1989).
23. Raja Rao, *Kanthapura* (New York: New Directions, 1967).
24. 'Post-Colonialism, Post-Modernism and the Rehabilitation of Post-Colonial History', *The Journal of Commonwealth Literature*, 23 (1988), 169–81.

PART 6
JAMES JOYCE:
ULYSSES

INTRODUCTION

Joyce's novel was published in the year that Ireland was partitioned: 1922. Rooted in Dublin, which Joyce described as the second city of the British Empire, *Ulysses*' concern with 'racial' identity and xenophobia, nationalism and anti-colonialism, has long been commented upon within critical studies, yet books have appeared only recently with the focus of Vincent Cheng's *Joyce, Race and Empire* and Emer Nolan's more trenchant and indeed nationalistic *Joyce and Nationalism* (cf. Declan Kiberd's assertion in one introduction to the novel that 'Joyce believed that a writer's first duty might be to insult rather than to flatter national vanity ... [and] saw himself as a national rather than a nationalist patriot').[1] The influence of Edward Said's work and of post-colonial studies is found in obvious places, as in Cheng's section on Orientalist discourses in *Ulysses* (pp. 169–84), but also across the range of work on Joyce, which is now almost as likely to reference the novel's representation of black or Jewish identity as the Land League and the Easter Rising.

It is also true that modernism's debt to the colonial project, so clear in the rise of the realist novel, has been increasingly foregrounded in recent work. David Trotter has argued that modernism had two motives: the desire to establish artistic thresholds and the drive to exploit new subject matter thrown up by the speed of 'economic, political, and social change'.[2] The forces behind both the desire and the drive were not generated predominantly let alone exclusively within Europe, however; Ashcroft, Griffiths and Tiffin representatively argue that many of the various forms of literary experimentation at the turn of the century were products of 'the discovery of cultures whose aesthetic practices and cultural models were radically disruptive of the prevailing European assumptions'.[3] The confrontation with African art, Indian philosophy and the alternative aesthetic principles of non-Western countries led to a rejuvenation of European culture but also infused the crisis represented by modernism in European colonialism, as social, national and religious certainties, weakened by new movements predicated upon gender and class, were also being undermined by exposure to a colonial Other.

Much recent analysis has also been concerned with Joyce's, Ireland's and *Ulysses*' position in terms of Imperialism and First/Third World divisions. This has often concentrated on issues of liminality: the threshold occupation of a both/and identity of the Irish as colonised Europeans, as Imperial insiders and outsiders. The frustration and ambivalence of such a position is present at the end of Joyce's short story 'Araby', in which a romantic young Dubliner finds his reverential dream of the almost-sacred Oriental bazaar brought down to earth by the taint of economic and linguistic colonial corruption he senses before the English stallholders at the Royal Dublin Society showgrounds.

From another perspective, and with an eye on the formal experimentations of the turn of the century, Fredric Jameson argues in an important essay that imperialism is not found in modernism in the obvious places (symbolism, content, representation and so forth) but in its use of space.[4] He discusses Imperial mapping in Forster's *Howards End* and in *Ulysses*, finding throughout Joyce's text an in-between spatialised modernism appropriate to a writer who has moved away from the Imperial metropolis but who is not relocated in the 'Third World'. More broadly, the book's engagement with English occupation in its early chapters, its various perspectives on nationalism and ethnic identity in the middle chapters, and its constant toying with racial representations and colonial allusions, make *Ulysses* as rich a text for post-colonial analyses as it has proved for other critical approaches.

In the essays below, Carol Schloss, in 'Molly's Resistance to the Union: Marriage and Colonialism in Dublin, 1904', reads Anglo-Irish politics at the turn of the century through Molly Bloom's monologue in the 'Penelope' section at the end of *Ulysses*. A feminist reading of the novel, Schloss's argument considers the relation between imperial and gender oppression by asking how the institution of marriage in Ireland was affected by the country's position as a colonial nation.

David Lloyd, in an extract from *Anomalous States: Irish Writing and the Post-Colonial Moment*, considers the role of adulteration (Lloyd's term for hybridity but incorporating notions of modification, contamination, miscegenation and other fusings) in Irish literature and in *Ulysses* in particular. Lloyd contends that 'adulteration', sexual and 'racial', is the constitutive anxiety of an Irish nationalism which both fears contamination and accuses the nation of it. By contrast, Irish writing from street ballads through to Joyce has been heterogeneous, parodic, assimilating and characterised by this 'adulteration'. Such strategies are opposed to nationalist constructions but also to imperial identifications, and they constitute an anti-colonial resistance. It is *Ulysses*' hybrid position that makes it a contested object of persistent political struggles over meaning. For Lloyd, it is the text's ambiguity between imperialism and post-colonial nationalism which makes it so contentious but which also makes it disruptive of fixed identities, whether promulgated by imperialist or nationalist ideologies.

The extract from Vincent Cheng's *Joyce, Race and Empire* is from the section entitled '"What is a Nation?" Nationalism, Ireland, and "Cyclops"' and considers, in the light of theories by Benedict Anderson and Homi Bhabha, the way in which the Citizen and others imagine the Irish nation, in distinction from Bloom's questioning of nationalism from his marginalised position.

Finally, Declan Kiberd's 'James Joyce and Mythic Realism' sees *Ulysses* as an anticipation of later post-colonial writings. He situates it as a polyphonous, multicultural text, without final authority, anchored by no convictions of generic, narratorial or authorial integrity. The novel's treatment of (anti-realist) mythology and (anti-)colonialism anticipates magic realism in its easy yet strained conjunction of pre-modern beliefs with the formation of the nation state, however 'insufficiently imagined'. The novel, amongst many other things, amounts to a rebuttal of the colonisation of the English language and the usurpation of oral traditions by written literature, such that Joyce, like Homer, invents a tradition for himself.

NOTES

1. Emer Nolan, *Joyce and Nationalism*, London: Routledge, 1995. Declan Kiberd, 'Introduction', *Ulysses*, Harmondsworth: Penguin, 1990, p. xiii–xiv.
2. David Trotter, *The English Novel in History, 1895–1920*, London: Routledge, 1993, p. 290.
3. Bill Ashcroft, Gareth Griffiths and Helen Tiffin, *The Empire Writes Back*, London: Routledge, 1989, p. 156.
4. Fredric Jameson, 'Modernism and Imperialism', in Seamus Deane (ed.), *Nationalism, Colonialism, and Literature*, Field Day Minneapolis: University of Minnesota Press, 1990.

6.1

'MOLLY'S RESISTANCE TO THE UNION: MARRIAGE AND COLONIALISM IN DUBLIN, 1904'

Carol Schloss

What can James Joyce's character, Molly Bloom, tell us about Anglo-Irish politics at the turn of the century? If we agree with M. M. Bakhtin that the 'internal politics of [a novel's] style (how the elements are put together) is determined by its external politics (its relation to alien discourse)' (284), then it is interesting to ask what elements of Molly's soliloquy at the end of *Ulysses* can act as indexes of the external political situation of women in Dublin in 1904. A soliloquy is not a dialogue, but it can be a form of responsive speech that reacts to and reflects upon other relationships. Seen dialogically, Molly's knowledge, her silence, her biases, and her dissatisfactions can all signal much more than they might if we considered them in isolation. Even her relationships with men can reveal something about the conjugal suppression of Irish women in 1904 as well as the more general civil suppression of the Irish under George Wyndham's Unionist government during this part of her lifetime.

Not surprisingly, Ireland's status as a colonial nation, with England playing 'the predominant partner' in the Empire, affected the institution of marriage within Ireland where questions of autonomy within partnership could also be at issue. We might say that the Irish nationalist drive toward Home Rule in the early 1900s left its mark on the ideas of individual men and women who were faced in the private sphere with home rule issues of their own: to what extent did one cooperate in the success of one's marriage, actively sorting out the differences between reciprocal obligations, legitimate grievances, and oppression? At what point and in what ways did one withdraw from or protest the

Modern Fiction Studies, 35:3, Autumn 1989, pp. 529–41.

inequitable demands of union? Ultimately Molly's rambling thoughts and reflections raise a question that is central to all people to whom effective political self-definition is denied: what strategies of resistance can be used when the means of redressing perceived inequities are not immediately at hand?

At first this seems to be a particularly elusive question to answer, for Molly Bloom gives the impression of being apolitical and even hostile to the problems of collective life. She disparages Mrs Riordan for having 'too much old chat in her about politics' (*U* 738), and although we could read this as a mark of her unhappiness about Mrs Riordan's former intimacy with Bloom, Molly insists on separating herself from women who speak their minds in public: 'Miss This Miss That Miss Theother lot of sparrowfarts skitting around talking about politics they know as much about as my backside' (762).[1] Priding herself on knowing 'more about men and life when I was 15 than theyll all know at 50' (762), she turns her attention to the lover who has just left her, to the idiosyncracies of her husband and to memories of girlhood, courtship, and the early years of her marriage.

Despite these disclaimers, Molly Bloom is not without knowledge of political life, and, in fact, it is often dislike of what she knows that turns her back to the private sphere and into its implicit possibilities for change and renewal. 'I hate the mention of politics' (748), she repeats as she goes into the details of war in the Transvaal: 'Pretoria and Ladysmith and Bloemfontein where Gardener Lieut Stanley G 8th Bn 2d East Lancs Rgt ... they could have made their peace in the beginning ... the old Krugers go and fight it out between them instead of dragging on for years killing' (748–749). It is only later that we learn that Gardner was someone she had once known who was killed in South Africa.

Other parts of her political awareness seem to have come either from reading newspapers (she mentions *The Irish Times*, *Lloyd's Weekly News*, *Freeman's*, *Photo Bits*, and *The Gentlewoman's Chronicle*) or from conversations with her husband about everything from Christ's status as the first socialist (742) to British field marshal Sir Garnet Wolseley's maneuvers at Khartoum in the Sudan (757). Her most recurrent thoughts are those that deal with problems closer to home which both originate with Bloom and take issue with his assessment of them. At one point she remembers that 'all the Doyles said he was going to stand for a member of Parliament O wasnt I the born fool to believe all his blather about home rule and the land league ... [and] rigmaroling about religion and persecution' (771).

At another time, she speaks about Arthur Griffith, whose newspaper articles about 'The Resurrection of Hungary' were appearing in *The United Irishman* in 1904. Griffith had written these essays to suggest a parallel between the Hungarians, who had used a unified passive resistance to secure their independence from the Austrian Empire, and the Irish, who might use a similar pacifism as an alternative to the physical force policy of the Irish Republican Army or the cooperative incremental policy of the Irish Parliamentary Party (O'Neal 49). Bloom, as we know from his musings during the day, concurs with Griffith, and rumor has it that 'Bloom gave the idea for Sinn Fein to Griffith' (335; 436). It is through her husband's eyes that Molly sees him: 'he says that little man he showed me without the neck is very intelligent the coming man Griffith is he' (748).

But these instances of specific political knowledge do not negate the generally private nature of Molly's thought during the night. She remains primarily concerned with men, with issues of relationship, and with a sense of being that is firmly rooted in the body. Never unaware of the husband who is sleeping 'upside down' beside her, her thoughts return to him, to the sexual experience she has just had with Blazes Boylan, and to the significance of her own behavior. Her memories bring pleasure as well as dissatisfaction, and, indeed, it is the interplay between these poles of feeling that lends Molly's reveries special interest. For in her rambling assessment of her situation, we can see a pattern of response, which far from being irrelevant to the Irish political situation, acts as a gauge for it. Although private and public remain separate domains in Molly's consciousness, it is nonetheless true that her sensitivity to the issues of authority, privilege, and financial dependence in her relationships with men corresponds with sentiments held by Irish nationalists in their dealings with England. Both women in marriage and the Irish population in thrall to a colonial government faced a kind of benevolent paternalism that sought to disguise the internal contradictions of union in the language of equity and concern. For both groups, responses to domination had to be forged without any general agreement about what constituted an effective strategy of resistance or even a consensus about how to articulate grievances clearly. 1904 found both groups disorganized and emerging out of silence, poised before the 'speech act' of 1916 when the Easter Rising made clear the limits of nationalist patience and before the long road to female suffrage, which was not effectively organized until the Irish Women's Franchise League (I.W.F.L.) was formed in 1908.

The social and legal parameters of Molly's life would have been shaped by George Wyndham who, in 1904, had been Chief Secretary in Ireland for four years. The friend and successor of Gerald Balfour, he believed that the policy that he inherited could be 'progressively developed' (O'Halpin 24). He focused his attention on the land issue, on the demand for university education for Catholics, and somewhat later, on bureaucratic reorganization and the 'devolution' of political power to local boards. Like the Balfours, he believed that the reason for Irish restlessness within the Empire lay in a series of widespread social and economic grievances; and, like them, he believed that disposing of or 'ameliorating' these grievances would guarantee acquiescence in the union.

Balfour's most famous (notorious) statement of purpose had been produced in 1895 for a *National Review* symposium on 'Unionist Policy for Ireland.' It was here that he generated the phrase 'kill[ing] home rule with kindness' to describe the intentions of his party:

> I do not for a moment suggest that that implies that the majority of the Irish people have lost their desire for home rule. On the contrary, I have not the slightest doubt that, if they had to vote again on the subject tomorrow, they would again vote for home rule as they voted for it at the last election ... We should be glad enough, no doubt, to kill home rule with kindness if we could, but, whatever may be the result of our efforts, our intention is to do our utmost to introduce and pass such measures as will really promote the interests of the material prosperity of Ireland. (*The Times*, 17 Oct. 1895, cited in Gailey 35)

Although his statement clearly distinguished between the innate rightness of his remedial measures (they will 'promote the interests of the material prosperity of Ireland') and the intent to 'kill' Home Rule, it was the phrase itself that was decontextualized and remembered by nationalists and unionists alike. Wyndham knew that the heart of Balfour's strategy had been 'coercion and conciliation,' that is, that he had tackled the root economic causes of unrest in Ireland while dealing severely with disorder. Although he modified the balance of Balfour's plan, leaning more on concession than on force for the containment of disorder, he essentially carried forward the practical commitments and political philosophy of his predecessor. Both men were imperialists who believed fervently in the moral rightness of the British Empire.

Judging the greatest agitation in Ireland to be provoked by the issues of land ownership, Wyndham first turned his attention in 1901 to major land reform. In doing this, he was opposing party feeling in Britain, where issues of law and order were more popular than the '"invisible" economic measures of official policy' (Gailey 176). He was in turn opposed by the Irish Parliamentary Party which, 'spurred on by the United Land League [U.I.L.] on its flank, indulged in obstructive tactics not seen since Parnell's heyday' (177). Writing to the editor of *The Spectator*, a Professor Dicey of Magee College expressed British sentiments when he observed that 'it is the merest delusion that we can keep on friendly terms with nationalists. There must be fighting and incessant fighting, though the fight must be carried on fairly' (178). Wyndham was fully aware of these English attitudes, but he felt that relentless coercion would throw Redmond's Parliamentary Party fully to the U.I.L. and in the end strengthen his Irish opposition. Consequently, he stalled on implementing coercive measures, but by 1902 the British cabinet had compelled him to put the Crimes Act into effect, 'proclaiming' fully half the country including Dublin (182). What he feared happened, for the alienated Irish withheld their support of his first land bill which had to be withdrawn from Parliament.

This stalemate was partially resolved by changes in government personnel: Arthur Balfour became Prime Minister; C. T. Ritchie took over the Irish Office of the Treasury, and Anthony MacDonnell became his new undersecretary. MacDonnell, a forty-year veteran of the Indian civil service, not only shared Wyndham's imperialist perspective but was also an expert on land reform and famine prevention. He seemed a superb ally to have at this moment, for he had already dealt successfully with the problems that faced Wyndham in Ireland, a 'cycle of famine, popular agitation and political terrorism' (Gailey 184). Together they reapproached the British cabinet to urge its support for land reform, tax relief, and a Catholic university as the basis for future Irish loyalty to the Empire.

When John Shawe-Taylor called for a conference of landlord and tenant representatives in 1902, Wyndham saw this as an opportunity to win back his initiative in Irish politics. When John Redmond (I.P.P) and William O'Brien (U.I.L.) also came out in support of such a conference, Wyndham felt, once again, that the 'land war' in Ireland could be settled definitely. By 1903 negotiations over the legal and financial terms of the bill were accomplished: essentially the imperial Treasury would make up the difference between what the tenant could pay and what the landlord could afford. With this, the land structure of rural Ireland was transformed.

This abbreviated account of land reform in 1903 leaves out the intricacies of persuading the cabinet, the Treasury, and the party to act together, but it does let us see a structure of decision-making and a concomitant set of social attitudes. For this plan to work, the Chief Secretary had to usurp some of the Treasury's authority for financing Irish programs, but he remained antagonistic to any Irish attempts to wrest authority for self-governance from him.

Although there was undoubted good will and British consensus involved in this piece of legislation, Wyndham never forgot that the ultimate goal of such reform measures was the acquiescence of the Irish to beneficent British rule. He did not really want the cooperation of the two countries as partners with full parity, but he saw the measure, instead, as a sign that the Irish would henceforth consider the Castle a 'remedial and beneficent instrument' (Gailey 187) responsible to Irish needs and would cease to press for independent decision-making powers. 'Ireland is in a plastic state,' he wrote to Balfour on 4 November 1903. 'We can mould her almost at will provided that we go on doing something over here. We must give the Irish something sensible to think about and work for. Otherwise they relapse into a position of being mere pawns in a game between rival politicians' (quoted in Gailey 198).

His predictions about future consensus proved to be wrong—both because he had not fully quieted the Irish opposition (Michael Davitt, for example, remained against the bill) and because his future dealings with his own under-secretary on the 'devolution issue' (which came to a head in 1904) made clear his essential opposition to Home Rule and his continued belief in an all-powerful paternalistic state that would rule in the 'best interests' of the ruled (Gailey 187).

Without delving more deeply into the conflict of internal loyalties and prejudices that characterized the Unionist government in these years, it is still possible to see the strategic position that was left to Irish nationalists as a consequence of these kinds of policy-making procedures. Because they were designed to coopt opposition by material benefit, one could acquiesce in gratitude for gain, or one could resist. One could accept a consultative role, or one could agitate. But in no circumstance could the Irish initiate national policy with the expectation of success. The effect of Wyndham's mode of governance was to leave people in better material circumstances but powerless to insure their own continued self-interest.

It is this situation of corporate powerlessness within a supposedly benign partnership that provides, for me, the most interesting context for Molly Bloom's grumblings on the evening of 16 June. For, seen in this light, her speech acquires a political status simply by being the kind of 'guerilla' tactic that was, in 1904, common to any Irish resistance to unionism.

Joyce could not have been unaware of the rhetorical implications of such heckling, of 'speech acts' like Molly's that are inherently political but that lack the power to make effective change. Indeed, one way to read Joyce's earlier work, *A Portrait of the Artist as a Young Man*, is to follow Stephen Dedalus' assault upon different kinds of corporate authority as he attempts to reconstitute his own power, or, as Vicki Mahaffey has argued so persuasively, to 'reauthorize' himself by noncompliance.

This relationship between authority and verbal noncompliance is one of the issues that underlies Stephen's reflections on the English priest's insistence that a 'tundish' is really a 'funnel.' He is confronted with one language that, in seeming to represent two cultures—the English and the Irish—succeeds only in expressing the voice of oppression:

> —The language in which we are speaking is his before it is mine. How different are the words *home*, *Christ*, *ale*, *master*, on his lips and on mine! I cannot speak or write these words without unrest of spirit. His language, so familiar and so foreign, will always be for me an acquired speech. I have not made or accepted its words. My voice holds them at bay. My soul frets in the shadow of his language. (189)

In this passage, Joyce articulates the linguistic dilemma of a colonial nation whose own cultural identity has been eclipsed by an invading authority. Stephen knows that English precludes Gaelic and that its ascendancy places him in history at a point when he, as a writer, can only borrow the words of one language and seek darkly for the older tongue whose use has been denied him. Caught between the foreign and the unknown, he locates authenticity in an 'unborn' future that his writing will help to create.

What Stephen and the priest do in the face of their unvoiced antagonism is important to notice, for their behavior is emblematic of a strategy that many people, both men and women, use to negotiate unequal power relationships: knowing nothing of Stephen's bitterness, the priest urges him to persevere and to anticipate a successful end to his studies. A Belvedere professor then comes into the room to begin a lecture on applied science, while Stephen fades into the company of his fellow schoolmates who listen with increasing restlessness and ill-concealed rudeness:

> Moynihan leaned down towards Stephen's ear and murmured:
> —What price ellipsoidal balls! Chase me, ladies, I'm in the cavalry!
> . . . Moynihan . . . began to call with the voice of a slobbering urchin:
> —Please, teacher! Please, teacher! This boy is after saying a bad word, teacher. (192–193)

Amid this heckling,

> The droning voice of the professor continued to wind itself slowly round and round the coils it spoke of, doubling, trebling, quadrupling its somnolent energy as the coil multiplied its ohms of resistance. (194)

Like the electrical demonstration that he conducts in front of the students, the professor's voice coils and is met by recoil. Although he has control of the discourse, his speech engenders its own resistance. The young men in the gallery show their unwillingness through 'guerilla' tactics similar to the ones Molly Bloom uses at the end of the day: knowing that their conflicts with this particular representative of English authority cannot be resolved through argument and rebuttal, they snipe, they heckle, they mock. They refuse to acquiesce, but they stop short of open rebellion. Stephen dislikes his classmates. 'Can you say with certitude,' he asks, 'by whom the soul of your race was bartered and its elect betrayed—by the questioner or by the mocker?' (193–194); but we should remember that it is his denigration of Others, it is his decision to give up on them and to leave, that has led us to ignore the unexpressed, or barely expressed, or badly expressed, desperation of those who are left behind in Ireland and who remain below the level of political discourse. Like rude and ineffectual children, Stephen's Irish compatriots whisper 'two and two behind their hands' (192).

Molly's disorganized speech can be read, then, in the terms established by the classroom in *Portrait*, where science and nonscience, authority and a discredited Other confront one another in unequal battle. The distinction lies, of course, in the issue of gender, for the terms of domination and suppression, of expression and silence, have been transformed from 'England' and 'Ireland' in their struggle with the union to 'male' and 'female' without changing the issues of marginality and the inadequacy of cultural representation that remain at the heart of Joyce's concern in both books. In fact, what remains in *Ulysses* is evidence of the double alienation that history has generally bestowed upon women under colonial rule, where gender has established yet another mode of dispossession from the political and cultural arena. 'How different are the words . . . on his lips and on mine! I cannot speak or write these words without unrest of spirit' (*P* 189) might serve to express Molly's sentiments as well as those of Stephen Dedalus. 'His language,' he or she might say, 'so familiar and so foreign, will always be for me an acquired speech. I have not made or accepted its words' (*P* 189).

Certainly these are the thoughts of anyone who has been dispossessed by the world he or she is forced to inhabit or who understands, however obliquely, that the script of the dominant culture precludes authentic self-expression. Like

Stephen who uses language as a weapon, Molly drones on at the end of *Ulysses*. 'My voice holds them at bay' (*P* 189). For each of them, the act of speaking, however inchoately, is itself a political act, an act of assertion, a search for definition in the face of a domineering Other.

What else could Molly Bloom have done in 1904 had she wanted to assert herself more effectively in the world? Neither her legal position nor her status as a citizen, wife, and mother would have empowered her. If we look at 1904 not only as a year in the struggle for Irish independence from England but also as a year in the movement of women for citizenship in the British Isles, we would find an equally compelling (and discouraging) set of circumstances that would have confronted Molly. All of them would have affected the way that she experienced her marriage and, indeed, her very sense of the reaches of her own authority in life.

She would have had some rights and protections.[2] The 'Poor Law Guardian, Ireland (Women) Act' of 1896 would have made her eligible to be a Poor Law Guardian, and the 'Irish Local Government Act' of 1898 had reorganized local government so that women who had been previously excluded from the municipal franchise were made eligible for Rural and District Councils (Blackburn 270). But, even barring the great issue that faced British and Irish women alike—the right to vote in national elections—Ireland lagged far behind England in other matters of legal concern for women. Molly would not have been allowed, even in cases of aggravated assault, to get a separation order; she would not have been given custody of Milly, had divorce been possible; she had no right to the money she earned by singing in concert, nor could she have invested money or held property in her own name. 7 Eccles Street did not belong to her. Had Bloom died, the court would not have appointed her guardian of her own child unless he had specified it as his wish, nor would she have had claim to even a minimum share in his estate had he died intestate.[3] In short, quite apart from the fact of her political disenfranchisement on the national level, Molly would have known herself to be the lesser member of a marital union with a male 'predominant partner.' This would have been so no matter how much kindness or private affection may have tempered Bloom's responses to her. In 1904 Irish marriage was from the legal perspective very much like Wyndham's unionist rule of Ireland. Both were institutions predicated on an unequal distribution of power over property, finance, inheritance, and 'voice,' and both sought to finesse, accommodate, and neutralize resistance by means of conciliatory gestures.

Given her unequal status in so intimate an institution as marriage, it is little wonder that Molly's thoughts remain so consistently rooted in the intricacies of personal relationships, for they were the very forms through which the political world made its power known to her. She had no direct access to authority nor even an organization for voicing opposition. The movement to make Irish women citizens lay several years in the future, and even its later vicissitudes showed how fully issues of parity between the two genders informed the nationalist drive for Home Rule.

Far from being 'acutely sensitive to the relativity of language ... to political power,' as Joseph Valente has argued (59),[4] the Irish Nationalists would prove to be as determined to keep women voiceless as the English had been with regard to them. When the general election of February 1910 shifted the balance of power between the Liberal government and the Unionists in England, the Irish Party found itself able to press the Liberals for another Home Rule Bill as a condition for their continued support (Ward 22). Clearly British 'kindness' had not succeeded in mitigating their desire for independence.

But as Anna Haslam, Hanna Sheehy-Skeffington, and Gretta Cousins, all active Dublin feminists, were to discover, this did not prevent the Party's being unkind to them. Not only did the Irish Party reject the idea of a 'predominant partner,' but they also rejected the idea of partnership altogether. John Redmond, the leader of the Irish Nationalists, was vehemently opposed to women's enfranchisement, and although the Irish Women's Franchise League, founded in 1908, was intent on insuring that votes for women be incorporated within the proposed Home Rule Bill (Ward 24), he persisted in believing that including women in the bill would divide the nationalist ranks and also lead to the resignation of the British Prime Minister, Asquith. Should the Liberal government fail, Redmond reasoned, the Home Rule Bill would be jeopardized just as completely as it had been in the time of Parnell. Kitty O'Shea, in one generation, and the women suffragists in the next, played the role of demon lovers whose acknowledgment had broken/would break the solidarity and effectiveness of the Irish Party. Despite a variety of tactics on the part of women—some of them rhetorical and some of them violent[5]—the Home Rule Bill of 1913 left the women of Ireland without a vote.

C. P. Scott, editor of *The Manchester Guardian*, 'tried to urge [Redmond] to reconsider his attitude by pointing out the inconsistency of a Home Rule party betraying the very principle of Home Rule—"that emancipation for Irish men [would be] purchased at the cost of its refusal for women"' (David Morgan, quoted in Ward 26), and the Irishwomen's Suffrage Federation reiterated his view, saying 'that nationalist opposition to the principle of woman suffrage contained in the Conciliation Bill would be "an act of hostility to Irish women"' (Ward 26), but to no avail. Under Home Rule, women were to suffer from circumstances analogous to the repression that men and women had both endured under the English Unionist Party. Only when Padraic Pearse read the Republican Proclamation in front of the General Post Office at the Easter Rising of 1916 was the principle of equal citizenship for Irish men and Irish women reaffirmed. In 1922 the franchise was finally extended to women.

All of these struggles for women's independence lay ahead of Molly in 1904. Anna Haslam, a Quaker woman whose interest in higher education and employment for women had resulted in the foundation of the Queen's Institute (Molesworth Street), was active in her support of women's suffrage in Dublin (Blackburn 129), but no organized, vocal group existed for Molly to join, even had she possessed a more militant temperament.

Instead, Molly's resistance to the union—whether we understand 'union' to mean the tie between England and Ireland or that between Bloom and herself—has been reduced to insurgency: she can withhold consent, she can complain, and she can engage in acts of subterfuge that undermine the structures of authority that bind her life. She does all three.

If she has not understood how to use knowledge or power or even how to imagine the full ramifications of her own cultural position, she has mastered a more fragmentary critical art. Like the students in Stephen Dedalus' physics lecture, she has learned how to heckle, to snipe, and to mock the script that continues to write limited cultural roles for her: 'we have to be thankful for our mangy cup of tea itself as a great compliment to be noticed the way the world is divided' (750). Her dissatisfactions can be considered the beginning signs of insurrection, just as, on another level, her decision to take a lover is a second refusal of paternalistic tradition. Seen in this light, the political importance of Molly's affair with Blazes Boylan lies precisely in its symbolic 'uncoupling' of that which has coupled her unjustly. It is a 'speech act' against marriage, a refusal of its bonds.

To say this is not to make any claims about Leopold Bloom's strengths or deficiencies as a husband. But it is to notice the complexity of Irish marriage at the turn of the century, to insist on its analogy to colonial rule, and to see the structural inequities of both institutions with regard to women. If Molly's soliloquy is a catalogue of vigorous complaints and a litany of vague hopes for more autonomy ('they darent order me about the place its his fault' [768]), and if it only contains the rudiments of a narrative construct that might serve as a counterpart to Bloom's view of their marriage ('I declare somebody ought to put him in the budget if I only could remember the one half of the things and write a book out of it' [754]), it nonetheless shows the possibility of female resistance to male domination in 1904. The French historicist Michel Foucault would call Molly's coming-into-speech, in whatever halting way, 'an insurrection of subjugated knowledge.' Similarly, the American feminist Adrienne Rich would call it a 're-vision' or a seeing-again of cultural institutions that have seemed immutable but that are, in fact, the consequences of patriarchal modes of organizing structures of knowledge, structures of art, and structures of social engagement. When Foucault was asked to explain the meaning of his terminology, he said:

> I believe that by subjugated knowledges one should understand . . . a whole set of knowledges that have been disqualified as inadequate to their task or insufficiently elaborated: naive knowledges, located low down on the hierarchy, beneath the required level of cognition or scientificity. I also believe that it is through the re-emergence of these low-ranking knowledges, these unqualified, even directly disqualified knowledges . . . that criticism performs its work . . . (82)
>
> To emancipate [them] from that subjection [is] to render them . . . capable of opposition and of struggle . . . (85)

Adrienne Rich, whose interest in subjugated knowledge is more directly focused on the suppression of women's knowledge of themselves, is, perhaps, a more appropriate critic to call on here, for she took the inspiration for one of her most influential essays from Henrik Ibsen, the dramatist who so deeply influenced Joyce. Amplifying the themes that she saw in Ibsen's *When We Dead Awaken*, she contended that 'the sleepwalkers are coming awake.'

> Until we can understand the assumptions in which we are drenched we cannot know ourselves. [We should ask] how we have been led to imagine ourselves, how our language has trapped as well as liberated us; and how we can begin to see . . . afresh. (35)

Rich's project was not, and is not, one that has been completed; and it was certainly not achieved by the Molly Bloom whom Joyce gives to us in the midst of tired, nighttime musings.

But both Foucault and Rich help us to understand how Molly's soliloquy is a kind of speech that is beginning to emerge and to be 'capable of opposition and of struggle.' Given the limited political choices that she faced in 1904, we can see that 'struggle'—the ability to say 'no'—was as important to Molly as the ability to say 'yes.' And to be able to say 'yes' need not have been an overwhelming endorsement of 'love,' even though Richard Ellmann would have liked us to think that.

Marriage demands loyalty that is inevitably divided between self-interest and the desires of the Other; it requires mediation between corporate and individual welfare; it is supported by the ability to negotiate differences. Domination rarely serves these goals, nor does unquestioned yielding. That Molly withholds consent from the terms of her marriage on Bloomsday is as significant as remembering that she said 'yes I will' to Bloom years earlier on the Hill of Howth.

Foucault, Rich, and Bakhtin would all have endorsed her contrariness. Bakhtin called these tendencies toward disunification 'heteroglossia' or 'dialogue' (272). He recognized that such verbal strategies, however disruptive, were at the same time dynamic, the sign that language 'is alive and developing' as it must be in any union that strives to obliterate the need for a 'predominant partner' and to maintain the social life of gendered languages.

NOTES

1. In 'Women, the Vote and Revolution,' M. MacCurtain reports the comment of a parish priest in Ventry, County Kerry, who said 'it was a sure sign of the break-up of the planet when women took to leaving their homes and talking in public' (49). This remark tells us not only that the priesthood opposed women's voices in political life at this time but also that Molly's view is a male-identified one, one acquired from the clergy. Her comment is also interesting in light of John Redmond's (the leader of the Irish Parliamentary Party) fear, articulated in 1911, that votes for women would increase the power of the Church.
2. As Countess Markievicz asserted in *The Irish Citizen*, 'three great movements were going on in Ireland in those years, the national movement, the women's movement

and the industrial one.' To the students of the National Literary Society, Markievicz said in 1909, 'Fix your minds on the ideal of Ireland free, with her women enjoying the full rights of citizenship in their own nation' (quoted in MacCurtain 52, 53).

3. Compare 1830 and 1873 Custody of Infants Acts; 1878 Matrimonial Causes Act; 1870 Married Women's Property Act; 1886 Guardianship of Infants Act; and 1890 Intestates Act (Blackburn 271–272).
4. The full quotation is: 'A national culture rediscovering itself amid another dominant one, awakening to its long-alienated language and customs, and feeling its everyday lifestyle correspondingly alien, will be even more acutely sensitive to the relativity of language, especially its relativity to political power' (Valente 59).
5. For an excellent discussion of the various suffrage movements in Ireland and the varieties of political strategies they chose, see Margaret Ward.

WORKS CITED

Bakhtin, M. M. *The Dialogic Imagination*. Austin: U of Texas P, (1981).

Blackburn, Helen. *Women's Suffrage: A Record of the Women's Suffrage Movement in the British Isles*. Oxford: Williams and Norgate, (1902).

Foucault, Michel. 'Two Lectures.' *Power/Knowledge*. New York: Pantheon, (1980). 78–108.

Gailey, Andrew. *Ireland and the Death of Kindness: The Experience of Constructive Unionism, 1890–1905*. Cork: Cork UP, (1987).

Ignota. 'The Present Legal Position of Women in the United Kingdom.' *Westminster Review* 163 (1905): 513–529.

MacCurtain, M. 'Women, the Vote and Revolution.' *Women in Irish Society: The Historical Dimension*. Ed. Margaret MacCurtain and Donccha O'Corrain Westport: Greenwood, (1979). 46–64.

Mahaffey, Vicki. *Reauthorizing Joyce*. Cambridge: Cambridge UP, (1988).

O'Halpin, Eunan. *The Decline of the Union: British Government in Ireland, 1892–1920* Syracuse: Syracuse UP, (1987).

O'Neal, Daniel. *Three Perennial Themes of Anticolonialism: The Irish Case*. Denver: U of Denver Monograph Series in World Affairs, (1976).

Rich, Adrienne. 'When We Dead Awaken: Writing as Revision.' *On Lies, Secrets and Silence*. New York: Norton, (1979). 20–35.

Valente, Joseph. 'The Politics of Joyce's Polyphony.' *New Alliances in Joyce Studies*. Ed. Bonnie Kime Scott. Newark: U of Delaware P, (1988). 56–72.

Ward, Margaret. '"Suffrage First—Above All Else!" An Account of the Irish Suffrage Movement.' *Feminist Review* 10 (1982): 21–36.

6.2

FROM *ANOMALOUS STATES: IRISH WRITING AND THE POST-COLONIAL MOMENT*

David Lloyd

I

Irish cultural nationalism has been preoccupied throughout its history with the possibility of producing a national genius who would at once speak for and forge a national identity. The national genius is to represent the nation in the double sense of depicting and embodying its spirit – or genius – as it is manifested in the changing forms of national life and history. The idea could be reformulated quite accurately in terms derived from Kantian aesthetics: the national genius is credited with 'exemplary originality'.[1] That is to say, the national genius not only presents examples to a people not yet fully formed by or conscious of their national identity, but does so by exemplifying in himself the individual's ideal continuity with the nation's spiritual origins. True originality derives from the faithful reproduction of one's origins. Thus far, Irish nationalism represents, as indeed does Kant, merely another variant on the Enlightenment and Romantic critical tradition for which the originality of genius is understood as the capacity to reproduce the historical or individual sources of creativity itself. The Irish nationalist merely insists on a different notion of what is to be formed in the encounter with genius: not so much the intermediate subject of taste as, directly, the political subject, the citizen-subject, itself.

Unlike Kant, however, the Irish nationalist is confronted with a peculiar dilemma, succinctly expressed by Young Ireland's most influential aesthetician, D. F. MacCarthy, as the great national poet's being 'either the creation or the

Dublin: Lilliput, 1993, pp. 88–9 and 100–15.

creator of a great people'.[2] The expression points to an unavoidable aporia for the doubly representational aesthetics of nationalism, since the poet must either be created by the nation which it is his (always his) function to create, or create it by virtue of representing the nation he lacks. Neither a continuous national history, which could connect the individual to the national genius, nor even nature, on whose invocation in the form of *Naturgabe* the category of genius has traditionally been grounded, are easily available to the Irish nationalist.[3] For the nationalism of a colonized people requires that its history be seen as a series of unnatural ruptures and discontinuities imposed by an alien power while its reconstruction must necessarily pass by way of deliberate artifice. Almost by definition, this anti-colonial nationalism lacks the basis for its representative claims and is forced to invent them.[4] In this respect, nationalism can be said to require an aesthetic politics quite as much as a political aesthetics.

Historically, this constitutive paradox of Irish nationalism has not been practically disabling, though in cultural terms it leaves the problem that Ireland's principal writers have almost all been remarkably recalcitrant to the nationalist project. I have discussed this more extensively elsewhere in relation to the extreme demand for identification with the nation that nationalism imposes upon the Irish writer.[5] Here, I wish to explore more fully how not only the anti-representational tendency in Irish literature but also the hybrid quality of popular forms constantly exceed the monologic desire of cultural nationalism, a desire which centres on the lack of an Irish epic. Both the popular and the literary forms map a colonial culture for which the forms of representational politics and aesthetics required by nationalism begin to seem entirely inadequate, obliging us to conceive of a cultural politics which must work outside the terms of representation.

. . .

Unsurprisingly, given the virtually aporetic status of its contradictions, the terms of mid-nineteenth-century nationalist cultural discussions are reproduced half a century later in the Irish Literary Revival. James Joyce presents them prominently in *Ulysses* as a prelude to Stephen Dedalus's development of his own conception of genius out of Saxon Shakespeare:

> —Our young Irish bards, John Eglinton censured, have yet to create a figure which the world will set beside Saxon Shakespeare's Hamlet though I admire him, as old Ben did, on this side idolatry.
>
> . . .
>
> Mr Best came forward, amiable, towards his colleague.
>
> —Haines is gone, he said.
>
> —Is he?
>
> —I was showing him Jubainville's book. He's quite enthusiastic, don't you know, about Hyde's *Love Songs of Connacht*. I couldn't bring him in to hear the discussion. He's gone to Gill's to buy it.

> *Bound thee forth, my booklet, quick*
> *To geet the callous public,*
> *Writ, I ween, 'twas not my wish*
> *In lean unlovely English.*
>
> —The peatsmoke is going to his head, John Eglinton opined.
>
> ...
>
> —People do not know how dangerous lovesongs can be, the auric egg of Russell warned occultly. The movements which work revolutions in the world are born out of the dreams and visions in a peasant's heart on the hillside. For them the earth is not an exploitable ground but the living mother. The rarefied air of the academy and the arena produce the sixshilling novel, the musichall song. France produces the finest flower of corruption in Mallarmé but the desirable life is revealed only to the poor of heart, the life of Homer's Phaeacians.[6]

It is not merely that Joyce alludes here, in compressed fashion, to the principal concerns that continue to play through Irish cultural nationalism: the desire for the masterwork; the opposition between the spirit of peasant song, 'racy of the soil', and the hybrid 'flowers of corruption'; the turn to Homer as the figure representing the unification of the work of genius with the 'genius of place'. Furthermore, he indicates the complexity of the cultural transactions that take place in the thoroughly hybridized culture of 'West Britain', where Irishmen discourse on English, German and Greek culture while an Englishman, Haines, studies the Celtic element in literature and Hyde regrets the necessity that forces him to exemplify a Gaelic metre in lean, unlovely English.

Joyce's evocation of Hyde at this juncture allows us to grasp both the extent to which turn-of-the-century cultural nationalism recapitulates its earlier forms and the extent to which its terms had become at once more sophisticated and more problematic. Douglas Hyde, founder-president of the Gaelic League, was a principal advocate of the Irish-language revival, a scholar, poet-translator and folklorist. His most famous single essay, 'The Necessity for De-Anglicising Ireland' (1892), resumes Young Ireland's attacks on the penetration of Ireland by English culture as well as capital, and on the consequent emergence of an entirely 'anomalous position' for the Irish race, 'imitating England and yet apparently hating it'.[7] In large part, this essay presents a dismal catalogue of hybridization which ranges through place and family names to musical forms and clothing. Its conclusion, that a de-anglicization of Ireland is the necessary prelude to and guarantee of eventual Irish autonomy, is prescriptive for efforts like Hyde's own laborious collection and translation of Irish folk-songs and poetry. In these, as he had already argued in his essay 'Gaelic Folk Songs' (1890), the Irish genius was properly to be deciphered:

> We shall find that, though in their origin and diffusion they are purely local, yet in their essence they are wholly national, and, perhaps, more

> purely redolent of the race and soil than any of the real *literary* productions of the last few centuries.[8]

When it comes to deciphering that essence, nonetheless, Hyde is confronted with the dilemma that led to Young Ireland's translational aesthetic: there remain 'great gaps in Irish song'. For Hyde, however, as a scholar whose intimacy with the Gaelic material was far greater than Davis's or MacCarthy's, the question as to whether the 'gapped' nature of Irish folk-song was of its essence or an accident based upon the contingent, historical determinants of an oral culture, remains correspondingly more difficult to resolve. After giving a number of instances from Gaelic love songs, he pauses to remark on the necessity to cite examples in order to represent the nature of these songs in general. The ensuing reflections lead him to an unusually complex rendering of the 'nature' of the Gaelic spirit, leaving him unable to decide between the historical and the essential:

> It may appear strange, however, that I have only given stray verses instead of translating entire songs. But the fact is that the inconsequentness of these songs, as I have taken them down from the lips of the peasantry, is startling.
>
> Many adjectives have been applied by many writers to the Gaelic genius, but to my mind nothing about it is so noticeable as its inconsequentness, if I may use such a word – a peculiarity which, as far as I know, no one has yet noticed. The thought of the Irish peasant takes the most surprising and capricious leaps. Its movement is like the career of his own goblin, the Pooka; it clears the most formidable obstacles at a bound and carries across astonishing distances in a moment. The folk-song is the very incarnation of this spirit. It is nearly impossible to find three verses in which there is anything like an ordinary sequence of thought. They are full up of charms that the mind must leap, elipses [*sic*] that it must fill up, and detours of movement which only the most vivid imagination can make straight. This is the reason why I have found no popular ballads amongst the peasantry, for to tell a story in verse requires an orderly, progressive, and somewhat slow sequence of ideas, and this is the very faculty which the Gael has not got – his mind is too quick and passionate . . .
>
> But even this characteristic of Gaelic thought is insufficient to account for the perfectly extraordinary inconsequentness and abruptness of the folk-songs, as I have found them, I imagine that the cause of this peculiarity is not to be ascribed wholly to the authors of the songs, but also in great part to the medium which the songs passed through before they came to us – that medium, of course, being the various generations of local singers who have perpetuated them. These singers often forgot, as was natural, the real words of the song, and then they invented others, but more frequently they borrowed verses from any other piece that came into their head, provided it could be sung to the same tune, and hence the songs as we have them now are a curious mixture indeed. What between the 'unsequacious'

> mind of the original makers, the alterations made by generations of singers who forgot the words, and the extraneous verses borrowed from completely different productions, two out of three of the folk-songs which I have collected, resemble those children's toys of paper where when you pull a string you get a different pair of legs or a different head, joined to a different body. The most beautiful sentiments will be followed by the most grotesque bathos, and the tenderest and most exquisite verses will end in the absurdest nonsense. This has been done by the singers who have transmitted them. (pp. 113–14)

The folk-songs appear here as at once the representation of an essence, the Gaelic spirit, and the products of the specific and contingent conditions of their transmission. But if we take these representations as those of an essence, then the essence itself makes it impossible to define any essential character of the race, since a character, to have any identity at all, must be consistent, as Young Ireland and their followers in the Literary Revival consistently argued. On the other hand, the historical argument in its turn, recognizing the sheer contingency that has conditioned the forms and peculiarities of the folk-songs, would make it impossible to derive a national character from them.

Despite his momentary hesitation at this acknowledgment of the over-determined grounds for the 'great gaps in Irish song', Hyde rapidly recuperates the Irish identity by offering, after citing a thoroughly adulterated verse, 'one specimen of a comparatively perfect folk-song which has not been interfered with' (p. 115). The song, 'Mo bhrón ar an bhfarraige' ('Oh, my grief on the sea!'), which concludes with the lines,

> And my love came behind me –
> He came from the south –
> With his breast to my bosom,
> His mouth to my mouth,

appears as a perfect because consistent expression of 'genuine passion', lacking any of the marks, 'the alliteration, adjectives, assonance, and tricks of the professional poet' (p. 117). Hyde's 'restoration' of the essential folk-song requires, in other words, not only its purification from hybridization internal to the culture or resulting from external influence, but even the representation of the work of the Gaelic bards as a deviation from the true passion of the people. Irish folk culture is transformed into an ahistorical ground on which the defining difference of 'Irishness' can be established over against the homogenizing/hybridizing influence of 'Anglicization'. Ironically, the values by which the genuine item is identified and canonized themselves derive, perhaps by way of earlier translators, like the unionist Samuel Ferguson, from the 'common language' of British Romanticism.

It is more than probable that Joyce knew Hyde's essays, and certain that he knew this particular song, if only from the slightly revised version in *The Love*

Songs of Connacht, since it appears transformed early in *Ulysses*. It reappears, however, not in the context of 'genuine passion', but in the course of Stephen's 'morose delectation' on Sandymount Strand as his thoughts shift back and forth between the cockle picket's woman passing him and the memory of his dead mother:

> She trudges, schlepps, trains, drags, trascines her load. A tide westering, moondrawn, in her wake. Tides, myriadislanded, within her, blood not mine, *oinopa ponton*, a wine-dark sea. Behold the handmaid of the moon. In sleep the wet sign call her hour, bids her rise. Bridebed, childbed, bed of death, ghostcandled. *Omnis caro ad te veniet*. He comes pale vampire, through storm his eyes, his bat sails bloodying the sea, mouth to her mouth's kiss. (*Ulysses*, p. 40)

The verses emerging here recur somewhat later, in the 'Aeolus' section, in a form closer to that given by Hyde:

> *On swift sail flaming*
> *From storm and south*
> *He comes, pale vampire,*
> *Mouth to my mouth.*
>
> (*Ulysses*, p. 109)

We may read in the gradual transformation of the folk-song a representation at several levels of the processes of hybridization as they construct the individual consciousness. Many of the elements of that hybridization are superficially evident: the chain of foreign, or rather 'anglicized', words used to describe the cockle picker's woman, the phrases from Homer and from the Latin of Catholic ritual, or the parody of biblical invocations. The *effect* of hybridization, however, needs more careful analysis, both at the formal literary level and at that of the representation of an individual subjectivity which it entails. The most familiar stylistic term in Joyce criticism used to describe the representation of subjective interiority is 'stream of consciousness', which implies a certain consistency within the representation as well as a relative transparency and evenness among the elements. As such, the term is largely inadequate, even in the earlier sections of the novel, to describe the staccato or interrupted rhythms, the varying accessibility of the allusions, whether to different readers or to the represented subject (Stephen or Bloom), or to the several levels of implicit 'consciousness' that these stylistic effects constitute.

Equally inadequate would be any description of these effects as instances of 'assimilation' or 'appropriation', terms employed by Bakhtin in his description of the normative dialogical formation of the subject:

> As a living, socio-ideological concrete thing, as heteroglot opinion, language, for the individual consciousness, lies on the borderline between oneself and the other. The word in language is half someone else's. It

> becomes 'one's own' only when the speaker populates it with his own intention, his own accent, when he appropriates the word, adapting it to his own semantic and expressive intention. (p. 293) ... One's own discourse is gradually and slowly wrought out of others' words that have been acknowledged and assimilated, and the boundaries between the two are at first scarcely perceptible. (p. 345n)

Despite the difficulties he recognizes as afflicting these processes, Bakhtin is clearly operating here with an at least residually Kantian subject, one existent as potential prior to any engagement with word or object, and, perhaps more importantly, on its way to conformity with those maxims of enlightenment that for Kant define the autonomous subject: independence, consistency, and formal, universal identity.[9]

It is, of course, towards the production of such a subject, capable, for example, of assimilating the alien English language to Irish identity or the equally alien Gaelic language to the English 'mother-tongue', that Irish nationalism is directed. What it constantly diagnoses, however, is a subject-people always the *object* of imperfect assimilation to either culture, in a state, that is, of continuing *dependence*. It is for this reason that Joyce's 'citational' aesthetic in *Ulysses* cuts so strongly against both Bakhtin's description of the subjective processes which the novel typifies, and the translational aesthetic of Irish nationalism. One could, indeed, argue that Bakhtin's assimilation is itself a version of a generally translational aesthetic for which the subject is formed in a continual appropriation of the alien to itself, just as translation, as opposed, for example, to interpretation or paraphrase, is seen as essentially a recreation of the foreign text in one's own language.[10] Joyce's, or Stephen's, version of this love song of Connacht rather insists on its heterogeneity in the course of an essentially 'inconsequential' meditation or miscegenates it with an entirely different – but no less 'Irish' – tradition of Gothic vampire tales.[11]

Accordingly, where the principal organizing metaphor of Irish nationalism is that of a proper paternity, of restoring the lineage of the fathers in order to repossess the motherland, Joyce's procedures are dictated by adulteration. Joyce's personal obsession with adultery is well documented and it is a commonplace that the plot of *Ulysses* itself turns around Molly Bloom's adulterous relationship with Blazes Boylan.[12] That the figure of the nineteenth-century leader of the Home Rule party, Charles Stewart Parnell, recurs from Joyce's earliest works as a victim of betrayal consequent on his adulterous relationship with Kitty O'Shea underlines the extent to which adultery is also an historical and political issue for Irish nationalism. The common tracing of the first Anglo-Norman conquest of Ireland in 1169 to the adulterous relationship between Diarmaid MacMurchadha, King of Leinster, and Dearbhghiolla, the High King's wife, establishes adulteration as a popular myth of origins for Irish nationalist sentiment. As the Citizen puts it, in the 'Cyclops' chapter of *Ulysses*: 'The adultress and her paramour brought the Saxon robbers here ... A dishonoured wife ... that's what's the cause of all our misfortunes' (*Ulysses*, p. 266).

For the nationalist citizen, the identity of the race is adulterated by 'la belle infidèle' and, as in the old expression, the restoration of that identity by translation (*traditore*) is haunted by the anxiety of a betrayal (*traduttore*). This chapter, that in *Ulysses* in which issues of nationalist politics and culture are played out most intensely and in which the various elements of Irish culture are most thoroughly deployed, circulates not only thematically but also stylistically around adulteration as the constitutive anxiety of nationalism. For while the citizen is militant against the hybridization of Irish culture, the chapter itself dramatizes adulteration as the condition of colonial Ireland at virtually every level. Barney Kiernan's pub is at the heart of Dublin, but also located in Little Britain Street, in the vicinity of the Linenhall, the law courts and the Barracks, and across the river from Dublin Castle, the centre of British administration. Most of the characters who pass through the bar (already a parodic form of the legal bar, both being sites of censure and debate) are connected in one or other way with these institutions, while the legal cases cited continually associate the influence of British institutions with economic dependency in the form of debt, and that in turn with the stereotype of financial and cultural instability, the Jew.[13] The slippage among institutional, cultural, racial and political elements is a function of a stylistic hybridization that refuses to offer any normative mode of representation from which other modes can be said to deviate.

These features of the 'Cyclops' chapter have been noted in different ways by many commentators. What needs to be stressed, however, is that by and large the mingling of stylistic elements is rendered by critics in terms which reduce the process of hybridization to the juxtaposition of a set of equivalent representational modes, a reduction which, even where it refuses to posit the register of colloquial speech as an 'original' of which all other modes are 'translations', implies the essential coherence or integrity of each mode in itself. To do so is to leave fundamentally unchallenged the principle of equivalence on which the translational aesthetic is based. This is the case even in one of the most astute accounts of the chapter. After rewriting a passage from 'Cyclops' in what is effectively parallel text, Colin MacCabe comments:

> Ignoring for the moment that part of the second text which has no parallel in the first, what is important in this passage is not the truth or falsity of what is being said, but how the same event articulated in two different discourses produces different representations (different truths). Behind 'an elder of noble gait and countenance' and 'that bloody old pantaloon Denis Breen in his bath slippers' we can discern no definite object. Rather each object can only be identified in a discourse which already exists and that identification is dependent on the possible distinctions available in the discourse.[14]

MacCabe's description of Joyce's procedures at this juncture is comparable to Bakhtin's general description of the novel as a genre:

> The novel can be defined as a diversity of social speech types (sometimes even diversity of languages) and a diversity of individual voices, artistically organized. The internal stratification of any single national language into social dialects, characteristic group behaviour, professional jargons, generic languages, languages of generations and age groups, tendentious languages, languages of the authorities, of various circles and of passing fashions, languages that serve the specific sociopolitical purposes of the day, even of the hour (each day has its own slogan, its own vocabulary, its own emphases) – this internal stratification present in any given language at any given moment of its historical existence is the indispensable prerequisite for the novel as a genre.
>
> (pp. 262–3)

Adequate so far as they go, neither description is capable of grasping the internal heterogeneities, the adulteration of discourses as Joyce constructs them in 'Cyclops' and throughout *Ulysses*. This process of adulteration ranges from a phenomenon of colloquial Irish speech to which Oscar Wilde gave the name of 'malapropism' to the ceaseless interpenetration of different discourses. Malapropism varies from casual misspeaking, sometimes intentional, sometimes based on mishearings of an improperly mastered English ('Don't cast your nasturtiums on my character' [p. 263]), to deliberate and creative polemical wordplay (as in English 'syphilisation')[15] As a larger stylistic principle, the adulteration of interpenetrating discourses is unremitting, blending, among other things, pastiches of biblical/liturgical, medieval, epic (based in large part on Standish O'Grady's already highly stylized versions of old Irish heroic cycles), legal, scientific and journalistic modes. Frequently, the legal and journalistic discourses at once contain and disseminate adulteration, representing as institutional formations material sites for the clash of heterogeneous languages and interests. The following example instantiates the possible modulations among different registers:

> And whereas on the sixteenth day of the month of the oxeyed goddess and in the third week after the feastday of the Holy and Undivided Trinity, the daughter of the skies, the virgin moon being then in her first quarter, it came to pass that those learned judges repaired them to the halls of law. There master Courtenay, sitting in his own chamber, gave his rede and master Justice Andrew, sitting without a jury in probate court, weighed well and pondered the claim of the first chargeant upon the property in the matter of the will propounded and final testamentary disposition *in re* the real and personal estate of the late lamented Jacob Halliday, vintner, deceased, versus Livingstone, an infant, of unsound mind, and another. And to the solemn court of Green street there came sir Frederick the Falconer. And he sat him there about the hour of five o'clock to administer the law of the brehons at the commission for all that and those parts to be holden in and for the county of the city of Dublin. And there sat with him

> the high sinhedrim of the twelve tribes of Iar, for every tribe one man, of the tribe of Patrick and of the tribe of Hugh and of the tribe of Owen and of the tribe of Conn and of the tribe of Oscar and of the tribe of Fergus and of the tribe of Finn and of the tribe of Dermot and of the tribe of Cormac and of the tribe of Kevin and of the tribe of Caolte and of the tribe of Ossian, there being in all twelve good men and true ... And straightway the minions of the law led forth from their donjon keep one whom the sleuthhounds of justice had apprehended in consequence of evidence received. (p. 265)

Categorization of this and similar passages as 'dialogic' would be limited insofar as what occurs here is not an opposition, conversational or polemical, between coherent 'voices', but their entire inter-contamination. Indeed, precisely what is lacking or erased here is *voice*, which, as Bakhtin remarks, is a category fundamental 'in the realm of ethical and legal thought and discourse ... An independent, responsible and active discourse is *the* fundamental indicator of an ethical, legal and political human being' (pp. 349–50).

It is through the question of voice and its dismantling that we can begin to grasp the complex ramifications of Joyce's deployment of adulteration as both motif and stylistic principle in *Ulysses*. Where nationalism is devoted to the production, in stylistic terms, of a singular voice, and to the purification of the dialect of street ballads or Gaelic songs, it produces equally what we might envisage as a matrix of articulated concepts which provide the parameters of its political aesthetic or aesthetic politics. Thus this singular voice correlates with the formation of the Irish subject as autonomous citizen at one level and with a collective Irish identity at another. That analogical relation between the individual and the national moments is permitted by a concept of representation which requires a narrative movement between the exemplary instance and the totality that it prefigures. The identification of each representative individual with the nation constitutes the people which is to claim legitimate rights to independence as an 'original', that is, essential, entity. Consistent representation of that essence underwrites simultaneously the aesthetic originality, or autonomy, of the literary work that takes its place as an instance of the national culture. Such a self-sustaining and self-reinforcing matrix of concepts furnishes the ideological verisimilitude of cultural nationalism, permitting its apparent self-evidence.

Joyce's work, on the contrary, deliberately dismantles voice and verisimilitude in the same moment. Even if, as MacCabe has suggested, particular discourses attain dominance at given points in the text, the continual modulations that course through 'Cyclops', as indeed through the work as a whole, preclude any discursive mode from occupying a position from which the order of probability that structures mimetic verisimilitude could be stabilized. But even beyond this, the constantly parodic mode in which given discourses are replayed prevents their being understood as internally coherent, if rival, systems of verisimilitude. The double face of parody, at once dependent on and antagonistic to its models, constantly undercuts both the production of an autonomous voice and the stabilization of a discourse in its 'faithful' reproduction.[16] Adulteration as a stylistic principle institutes a multiplication of possibility in place of an order of probability and as such appears as the exact aesthetic correlative of adultery in the social sphere. For if adultery is forbidden under patriarchal law, it is precisely because of the potential multiplication of possibilities for identity that it implies as against the paternal fiction, which is based on no more than legal verisimilitude. If the spectre of adultery must be exorcized by nationalism, it is in turn because adulteration undermines the stable formation of legitimate and authentic identities. It is not difficult to trace here the basis for nationalism's consistent policing of female sexuality by the ideological and legal confinement of women to the domestic sphere.[17] Nor is there any need to rehearse here the anxieties that Bloom raises for the Citizen on racial as well as sexual grounds, or the extent to which the narrative as a whole occupies aesthetic, cultural and sexual terrains in a manner that continually runs counter to nationalist ideology.[18] What must be noted, however, is the extent to which its anti-representational mode of writing clashes with nationalist orders of verisimilitude precisely by allowing the writing out of the effects of colonialism that nationalism seeks to eradicate socially and psychically. This is not merely a matter of the content of a representation but also inseparably an issue of stylistics. Thus, for instance, Bloom cannot be the exemplary hero of what might be an Irish epic, not only because of his status as 'neither fish nor fowl', to quote the Citizen, but because *Ulysses* as a whole refuses the narrative verisimilitude within which the formation of representative man could be conceived. The aesthetic formation of the exemplary citizen requires not alone the selection of an individual sociologically or statistically 'normative', but the representation of that individual's progress from unsubordinated contingency to socially significant integration with the totality. This requires in turn what Bakhtin describes as 'a combining of languages and styles into a higher unity', the novel's capacity to 'orchestrate all its themes' into a totality (p. 263). *Ulysses*' most radical movement is in its refusal to fulfil either of these demands and its correspondent refusal to subordinate itself to the socializing functions of identity formation.[19] It insists instead on a deliberate stylization of dependence and inauthenticity, a stylization of the hybrid status of the colonized subject as of the colonized culture, their internal adulteration and the strictly parodic modes that they produce in every sphere.

III

> We will become, what, I fear, we are largely at present, a nation of imitators, the Japanese of Western Europe, lost to the power of native initiative and alive only to second-hand assimilation. (Douglas Hyde)

> Everywhere in the mentality of the Irish people are flux and uncertainty. Our national consciousness may be described, in a native phrase, as a

> quaking sod. It gives no footing. It is not English, nor Irish, nor Anglo-Irish . . . (Daniel Corkery)
>
> [The *pachuco*'s dangerousness lies in his singularity. Everyone agrees in finding something hybrid about him, something disturbing and fascinating. He is surrounded by an aura of ambivalent notions: his singularity seems to be nourished by powers that are alternately evil and beneficent. (Octavio Paz)
>
> We Brazilians and other Latin-Americans constantly experience the artificial, inauthentic and imitative nature of our cultural life. An essential element in our critical thought since independence, it has been variously interpreted from romantic, naturalist, modernist, right-wing, left-wing, cosmopolitan and nationalist points of view, so we may suppose that the problem is enduring and deeply rooted. (Roberto Schwartz)
>
> A European journalist, and moreover a leftist, asked me a few days ago, 'Does a Latin-American culture exist?' . . . The question . . . could also be expressed another way: 'Do you exist?' For to question our culture is to question our very existence, our human reality itself, and thus to be willing to take a stand in favor of our irremediable colonial condition, since it suggests that we would be but a distorted echo of what occurs elsewhere. (Roberto Fernández Retamar)
>
> The danger is in the neatness of identifications. (Samuel Beckett)
>
> Riding on the train with another friend, I ramble on about the difficulty of finishing this book, feeling like I am being asked by all sides to be a 'representative' of the race, the sex, the sexuality – or at all costs to avoid that. (Cherrié Moraga)[20]

Since there is insufficient space for a more exhaustive account, the above citations must serve as indicators of a recurrent and problematic set of issues that course through numerous colonial situations, perhaps especially in those where an 'original' language has been displaced by that of the colonizing power.[21] This problematic can be described as a confrontation with a cultural hybridization which, unlike the process of assimilation described by Bakhtin and others, issues in *inauthenticity* rather than authentic identity. To describe this confrontation as problematic is to insist that the experience of inauthenticity intended here is not to be confused with that of the celebrated post-modern subject, though clearly the overlapping geographical and historical terrain of each ultimately requires that they be elaborated together. For the aesthetic freedom of the post-modern subject is the end-product of a global assimilation of subordinated cultures to the flows of multinational capital in the post-colonial world, and to fail to specify that subject is to ignore equally the powerful dissymmetry between the subject who tastes and the indifferent, that is, interchangeable objects of his/her nomadic experience.[22] It should be recalled that the experience of colonized cultures such as Ireland's, with differing but increasing degrees of intensity, is to be subjected to an uneven process of assimilation. What is produced, accordingly, is not a self-sustaining and autonomous organism capable of appropriating other cultures to itself, as imperial and post-modern cultures alike conceive themselves to be, but rather, at the individual and national-cultural level, a hybridization radically different from Bakhtin's in which antagonism mixes with dependence and autonomy is constantly undermined by the perceived influence of alien powers.

A complex web of specular judgments constructs this problematic. On the side of the colonizer, it is the inauthenticity of the colonized culture, its falling short of the concept of the human, that legitimates the colonial project. At the other end of the developmental spectrum, the hybridization of the colonized culture remains an index of its continuing inadequacy to this concept and of its perpetually 'imitative' status. The colonizer's gaze thus overlooks the recalcitrant sites of resistance that are at work in hybrid formations such as those we have been analysing. From the nationalist perspective, hybridity is no less devalued; the perceived inauthenticity of the colonized culture is recast as the contamination of an original essence, the recovery of which is the crucial prerequisite to the culture's healthy and normative development. The absence of an authentic culture is the death of the nation, its restoration its resurrection. In this sense, nationalist monologism is a dialogic inversion of imperial ideology, caught willy-nilly in the position of a parody, antagonistic but dependent.[23]

These remarks need to be qualified, however, by reiterated stress upon the dissymmetry of the specular relation. Nationalism is generated as an oppositional discourse by intellectuals who appear, by virtue of their formation in imperial state institutions, as in the first place subjected to rather than the subjects of assimilation. Their assimilation is, furthermore, inevitably an uneven process: by the very logic of assimilation, either the assimilated must entirely abandon their culture of origins, supposing it to have existed in anything like a pure form, or persist in a perpetually split consciousness, perceiving the original cultural elements as a residue resistant to the subject formed as a citizen of the empire. Simultaneously, the logic of assimilation resists its own ideal model: since the process is legitimated by the judgment of the essential inferiority of the colonized, its very rationale would be negated in the case of a perfect assimilation of colonized subjects without remainder. Therefore, it is at once the power and the weakness of assimilation as the cultural arm of hegemonic imperialism that a total integration of the colonized into the imperial state is necessarily foreclosed. Recognition of this inescapable relegation to hybrid status among 'native' intellectuals formed by the promise of an ever-withheld subjecthood is a principal impulse to nationalism at the same time as it determines the monologic mode of nationalist ideology.[24]

We should recall, however, that the desire for the nation is not merely to be formative of an authentic and integral subjecthood, but also the means to capture the state which is the nation's material representation. This fact has crucial theoretical and practical consequences. The formation of nationalist intellectuals takes place through both the repressive and the ideological state apparatuses of the empire, the army and police forces being as instrumental as the schools or recreationary spaces. This entails the space of the nation itself being constituted through these apparatuses which quite literally map it and give it its unity in the form of the state. Accordingly, just as the state form survives the moment of independence, the formation of the citizen-subject through these apparatuses continues to be a founding requirement of the new nation state.[25] What is time and again remarked of the post-colonial world, that 'independent' states put in place institutions entirely analogous to those of the colonial states that dominated them, is not merely to be explained as a ploy by which the defeated empires continue their domination in renovated guise. For the state form is a requirement of anti-colonial nationalism as it was its condition. By the same token, post-colonial nationalism is actively engaged in the formation of citizen-subjects through those institutions and thereby on the analogy of the metropolitan subject. This is an instance of the 'modernizing' effect of the state as the ensemble of institutions which ensures the continuing integration of the post-colonial state in the networks of multinational capital. But it is no less an instance of the modernizing effect of nationalism itself.

The terrain of colonial hybridization here analysed in the Irish context but with specific counterparts virtually everywhere in the colonial world falls in a double and, for the new nation, contradictory sense under the shadow of the state. Even where its most immediate instruments seem to be economic or cultural forces remote from the purview of the state, hybridization is impelled and sustained by the intervention of the imperial state – by its commercial and criminal laws, its institutions, its language, its cultural displays. Against this process reacts a monologic nationalism which, though already marked by hybridization, seeks to counter it with its own authentic institutions. In the post-independence state, these very institutions continue to be the locus of a process of hybridization despite the separation out of a more or less reified sphere of 'national culture' whose functions, disconnected from oppositional struggle, become the formal and repetitive interpellation of national subjects and the residual demarcation of difference from the metropolitan power. In this respect also, the post-independence state reproduces the processes of metropolitan culture, the very formality of the 'difference' of the national culture ensuring that the interpellation of its citizens always takes the 'same form' as that of the metropolitan citizen.

Consequently, the apparatuses of the state remain crucial objects for a resistance which cannot easily be divided into theoretical and practical modes, not least because what determines both is an aesthetic narrative through which the theoretical is articulated upon the practical and vice versa. What begins as a Kantian precept finds specific material instantiation in post-colonial politics. For though the mode of formation of the citizen-subject may appear as a merely theoretical issue, the narrative of representation on which it depends for the principle by which individual and nation can be sutured determines equally the forms of schooling and of political institutions adopted. These in turn demarcate the limits of what can properly, in any given state, be termed a political practice. For, like any other social practice, politics is an effect of an ideological formation obedient to specific laws of verisimilitude. To have a voice in the sphere of the political, to be capable either of self-representation or of allowing oneself to be represented, depends on one's formation as a subject with a voice exactly in the Bakhtinian sense.

I have been arguing throughout that the processes of hybridization active in the Irish street ballads or in *Ulysses* are at every level recalcitrant to the aesthetic politics of nationalism and, as we can now see, to those of imperialism. Hybridization or adulteration resist identification both in the sense that they cannot be subordinated to a narrative of representation and in the sense that they play out the unevenness of knowledge which, against assimilation, foregrounds the political and cultural positioning of the audience or reader. To each recipient, different elements in the work will seem self-evident or estranging. That this argument does not involve a celebration of the irreducible singularity of the artistic work, which would merely be to take the detour of idealist aesthetics, is evident when one considers the extent to which *Ulysses* has been as much the object of refinement and assimilation in the academy as were the street ballads before. This is, after all, the function of cultural institutions, metropolitan or post-colonial, which seek to reappropriate hybridization to monology. By the same token, such works are continually reconstituted as objects in a persistent struggle over verisimilitude.

It is precisely their hybrid and hybridizing location that makes such works the possible objects of such contestations, contestations that can be conducted oppositionally only by reconnecting them with the political desire of the aesthetic from which they are continually being separated. The same could be said for the multiple locations that make up the terrain of a post-colonial culture: it is precisely their hybrid formation between the imperial and the national state that constitutes their political significance. If, as post-colonial intellectuals, we are constantly taunted – and haunted – by the potentially disabling question, 'Can the subaltern speak?', it is necessary to recall that to speak politically within present formations one must have a voice and that the burden of the question here cited is to deprive two subjects of voices: the subaltern, who cannot speak for herself, and the intellectual, who, by speaking for him or herself, is deprived of the voice that would speak for others. The post-colonial intellectual, by virtue of a cultural and political formation which is for the state, is inevitably formed away from the people that the state claims to constitute and represent and whose malformation is its *raison d'être*. What this entails, however, is not occasion for despair and self-negation but rather that the intellectual's own hybrid formation become the ground for a continuing critique of the narrative of representation that legitimates the state and the double disenfranchisement of subaltern and citizen alike. Within this project, the critique of nationalism is inseparable from the critique of post-colonial domination.[26]

NOTES

1. See Immanuel Kant, *The Critique of Judgement*, James Creed Meredith (trans.) (Oxford 1952), p. 181. I have discussed the ramifications of the concept of exemplarity for politics and pedagogy in 'Kant's Examples', *Representations*, 28 (Autumn 1989), pp. 34–54.
2. D. F. MacCarthy, cited in Charles Gavan Duffy, *Four Years of Irish History, 1845–1849* (London 1883), p. 72.
3. On the concept of *Naturgabe* as grounding the economy of genius, see Jacques Derrida, 'Economimesis', Richard Klein (ed.), *Diacritics*, 11.2 (Summer 1981), pp. 10–11.
4. Jacques Derrida explores the logical paradoxes involved in the founding of the state in the name of the people in 'Déclarations d'indépendance' in *Otobiographies: l'enseignement de Nietzsche et la politique du nom propre* (Paris 1984), pp. 13–32. The consequences of these logical paradoxes are worked out later in Ireland's own declaration of independence in 1916, as I have tried to show in 'The Poetics of Politics' above.
5. See especially chapter 2 of my *Nationalism and Minor Literature* (Berkeley and Los Angeles 1987).
6. James Joyce, *Ulysses* (New York 1986), pp. 152–3.
7. Douglas Hyde, 'The Necessity for De-Anglicising Ireland' in Breandán Ó Conaire (ed.), *Language, Lore and Lyrics: Essays and Lectures* (Blackrock 1986), p. 154.
8. Douglas Hyde, 'Gaelic Folk Songs', in *Language, Lore and Lyrics*, p. 107.
9. In both *Anthropology from a Pragmatic Point of View*, pp. 96–7, and *The Critique of Judgement*, pp. 152–3, Kant describes the enlightened subject as adhering to three precepts: to think for oneself; to think consistently; and to think from the standpoint of all mankind. Though Bakhtin's formulation apparently abandons the final maxim, it is formally and therefore universally prescriptive in exactly the same manner as Kant's. Samuel Beckett's terse formulation, 'I'm in words, made of words, others' words,' is perhaps the most succinct deconstruction of both. See *The Unnamable* (London 1959), p. 390.
10. I have discussed the complexities, largely resistant to nationalist aesthetics, of the process of translation in chapter 4 of *Nationalism and Minor Literature*.
11. Robert Tracy, in his essay 'Loving You All Ways: Vamps, Vampires, Necrophiles and Necrofilles in Nineteenth Century Fiction', in Regina Barreca (ed.), *Sex and Death in Victorian Literature* (London 1990), pp. 32–59, gives an excellent account of the social and political background to the vampire tales of Irish writers like Sheridan Le Fanu and Bram Stoker, creator of Dracula. Alan Titley, *Dublin and Dubliners*, derives the name Dracula itself from the Gaelic Droch-Fhola, or bad blood, confirming its Irish origins. I am indebted to Kevin Whelan for this reference.
12. On Joyce's personal obsession with adultery and betrayal, see for example Richard Ellmann, *James Joyce* (Oxford 1959), pp. 255, 288–93. This obsession was written out not only in *Ulysses*, but also in 'The Dead', the last story of *Dubliners*, and *Exiles*, Joyce's only play.
13. On the question of the hybridization of Irish culture, the most useful study is Cheryl Herr's *Joyce's Anatomy of Culture* (Urbana/Chicago 1986), which analyses in detail the various institutions which compose and interact within colonial Ireland. As she remarks, 'The distortions of reality which one institution imposes on a semantic field operate endlessly in a culture composed of many competing institutions' (p. 14). The chapter pivots around Leopold Bloom's scapegoating as an alien Jew, and

opens with the figure of the Jewish money-lender, Moses Herzog, whose name connects directly with the identically named Zionist leader. Since in this chapter Bloom is also given credit for Sinn Féin leader Arthur Griffith's adaptation of Hungarian nationalist strategies, it is clear that Joyce is deliberately playing up the paradox that lies at the heart of nationalism, namely, its dependence on the dislocatory forces of modernization for its 'local' appeal. If Leopold Bloom be considered Everyman, that is, in Odysseus's own formulation to the Cyclops, 'Noman', then he is so only in the sense that he fulfils Karl Marx's prediction in 'On the Jewish Question', that the principle of exchange for which anti-Semitism castigates the Jew will be most fully realized in 'Christian' civil society. See especially the second essay in *Early Writings*, Rodney Livingstone and Gregor Benton (trans.) (New York 1975). Morton P. Leavitt, in 'A Hero for our Time: Leopold Bloom and the Myth of Ulysses', in Thomas F. Staley (ed.), *Fifty Years Ulysses* (Bloomington, Indiana 1974), p. 142, makes a representative claim for the notion that 'In the urban world in which we all live, no man could be more representative.' For J. H. Raleigh, 'he is modern, secular man, an international phenomenon produced in the Western world at large in fairly sizable numbers by the secular currents of the eighteenth, nineteenth and twentieth centuries, a type often both homeless in any specific locale and at home in any of the diverse middle-class worlds in the Europe and America of those centuries.' See 'Ulysses: Trinitarian and Catholic' in Robert D. Newman and Weldon Thornton (eds), *Joyce's Ulysses, The Larger Perspective* (Newark 1988), pp. 111–12.

14. See Colin MacCabe, *James Joyce and the Revolution of the Word* (London 1979), p. 92. See also Karen Lawrence, *The Odyssey of Style in Ulysses* (Princeton 1981), whose excellent analysis of the 'Cyclops' chapter recognizes its hybrid or uneven character stylistically (especially pp. 106–7), but confines its implications to a modernist problematic of style and to 'Joyce's skepticism about the ordering of experience in language *and* a personal desire to be above the constraints that writing usually imposes' (p. 119). The nature of this chapter has best been described, in terms that would be quite critical of MacCabe's rendering of it, by Eckhard Lobsien, *Der Alltag des Ulysses: Die Vermittlung von ästhetischer und lebensweltlicher Erfahrung* (Stuttgart 1978), p. 106: 'Die zunächst so selbstverständlich anmutende Perspektive des Ich-Erzählers zeigt sich alsbald ebenso verformt und von undurchshauten Spielregeln eingeschränkt wie die Interpolationen' ('The at first apparently self-evident perspective of the first person narrator reveals itself directly to be just as deformed and restricted by inscrutable rules as the interpolations'); and p. 110: 'Die verschiedenen, in sich geschlossenen Versionen von Alltagswelten werden derart in Interferenz gebracht, daβ die Leseraktivität auf die Aufdeckung der geltenden Spielregeln und damit eine Desintegration des Textes abzielt' ('The various, self-enclosed versions of everyday worlds are thus brought into interference with one another so that the reader's activity aims at discovering the appropriate rules and thereby a disintegration of the text'). Lobsien emphasizes throughout the 'interference' that takes place at all discursive levels in 'Cyclops' and its effect of relativizing the 'Repräsentationsanspruch jeder einzelnen Sprachform' ('representational claims of every individual form of language') (p. 108). In the present essay, I seek to give back to that 'claim to representation' its full political purview.

15. Joyce's fascination with malapropism is evident from as early as the first story of *Dubliners*, 'The Sisters', in which Eliza speaks of the new carriages' 'rheumatic wheels', to *Finnegans Wake*, for which it might be held to be a stylistic principle. Unlike the pun, which generally is more likely to be 'forced', i.e. the product of an eager intention to subvert, malapropism (as the name nicely implies) evokes a subject not entirely in control of the metonymic productivity of language. If puns condense, malapropisms displace. *Finnegans Wake* clearly plays on the borderline between the two, generating more displacements than an individual subject can master. The Citizen's pun on 'civilisation' and 'syphilisation' is especially interesting

insofar as it invokes standard nationalist attacks on the corrupting effects of English civilization on a morally pure Irish culture in the form of a verbal corruption. The movements of displacement or dislocation that construct colonized society are grasped in the displaced language of the colonized. Both are at once indices of damage and impetuses to the dismantling of the appropriative autonomous speaking subject.

16. See Lloyd, *Nationalism and Minor Literature*, pp. 113–15, for a fuller discussion of the oscillation between antagonism and dependence in parody. An excellent study of the dynamics of parodic forms is Margaret A. Rose, *Parody/Metafiction: An Analysis of Parody as a Critical Mirror to the Writing and Reception of Fiction* (London 1979).
17. In first writing this essay for a publication on Chicano culture, I was forcibly reminded of the figure of La Malinche in Mexican/Chicano culture, who, as Cortez's mistress and interpreter, condenses with exceptional clarity the complex of racial betrayal, translation and adultery that Joyce equally seeks to mobilize in 'Cyclops'. On La Malinche, see Octavio Paz, 'The Sons of La Malinche' in *Labyrinths of Solitude* (New York 1961), pp. 65–88; Norma Alarcón, 'Chicana Feminist Literature: Re-vision through Malintzin/or Malintzin: Putting Flesh Back on the Object' in Cherrié Moraga and Gloria Anzaldua (eds), *This Bridge Called My Back: Writings by Radical Women of Color* (New York 1983), pp. 182–90; and Cherrié Moraga, 'A Long Line of Vendidas' in *Loving in the War Years: lo que nunca pasó por sus labios* (Boston 1983), especially pp. 113–14 and 117. In his essay 'Myth and Comparative Cultural Nationalism: the Ideological Uses of Aztlan', in Rudolfo A. Anaya and Francisco Lomeli (eds), *Aztlan: Essays on the Chicano Homeland* (Albuquerque 1989), Genaro Padilla provides a valuable critical history of such recourses to mythic figures in Chicano cultural politics and indicates the similarities in political tendency and value of such tendencies across several cultural nationalisms, including Ireland's. In the Chicano as in the Irish context, what is politically decisive is the appropriative or malapropian displacing effect of the mythic gesture with regard to dominant culture.
18. Colin MacCabe explores all these issues in Joyce's writings throughout *James Joyce and the Revolution of the Word*. See also Bonnie Kime Scott, *Joyce and Feminism* (Bloomington, Indiana 1984), especially chapter 2, 'Mythical, Historical and Cultural Contexts for Women in Joyce', pp. 9–28; Dominic Manganiello, *Joyce's Politics* (London 1980); Hélène Cixous, *L'Exil de James Joyce ou l'art du remplacement* (Paris 1968), especially *II*.1, 'Le réseau des dépendances', is a valuable exploration of the linkages between family, church and nation, which perhaps surprisingly takes the father's rather than the mother's part.
19. On the socializing function of the novel, see especially Moretti, *The Way of the World*, pp. 15–16. Even where he lays claim to Irish identity ('I'm Irish; I was born here'), or where he seeks to define a nation ('The same people living in the same place'), Bloom appeals to the contingencies of merely contiguous relationships as opposed to the nationalist concern with a lineage of spirit and blood which must be kept pure. Bloom's insistence on contiguity underwrites his own figuration as a locus of contamination or hybridization as against the assimilative principles of nationalist ideology.
20. See respectively: Hyde, 'The Necessity for De-Anglicising Ireland', p. 169; Daniel Corkery, *Synge and Anglo-Irish Literature* (Cork 1931), p. 14; Paz, 'The Pachuco and Other Extremes' in *Labyrinths of Solitude*, p. 16; Roberto Schwarz, 'Brazilian Culture: Nationalism by Elimination', *New Left Review*, 167 (January/February 1988), p. 77; Roberto Fernández Retamar, 'Caliban' in *Caliban and Other Essays*, Edward Baker (trans.) (Minneapolis 1988), p. 3; Samuel Beckett, 'Dante . . . Bruno. Vico . . . Joyce' in Ruby Cohn (ed.), *Disjecta: Miscellaneous Writings and a Dramatic Fragment* (New York 1984), p. 19; Cherrié Moraga, *Loving in the War Years*, p. vi.

21. Retamar writes in 'Caliban' (p. 5) of the singularity of Latin American post-colonial culture in terms of its having always to pass through metropolitan languages, those of the colonizer. In this, as in many other respects, there are evidently close affinities between the Irish and the Latin American experience. But this appeal to specificity may in fact be spurious. As Ngugi Wa Thiong'o has pointed out, African literature has also by and large been written in the colonizer's languages despite the ubiquitous survival of African vernacular languages. See *Decolonising the Mind: The Politics of Language in African Literature* (London 1986), pp. 4–9. What this indicates, as I shall argue in what follows, is that the crucial issue is the space constituted for the citizen-subject in the post-colonial nation not only by the languages but also by the institutional and cultural forms bequeathed by the departing colonizer. As Thiong'o grasps, these are the sites and the subjects in which colonialism continues to reproduce itself.
22. See for example Jean-François Lyotard, *The Postmodern Condition: A Report on Knowledge*, Geoff Bennington and Brian Massumi (trans.) (Minneapolis 1984), p. 76:

> When power is that of capital and not that of a party, the 'transavantgardist' or 'postmodern' (in Jenck's sense) solution proves to be better adapted than the antimodern solution. Eclecticism is the degree zero of contemporary general culture: one listens to reggae, watches a western, eats McDonald's food for lunch and local cuisine for dinner, wears Paris perfume in Tokyo and 'retro' clothes in Hong Kong; knowledge is a matter for T.V. games. It is easy to find a public for eclectic works . . . But this realism of anything goes is in fact that of money; in the absence of aesthetic criteria, it remains possible and useful to assess the value of works of art according to the profits they yield. Such realism accommodates all tendencies, just as capitalism accommodates all 'needs', provided that the tendencies and needs have purchasing power. As for taste, there is no need to be delicate when one speculates or entertains oneself.

Perceptive as this critique is of a vulgar post-modernism's 'cosmopolitanism', we might note that the 'one' of 'general culture' is restored at a higher level only by the invocation of 'taste' and 'aesthetic criteria', that is, at the level of the cosmopolitan point of view of the Subject.

For an excellent critique of the confusion between post-colonial and post-modern forms, see KumKum Sangari, 'The Politics of the Possible', *Cultural Critique*, 7 (Autumn 1987), pp. 157–86. Both she and Julio Ramos, in his 'Uneven Modernities: Literature and Politics in Latin America', forthcoming in *Boundary*, 2, have pointed out that many of the distinguishing characteristics of Latin American literature, which often appear as post-modern effects, can in fact better be derived from the uneven processes of modernization that have occurred there. This is not, of course, to suggest a single developmental model for all societies but, on the contrary, to suggest the radical variability of modes as well as rates of change. Given the contemporary allure of the 'nomadic subject' or of 'nomadic theory', it is perhaps cautionary to recall that the legitimating capacity of the imperial subject is his ability to be everywhere (and therefore nowhere) 'at home'. For some exploration of this notion as it structures imperialist and racist representations, see Satya Mohanty, 'Kipling's Children and the Colour Line', in *Race and Class*, special issue, 'Literature: Colonial Lines of Descent', 31, no. 1 (July/September 1989), especially pp. 36–8.

23. Early-twentieth-century nationalist appeals to Celticism are an excellent instance of this process, reversing the value but retaining the terms of stereotypes of the Celt first promulgated systematically by Samuel Ferguson and then extended by Matthew Arnold. I have discussed the formation of this stereotype in Ferguson's

writings of the 1830s and Arnold's in the 1860s in 'Arnold, Ferguson, Schiller: Aesthetic Culture and the Politics of Aesthetics', *Cultural Critique*, 2 (Winter 1986), pp. 137–69.

24. Homi Bhabha has explored the hybrid status of the colonized subject in 'Of Mimicry and Man: The Ambivalence of Colonial Discourse', *October*, 28 (Spring 1984), pp. 125–33. On the foreclosure of the native intellectual's assimilation to the imperial state, see Benedict Anderson, *Imagined Communities* (London 1983), p. 105. I owe the distinction between the dominant and hegemonic phases of colonialism to Abdul Jan Mohamed's powerful essay, 'The Economy of Manichean Allegory: The Function of Racial Difference in Colonial Literature', in Henry Louis Gates, Jr (ed.), *'Race', Writing, and Difference* (Chicago 1985), pp. 78–107. Jan Mohamed criticizes Bhabha in this essay for failing to respect the dissymmetry between the colonizing and colonized subject in the Manichean social relations of colonialism. I try to show here that the two positions are intervolved, insofar as any nationalist opposition to colonialism is first articulated through the transvaluation of forms furnished by the colonial power. The moment of dependence in the relationship in no way diminishes the force of the antagonism in the national struggle for independence, but it does determine the forms taken by the post-colonial state and the necessity for a continuing critique of nationalism as a mimicry of imperial forms. On these aspects of nationalism, see Partha Chatterjee's *Nationalism and the Colonial World, A Derivative Discourse*? (London 1986), especially chapters 1 and 2. With regard to the logic of assimilation and its perpetual production of residues, I am greatly indebted to Zita Nune's analysis of the formation of Brazilian national identity in literary modernism and anthropology of the 1920s and 1930s. Her work lucidly shows how the Manichean construction of otherness and the hybrid forms produced by colonialism are logically interdependent moments in the process of assimilation. It thus provides a means to repoliticizing Bhabha's understanding of 'hybridization', since that process is shown to be captured in the hierarchic movement of assimilation which necessarily produces a residue that resists. Hybridization must accordingly be seen as an unevenness of incorporation within a developmental structure rather than an oscillation between or among identities. Nunes also demonstrates clearly the necessarily racist constructions implicit in cultural solutions to problems of national identity, thus introducing an invaluable corrective to concepts such as *mestizaje* which continue to be uncritically espoused even by thinkers such as Retamar. See Nunes, 'Os Males do Brasil: Antropofagia e Modernismo', Papeis Avulsos do CIEC (Rio de Janeiro), no. 22.

25. My terms here are indebted to Louis Althusser's essay 'Ideology and Ideological State Apparatuses (Notes towards an Investigation)' in *Lenin and Philosophy and Other Essays*, Ben Brewster (trans.) (New York 1971), pp. 127–86. Anderson, *Imagined Communities*, pp. 108–9, indicates the extent to which nationalist intellectuals are formed within the colonial state apparatus, a perception borne out in the case of Young Ireland by Jacqueline Hill's analysis of the social composition of the movement in 'The Intelligentsia and Irish Nationalism in the 1840s', *Studia Hibernica*, 20 (1980), pp. 73–109. See also Frantz Fanon's essays 'The Pitfalls of National Consciousness' and 'On National Culture' in *The Wretched of the Earth* (New York 1963), pp. 148–205 and 206–48 respectively. These essays analyse the dialectical process by which a bourgeois anti-colonial nationalism may give way to a popular nationalism in the post-independence state which is not subordinated to a fetishized 'national culture'. As such, they provide the ground for a critique of intellectual tendencies such as Irish revisionist history which criticize the anti-modernist and Manichean tendencies of nationalism only to valorize British imperialism as an essentially modernizing force.

26. I allude of course to Gayatri Chakravorty Spivak's seminal essay 'Can the Subaltern Speak?' in *Marxism and the Interpretation of Culture*, Cary Nelson and Lawrence

Grossberg (eds) (Urbana and Chicago 1988), pp. 271–313. I make no attempt to paraphrase this essay here, wishing only to suggest that the opposition it establishes between *Darstellung* and *Vertreten* requires to be transformed dialectically through the concept of the state in which both are subsumed into a unity of being and of being capable of being represented. That the subaltern cannot speak in our voice is a problem only insofar as the post-colonial intellectual retains the nostalgia for the universal position occupied by the intellectual in the narrative of representation. Similarly, the inevitability of employing Western modes of knowledge is a critical condition of the intellectual's formation and inseparable from his/her occupation of a national space. The logical inverse of these propositions is that the contradictory existence of the post-colonial intellectual equally affects the coherence of Western modes of knowledge which are necessarily reformed and hybridized in other locations. The most interesting discussion of these issues is Homi Bhabha's 'The Commitment to Theory', *New Formations*, 5 (1988), pp. 5–24. In all this, as in the composition of this essay as a whole, I am indebted to conversations with Dipesh Chakrabarty.

6.3

FROM *JOYCE, RACE AND EMPIRE*

Vincent Cheng

'What is a Nation?': Nationalism, Ireland, and 'Cyclops'

What does it mean to be Irish? Who qualifies as 'Irish?' What *is* Ireland? What is a nation? These are crucial questions which Bloom's mental observations about himself and the 'Italian' Nannetti ('Ireland my country') invoke; they form a key subtext of *Ulysses*, especially in the 'Aeolus' and 'Cyclops' episodes, evoking the controversy then raging in Ireland regarding who could qualify as being 'truly' Irish. This was an issue frequently discussed in Arthur Griffith's *United Irishman*, articulating the Celticist debate in the Nationalist revival – in which the racial purists argued that 'only Gaels' were truly Irish, as opposed to the more liberal viewpoint that any 'Irish-born man' should be considered Irish. As Gifford (130) points out: 'It is interesting that the purist position would deny the distinction "Irish" to many outstanding Irish-born people, including Swift, Sheridan, and Burke, Grattan and the members of his Parliament, Wolfe Tone and most of the United Irishmen, Parnell, Yeats and Synge, the Irish-born Italian Nannetti, and of course, the Irish-born Bloom.' Joyce found such arguments for racial purity ridiculous; he had written to Stannie from Trieste that he would consider himself a Nationalist if it weren't for the Celticist insistence on the Irish language (Gaelic) – and if Griffith's newspaper weren't, in Joyce's words, 'educating the people of Ireland on the old pap of racial hatred' (*Letters II*, 187).

In the 'Cyclops' episode's debate between Bloom and the Citizen, Bloom is asked to define what a nation is ('do you know what a nation means?' in *U* 12.1419), echoing the famous question (and essay), '*Qu'est-ce qu'une nation?*'

Cambridge: Cambridge University Press, 1995, pp. 191–8 and 211–18.

by Ernest Renan (whose work Joyce was familiar with and whose birthplace he visited; Ellmann, *III*, 567). With that debate (in 'Cyclops') in mind, I would like first to contextualize my reading of that episode (and of *Ulysses* in general) by briefly discussing the concept of Nation within some recent ideological studies on nationalism. The existence of one's 'nation' as a natural trait that we are born into – like one's epoch, sex, 'race,' or gender – is for most of us an unquestioned fact so taken for granted that we seldom if ever wonder what it is that we may mean by our 'nation' (though the recent breakdown of Eastern Europe into ethnic warfares and new nationalisms has focused renewed attention on that elusive concept of 'nation').

In his provocative study *Imagined Communities: Reflections on the Origin and Spread of Nationalism*, Benedict Anderson suggests that 'nation-ness is the most universally legitimate value in the political life of our time' (3), able to 'command such profound emotional legitimacy,' in spite of the fact that 'nation-ness, as well as nationalism, are cultural artefacts' which have emerged only in relatively recent history, products of discursive and ideological formations (3–4) – and in spite of the fact that, to cite Hugh Seton-Watson, 'no "scientific definition" of the nation can be devised; yet the phenomenon has existed and exists' (Anderson, 3). In view of this phenomenon, I would like to invoke Anderson's important and thought-provoking formulation of 'nation' in terms of the concept of an 'imagined community.' Anderson begins:

> In an anthropological spirit, then, I propose the following definition of the nation: it is an imagined political community – and imagined as both inherently limited and sovereign.
>
> It is *imagined* because the members of even the smallest nation will never know most of their fellow-members, meet them, or even hear of them, yet in the minds of each lives the image of their communion ... In fact, all communities larger than primordial villages of face-to-face contact (and perhaps even these) are imagined. Communities are to be distinguished, not by their falsity/genuineness, but by the style in which they are imagined. (6)

While a lot of Joyce's Dubliners do in fact seem to know each other (but they certainly know no more than a very small slice of the heterogeneity and variety of the entire country), nevertheless they are capable of imagining an Irish nation as a cohesive community of Celtic racial origins and Irish national character – in spite of the palpable, material reality and presence within their midst of variants such as Leopold Bloom, Reuben J. Dodd, Joseph Nannetti, W. B. Yeats, and Charles Stewart Parnell. Anderson continues:

> The nation is imagined as *limited* because even the largest of them ... has finite, if elastic, boundaries, beyond which lie other nations. No nation imagines itself coterminous with mankind. The most messianic nationalists do not dream of a day when all the members of the human race will join

> their nation in the way it was possible, in certain epochs, for say, Christians to dream of a wholly Christian planet.

Although the entire community of a nation necessarily encompasses a great spectrum of heterogeneous characters and difference, yet nations imagine themselves as somehow inherently (and essentially) different from each other, and therefore rivals and competitors. As Anderson notes, even messianic nationalists don't dream of all members of the human race becoming one nation; but messianic Leopold Bloom, the utopian prophet of the New Bloomusalem, will, in his fantasies in 'Circe' – as does, to a more limited degree, James Joyce, who, I would argue, does at least posit the desirability of a more culturally inclusive alternative to the limits of Irish Nationalism.

> It is imagined as *sovereign* because the concept was born in an age in which Englightenment and Revolution were destroying the legitimacy of the divinely-ordained, hierarchical dynastic realm . . . nations dream of being free . . . The gage and emblem of this freedom is the sovereign state.

I will have more to say on this idea (a truly imagined one) of Ireland as a 'sovereign' state later, and would like to bracket this till our reading of 'Cyclops.'

> Finally, it is imagined as a *community*, because, regardless of the actual inequality and exploitation that may prevail in each, the nation is always conceived as a deep, horizontal comradeship. Ultimately it is this fraternity that makes it possible, over the past two centuries, for so many millions of people, not so much to kill, as willingly to die for such limited imaginings. (Anderson, *Imagined Communities*, 7)

Which is to say that the imagined horizontal community allows for imaginary constructs – such as 'national character' or national identity and values – to be reified, which in turn makes it possible for patriotic sentiments and identifications to attach themselves to such reified constructs, to such an extent that people are willing to go to war or to die for these imaginary inventions.

In such a perspective, the idea of 'nation' leads to the discursive reification of a rather arbitrary and homogeneous 'national character' imposed upon a necessarily very heterogeneous collection of different people(s) over a wide expanse of territory, a notion that thus – in the process which Anderson calls 'imagining the nation' and which Homi Bhabha calls 'writing the nation' – writes out (erases) difference and the realities of a pluralistic and culturally diverse 'contact zone' (to use Mary Pratt's term), so as to establish an essentialized (but largely imaginary) 'national character.' The nation is thus imagined as 'a solid community moving steadily down (or up) history'; as Anderson points out, 'An American will never meet, or even know the names of more than a handful of his 240,000,000-odd fellow-Americans. He has no idea of what they are up to at any one time. But he has complete confidence in their steady, anonymous, simultaneous activity' (26). As a result, the nation becomes a totalized version of the universal-particular,[1] an attempt to universalize individual difference, to homogenize heterogeneity: nation-formation leads to the imagined/imaginary collectivity which results in essentialism – so that 'Finally, the imagined community . . . thinks of the representative body, not the personal life' (*Imagined Communities*, 32).

This totality is, as Homi Bhabha points out in his collection *Nation and Narration*, 'an idea whose cultural compulsion lies in the impossible unity of the nation as a symbolic force' (1), based on the imagined premise of 'the many as one'. 'We may begin by questioning that progressive metaphor of modern social cohesion – *the many as one* – shared by organic theories of the holism of culture and community, and by theorists who treat gender, class, or race as radically "expressive" social totalities' (294).

Such a totalizing movement was very much behind the Irish Nationalist construction of an Irish/Celtic national character, as Seamus Deane has argued in his essay on 'National Character and National Audience: Races, Crowds, and Readers.' Deane points out:

> In almost all the literature of nineteenth century Ireland, national character and the appeal of its various embodiments to a new national audience, is a constant refrain. Maria Edgeworth, Lady Morgan, Thomas Moore, Gerald Griffin, the Banim brothers, Mrs Hall; William Carleton, Father Prout, William Maginn, Somerville and Ross, the Young Irelanders, Standish O'Grady, the young Yeats, and Shaw . . . all give it prominence. ('National,' 40–41)

Deane shows how the leading nineteenth-century Irish authors – up to and including Yeats, Shaw, Synge, and Douglas Hyde (in trying, as Yeats put it, 'To write for my own race') – tried repeatedly to imagine (both for their subject matter and as their ideal audience) 'imagined communities' which they defined as the Irish nation and race, with all the desired 'national character' and radical uniqueness which each one fantasized (and endowed their writing with).

This is very much part of the process that Bhabha calls 'writing the nation':

> The scraps, patches, and rags of daily life must be repeatedly turned into the signs of a national culture, while the very act of the narrative performance interpellates a growing circle of national subjects – It is through this process of splitting that the conceptual ambivalence of modern society becomes the site of *writing the nation*. ('DissemiNation,' 297)

In such a process, the ambivalence involves a discursive occlusion (in both the present and past history) of the internal cultural differences which exist within any large and heterogeneous contact zone: 'The barred Nation *It/Self*, alienated from its eternal self-generation, becomes a liminal form of social representation, a space that is *internally* marked by cultural difference and the heterogeneous histories of contending peoples, antagonistic authorities, and tense cultural locations' (Bhabha, 'DissemiNation, 299). The result is essentialized national stereotypes (of both the national Self and of its Others), constantly driven by a nostalgia for pure origins in an 'attempt to hark back to a "true" national past, which is often represented in the reified forms of realism and stereotype' (Bhabha, 'DissemiNation,' 303).

As a result, we have the popular investments in an imagined and essentialized national identity; as Anderson points out, 'each communicant' in such a national community assumes that his daily experience is more or less typical of those of 'thousands (or millions) of others of whose existence he is confident, yet of whose identity he has not the slightest notion,' for he/she has been 'continually reassured that the imagined world is visibly rooted in everyday life, creating that remarkable confidence of community which is the hallmark of modern nations' (*Imagined Communities*, 35–36). Anderson's observations about 'imagined communities' (like most important discoveries) seem almost obvious once they are pointed out. Yet the point is brilliant and important – and reflects an experiential reality we have each discovered in getting to know other people: for the fact is that I, for example – as a Chinese male who grew up in various countries overseas but who am now a naturalized American – have perhaps much more in common with, say, certain individual Canadian women, or individual Dutch nationals, or individual black Americans, or individual gay males – than with most other heterosexual Chinese-American males. Any large and heterogeneous group with whose individual gay membership one cannot be personally familiar, but which is nonetheless characterized or shaped in terms of presumed shared traits, is, finally, an essentialized and imagined/imaginary community.

Nevertheless, so strong is this neo-religious impulse towards nation-ness, that the nations to which these 'imagined communities' give political expression are then conceived so as to 'always loom out of an immemorial past, and, still more important, glide into a limitless future. It is the magic of nationalism to turn chance into destiny' (Anderson, *Imagined Communities*, 11–12). Like Jay Gatsby (and like the imagined American 'national character' he represents), nations – once born – tend to create an immemorial past for themselves, as if they had always been there, and a limitless future whose destiny has always been written; as Bhabha puts it, 'Nations . . . lose their origins in the myths of time and only fully realize their horizons in the mind's eye' (*Nation*, 1).

The sentimental vocabulary for patriotic love-of-one's-nation suggests to what extent 'nation' becomes internalized as a natural and unquestioned condition of essence and destiny, often 'either in the vocabulary of kinship (motherland, *Vaterland*, *patria*), or that of home (*heimat* or *tanah air*)' – for both idioms 'denote something to which one is naturally tied' and 'In this way, nation-ness is assimilated to skin-colour, gender, parentage and birth-era – all those things one cannot help . . . To put it another way, precisely because such ties are not chosen, they have about them a halo of disinterestedness' (Anderson, 143). This halo of 'natural' inevitability surrounding one's nation-ness is patently ludicrous to any marginal or diasporic peoples, or to anyone living by choice in a 'contact zone,' for they have not been granted such an aura – people (like myself) who, whether by choice or circumstance, do not assume that 'Chinese' (or whatever) is a nationality by destiny, but instead might opt to become American, Brazilian, Swazi, or whatever. Joyce's Bloom, by contrast, is in the unenviable position of being unable to *choose* (or even to wish) to become Irish, since he was born in Ireland and already *is* Irish; yet he is, nonetheless, unceasingly typed as a foreigner always belonging somewhere else, essentialized within another static, reified 'natural' state (Jewish heritage) that he didn't choose either. The absurdity of such presumed inevitability is mocked by the very fact that almost every nation has an institutional process by which foreigners *can* become nationals: but even the term we use for that process – 'naturalization' ('wonderful word!' as Anderson [145] notes) – is an attempt linguistically to deceive ourselves into imagining the acquired identity as something eternal and natural.

The effect of such an imagined national character and community is, in Anderson's term, 'unisonance': 'Singing the Marseillaise, Waltzing Matilda, and Indonesia Raya provide occasions for unisonality, for the echoed physical realization of the imagined community' – when, perhaps, in truth 'Nothing connects us all but imagined sound' (*Imagined Communities*, 145). The composite reality of, say, 'France,' in the full range of its internal cultural/ethnic/individual heterogeneity and difference, may not be very much different from the corresponding heterogeneous ranges and realities of any (not purely tribal) nation – whether Indonesia, Algeria, Australia, the United States, Canada, and so on. It is the tragedy of a unisonant, monologic perspective that it is blind to the pluralism, heterogeneity, and multivalence of perspectives available – even within one's own nation. It is for this reason that Joyce's representation of nationalistic xenophobia and chauvinistic myopia through the trope of the one-eyed Cyclops is such a brilliantly effective and resonant choice.

The 'Cyclops' episode of *Ulysses* presents and explores many of the above issues and ideas about Nation. Throughout the episode, the increasingly drunken men at Barney Kiernan's pub repeatedly slander Bloom with racial slurs on his Jewishness – 'A bit off the top' (*U* 12.20), 'the little jewy' (*U* 12.31), 'the prudent member' (*U* 12.211), 'those jewies does have sort of a queer odour' (*U* 12.452–53), 'old shylock' (*U* 12.765), 'the bottlenosed fraternity' (*U* 12.1086), and so on. At the same time, such slurs, ironically, are often immediately followed by unconscious references such as 'How are the mighty fallen!' taken from the Jewish Old Testament or, more consciously, repeated comparisons of the situation of the Irish to that of the exiled Israelites under Pharoah (as already manifest in 'Aeolus'), such as the following description of Irish heritage in terms of Judaic tribes: 'the high sinhedrim of the twelve tribes of Iar, for every tribe one man, of the tribe of Patrick and of the tribe of Hugh and . . .' (*U* 12.1125) – for Iar was one of the three sons of Mileadh and the legendary Milesian ancestor of the Irish clans, of 'Iar-land' (Gifford, '*Ulysses*' *Annotated*, 347). The men in the pub, however, are blind to the self-contradicting irony inherent in such anti-Semitism – for they have the limited, monologic, cycloptic vision of an ethnocentric and xenophobic nationalism. This is true of the various men drinking in the pub – but especially of the Citizen, based on Michael Cusack (1847–1907), the founder of the Gaelic Athletic Association, that 'notably contentious' association 'dedicated to the revival of Irish sports such as hurling, Gaelic football, and handball' (Gifford, '*Ulysses*' *Annotated*, 316). Cusack, who referred to himself as 'Citizen Cusack,' was notoriously contentious himself, greeting people thus: 'I'm Citizen Cusack from the Parish of Carron in the Barony of Burre in the County of Clare, you Protestant dog!' (Ellmann, *JJII*, 61) As the episode opens, its curmudgeonly narrator notices the Citizen in the bar: 'There he is . . . working for the cause' (*U* 12.123–24); ironically, the only cause the Citizen seems to be working for the entire episode is cadging free drinks, while it is Bloom who is actively engaged in a humanitiarian activity at the moment (meeting Cunningham and Power to set up a charity for the Dignam family).

Right away the episode's narrator mockingly describes the Citizen as 'Doing the rapparee and Rory of the hill' (*U* 12.134) – 'rapparees' (Irish for robbers or outlaws) were originally Catholic landlords displaced by Cromwell who turned to blackmailing and plundering the Cromwellian Protestants who had taken over their lands; they were idealized in the nineteenth century by Charles Gavan Duffy in 'The Irish Rapparees: a Peasant Ballad' praising their retributive violence in response to the Cromwellers. 'Rory of the hill' was the signature 'adopted in about 1880 by letter writers who threatened landlords and others in the agitation for land reform'; it was also the title of a nineteenth-century poem by Charles Joseph Kickham sentimentally avowing that 'dear Ireland's strength / Her honest strength – is still / The rough-and-ready roving boys, / Like Rory of the Hill' (Gifford, '*Ulysses*' *Annotated*, 320). Thus, from the start of 'Cyclops,' Joyce illustrates how the Citizen's prototypically macho qualities of physical strength and retributive violence 'rough-and-ready roving boys') get sentimentalized and idealized into national legendry, the very stuff Joyce is parodying in the episode.

. . .

– Persecution, says he, all the history of the world is full of it. Perpetuating national hatred among nations.
– But do you know what a nation means? says John Wyse.
– Yes, says Bloom . . . A nation is the same people living in the same place . . . Or also in different places.
– What is your nation if I may ask? says the citizen.
– Ireland, says Bloom. I was born here. Ireland.

(*U* 12.1417–31)

This is an important passage about the difficult issue we have been exploring, 'what is a nation?' As we have seen, nations tend to construct themselves as imagined communities with a national essence, character, and identity, resulting in a value-laden hierarchy that writes out or homogenizes non-conforming 'others.' Bloom, as one of those 'others' which Celticist nationalism would write out (even though, as he points out, he was born Irish), responds simply that 'A nation is the same people living in the same place' – or, in some cases, 'in different places.' While his flustered answer is one the men make fun of, it is nonetheless significant (and powerful) in its tolerant breadth: by defining a nation simply as a people generally within a geographical location, Bloom's answer refuses either to hierarchize or to 'imagine' an essentialized community, but rather allows for personal or ethnic difference and heterogeneity without denying the status of 'citizens' or 'nationals' to anyone within the community.

Speaking himself into boldness, Bloom points out that the Irish aren't the only people being persecuted:

– And I belong to a race too, says Bloom, that is hated and persecuted. Also now. This very moment. This very instant . . . Taking what belongs to us by right. At this very moment, says he, putting up his fist, sold by auction in Morocco like slaves or cattle.
– Are you taking about the new Jerusalem? says the citizen.
– I'm talking about injustice, says Bloom.

(*U* 12.1467–74)

Although it sounds like Bloom is merely waxing melodramatic here, he is actually right on two counts: first, he is of course being hated and persecuted by the Citizen and his cohorts at 'this very moment'; but also, Bloom is aware that in 1904 Jews were in fact still being bought and sold by the Moslem majority of Morocco to perform so-called 'compulsory service,' a practice of slavery not abolished till 1907 (Gifford, '*Ulysses*' *Annotated*, 364); in fact there had been some massacres of Jews in Morocco recently reported in the international newspapers.[2]

Having argued for non-violence, Bloom has restrained himself thus far from the Citizen's blatant provocations. Now, Nolan tells him: '– Right, says John Wyse. Stand up to it then with force like men.' But if that is what it means to be manly ('like men'), Bloom rejects it:

But it's no use, says he. Force, hatred, history, all that. That's not life for men and women, insult and hatred. And everybody knows that it's the very opposite of that that is really life . . . Love . . . I mean the opposite of hatred. I must go now.

(*U* 12.1476–85)

And off he runs in search of Martin Cunningham, while the Citizen mocks him: '– A new apostle to the gentiles . . . Universal love . . . Beggar my neighbour is his motto' (*U* 12.1489–91). But, in spite of the narrator's hilarious parody of 'universal love' (Love loves to love love' and so on), Bloom's action speaks louder than their mockery – for he is in fact off on an errand of *caritas* ('love,' 'the opposite of hatred') to help the Dignam family, proving himself a much better citizen than the 'Citizen' and his drunken fellows 'stand[ing] up to it ... like men' – at the bar.

While Bloom is out looking for Cunningham, the men in the pub – thinking Bloom has gone to cash in his 'shekels' on Throwaway but being too cheap to stand them drinks – continue slandering him: 'Ireland my nation says he ... never be up those bloody ... Jerusalem ... cuckoos'; 'Defrauding widows and orphans', and so on (*U* 12.1570–72, 1622). John Wyse Nolan tries to defend Bloom, 'saying it was Bloom gave the ideas for Sinn Fein to Griffith to put in his paper all kinds of jerrymandering, packed juries and swindling the taxes off of the government and appointing consuls all over the world to walk about selling Irish industries' – a claim Martin Cunningham, who works in Dublin Castle, corroborates as he now joins the group: 'it was he drew up all the plans according to the Hungarian system. We know that in the castle' (*U* 12.1574–77, 1633–37). They believe this about Bloom because of his Hungarian background: the Hungarian resistance to Austrian imperial domination had followed tactics similar to those now advocated by Griffith, who was also 'rumored to have a Jewish adviser-ghostwriter' (Gifford, '*Ulysses*' *Annotated*, 366). As Nolan points out: '– And after all, ... why can't a jew love his country like the next fellow?' (*U* 12.1628–29)

Whereas it is quite unlikely that Bloom (even in fiction) was the man behind Arthur Griffith's ideas, Nolan is correct at least to claim that Bloom is a Jew who loves his country – and, in spite of the attacks on him as a 'foreigner,' quite a conscientious patriot in his own ways. Bloom is, as we shall later learn, a big fan and advocate of Arthur Griffith's ideas. Indeed, in his youth (Molly recalls and derides his 'socialist' ideas in 'Penelope'), Bloom apparently had radical sympathies and was involved in anti-English activism. In 'Lestrygonians' he thinks of 'The patriot's banquet. Eating orangepeels in the park' (*U* 8.516–17), a gesture employed by Nationalists at patriotic assemblies in Phoenix Park so as to irritate Orangemen (Gifford, '*Ulysses*' *Annotated*, 172–73); he thinks of James Stephens, Garibaldi, Parnell, Griffith, and Irish Nationalist debates, such as 'That the language question should take precedence of the economic question' (we will later learn that Bloom favors the reverse); and he recalls the time he was involved in a protest against Joseph Chamberlain at Trinity, almost getting beaten up in the process by mounted policemen: 'That horsepoliceman the day Joe Chamberlain was given his degree in Trinity he got a run for his money ... His horse's hoofs clattering after us down Abbey street. Lucky I had the presence of mind to dive into Manning's or I was souped' (*U* 8.423–26). Chamberlain, a foe of Home Rule and an aggressive imperialist associated with the English policies in the Boer War, was understandably hated in Ireland. On December 18, 1899 he came to Dublin to receive an honorary degree at Trinity College; O'Leary, Maud Gonne, and other radicals organized a pro-Boer demonstration which resulted in the clashes with the police which Bloom recalls (Gifford, '*Ulysses*' *Annotated*, 168). We will encounter considerably more evidence of Bloom's patriotic sentiments and activities in later episodes.

But the Citizen's polarized system of absolute differences cannot accommodate for a Bloom or a Jew who is an Irish patriot; he continues mocking Bloom ('the new Messiah for Ireland!'; *U* 12.1642) in his xenophobic obsession with racial purity: '– Saint Patrick would want to land again at Ballykinlar and convert us, . . . after allowing things like that to contaminate our shores' (*U* 12.1671–72). When Bloom returns to find Cunningham at last, the Citizen now lashes out at him so viciously that Bloom can no longer restrain himself: as Cunningham and Power drag him away from the Citizen's violence (while the bystanders again racialize him as a 'coon' by singing '*If the man in the moon was a jew, jew, jew*' – echoing a popular American tune of the time, 'If the man in the moon were a coon, coon, coon'; Gifford, '*Ulysses*' *Annotated*, 378), Bloom retorts proudly in defence of his Judaic heritage: '– Mendelssohn was a jew and Karl Marx and Mercadante and Spinoza. And the Saviour was a jew and his father was a jew. Your God . . . Christ was a jew like me.' Typically, Bloom gets it only approximately right – for Mercadante was not a Jew and, as Cunningham reminds him, the Saviour 'had no father', but Bloom's basic point is quite correct and eloquently driven home. This is too much for the Citizen – but, ironically, even his very words of emotive anger unconsciously prove Bloom's point, for in responding to the perceived insult to his god (Christ) he takes His name in vain, swearing (by Jesus) that he will do to Bloom ('crucify') precisely what the Jews did to the Christ he holds so sacred: '– By Jesus, says he, I'll brain that bloody jewman for using the holy name. By Jesus, I'll crucify him so I will' (*U* 12.1801–12). It is a wonderfully concise illustration of the cycloptic myopia of polarized binarities.

Meantime, as the 'new Messiah' and 'apostle to the gentiles,' Bloom (in narrative parody) ascends to heaven like Elijah, only to return later in 'Circe' as the Messiah of the New Bloomusalem and the Nova Hibernia of the future. Significantly, the fantasized New Bloomusalem is a tolerant nation whose characteristics are pluralistically inclusive rather than exclusive: 'Union of all, jew, moslem and gentile . . . universal brotherhood . . . Mixed races and mixed marriage' (*U* 15.1686–99).

We have been exploring the arguments in 'Cyclops' within the discourse of Nation. As Anderson pointed out, nations tend to construct themselves as imagined communities with a cohesive national character, sovereignties retrospectively endowed with a revisionist history of antiquity and racial purity: for they 'always loom out of an immemorial past, and, still more important, glide into a limitless future. It is the magic of nationalism to turn chance into destiny' (*Imagined Communities*, 11–12). Thus, the favorite metaphor of emerging nations 'discovering' their forgotten but ancient past (consider the Celtic 'Revival') – as Anderson points out in his resonant discussion of Renan's use of 'memory' and 'forgetting' within the dynamics of a national consciousness – 'sleep' (or 'remembering'/reviving what had been forgotten): '[No other metaphor] seemed better than "sleep," for it permitted those intelligentsias and bourgeoisies who were becoming conscious of themselves as Czechs, Hungarians, or Finns [or Celts] to figure their study of Czech, Magyar, or

Finnish languages, folklores, and musics as "rediscovering" something deep-down always [already] known' (196). As a result, this 'destiny' of one's nationality acquires a quasi-religiosity about it that seems natural, eternal, and even worth dying for: 'Dying for one's country ... assumes a moral grandeur which dying for the Labour Party, the American Medical Association, or perhaps even Amnesty International can not rival, for these are all bodies one can join or leave at easy will' (Anderson, *Imagined Communities*, 144). Just as ethnocentric nationalism endows the Self with a somehow unchanging racial purity and essence (in spite of centuries of invasion and intermarriage), so it endows the other with a static stigma of racial Otherness: a Jew is a 'Jew' (with all the attendant stereotypes) no matter where he is born (even Ireland); one drop of African blood makes you a 'black'; and so on. Race and nation-ness acquire the essentialized aura of destiny.

At this point I would like to return to the part of Anderson's definition of a nation that we had earlier bracketed: 'it is imagined as *sovereign*' (*Imagined Communities*, 7). If the sovereignty of Ireland seems like immemorial destiny and nature, as Celticists like the Citizen argued, it is indeed a very strange sort of sovereignty and of destiny. In waxing nostalgic about recovering the 'sovereignty' of 'Ireland' as a 'nation' – *A Nation Once Again*, as in the patriotic song by Thomas Osborne Davis sung by the men in 'Cyclops,' with its refrain 'And Ireland, long a province, be / A nation once again!' – we might do well to reflect on what that means, on the inherent contradiction in such a desire for a return to being a 'nation' called Ireland. For the fact is that (at least before 1922) there never has been such a thing;[3] 'Ireland' as such has *never* been a nation! Unlike, say, the condition of France under German occupation during the Second World War (dreaming of a return to national sovereignty), this patriotic Irish dream of a return to Irish national sovereignty which so many of the Irish had and have been willing to die for – while arguably a worthy cause – is a purely imagined construct introduced into the retrospectively revisionist 'memory' of the culture's historical consciousness. When was Ireland ever *not* either a colony of some foreign power or other, or else a loose collection of rival and warring tribes or kingdoms? From the prehistoric islanders to the times of the Celtic migrations or the Belgae/Fir-Bolgs (each group itself steeped in internecine tribal warfare) to the resultant 'Gaels' (a term denoting the peoples of the island, never a nation) to the Viking and Danish invaders to the many small warring kingdom-states (occasionally joining under a High King to fight the Danes) to the Norman invasions and then the Saxons: when was the island ever a *sovereign* state, 'Ireland'? And so what can one mean in arguing so passionately and 'patriotically' (imagining *patria*) for the solidarity and integrity of Ireland and of its 'national' purity (within the logic even of 'ethnic cleansing')? Even to the point of denying some of its own native citizens (like Bloom or Parnell) the mythical status of true 'Irishness' – when such a citizenship or thing has never existed? In invoking Irish racial purity by invoking Celtic, Gaelic, or Milesian roots, racial purists necessarily occlude the fact that the Milesians and Gaels and Celts were themselves engaged in internecine tribal warfare, none holding a cohesive sovereignty over the island – and certainly none of them thought of themselves as 'Irish'! The terms 'Irish' and 'Ireland' as *national* signifiers are purely retrospective constructs imposed upon an earlier (and unsuspecting) history by 'imagining' for the island a historically-continuous community with a homogenous national character, whereas such a sovereign community has never existed in history. But history rewrites itself as one long 'Irish' tradition (with mists of inevitability) – in which the differences between Milesians, Gaels, Celts and even Danes and Spaniards get written out; in which the Anglo-Irish get bracketed; in which Jews get written out altogether (in spite of their material presence in one's midst); and in which the purity of an Irish 'race' is proclaimed in spite of the fact that there never was such a thing as an Irish 'nation' and in spite of the many racial/ethnic interminglings of the extended, pluralistic contact zone known as 'Ireland.'

Joyce, who had decried what he called 'the old pap of racial hatred' on which such militant Irish Nationalism was founded, had – in his 1907 essay in Trieste on 'Ireland, Island of Saints and Sages' – rejected wholesale the Celticist argument for racial purity and national characteristics, which he found to be as specious as the English stereotyping of the Irish character as apes and Calibans, reminding us that 'the Celtic race' was 'compounded of the old Celtic stock and the Scandinavian, Anglo-Saxon and Norman races ... with the various elements mingling and renewing the ancient body.' The Irish, Joyce argued, are in fact a very mixed people – 'Do we not see that in Ireland the Danes, the Firbolgs, the Milesians from Spain, the Norman invaders, and the Anglo-Saxon settlers have united to form a new entity?' (CW 161–62; the present mayor of Dublin, Mr Nannetti, he informs his Triestine audience, is Italian). Joyce's representation of the Irish, cogently articulated in a significant passage, is very much a vision of a complex mix of racial and cultural strains operating within a fluid 'contact zone':

> Our civilization is a vast fabric, in which the most diverse elements are mingled, in which nordic aggressiveness and Roman law, the new bourgeois conventions and the remnants of a Syriac religion [Christianity] are reconciled. In such a fabric, it is useless to look for a thread that may have remained pure and virgin without having undergone the influence of a neighbouring thread. What race, or what language ... can boast of being pure today? And no race has less right to utter such a boast than the race now living in Ireland. (CW 165–66)

Joyce – in first noting the absurdities of such Nationalist imaginings in his 1907 essay and then in displaying them so fully and symptomatically in *Ulysses* – did not (unlike Renanesque national consciousness) 'forget to remember' the actual racial heterogeneities that were occluded by the imagined 'Irishness.' While Joyce's writings, both fiction and non-fiction, are often arguably 'nationalist' in intention[4] and certainly do not deny the vital importance and necessity of nationalism and nationalist feeling in mobilizing resistance to English oppression – *Ulysses* repeatedly reminds us that it is very important to be self-consciously vigilant about the *forms* such 'national consciousness' (to use Fanon's phrase) takes, within the range of possible nationalisms in the plural: for one must be aware of the pitfalls and limits of certain very alluring but limited nationalist visions – or else one is doomed to failure by reproducing the same binary hierarchies inherited from one's oppressors.[5]

NOTES

1. Cf. *FW* 260.R3: 'THE PARTICULAR UNIVERSAL.'
2. Erwin R. Steinberg has shown that in the months preceding June 1904, Jews were being massacred in Morocco; the reports made headlines in both the London *Times* and *The New York Times*. Steinberg, '"Persecuted . . . sold . . . in Morocco like slaves",' 615–22.
3. One could argue, even after 1922, that 'Ireland' still has not existed as a sovereign nation – for the Republic continues to claim Northern Ireland as part of its national sovereignty and thus as part of the 'imagined' community of 'Ireland.' Such an 'Ireland' – which is to say, the entire island as one sovereign community – has never existed in history.
4. As Seamus Deane points out: 'In revealing the essentially fictive nature of political imagining, Joyce did not repudiate Irish nationalism. Instead he understood it as a potent example of a rhetoric which imagined as true structures that did not and were never to exist outside language' (*Celtic*, 107).
5. David Lloyd writes: 'Even in its oppositional stance, nationalism repeats the master narrative of imperialism, the narrative of development that is always applied with extreme rigor and priority to colonized peoples . . . The nationalist desire to develop the race into authenticity, borrowed already from a universalist ideology, produces the hegemonic conditions for the ultimate perpetuation of imperial domination even after independence is achieved' ('Writing,' 83–84).

   As G. J. Watson suggests, it was 'perhaps inevitable that the tides of nationalism which swept all of Europe in the nineteenth century should have led, in Ireland, to the construction of a set of compensatory myths which would appropriate, shape, and glamorize the dismal story. This version of Irish history is powerfully teleological, even apocalyptic' ('Politics,' 51). *Ulysses*, Watson agrees, 'presents a powerful critique of this unholy alliance of romanticism, nationalism, and aestheticized history' (52).

   On the other hand, Terry Eagleton has argued in an essay on 'Joyce and Mythology' (310) that:

   > If colonialism tends to deprive those it subjugates not only of their land, language, and culture but of their very history . . . then it is arguable that the mythological image of Ireland . . . is itself a markedly historical phenomenon. A people robbed of their sense of agency and autonomy, unable to decipher the social institutions around them as expressions of their own life-practice, may tend quite reasonably to read their collective experience through the deterministic optic of mythology, with its sense of human life as shaped by the mighty forces of some process quite hidden to consciousness. Myth is in this sense less some regrettable, primitive irrationalism than a kind of historical truth.

BIBLIOGRAPHY

Anderson, Benedict. *Imagined Communities: Reflections on the Origin and Spread of Nationalism*. Revised edition. London: Verso, 1991.

Bhabha, Homi. 'DissemiNation: Time, Narrative, and the Margins of the Modern Nation.' In Bhabha, ed., *Nation and Narration*. 291–322.

—— *Nation and Narration*. London: Routledge, 1990.

Deane, Seamus. 'National Character and National Audience: Races, Crowds, and Readers.' In *Critical Approaches to Anglo-Irish Literature*, eds. Michael Allen and Angela Wilcox. Totowa, NJ: Barnes & Noble, 1989. 40–52.

—— *Celtic Revivals: Essays in Modern Irish Literature 1880–1980*. London: Faber and Faber, 1985.

Eagleton, Terry. 'Joyce and Mythology.' In *Omnium Gatherum: Essays for Richard Ellmann* eds. Susan Dick, Declan Kiberd, Dougald McMillan, and Joseph Ronsley. Gerrards Cross: Colin Smythe, 1989. 310–19.

Ellmann, Richard. *James Joyce*. (*JJI*) first edition. Oxford: Oxford University Press, 1959.

—— *James Joyce*. Revised edition. (*JJII*) Oxford: Oxford University Press, 1982.

Gifford, Don. *Joyce Annotated: Notes for 'Dubliners' and 'A Portrait of the Artist as a Young Man'*. Berkeley: University of California Press, 1982.

—— and Robert J. Seidman. *'Ulysses' Annotated: Notes for James Joyce's 'Ulysses'*. Revised edition. Berkeley: University of California Press, 1982.

Joyce, James. *Finnegan's Wake*. (FW). New York: Viking, 1939.

—— *The Critical Writings of James Joyce*. (CW). Ed. Ellsworth Mason and Richard Ellmann. New York: Viking, 1959.

—— *Letters of James Joyce*, II and III. (*Letters*). Ed. Richard Ellmann. New York: Viking, 1966.

—— *Ulysses*. (U). Eds. Hans Walter Gabler et al. New York: Vintage, 1986.

Lloyd, David. 'Writing in the Shit: Beckett, Nationalism and the Colonial Subject.' *Modern Fiction Studies*, 35.1 (Spring 1989).

Steinberg, Erwin R. '"Persecuted ... Sold ... in Morocco like Slaves".' *James Joyce Quarterly*, 29.3 (Spring 1992). 615–22.

Watson, G. J. 'The Politics of *Ulysses*.' In *Joyce's 'Ulysses': The Larger Perspective*. Eds. Robert D. Newman and Weldon Thornton. Newark: University of Delaware Press, 1987.

6.4

FROM 'JAMES JOYCE AND MYTHIC REALISM'

Declan Kiberd

Benedict Anderson has observed that the problem which besets many a partitioned state is of having been 'insufficiently imagined'.[1] That is hardly surprising, for the builders of modern nation-states were expected to dismantle the master's house and replace it with a better one, using only what tools the master cared to leave behind. A similar issue is raised in the opening chapters of *Ulysses*, where Stephen's problem is a version of Joyce's: he wears the second-hand trousers cast off by Mulligan, and yet somehow in them he must learn to cut a dash. The search for a true home is conducted in inappropriate, inherited forms. The first chapter of *Ulysses* is set in the Martello Tower in Sandycove, built by the British authorities to forestall a possible French invasion in support of Irish republicans. A colonial structure, it nonetheless allows the youths to improvise what freedoms they can. If Joyce adopts a somewhat incongruous scaffolding of Homer's *Odyssey* for a subversive narrative, then Stephen and Mulligan attempt a similar transformation of the tower, which they plan to make the centre of a modern Irish culture. All are compelled to reshape past forms in keeping with the needs of the present. Joyce's initial chapter is named for Telemachus, the embittered son in *The Odyssey* who was angry because the land of his father was occupied by foreign warriors: in the story, false suitors of his mother shamelessly waste his patrimony, while the goddess Athene (disguised in *Ulysses* as an old milkwoman) advises him to leave his mother and seek the absent father.

In *Inventing Ireland*, London: Jonathan Cape, 1995, pp. 338–55

Even at this early stage, Joyce employs the technique of mythical realism, juxtaposing Odyssean marvels against the Irish quotidian. This method has been shown to have been implicit in many texts of the Irish revival, especially the early plays of the Abbey Theatre, whose writers were among the first to grasp that fantasy, untouched by any sense of reality, is only a decadent escapism, while reality, unchallenged by any element of fantasy, is a merely squalid literalism. Joyce's early books, with their unusual blend of symbolism and naturalism, added much to this method: but it was in *Ulysses* that it reached its apogee. Henceforth, Joyce would equate realism with the imperial/nationalist narrative: it was the favoured mode for chronicling the fate of the European bourgeoisie. The Irish experience, however, was not fully comparable with the European in this respect, because the Irish middle class was not yet fully formed. The split between modernity and undevelopment was obvious to Joyce within Ireland itself in the almost surreal juxtapositions of affluence and dire poverty, of ancient superstition and contemporary *anomie*. No merely realist method could do full justice to that. A form had to be created which would, is the words of Salman Rushdie 'allow the miraculous and the mundane to coexist at the same level – as the same order of event'.[2] That form was adumbrated in *Ulysses*.

The modernism of Joyce was not only that of Mann, Proust or Eliot: even more it anticipated that of Rushdie, Márquez and the post-colonial artists. For them, modernism did not signalize a move from univocal realism to multivocal hyperreality, but from a realism which never seemed real at all to a pluralism which did try to honour the many voices raised after independence.[3] European radicals still followed Rousseau in asking how it was that, born originals, people still died as copies. However, the post-colonial artists, born as copies, were determined to die originals. The modernizers from Europe sought to expose the myths of traditional societies to the scrutiny of analytic reason, but they never dismantled the myths which bound them to their own culture. Joyce's canny blend of myth and realism did just that, using each term as a critique of the other, so that neither could achieve its goals. Rather than levelling all differences, however, he produced in *Ulysses* a genuinely multicultural text, which didn't just redraw the boundaries between discourses at some other point. And he provided a model for the magic realists in the refusal of *Ulysses* to ground itself in a narrating subject or an identifiable author: instead he offered a text without any final authority.

The risks of such a venture are still huge, and must have been all but unimaginable when Joyce wrote. Joyce's answer was to seek a tradition and, in that very act of seeking, to invent it.[4] Such a tradition exists more in its absence than in its presence: it is its very lack which constitutes an artist's truest freedom, for nothing could be more deadening than the pull of the past. Yet the very denial of tradition can become the most potent tradition of all, the tradition of inherited dissent, which is all the more powerful for being paradoxical. Borges denounced the conceit of his fellow-Argentinian writers that they were creating *ex nihilo* as reminiscent of that moment in history when the Emperor of China ordered the Great Wall to be built and all books written before its commencement to be burnt.[5] Joyce was quite open in his admiration for, and rapturous devotion to, the European classics. 'Apart from a few professors of philology, who receive a salary for it', writes Roberto Retamar, 'there is only one type of person who really knows in its entirety the literature of Europe: the colonial'.[6] These elements are present also in Joyce, but with a difference: he mocked them to perdition in the bookishness of Stephen and, again, in the writerly exchanges of the men in the National Library. In that scene, most of them speak in dead quotations and citations, as they are surrounded by the 'coffined thoughts' of a cultural cemetery.[7]

Joyce, therefore, adopted an attitude of lofty condescension to the European realist novel. He sought a method which could treat of the superstitions of a premodern community, which existed alongside and within a society already developed beyond the confining outlines of the nation-state. He did this in the conviction that the religious sensibility can sometimes survive more honestly outside of church structures and official dogma: for him art could be the third principle which, mediating between the material and sacred worlds, offered that new thing, 'a secular definition of transcendence'.[8]

By setting the past and present into dialectical tension, the mythic method undermined the European enlightenment's notions of time and linear progress. Instead, it evoked a world of cycles and spirals, which mocked the view of history as a straight line and they set in its place another, very different model. Separate chapters of *Ulysses* overlap in chronology, and even separate sections of the 'Wandering Rocks' chapter narrate the same events in time as seen from different perspectives, rendering by this means a most varied set of voices and experiences. The linear time of the realist novel denied all this and sought to dispose of time in neat parcels, but Joyce, in restoring a sense of an Eternal Now, also restored time's mystery.

One explanation of this return to the mythical is the conviction that the enlightenment project in its merely European form was incomplete. Yeats, complaining that nineteenth-century meliorists lacked the vision of evil, prayed for delivery from a mechanistic rationalism. The darker forces thus excluded were bound to reassert themselves on the peripheries: Ireland – like Africa, India or Latin America – was bound to become a sort of fantasy-land, as a result of psychological self-repression at the imperial centre, a repression crucial to the imperial enterprise. In Yeats and Joyce, and in many writers of the developing world, certain themes and images seem to recur, as if inevitably: the self as labyrinth, the notion of the environment as a place calibrated to solitude, the sense that all texts are psychological rather than social explanations.

The critique of imperial educational methods in the chapter known as 'Proteus' perfectly accords with Yeats's attack on rote memory-work and on that compilation of facts which excluded all feeling and emotion. In later sections of *Ulysses*, especially 'Circe', Joyce would explore the forbidden night-world of the dreamer whose censors have been freed. In a more general way, his book deliberately utilized all the discredited materials and despised potentials banished from the European mind-set, in a manner similar to the Abbey playwright's adoption of the superstitions and folk beliefs of a derided native culture. Clearly, a realist text, with its narrative stability and its depiction of intense personal relations in an ordered society, would have been inadequate to Joyce's needs: what he faced was an under-developed country under the yoke of empire and a people's culture which was oral rather than written in its predominant forms.

To understand the evolution of mythical realism, it must be seen as the outcome of a desperate refusal by native artists of the recommended European novel. In eighteenth-century Ireland, for instance, the tellers of romantic tales responded to the challenge in predictable ways. The anti-hero made his first appearance in Gaelic Ireland in *Stair Eamuinn UíChléire* (The Story of Eamonn O'Clery, 1710), a parodic reworking by Seán Ó Neachtain of medieval texts. The author, dissatisfied with the two-dimensional characters of the romances, seemed caught between the desire to mock them in a hilarious send-up and the wish to supply a more realistic motivation for the virtues and weaknesses of the central character.

Modern Gaelic scholars tend to see in the emergence of such an anti-hero 'a noteworthy phenomenon which suggests a decline in cultural standards',[9] but it really represents the attempt by artists in the Irish language to marry their oral narratives to the forms of Cervantes and Fielding. The attempt failed mainly because there were few Gaelic printing-presses in eighteenth-century Ireland. England was undergoing an industrial revolution and a massive growth in towns, as Fielding produced his masterpieces for the expanding middle class. In Ireland, speakers of the native language still told the old romantic tales, which were filled with supernatural wonders and were recited in public to a credulous audience. The European novel, on the other hand, was a realistic account of everyday life, to be read in silence and in private by the sceptical, solitary reader. It dealt in private emotions and psychological analyses which were lacking in the world of most storytellers.

Ó Neachtain and his contemporaries did their best to conflate the two modes, but without a printing-press could go no further;[10] and nineteenth-century Irish novelists in English simply repeated the prevailing English methods, in a tradition which stretched from Edgeworth to Griffin, from Carleton to Moore. Only Joyce in *Ulysses* managed to take the form out of that rational, middle-class world and to restore some of the magical elements of the romances – as when Mr Bloom ascends into heaven, at the close of 'Cyclops', 'like a shot off a shovel', thereby escaping his pursuers.[11] The deadpan narration of the attendant factual details 'at an angle of forty five degrees over Donohoes' in Little Green street') anticipate by some decades the somewhat similar ascension of Remedios the Beauty in *One Hundred Years of Solitude*. In both cases, the writers achieve their characteristic effect by a subversive *combination* of the mythical and the real.

Whether the results of their labours should be called 'novels' is a highly debatable point: it is more likely that they are written in new forms for which there is, as yet, no agreed generic name. There is a strongly parodic element at work in *Ulysses*, mocking the heroic militarism of epic, the supernatural wonders of folk-tale, the psychological verisimilitude of the novel, but the form which results is in no way confined by these targets. Due homage is paid to those targets: their working conventions are laid bare, in an active exploration of each mode which is also an exercise in literary criticism: however, the parody is no merely temporary transgression, but a gesture which precedes a radical break. *Ulysses* illustrates the dictum that every great work of literature not only destroys one genre but helps to create another. Radical parody of this kind has the effect of speeding up this natural development of literary form: its ensuing narrative frees itself sufficiently from the targeted texts to constitute a fresh and autonomous form,[12] a further proof that (in literature, as in politics) the urge to destroy may also be a creative urge.

What is enacted is an energetic protest against those who would convert a once-enabling form into a life-denying formula: and that protest is based on the conviction that all genres – not just the epic basis of *Ulysses* are mere scaffoldings, which may permit a new text to be created, but which should be unsentimentally dismantled when the work is well done. On this marvellous mutation, Fredric Jameson has a pertinent comment:

> The failure of a generic structure, such as epic, to reproduce itself not only encourages a search for those substitute textual functions that appear in its wake, but more particularly alerts us to the historical ground, now no longer existent, in which the original structure was meaningful.[13]

Yet even this statement is scarcely enough for, despite all the mockery of those militarist elements of *The Odyssey* which have been superannuated, there is also in *Ulysses* a genuine refunctionalization of other, less disposable aspects. If classical epic depicted an individual risking all for the birth of a nation, *Ulysses* will instead present a hero living as the embodiment of community values. If bodies were pulverized in ancient epic to support its ideals, *Ulysses* will, chapter by chapter, celebrate each distinctive organ, offering an 'epic of the body' as an image of the restored human community.

A *part* of each earlier form survives in the assemblage that is *Ulysses*, but it would be foolish to name the book for one or other of these genres. Insofar as it is susceptible of generic analysis, it might dynamically interrelate not just with Homer or Rabelais but also with Borges or Rushdie, serving as a rallying-point for the emergence of a new narrative mode. For Joyce, the shattering of older forms permitted the breakthrough of a new content, a post-imperial writing. The danger, as always, is that conventional critics will seek to recolonize that writing, or any other baffling text by an Irish artist or a Latino or an Indian, translating its polyvocal tones back into the too-familiar, too-reassuring terms of the day-before-yesterday.

Another, even greater, danger in interpreting *Ulysses* would be to treat it as a

'Third World' text which is, in *all* aspects, the very antithesis of a 'First World' narrative.[14] Yet the Ireland which Joyce chronicled had its share in the making of empire, as well as of its victims. It was, in that respect, a vivid reminder of the relentless reciprocity by which one set of experiences is bound to the other. If Europe scarcely has any meaning without the suffering of the native peoples who contributed to its opulence, and if the 'Third World' is but an effect of European desires, then Ireland affords a field of force in which the relation between the two is enacted within the community.

Europe, after all, was the creator of both the dialectics of liberation *and* the ethic of slave-holding: what characterizes Joycean modernism is its awareness of the need to write both of these narratives *simultaneously*. Each situation has its unique aspects and to construct the 'Third World' exclusively as a manageable other of the 'First' is, at a certain point, to submit to the very tyranny the phrase was designed to deplore. There is, however, a linked and even greater danger: that of conceiving the encounter as of two *distinct* worlds facing each other, rather than as social worlds which are part of one another, though differently constituted. Ireland's historical disadvantage, being a European people who were nonetheless colonized, afforded it a remarkable *artistic* advantage. The country was, and still is, one of those areas where two codes most vividly meet: and, as such, its culture offers itself as an analytical tool at the very twilight of European artistic history. It, too, was asked to remain marginal, so that other peoples could feel themselves central. Now in a position to negotiate between colonizer and colonized, it could be forgiven for strategically seeing itself as a centre. If the 'west' turns to the exploited peripheries in the desire for a return of all that it has repressed in itself, the post-colonies turn to the west as to yet another command.[15] Ireland, in between, provided Joyce with a more visibly open site of contest, and a reminder that each side in that contest needed the other for a completed account of its own meanings.

The great absences in the texts of European modernism are those native peoples whose exploitation made the representations of European magnificence possible. Even writers such as Conrad or Forster who showed some awareness of the issue were unable to render with comprehensive conviction the lives of Africans or Indians.

Irish writers of the time gave English readers some inkling of the life behind that blankness: and they could do this because they wrote in the language of the imperialist, about what it was like to grow to maturity in an occupied country. Radical modernism, as practised by a Joyce or a Rushdie, has been a prolonged attempt to render this accounting, to write a narrative of the colonizers and colonized, in which the symbiotic relation between the two becomes manifest. This is usually based on a recognition by the members of a nomadic native intelligentsia of all that has been repressed in the imperial texts and all that has gone uncomprehended in the native fables. The two orders of reality, when taken together onto a third plane, make for a new level of meaning.

Ireland, in Joyce's schema, was one of those liminal zones, between old and new, where all binary thinking was nullified, and where there could be a celebration of manly women and of womanly men. He recognized the extent to which nationalism was a necessary phase to restore to an occupied people a sense of purpose: and he distinguished sharply between the xenophobic nationalism of the imperial powers and the strategic resort to nationalism by the forces of resistance. The men in the pub in 'Cyclops' are a case in point. They mimic English Francophobia ('set of dancing masters'), but they are not anti-foreign, evincing a real sympathy for people of colour living under the lash in other corners of empire. Humanist critics like Richard Ellmann who castigate their chauvinism have failed to note that their range of reference is not Eurocentric, but far wider than that of most humanists themselves.[16] The law, which seems established to many Anglo-American readers of *Ulysses*, did not appear as such to Joyce, being merely a tyranny based on official terror.

Nevertheless, Joyce in *Ulysses* never fell into the trap of equating nationalism with modernization: indeed, his spiritual project was to attempt to imagine a meaningful modernity which was more open to the full range of voices in Ireland than any nationalism which founded itself on the restrictive apparatus of the colonial state. If the patriots cloaked the fundamental conservatism of their movement in a rhetoric of radicalism, Joyce more cannily chose to dress his utterly innovative narrative in the conservative garb of a classical narrative. This led many critics to the mistaken view that he offered his critique of nationalism from the vantage-point of a European humanist. A close reading of *Ulysses* will, however, throw up far more evidence of its anti-colonial themes.

As one of a subject people, Stephen can empathize fully with the Jews, whose behaviour he recalls from his time in Paris: 'Not theirs: these clothes, this speech, these gestures'.[17] Here is another oppressed, landless people, whose gestures, clothing and inherited structures are not their own, but the cast-offs of overlords. One of these overlords, Mr Deasy, repeats Haines's view of history as a perpetual search for scapegoats, and he too blames various women (McMurrough's wife, and Kitty O'Shea) for Irish wrongs. The repeated offloading of blame emphasizes the need for one who will incorporate all the despised elements in himself: Leopold Bloom.

Before his advent, however, Stephen takes his walk along Sandymount Strand, dragging up ideas and images from his unconscious as he looks out over the sea. Rejecting the ideal of a restored Gaelic culture, he prefers creation *ex nihilo*. Tramping on the dead shells of the past, he intuits a radically different future, and so he rejects Mr Deasy's stasis for a world of flux. At present, he seems able to play every part except his own, but the attempt to seize power by the act of writing has begun. Stephen's weighty self-consciousness has often intimidated readers, who may not appreciate that the portraiture is largely satiric. Joyce is dramatizing a consciousness suffering the over-effects of a recent university education, and immobilized accordingly.

Stephen's style of interior monologue is 'writerly', developing at the instigation of words, unlike that of Bloom which will respond to the pressure of actual experience. Stephen's rejection of the quotidian ('Houses of decay . . .')[18] is most unJoycean, and will not be ratified by Bloom. A painfully provincial intellectual, Stephen strikes aesthetic poses in hopes of investing himself with an innate authority, but he has been slighted even by a serving-woman. He is shrewd enough in his impersonations, however, to sense an echoing falseness in the bravado of his English rulers, all mimicking the ideal type (which they are not) in a 'paradise of pretenders'.[19] Mulligan, a degraded instance, has seized the key to the tower, whose rent Stephen nevertheless pays, while the Englishman goes free of charge. This overlord and his Irish toady strike Stephen as a neo-colonial act, 'the panthersahib and his pointer'.[20]

At this stage, after just three chapters, Stephen disappears into the book, which becomes thereafter an account of why his consciousness cannot be further elaborated in that society. The consciousness of Stephen certainly exceeds all available literary styles, which it wears with a richly ironic sense of their formal inappropriateness. Where a youth in an English novel would probably quantify and test the solidity of the landscape, Stephen sees it as a mere theatre for the improvisation of a free consciousness, a summons to reverie. He is the first instance in *Ulysses* of a succession of characters – Bloom, Gerty MacDowell, various unnamed narrators, Molly – all of whom will be doomed to express real enough feeling in inauthentic form.

Finding himself nowhere, Stephen attempts to fabricate an environment: 'signatures of all things I am here to read'.[21] But the problem is that his learning is more dense than his setting. He is a dire example of the provincial intellectual weighed down by the learning of the European literary tradition. His world, like that of his colleagues later in the National Library, is a parade of second-hand quotations, of gestures copied from books, of life usurped by art. Joyce may have used English with a lethal precision impossible to most of his English rivals, but he was well aware of the humiliation felt by the *assimilé* who speaks the language with a degrading, learned correctness: and he had a corresponding sense of the ways in which such persons softened raw realities by the euphemisms of art. Here he mocks the manner in which Stephen's consciousness is at the mercy of literature. Joyce was himself often accused of developing his narrative at the instigation of words rather than felt experience, but this is true strictly and only of Stephen. Joyce's own texts are profoundly dissatisfied with available forms and words, and they refuse any final homage to art, celebrating instead those aspects of life which generally elude literature.

Far from being an autistic surrealist, as early detractors complained, Joyce felt that he struggled under far too many controls. Like Stephen, he tried in his art to reconstruct a world out of barbarism, to begin again with Finn again. His problem in handling Stephen was that faced before him by Synge with Christy Mahon, by Shaw with Keegan, by Yeats with his *personae*: to return a figure of such renovated consciousness back into an unredeemed community would be tantamount to humiliating that figure and destroying that consciousness. Previous writers had solved that problem by refusing the return: the sensibility of their heroes became an end in itself rather than a way of reshaping a world, and their final glamour resided in the audience's awareness that no form could be found commensurate with their own capacity for wonder, that no words could represent their heightened inner state. Joyce, however, came to this point relatively early in *Ulysses*, and so, in the fourth chapter, with the onset of Bloom, he shifted his investigation from the mind of Stephen Dedalus to the setting which thwarts its articulation.

Yet what he finds, almost at once, is that there is no 'society' to report, even within Bloom's own household in Eccles Street. A few pages of interior monologue are sufficient to make clear that the Blooms can never know one another as the reader will come to know each of them. Indeed, the tragedy of the interior monologue will be revealed to lie in the counterpoint between the richness of a person's thoughts and the slender opportunities for sharing those thoughts with others in conversation. What is depicted in the ensuing chapters could hardly be called a society in the conventional sense, being rather a gathering of fugitives, of submerged groups, of clamorous competing voices and of speakers who do not often listen to one another. If the traditional European novel has a plot which hinges on a number of crucial dialogues, then this is not such a narrative at all, being constructed more around monologues, soliloquies and reveries.

What is evoked in 'Calypso' is the world of the outsider Bloom, who registers his distance from the social consensus by use of the word 'they' to describe his fellow humans. His Jewishness, like his Irishness and his femininity, resides in the experience of being perpetually defined and described by others, as whatever at any given moment they wish him to be. In part, this is because he remains an enigmatic open space. There is no initial physical description of him and, over the hundreds of pages to follow, scant details are let slip, beyond the fact that he has a gentle voice, sad eyes, and is of medium height and weight. If acquaintances are more readily classifiable than intimates, he retains some of the mystery and indescribability of a close friend.

Something similar might also be said of the Dublin through which he moves: its settings are only shadowily evoked, and a knowledge of them is assumed. This was a recognized feature of epic narrative, whose environments were well-known to auditors in no need of predictable descriptions. The assumed intimacy of oral narration is even more blatantly a feature of a printed text like *Ulysses*. To address *anyone*, a person must presume to be already inside another mind even before conversation begins, and so Joyce must fictionalize his reader. Yet, though he knows the traditional protocols which permit entry, his whole enterprise is to subvert them: for he wants not only to enter his reader's consciousness, but to *alter* it.

Bloom is rather wary of literature and of its tendency to soften hard realities. No sooner does he enjoy a vision of an eastern girl playing a dulcimer, as in Coleridge's 'Kubla Khan', than he applies the brakes to that vision. Yet, although he refuses to use books to 'read' life, he is quite keen to convert experience into metaphor, likening a poster on a nearby window to a patch over an eye. He thinks of jotting his wife's sayings onto his shirt cuff, as a prelude to including them in a story: but Joyce's own reservations about written literature beautifully negate all this, when he ends the chapter with Bloom wiping his bottom clean in the toilet with a page from *Titbits*. Writing is deathly, and in this book, the letter kills; while it is speech, especially the silent speech of thought, which seems to issue from the uncensored depths of the unconscious. Bloom's language is as oral as Stephen's writerly: like all adepts of an oral culture, he uses balanced, rhythmic language and cites proverbs and old saws as an aid to memory and adjudication.

Perhaps the most significant oral narrative cited in *Ulysses* is John F. Taylor's speech on imperialism and dispossession, a speech which described Moses bringing 'the tables of the law in the language of the outlaw'[22] – and the phrase might be taken to indicate a new dispensation for literature, written, however, in the experimental language of the rebel. Yet the speech is couched in pure Victorianese, scarcely an assured basis for its own separatist argument, and admired more for its style than its content. Joyce may imply that the Celtic love of style for its own sake is masturbatory. He makes equally clear that the fragments of endless quotation ('Lay on Macduff') bespeak a nervous provincialism and the pedantry practised by a repressed people who fear that they may be second-rate. Stephen, of course, is affected by the same virus, but at least his quotations generally occur in internal monologue. Vast learning in the newspaper office is put in the service of futility, in a world where conversations lack a central set of overarching themes.

In the National Library scene of 'Scylla and Charybdis', the narrator manages to mangle the names of the protagonists and to mock the widespread fashion for pseudonyms among men who fear to become themselves. The conversation, accordingly, is smothered by quotations. The Quaker librarian Lyster is treated as a man more concerned to drop names than advance arguments. He talks in essayistic clichés which show how writing can corrupt speech. In his library, as in so many others, little reading but much talking ensues. Joyce presents its 'coffined thoughts' in 'mummycases'[23] as deathly (in keeping with the earlier link made between printed sheets and defecation). Stephen complained in 'Proteus' of having to breathe 'dead breaths', which might now in the library be seen as the endless quotations from the dead authors that swirl all around him. His own refusal to publish his theory of *Hamlet* is his way of refusing to embalm his idea. The library in this chapter parallels the graveyard in 'Hades', with the librarian in the role of the gate-keeper and Stephen's review of the coffined thoughts recalling Bloom's musings over the dead.

The librarian echoes Goethe's view of Hamlet: 'the beautiful ineffectual dreamer who comes to grief against hard facts'[24]; but this is the purest Celticism. Stephen – and, we may assume, Joyce – is not convinced at all, pitting the brute realities of Shakespeare's actual history ('he drew a salary equal to that of the lord chancellor of Ireland')[25] against all Yeatsian attempts to Celticize a poet, whose most famous creation he sees in a more imperialist light:

> Not for nothing was he a butcher's son, wielding the sledded poleaxe and spitting in his palms. Nine lives are taken off for his father's one. Our Father who art in purgatory. Khaki Hamlets don't hesitate to shoot. The bloodboltered shambles in act five is a forecast of the concentration camp sung by Mr Swinburne.[26]

In open revolt against that Celticism which was patented by Matthew Arnold out of the pages of Ernest Renan, Stephen sarcastically notes the latter's relish of the later writings of Shakespeare: but he proceeds to reinvent a bard more serviceable to himself, one in whom the 'note of banishment' can be heard from start to finish.[27]

The trouble to which Joyce went in 'Wandering Rocks' to invent a vice-regal cavalcade (which never actually happened) suggests his continuing anxiety to emphasize the colonial theme. The other procession recorded is that of Father Conmee, whose identification with members of the declining aristocracy is as notable as his relationship with the rising nationalists. The atmosphere of toadying and deference, which surrounds both figures, had dissolved by the end of the Great War and the victory of Sinn Féin in 1918. Joyce must have known that the manners, which he correctly attributed to 1904, were largely historical by the time he published *Ulysses*.[28] The respective paths of church and state do not cross at any point in the chapter, as if to suggest the tacit truce which has permitted them to carve up Ireland between them; but Joyce is also at pains to suggest that neither Stephen nor Bloom pays homage to the colonial power. Whereas others 'smiled with unseen coldness', or provocatively stroked a nose, the two men are neither insolent nor craven (the usual polarity of reactions as reported, for instance, by Forster in *A Passage to India*, 1924). Already acting with an unconscious affinity, they have embarked on the mission set down by Stephen: to kill, not in bloody battle but in the depths of the mind, the twin tyrannies of priest and king.

Half-way through *Ulysses*, in a chapter of fragments, each of which represents *in parvo* a chapter of the book, Joyce adopts a god's eye view of Dublin, from which distance both men appear (like everyone else) as mere specks on the landscape. This serves to remind us that thousands of other lives and monologues had been proceeding as we read the earlier chapters; and that any might have been centralized in the book. Joyce's assumption of intimacy with the streetlife of Dublin now grows a mite treacherous, as the reader is fed a series of false leads. For example, the Viceroy who passes in cavalcade is given many titles, but never the correct one: Gerty MacDowell thinks him the Lord Lieutenant, two old ladies fancy he is Lord Mayor, and Mr Kernan is convinced that he has just seen Long John Fanning. Though the king's man scrupulously acknowledges the salutes (which come, absurdly, even from the singers of rebel ballads), he remains as unknown to any of his subjects as they to him.

The 'Cyclops' chapter, set in a pub rather symbolically sited in Little Britain Street, is Joyce's most trenchant exposure of the psychology of narrow-gauge nationalism, though it would be foolish to ignore its equal critique of imperialism. The patriotic Citizen (loosely modelled on Michael Cusack, founder of the Gaelic Athletic Association in 1884) possesses a one-track mind, which leaves him intolerant of all foreigners among whom, of course, he includes the Jews. Bloom, as an internationalist, profoundly tests the Citizen's tolerance, enabling Joyce to do two things with their scenes – to distinguish Bloom's liberationism from the Citizen's nationalism, and to show how closely the latter's ideas were based on English models which he claimed to contest. Against that backdrop, Bloom emerges as much 'more Irish' than the Citizen.

The Citizen denounces British violence, but re-enacts it in his own brutality towards Bloom. He was once a Fenian, until he violated those principles by grabbing the land of an evicted tenant. His cronies, though scornful of the British parliamentary system, mimic its procedures, preferring not to call one another by name and often referring to Bloom as 'him'. The boxing-match between Myler and Percy is a comment on the vicarious taste for violence among Dubliners, who can nonetheless appear genuinely appalled by British military cruelty. Bloom alone is upset by these tastes, and upset in a way which links him back to Stephen, who saw the school playing-field as the source of history's nightmare. Bloom (though he rather inconsistently favours capital punishment for certain crimes) can see nothing superior in employing Irish violence against its colonial counterpart: 'Isn't discipline the same everywhere? I *mean*, wouldn't it be the same *here* if you put force against force?'[29] (These views, which link him to the anarchists, will be fleshed out by later revelations that he went even further than Michael Davitt, favouring the expropriation of private property.) It is at this point that he asserts that love is the very opposite of 'force, hatred, history, all that'.[30] The price of uttering such a truism is eviction, as Bloom hurriedly adds: 'I must go now', in the manner of a departing Christ. Later, the Citizen will threaten to 'crucify him'[31] and Bloom will indeed ascend into the skies, like Christ from Mount Olivet. This man, who will finally be embraced at their meeting by Stephen as 'Christus, or Bloom his name is, or after all any other' has many analogies with Jesus, a figure born in a colony to a marginal family and destined to be a scapegoat for communal violence.

Linked to this in Joyce's mind was the masochistic element in the Irish character, whether reliving the legend of the Croppy Boy (betrayed by a soldier dressed in the garb of a bogus priest) or of Robert Emmet's execution. At the climax of the hanging of the rebel, a 'handsome young Oxford graduate'[32] offers his hand to the condemned man's lover: clearly, he is a version of Haines, and the epitome of the English forces now taking over the Irish Revival on their own terms. In the figure of the woman who willingly hands herself over to the Oxonian, Joyce indicates a sell-out of national interests in a moment of apparent patriotism, to the English scheme of things. He seems to have been troubled by the frequent assertion that Ireland was subdued only because the Irish were inherently subduable.

This might, by extension, be a way of suggesting that the Jews were used as a scapegoat for Ireland's problems, just as they were used by Haines and Deasy to account for England's economic woes. In this, too, Irish nationalism could be a depressing image of its English parent. Joyce might, therefore, be implying that the real problem is the failure of timid men (like the Citizen or the singers in the Ormonde bar) to tackle the British, and that they have failed in this because they are secretly in awe of them. It thus becomes easier to create a knock-on Jewish victim from within their own ranks than to face the full implications of their own victimage. So the Citizen ends up persecuting the man who gave the idea for Sinn Féin to its founder.

This is not as paradoxical as it seems, for the nationalists appear to Joyce as analogous to the leaders of African tribes who manage, in the end, to co-operate with the imperial mission. The passage read out from a newspaper by the Citizen reflects – though this would never strike him – very badly on himself:

> – The delegation partook of luncheon at the conclusion of which the dusky potentate, in the course of a happy speech, freely translated by the British chaplain, the reverend Ananias Praisegod Barebones, tendered his best thanks to Massa Walkup and emphasized the cordial relations existing between Abeakuta and the British Empire, stating that he treasured as one of his dearest possessions an illuminated bible, the volume of the word of God and the secret of England's greatness, graciously presented to him by the white chief woman, the great squaw Victoria, with a personal dedication from the august hand of the Royal Donor.[33]

The mockery of the willingness of a Protestant clergy to legitimize British imperialism is put to double-edged use by Joyce, given his caustic treatment earlier in the chapter of the Catholic clergy's endorsement of the Gaelic League: the priests listed at its meeting were, variously, academics, leaders of religious orders, parish controllers and so on. In this, as in much else, one tyranny is seen to duplicate another, though the fellow-feeling of the drinkers in the pub with the victims of imperialism in the Belgian Congo seems real enough:

> Did you read that report by a man what's this his name is?
> – Casement, says the citizen. He's an Irishman.
> – Yes, that's the man, says J. J. Raping the women and girls and flogging the natives on the belly to squeeze all the red rubber they can out of them.

However, the drinkers bring an equal moral outrage to bear on the holders of petty official jobs, always a source of resentment in a city of high unemployment:

> Sure enough the castle car drove up with Martin on it and Jack Power with him and a fellow named Crofter or Crofton, pensioner out of the collector general's, an orangman Blackburn does have on the registration and he drawing his pay or Crawford gallivanting around the country at the king's expense.[34]

Though the Homeric parallel is manipulated with great deftness in every chapter, Bloom remains quite unaware of it. Joyce, committed to the ordinary, finds him admirable in his refusal to mythologize either himself or others. In a book where both Stephen and Gerty try unsuccessfully to emulate approved patterns, Bloom unknowingly achieves their desire. Refusing to conform to the prescriptions of a text, he reserves his small measure of freedom, and through his unconscious deviations, he establishes the lineaments of an individual personality. He creatively misinterprets past moments, in keeping with his current needs. Moreover, his is a 'repetition with difference' and out of those differences he constructs a system of resistance to literature. This becomes the basis for a new kind of hope in an Ireland too rich in examples of characters who make themselves willing martyrs to ancient texts. Though repetition is a crucial theme throughout the book, what saves Bloom is his conviction that things can be different, while somehow remaining the same. In a somewhat similar way, what animates Joyce is his conviction that Homer can be rewritten. It would not be excessive to read *Ulysses* as a deliberate attack on *The Odyssey*, which it divests of its ancient authority by converting it into a botched-up version of *Ulysses*. The audacious assumption is that *The Odyssey* will henceforth be read mostly by those who have first learned of its importance through a reading of Joyce's book.

Accordingly, later chapters like 'Oxen of the Sun' find in the rise and fall of the Irish nation echoes of a more general decline of European civilization. In a voice parodic of Haines, an Englander confesses his imperial crimes. Joyce plays with the notion that the self-discipline needed to run an empire finally drove many of its rulers mad, or into drug-dependency:

> – My hell, and Ireland's, is in this life. It is what I tried to obliterate my crime. Distractions, rookshooting, the Erse language (he recited some), laudanum (he raised the phial to his lips), camping out. In vain! His spectre stalks me. Dope is my only hope . . . Ah! Destruction! The black panther![35]

Within the chapter is enacted the rise and decline of English literary tradition also.

The shipwreck in Homer's Book Twelve is re-enacted in the disintegration of all major literary styles of English literature, from Anglo-Saxon to the present. But the mockery of the Holy Family myth of Christendom extends the attack to western civilization as a whole: *everything* is negated. Early critics, in their terror at this, devoted themselves to the analytical pleasures of hidden symmetry in order to absolve themselves of the search for meaning, perhaps because they suspected in their hearts that there might be no meaning at all. *Ulysses*, therefore, offers a challenge more difficult than that held out by any sacred text, yet it refuses to become a sacred text itself.

To confront the void within the self is the awesome task addressed in the final chapters. Their schematizing of experience is intentionally excessive on Joyce's part – for example, the catechism form of 'Ithaca' parodies the attempt by the Catholic Church to ravish the ineffable and to submit the mystery of life to a form imposed from without. Society is increasingly experienced by Bloom and Stephen as an autonomous, external force; and though both men meet, they feel less in direct relation to one another than they feel towards the force which oppresses them and prevents them from becoming themselves. Joyce concludes that there can be no freedom for his characters within that society: they exist in their interior monologues with a kind of spacious amplitude which proves impossible in the community itself. So his refusal to provide a 'satisfactory' climax in their final meeting is his rejection of the obligation felt by realists to present a coherent, stable, socialized self.

In the macrocosm of Joyce's world is a 'principle of uncertainty' which leads him and his characters to attempt an almost manic precision in the microcosm. The attempt at rigid control of the empty space which mocks all human life is a colonization by the masculine principle which loves to order, to tabulate, to map and to judge – the tradition represented by the written book. 'Oxen of the Sun' had thrown that tradition into deep question: now the large full-stop at the close of 'Ithaca' may signalize the cessation of the written word, the better to make way for the oral, feminine narrative of Molly Bloom and Anna Livia Plurabelle.

What Yeats wrote in another context in 1906 might be apposite here: 'In Ireland today, the old world that sang and listened is, it may be for the last time in Europe, face to face with the world that reads and writes, and their antagonism is always present under some name or another in Irish imagination and intellect ... The world soon tires of its toys, and our exaggerated love of print and paper seems to me to come out of passing conditions'.[36] Joyce concurred: his own texts increasingly substituted a sentient ear for an imperial eye, and, like his disciple Beckett, he trained himself to process the voices which came, as if unbidden, from his unconscious. *Ulysses*, judged in retrospect, is a prolonged farewell to written literature and a rejection of its attempts to colonize speech and thought. Its mockery of the hyper-literary Stephen, of the writerly talk of librarians, of the excremental nature of printed magazines, is a preparation for its restoration of the human voice of Molly Bloom; and, in a book where each chapter is named for a bodily organ, the restoration of her voice becomes a synecdoche for the recovery into art of the whole human body, that body which always in epic underwrites the given word. A restored body becomes an image of the recovered community, since the protection of a body from outside contact has often been the mark of a repressive society.

Like Yeats, Joyce presented himself as a modern Homer, a type of the epic narrator even in his reluctance to begin ('Who ever anywhere will read these written words?').[37] He knew that his national culture, in which a centuries-old oral tradition was challenged by the onset of print, must take due account of both processes. *Ulysses* paid a proper homage to its own bookishness, but, caught on the cusp between the world that spoke and the world that read, Joyce tilted finally towards the older tradition. Like all epics, his would only be given its full expression in the act of being read aloud.

NOTES

1. Benedict Anderson, *Imagined Communities*, London 1983, 127–46.
2. Salman Rushdie, *Imaginary Homelands*, London 1992, 376.

3. Gerald Martin, *Journeys Through the Labyrinth: Latin American Fiction in the Twentieth Century*, London 1989, 206.
4. Octavio Paz, 'A Literature of Foundation', in J. Donoso and W. Henkins eds., *The Triquarterly Anthology of Latin American Literature*, New York 1969, 8 (tr. Laysander Kemp).
5. Jorge Luis Borges, *Labyrinths*, Harmondsworth 1970, 221–4.
6. Roberto Fernández Retamar, *Caliban and Other Essays*, tr. Edward Baker, Minneapolis 1989, 28.
7. James Joyce, *Ulysses*, Harmondsworth 1992, 248.
8. Rushdie, *Imaginary Homelands*, 420.
9. R. A. Breatnach, 'The End of a Tradition', *Studia Hibernica*, 1961, 142.
10. On this see Cathal Ó Háinle, 'An tÚrscéal nár Tháinig', *Promhadh Pinn*, Dublin 1978, 74–98.
11. *Ulysses*, 449.
12. Linda Hutcheon, *A Theory of Parody: The Teaching of Twentieth Century Art Forms*, London 1985, 35.
13. Fredric Jameson, *The Political Unconscious: Narrative as a Socially Symbolic Act*, London 1981, 146.
14. Vincent Tucker, 'The Myth of Development', Unpublished paper, Dept. of Sociology, University College Cork 1993.
15. Gayatri Spivak, *The Postcolonial Critic*, London 1990, 8.
16. See Emer Nolan, *James Joyce and Nationalism*, London 1994.
17. *Ulysses*, 42.
18. Ibid., 49.
19. Ibid., 56.
20. Ibid., 55.
21. Ibid., 45.
22. Ibid., 181.
23. Ibid., 248.
24. Ibid., 235.
25. Ibid., 258.
26. Ibid., 239–40.
27. Ibid., 272.
28. On the decline in deference see David Fitzpatrick, *Politics and Irish Life 1913–21*, Dublin 1977; and J. J. Lee, *The Modernisation of Irish Society 1848–1918*, Dublin 1973.
29. *Ulysses*, 427.
30. Ibid., 432.
31. Ibid., 445.
32. Ibid., 401.
33. Ibid., 434.
34. Ibid., 435–6.
35. Ibid., 539.
36. W. B. Yeats, *Samhain*, December 1906, 6.
37. *Ulysses*, 60.

PART 7
E. M. FORSTER:
A PASSAGE TO INDIA

INTRODUCTION

In the main, reviews of *A Passage to India* in 1924 were very favourable, praising the novel's fairness, characterisation and verisimilitude. Hostile reactions were only found among reviews by the Anglo-Indian press. The *Calcutta Statesman* thought the trial scene preposterous and 'full of technical error' while the *Calcutta Englishman* took the book to be a tissue of prejudices. The contemporary response from the Indian press was generally sympathetic and acknowledged that Forster's novel would provoke hatred among the British in India. One critic, Bhupal Singh, wrote that it contained a 'a subtle portraiture of the Indian', while another, Nihal Singh, thought it showed 'how the British in India despise and ostracise Indians, while on their part the Indians mistrust and misjudge the British'.[1] However, in 1954, the first substantial strike in the backlash against Forster was made by Nirad Chaudhuri, who, in his article 'Passage to and From India', criticised the book for its Muslim protagonist (unrepresentative of a predominantly Hindu country or of the 'India question' the novel sought to address), and for its reduction of political history to a liberal's preoccupation with personal relationships. Since then discussion of the novel has shifted gradually away from its presentation of the 'twilight of the double vision' to its representation of Indo-British relationships.[2] An important early essay in terms of post-colonial theory is Abdul R. JanMohamed's 'The Economy of Manichean Allegory: The Function of Racial Difference in Colonialist Literature'.[3] JanMohamed posits 'imaginary' and 'symbolic' kinds of colonialist writing, instancing Forster's novel (and *Kim*) as examples of 'symbolic' literature, which shows an awareness of 'potential identity' (while 'imaginary' literature is characterised by aggression and a projection of the coloniser's self-alienation onto the colonised).

He discusses *A Passage to India* and *Kim* as the two English novels which 'offer the most interesting attempts to overcome the barriers of racial difference.'

The politics of those attempts have been debated in terms of aspects such as geography, sexuality, gender, history and metaphysics; and so I would like to say a little about each. In terms of geography, although the novel begins after Adela and Mrs Moore's P&O crossing, *A Passage to India* advertises itself as a 'journey' through its title, and its chief incident is the expedition to the caves. It begins with a description of Chandrapore and the Marabar caves, delineating differences between places and cinematically describing the town from its central point on the Ganges up through human and animal habitation to the overarching sky and, finally, the domes beyond that signify for Forster both a cold, empty universe and the all-encompassing inclusiveness of Hinduism (opposed to the separation into saved and damned of Christianity). The novel's three sections are titled 'Mosque', 'Cave' and 'Temple'; each begins with a comment on the dislocation in time or space of the Marabar Caves. Throughout the text there are references to the 'real India', England, the Mediterranean 'norm', the Orient as opposed to Europe, and so on.[4] One of Forster's aims in writing his 'Indian novel' was to convey the empty vastness of a Godless universe through the image of English people dwarfed by the size of the subcontinent. The book, more than almost any other British novel, insists to its readers that the impact the English made on India was not great or even significant for a huge number of Indians. At its height British rule covered only 61.5 per cent of India, whose population, taken in the census of 1901, was approaching 300 million. Most of these, as now, lived in villages remote from the signs of Imperial authority. As the Collector concludes in Farrell's *The Siege of Krishnapur*, 'The British could leave and half India wouldn't notice us leaving just as they didn't notice us arriving. All of our reforms of administration might be reforms on the moon for all it has to do with them.'[5] To village India, the English played far less of a role in their sense of identity or in their way and standard of life, than India did in the lives of English villagers who, dismissive of India, will have used its words, consumed its goods and prospered by its possession.

In terms of gender and sexuality, we have to begin by noting that the novel's plot hinges on an alleged sexual assault on a British woman by an Indian man. This links with English narratives of the 1857 rebellion or 'Mutiny' (a key moment in Indo-British history) and with metaphors of Imperial and personal 'rape'. The novel also confronts stereotypes of the 'lascivious Oriental' and the 'mysterious East', opposed to the cool, reserved and repressed English. To many critics, the book is structured around the (homosexual) relationship between Fielding and Aziz ('beloved' in Arabic and Urdu), which is arguably an image of the friendship between Forster and the book's dedicatee, Syed Ross Masood, whom Forster taught.[6]

A Passage to India gestated in Forster's mind over ten years which spanned the First World War, the Rowlatt Acts (extending repressive wartime measures – including imprisonment without trial – to postwar India), Gandhi's return from

South Africa, an upsurge in Nationalist feeling in India, British promises of Independence and the Amritsar massacre.[7] It is firmly rooted in its history even though Forster argued that his book was about the human race's attempt to find a 'more-lasting home': that it was at its core about religion and metaphysics. The first and third sections of the novel foreground religion in their titles ('Caves' is a reference to the Jain religion, a sect founded in the sixth century BC by the reformer Mahavira. Jains stress the sanctity of all life [*ahimsa*], and place special emphasis on non-violence). The third section transcribes Forster's experience of the Hindu Gokul Astami festival (as described in his autobiographical account *The Hill of Devi*) into fiction, and repeatedly teases the reader with Forster's understanding of India as an especially spiritual country, in notions such as the transposed 'God si love', in telepathy and in transcendence.[8]

The essays and extracts below are a selection from the wide range of recent essays about Forster's novel. Teresa Hubel's discussion from *Whose India?* considers the confluence of the erotic and the exotic in the novel: Forster's nexus of an otherness that shifts between gender, ethnicity and sexuality. Using Fanon and Said, Brenda R. Silver's essay 'Periphrasis, Power and Rape in *A Passage to India*' also analyses issues of control and resistance throughout the novel in terms of gender, race and sex (e.g., Indian women are figured as rapable, Indian men are metonymically represented as penises). Where Sara Suleri has argued that the centre of the book is the vacancy of the Marabar Caves (mirroring European beliefs about the emptiness of India, a land simply of heat and dust), Silver maintains that at its heart is the 'unspeakable' colonial trope of rape.

The article by Zakia Pathak et al., 'The Prisonhouse of Orientalism', is again one of those which use Said's *Orientalism*: here, to inform a reading of *A Passage to India* in relation to a recent collection of Indian criticism. The extract also offers a critique of the shortcomings of Said's approach and of *Orientalism* as a 'white text'. Homi Bhabha's less direct analysis in 'Articulating the Archaic' reads Forster's novel and others such as *Heart of Darkness* as texts which exhibit their incomprehension of other cultures through their (non-)representations of language and their descent into incoherence.

Finally, when analysing *A Passage to India*, we must remember that Forster's novel is itself concerned with interpretation and the problem of negotiating cultural difference. The narrative is littered with misunderstandings and misreadings: over the invitation from Mrs Bhattacharya, Aziz's collar stud, the reasons for the 'bridge party', who Fielding has married, and, of course, what happened in the Marabar Caves. The novel repeatedly uses words such as 'muddle' and 'mystery' to characterise what is happening in the narrative, but it is a matter of interpretation how far this is a reflection of Forster's pessimism, of Imperial uncertainty, or of British-Indian relationships.[9]

NOTES

1. For reviews of all of Forster's novels see Philip Gardner (ed.), *E. M. Forster: The Critical Heritage*, London: Routledge, 1973.

2. For example, the large number of sociological and political readings of the novel includes G. K. Das, '*A Passage to India*: A Socio-Historical Study', in John Beer (ed.), *A Passage to India: Essays and Interpretations*, London: Macmillan, 1985, pp. 1–15, and Benita Parry, 'The Politics of Representation in *A Passage to India*', also in Beer's edited collection, pp. 27–43.
3. In Henry Louis Gates jnr. (ed.), *'Race', Writing, and Difference*, Chicago: University of Chicago Press, 1986, pp. 78–106.
4. See, for example, Sara Suleri, 'The Geography of *A Passage to India*', in D. Walder (ed.), *Literature in the Modern World*, Milton Keynes: Open University Press, 1991.
5. J. G. Farrell, *The Siege of Krishnapur*, London: Flamingo, 1985, p. 210.
6. See, for example, Jenny Sharpe, 'The Unspeakable Limits of Rape: Colonial Violence and Counter-Insurgency', in P. Williams and L. Chrisman (eds), *Colonial Discourse and Post-colonial Theory*, Hemel Hempstead: Harvester, 1993 and Bette London, 'Of Mimicry and English Men: E. M. Forster and the Performance of Masculinity', in Tony Davies and Nigel Wood (eds), *A Passage to India: Theory into Practice*, Milton Keynes: Open University Press, 1994, pp. 90–115.
7. See, for example, Frances B. Singh, '*A Passage to India*, the National Movement, and Independence', *Twentieth-Century Literature*, 31: 2&3, Summer/Fall 1985, pp. 265–77.
8. See, for example, Nirad C. Chaudhuri, 'Passage to and From India', in A. Rutherford (ed.), *Twentieth-Century Interpretations of A Passage to India*, Prentice-Hall, 1970 and Harish Trivedi, *Colonial Transactions: English Literature and India*, Manchester: Manchester University Press, 1995.
9. See, for example, Paul B. Armstrong, 'Reading India: E. M. Forster and the Politics of Interpretation', *Twentieth-Century Literature*, 38:4, Winter 1992, pp. 365–85.

7.1

FROM 'LIBERAL IMPERIALISM AS A PASSAGE TO INDIA'

Teresa Hubel

A Passage to India has been privileged over virtually all other British fiction about India. It has been repeatedly proclaimed a masterpiece, a declaration which invariably discourages the kind of critique I am offering here. For the reputation of this novel gets in the way of seeing the process of its construction—the historical, social and political allegiances which contributed to its making. Western readers have placed a great deal of trust in Forster's vision of India because it is thrilling and provocative and because it tries to be a generous vision. It does not always succeed. My reading focuses on those moments in the text when Forster's generosity fails him, when *A Passage to India* is unable to encounter the other without somehow undermining it or him or her. These failures are important; they point us toward the novel's sad suspicion that the liberal ethic did not live up to its ideals in India.

A Passage to India is hard on women. It portrays them unfavorably—as shrewish harpies, silly gigglers, confused spinsters, and cranky old ladies; it accords them only one outlet, marriage, for meaning and value within a patriarchal system, and then it persistently undermines that outlet; and it valorizes the cross-national alliance of men at their expense. When Elaine Showalter writes, 'I think we must accept the fact that Forster often saw women as part of the enemy camp' (7), I can hardly help but agree with her. Yet the novel is not so much a record of Forster's animosity toward women in general, as Showalter's use of the word 'enemy' suggests; it is a record of his indifference.

In *Whose India? The Independence Struggle in British and Indian Fiction and History*, London: Leicester University Press, 1996, pp. 95–108.

Women don't really count in the patriarchal economy of *A Passage to India*. Certainly Forster lavishes much careful expository detail on Adela's sexual angst and Mrs Moore's dark night of the soul, but these female characters and issues by and large lie outside the orbit of the novel's course.

A Passage to India is a novel principally about men, about their attempts to reach across continents, across cultures, across race in order to understand and even to love one another. It announces this intention in its title, which is a reference to Walt Whitman's poem of the same name. Whitman's 'Passage to India' celebrates, with feverish intensity, the history of man's explorations to the New and the Old World. Christopher Columbus is its muse ('Ah Genoese thy dream! thy dream' [l. 65]), and Vasco da Gama, Alexander the Great, Tamerlane, the Mughal Emperor Aurungzebe, Marco Polo, and Batouta the Moor are its heroes. Notably, each of these characters from history was a conqueror or a merchant, and all of them were engaged in the task of colonization, either for the purposes of political power or for trade. As much as anything Kipling ever wrote, Whitman's 'Passage to India' is a poem that glorifies imperialists and their mission to the world:

> Passage to India!
> Lo, soul, seest thou not God's purpose from the first?
> The earth to be spann'd, connected by network,
> The races, neighbors, to marry and be given in marriage,
> The oceans to be cross'd, the distant brought near,
> The lands to be welded together.
> A worship new I sing,
> You captains, voyagers, explorers, yours,
> You engineers, you architects, machinists, yours,
> You, not for trade or transportation only,
> But in God's name, and for thy sake O soul.
>
> (ll. 30–40)

Whitman's vision addresses itself almost exclusively to men. It praises male professions (or what would have been male professions in 1871 when 'Passage to India' was first published) and depicts the journey implicit in its title as a predominantly male endeavor. Women are hardly present in the poem. The 'marriage of continents' (l. 118), which he holds up as an ideal, must therefore be read as a union between men and between masculine knowledges, powers, and discoveries.

Forster's novel is much less blind to the feminine presence, but it nevertheless shares Whitman's vision. The narrator makes this clear when he describes Fielding's approach to life: 'The world, he believed, is a globe of men who are trying to reach one another and can best do so by the help of goodwill plus culture and intelligence ...' (80). One can make too much of the connections between Fielding and Forster or between Fielding and the general attitude of the novel itself. However, events in the novel repeatedly lend support to Fielding's belief. At one point in the story, Aziz and an unidentified Englishman develop a brief affection for one another while playing a game of polo. When it is over, the narrator tells us, 'Nationality was returning, but before it could exert its poison, they parted, saluting each other. "If only they were all like that," each thought' (76). The famous moment at the end of the novel when Aziz and Fielding attempt to embrace and are prevented from doing so by the hundred voices of the Indian landscape, which announce 'No, not yet ... No, not there' (316), relies for its emotional efficacy on the notion that a loving relationship between the two men *should* be possible and *would* be, if the time were right. Both of these events, and numerous others in the novel, assume that it is the friendship of men that will bring about the union of the nations.

Women are not included in this union because they tend to function in the novel not as active participants in the creation of these friendships but instead as obstacles to them or, conversely, as conduits, which enable the friendship to come about or continue. Wives in particular serve this latter purpose. Aziz's relationship with Fielding achieves a depth and permanence by means of his dead wife. A photograph of her, which he allows Fielding to see, becomes a token of Aziz's trust and affection for the Englishman. When Fielding responds with gratitude to the gesture, Aziz tells him that had his wife been alive, he would have been permitted to see her in spite of the purdah (seclusion of women). He adds, 'All men are my brothers, and as soon as one behaves as such he may see my wife,' to which Fielding answers, 'And when the whole world behaves as such, there will be no more purdah' (128). Beyond being a vague memory which Aziz calls up when he is feeling poetic, his wife has no autonomous existence in the story. Her primary function is to serve as a vehicle for the affection of her husband and his friend. Furthermore, the act of viewing her photograph is linked to the utopian possibilities that the friendship of Aziz and Fielding represents. When Whitman's and Forster's vision is realized and all men recognize their brotherhood, purdah will end because men will no longer feel the need for it. There is, of course, an erasure here of the wife's will. Were she alive, she would apparently have no say either about meeting Fielding or about the practice of purdah in her household.

Despite the importance of the purdah custom to the workings of this paradigm in which females are tokens, such nullification of women is not confined solely to Indian culture. Englishmen also have wives to exhibit. Fielding returns Aziz's compliment toward the end of the novel when he uses his wife, or, more accurately, information about his wife as a means of demonstrating his feelings for the other man. One of the narrator's comments establishes that this is indeed his motive in revealing Stella's spiritual restlessness to Aziz: 'And, anxious to make what he could of this last afternoon, he forced himself to speak intimately about his wife, the person most dear to him' (313). In *A Passage to India*, wives, or at least 'good' wives, seem to exist to further the friendship between husbands and the ties between nations. Speaking about the discourse of *sati*, to which Indian men of the upper caste and English ICS officers contributed but from which the testament of the widows who practiced it is entirely left out, Spivak observes that, 'Between patriarchal subject-formation and imperialist object-constitution, it is the dubious place of the free will of the sexed subject as female that is successfully effaced' ('Rani' 144). Spivak's widows and Forster's wives are caught between these two mutually supportive systems and effectively silenced.

The female characters in the novel who refuse to be silenced earn the resentment of their men and the narrator's disapproval as well. These are the Anglo-Indian wives, and they are the characters we are least encouraged to like. Forster's condemnation of Anglo-Indian women has a discursive history that goes back before *A Passage to India* was published. In a 1922 article for the journal *The Nation & the Athenaeum*, Forster lambastes all Anglo-Indians for the social ineptitude toward Indians for which they have become renowned. But he saves his most scathing reproof for Anglo-Indian women:

> If the Englishman might have helped the Indian socially, how much more might the Englishwoman have helped! But she has done nothing, or worse than nothing. She deserves, as a class, all that the satirists have said about her, for she has instigated the follies of her male when she might have calmed them and set him on the sane course. (615)

In Forster's eyes the Anglo-Indian woman is more responsible than her male counterpart for the appalling racial situation in India, and, therefore, all the social blunders of the British Empire are laid at her feet. The attitude toward these women in the novel is much more calm, much less vociferous, but nevertheless hostile. Throughout the novel, they are blamed for standing in the way of their men. We are told on one occasion that the men would have made a greater effort to socialize with the Indian guests at the Turton's 'bridge' party but were 'prevented from doing so by their womenfolk whom they had to attend, provide with tea, advise about dogs, etc.' (66) Moreover, at a particularly crucial time for the Anglo-Indian society in the novel—when the women feel threatened because of Adela's experience (or imagined experience) of attempted rape and the men have assumed roles as their protectors—the novel relays the Collector's inmost thought, and it is, not surprisingly, a misogynistic one: 'After all, it's our women who make everything more difficult out here' (217). Anglo-Indian women are the novel's scapegoats; they bear the brunt of Forster's anger about English conduct in India. The Anglo-Indian men, on the other hand, are criticized but are usually accorded some sympathy because of the difficult jobs they are required to do.

The text's resentment toward these women may also be a part of their refusal to accommodate its utopian ideal. For whatever reasons, they will not do what is expected of them, that is, be a passageway for the easy flow of friendship between English and Indian men. On the contrary, the women force their men to choose sides. Fielding recognizes this early in the novel: 'He had discovered that it is possible to keep in with Indians and Englishmen, but that he who would also keep in with Englishwomen must drop the Indians. The two wouldn't combine' (80). Fielding initially chooses Aziz and his Indian friends, but when he marries an Englishwoman, his continued relationship with Indian men becomes an impossibility. His marriage to Stella constitutes both a political and emotional betrayal of Aziz—political because Fielding has thrown his lot in with a community that Aziz and *his* community have sworn to defeat and emotional because the novel is grounded in the belief that love between men of different races is the solution to the problem of international conflict.

But where do Adela and Mrs Moore fit into the picture, since neither of them are Anglo-Indian wives? Initially, Mrs Moore appears to be someone who will disrupt the pattern, for she is a woman who maintains a friendship with an Indian man independently of the Englishmen around her. What occurs between her and Aziz—the tender friendship which finds expression first at the mosque, later at Fielding's tea party, and finally at the caves—does not require the presence of an Englishman to give it meaning. But Mrs Moore's descent into meaninglessness, which turns her into a cranky and petulant old woman, removes her from the stage of inter-racial friendship altogether. She withdraws so far into herself that she is unable to see any longer the relevance of such friendship, and at Aziz's lowest moment, she leaves both him and India to their respective fates. Her actions just prior to her death at sea cast a shadow back over her earlier pleasant encounters with Aziz. Readers may conclude that she is not capable of participating in the ideal union of nations.

As for Adela, she exists on the margins of this ideal throughout the story, because she seems to lack the ability to enter into friendships with Indians. From the beginning, it is clear that she does not possess the understanding necessary to bridge the gap between these cultures. For instance, in spite of her good will, she repeatedly makes errors in judgment and in feeling during her conversations with Aziz and with other Indians, and the result is she never wins anybody's affection. Her moment of truth in the courtroom, when she courageously retracts her accusation, goes unappreciated by the Indian characters in the novel. The action elicits their hostility, in fact, because of the unemotional way in which it is accomplished:

> For her behaviour rested on cold justice and honesty; she had felt, while she recanted, no passion of love for those whom he had wronged. . . . And the girl's sacrifice—so creditable according to Western notions—was *rightly* rejected, because, though it came from her heart, it did not include her heart. A few garlands from students was all that India ever gave her in return. (245, emphasis mine)

This is the narrator speaking, and it is interesting that he is in complete accord with the Indians' reaction. Indeed the novel seems generally bent on demonstrating the shallowness of Adela's behavior in India. She is well meaning but, unlike Fielding, quite incapable of establishing anything beyond superficial connections with Indians. The fault lies in Adela's deficient vision of India, and this is most apparent in the beginning when she announces her desire to see the 'real India.' Such a goal is shown finally to be pathetically misguided, since one of the main points of the novel is that the 'real India' is unapprehendable; it might not even exist. And Adela never acquires and ultimately does not seem to want the knowledge that Fielding possesses from the start—that Indians themselves are all that anyone can know of 'the real India.' Thus the novel suggests that if Indians gave Adela almost nothing in return for her courage in the courtroom, because of her mistaken notions about India, it was all that she deserved.

Despite her inadequacy, Adela does function as the person through whom Fielding and Aziz meet and whose misfortune causes their friendship to deepen. It is as a result of Adela's desire to see the 'real India' that the two men embark on their cross-cultural relationship. When Fielding organizes a tea party for Mrs Moore and Adela, Aziz is invited because of Adela's interest in him. He arrives early, before Mrs Moore and Adela, and immediately strikes up a friendship with Fielding. Once Aziz learns that the two women will be coming to tea as well, he is disappointed, because, as the narrator explains, 'he preferred to be alone with his new friend' (84). At the outset of this party, the women are made to seem superfluous.

Adela's frightening experience in the cave serves to cement even further the friendship between the two men, since it is because of Aziz's arrest that Fielding is forced to take a public stand in favor of his friend and against Adela and the Anglo-Indian community. But at the same time that the novel documents their increasing intimacy, it simultaneously invalidates Adela's experience of sexual assault.

Aziz and Fielding grow closer as Adela's memory of the incident seems to blur. Although she is at first certain of what has happened to her in the cave, eventually she is forced to entertain the possibility—an idea implanted by Fielding—that she had hallucinated the entire experience; 'the sort of thing,' she herself draws the comparison, 'that makes some women think they've had an offer of marriage when none was made' (240). Fielding also suggests that it was the Indian guide who entered the cave after Adela and attempted to assault her, but Aziz's friend Hamidullah angrily dismisses that possibility: 'I gather you have not done with us yet, and it is now the turn of the poor old guide who conducted you round the caves' (243). Finally, in her last conversation with Fielding, when he presses her to examine the moment in the cave once more, she closes the subject for good by complacently adopting his suggestion about the guide. We are told that 'the question had lost interest for her suddenly' (242). Every opinion in the text, even Adela's, conspires to relegate her experience of sexual assault to the edges of the story, and the reason for this resides in something I have mentioned earlier, namely, Forster's indifference to women. I should make it clear that this indifference does not prevent Forster from constructing women as characters with interesting stories and experiences of their own. Mrs Moore and Adela are both central figures in the novel, and their separate approaches to India in particular and life in general are delineated with careful detail and with sympathy. What Forster is indifferent to are those aspects of these women's characters that exist apart from and even in spite of their roles in patriarchal and imperialist structures.

Although she is not a wife, Adela functions like so many female characters in *A Passage to India*, as a conduit or even a cipher. She provides the opportunity for Fielding and Aziz to meet and later the means through which their friendship is tested and strengthened. It is largely at her expense that they are friends at all, since in order for them to retain their friendship, her account of the event in the cave must be retracted. Once Adela withdraws her accusation of Aziz and his innocence is no longer in question, the incident in the cave moves into a new area of significance. As a personal experience, it recedes into unimportance. In the end, it does not matter to any of the characters what actually happened in the cave. Adela's experience of sexual assault is elided to make way for another reading, a reading that transforms the personal into the transpersonal and the universal. The incident becomes a moment of supreme mystery and represents, therefore, one more testament to the unreality, the 'muddle' that the novel posits as India.

Forster's treatment of womanhood is even more fascinating and problematic when analyzed alongside the feminized image of India that the text appears on the surface to affirm. As in much British fiction about India, in Forster's novel the country is depicted as a seductive and alluring female. Various moments throughout the text contribute to this conception of India, particularly the Caves section. This passage follows Adela's contemplation of her future life in British India, but it is evident from both the content, which proclaims its speaker as a person with more than a superficial knowledge of India, and the masculine gaze, which fixes India as a female object, that it is not Adela who is speaking. It is a male voice:

> How can the mind take hold of such a country? Generations of invaders have tried, but they remain in exile. The important towns they build are only retreats, their quarrels the malaise of men who cannot find their way home. India knows of their trouble. She knows of the whole world's trouble, to its uttermost depth. She calls 'Come' through her hundred mouths, through objects ridiculous and august. But come to what? She has never defined. She is not a promise, only an appeal. (148–49)

Such a construction seems to have been irresistible during the colonial period. Almost every novel and a number of poems written about India by Englishmen in the nineteenth and first half of the twentieth century contain some vision of India or of the East as a magnetically attractive female figure.[1] Forster taps into an Anglo-Indian tradition when he uses this image in his novel. But a close look at Forster's construction reveals something radically different.

In other British writing, this trope is invariably composed of a catalog or lavish descriptions of much-loved Indian things. Kipling's 'Mandalay,' about a

London man pining for his beloved and for her country, contains the best-known example of this discursive practice:

> 'If you've 'eard the East a-callin', you won't never 'eed naught else.'
> No! you won't 'eed nothin' else
> But them spicy garlic smells,
> An' the sunshine an' the palm-trees an' the tinkly temple-bells;
> On the road to Mandalay . . .
>
> (189)

But in Forster's construction, there is no catalog because there is nothing to inscribe; India has no substance. 'She is not a promise, only an appeal,' the narrator tells us, a siren who calls to men and then disappears when they reach her. We can understand why Kipling's Londoner is drawn back to the East because we are given the details of his longing and a list of her attractions. Forster's India, however, is apparently an empty show. If we read Forster against Kipling, we recognize that Forster is implicitly criticizing those who, hearing India call 'through objects ridiculous and august,' actually believe that she has something to offer. In *A Passage to India*, the otherness of the East, 'the sunshine an' the palm-trees an' the tinkly temple-bells,' is subsumed by the modern writing mind of the West, which is determined to find not difference but an extension of its exiled self in India.

The male narrator's refusal or inability to see the difference of India has everything to do with the fact that India is constructed as a woman. *A Passage to India* is a narrative in which it is nearly impossible to discern any perspective but a western perspective or any gender but the masculine gender. Thus the women characters and female figures in the novel tend to function as conduits or as obstacles to the friendship of Fielding and Aziz. In a similar manner, when Forster adopts the traditional Anglo-Indian image of India as a seductive female, her magnetism is shown to be a ruse, since she is all appeal and no substance, and her meaning is made dependent on the masculine mind that apprehends her. Images of India as an other who possesses an autonomous existence outside the western writing mind, who is not an extension of that mind nor is fully apprehendable by it, are available in the text, but they are not female images.

As in many western novels written during the colonial period, for example, Joseph Conrad's *Heart of Darkness*, the image of the colonized country is a construction which participates in the mutually constitutive discourses of both exoticism and eroticism. However, while Conrad's Africa comes to be represented most poignantly by the proud and alluring African woman who emerges out of the jungle to bid farewell to Kurtz, Forster's India is a masculine one. It is not the seductress calling to troubled men with her hundred mouths who claims the narrator's most careful and loving attention. It is, rather, the punkah puller described so painstakingly during the scene in the court room and later the servitor whose floating village of Gokul causes the collision of Aziz's and Fielding's boats at the end of the novel. Of all the emblems of India in the text, these portraits of Indian maleness come closest to embodying Forster's conception of and affection for the country. Unlike the female siren figure of the Caves section, the punkah puller and the servitor are not subject to the narrator's philosophical skepticism, which neutralizes otherness through an elaborate and ultimately dismissive analysis. On the contrary, these images somehow cannot be explained away or made to seem nebulous and ungraspable. In their concrete impenetrability, they lead the text out of the discourse of liberal imperialism because they are never subsumed by the western writing mind, which dominates every other Indian image in *A Passage to India*.

The punkah wallah and the temple servitor are notable in the novel because of the control that they, as Indians, are allowed to exercise over their environments. The servitor holds this authority by virtue of 'his hereditary office to close the gates of salvation.' It is his job during the celebration of Krishna's birthday to bring the festivities to an end by pushing the clay image of the god's village into the lake. At the moment that the clay dolls of Krishna's family begin to collide and sink, the two boats containing Fielding and his wife, Stella, and Aziz and Stella's brother, Ralph, replicate the action. The four outsiders drift 'helplessly' toward the servitor, who 'awaited them, his beautiful dark face expressionless, and as the last morsels melted on his tray it struck them' (309). This causes the boats to capsize and Aziz and Fielding to become friends once again. 'That was the climax, as far as India admits of one,' the narrator announces (310). Although the servitor stands outside the story's climax, in that he is not part of the reconciliation, he is responsible for having brought it about. Moreover, in the midst of much confusion and helplessness, he is represented as a figure of calm supremacy, who—depending on how one interprets the word 'awaited' quoted above—even seems to have some foreknowledge of the event. The discourse of power and knowledge is more pronounced in the description of the punkah puller. He is officially the least important of all the characters in the court room, yet in Adela's eyes, 'he seemed to control the proceedings' (220). Like the servitor, he is depicted as outside the course of the story but as somehow its director: 'Pulling the rope towards him, relaxing it rhythmically, sending swirls of air over others, receiving none himself, he seemed apart from human destinies, a male Fate, a winnower of souls' (221). This metaphor of the punkah wallah as a 'male Fate' is confirmed when Adela, whose vision of him incites her to question her own sense of self-importance, eventually recognizes the mistake she has made about Aziz, a moment which then serves as the central turning point in the novel. It takes the presence of the punkah puller at one point and the temple servitor at another to provide the necessary plot complications and finally to bring the story to its conclusion.

These two masculine figures function as the embodiment of their author's feelings about India, about India's attractions and its relationship to the West. That these feelings are sexual is evident in the eroticization of both the punkah puller and the servitor. The narrator delineates the servitor as 'naked, broad-shouldered, thin-waisted—the Indian body again triumphant' (309), the 'again' referring back to the punkah wallah. The narrator's gaze seems homoerotic. Similarly, in the description of the punkah wallah, although it is Adela's eyes that we are following, it is the male narrator's or perhaps the author's desire that we hear:

> Almost naked, and splendidly formed, he sat on a raised platform near the back, in the middle of the central gangway, and he caught her attention as she came in ... He had the strength and beauty that sometimes come to flower in Indians of low birth. When that strange race nears the dust and is condemned as untouchable, then nature remembers the physical perfection that she accomplished elsewhere, and throws out a god. ... This man would have been notable anywhere; among the thin-hammed, flat-chested mediocrities of Chandrapore he stood out as divine. (220)

There is no indication anywhere in the text that Adela has noticed other Indian men in Chandrapore, described here as 'thin-hammed, flat-chested mediocrities.' Indeed, Adela's own asexuality and her non-sexual approach to the world, both of which are made much of in the novel, would undoubtedly render her incapable of such an erotic perception.

What is remarkable about these eroticized, male images of India is that they seem to emerge out of an Orientalist perspective.[2] Earlier, I examined this perspective at work in Kipling's short stories and even to some extent in Duncan's novel. Orientalism, both in Edward Said's explication of the term in his book of the same name and in older scholarship about imperialism, such as Francis G. Hutchins's *The Illusion of Permanence*, which defines Orientalism —or what he calls 'Orientalization'—as a politics standing in opposition to liberalism, is a way of seeing the East entirely as the other, as that which is not the West. In order to preserve this dichotomy, Orientalist or conservative politicians of the colonial period had also to preserve the separateness of the East. Hence, the westernization program, which liberal policy encouraged, was criticized by the Orientalists for much the same reasons that Kipling belittles Wali Dad in 'On the City Wall'—because it robbed the colonized of their own culture and replaced it with a watered-down version of the West. Implicit in Orientalism is a certain respect for the indigenous culture. But, as Hutchins observes, this respect was frequently translated into a refusal on the part of the Orientalists to acknowledge or allow change to occur in the East:

> An India of the imagination was created which contained no elements of either social change or political menace. Orientalization was the result of this effort to conceive of Indian society as devoid of elements hostile to the perpetuation of British rule, for it was on the basis of this presumptive India that Orientalizers sought to build a permanent rule. (157)

Fittingly, the predominant Orientalist image of the East is one that emphasizes its timelessness.

The figures of the punkah wallah and the temple servitor in *A Passage to India* are both products of Orientalism, for both are imaged as somehow existing outside time, in that eternal and changeless India that the West cannot and should not touch. As such, they are exempt from the narrator's sceptical analysis, which usually examines the objects, people, and beliefs of India in order to absorb them into a western narrative. Still, it can be argued that the existence of these pristine Orientalist images in a text that tends to flatten out difference does not take us very far. Although they lead us away from the liberal paradigm that dominates the novel, we are, nevertheless, still within an imperialist discourse. Forster has simply switched camps from the liberal to the conservative.[3] I think, however, that we can interpret these glimpses of Orientalism in light of a much more radical thesis. The inappropriateness of their presence in this novel encourages us to do so. Instead of seeing these images as turning us back to an imperialist arena, we can allow them to point us to a perspective that the text obliquely endorses but is completely unable to articulate given the limits of its vision. This is the perspective of the peasant or the subaltern.

A Passage to India is primarily concerned with valorizing the interracial dialogue between men, and those voices which might get in the way of this ideal are either incorporated, that is made to work on its behalf, or rendered irrelevant. Somehow the punkah wallah and the temple servitor escape this treatment. They are, in fact, accorded the deepest respect and admiration that the novel has to offer. The reason that they cannot be recuperated in the interests of the prevailing liberal reformative ideology is that they stand too far outside the novel's ideal. The interracial dialogue toward which the text strives is a closed conversation. Only the ruling Englishmen and the Indian elite, such as the western-trained doctor, Aziz, and the lawyer, Hamidullah, are capable of participating, since they have acquired the language in which the dialogue is conducted. The punkah wallah and the servitor have no access to this language. That the text nevertheless accords a place to these subaltern figures, a place that it does not subsequently colonize, suggests that another kind of dialogue is possible.

The so-called Indian masses—the workers, the peasants, and the untouchables—have been the subject of much elite writing about India, both historiography and literature. Gandhi, imperialists such as ICS officials and viceroys, Anglo-Indian novelists, and most recently the subaltern historians, all have laid claim to the places that these people who apparently do not write are supposed to occupy. All have endeavored to construct their history and to speak on their behalf. Forster does not do this. His male subalterns are silent but still authoritative. If there is a non-imperialist perspective in *A Passage to India*, it is not the women characters who provide it because their voice is entirely appropriated. Nor is it Aziz with his brand of nationalism, which, so far as it is examined at all, is shown to be simply the inverse of imperialism, the other side of an elite dialogue. If there is a passage to India which might be able to take us beyond the novel's imperialist structures, it is through the powerful silences of the punkah wallah and the temple servitor.

NOTES

1. Without undermining the genuine emotion that has gone into the creation of this image, it is important that we understand how convenient it is as an explanatory trope. It is convenient because it explains away the Englishman's attraction to India, without making him examine his part in that attraction. Englishmen come because India calls. That there might be some other motive behind the Englishman's residence in India, for instance, that Englishmen stood to gain financially by living in India, is an issue that is suppressed by this romantic trope of India's seductiveness.
2. I am indebted to Jenny Sharpe's article 'Figures of Colonial Resistance' for making this connection between the punkah wallah and Orientalism.
3. Throughout this chapter, I have argued that English imperialism manifested two separate and distinct forms in India, the liberal reformative ethic and conservative Orientalism. I am convinced that this bipartite understanding of imperialism accounts for many apparently contradictory events and their accompanying attitudes—such as the social reform movement of the early and middle nineteenth century, with its openness to change, followed by the later reaction to reform after the Mutiny or Indian Revolt of 1857, which enshrined India as unchangeable. It is not enough to interpret imperialism, as Said often does in *Orientalism*, as stable and static, an ethos which simply grew more intractable as the Empire expanded, because such an interpretation ignores the rhythms through which English imperialism in India expressed itself. The one aspect of imperialism which remained constant, however, was the desire of the English to rule the Indians, though that rule was occasionally liberal and at other times conservative in tone. In the pursuit of this desire, the two streams frequently merged or subtly and unresistantly gave way to one another. Liberalism was frequently informed by conservative Orientalism and vice versa. When I say, therefore, that Forster switches camps from the liberal to the conservative through the introduction of the figures of the punkah wallah and temple servitor, I am acknowledging the tendency of English imperialism to move back and forth between these streams.

BIBLIOGRAPHY

Forster, E. M. *A Passage to India*. 1924. Harmondsworth: Penguin, 1980.

——'Reflections in India: I—Too Late?' *The Nation and the Athenaeum*. 30 Jan. 1922: 614–5.

Hutchins, Francis G. *The Illusion of Permanence: British Imperialism in India*. Princeton: Princeton UP, 1967.

Kipling, Rudyard. 'Mandalay.' *A Choice of Kipling's Verse*. London: Faber, 1987.

Said, Edward. *Orientalism*. 1978. New York: Vintage, 1979.

Sharpe, Jenny. 'Figures of Colonial Resistance.' *Modern Fiction Studies*. 35.1 (1989): 137–55.

Showalter, Elaine. '*A Passage to India* as "Marriage Fiction": Forster's Sexual Politics.' *Women & Literature*. 5.2 (1977): 3–16.

Spivak, Gayatri. 'The Rani of Sirmur.' *Europe and its Others*. Vol. I: Proceedings of the Essex Conference on the Sociology of Literature July 1984. Eds. Francis Barker et al. Colchester: U of Essex, 1985: 128–51.

7.2

FROM 'PERIPHRASIS, POWER AND RAPE IN *A PASSAGE TO INDIA*'

Brenda R. Silver

Periphrasis, defined most simply as 'the use of many words where one or a few would do,' has, like all figures, a more devious side. Rooted in the Greek 'to speak around,' described variously as a figure that simultaneously 'under- and over-specifies,' or 'the use of a negative, passive, or inverted construction in place of a positive, active or normal construction,' the circumlocution associated with periphrasis begins to suggest a refusal to name its subject that emphasizes the fact of its elision.[1] If we go further and describe it in Gerard Genette's terms as a figure that both opens up and exists in a gap or space between sign and meaning, a figure that is moreover 'motivated' in its usage,[2] then we arrive at the association between periphrasis, power, and rape that structures both linguistic and social relations in *A Passage to India* and provides the space for re-reading E. M. Forster's most enigmatic novel.

To introduce this association, we must move immediately to the event at the heart of the novel, Adela Quested's experience in the Marabar caves that leads to the trial of the Indian doctor Aziz for attempted rape. Or so we assume: the charge, like the event, is either elided completely or referred to by the English as an 'insult,' a clearly motivated circumlocution. Later, in a moment of vision during the trial, Adela returns to the caves and retracts her accusation of Aziz, but the reader never learns what if anything actually happened there. Where we would have the naming of the crime and its perpetrator, exists only a periphrasis, a gap. That Forster deliberately created this gap is clear from the original version

Novel: a forum on fiction 22.1, Fall 1988, pp. 86–105. Extract: pp. 86–8 and 91–100.

of the scene, where an assault definitely occurs: the reader is in the cave with Adela and feels the hands that push her against the wall and grab her breasts; we too smash the assailant with the field glasses before running out of the cave and down the hill.[3] In the published version, not just the violent physical attack but the entire scene in the cave is elided. Into the interpretive space opened by this elision, critics have not feared to rush, supported by Forster's statement that 'in the cave it is *either* a man, *or* the supernatural, *or* an illusion.'[4] Many, choosing to explore the 'illusion,' read the experience in psychological terms, basing their reading on Fielding's description of Adela as a prig, and on her realizations just before entering the cave that she has no love or sexual passion for Ronny, the man she is engaged to marry, and that Aziz is 'a handsome little Oriental.'[5] At one point after her retraction, moreover, she responds to Fielding's hallucination theory by comparing her experience to 'the sort of thing . . . that makes some women think they've had an offer of marriage when none was made' (240). Thus it is that sexuality and repression enter the gap at the center of the novel. In this reading, Adela becomes a later version of Henry James's governess in *The Turn of the Screw*: a hysterical, repressed, overly-intellectual New Woman who fantasizes and is haunted by sex ghosts. In this reading, we might add, Adela wants to be raped.[6]

That Forster used his fiction to explore and expose prevailing sexual attitudes is a commonplace. On one level, he recognized the way in which society, in Michel Foucault's terms, had appropriated bodies and pleasure and deployed a sexuality that served to control individuals; he certainly would have understood the strategies, such as 'a hysterization of women's bodies' and 'a psychiatrization of perverse pleasure,' that Foucault associated with this deployment.[7] At another level, however, Forster's resistance to the system and his imagination were shaped by the sexual discourse of the period, including the concept of repression. In his fiction he continually evokes a scenario in which a darker, more sensual, usually foreign and/or lower class character initiates the repressed, often intellectual English man or woman into an awareness of his or her sexuality. An explicit example occurs in the heavily ironic fantasy entitled 'The Torque,' which hinges on the homosexual rape of a Christianized Roman by a Goth: an act that undercuts the power of institutionalized chastity (the Church) and precipitates a realm of sexual freedom and fulfillment. Rape in this story becomes the pleasurable consummation of illicit desires experienced without guilt or subsequent suffering, a transgression of racial and sexual boundaries that unites rather than separates the two races.[8]

But *A Passage to India* tells a different story. For here, as Patricia Joplin would argue, rape becomes an act of violence, a transgression of boundaries, that enacts the rivalries at work within the culture and the novel upon the body of a woman who is herself potentially silenced, elided.[9] With this in mind, we can return to Adela's 'unspeakable' experience in the cave—and the word is Forster's (208)—the experience that she speaks as violation or rape, and read it not in terms of sexual desire or repression, but in terms of a deployment of sexuality within a discourse of power that posits a complex network of sameness and difference. Within this discourse, what is at stake is both gender difference and racial difference, with manifold lines of power, 'a multiplicity of force relations' (Foucault, *Sexuality*, 92), criss-crossing the textual and social field. To read the novel from this perspective is to see it as a study of what it means to be *rapable*, a social position that cuts across biological and racial lines to inscribe culturally constructed definitions of sexuality within a sex/gender/power system.

. . .

When applied to social relations in *A Passage to India*, the construction of the class, or category, woman criss-crosses racial as well as sexual lines. This intersection illustrates both Foucault's conception of power as the 'interplay of nonegalitarian and mobile relations' and his description of 'relations of power' as 'immanent in' rather than 'in a position of exteriority with respect to other types of relationships,' even as it revises his formulation by inserting in it the crucial role of social sexing, of gender. And like other relations of power, gender has 'a directly productive role, wherever [it comes] into play,' producing among other things the discourses that simultaneously shape and sustain it.[10] Within this mobile discursive field, subject and object may shift, but the category of object and the category of woman remain identical.

For the first part of the novel English and Indian are locked into a power relationship and a discourse of race in which each objectifies the other, although in any direct confrontation the English maintain the position of subject. At the same time, however, English and Indian *men* share a discourse of sexuality that inscribes their subjectivity by objectifying and silencing women. After the 'insult,' relations shift to place the Indians explicitly in the category of woman, where their bodies and their subjectivity are appropriated for social ends. Within this latter discourse, both Adela, the Englishwoman, and Aziz, the Indian man, are elided in the English construction of the event through a deliberate act of periphrasis said by the narrator to be the result of the rape. When Fielding, the liberal schoolteacher who sides with the Indians, produces a 'bad effect' at the English club by asking about Miss Quested's health, his transgression consists of pronouncing her name: for since the 'insult' 'she, like Aziz, was always referred to by a periphrasis' (182). By reversing the figure, however, we can perceive the periphrasis as embedded in the *cause* rather than the *effect* of the rape. For periphrasis, the elision or negation of the individual human being, functions as part of a rhetoric of difference and power that objectifies the other and creates the space for rape to occur.

To a great extent, the rhetoric of power manifests itself within the novel in the use of synecdoche and metonymy to reduce the other, the signified, to a materiality, a physicality, that denies the irreducibility and multiplicity of the individual subject. Rather than suggesting 'relationship' or 'connectedness,'[11] synecdochal representation opens up unbridgeable gaps. Ironically, the Indians introduce this reductive rhetoric in the opening dialogue of the novel when they refer to Ronny, the new City Magistrate, as 'red-nosed boy' (10), a usage motivated by the belief, stated repeatedly in this conversation and confirmed by the text, that the English are essentially indistinguishable: '"They all become exactly the same, not worse, not better. I give any Englishman two years, be he Turton or Burton. It is only the difference of a letter. And I give any Englishwoman six months"' (11). What differences the Indians sardonically allow are physical, not moral, a representation of the political reality that the presence of the English in India was itself immoral: '"Red-nose mumbles, Turton talks distinctly, Mrs Turton takes bribes, Mrs Red-nose does not and cannot, because so far there is no Mrs Red-nose"' (11). Paradoxically, the '"difference of a letter"' in the first figure suggests the possibility of opening a space between signifier and signified, individual and group, where individuals might meet; but when exceptions are introduced, they are immediately elided. As the narrator remarks, they 'generalized from [their] disappointments—it is difficult for members of a subject race to do otherwise' (13).

But what of the masters, the English? Caught up in a rhetoric of power they initiated and control, they too generalize, unwilling to break free of the by then historically well-inscribed characteristics of the category 'Indian' constructed through the representations of generations of Orientalists. To the English the Indians are 'types' and they 'know' them all, as well as how to handle them. Equally important, within this conceptual and stylistic framework, the English themselves become a type, the White Man, with a fixed set of judgments, gestures, and language; those who do not conform are not pukka.[12] Thus, the first mention of Aziz by the English, set within the confines of the club, the locus of linguistic and social conformity, reduces the man, so vividly alive while chattering with his friends and in the intervening encounter with Mrs Moore, to 'some native subordinate or other' who had, typically, failed to show up when needed; in the same breath Ronny is referred to as 'the type we want, he's one of us' (25).

The mode on both sides, then, is reduction, a reduction that claims as well the privilege of totalizing the other group. In addition, both groups represent their synecdochal reductions as capturing 'the truth,' including the truth of the other's moral state. For the English, however, the rulers, the mania for reductive categorizing goes hand in hand with a dramatization of difference and superiority inherent in their position of power: power not only to define the categories but to enforce the 'truths' they supposedly convey; for the English, knowledge, representation, and power are one. Fielding, a linguistic renegade long before the scene in the club following the 'insult' experiences the strength of this discursive system, and his alienation from it, when he comments that 'the so-called white races are really pinko-grey. He only said this to be cheery, he did not realize that "white" has no more to do with a colour than "God Save the King" with a god, and that it is the height of impropriety to consider what it does connote' (62). More than a 'manner of being-in-the-world' or a style (Said 227), the linguistic structures practiced by the English inscribe the oppression of the Indians, both individually and as a group. The Indians' subversive rhetoric, at least in the early stages of the novel, produces rhetoric alone.

Ronny, the newcomer, enacts the linguistic and ideological power inherent in the racial discourse most explicitly, thereby satisfying the English desire for conformity and proving the Indians' perception of the English correct. To Ronny, the 'higher realms of knowledge' to which he aspired were 'inhabited by Callendars and Turtons, who had been not one year in the country but twenty and whose instincts were superhuman' (81). In his zeal to learn the lingo and show his orthodoxy, he continually uses 'phrases and arguments that he had picked up from older officials' (33) to describe the Indians, phrases that simultaneously reduce them to a material state and equate this with their defective mental and moral character. In this way he illustrates the process by which synecdochal representation crosses the line described by Kenneth Burke between figurative language as used by poets and the scientists' belief that their representations are 'real' (507). At its most extreme, as in Ronny's remark during the Bridge Party that 'no one who's here matters; those who matter don't come' (39), this rhetoric effectively reduces the Indians present from the status of objects to non-existence. The result is 'to wipe out any traces of individual[s] . . . with narratable life histories' (Said 229). Conscious only of the official link that ties him to the Indians, 'as private individuals he forgot them' (77).

Nevertheless, Ronny, like the other English, 'knows' the Indians, a knowledge premised on his access to the rhetoric of power. After his disruption of the tea party at Fielding's, for example, where he pointedly treats Aziz and Godbole as if they were invisible, he 'knows' Aziz to be the 'spoilt Westernized' type (77). In the manuscript version of the Bridge Party, the linguistic and social event that is meant to bring Indian and English together but only widens the gap, Ronny's exaggerated use of synecdoche and his claim to absolute representation are even more pronounced. Whereas Mr Turton had told Adela he could provide her with 'any type' of Indian she wanted (27), Ronny 'explained the various types' by their head dresses, 'and to each . . . he appended a few observations: you might expect such thoughts beneath a turban of such a shape, beneath a fez, beneath a mush-room topi' (*Manuscripts* 46). Ultimately, inevitably, it is Ronny who provides the most painfully ironic example of synecdochal reduction masquerading as truth in the novel, the representation of Aziz and all Indians by his missing collar stud—missing because he gave it to Fielding. To Ronny, this detail signifies 'the Indian all over: inattention to detail; the fundamental slackness that reveals the race' (82).

Within the gap opened by synecdochal reduction of the other to object, rape finds its material and linguistic space. And when race is involved, the space increases exponentially. From Ronny's statement of the 'fundamental slackness of the race' it is just a short step to the policeman McBryde's theory of the depravity of Indian men, which includes their sexual promiscuity and their attraction to white women. In this construction, the Indian man, reduced to his sexuality, becomes simultaneously rapist and object of rape.[13] No matter that Aziz's missing collar stud signifies the space in which he and Fielding break free of the reductive generalities of the racial discourse to initiate their friendship; the established mode swallows such resistances in its representation of the Indian male. In *Black Skins, White Masks*, Frantz Fanon offers an explanation for this phenomenon when he argues that the black man exists for whites *as* a synecdoche, in particular a penis, which eclipses the black man himself. Citing as his example a passage that includes descriptions such as, '"Four Negroes with their penises exposed would fill a cathedral. They would be unable to leave the building until their erections had subsided,"' the Negro, he argues, 'is turned into a penis. He *is* a penis.'[14] This passage occurs in a chapter in which Fanon describes negrophobia on the part of both white men and white women as fear of rape. 'Whoever says *rape* says *Negro*,' Fanon writes (166), exploring in depth the psychopathology that underlies the complicated intertwining of fear and desire that he believes structures relationships between whites and black men. 'The woman of color,' Fanon tells us, is deliberately elided from his discussion (179–80).

When Adela speaks rape, however, she says more than Negro; she speaks from within a discourse of sexuality that crosses racial lines and objectifies all women. While resting on similar rhetorical strategies as the discourse of race, this discourse shifts the axis of sameness and difference, subject and object, from race to gender. Look, for example, at the moment during the Bridge Party when Mr. Turton, the highest ranking Englishman, indicates to his wife her duty (that is, to speak to the Indian women): '"To work, Mary, to work," cried the Collector, touching his wife on the shoulder with a switch' (41). The synecdochal details here, the shoulder and the switch, serve to place her in the subservient position of his horse, reducing her to a material adjunct of both the man, her master, and the empire he represents. Next to this moment we can place Turton's thought after the 'insult' when his wife, voicing her hatred for the Indians, calls for the use of violence: '"After all, it's our women who make everything more difficult out here. ... Beneath his chivalry to Miss Quested resentment lurked. ...' 'Perhaps,' the narrator comments, 'there is a grain of resentment in all chivalry' (214). Perhaps, we could add, what we have here is the most significant aside in the novel, a glimpse into the misogyny, the contempt, characteristic of those who use '"women and children"' (183) as the rallying cry for their defence of women whom they in fact subordinate and elide by touches, however light, with a switch.

What, then, do these men resent? The rare moments when women, rather than allowing themselves to be objects of protection or exchange among those who have power, resist this structure by acting or speaking for themselves? In the case of Mrs Turton and the other seasoned Englishwomen, the confinement of their roles and their limited contact with Indians evoke a racism more extreme than their husbands', but their outbursts only serve to underline the men's 'contemptuous affection for the [Indian] pawns [they] had moved about for so many years' (214). The threat posed by Adela and Mrs Moore, however, differs, for their resistance threatens to destroy the status quo through intimacy, not hatred. One such moment of resistance occurs during the Bridge Party. Unlike Mrs Turton, whose knowledge of Urdu consists only of the imperative mood and whose comments in English about the Indian women are glaringly reductive (42), the two newcomers attempt to initiate a conversation with the Indian women, who form a third group in the social fabric, distinct from their men and the English alike. But the attempt fails; the Indian women remain silent. For one thing, the Indian men insist on talking for them. More significant, however, is the narrator's comment that 'they sought for a new formula which neither East nor West could provide' (42). Perhaps, then, men resent women as a disruption within the male discourse that controls social exchange, whether this exchange occurs officially or unofficially.[15] Here, even Fielding, capable as he is of seeing Indians as individuals, shares Turton's resentment. Motivated by his desire for the picnic at the caves to be a success for Aziz's sake, Fielding thinks, '"I knew these women would make trouble."' Mrs Moore accurately identifies this reaction for what it is, scapegoating women: '"This man, having missed the train, tries to blame us"' (158).

A similar pattern of attributing power to women who in relationship to their men have little or none occurs within the Indian community as well. For the most part, Indian women in the novel are nameless and invisible, represented only through their relatives' conversation about them. When we do go behind the purdah, as in the opening scene, we find Hamidullah's wife indicating her inferiority by the endless talk she sustains in order to show that she is not impatient for the dinner she cannot eat until her husband has eaten his (13). Equally telling is her long tale about the horrors awaiting women who do not marry, her attempt to urge Aziz to remarry. Worried as Aziz might be by this tale, he has the power to act or not act, and Hamidullah considerately '[wipes] out any impression that his wife might have made' (14). The woman is left behind the purdah with nothing but empty words at her command. Yet later, when his wife refuses to see Fielding—or more accurately, refuses to let Fielding see her—Hamidullah claims that she wields the real power in the relationship (271), a power we can define as the power to choose to remain invisible and thus to disrupt, however slightly, the male bonding achieved in this novel, as in patriarchal societies in general, through the exchange or mediation of women. Perhaps the clearest representation of women's power as refusal or negativity, however, occurs in the discussion of the 'queer' events surrounding Aziz's trial. Here we learn that 'a number of Mohammedan ladies had sworn to take no food until the prisoner was acquitted; their death would make little difference, indeed, being invisible, they seemed dead already, nevertheless it was disquieting' (214).

Women, then, can disrupt or cause disquietude by their refusals, but their resistance is severely limited by the dominant rhetoric of power that reinscribes them as object of exchange or catalyst for rivalry within male conversation and male power struggles. Thus, the alleged 'insult' of one English woman becomes the occasion for cloistering all Englishwomen, simultaneously reducing them to objects of protection and using them as an excuse to reassert white male power over both their women and their potential attackers. The pattern enacted in the novel is familiar to us from the South, a pattern that attaches itself to interracial rape and power relationships and works to intimidate and coerce both black men and women and white women into accepting their subordinate positions.[16] Within this context, Fielding's refusal to elide Adela's name amidst the hysteria at the club surrounding 'women and children' takes on heroic proportions. By speaking of her by name, by trying to reach her directly, he resists the periphrasis that destroys subjectivity and identity and reduces both her and Aziz to metonymic figures in a morality play of violated innocence and evil, whose end is to reaffirm the power of the white male. He refuses, that is, their reduction to ciphers in the lengthening chain of periphrases leading to one possible closure only; he returns Adela to a virtual level of existence and focuses on the particular event.

When his attempt fails, however, Fielding, knowing the code, enacts his resistance to the group fiction by refusing to stand up for Ronny, the 'insulted' fiance, the 'martyr' (185) in this as in every drama of rape, in which the true victim is perceived to be the man whose boundaries and property have been violated through the usurpation of his woman's body.[17] His resistance, that is, occurs within and is contained by a social system and a discourse of sexuality predicated on male bonding and male rivalry, in which the woman's experience, even of rape, is elided. Forced to choose sides, Fielding chooses Aziz, and in doing so, he reaffirms the discourse of sexuality, a discourse in which their shared gender mediates—at least potentially—racial difference.

Within this discourse, Aziz and Fielding speak equally as subjects, as men, from the position of power, including the power to objectify and appropriate women. Thus, Aziz, in his attempt to seal the intimacy between the two men, comments unabashedly that Adela '"was not beautiful. She has practically no breasts . . .,"' a synecdochal representation that reduces women to their physical attributes alone. For Fielding, he will '"arrange a lady with breasts like mangoes . . ."' (120). In this scene, as elsewhere in the novel, Aziz's sexual objectification of women, the 'derived sensuality—the sort that classes a mistress among motor-cars if she is beautiful, and among eye-flies if she isn't' (241) alienates Fielding, who sees Aziz's valuation of women as commodities as a sign of 'the old, old trouble that eats the heart out of every civilization: snobbery, the desire for possessions, creditable appendages' (241). But however admirable this statement appears—however blind Fielding may be to his own ethno-centric biases—in committing himself to Aziz Fielding acknowledges as well his place within the discourse of sexuality. When Aziz initiates their intimacy by showing Fielding the photograph of his dead wife, Fielding regrets that he has no woman or story of a woman to offer in exchange. The 'compact . . .

subscribed by the photograph' (122) is completed by Aziz's statement that had his wife been alive, he would have shown the woman herself to Fielding, justifying this transaction to her by representing Fielding as his brother. Fielding feels honored.

It is not surprising, then, that in his attempt to reclaim Aziz from the periphrasis that threatens to engulf him after his arrest, Fielding tries to restore his status as subject by restoring his place within the sexual discourse shared by men. When McBryde, described as one of the most reflective and best educated of the English officials, offers Fielding a letter planning a visit to a brothel as evidence of Aziz's—and all Indians'—innate sexual depravity, Fielding responds within the sexual discourse, claiming that he had done the same thing at Aziz's age. 'So had the Superintendent of Police,' the narrative continues, 'but he considered that the conversation had taken a turn that was undesirable' (169). Why? Because by minimizing racial difference Fielding is '[leaving] a gap in the line' that these 'jackals,' the Indians, would exploit (171). Fielding, that is, fills or bridges the gap generated by and necessary to the rhetoric of power by creating a gap in the barrier that ensures English self-representation and dominance.

But as Fielding learns from this exchange, more than racial stereotyping is in play here; social sexing is as well. In denying his complicity with Fielding and Aziz, in denying the sexual discourse that men share, McBryde refuses to recognize Aziz as man, as subject. And whatever Aziz's power to reduce women to commodities, when spoken of as Indian within the discourse of English and Indian, sahib and native, he himself is objectified; he enters the 'category' woman and becomes rapable. From the moment of his arrest, from the moment the door of the carriage is thrown open and the power of the state intrudes, Aziz is absorbed into a discourse that simultaneously defines him as penis and castrates him, equating castration and rape.

However powerful the representation of the black man as penis, illustrated by Fanon, may appear to the English, it functions as well to reduce Aziz to a physicality that can then be subordinated to the authority vested in the greater power of the (phallic) legal system and the symbolic order that engenders and supports it. In contrast to the white man's position, which is coterminous with the power of 'the law,' the position of the Indian man is to be symbolically 'raped' by the accusation of rape, a position crucial for maintaining the white man's power and one that carries as much centrality in the intertwined discourses of sex and race as rape itself.[18]

Once accused of rape, Aziz disappears as speaking subject, appearing only as the object of discourse and power; both his body and his possessions, including his letters, are appropriated by the police and used against him. For one thing, McBryde reduces Aziz to his body, his skin color, by implication his sexuality, which is by definition depraved. In discussing Aziz with Fielding, McBryde asserts that while the schoolmaster sees the Indians at their best, when they are boys, he, the policeman, '"[knows] them as they really are, after they have developed into men"' (169). Later, in Court, 'enunciating a general truth,' he will state the 'fact which any scientific observer will confirm,' that 'the darker races are physically attracted by the fairer, but not *vice versa*' (218–19).

From the perspective of McBryde's objective, 'scientific,' epistemological system Aziz, the object known by the observer, loses his status as man and with it the power to protect women, even his dead wife. When McBryde appropriates the photograph along with his other possessions, it ceases to signify Aziz's ability to exchange women in a ritual of male bonding; instead it indicates his reduction to sexual object. In response to Fielding's identification of the photograph, McBryde 'gave a faint, incredulous smile, and started rummaging in the drawer. His face became inquisitive and slightly bestial. "Wife indeed, I know these wives!" he was thinking' (172). If the Indian man is a penis, Indian women are whores.[19]

The photograph of Aziz's wife, then, become emblematic of woman both as object of exchange and as object of violation—violated here by McBryde's reading of her. He 'knows' her, a metaphor that suggests clearly the relationship between knowledge, sexuality, and power—including the power to define, or name, the truth. While McBryde's statement illustrates the specific construction that metaphorizes the Orient as female, penetrated by the knowledge of the Western male Orientalist, the use of metaphors associated with sexuality or the violation of boundaries in discussions of the acquisition of knowledge is common in all 'objective' or 'scientific'—by definition 'male'—discourses.[20] Within these discourses, the claiming of knowledge, the appropriation and objectification of the woman, is frequently visual. For Susan Sontag, writing of photography as knowledge, the link between visual appropriation and rape is clear: 'The knowledge gained through still photographs will always be ... a semblance of knowledge, a semblance of wisdom, as the act of taking pictures is a semblance of wisdom, a semblance of rape.'[21]

Photographs, if silent themselves, can be named; and the woman in this photograph is twice named and twice silenced—first by Aziz as woman, as object of exchange, and later by McBryde as object of an object, the sexualized Indian male. As such, her circulation reveals the shifting network of signification that elides the reality of the violation of woman and Indian through the periphrases at the heart of the novel. For if as woman she signifies the way in which all women are subject to rape by virtue of their gender—their sexual objectification and powerlessness to define themselves—she also signifies the rape practiced upon the Indians by virtue of their objectification and powerlessness. Her violation in her own right, however, remains an untold tale.

When Aziz regains his freedom, he reclaims his violated wife and with her his manhood (261), setting the stage for the separation that ensues between Fielding and him, a separation precipitated first by Fielding's friendship with Adela after the trial and later by his marriage not to Adela—which is what Aziz mistakenly believes—but to Stella, Ronny's sister. Once the misunderstanding is cleared up, Fielding tries to recapture their previous closeness by '[forcing] himself to speak intimately about his wife'—by evoking, that is, the sexual discourse that had united them before. By now, however, Aziz no longer wishes intimacy with any English person and Fielding has 'thrown in his lot with Anglo-India by marrying a country woman' (319). However great Fielding's initial disregard of the racial discourse, he perceives his marriage as committing him to the system that defines him as English and male, and he accepts its limitations; he can no longer, in his words, 'travel as lightly' (317), nor can he risk flirting with the other. Aziz is reduced to a 'memento, a trophy' (319). Just as Fielding's defiance after Aziz's arrest was contained by the relations of power that made Ronny and him antagonists who spoke the same language, the form of his resistance corroborates rather than undermines the system. In this way it illustrates Foucault's belief that 'resistance is never in a position of exteriority in relation to power'; it exists within the power/knowledge apparatus that 'depends' upon it and is subject to its discourses.[22] In his defense of Aziz, for example, Fielding relies on the power of evidence and knowledge, which he believes will triumph, unable to recognize, as Hamidullah and the Indians do from the position of the feminized and colonized object, that even evidence and knowledge would not work to free them (73; 269: '"If God himself descended . . . into their club and said you [Aziz] were innocent, they would disbelieve him"). Unable to cross the boundaries that separate subject and object, to enter fully into the category woman, Fielding, for all his good intentions and his exposure of the system, enacts the story of the failure to identify with otherness.

Ultimately, it is Adela Quested, the woman, not Fielding, the man, who resists the 'scientific truths' put forward by McBryde, simultaneously revealing and disrupting the mastery and violation that function as part of the rhetoric of knowledge and power. It is Adela who comes to represent the form of resistance described as 'less a resistance, a force that can be set against power, than a non-force, an absolute difference with respect to power' (De Lauretis 93). Edward Said has argued that the ending of the novel, where the landscape of India prevents Fielding and Aziz from bridging the gap that divides them, reinforces 'a sense of the pathetic distance still separating "us" from an Orient destined to bear its foreignness as a mark of its permanent estrangement from the West' (244). But when viewed through the prism of gender, of social sexing, what separates the two men are their positions within the power grid that lock them into the discourse of male bonding and male rivalry, including racial rivalry. Adela, however, speaking from the gaps or interstices of the shifting power networks, speaks as woman for the category woman. In this reading, the 'mark of . . . permanent estrangement' that separates the two cultures is inscribed in the woman who enters the caves and returns speaking rape.[23]

NOTES

1. In, respectively, *Webster's New World Dictionary of the American Language*, 2nd College ed. (New York: Collins, 1978); Geoffrey Hartman, 'The Voice of the Shuttle: Language from the Point of View of Literature,' *Beyond Formalism*,

Literary Essays 1958–1970, (New Haven: Yale UP, 1970), p. 352; *Webster's Third New International Dictionary* (Springfield, MA: Merriam, 1971). For a discussion of periphrasis as a figure of emphasis, in opposition to ellipsis, a figure of understatement, see Nancy K. Miller, 'Writing (from) the Feminine: George Sand and the Novel of Female Pastoral,' *The Representation of Women in Fiction*, ed. Carolyn G. Heilbrun and Margaret R. Higgonet (Baltimore: Johns Hopkins UP, 1983), pp. 134, 149.

I am grateful to Nancy Miller and to Louise Fradenburg, Marianne Hirsch, Patricia McKee, Sandy Petrey, and Nancy Vickers for their valuable criticism and suggestions.

2. 'Figures,' *Figures of Literary Discourse*, trans. Alan Sheridan (New York: Columbia UP, 1982), pp. 47–49, 57.
3. E. M. Forster, *The Manuscripts of A Passage to India*, ed. Oliver Stallybrass (London: Edward Arnold, 1978), pp. 242–43; hereafter cited in the text as *Manuscripts*.
4. Letter to G. L. Dickinson, June 26, 1924; quoted in Oliver Stallybrass, ed., *A Passage to India*, by E. M. Forster, Abinger Ed. (London: Edward Arnold, 1978), p. xxvi.
5. E. M. Forster, *A Passage to India* (1924; New York: Harcourt, 1984), p. 152. Further references to this, the Harvest edition, will appear in the text.
6. The phrase 'sex ghosts' comes from Mark Spilka's analysis of the governess's 'prurient sensibility' as indicative of 'the impasse in Victorian attitudes toward sex and innocence': 'Turning the Freudian Turn of the Screw: How Not to Do It,' *Literature and Psychology* 13 (1963), 105–11. V. A. Shahane, summarizing various interpretations of Adela's experience, cites as 'a minority critical view' that 'Adela is sexually charmed by Aziz and that in her subconscious self she desires to be raped by him': *E. M. Forster. 'A Passage to India': A Study* (Delhi: Oxford UP, 1977), p. 31. Those who contribute to this view include Frederick C. Crews, *E. M. Forster: The Perils of Humanism* (Princeton: Princeton UP, 1962), pp. 159–60; Ted E. Boyle, 'Adela Quested's Delusion: The Failure of Rationalism in *A Passage to India*' (1965), *Perspectives on E. M. Forster's 'A Passage to India*,' ed. V. A. Shahane (New York: Barnes, 1968), pp. 73–76; Louise Dauner, 'What Happened in the Cave? Reflections on *A Passage to India*' (1961), *Perspectives*, ed. Shahane, pp. 51–64; and Benita Parry, *Delusions and Discoveries: Studies in India in the British Imagination 1880–1930* (Berkeley: U of California P, 1972), pp. 294–95.

The reading of Adela's experience in terms of repression, sexual hysteria, frigidity, or fear of the body is, in fact, widespread. See, e.g., Keith Hollingsworth, '*A Passage to India*: The Echoes in the Marabar Caves' (1962), *Perspectives'* . . ., ed. Shahane, pp. 35–50; Wilfrid Stone, *The Cave and the Mountain: A Study of E. M. Forster* (Stanford: Stanford UP, 1966), pp. 317, 335; Bonnie Blumenthal Finkelstein, *Forster's Women: Eternal Differences* (New York: Columbia UP, 1975), pp. 128–34; G. S. Amur, 'Hellenic Heroines and Sexless Angels: Images of Women in Forster's Novels,' *Approaches to E. M. Forster: A Centenary Volume*, ed. V. A. Shahane (Atlantic Highlands, N.J.: Humanities Press, 1981), pp. 25–34: and Barbara Rosencrance, *Forster's Narrative Vision* (Ithaca: Cornell UP, 1982), p. 207. In addition, many critics associate Adela's experience with the condition of modern rationalism and the failure to recognize the importance of the heart, or the passions, or the instincts (revealed in part by the 'new psychology' of Freud and Jung), but even here sexual repression enters the argument. Comparing Adela to D. H. Lawrence's Hermione Roddice, Stone writes, 'Both are catastrophes of modern civilization—repressed, class-bound, over-intellectualized' (382). A different perspective on Adela's perception of the experience as a rape, one closer to my own, associates it with the loveless or forced union symbolized by her engagement to Ronny: Shahane, *E. M. Forster*, p. 30; Gertrude M. White, '*A Passage to India*: Analysis and Revaluation,' *PMLA*, 68 (1953), 641–657; Elaine Showalter, '*A Passage to India* as "Marriage Fiction". Forster's Sexual Politics,' *Women and Literature*, 5.2 (1977), pp. 3–16. White also suggests an analogy between the relationship of Ronny and Adela and that of English and Indian in the novel.

One glaring contribution to the reading of Adela as sexually repressed is David Lean's film version of the novel. In an interview about the film, Lean remarked, 'And Miss Quested ... well, she's a bit of a prig and a bore in the book, you know. I've changed her, made her more sympathetic. Forster wasn't always very good with women': *The Guardian* (January 23, 1984); quoted in Salman Rushdie, 'Outside the Whale,' *American Film* 10.4 (1985), p. 70.

7. Michael Foucault, *The History of Sexuality, Vol. 1: An Introduction*, trans. Robert Hurley (1978; New York: Vintage, 1980), pp. 44, 47, 104–05; hereafter cited in the text as *Sexuality*.
8. *The Life to Come and Other Stories* (1972; New York: Avon, 1976), pp. 160–76.
9. Patricia Klindeist Joplin, 'The Voice of the Shuttle is Ours,' *Stanford Literary Review*, 1.1 (1984), pp. 25–53.

   For a history of the discourse of interracial rape in America and its problematic nature, see Angela Davis, *Women, Race and Class* (New York: Random House, 1981), ch. 11; Jacqueline Dowd Hall, *Revolt Against Chivalry: Jessie Daniel Ames and the Women's Campaign Against Lynching* (New York: Columbia UP, 1979), ch. 5, and '"The Mind that Burns in Each Body". Women, Rape, and Racial Violence,' *Powers of Desire: The Politics of Sexuality*, ed. Ann Snitow, Christine Stansell, and Sharon Thompson (New York: Monthly Review, 1983), pp. 328–49.
10. *The History of Sexuality*, p. 94. See as well Foucault's analysis of the 'will to knowledge' and the 'will to truth' inherent in power in *The Discourse on Language*, trans. Rupert Swyer, 1971, in *The Archaeology of Knowledge* (New York: Pantheon, 1972), pp. 215–37. Commenting on the complex web of prohibitions at work in controlling a society's discourse, Foucault notes that 'the areas where this web is most tightly woven today ... are those dealing with politics and sexuality' (216).
11. I am following here Kenneth Burke's designation of synecdoche in 'Four Master Tropes,' *A Grammar of Motives* (New York: Prentice-Hall, 1945), p. 507, 509; hereafter cited in text. In the sense that synecdoche in this novel works towards reduction, it tends towards Burke's definition of metonymy.
12. 'Being a White Man was ... an idea and a reality ... It meant—in the colonies—speaking in a certain way, behaving according to a code of regulations, and even feeling certain things and not others ... It was a form of authority ... Being a White Man, in short, was a very concrete manner of being-in-the-world, a way of taking hold of reality, language, and thought. It made a specific style possible' (Edward Said, *Orientalism* [1978; New York: Vintage, 1979], p. 227); further references appear in the text.
13. This is also the position of Hari Kumar in Paul Scott's *Raj Quartet*, both figuratively and, in his encounter with Superintendent of Police Merrick after his arrest, literally. See *The Day of the Scorpion* (1968; New York: Avon, 1979), pp. 273–74, 292–302, 309–12.
14. *Black Skins, White Masks*, trans. Charles Lam Markmann (New York: Grove, 1967), pp. 169–70; hereafter cited in text.
15. To the extent that women, like 'words in conversation,' are the object of exchange between men in the establishment of social relationships, as Claude Levi-Strauss has argued, they are theoretically unable to initiate such exchanges (see the extract from *The Scope of Anthropology*, in *20th Century Literary Criticism*, ed. David Lodge [London: Longman, 1972], p. 550 for the quotation). My reading of the male bonding and male rivalry that structures social relations in the novel, as in patriarchal society, draws upon feminist analyses of both Levi-Strauss and René Girard. The point emphasized is the position of women as objects of exchange, mediation, or protection in what Gayle Rubin calls 'the traffic in women' and Eve

Sedgwick describes as 'the use of women as exchangeable, perhaps symbolic, property for the primary purpose of cementing the bonds of men with men' (*Between Men*, New York: Columbia UP, 1985, pp. 25–26). Sedgwick has termed this relationship between men 'homosocial.' In Luce Irigaray's formulation, 'The use and traffic in women subtend and uphold the reign of masculine hom(mo)-sexuality,' which is 'played out through the bodies of women, matter, or sign ...' 'Women on the Market,' *This Sex Which is Not One*, trans. Catherine Porter [Ithaca: Cornell UP, 1985], p. 172).

16. See the two works by Hall, n. 9 above; Ida B. Wells-Barnett, 'Lynching, Our National Crime,' *The Voice of Black America*, ed. Philip S. Foner (New York: Simon and Schuster, 1972), pp. 687–91; Davis, pp. 183–96. As recent analyses of the southern situation make clear, the myth and reality of the rape of white women by black men and its punishment, lynching, served this dual function well: 'the two phenomena were intimately connected, for the fear of rape, like the threat of lynching, served to keep a subordinate group in a state of anxiety' and placed the white woman who needed 'protection' in the position of 'paying with a lifetime of subjugation to the men gathered in her behalf' (Hall, *Revolt Against Chivalry*, pp. 153, 151). Sedgwick's reading of the assault on Scarlett in *Gone with the Wind* illustrates this point as well (pp. 9–10). Mrs Turton's belief in the novel that Indian men 'ought to crawl from here to the caves on their hands and knees whenever an Englishwoman's in sight' (216) reflects another of the negative effects of this 'chivalry' on white women (as well as alluding to the actual treatment of Indians during the Amritsar riots after a white woman was attacked). Hall's work examines the efforts of southern white women to destroy the code of chivalry, founded among other things on the fear of rape, that was used to justify lynching and other racial injustices.
17. See Joplin, pp. 32–35; Susan Brownmiller, *Against Our Will: Men, Women and Rape* (London: Secker, 1975), pp. 16–18; and Lorenne Clark and Debra Lewis, *Rape: The Price of Coercive Sexuality* (Toronto: Women's Press, 1977), chs. 7–8.
18. I am grateful to Evelyn Fox Keller for her insights on how Aziz can be both 'penis' and 'castrated,' that is, 'woman,' as well as her reading of the social significance of this position.
19. For an analysis of the connection between the portrayal of black men as rapists and animals and black women as whores, see Davis, p. 182, and Hall, *Revolt Against Chivalry*, pp. 155–56.
20. Evelyn Fox Keller extensively documents these interconnections in the language of science and 'objectivity' in *Reflections on Gender and Science* (New Haven: Yale UP, 1985).
21. *On Photography*; cited in MacKinnon, 'Feminism, Theory, Marxism and the State: Toward Feminist Jurisprudence,' *Signs*, 8 (1983), 637.
22. *The History of Sexuality*, p. 95. See also De Lauretis' exploration of Foucault's formulation in her discussion of male power and male resistance as playing by the same rules in *Alice Doesn't*, Bloomington: Indiana UP, 1984, pp. 91–92. Her text is Nicolas Roeg's film *Bad Timing*, which has a rape as a central narrative impetus.
23. Forster's '"No, not yet" ... "No, not there,"' the message at the end of the novel, is echoed in Julia Kristeva's definition of women's practice as 'negative, in opposition to that which exists, to say that "this is not it" and "it is not yet."' Kristeva's definition is cited by De Lauretis (95) in her reading of the violated woman in *Bad Timing* who asks, '"What about my time"' and '"what about now ..."' (pp. 98–99).

7.3

FROM 'THE PRISONHOUSE OF ORIENTALISM'

Zakia Pathak, Saswati Sengupta and Sharmila Purkayastha

No, it is not our intention to provoke. The metaphor is heuristic. We teach English literature at graduate level at a women's college in Delhi University: for three years to those who major in the subject and to all students of the first year, science and humanities, as a compulsory subject. It is a pedagogical imperative with us that the teaching of literature should negotiate a discursive relation with the world outside the classroom. And texts must be read 'ethically':

> When we connect the text of the book to the text of our lives, the world of choice and action opens before us ... The word ethics is a mockery ... where the question of the relationship between reading and any form of action beyond discussing one's reading is never even raised.[1]

Given the increasing marginalization of literature in the culture, this might appear to be a quixotic enterprise. The problem is compounded by our having to teach a literature that is not our own.

Said's *Orientalism* was an epistemological intervention in this fraught distraught enterprise.[2] To deconstruct the text, to examine the process of its production, to identify the myths of imperialism structuring it, to show how the oppositions on which it rests are generated by political needs at a given moment in history, quickened the text to a life in our world. An immediate taxonomic impulse – with implications for an indigenously constructed canon – was to identify what we shall call white texts, i.e. literary texts by white writers dealing

Textual Practice, 5:2, Summer 1991, pp. 195–218. Extract: pp. 195–202 and 214–6.

with the colonial encounter, and to constitute them as a strategic formation answerable to an orientalizing interpretation. From our location in this formation we could participate in the major debates on nationalism, on tradition and modernity which are engaging this country. A study of the white texts could even, hopefully, activate our students to consider how a national identity can be formulated in troubled times. Certainly the project would enable us to engage with English literature more authoritatively than had been granted to us before, since it would create a space from which we could speak as privileged, first-order critics.

In the course of time, however, this project came to be riddled with reservations. The concept of a national identity in the vast, multi-religious, multi-cultural subcontinent that is India has always been contentious at the conceptual and action levels. It seeks to homogenize differences of religion, class and caste, region, and gender; differences which, when suppressed, implode within any nationalistic formulation. Yet such a formulation is implicated in our project. The homogenization of differences seems to force upon us as a condition of its possibility a binary opposition in which the Occident is opposed by a western-educated, secularized, urban, middle class. This class is increasingly being viewed by those outside it – the vast majority in this country – as spawned by our erstwhile rulers and baptized in their image. To construct a national identity on such precarious ground is, on the one hand, to marginalize ourselves in the national debate, as neo-colonialists. On the other hand, it is to remain within the oppositions of colonial discourse, in a structure which we began, in our titular metaphor, by refusing. In fact, we found the driving power of our deconstructive project to be such that it collapses taxonomic categories. Every text becomes a white text. In every text from a Donne poem to *Wuthering Heights* are clues that yield a narrative which might well become narcissistic or paranoid. In such re-readings of the English literary text which privilege Orientalist discourse as an interpretative grid, the whole of English literature may be reduced to a ground on which racial identities are contested. We remain trapped in the prisonhouse.

Finally, to read the text in ways which inevitably construct the west as Other to be exorcised is to be insensitive to the complex and troubled relations which govern the East–West encounter in Indian society today. The prestige of the English language has, if anything, soared since independence. English has now the status of an associative language, recognized by the Constitution of India. After the United Kingdom and the United States, India has the largest English-speaking population. Many religious and political leaders who condemn the hegemony of English from public platforms ensure that their children are admitted to English-medium schools. Recent attempts by the governments of Uttar Pradesh and Goa to withhold financial grants from these schools has led to widespread protest. In the national education system, English is one of the languages in the three-language formula. (And it is still widely held that a language is best taught through its imaginative literature.) The Sahitya

Akademi, the Central Government-sponsored academy for the promotion of Indian literatures, has now recognized that English is one of the languages in which Indian literature may be written.

This hegemony of the west in several fields was sharply brought home to us by the response of our students to our orientalizing project. It ranged from resistance to indulgence of the pedagogue. Irresistibly drawn to the electronic and consumer goods made possible by western technology, avidly reading western magazines from *Time* and *Newsweek* to women's and fashion magazines, their perception of the west is marked by desire. The anxiety and threat as they are experienced by the Indian expatriate cannot effectively communicate a warning to those back home because of the obstinate fact of the expatriates' continuing to prefer their domicile there. In fact, the green-card holder seems to have displaced the Indian Administrative Services Officer in the hierarchy of the marriage market. In these circumstances, to sensitize the student to the ugliness of the colonial encounter by constructing the west as Other is to indulge in an artificial exercise that remains confined to the classroom and defeats the pedagogical objective of connecting it to the world.

In the case of texts which remain outside the formation of white texts, we think that the pedagogical imperative can be more effectively served by inserting them into our cultural practices as a means of estrangement or *ostranenie*; as a means by which we defamiliarize our customs and make them ideologically visible. It seems to us that this would be responsible to both the producing and receiving cultures. By historicizing the text in the one, we would escape narcissism and paranoia; by using it as estrangement, we could make it relevant to our culture and retain our space as privileged critics. We quote an example of how this may be done from the experience of our colleague Rashmi Bhatnagar in the course of her classes on Pope's *The Rape of the Lock*. The rape of Belinda's lock of hair was instrumental in creating a sense of shared humanity across gender.

> Briefly, the students began by recognizing the poet's theme to be what in India is euphemistically called eve-teasing. Meanwhile the massacre of Sikhs took place that winter (November 1984) on the streets of Delhi. When my students, many of whom were victims/spectators of the sadistic violence and humiliation came back to the poem after curfew was lifted, the cutting off of the lock of hair acquired new and painful associations. We remembered how rioters had desecrated the sacred symbols of the Sikhs by forcibly cutting off their hair in public. The poem thus became not only about the desecration of women but obliterated the sexual differential as Gayatri Spivak puts it and became a poem about the desecration that can be visited even on oppressed men.[3]

This article is concerned with the teaching of what we call the white text. We choose four white texts covering the syllabus from the first year honours to the M.Phil. programme: Forster's *A Passage to India*, Greene's *The Quiet Amer-*

ican, Thompson's *An Indian Day* and Conrad's *Lord Jim*. We do not propose a comprehensive reading, an in-depth analysis or an extensive history of previous and contemporary readings. Rather, we offer our reading as an incision into the text which opens up its politics to pedagogical practice. We begin with *A Passage to India* and plot the complicity of the liberal humanist tradition of interpretative criticism with orientalist assumptions. We go on to show how the 'Indian' response which sets out to disrupt the hegemony of this tradition succeeds only in replacing colonialist with neo-colonialist discourse. Moving on to *The Quiet American*, we carry forward the subaltern representation of silence as a site for the ethnological encounter from the racial politics of Forster's novel to the sexual politics of Greene's. And we find Said's assessment of western notions about oriental sexuality inflected by a gender bias. In our reading of *An Indian Day* we refuse the monologic history that orientalism recovers and recuperate the multiple narratives which interrupt it. Finally, in our reading of *Lord Jim*, we argue for a reading as polymorphous, provisional, and sensitive to the space of the subject as interdiscourse.

It will become clear in the course of this article how *Orientalism* functioned for us as a theory of reading which transformed our classroom practice by alerting us to the workings of the colonized consciousness and to our interpellation as the colonized reader. But a certain distance from Said began to formulate as we let the world into the classroom; at this juncture we found the work of the Indian subaltern historians to be a sobering corrective to our uncritical orientalizing of white texts. We hope thus to have escaped the prisonhouse of self and other, east and west, us and them.

It will be obvious that we have not been concerned to propagate taste, create a canon, or otherwise endorse an aesthetic. Our critical practice has been 'to release the positions from which the text is intelligible.'[4] We believe that the task of criticism is 'that of actively politicising the text, of making its politics for it, by producing a new position for it within the field of cultural relations'.[5] And we offer as a political reading one that is multiply determined by concerns of race, class, caste, religion and gender; never finished, always in process.

I

We enter *A Passage to India* (hereafter API) through a collection of essays by Indian critics entitled *A Focus on 'A Passage to India'*.[6] We briefly examine these essays before concentrating on the one by M. K. Naik, to plot the complicity of these critics with Orientalist discourse even when their avowed purpose is to articulate an 'Indian' response in distinction to the western.

A pedagogical practice that is alert to the career prospects of our students which depend on the grading of examination scripts cannot ignore the critical tradition canonized in Delhi University; a detour through criticism based on liberal humanist premises is therefore *de rigueur*. Such criticism foregrounds, in the case of API, the metaphysical dimension of the novel and the non-mimetic mode. A quick glance at the essays in the *Twentieth Century Views* and

Casebook volumes, which form the staple of our student's reading, shows that the Caves section preoccupies most critics and Mrs Moore is the privileged character here.[7] She has the Hindu vision of life and it crushes her (Trilling). It is the experience of the wasteland; there is scepticism as to whether union can ever be achieved (Breuer). The highest experience is to perceive the annihilation of value: Mrs Moore does (Crews). Individual studies repeat the theme. There is a split between reality and inward vision; intensity, almost hysteria, is Mrs Moore's experience of the caves.[8] The India of Forster is the modern world in epitome.[9]

The Indian collection of essays is introduced by the editor as the 'genuine' Indian response as opposed to the 'fake' response which places undue emphasis on 'the patterns of common heritages and parallelisms in the theories of East and West'.[10] What becomes clear on reading the essays, however, is that the difference rests simply on the insertion of *Indian* philosophy, more particularly the Bhakta philosophy, into the spiritual dimension. The crucial concern is still with the metaphysical. Post-Said, these essays can be read as emanating from a colonized consciousness. Published almost thirty years after the British imperial presence had been removed from India, they have not broken out of the paradigm of interpretation legitimized by western critics. Indeed they are complicit with Orientalist discourse. First, they subordinate the political story to the philosophy. Nageswar Rao goes so far as to say that the novel is not about race relations at all but about 'fundamental experience' and is 'symbolic of the contemporary situation'.[11] Second, they implicitly glorify the golden past of India's history while resolutely looking away from the ugliness of the contemporary reality of colonial subjection. The uncritical boast that on the spiritual plane India can regenerate the west, that Hinduism made Forster aware of the gap in Christianity and gave promise of hope in a nihilistic world, is complicit with imperialist interests. Third, none of the writers disputes the claim of the white man to speak for the natives. 'Whether Forster speaks of Hindus or Muslims he gets into their hearts ... the sheer authenticity of the dialogue is staggering.'[12]

We shall focus in detail on the essay by M. K. Naik because it specifically addresses the problem of race relations. Ironically, it is the most colonized of the lot. Naik appears to rely on the principles of classic historiography which tie the writing of history to the realistic mode of representation. He finds *API* inadequate and even misleading as a historical document of race relations in the 1920s in India. To qualify as a history, Naik requires that *API* have a historical setting, whereas the novel does not so much as mention the Civil Disobedience Movement which was particularly successful in British, as distinct from princely, India where the novel for the most part is set. Also, it does not mention such towering political personalities as Mahatma Gandhi. These are a 'serious omission'. Next, Naik requires rounded 'living' characters, not 'sheep and goats' as most of the British characters are depicted as being – and not caricatures like Godbole and Pannalal. He requires 'representative' worthy

Indians, not Indians like Aziz with his face turned nostalgically to the past instead of determinedly to the future. Finally, he cannot find a teleological progression where the problems raised in the first two sections are on the way to being solved in the final one; the Temple section, disappointingly, is 'sketchy', Forster is 'out of his depth'.

In thus privileging the protocols of realistic representation Naik is blind to the various modes in which reality can be represented. Said's *Orientalism* inspired us to read the novel's non-mimetic mode historically; and the Indian subaltern historian Ranajit Guha helped us to disperse the primordial miasma of the caves and recuperate history.[13] The caves are described in the novel as 'older than all spirit'; without a history – 'Nothing, nothing attaches to them' – in other words, without a past.[14] What *we* read into the representation of the caves is not the absence of history but the *suppression* of history which marks the paranoid response of the Orientalists to processes which they could not understand, since, as Guha points out, this knowledge was withheld from them by the natives. 'Primal', 'dark', 'fists and fingers', 'unspeakable', fearsomely advancing to the town with the sunset – these phrases signal the fear and insecurity the imperialists experienced, confronted with what they could not master; to reduce it to stasis was to contain that fear and hold that threat at bay. The stereotype of Godbole as 'the inscrutable Oriental', 'enigmatically silent', must be unpacked. The silence of the native has been represented by Guha as a site for 'the ethnological encounter'.

> It is significant ... that some of the resistance to the formation of the colonial state in India should have been identified by the first colonialists as a refusal on the part of the natives to share a certain kind of knowledge with them ... a knowledge of the Indian past.[15]

Godbole is described by Forster as 'Ancient Night' – native cunning, secrecy and deception were generally seen as the reasons why the natives withheld knowledge. Aziz, however, understands Godbole's silence – for he too has experienced the need in his relations with Major Callendar: 'a power he couldn't control which capriciously silenced his mind. Godbole had been silenced now; no doubt not wittingly, he was concealing something' (p. 74). Thus Godbole, far from being 'a clown' or, for Naik, 'disaster', is an instance of the resistance to colonial subjection.[16] Similarly, Aziz's nostalgia for his Moghul past, Afghan ancestors and Persian poetry is also a site for the ethnological encounter. As Guha puts it, the domain of Clio and Mnemosyne intersect. The remembrance of things past, he states, is informed by the notion of the Other. By designating his past as Muslim, Aziz constitutes it as not-British, not-colonial. When towards the end of the story he decides to renounce the glories of Cordoba and Samarkhand, he concludes that 'The song of the future must transcend creed' (p. 261). He is led to 'a vague and bulky figure of a Motherland' (p. 262).

Finally, our reading of the novel disputes both Naik's contention that the ending is sketchy, that Forster is out of his depth, as it also disputes Said's opinion that it is 'a disappointing conclusion'. 'We are left at the end with a sense of the pathetic distance still separating "us" from an Orient destined to bear the mark of its foreignness as a mask of its permanent estrangement from the west' (p. 244). Our reading of the concluding 'Not now, not yet' constructs a Forster who displaces the estrangement the permanence of which is premised on racial grounds and relocates it on the axis of power. *API* is not addressed to its Indian readers. It is part of the formation of texts which critique liberal humanism. Forster's location within this formation pleads for a dialogue with those who believe that friendship between individuals is possible within structures of power in which they are unequally placed because the individual is capable of transcending these limitations. *API* works to undermine this belief. Slowly but relentlessly the novel charts the construction of the colonial subject in the three individuals who consider themselves impervious to such construction – Fielding, Adela and Aziz. 'At the moment when he was throwing in his lot with them, he realized the profundity of the gulf which separated them. They always do something disappointing' (p. 170). The masterly fading into the free indirect speech of the last sentence has Fielding wriggling on the colonial pin. The tourist of the Temple section, worried about eggs for breakfast and mosquitoes at night, is foreshadowed. With Adela, the process starts earlier, even as she expresses to Aziz her fear of being drawn into the Anglo-Indian mentality. '"Women like –" she stopped, not quite liking to mention names. She would boldly have said Mrs Turton and Mrs Callendar a fortnight ago' (p. 144). On the other side of the gulf, Aziz, who started out in the transcendent belief of 'the secret understanding of the heart' (p. 63) ends up by finding a national identity in hatred of the British. 'My heart is for my own people henceforward' (p. 198). Slowly and surely the three have been sucked into the subject spaces created by the discourse of imperialism. The trial is the site for the violent constitution of the colonial subject. It is not an instance of the reformed British policy of sharing power with native judges.[17] Ronny's faith in British fair play as imparted to Indian Civil Servants: 'My old Das is alright', is derided by Callendar: 'You mean he's more frightened of acquitting than convicting, because if he acquits he'll lose his job.' Das's own illusions are blown apart by his countryman Mehmoud Ali: 'I am not defending a case, nor are you trying one. We are both of us slaves' (p. 218).

Macaulay's Minute on Education of 1835 had urged the creation of 'a class of interpreters between us and the millions whom we govern – a class of persons Indian in blood and colour, but English in tastes, in opinions, in morals and in intellect ... almost the same but not quite.'[18] The agent of this change, as his brother-in-law Charles Trevelyan stated, was to be English Literature. Naik's political essay on race relations exemplifies the success of this programme. For Naik, the representative Indian intellectual is one who has enjoyed the benefits of 'western education', primarily enabling him to look forward to India's 'destiny in the modern world'. Aziz is, on this count, 'totally unrepresentative'. 'Morals' – Naik's Forster attempts to be just to his British and Indian characters because of 'his typically British sense of fair play'. 'Opinions' – there are two types of Britishers: those administrators with the 'pukka Sahib' mentality and 'the opposite type . . . the liberal minded Briton who hates the notion of the white man's burden'. 'Tastes' – those of polite British society: Godbole 'even fails to get up when the ladies rise – a crudity hardly credible in a man of his culture and position'. Here is Trevelyan's Improved Hindu: 'the summit of their ambition is to resemble us.'[19]

Shahane had stressed that the purpose of this collection of essays was to present 'the Indian image' – it is the image of a deracinated, decultured Indian. Disturbingly, circulating through Naik's essay is the desire and grasping for power after the departure of the imperialists by the arrogation of representative Indian-ness to a class, a creed and a caste who eventually became the nucleus of the new oppressors: western-educated, Hindu, and upper-caste. Both Aziz and Panna Lal are trained in the western system of medicine. But the former's nostalgia for his Moghul past, Afghan ancestors and Persian poetry constitute him as a Muslim and *ipso facto* not Indian. As for the latter: why, asks Naik, did Forster choose 'this cowardly, low-born man as the representative Hindu?'

. . .

Identity is a matrix of subject positions which may contradict one another.[20] Indian subject-identities are constituted in a multiplicity of discourses arising out of structures of religion, class, caste and gender. If *Orientalism*'s foregrounding of the colonial identity made so strong and immediate an appeal to us, it was testimony to the strength of our need in the present troubled times to produce a national identity which could defuse divisive tendencies. Precisely for that reason, however, it imperilled our pedagogical imperative of connecting the classroom to the world; for it is not our colonial identity that operates in negotiating the business of living. *Orientalism*, then, could neither bring our hegemonic relationship with the west to a crisis nor could it help to deconstruct existing structures of exploitation.

The history that *Orientalism* helps recover from the white text is thus monologic; it does not help us to recuperate the other narratives which interrupt the hegemony of the narrative of imperialism. 'Islam excepted, the Orient was for Europe until the nineteenth century, a domain with a continuous history of unchallenged western dominance' (Said, p. 73). 'India itself never provided an indigenous threat to Europe' (p. 75). There are modes of resistance other than military intransigence, as we have shown in our reading of the white texts. What concerns us is the contradiction involved in lauding, in the white text, counter-discursive strategies which in the context of nationalism are clearly discriminatory and retarding. An example is the orthodoxy of the Hindu caste system and its rituals of purification. Such strategies today are exploited by the forces of secession. The fundamentalism of religious establishments and the terrorism of its militant wings are threatening to split the country.

Finally, as students of literature, we take issue with Said's conception of imaginative literature. He pays lip-service to 'the mythology of creation, in which it is believed that artistic genius . . . can leap beyond the confines of its own time and place' (p. 202) but in tracing the history of such intervention, the influence exerted by Orientalist discourse is projected as deterministic: 'the words of even the most eccentric artist are constrained and acted upon by society, by cultural tradition, by worldly circumstance and by stabilizing influences like schools, libraries and governments' (p. 201). We produce a few sentences that will show how Said leans on the side of determinism. 'The official intellectual genealogy of Orientalism . . . might neglect the great contribution of imaginative and travel literature which strengthened the divisions established by Orientalists . . . for the Islamic Orient this literature is especially rich and makes a special contribution to building the Oriental discourse' (p. 99). 'What Orientalists . . . made available, the literary crowd exploited' (p. 168). Said's notion of perceiver and object seems to fit in with the unproblematic subject–object paradigm. 'Chateaubriand came to the Orient as a constructed figure, not as a true self'; this impelled him 'to see things, not as they were, but as he supposed they were' (p. 171). With Kinglake, 'it is interesting how little the experience of actually seeing the Orient affected his opinions. Like many other travellers he is more interested in remaking himself and the Orient than he is in seeing what there is to be seen' (p. 193). With Burton the voice of 'individuality' struggles with the 'voice of empire' but he is eventually reduced to 'the imperial scribe . . . as the scene required management, it became clear that institutions and governments were better at the game of management than individuals'. 'This is the legacy of nineteenth-century orientalism to which the twentieth century has become inheritor' (p. 197).

The double movement, to make a space for a counter-discourse and then to collapse it into the dominant, is a characteristic of Said's treatment of official discourse as well. Theorized as latent and manifest Orientalism, this invariant structure takes no cognizance of the politics of reading. On another reading, for example, a counter-discourse might be seen as functioning within the official discourse of Orientalism as Said himself describes it: Whiston against Ockley in the eighteenth century, Flaubert and Nerval against Lane and Burton in the nineteenth, and Massignon against Gibbs in the twentieth. Said struggles desperately to be fair, to make discriminations, but the cumulative pressure of his modifiers – however, nevertheless, yet, on the other hand, even so, none the less – have the effect of repressing the 'randomness' of his material in the interests of an 'anasemic' reading, where 'the glue of chance is not allowed to make sense'; thus Orientalism operates according to 'the law of dialectics' which always 'synthesizes and closes'.[21]

If style is the 'recognizable, repeatable and presentable sign of an author who reckons with an audience',[22] then, as the blurb on the back cover of *Orientalism* recognizes, it is pugnacity and fury which are Said's style. He had several audiences in mind: 'students of literature and criticism, contemporary students of the Orient, the general reader and lastly readers in the third world' (pp. 24–5).

This categorization does not in effect reckon with us. *Orientalism* is addressed to the white reader; which explains its pugnacity and fury. But this is the fury of the expatriate, invested with desire; it is a demand for love which the other does not have it in him to give. It is doubtful if this obsession can ever be broken out of from a place in the first world.

NOTES

1. Robert Scholes, 'The pathos of deconstruction', *Novel: a Forum on Fiction*, 22 (Winter 1989), p. 227.
2. Edward Said, *Orientalism* (London: Routledge & Kegan Paul, 1978). All subsequent citations are from this edition.
3. Rashmi Bhatnagar, 'A reading of Pope's *The Rape of the Lock*', in Lola Chatterji (ed.), *Woman, Image, Text* (New Delhi: Trianka Publications, 1986), p. 51.
4. Catherine Belsey, *Critical Practice* (London: Methuen, 1980), p. 4.
5. Tony Bennet quoted in A. P. Foulkes, *Literature and Propaganda* (London: Methuen, 1983), p. 19.
6. Vasant Shahane (ed.), *A Focus on 'A Passage to India'* (Bombay: Orient Longman, 1975).
7. See Malcolm Bradbury (ed.), *Forster: A Collection of Essays*, 'Twentieth Century Views' series (New Delhi: Prentice-Hall of India, 1979); Malcolm Bradbury (ed.), *E. M. Forster: A Passage to India*, a 'Casebook' series (London: Macmillan, 1970).
8. See John Beer, *The Achievement of E. M. Forster* (London: Chatto & Windus, 1963), Chapter 1.
9. John Sayre Martin, *E. M. Forster* (Cambridge: Cambridge University Press, 1976), Chapter 7.
10. Shahane, *A focus on 'A Passage to India'*, p. 25.
11. Ibid., p. 34.
12. Ibid., p. 4.
13. Ranajit Guha, *An Indian Historiography of India; A Nineteenth-century Agenda and its Implications* (Calcutta and New Delhi: K. P. Bagchi, 1988).
14. E. M. Forster, *A Passage to India* (Harmondsworth: Penguin Books, 1954). All subsequent citations are from this edition.
15. Guha, *An Indian Historiography of India*, p. 6.
16. Nirad C. Chaudhuri, 'Passage To and From India', *Encounter*, II (June 1954).
17. See G. K. Das, *E. M. Forster's India* (London: Macmillan, 1977).
18. Minute of 2 February 1835, in G. M. Young (ed.), *Macaulay: Prose and Poetry* (Cambridge, Mass.: Harvard University Press, 1967), p. 729.
19. Quoted in Tejaswani Niranjana, 'Translation, colonialism and rise of English', *Economic and Political Weekly*, XXV (April 1990), Bombay.
20. Belsey, ibid., ch. 3.
21. Jacques Derrida, quoted in Claudette Sartiliot, '"Reading with an other ear": Derrida's Glas in English', *New Orleans Review*, 15, (Fall, 1988) 3, pp. 18–29.
22. Edward Said, *The World, the Text and the Critic* (Cambridge, Mass.: Harvard University Press, 1983) p. 33.

7.4

FROM 'ARTICULATING THE ARCHAIC'

Homi Bhabha

> How can the mind take hold of such a country? Generations of invaders have tried, but they remain in exile. The important towns they build are only retreats, their quarrels the malaise of men who cannot find their way home. India knows of their trouble . . . She calls 'Come' through her hundred mouths, through objects ridiculous and august. But come to what? She has never defined. She is not a promise, only an appeal. (E. M. Forster, *A Passage to India*)[1]

> The Fact that I have said that the effect of interpretation is to isolate in the subject a kernel, a *kern*, to use Freud's own term, of *non-sense*, does not mean that interpretation is in itself nonsense. (Jacques Lacan, 'The Field of the Other')[2]

There is a conspiracy of silence around the colonial truth, whatever that might be. Around the turn of the century there emerges a mythic, masterful silence in the narratives of Empire, what Sir Alfred Lyall called 'doing our Imperialism quietly', Carlyle celebrated as the 'wisdom of the Do-able – Behold ineloquent Brindley . . . he has chained the seas together',[3] and Kipling embodied, most eloquently, in the figure of Cecil Rhodes – 'Nations not words he linked to prove / His faith before the crowd.'[4] Around the same time, from those dark corners of the earth, there comes another, more ominous silence that utters an archaic colonial 'otherness', that speaks in riddles, obliterating proper names and proper places. It is a silence that turns imperial triumphalism into the testimony of colonial confusion and those who hear its echo lose their historic memories.

In Peter Collier and Helga Geyer-Ryan (eds), *Literary Theory Today*, Ithaca: Cornell, 1990, pp. 203–18. Extract: pp. 203–8.

This is the Voice of early modernist 'colonial' literature, the complex cultural memory of which is made in a fine tension between the melancholic homelessness of the modern novelist, and the wisdom of the sage-like storyteller whose craft takes him no further afield than his own people.[5] In Conrad's *Heart of Darkness*, Marlow seeks Kurtz's Voice, his words, 'a stream of light or the deceitful flow from the heart of an impenetrable darkness' and in that search he loses 'what is in the *work* – the chance to find yourself'.[6] He is left with those two unworkable words, 'the Horror, the Horror!' Nostromo embarks on the most desperate mission of his life with the silver tied for safety around his neck 'so that it shall be talked about when the little children are grown up and the grown men are old', only to be betrayed and berated in the silence of the Great Isabel, mocked in the owl's death call 'Ya-acabo! Ya-acabo! – it is finished; it is finished.'[7] And Aziz, in *A Passage to India*, who embarks jauntily, though no less desperately, on his Anglo-Indian picnic to the Marabar caves is cruelly undone by the echo of the Kawa Dol: 'Boum, ou-boum is the sound as far as the human alphabet can express it ... if one spoke silences in that place or quoted lofty poetry, the comment would have been the same ou-boum.'[8]

As one silence uncannily repeats the other, the sign of identity and reality found in the work of Empire, is slowly undone. Eric Stokes, in *The Political Ideas of English Imperialism*[9] describes the mission of work – that medium of recognition for the colonial subject – as a distinctive feature of the imperialist mind which, from the early nineteenth century, effected 'the transference of religious emotion to secular purposes'. But this transference of affect and object is never achieved without a disturbance, a displacement in the representation of Empire's work itself. Marlow's compulsive search for those famous rivets, to get on with the work, to stop the hold, gives way to the compulsive quest for the Voice, the words that are half-lost, lied about, repeated. Kurtz is just a word, not the man with the name; Marlow is just a name, lost in the narrative game, in the 'terrific suggestiveness of words heard in dreams, of phrases spoken in nightmares'.

What emerges from the dispersal of work is the language of a colonial nonsense that displaces those dualities in which the colonial space is traditionally divided: nature/culture chaos/civility. Ou-boum or the owl's deathcall – the horror of these words! – are not naturalized or primitivistic descriptions of colonial 'otherness', they are the inscriptions of an uncertain colonial silence that mocks the social performance of language with their non-sense; that baffles the communicable verities of culture with their refusal to translate. These hybrid signifiers are the intimations of a colonial Otherness that Forster describes so well in the beckoning of India to the conquerors: 'She calls "Come" ... But come to what? She has never defined. She is not a promise, only an appeal.' It is from such an uncertain invitation to interpret, from such a question of desire, that the echo of another significant question can be dimly heard, Lacan's question of the alienation of the subject in the Other: 'He is saying this to me, but what does he want?[10] Ya-acabo! Ya-acabo! – it is finished ... finished': these words stand not for the plenitudinous place of cultural diversity, but at the point of culture's 'fading'. They display the alienation between the transformational myth of culture as a language of universality and social generalization, and its tropic function as a repeated 'translation' of incommensurable levels of living and meaning. The articulation of nonsense is the recognition of an anxious contradictory place between the human and the not-human, between sense and non-sense, which no dialectic can deliver. In that sense, these 'senseless' signifiers pose the question of cultural choice in terms similar to the Lacanian 'vel', between being and meaning, between the subject and the other, 'neither the one nor the other'. Neither, in our terms, 'work' nor 'word' but precisely the work of the colonial word that leaves, for instance, the surface of Nostromo strewn with the detritus of silver – a fetish, Emilia calls it; an evil omen, in Nostromo's words; and Gould is forever silent. Bits and pieces of silver recount the tale that never quite adds up either to the narcissistic, dynastic dream of Imperial democracy, nor to Captain Mitchell's banal demand for a narrative of 'historical events'.

The work of the word impedes the question of the transparent assimilation of cross-cultural meanings in a unitary sign of 'human' culture. In-between culture, at the point of its articulation of identity or distinctiveness, comes the question of signification. This is not simply a matter of language; it is the question of culture's representation of difference – manners, words, rituals, customs, time – inscribed without a transcendent subject that knows, outside of a mimetic social memory, and across the – Ou-boum – kernel of non-sense. What becomes of cultural identity – the ability to put the right word in the right place at the right time – when it crosses the colonial non-sense – neither the one – meaningful – nor the other – meaningless? Such a question impedes the language of relativism in which cultural difference is usually disposed of as a kind of ethical naturalism, a matter of cultural diversity. 'A fully individual culture is at best a rare thing' Bernard Williams writes in his interesting new essay *Ethics and the Limits of Philosophy*.[11] Yet, he argues, the very structure of ethical thought seeks to apply its principles to the whole world. His concept of a 'relativism of distance', which is underwritten by an epistemological view of society as a given whole, seeks to inscribe the totality of other cultures in a realist and concrete narrative that must beware, he warns, the fantasy of projection. Surely, however, the very project of ethical naturalism or cultural relativism is spurred precisely by the repeated threat of the *loss* of a 'teleologically significant world', and the compensation of that loss in projection or introjection which then becomes the *basis* of its ethical judgement. From the margins of his text, Williams asks, in parenthesis, a question not dissimilar from Forster's India question or Lacan's question of the subject; 'What is this talk of projection [in the midst of naturalism] really saying? What is the screen?' He makes no answer.

The problematic enunciation of cultural difference becomes, in the discourse of relativism, the perspectival problem of temporal and spatial distance. The threatened 'loss' of meaningfulness in cross-cultural interpretation, which is as much a problem of the structure of the signifier as it is a question of cultural codes (the *experience* of other cultures), then becomes a hermeneutic project for the restoration of cultural 'essence' or authenticity. The issue of interpretation in colonial cultural discourse is not, however, an epistemological problem that emerges because cultural objects appear *before* (in both senses) the eye of the subject in a bewildering diversity. Nor is it simply a quarrel between pre-constituted holistic cultures, that contain within themselves the codes by which they can legitimately be read. The question of cultural difference as I want to cast it, is not what Adela Quested quaintly identified as an 'Anglo-Indian difficulty', a problem caused by cultural plurality. And to which, in her view, the only response could be the sublation of cultural differentiation in an ethical universalism: 'That's why I want Akbar's "universal religion" or the equivalent to keep me decent and sensible.'[12] Cultural difference, as Adela experienced it, in the nonsense of the Marabar caves, is not the acquisition or accumulation of additional cultural knowledge; it is the momentous, if momentary, extinction of the recognizable object of culture in the disturbed artifice of its signification, at the edge of experience.

What happened in the caves? *There*, the loss of the narrative of cultural plurality; *there* the implausibility of conversation and commensurability; *there* the enactment of an undecidable, uncanny colonial present, an Anglo-Indian difficulty, which repeats but is never itself fully represented: 'Come ... But come to what?'; remember India's invocation. Aziz is incurably inaccurate about the events, because he is sensitive, because Adela's question about polygamy has to be put from his mind. Adela, obsessively trying to think the incident out, somatizes the experience in repeated, hysterical narratives. Her body, Sebastian-like, is covered in colonies of cactus spines, and her mind which attempts to disavow the body – hers, his – return to it obsessively: 'Now, everything transferred to the surface of my body ... He never actually touched me once ... It all seems such nonsense ... a sort of shadow.' It is the echochamber of memory: '"What a handsome little oriental ... beauty, thick hair, a fine skin ... there was nothing of the vagrant in her blood ... he might attract women of his own race and rank: Have you one wife or many? ... Damn the English even at their best," he says ... "I remember, remember scratching the wall with my finger-nail to start the echo ..." she says ... And then the echo ... "Ou-boum".'[13]

In this performance of the text, I have attempted to articulate the enunciatory disorder of the colonial present, the writing of cultural difference. It lies in the staging of the colonial signifier in the narrative uncertainty of culture's in-between: between sign and signifier, neither one nor the other, neither sexuality nor nationality, neither, simply, memory nor desire. The articulated opening in-between that I am attempting to describe, is well brought out in Derrida's placing or spacing of the hymen. In the context of the strange play of cultural memory and colonial desire in the Marabar caves, Derrida's words are uncannily resonant. 'It is neither desire nor pleasure but between the two. Neither future nor present, but between the two. It is the hymen that desire dreams of piercing, of bursting in an act of violence that is (at the same time or somewhere between) love and murder. If either one *did* take place, there would be no hymen . . . It is an operation that both sows confusion between opposites and stands *between* the opposites 'at once'.[14] It is an undecidability that arises from a certain culturalist substitution that Derrida describes as 'anti-ethnocentrism thinking itself as ethnocentrism . . . silently imposing its standard concepts of speech and writing'. For neither can the epistemological object of cultural identity nor the dialectical, structuralist sign of arbitrary difference contain the effect of such colonial nonsense.

In the language of epistemological cultural description, the object of culture comes to be inscribed in a process that Richard Rorty describes as that confusion between justification and explanation, the priority of knowledge 'of' over knowledge 'that': the priority of the visual relation between persons and objects above the justificatory, textual relationship between propositions. It is precisely such a priority of eye over inscription, or Voice over writing, that insists on the 'image' of knowledge as confrontation between the self and the object of belief seen through the mirror of Nature. In such a visibility of truth the metonymy of the colonial moment comes to be disavowed because its narrative ruse lies in proferring a visibility or totality of the event of cultural authority, or the object of race, only to alienate it from itself, to replicate identity as iteration. The signifiers of ambivalent, hybrid, cultural knowledges – neither 'one' nor 'other' – are ethnocentrically elided in the search for cultural commensurability, as Rorty describes it: 'to be rational is to find the proper set of terms into which all contributions should be translated if agreement is to become possible'.[15]

And such agreement leads inevitably to a transparency of culture that must be thought outside of the signification of difference; what Ernest Gellner has simplistically resolved in his recent work on relativism, as the diversity of man in a unitary world. A world which, if read, as 'word' in the following passage illustrates the impossibility of signifying, within its evaluative language, the values of anteriority and alterity that haunt the colonial non-sense.

Gellner writes: 'Assume the regularity of nature, the systematic nature of the world, not because it is demonstrable, but because anything which eludes such a principle also eludes real knowledge; if cumulative and communicable knowledge is to be possible at all, then the principle of orderliness must apply to it . . . Unsymmetrical, idiosyncratic explanations are worthless – they are not explanations.'[16]

It is the horizon of holism, towards which cultural authority aspires that is made ambivalent in the colonial signifier. To put it succinctly, it turns the dialectical 'between' of culture's disciplinary structure – *between* unconscious and conscious motives, *between* indigenous categories and conscious rationalizations, *between* little acts and grand traditions, in James Boon's[17] words – into something closer to Derrida's 'entre', that sows confusion between opposites and stands between the oppositions at once. The colonial signifier – neither one nor other – is, however, an act of ambivalent signification, literally splitting the difference between the binary oppositions or polarities through which we think cultural difference. It is in the enunciatory act of splitting that the colonial signifier creates its strategies of differentiation that produce an undecidability between contraries or oppositions.

Marshall Sahlins' 'symbolic synapses'[18] produce homologous differentiations in the conjunction of oppositions from different cultural planes. James Boon's cultural operators produce the *Traviata* effect – when Amato del Passato turns into the sublime duet Grandio – as moment that recalls, in his words, the genesis of signification. It is a moment that matches the right phones to the language system, producing from different orders or oppositions a burst of cross-referencing significance in the 'on-going' cultural performance. In both these influential theories of the culture-concept, cultural generalizability is effective to the extent to which differentiation is homologous, the genesis of signification recalled in the performance of cross-referencing.

What I have suggested above, for the colonial cultural signifier, is precisely the radical loss of such a homologous or dialectical assemblage of part and whole, metaphor and metonymy. Instead of cross-referencing there is an effective, productive cross-cutting across sites of social significance, that erases the dialectical, disciplinary sense of 'Cultural' reference and relevance. It is in this sense that the culturally unassimilable words and scenes of nonsense, with which I started – the Horror, the Horror, the owl's death call, the Marabar caves – suture the colonial text in a hybrid time and truth that survives and subverts the generalizations of literature and history.

NOTES

1. E. M. Forster, *A Passage to India*, (Harmondsworth: Penguin) 1979, p. 135.
2. J. Lacan, *The Four Fundamental Concepts of Psycho-Analysis*, (Harmondsworth: Penguin, 1979), p. 250.
3. Carlyle, *Essays*.
4. Rudyard Kipling, 'The Burial' quoted in Eric Stokes, *The Political Ideas of English Imperialism* (London: Oxford University Press, 1960) p. 28. I am indebted to Stokes' suggestive remarks on the value of 'inarticulateness' attributed to the mission of colonial enterprise.
5. W. Benjamin, *Illuminations*, trans. Harry Zohn (London: Jonathan Cape, 1970), pp. 98–101.
6. J. Conrad, *Heart of Darkness* (Harmondsworth: Penguin, 1979).
7. J. Conrad, *Nostromo* (Harmondsworth: Penguin, 1979) p. 345.
8. E. M. Forster, *A Passage to India* (Harmondsworth: Penguin, 1975), p. 145.
9. E. Stokes, *Political Ideas*, p. 29.
10. J. Lacan, *The Four Fundamental Concept of Psycho-Analysis*, p. 214.
11. B. Williams, *Ethics and the Limits of Philosophy* (London: Fontana, 1985).
12. E. M. Forster, *Passage to India*, p. 144.
13. This is a collage of words, phrases, statements made in/around the entry to the Marabar caves. They represent a fictional re-enactment of that crucial moment as an act of memory.
14. J. Derrida, *Dissemination*, trans. Barbara Johnson (Chicago: Chicago University Press, 1981), pp. 212–3.
15. R. Rorty, *Philosophy and the Mirror of Nature* (Princeton: Princeton University Press, 1979), p. 318.

16. E. Gellner, *Relativism and the Social Sciences* (Cambridge: Cambridge University Press, 1985), p. 90.
17. J. Boon, 'Further operations of "culture" in anthropology: a synthesis of and for debate', *Social Science Quarterly*, vol. 52, pp. 221–52.
18. M. Sahlins, *Culture and Practical Reason* (Chicago: Chicago University Press, 1976.

PART 8
SALMAN RUSHDIE:
THE SATANIC VERSES

INTRODUCTION

In *Midnight's Children* the West hangs over Rushdie's characters with the full force of English literature and historiography weighting it down from the start, when '[Aadam Aziz] learned that India – like radium – had been "discovered" by the Europeans.'[1] In Rushdie's fourth novel, *The Satanic Verses*, the Empire comes home to roost. The novel's chief literary concern is not with 'English' literature but the Koran, and the setting is not India but Ellowen Deeowen – London.

Rushdie's writings have become the focus of a certain kind of struggle for cultural identity in Britain, which is the reason why, for example, arguments over *The Satanic Verses* are used in Hanif Kureishi's novel of London conflict between white liberal academics and militant Muslim students, *The Black Album*;[2] and David Caute's self-published but critically acclaimed 1998 novel *Fatima's Scarf* also uses the Rushdie affair as its blueprint for a plotline concerning the burning of a blasphemous novel by Muslims in a northern English town, and a later *fatwa* declared from Iran on the book's Anglo-Indian author.

The publication of *The Satanic Verses* in 1988 led to fierce debate and street violence, death threats and even murder. Such contention was not over just literature but religious tolerance, free speech and international politics. Charges of apostasy levelled against Rushdie were followed by the Ayatollah Khomeini's *fatwa*. This judgement, placing Rushdie under a death sentence, supported the interpretation that he had unforgivably blasphemed against Islam. By contrast, the Al Azhar Seminary of Cairo, the Muslim religious ruling body, has at no time passed any decree on *The Satanic Verses*.[3] In Britain, calls to ban the book were supported by public demonstrations against Rushdie, including ritualised book burnings. Suspected racist attacks against Muslim offices followed.

A key issue in 1988 was the law of blasphemy, which protects the Christian faith but not other religions (e.g., *Gay News* has been prosecuted for suggesting Jesus could have been homosexual). Such discrepancies reveal the tensions between understandings of Britain as a multicultural society encompassing a variety of religious faiths and more traditional opinions of a 'central' British culture, which includes Christianity. Opposed to this, but also resting an argument on ideas of democratic rights, supporters of *The Satanic Verses* often emphasise, in addition to the importance of free speech, the question(ability) of literature's accountability to non-fictional realms of discourse.

Readings of the novel and of the significance of the debate surrounding it vary greatly. Satendra Nandan writes that

> Any attempts to go *before* these colonial, canonical texts [the Mahabharata, the Ramayana, the Bible, the Koran] often create havoc. Isn't that the fundamental issue of *The Satanic Verses*? The current preoccupation with post-colonialism prevents us from exploring, exposing the ancient, internal colonialism of the 'traditional order'.[4]

By contrast, Gayatri Spivak's essay, 'Reading *The Satanic Verses*', offers an interpretation of the novel in terms of national fragmentation, the heterogeneity created by migrancy to the metropolis, and the way that, in post-coloniality, aesthetic objects are forced into a particular register of the political.[5]

The book and the Rushdie Affair that followed its publication have met with a variety of lengthy responses. In India, for example, Chandrashekhar Sastry included a chapter on '*The Satanic Verses* and Islamic Response' in his book on *The Non-Resident. Indian* in 1991, while in the West Malise Ruthven's book-length review of the storm raised by the novel was published as *A Satanic Affair*, and, in 1990, the London-based journal *Third Text* published a special issue devoted to the novel's reception, 'Beyond the Rushdie Affair'.[6] Another useful article, in terms of Britain's post-colonial position since 1989, is Talal Asad's 'Multiculturalism and British Identity in the Wake of the Rushdie Affair', while, in the context of Islam, an especially insightful essay is Feroza Jussawalla's 'Rushdie's *Dastan-e-dilruba*: *The Satanic Verses* as Rushdie's love letter to Islam'.[7]

The essays included below offer a range of different perspectives. Amin Malak's 'Reading the Crisis: The Polemics of Salman Rushdie's *The Satanic Verses*' is first of all useful because, published a year after the novel, it takes the trouble to explain the reasons why the book became so controversial. The essay speculates that the furore, which much of the West found so incomprehensible over a 'mere' novel, occurred precisely because Islam was satirised in a work of fiction. It ends by suggesting five hypotheses concerning the novel's reception in the light of Western stereotypes, Orientalism and postmodernism. The extract from Timothy Brennan's *Salman Rushdie and the Third World: Myths of the Nation* tenders a long reading of several aspects of the novel to do with its many parodies and satires but also criticises Rushdie for the limitations of his 'levity' (the novel arguably lacks any kind of positive aspect, in terms of black culture or resistance to racism). Brennan sees *The Satanic Verses* as a text of decolonisation and migrancy, but one which still leaves the (ex-)colonised without a voice that is demonstrated to matter. Michael Gorra's afterword from *After Empire* was first written in 1989 soon after the *fatwa*. His essay considers the way the novel prefigures the response that it itself received, and interrogates the issues that the book generated, of blasphemy, omnipotence, truth and the relationship between writing and religion, fiction and myth. At the same time, Gorra shows an awareness of his own position as a Western writer in a secular society, for whom the questions raised by the book are inevitably different from those perceived by 'the Islamic world'.

Lastly, Vijay Mishra's 'Postcolonial Differend: Diasporic Narratives of Salman Rushdie' scrutinises the importance of diaspora to constructions of national and religious identity. His discussion of post-colonial identity politics and nationalism starts from sixties Powellism and moves forward through the theories of Benedict Anderson and Homi Bhabha, to end with a consideration of the tension (which the essay later explores in terms of Lyotard's differend) between diasporic aesthetics and ideas of the sacred.

The Satanic Verses is of course also deeply critical of the West and of neo-colonial attitudes – the new empire within Britain. Like other post-colonial writers, one of Rushdie's most basic moves is to switch positions around, as when he writes: 'Native and settler, that old dispute, continuing now upon soggy streets, with reversed categories.'[8] Again inverting colonial mimicry, Rushdie has his chief anglophile in *The Satanic Verses* observe that it is the English who are unable to live up to the standards of their national identity: 'For a man like Saladin Chamcha the debasing of Englishness by the English was a thing too painful to contemplate.'[9] Chamcha's received colonial and stereotypical Englishness is something he himself has to maintain as the English do not: 'The Alps, France, the coastline of England, white cliffs rising to whitened meadowlands. Mr Saladin Chamcha jammed on an anticipatory bowler hat.'[10]

Similarly, Rushdie turns the theory of a national personality determined by climate against the ex-colonisers, invoking all the tropes of weather, countryside and temperament that contemporaries from Powell through David Lean to Ruth Jhabvala still use to delineate an Indian character:[11] 'Gibreel Farishta floating on his cloud formed the opinion that the moral fuzziness of the English was meteorologically induced. "... City," he cried, and his voice rolled over [London] like thunder, "I am going to tropicalise you."'[12]

Rushdie's other obvious reaction to white racism is to take its fantasy and make it fact. The novel's first section ends with Saladin Chamcha, British citizen, arrested for being an illegal immigrant, looking like the devil (and the animal images that abound in even so anti-Imperial a novel as George Orwell's *Burmese Days* are used literally by Rushdie in *The Satanic Verses* as Senegalese vacationers turn into snakes and Nigerians grow tails).

Rushdie says of *The Satanic Verses* that it is a celebration of miscegenation, it 'is for change-by-fusion, change-by-conjoining. It is a love-song to our mongrel selves.'[13] He has variously spoken against those who have denounced the book but, most often, he has seen outcries in terms of a fear of impurity and intermingling, of newness entering the world.[14] However, what is perhaps most important in his work is the complication and revision of national identity in the light of post-colonial migrations, and selves constituted more by displacement and diaspora than by notions of 'home' and 'belonging'. That revision has also been fought over since 1989 in the wake of the Rushdie Affair. Paul Gilroy writes:

> Whatever view of Rushdie one holds, his fate offers another small, but significant, omen of the extent to which the almost metaphysical values of England and Englishness are currently being contested through their connection to 'race' and ethnicity. His experiences are also a reminder of the difficulties involved in attempts to construct a more pluralistic, post-colonial sense of British culture and national identity.[15]

NOTES

1. Salman Rushdie, *Midnight's Children*, London: Picador, 1982, p. 11.
2. Hanif Kureishi, *The Black Album*, London: Faber, 1995.
3. For contemporary views and accounts, see Lisa Appignanesi and Sara Maitland (eds), *The Rushdie File*, London: Fourth Estate, 1989.
4. Satendra Nandan, 'The Diasporic Consciousness', in Harish Trivedi and Meenakshi Mukherjee (eds), *Interrogating Post-Colonialism: Theory, Text and Context*, Shimla: Indian Institute of Advanced Study, 1996, p. 15.
5. G. C. Spivak, 'Reading *The Satanic Verses*', in *Outside in the Teaching Machine*, London: Routledge, 1993, pp. 217–42.
6. Chandrashekhar Sastry, *The Non-Resident Indian*, Bangalore: Panther, 1991 and Malise Ruthven, *A Satanic Affair*, London: Heineman, 1991.
7. Talal Asad, 'Multiculturalism and British Identity in the Wake of the Rushdie Affair', *Politics and Society*, 18:4, 1990, pp. 455–80 and Feroza Jussawalla, 'Rushdie's *Dastan-e-dilruba*: *The Satanic Verses* as Rushdie's love letter to Islam', *Diacritics*, 26:1, Spring 1996, pp. 50–73.
8. Salman Rushdie, *The Satanic Verses*, London: Viking, 1988, p. 353.
9. Ibid, p. 75.
10. Ibid, pp. 86–7.
11. Lean in the comparisons between cool, rainy England and dry, inhospitable India in his film of *A Passage to India* and Jhabvala in her comparison of the plains and hills in terms of Indian and English characters in *Heat and Dust* (for a discussion of this, see Laurie Suchers *The Fiction of Ruth Prawer Jhabvala*, London: Macmillan, 1989).
12. Rushdie, *The Satanic Verses*, p. 354.
13. Salman Rushdie, *In Good Faith*, London: Viking, 1990, p. 4.
14. Ibid. See also Bhabha's support for this reading and approach in his 'Down Among the Writers', *New Statesman and Society*, 28 July 1989, pp. 16–18.
15. Paul Gilroy, *The Black Atlantic*, London: Verso, 1993, pp. 10–11. See also Talal Asad, 'Multiculturalism and British Identity in the Wake of the Rushdie Affair', *Politics and Society*, vol. 18, 4, 1990, pp. 455–80. Asad speaks against Gilroy's and Bhabha's position, arguing that distinct cultural traditions need to be acknowledged, for both logical and political reasons.

8.1

'READING THE CRISIS: THE POLEMICS OF SALMAN RUSHDIE'S *THE SATANIC VERSES*'

Amin Malak

I

To begin with, life in the literary world has never been the same ever since the publication of *The Satanic Verses* (1988). What we have witnessed has been an overwhelming crisis of reading, interpreting, and responding to a troubled, troubling text.[1] As such, *The Satanic Verses* daringly and ambitiously presents itself as a historiographical metafiction, deploying various tropes and encompassing multiple layers of signification, while operating within a postmodernist, counter-culture context. Rushdie's strategy involves 'pitting levity against gravity' (*Satanic* 3); its narratological slogan, inspired by *The Arabian Nights*, declares 'it was and it was not ... it happened and it never did' (35). Transcending time and space, the narrative moves synchronically (between England, India, and Argentina) and diachronically (between the present and the early days of Islam). Yet this impressively expansive narrative is consciously bounded by the *doppelgänger* motif, embodied by two survivors of a blown-up plane: Saladin Chamcha and Gibreel Farishta. These dual 'angeldevilish' (5) heroes experience a series of tragi-comic, fantastic-realistic episodes narrated in the usual Rushdiesque multi-layered, multi-toned fashion.

While Rushdie's two preceding novels, *Midnight's Children* (1981) and *Shame* (1983), touched off some controversy in India and Pakistan respectively, the crisis caused by *The Satanic Verses* excessively and intensely surpassed the previous reactions; it assumed an unprecedented violence whose universal

ARIEL, 20:4, October 1989, pp. 176–86.

implications are bound to be damaging. Deplorably, the crisis has resurrected ancient cultural enmities (if ever they were dormant), provoked an ugly orgy of accusations, name-calling, and racism, in the midst of which the West (to use those grand, binary divides) has once again misread the East, and the East has once again misrepresented itself. More seriously and closer to my concerns, we risk, in this sorry situation, contaminating our discourse—whether literary or religio-political—with intolerance, transgression, and disturbingly presumptuous assumptions about the superiority of *one* value system over another. What we acutely need in the process of reading (and hopefully riding) the crisis is a genuine, mutual (at times heroic) exercise of sympathetic imagination, whereby the concerns and sensitivities of the *other* are recognized.

II

> Philosophe, orateur, apôtre, législateur, guerrier, conquérant d'idées, restaurateur de dogmes rationnels, d'un culte sans images, fondateur de vingt empires terrestres et d'un empire spirituel, voilà Mahomet! A toutes les échelles où l'on mesure la grandeur humaine, quel homme fut plus grand? (Alphonse de Lamartine)

> Our current hypothesis about Mahomet, that he was a scheming Imposter, a Falsehood incarnate, that his religion is a mere mass of quackery and fatuity, begins really to be now untenable to any one. The lies, which well-meaning zeal has heaped round this man, are disgraceful to ourselves only. (Thomas Carlyle)

Any reader of Rushdie's earlier works, especially his critically acclaimed *Midnight's Children*, has, like myself, looked forward with excitement and eager anticipation to reading another novel by a writer of such creative energy and fertile imagination. However, anyone who has even a rudimentary knowledge of the culture and civilization of Islam would immediately realize on encountering certain passages in the text that the book contains a bombshell. The most offensive part of the novel centres on the historical portion in which the narrative turns into a *roman à clef*, depicting in a deliberately convoluted way the life of the Prophet Muhammad, referred to as Mahound. Obviously the choice of this name is anything but innocent. As the OED tells us 'Mahound' signifies, especially for Western medievalists, four meanings, all offensive: 'false prophet'; 'a false god'; 'a hideous creature'; and 'a name for the devil.'

More particularly, the offensive parts are contained in Chapter II, 'Mahound' (89–126), and Chapter VI, 'Return to Jahilia' (357–94). Rushdie's deliberate discourse, couched in a thinly veiled dream sequence, suggests three offensive things about this 'Mahound-Mahon-Muhammad' (401). First, Mahound, a calculating businessman-turned-prophet, founds a religion called 'Submission' (a literal translation for the Arabic word 'Islam') in the desert city of Jahilia (which literally means 'ignorance' but here stands for pre-Islamic Mecca). Charismatic and determined, Mahound seems mainly engaged in a personal pursuit of power. This 'fit man, no soft-bellied usurer he' (93) has three powerful opponents: the poet Baal, 'the precious polemicist' and one of Jahilia's 'blood-praising versifiers' (98); the wealthy businessman Abu Simbel, the plutocrat whose manipulative skills enable him to 'make his quarry think he has hunted the hunter' (98); and Abu Simbel's wife Hind, a towering, lustful figure whose seductive powers are rooted in wealth, status, and physical charm. Nevertheless, Mahound's crafty, at times cruel, schemes triumph over these formidable foes, since he has 'no scruples ... no qualms about ways and means' (363).

Second, this businessman-turned-prophet cunningly contrives 'those matter-of-fact revelations' (366), claiming them to be delivered to him by the archangel Gibreel (Gabriel). These speculations are uttered by Mahound's intoxicated scribe, Salman the Persian (again an irreverent depiction of one of the Prophet's companions by the same name):

> And Gibreel the archangel specified the manner in which a man should be buried, and how his property should be divided, so that Salman the Persian got to wondering what manner of God this was that sounded so much like a businessman. This was when he had the idea that destroyed his faith, because he recalled that of course Mahound himself had been a businessman, and a damned successful one at that, a person to whom organization and rules came naturally, so how excessively convenient it was that he should have come up with such a very businesslike archangel, who handed down the management decisions of this highly corporate, if non-corporeal, God. (364)

Proceeding with this implicit/explicit notion of the aprocrypha of *The Qur'an*, Muslims' holy book, Rushdie revives the long dead issue of the so-called 'Satanic Verses' from which the novel's title is derived. The title alludes to an incident that two Muslim historians (who lived about two centuries after the Phophet's death) report to have occurred: Muhammad, allegedly, made a concession to the oligarchy of pre-Islamic Mecca, accepting three idols as divine intercessors.[2] In the course of the novel, the wily Mahound becomes partly tempted, partly pressured into a deal with Abu Simbel to compromise the new religion's categorical monotheism by accepting three idols (Al-Lat, Al-Uzza, and Manat) as intermediaries between worshipping, revenue-generating pilgrims and God. The deal gives crucial political and practical advantages to Mahound's new religion; simultaneously, it secures profit for Jahilia's business establishment. However, Mahound revokes the deal and recants the *ayāt* (verses) that endowed the idols with intercessionary powers, claiming that the verses were deliberately altered, falsified, and delivered to him by Shaitan (Satan). This disputable episode—as well as others that Rushdie appropriates—is capitalized on by some Orientalists, even though almost all Muslim scholars reject it. By adopting and dramatizing this episode, Rushdie highlights it as a version of truth that may have been deliberately ignored by the sanitized and 'sanctified' chronicles of history. The ultimate implication of this narrativized incident is that *The Qur'an* is not the holy, definitive book that all Muslims believe to be God's exact words, *ipsissima verba*, but a text conveniently faked by the Prophet.

Third, and more seriously, Rushdie portrays an elaborate scene at 'the most popular brothel in Jahilia' (376) called the Curtain, 'Hijab' (which also means in Arabic 'veil,' a suggestion that Muslims treat their women, some of whom may wear veils, as prostitutes). The female workers at the Curtain impersonate the Prophet's wives to improve business. The idea is the fruit of Baal's depraved poetic imagination:

> How many wives? Twelve and one old lady, long dead. How many whores behind the Curtain? Twelve again; and, secret on her black-tented throne, the ancient Madam, still defying death. Where there is no belief, there is no blasphemy. Baal told the Madam of his idea; she settled matters in her voice of a laryngitic frog. 'It is very dangerous,' she pronounced, 'but it could be damn good for business. We will go carefully; but we will go.' (380)

In this segment of the novel, the real names of the Prophet's wives (whom Muslims reverentially call 'Mothers of the Believers') are used. Even a dead wife is not spared in this puzzling, bizarre segment, since catering to necrophilic customers can create profit:

> Strangest of all was the whore who had taken the name of 'Zainab bint Khuzaimah', knowing that this wife of Mahound had recently died. The necrophilia of her lovers, who forbade her to make any movements, was one of the more unsavoury aspects of the new regime at The Curtain. But business was business, and this, too, was a need that the courtesans fulfilled. (382)

Believers would legitimately consider such a wantonly contrived episode as the most vicious of Rushdie's offences. To them Rushdie's blend of blasphemy with quasi-pornography tastelessly verges on the obscene.

As an admirer of Rushdie's talent and a believer in the function and validity of literature, I can appreciate why a Western reader, educated in a secular, liberal-humanist culture, may be bedeviled by all the fuss and furor about a mere book, a work of fiction containing a troubling dream sequence. However, in order to understand the enormity of what has been done, a circumspect, tolerant reader needs to appreciate what the Prophet Muhammad means to Muslims all over the entire Muslim world: from Senegal to Kurdistan to Indonesia. The Prophet is not only a religious figure (the Messenger of the Faith) but also the symbol of the heroic tradition, the figure who epitomizes virtue, wisdom, love, compassion and courage. Fully human as he repeatedly affirmed, the Prophet has nevertheless become for over fourteen centuries a constant cultural focus in the collective consciousness of the masses. In short, he is the holiest figure that represents for over one-fifth of the earth's population the driving, enduring, cohesive centre. Is it any wonder then that Muslims (including liberal and secular Muslims) become puzzled, offended, or outraged when such a figure is so gratuitously and relentlessly ridiculed in a work of fiction?

Let us examine the issue from another angle. It is my belief that had Rushdie written a non-fictional work about the Prophet in which he engaged in a metaphysical or spiritual speculation, the anger would not have been so intense, nor would it have had such a regrettable level of demonization and counter-vilification. Rushdie's narrative strategy involves using subterfuge in the guise of fictionality. He cleverly immunizes his text against external charges by associating the offensive passages with the obsessive imagination of a possessed character. Moreover, he can always deploy the classic claim of authorial distance or demand multiple discourse about an ambivalent text by inviting other hitherto unarticulated layers of meaning. Here then is the sore point for the protesting Muslims: they feel frustrated and furious because the assault on the Prophet can be easily denied as a mere work of fiction, a mere dream sequence, or a mere statement uttered by a drunken character who does not represent the author's views. They see little room for meaningful, factual, point/counter-point debate.

III

> What the postmodern writing of both history and literature has taught us is that both history and fiction are discourses, that both constitute systems of signification by which we make sense of the past ('exertions of the shaping, ordering imagination'). In other words, the meaning and shape are not in the events, but in the systems which make those events into historical facts. This is not a 'dishonest refuge from truth,' but an acknowledgement of the meaning-making function of human constructs. (Linda Hutcheon)

In attempting to gauge our response to a complex text such as *The Satanic Verses*, we need to establish, as Bakhtin taught us, that literature is a process, not a final product, and that a novel is quintessentially polyphonic; that is, it cannot be reduced to a single voice: authorial, privileged, or otherwise. Moreover, the driving energy that propels the narrative in Rushdie's work is guided by postmodern views on history, which 'confront the problematic nature of the past as an object of knowledge for the present' (Hutcheon, 'Problematizing' 371). Here, history does not mean final, definitive renditions, nor does it involve the 'customary fetishizing of facts' (Hutcheon, 'Problematizing' 377); rather history is a selective, reconstructive, narrative discourse that challenges the dominant versions of representation and provokes a counter discourse. Moreover, if history, as Hayden White and others argue, is a form of narrative, the postmodern fiction that deploys and dramatizes historical figures or events can claim to be yet another version of the past that is entitled to legitimacy. The net result is that the postmodern version rivals or at least destabilizes the master narrative: self-consciously, tentatively, yet transgressively. Thus the postmodern historiographer reworks his material with characterological hubris and humility, affection and aversion, care and cruelty. Consequently, if the text affirms anything, it affirms its ambivalence, tentativeness and paradoxicality.

Such a paradoxical manner in the configuration and reshaping of history parallels, in Rushdie's *oeuvre*, a similar hesitant view towards history itself as an epistemological phenomenon to be contended with. On the one hand, history assumes a frightening kaleidoscopic totality over the individual's fate; as with Saleem Sinai, one is 'handcuffed to history' (MC 9). Likewise, Gibreel Farishta's obsession with history takes the form of a series of dreams that disturbingly infiltrate taboo territories. On the other hand, history represents a valuable source of inspiration, a liberator that can edify and enlighten us on complex, current issues. It functions as a crucial ideological ally that ultimately enriches the narrative of tentativeness and enhances the discourse of ambivalence: the primary aim is to probe rather than propound, question rather than confirm, doubt rather than dictate. History is in the eye of the beholder or projector; we do not have one history but *histories*. And Rushdie does not hide his hostility towards any belief system that posits 'history' on fixed, sanctified grounds. Like all postmodern writers, he sees reality (whatever that may mean) as an unfinished project, a flux phenomenon that resists containment or closure and remains open to multiple renditions and projections.

In order to prove his point, he accordingly selects his target most riskily and attacks ruthlessly and relentlessly the driving, enduring, cohesive centre of Muslim history and civilization, symbolized in the figure of the Prophet Muhammad. This may explain why the portrayal of the Prophet appears so inflammatory and offensive, since it entails ridiculing Islam's most sanctified figure. To Rushdie, as to all postmodernists, no one is sacred, nothing is static, and everything is open to question, to parody, and to subvert. Hence the clash of cultures and the conflict of representations.

IV

> The exteriority of the representation is always governed by some version of the truism that if the Orient could represent itself, it would; since it cannot, the representation does the job, for the West, and *faute de mieux*, for the poor Orient. (Edward Said)

Let me then conclude by venturing the following five *hypotheses*:

1. If the 'Rushdie Affair' proves anything, it affirms the inseparability of text and context. Any previous notions we might have had about the insularity of literature have been proven false. For, as Linda Hutcheon cogently argues, 'gone now is the belief that art is, or can be, autonomous, separate from the world. Postmodernist art situates itself squarely in the context of its own creation and reception in a social and ideological reality' ('Challenging' 34). In his article 'Outside the Whale,' Rushdie himself emphasizes that 'works of art, even works of entertainment, do not come into being in a social and political

vacuum; and that the way they operate cannot be separated from politics, from history' (130). We thus cannot divorce text from context. Put differently, the production of any literary work is culturally conditioned; subsequently the responses to the literary work are likewise culturally conditioned.[3]

2. The postmodernist impulse to articulate, appropriate, parody or subvert contexts has included foraying into the world of politics. *The Satanic Verses* does exactly that. It delves daringly and legitimately into various current political issues, because—as Rushdie lucidly and unequivocally argues—'politics and literature, like sport and politics, do mix, are inextricably mixed, and . . . that mixture has consequences' ('Whale' 137). Accordingly, one can qualify *The Satanic Verses* as a text permeated by politics from page one. The response (or responses) to such a polemical text is/are bound to be political too. We may not like some of the responses, but the text itself elicits and provokes a political response.
3. Starting with its title, *The Satanic Verses* unearths and copies some of the nastiest claims that a few Orientalists, be they missionaries or affiliates of colonial enterprises, have fabricated about the history and culture of Islam. Anyone familiar with Edward Said's compelling arguments in *Orientalism* (1978) and his subsequent works is aware of the weight and mass of what those 'experts' have propagated about Islam. The impact of their writings is still to a large extent dominant in Western views on Islam. Rushdie's utilization of those fabrications seems to the ordinary Muslim reader not only flattering to those pre-packed stereotypes about Islam, but also to signal the burning of bridges between the author and his own cultural roots.
4. By copying this reductively edited version of Islamic history, Rushdie, who should have known otherwise, has made his motives seem suspect to Muslims. Whether deliberately or inadvertently, he has turned his literary product into an attractive item (hot and rare) for Western consumers. Yet by doing so, Rushdie, the leftist polemicist, may have qualified himself for what the Marxist-feminist critic Gayatri Spivak calls 'the privileged native informant' (256). (She means by that those Third World writers who exploit their intimate knowledge of their culture to present unflattering images that endorse Western stereotypes: her two models are V. S. Naipaul and Bharati Mukherjee.)[4] In other words, Rushdie's narrative, if the hypothesis is valid, becomes in the final analysis alien to the Third World view of itself. Regrettably, he has, to apply Said's comment on Naipaul,'allowed himself quite consciously to be turned into a witness for the Western prosecution' ('Intellectuals' 53), and has thus rendered himself inoperative within the Third World literary discourse. As I see it, the dialectic of that discourse is critical (at times severely critical) of its cultural roots, yet

remains militantly committed to them. I am thinking of such committed writers as Naguib Mahfouz (the Egyptian novelist who won the Nobel Prize for literature in 1988) and Faiz Ahmad Faiz (the Pakistani poet).

5. While we may mildly or severely critique *The Satanic Verses*, while we may quibble with its contentious discourse, while we may impute all sorts of mercenary, conspiratorial, or blasphemous motives to its author, the book remains impressive. As Janette Turner Hospital puts it, this novel is 'a firecracker of a work whose every page fizzes with linguistic acrobatics and exuberance, with cross-language puns, with clichés suddenly rinsed and new[ly]-minted so that they shock and shimmer.' Besides, its author's energy, creativity and imagination have proven him to be one of the outstanding writers in the English language today. Given its profound literary value, its depth, its density, and above all its humour, *The Satanic Verses* does not deserve to be banned. It demands *debate*, not destruction.

NOTES

1. I wish to delineate three distinct aspects pertaining to the bizarre drama we call 'The Rushdie Affair.' The first relates to *The Satanic Verses* as a complex literary text. The second relates to the concept of freedom of expression championed by liberal-humanists as well as the literati. The third relates to the death sentence against the author, a move which compounded an already confusing situation and prompted the swift, sensational media to get on the bandwagon. The focus of this article is on the first aspect.
2. The two historians are Al-Waqidi (A.D. 747–823) and Al-Tabari (A.D. *c.* 839–923). The Prophet died in A.D. 632.
3. As an illustration of such a culture-specific response, let me excerpt Shahabuddin, who rhetorically asks Rushdie, 'You depict the Prophet whose name the practicing Muslim recites five times a day, whom he loves, whom he considers the model for mankind, as an impostor and you expect us to applaud you? You have had the nerve to situate the wives of the Prophet, whom we Muslims regard as the mothers of the community, in a brothel and you expect the Muslims to praise your power of imagination?'
4. Spivak has used the term '*false* native informants' in reference to the works of Naipaul and Mukherjee ('Scripts').

WORKS CITED

Bakhtin, Mikhail. *Problems of Dostoevsky's Poetics*. Ann Arbor: Ardis, (1973).

Carlyle, Thomas. *On Heroes, Hero-Worship and the Heroic in History*. (1841). London: OUP, (1928).

Hospital, Janette Turner, 'Angels in the Skies above England.' *Globe and Mail* 22 Oct. (1981): C17.

Hutcheon, Linda. 'Challenging the Conventions of Realism: Postmodernism in Canadian Literature.' *The Canadian Forum* (April 1986): 34–38.

———— 'The Postmodern Problematizing of History.' *English Studies in Canada* 14.4 (1988): 365–82.

Lamartine, Alphonse de. *Histoire de la Turquie*. Paris: Pagnerre, (1855).

'Mahound.' *The Oxford English Dictionary*. (1933). (1961).

Rushdie, Salman. *Midnight's Children*. (1981). London: Picador, (1982).

———— *The Satanic Verses*. London: Viking Penguin, (1988).
———— 'Outside the Whale.' *Granta 2* (1984): 125–38.
Said, Edward. *Orientalism*. (1978). New York: Vintage, (1979).
———— 'Intellectuals in the Post-Colonial World.' *Salmagundi* 70–71 (1986): 44–64.
Shahabuddin, Syed. 'You did this with Satanic foresight, Mr Rushdie.' *Times of India* 13 Oct. (1988): sec. 2:3.
Spivak, Gayatri Chakravorty. *In Other Worlds: Essays in Cultural Politics*. New York: Methuen, (1987).
———— 'Scripts of Feminism in a Divided World.' Distinguished Visitors Seminar. U of Alberta, Edmonton, 20 March (1986).
White, Hayden. *The Content of the Form: Narrative Discourse and the Historical Representation*. Baltimore and London: Johns Hopkins UP, (1987).

8.2

'REBIRTH, DISSENT AND THE THEORY OF ACQUIRED CHARACTERISTICS'

Timothy Brennan

The theodicy is at once, and usually in combination, played out at three levels. The first level is introduced in the book's title, which contains the principle of organisation for the entire novel. It alludes to an incident recorded by the ninth-century Arab historian Al-Tabari, in which the Prophet at first sanctioned, and later deemed corrupt, certain verses of the *Quran* that he believed had originated not from Allah but from the devil. As the novel explains, it was an act of religious tolerance and openness to alien intrusions that accounted for Muhammad's first satanic inspirations. Historically, the popular devotion among the pagan Meccans for the female deities Al-Lat, Al-Uzza and Al-Manat had prevented the peaceful expansion of Islam in its crucial early period; as a consequence, Muhammad at first believed it was God's will that their worship be permitted within the limits of Islamic doctrine. This concession, although apparently blasphemous (since Islam was nothing if not the discovery by the Meccans of the one true God), nevertheless ensured the new religion's success.

The novel is not really about these 'satanic verses', however. Much like *Shame*, it projects itself as a rival *Quran* with Rushdie as its prophet and the devil as its supernatural voice: '[God] moves in mysterious ways: men say. Small wonder then, that women have turned to me.' Or perhaps it is not the devil but only what the parasitical self-servers within the Faith call the devil by invoking God 'to justify the unjustifiable'. In this fertile indecision, this apotheosis of self-questioning, the counter-*Quran* of the novel finds its theology. To ask 'Is my

Salman Rushdie and the Third World: Myths of the Nation, London: Macmillan, 1989, pp. 152–66.

sense of right divine, or only a form of arrogance?' is to subscribe to the religion of doubt that Rushdie would like to see expand and flourish. Rushdie, then, takes on the features both of the Prophet and of Salman Al-Farisi, the Persian scribe to whom by legend Muhammad dictated the *Quran*. In the apocryphal passages of the *Satanic Verses*, this new Salman wilfully alters the words of his apparently unsuspecting (and illiterate) master. The novel thus floods into, overlaps with and creates anew the 'satanic verses' of tradition, although only in a world, as it argues, in which the supreme deity is both devil and God at once – both '*Ooparvala* ... the Fellow Upstairs' and '*Neechayvala*, the Guy from Underneath' (*SV*, p. 318).

Already familiar in the double characters of the earlier novels (Flapping Eagle and Grimus, Saleem and Shiva, Raza and Iskander), this twinning of opposites repeats itself in the heroes of *The Satanic Verses*, who are two famous Indian film and television stars recently relocated to England – Gibreel Farishta and Saladin Chamcha. The syncretism, however, is if anything more complex and more brilliant. The foreign vocabulary that dots the narrative has been meticulously gathered from Turkish, Persian, Egyptian, Indian and Arabian sources; it is not simply the Hindi, Urdu and Arabic that one growing up in Bombay might naturally come across. This linguistic polymorphism seems to realise what *Shame* only promised: the feeling of a genuine pan-Islam, especially of its non-Arabic peoples. Similarly, while a good deal has been written in reviews about the Islamic dimensions of the novel, the elaborate Indianness of the book has been forgotten. As much as *Midnight's Children* this is a book about India, especially the India of Bombay as seen by those who have just left it.

The clearest example of this lies in the contemporary identity of Gibreel Farishta, who in addition to all his other identities is meant to represent the great Bombay film idol, Amitabh Bachan.[2] The premier star of the Indian screen from the late 1960s until the early 1980s, Bachan also happened to be the product of the prestigious Doon School (the Indian Eton or Harrow), classmate of Sanjay Gandhi, a personal friend of the Nehru family, and later an elected member of Congress from Allahabad. Exactly as Rushdie describes in the book, Bachan became seriously ill in the early 1980s after a freak injury suffered while shooting a film. Like Gibreel he lingered between life and death for weeks as all of India held its breath, and Indira Gandhi cancelled scheduled visits abroad to fly to his bedside in Bombay. Similarly, the so-called 'theologicals' that Gibreel starred in are an actual genre in the Hindi cinema, especially popular in the Hindu south of India, and popularised recently by the actor N. T. Rama Rao, who is mentioned by name in the novel (although these films are called 'mythologicals' not 'theologicals' and Bachan did not star in them). Obviously, such films are drawn from Hindu, not Muslim, sources, since to represent the Prophet visually is taboo. As Firoze Rangoonwalla points out, however, 'the costume and fantasy films are often given a Muslim base to act as a countering influence and a way of catering to that section of the big Indian audience'.[3]

The syncretism can be seen also in the novel's startling opening passage, where

Gibreel and Chamcha tumble from the heavens in a great free-fall onto the shores of England, after the jumbo jet in which they were travelling is blown to pieces by Sikh terrorists. Plummeting together through the 'almost-infinity of the almost-dawn' these 'two real, full-grown, living men' rush towards their destinies in 'the great, rotting, beautiful, snow-white, illuminated city, Mahagonny, Babylon ... Proper London, capital of Vilayet' (p. 4). Jesting with Chamcha as he falls, flapping his arms and assuming foetal postures in mid-air – 'pitting levity against gravity' – Gibreel is strangely ecstatic, for he realises joyfully in the novel's opening lines the religious component of the novel's tripartite theodicy: 'to be born again ... first you have to die'. Naturally by this point we can only take these words as a collapsing together of Hindu reincarnation (strengthened by the Hindi film allusions in this predominantly Muslim imaginative terrain) and the metaphorical 'rebirth' that recent converts to Islam or Christianity speak of. Echoed repeatedly throughout the book, those hopeful lines build slowly to the triumphant conclusion that 'evil is never total, that its victory, no matter how overwhelming, is never absolute' (p. 467).

Taking its lead from the title, the scene of course re-enacts Shaitan's fall, which is cast here in the form of big-name celebrities from India being cut down to size in the alluring and indifferent Britain, where doctors and professors become publicans and janitors overnight. But the downward motion, as in the often adversity-filled life of the Prophet, is only a preparation for their ascension into heaven. As fall, the scene evokes the 'mutation' of the immigrants themselves, a change involving the 'debris of the soul, broken memories, sloughed-off selves, severed mother-tongues, violated privacies, untranslatable jokes [and] ... extinguished futures' (p. 4); as ascension, the new self, if any remains after the painful transformation. Here Rushdie plays with another allegorical level – the scientific – and asks whether the immigrant is contending with the barbarous survival strategies of 'natural selection', pitting a British master race against an inferior (tinted colonial) one; or whether, in a quite different option, the immigrants can give new life to the theories of Lamarck by consciously adopting the characteristics that their new environment demands; or (in the worst of the alternatives) they are merely the laboratory animals of a new technological 'creationism' – the playthings of a group of Western fanatics who through eugenics want to concoct a species of their own liking.

It is in this spirit that the many-levelled architecture of the novel works by reflecting each level off the other levels like the inverted images in a broken mirror: Gibreel is the angel Gibreel (the one who announces to the Prophet his mission, the biblical Gabriel) as well as that even better-known angel thrust out of heaven for daring to dissent – his heraldic brother, Shaitan (Satan). Ayesha – historically the favourite wife of Muhammad – is in the Titlipur dream-sequences also the Moses of Exodus, Gandhi on his famous march to the salt sea, the Ayatollah Khomeini's idea of the abominable Al-Lat, and Chamcha's lover Pamela; Jahilia is the spiritual state of immigration, the bad capital of corrupt pagan Mecca, the good (bad) capital of post-*hegira* Islam, and London.

Examples like this could be compounded throughout the novel: images of a single troubled mind freely associating.

Just as in the slogan of rebirth above, another slogan rings throughout the book, bringing us to the political level of the theodicy – to will is to dissent. Shaitan and Gibreel therefore belong together, for both can be seen to merge in tradition (both apocryphal and canonical) in the sense that both intercede with and ultimately affect the utterances of Muhammad. For in the tormented mind of Gibreel (who becomes certifiably insane after arriving in England) Muhammad is cast in the role of 'Mahound', an abusive name for Muhammad used by medieval European scholars who liked to portray the prophet as a crazed charlatan. In this sense, Rushdie's use of the term is precisely right and proper as an inevitable inversion of his own intentions: the act of turning 'insults into strengths' (*SV*, p. 93). At the same time, it is natural that Muslims would despise the book for its relativity and for reducing the prophetic legend to a psychological truth. All three identities – prophet, evil spirit and God's messenger – are assumed by Gibreel Farishta, who comes to London to blow the trumpet of doom in yet another incarnation: Azraeel, the exterminating Angel.

What we have in these images is more than an attempt to capture the immigrant's confused identity, or even an attempt to elaborate the by-now familiar point that the oppressed, simply because they are oppressed, are not necessarily 'angelic'. Beyond all the layerings of religious paranoia at the psychic level, what we have is a grotesque imaging of racist fantasies. For it is the British 'mainstream' that ascribes to the black newcomers a devil's role. Thus shortly after being washed up on the shore of England after his miraculous fall, Chamcha begins to sprout horns, grow goat hooves and display an immense erection. As his name implies, Chamcha had considered himself the perfectly acculturated Indian Englishman; he wears a bowler hat and pin-stripe suit and walks with fastidious carriage. No matter, though, since being (as Rushdie puts it) 'of the tinted persuasion', he embodies in the eyes of the police (who come to arrest him for entering the country illegally!) all the appropriate slanders levelled at the 'black beasts' in their midst: they are brutish, oversexed, unclean and (as the goatish incarnation implies) tragic. Later in the novel, as his bestial transformations progress, the black communities marvel at his Luciferian snortings and sulphurous breath, finally taking him as their own. Opposition to British hegemony within the black community takes the form of accepting the devil's role assigned to them by Britain, not passively but as a means of resistance. They show their defiance by fighting back in a distorted way appropriate to their commercialised surroundings – that is, with a fad, with pop tribal badges in the form of fluorescent halos and cheap clip-on devil's horns.

With the usual faithfulness to his sources, Rushdie closely interweaves the details of tradition into his modern rendering of politico-religious mission. Because Gibreel appears in both Bible and *Quran* as counsellor to the Prophet and inspirer of Moses, he 'became the guarantee of the coherence of Islam and the two older religions'.[4] The syncretic reference is repeated in the figure of the scribe Salman Al-Farisi, who first converted to Christianity, later travelled to Syria and Central Arabia in search of the Prophet, and was later still sold as a slave to a Jew. Both his obvious allusions to Rushdie himself and his Persian nationality perversely suggest the extremist brand of Shiite Islam in contemporary Iran, which Rushdie dislikes and which he describes briefly in the novel in a short section dealing with the exile of Khomeini in London before the Iranian revolution. As a contrast, Rushdie's secular attractions to the more artistic and personal brand of Islam found in Sufism is indirectly referred to in his use of Salman, who by tradition is said to be one of Sufism's founders.[5] As for Shaitan, the correspondences are even more elaborate. It is popularly thought that every poet requires a shaitan to inspire him, and that every person is 'attended by an angel and a shaitan who urge him to good and evil deeds respectively'.[6]

Gibreel and Chamcha, then, are the polarities of the novel – one, the self-anointed angelic/prophetic presence who hears infernal voices; the other, the 'good' immigrant turned Shaitan in the English metropolis. The narrative deliberately confuses the supernatural and the everyday precisely by switching rapidly between these characters' psychic imaginings and their normal activities as *actors* – that is, masters of disguise 'like much-metamorphosed Vishnu' (*SV*, p. 17). When, for example, in the second chapter, we suddenly find ourselves without explanation in eighth-century Mecca during the early days of Islam (although it is a parable whose characters have recognisable counterparts in the story proper) we do not yet know what we later learn: that it is not an historical flashback but the (imagined? dreamed?) contemporary set of a popular religious film being directed by Gibreel, whose career has floundered after coming to England and who is trying to make a comeback. There are two such stories taking up several chapters of the book. One dealing with 'Jahilia' (literally 'ignorance' and Islam's term of abuse for pre-Islamic Arabia) features the Prophet 'Mahound' – a story that introduces us to the scribe Salman and the court satirist Baal of which more later. The other is set in contemporary India, and involves the march of a small band of Muslim faithful to the shores of the Arabian Sea, the waters of which are made to part so that the pilgrims can walk unhindered to Mecca. The narrative rationale for these digressions is found in Gibreel's former status as a screen idol in India. His was a

> unique career incarnating, with absolute conviction, the countless deities of the subcontinent in the popular genre movies known as 'theologicals' . . . For over a decade and a half he had represented, to hundreds of millions of believers in that country – in which, to this day, the human population outnumbers the divine by less than three to one – the most acceptable, and instantly recognizable, face of the Supreme. (*SV*, p. 16)

We have, in other words, a motive for the lengthy narrative shifts in the mind of Gibreel himself, who recasts the characters of the novel into a context appropriate to his own tormented psychology, and who, as if in a vision, 'dreams' the Jahilia and Arabian Sea episodes as part of his mission to bring religion to the irreligious land of Vilayet (England). He had, it is said, 'played too many of those winged figures for his own good'. On the other hand, and at the same time as events portrayed in the popular cinema, these moments of high religious significance for Muslims are being trivialised in just the way that everything meaningful is trivialised by the vulgar market mentality of capitalist England.

Chamcha's acting career demonstrates this vulgarisation even more clearly for he had flourished as the 'Man of a Thousand Voices and Voice', an actor whose talent for voice-overs was used in television commercials to make such things as garlic crisps, baked beans and frozen peas seem more appealing. In an even more embarrassing case of salesmanship, he becomes the star of a popular children's television programme *The Aliens Show*.

> It was a situation comedy about a group of extraterrestrials ranging from cute to psycho, from animal to vegetable, and also mineral, because it featured an artistic space-rock that could quarry itself for its raw material, and then regenerate itself in time for the next week's episode; this rock was named Pygmalien . . . and there was a team of Venusian hip-hoppers and subway spray-painters and soul-brothers who called themselves the Alien Nation . . . The stars of the show, its Kermit and Miss Piggy, were the very fashionable, slinkily attired, stunningly hairstyled duo, Maxim and Mamma Alien, who yearned to be – what else? – television personalities. They were played by Saladin Chamcha and Mimi Mamoulian. (SV, p. 62)

If the theme of 'rebirth' applies here in obvious ways, the much more dangerous transformation of species to species is ever present as a threat. 'Creationism' as the West's own peculiar brand of religious demagogy is from the start allied with a spurious 'science' that challenges the more hopeful Lamarckianism of the true alien immigrants. Thus, on the plane to London, before the hijacking that eventually leads to his and Gibreel's miraculous fall, Chamcha meets an American 'creationist' by the name of Eugene Dumsday (eugenics, doomsday). A grating Christian lunatic and sworn enemy of Charles Darwin, he theorises that the ills of postmodern drug-and-sex culture are due to the pernicious influence of natural selection theories. As such, he introduces into the narrative the merging of 'advanced' Western technology and the West's frightful backwardness, a backwardness intensified by an assurance of superiority and the technological means to realise its ethnocentric vision.

In this vein, Chamcha, adrift in London, comes to appreciate the specifically mental eugenics at work on the inhabitants of a television culture:

> It seemed to him, as he idled across the channels, that the box was full of freaks: there were mutants – 'Mutts' – on *Dr Who*, bizarre creatures who appeared to have been crossbred with different types of industrial machinery: forage harvesters, grabbers, donkeys, jackhammers, saws,

> and whose cruel priest-chieftains were called *Mutilasians* . . . Lycanthropy was on the increase in the Scottish Highlands. The genetic possibility of centaurs was being seriously discussed . . . on *Gardeners' World* he was shown how to achieve a 'chimeran graft' . . . a chimera with roots, firmly planted in and growing vigorously out of a piece of English earth . . . he, too, could cohere, send down roots, survive. Amid all the televisual images of hybrid tragedies – the uselessness of mermen, the failures of plastic surgery, the Esperanto-like vacuity of much modern art, the Coca-Colonization of the planet – he was given this one gift. It was enough. (*SV*, pp. 405–6)

As Rushdie later shows, however, the crossbreeding of market and media produces an inhuman blob, as faceless as it is powerful. Chamcha's humanist resolve after his bout with television is everywhere challenged by the various antagonists he meets in real-life London. As the police raid a black nightclub, the television news cameras are said to stand aloof from the 'disordered shadow-lands' where people are being beaten, behind the protective wall of men in riot helmets, carrying shields. Although the reporters speak gravely under the Krieg lights, the fact is that a camera requires law, order, the thin blue line. Seeking to preserve itself, it remains behind the shielding wall, observing the shadow-lands from afar, and of course from above: that is, it chooses sides' (pp. 454–5).

Similarly, when faced with having to beg for his job back on *The Aliens Show*, Chamcha is told by producer Hal Valance that ethnic shows no longer sell. Valance is one of Rushdie's funniest and cruellest creations – the monstrous embodiment of the capitalist ad-man, the spawn of a society with throwaway ethics: 'With Hal, all explanations were *post facto* rationalization. He was strictly a seat of the pants man, who took for his motto the advice given by Deep Throat to Bob Woodward: *Follow the money*' (p. 265). Systematically eliminating all the blacks from this commercials because the commercials 'researched better' that way, he has a nose for the winds of change in the authoritarian populist climate of Thatcher's Britain. As he explains, 'I love this fucking country. That's why I'm going to sell it to the whole goddamn world, Japan, America, fucking Argentina. I'm going to sell the arse off it. That's what I've been selling all my fucking life: the fucking nation. The *flag*' (p. 268). In a typical reversal, the sentiments echo those of the neo-colonial elite satirised in the Third-World novels, and which are referred to earlier in the narrative in a reference to Sanjay Gandhi 'the airline pilot [who] flew back from the European conference chambers in which he had been negotiating the sale of the Indian economy to various transnational conglomerates.'[7]

The novel's essential anger is evoked by the ugliness of characterisations like these, which as usual are localised and theoretically accounted for in the specific monstrosity that Western capitalism has created. As one of the characters at one point explains, 'I . . . am conversant with postmodernist critiques of the West, e.g. that we have here a society capable only of pastiche: a "flattened" world'

(p. 261), or later: 'in this century history stopped paying attention to the old psychological orientation of reality. I mean, these days, character isn't destiny any more. Economics is destiny. Ideology is destiny. Bombs are destiny' (p. 432). At the fissure between old and new worlds, the immigrant consciousness rebels against this nightmare of the pre-fab soul – especially the older generation which has too many memories of a life in which family and community still mattered, even in the urban centres. The youth are caught between the attractions of subcultural style – the 'liberation' of punk hairdos and 'two-tone' music clubs (which gives the West a friendly face) – and an even more violent rejection, since as youth it is primarily they who are the targets of police harassment for having dark skins.

The repressive apparatus of the British state is therefore pictured relentlessly in the novel: Chamcha is beaten senseless by police officers in the back of a black maria, and forced to eat his own faeces; in the wake of mysterious serial killings, a black community activist is framed and, in the ensuing protests, a reign of official terror descends upon 'Brickhall' (Brixton, Southall, 'Brick Lane'): 'black youths hauled swiftly into unmarked cars and vans belonging to the special patrol groups and flung out, equally discreetly, covered in cuts and bruises' (p. 451). In this, as in other passages, the three motifs of immigration converge: the repressive science of 'creationist' racism in the sense that the freakish transformation of Chamcha – who despite his meticulous training to be English has been branded with the 'blacks' (even as he insists 'You're not my people. I've spent half my life trying to get away from you') – is viewed by his friends in Brickhall as the horrible outcome of vicious medical experiments performed on him while held in detention, a view everyone willingly believes remembering 'intra-vaginal inspections [upon entry into Britain], Depoprovera scandals, unauthorised post-partum sterilisations, and, further back, the knowledge of Third World drug-dumping' (p. 252).

Of course, in this case as in others, the victims believe what is reasonable but not real. Chamcha's bestialisation is not the crude work of scalpel and injection, but the no less dangerous work of organised bigotry. The inaccuracy, even the tragedy, of their mistake suggests for Rushdie the limitations of resistance, and he clarifies the point by reasserting the religious level of his allegory. For the scene briefly alludes to the Jahilia episode in which Jahilia, like immigrant London, is described as 'a city visible but unseen', which in turn reverberates with the Chamcha passage in the statement that one believes what one 'is prepared to look at'. The acceptance of a devil's role, under the pressure of an awareness that they are 'invisible', humanly speaking, leads the black communities to the empowering myth of a 'dream-devil', their own loyal Azraeel, whose vengeance is sweet even if it is blind. The problem is that their exterminating angel happens to be a deranged serial killer, whom the police want to believe is black, but who in fact has nothing to do with the black community. Sadly, 'the browns-and-blacks found themselves cheering, in their sleep, this what-else-after-all-but-Black-man, maybe a little twisted up by fate class race history, all that, but getting off his behind, bad and mad, to kick a little ass' (p. 324).

'To will is to dissent' – it is what separates humans from the angels. But unless the forms of dissent escape the polarisations of race, they compound the injuries. Rushdie's characteristic middle-ground is therefore located in what he considers to be the totality of English race relations. It cannot be total unless one factors in the part of the equation erased in black urban resistance:

> [England's] hospitality – yes! – in spite of immigration laws, and his own recent experience, he still insisted on the truth of that: an imperfect welcome, true, one capable of bigotry, but a real thing, nonetheless, as was attested by . . . the annual reunion, in Wembley, a stone's throw from the great stadium surrounded by imperial echoes – Empire Way, the Empire Pool – of more than a hundred delegates, all tracing their ancestry back to a single, small Goan village. (*SV*, p. 398)

This conjuration of a general guilt is the by-now familiar feature of Rushdie's fictional mood, which pulls back from the politics of conjuncture – specific responses to specific practices. The hegemonic and the subaltern are for him equally 'human'. Thus in an England that has recently seen the deportation and marginalisation of Asian and West Indian families, a press campaign directed against 'muggers' and the 'dole', he balances the politics of blame by evoking the vulnerability of white Britain. Just as in Derek Walcott's argument about the 'filial impulse' of violent rejection, he suggests that simple slogans of anger directed against the British state give away too much; they imply that official Britain and its 'mainstream' have more control and more self-assurance than they actually do. Thus, in one of many explanatory digressions, we find the story of an elderly British woman named Rosa Diamond, whose sole moment of pleasure in a long life – the memory that kept her going – was an affair she had with an Argentinian gaucho. Although he never mentions it, Rushdie obviously chooses Argentina as Rosa's mental refuge because of the dissonance the idea of 'Argentina' is bound to have in a country still high from its imperial adventures in the Falklands. At the personal level, Argentina (like the Caribbean and South Asia) has what England covets. As the gaucho puts it: 'Are you such exotics in your cold England? . . . señora, I don't think so. Crammed into that coffin of an island, you must find wider horizons to express these secret selves'. Rosa herself sadly concludes: 'passion was an eccentricity of other races' (p. 146).

In other ways, though, Rushdie comes to terms here for the first time with the escapism of his earlier work. The well-worked theme of writer as collaborator has matured into something more realistic. Hanging so much on the attractions of Western 'freedom' in the other novels, he sees in the British context some of the hollowness of its actual practice. It is, for example, a joke at his own expense when, in the Jahilia episode, he finds himself the offspring of both Salman the scribe and Baal the satirist. As the chapters explain, Salman was a reprobate who was both bold and cowardly – who without programme or conviction (only a kind of contrariness) dared to ignore the sacred words dictated to him by Mahound, and instead created his own. Baal, on the other hand, was the Jahilian Grandee's court hireling; he had been given a particular job, which was to satirise the village poor, the water-carriers and the homeless – to exercise, on behalf of the state, the 'art of metrical slander' (p. 98). Being the proud and arrogant poet that he is, he at first protests, saying 'It isn't right for the artist to become the servant of the state', at which point the Grandee observes that his only other option is to be the paid poet of professional assassins. Caught in that particular market/state dichotomy, Baal is forced to see the vanity of staying pure:

> Now that he had abdicated all public platforms, his verses were full of loss ... Figures walked away from him in his odes, and the more passionately he called out to them the faster they moved ... his language [was] too abstract, his imagery too fluid, his metre too inconstant. It led him to create chimeras of form, lionhead goatbodied serpenttailed impossibilities whose shapes felt obliged to change the moment they were set, so that the demotic forced its way into lines of classical purity and images of love were constantly degraded by the intrusion of elements of farce. (*SV*, p. 370)

Since *Grimus* at least, Rushdie has known that 'the public platform' was where writers ought to be, and in Baal's desperation we sense some of Fanon's observations on the rejection of farce among the Algerian storytellers under the impact of their own social upheavel. *The Satanic Verses* in fact problematises the colonial writer's metropolitan half, which is why for the first time Rushdie actually quotes approvingly, Gramsci and Fanon in the novel itself.

The hostile reception of the novel by Muslims has crowded out the legitimate anger that Britain's black communities as a whole – especially the Caribbean – might have had if given the chance. The book's characterisations of West Indians (like its characterisation of women) are often embarrassing and offensive. Although very much at home in the up-market publishing sphere, Rushdie nevertheless plays the role of court satirist too well. Some random examples might include the Sikh 'terrorist' Tavleen, who reveals beneath her gown a string of grenades bobbing like 'fatal breasts'; the comically stupid and overweight Afro-Caribbean community activist, Uhuru, given the last name 'Simba' after Tarzan's elephant; the clownish West Indian Underground employees speaking dialect as though it were fit for low comedy; the happy prostitutes of the Jahilia bordello who find pleasure in pretending they are the Grandee's harem for their fantasising clients, and who want their favourites to 'be the boss'; the West Indian lawyer Hanif, who is said to 'affect' a Trinidadian accent; Allie Cone, Pamela, Mishal, Rekha – the main characters' wives and lovers – all obsessed with childbearing or suicide at the loss of their men.

At one point, Rushdie's parody of 'dub' poetry (clever as it is) is misplaced and self-revealing. Its master is the repulsive Pinkwalla, a monstrous seven-foot tall albino, an 'East-India-man from the West Indies', a 'white black man', who entertains the customers of his Club Hot Wax with pseudo-radical raps: 'Now - mi - feel - indignation - when - dem - make - insinuation - we - no - part - a - de - nation - an - mi - make - proclamation - a - de - true - situation - how - we - make - contribution - since - de - Rome - Occupation' (p. 292). The humour is hollow and out of touch. Anyone familiar with the 'dub' poetry of Michael Smith, say, or Jean Binta Breeze – whose extraordinary images of cultural encirclement have given them an underground following on three continents – would know that far from being a kind of proxy politics or masturbatory venting of rage, their work has often been able to reach and affect the immigrant working classes. One thinks, for example, of Linton Kwesi Johnson's poem commemorating the arrest and frame-up of the trade unionist George Lindo, or of Michael Smith's 'Mi Cyaan Believe It' about the 'mad 'ouse' of black city life. Rushdie, however, places poets like these on the same parodic scale as *Midnight's Children*'s Cyrus, the guru sham. Rushdie does not seem to understand what others closer to the crucible of British expulsion/acculturation understand. In the words of Paul Gilroy in this study of the expressive black cultures of Britain:

> Black expressive cultures affirm while they protest ... Here, non-European traditional elements, mediated by the histories of Afro-American and the Caribbean, have contributed to the formation of new and distinct black cultures amidst the decadent peculiarities of the Welsh, Irish, Scots and English. These non-European elements must be noted and their distinctive resonance accounted for.[8]

That inability to protest and affirm at the same time, that peculiar attraction – repulsion complex with regard to the 'heroic narratives' of 'the people' as it has been elaborated in the discourses of decolonisation has consistently led in Rushdie's work to an aesthetic double-bind: an encyclopaedic frenzy, a narrative canvas packed with the colours and gestures of human 'stuff', and yet set within a horrifying narrative closure. The organic text, cleverly encircling a linear history of 'progress', consistently stifles the open-endedness of what Bakhtin called the 'still-unfolding present' and holds it captive within the structures of its own '*takallouf*'.

I have been trying to show both the advantages and the limitations of this kind of writing. Despite his interventions into the cloistered West and its book markets, Rushdie has been conditioned by them too. Despite the fresh thinking about national form, about a new homelessness that is also a worldliness, about a double-edged post-colonial responsibility, *The Satanic Verses* shows how strangely detached and insensitive the logic of cosmopolitan 'universality' can be. It may be, as he says, that 'bigotry is not only a function of power', but it does not seem adequate to argue in the particular immigration/acculturation complex of contemporary Britain that the central issue is one of 'human evil'. The means of distributing that evil are obviously very unequal, and the violence that comes from defending one's identity or livelihood as opposed to one's privileges is not the same.

By bringing to the surface for discussion all the interlocking debates of decolonisation, Rushdie, more than anyone else writing in English, has made English literary tradition international. And he has done this precisely by dramatising the totality of the components that make up that tradition – including those colonies and minorities until now referred to only from the safety of the 'centre'. But by doing so, he has also taken on another kind of responsibility, which is to the decolonisation struggles he interprets (and translates) for a Western reading public. The fulness and complexity of their collective visions are often foreshortened in the personal filter of Rushdie's fiction.

One only has to think, for example, of how Fanon – trained in the France of Sartre and Césaire, and the writer of a captivating and hallucinatory prose – was not, as one might expect in the company of Rushdie's Third-World postmodernism, an advocate of a literature of polemic. On the contrary – and in keeping with the (somewhat condescending) thrust of the *Satanic Verses*' reprimands against the actual forms of black British protest – his position was that 'stinging denunciations' are too easily welcomed by the occupying powers who recognise in them a form of catharsis.[9] And one could point also to Cabral, who as Basil Davidson points out, had 'no illusions about the incapacity of nationalism, as such, to solve the basic problems of post-colonial development'. What they did know, and insist on, was the necessity of national struggle. That is a point of view Rushdie shares in theory, but which he cannot bring himself to fictionalise. And it is in that sense that Bakhtin spoke of a 'laughter of all the people' as opposed to the 'negative and formal parody of modern times', and that Gramsci spoke of 'a new conformism from below [permitting] new possibilities of self-discipline, or perhaps of liberty that is also individual'.[10]

'Discipline', 'organisation', 'people' – these are words that the cosmopolitan sensibility refuses to take seriously. We get a sense in their work of the comic, but not of the comedic, which is so lively in the very unfunny work of some of the writers mentioned above – Roque Dalton, June Jordan, Obi Egbuna, with their imaginations of a future, and their portrayal of political activity as being at the heart of personal experience. We get protest, but not affirmation, except in the most abstractly 'human' sense. That is something, and it is perhaps even necessary as a mediation. For the greatest problem is still being unable to conceive of the colonial as even having a voice that matters.

NOTES

1. Salman Rushdie, *The Satanic Verses* (New York: Viking Penguin, 1988) p. 95. All further references to this book will be given in the text.
2. I thank Ketu Katrak for first pointing this reference out to me, and Suranjan Ganguly for supplying me with the sources to fill in the details.
3. Firoze Rangoonwalla, *A Pictorial History of Indian Cinema* (London: Hamlyn, 1979) p. 24.
4. B. Lewis, Ch. Pellat and J. Schact (eds), *The Encyclopedia of Islam, New Edition*

(London: Luzac, 1965) p. 363.
5. Ibid., p. 117.
6. Ibid., p. 286.
7. These lines can be found in Rushdie's manuscript of the novel on p. 32. They were edited out of the text before final publication.
8. Paul Gilroy, *There Ain't No Black in the Union Jack* (London: Hutchinson, 1987) pp. 155–6.
9. Frantz Fanon, *The Wretched of the Earth* (New York: Grove Press, 1963) p. 239.
10. Antonio Gramsci, 'Individual Man and Mass Man', *Antología* (La Habana: Instituto Cubano del Libro, 1973) p. 283.

8.3

'BURN THE BOOKS AND TRUST THE BOOK: *THE SATANIC VERSES*, FEBRUARY 1989'

Michael Gorra

The briefest of the dreams from which the Bombay film actor Gibreel Farishta suffers over the course of *The Satanic Verses* concerns a house in Kensington in which a 'bearded and turbaned Imam' in exile plans the overthrow of his country's wine-drinking Empress (205).[1] To the Imam such blasphemy 'is enough to condemn her for all time without hope of redemption.' He himself drinks only water, 'whose purity . . . communicates itself to the drinker' (209). And he is similarly determined to remain 'in complete ignorance' of London, that 'Sodom in which he had been obliged to wait; ignorant, and therefore unsullied, unaltered, pure' (206–7). The Imam relies on an 'American filtration machine' (209) to purify his water, on the radio his disciples use to broadcast the words I've taken for my title. Nevertheless he stands resolute against the idea of historical process that such technology implies, seeing it as the 'greatest of the lies—progress, science, rights—against which . . . [he] has set his face. History is a deviation from the Path, knowledge is a delusion, because the sum of knowledge was complete on the day Al-Lah finished his revelation to Mahound' (210).

But this vision of a Khomeini-like absolutism isn't the only place in which Salman Rushdie's novel seems to prefigure the Islamic world's response to it. In the Jahilia chapters that lie at the heart of what has now gone beyond a controversy, the poet Baal defines the writer's job: '"To name the unnamable, to point at frauds, to take sides, start arguments, shape the world and stop it from

In *After Empire*, Chicago University Press, 1997, pp. 149–56.

going to sleep." And if rivers of blood flow from the cuts his verses inflict, then they will nourish him' (97). Rushdie's work has always insisted on what in *Midnight's Children* he called the 'metaphorical content' of reality. Yet surely he couldn't have expected, or wanted, the wounds his own satire inflicts to come so grotesquely alive. Nourishment? Riots, bombs, bounties, rumors of death squads – they make Baal's thought too grim for me to enjoy the irony, in a way that reminds me that metaphors aren't finally real.

Or are they? Because that literalization seems to me what the quarrel is about. Is the book blasphemous, as so many Muslims have charged? The prophet that Rushdie calls Mahound has no use for Baal's satires; he compares writers to whores and has Baal beheaded. When I first heard the news of the February 12th riots in Islamabad, which seem to have sparked Khomeini's call for Rushdie's death, I was both moved and troubled by the fact that people had died in a protest about a book. I couldn't imagine anyone here taking any single book so seriously, and I recalled the comparison Philip Roth once made between the American writer, for whom 'everything goes and nothing matters,' and the Eastern European writer, for whom 'nothing goes and everything matters.'[2] Now I am not so sure. I believe there is such a thing as blasphemy. But I also believe that its definition lies so much in the beholder's eye that the punishment for it belongs to God alone and not to any man who claims to act for Him. As I write that sentence I'm struck by how Western, and how secular, such a thought is. And by the belief that the freedom to have such thoughts matters profoundly even if nothing else does.

It will be years—if ever—before we can separate *The Satanic Verses* from the storm around it. I was disappointed in the book at first. Its vision of good and evil seemed too cartoonish for what turned out to be a story of personal betrayal; as I read I kept thinking that a Jamesian psychological realism would have yielded a far more complex sense of evil, in particular, than Rushdie's reliance on fantasy was capable of. More tellingly, the book's thousand and one digressions made it seem not so much a loose and baggy as a bulbous monster: a structural mess, a book of brilliant pages—including those in which a group of prostitutes assume the names of Mahound's wives for business purposes, much as strip joints claim to feature 'college girls'—but not a whole. The main line of Rushdie's narrative deals with the fractured personal identities of the immigrants' London, that 'city visible but unseen' (241) by most whites, where teenagers may call their parents' homeland 'Bungleditch' (259) and yet settle into arranged marriages. But what relation did the Jahilia scenes, did the whole of Gibreel's dreams, have to that narrative? I didn't see much of one at first, but the events of the last ten days have made me think hard about that question. Looking back over the novel, I'm now struck more by its thematic consistency than by its heterogeneous structure; one could say, in fact, that that heterogeneity is itself the chief element in that consistency. *The Satanic Verses* is a thematic whole, and that whole does indeed offer a radically different vision of the world than that held by any Imam.

At issue are the two chapters in which Gibreel dreams about the birth of a monotheistic religion in the desert city of Jahilia, chapters that so heavily parody Islamic history and tradition as to puzzle most Western readers. The name 'Jahilia,' for example—to Muslims it means 'darkness' or 'ignorance' and is used with particular reference to pre-Islamic times. Here, however, the darkness doesn't vanish when Mahound proclaims the Word of the One God. Such sharp anticlerical satire has long been familiar in the West but remains foreign to the Islamic world. Too bad. The joke on 'Jahilia' isn't one that most Westerners will have the background to get, but the fact that Rushdie uses it anyway suggests that in some ways his ideal audience, however much the novel wounds them, might be precisely those British Muslims who burned his book in Bradford.

Muslims have found any number of other insults and blasphemies in these chapters. But the most important charge against Rushdie is that he suggests the Quran is not the uncreated Word of God, as dictated by the angel through the mouth of the prophet Mohammed, but was instead written by man. In Rushdie's novel the character Salman the Persian, who serves as Mahound's amanuensis—and a figure of that name was one of the actual Mohammed's earliest followers—grows suspicious of the way the revelations Mahound claims to receive from Gibreel accord too neatly with what the Prophet has already decided he wants to do. And so Salman begins to test Mahound, to change the dictation in subtle ways: 'If Mahound recited a verse in which God was described as *all-hearing, all-knowing*, I would write, *all-knowing, all-wise*. Here's the point: Mahound did not notice the alterations. So there I was, actually writing the Book, or rewriting, anyway, polluting the word of God with my own profane language. But good heavens, if my poor words could not be distinguished from the Revelation by God's own Messenger, then what did that mean?' (367). Salman hopes that Al-Lah, if there is an Al-Lah and if the Book is really His, will not allow Mahound to preach a mistaken Word, hopes that the Prophet will catch the error and so confirm his faith. But Mahound doesn't notice, and the substitutions remain, implying that the Word is not the only one, that the text of the Quran is not only human but corrupt. Or, as Salman says, 'It's his Word against mine' (368).

'Why do I fear Mahound?' the polytheistic merchant Abu Simbel asks himself in the first Jahilia chapter. 'For that: one one one, his terrifying singularity. Whereas I am always divided, always two or three or fifteen. I can even see his point of view' (102). The one one one truth sees any concept of pluralism, of conflicting and overlapping truths, of Salman's words rather than the Word, as an assault on its authority. It's of no use to say that Rushdie presents these scenes, which in themselves enact the conflict over *The Satanic Verses*, in the form of Gibreel Farishta's dreams, the dreams of a character who's going mad. For Islam's central belief that the Quran is not just divinely inspired but is itself Divine seems to demand a belief in the absolute integrity of words. It posits a virtual identity of words, belief, and action in a way that denies the Western distinction between the metaphoric and the literal, between character and author. If you accept that distinction, then you are already on the way to seeing Salman the Persian's point—already on the way to a belief in free speech.

But polytheists aren't the only ones who are 'always two or three or fifteen.' So are immigrants, who unlike the Imam can never remain in 'complete ignorance' of their new countries, who are never 'unsullied, unaltered, pure.' Their identity can never be fixed or singular but is instead fluid, plural, however much they cling to tradition or however much they try to shed it. But what's lost in shedding one life, one identity, to take up another? And how much of one's old identity remains? 'A man who sets out to make himself up,' Rushdie writes early in the novel, 'is taking on the Creator's role, according to one way of seeing things; he's unnatural, a blasphemer, an abomination of abominations. From another angle, you could see pathos in him, heroism in his struggle, in his willingness to risk: not all mutants survive' (49). The Muslim Gibreel Farishta has built a career out of playing Hindu gods in the 'theologicals' cranked out by the Bombay film industry. Yet he rejects that multiplicity in his own life, wants only to remain '*continuous*—that is joined to and arising from his past.' But the strain of maintaining that continuity, that oneness, proves too much. He dreams at night of the archangel whose name he bears, and his dreams keep leaking into and overwhelming his 'waking self' (427). The novel's other main character, the 'unnatural' Salahuddin Chamchawalla, has chosen a different sort of singular identity, doing his best to shed his Indianness and remake himself as an Englishman. When, for example, he's offered *masala dosa* for breakfast instead of 'packet cereal,' he complains about having 'to eat this filthy foreign food' (258). In coming to Britain he's even shortened his name, to Saladin Chamcha. (That's another of Rushdie's linguistic jokes, since *chamcha* means 'spoon' in Urdu and is slang for 'sycophant'—'Toadji' (58) as the Bombay art critic Zeeny Vakil calls him.) But while he aspires to singularity, Saladin earns his living as a mimic, whose thousand voices have made him much in demand for radio voice-overs—though sometimes, when he's with Indian friends, his perfect Oxbridge accent slips.

Rushdie takes as his epigraph this passage from Daniel Defoe's *The History of the Devil* (1726): 'Satan, being thus confined to a vagabond, wandering, unsettled condition, is without any certain abode; for though he has, in consequence of his angelic nature, a kind of empire in the liquid waste or air, yet this is certainly part of his punishment, that he is . . . without any fixed place, or space, allowed him to rest the soul of his foot upon.' After surviving his own miraculous fall from an exploding airplane at the start of the novel, Saladin finds himself briefly sprouting horns and growing hooves, until he looks so goatish that his British wife refuses to take him back into his house. The Devil is a wanderer, one without any fixed place or certain abode: stateless, fallen, no longer purely of one place or another, no longer purely one thing or another—an immigrant. And for the immigrant that Rushdie imagines, the Imam's purity of belief is impossible. He must live instead in the world of Salman the Persian, in which the conflicting demands and truths of different cultures must be weighed against each other. Devil? Yes, a 'foreign devil'; yes, in the sense that immigrants are often demonized by their new countries. Rushdie writes that he has given his prophet the name 'Mahound,' the 'demon-tag the farangis hung around his neck,' because 'to turn insults into strengths, whigs, tories, Blacks all chose to wear with pride the names they were given in scorn' (93). So too with Saladin, who through the literalized metaphor of those horns and hooves comes to learn both that he cannot so easily shed his past and that there are more ways than one of being British. He learns, for example, to accept the Indianness he has checked at the door of his beloved Garrick Club—and does so because the only people willing to accept his goatish self are the residents of that 'city visible but unseen,' the Asian East Enders he has always shunned.

Rushdie's character Zeeny Vakil has written a book attacking India's 'confining myth of authenticity, that folkloristic straitjacket which she sought to replace by an ethic of historically validated eclecticism, for was not the entire national culture based on the principle of borrowing whatever clothes seemed to fit, Aryan, Mughal, British, take-the-best-and-leave-the-rest?' (52). In *The Satanic Verses* those words stand most obviously as a reproof to Zeeny's friend Saladin, who has sought a different but no less confining 'myth of authenticity.' But they also describe the eclectic pluralism of Rushdie's vision of Indian identity in *Midnight's Children* and can serve as well for the bazaar of his style as a whole, in which British English gets fused with bits of Hindi, with Bombay film slang, with what used to be despised as 'babu English.' Such prose seems much closer to the inventive energy with which Indians actually speak the language than does the limpid English of an older writer like R. K. Narayan. And perhaps that style can offer a new and liberating model of postcolonial identity. For it suggests we learn to see that identity as a consciously created pastiche of 'whatever clothes [seem] to fit,' and in doing so it calls into question V. S. Naipaul's concept of the colonial as an essentially unthinking and impotent mimic man, condemned by history to ape the West. But Zeeny's words can also apply to *The Satanic Verse*'s vision of what Britain and being British should be, for both native and immigrant. *There Ain't No Black in the Union Jack*—so says the title of the sociologist Paul Gilroy's study of race in England. One of the challenges this novel offers is that it asks us to imagine the ways in which there might be. The sad irony, as Rushdie has noted, is that Muslim protests over his novel will 'confirm, in the Western mind, all the worst stereotypes of the Muslim world' and so make that act of imagination a more difficult one for whites and nonwhites alike.[3]

In *The Sense of an Ending*, Frank Kermode suggests that there is this difference between myth and fiction: 'Myth . . . presupposes total and adequate explanations of things as they are and were . . . Fictions are for finding things out . . . Myths are the agents of stability, fictions the agents of change. Myths call for absolute, fictions for conditional assent.'[4] Milan Kundera has written that the novel was born on the day Don Quixote looked out on the world and, finding he could no longer recognize it, began to conceive of that world as a question—not the answers of myth, of any totalizing system of belief.[5] What Salman

Rushdie has done in *The Satanic Verses* is set fiction against a particularly powerful, absolute, and peremptory myth—a myth that has governed a part of his own life. He has done it as a way of examining a conflict between two mutually exclusive ways of imagining the world: between purity and pluralism, monologue and dialogue, orthodox answers and skeptical questions – the very conflict that *The Satanic Verses* itself has provoked. In Gibreel's dreams, in Jahilia, the conflict takes a religious form; in London, that of examining what, in an interview, Rushdie has called the 'discomfort ... [of having] a plural identity . . . made up of bits and fragments from here, there.'[6] One wonders at the obliquity of this, in a writer whose earlier work has been about as subtle as a skyrocket. But it is the same issue throughout, and in fact the different ways in which Rushdie puts that issue serve in the end to underline the novel's essential unity, to emphasize its identity of theme and form.

Salman the Persian's rejection of the Word for words—of the Book for books—has a lesson for us. For it is in his world, and not the Imam's, that Saladin, that we all, must now learn to live. Nothing, paradoxically, demonstrates this better than British Muslims' 'discomfort' with their own inevitably plural identities, a discomfort that *The Satanic Verses* has made so many of them feel. Within the novel, the implicit conflict of values that Rushdie poses between Salman and the Imam is an unequal one. The battle outside will not be so easy.

NOTES

1. This essay originally appeared as a review essay in *Threepenny Review*, Summer 1989; my longer chapter on *Midnight's Children* returns at greater length to some of the same issues – and uses some of the same quotations – that I first developed here. Despite that repetition, the essay still seems to me to be relevant and to have, in its sense of immediacy and crisis, a kind of documentary value. In reprinting it, I have added citations and have made minor changes in punctuation and style. References to *The Satanic Verses* (New York: Viking, 1989) will be indicated by page numbers within parentheses.
2. Hermione Lee, 'The Art of Fiction *LXXXIV*: Philip Roth' (interview), *Paris Review* 26 (Fall 1984): 244.
3. Salman Rushdie, 'Choice between Light and Dark,' *Observer*, January 22, 1989.
4. Frank Kermode, *The Sense of an Ending: Studies in the Theory of Fiction* (Oxford: Oxford University Press, 1967), 39.
5. See 'The Depreciated Legacy of Cervantes' in Milan Kundera, *The Art of the Novel* (1986), trans. Linda Asher (New York: Grove Press, 1988).
6. Quoted in Gerald Marzorati, 'Salman Rushdie: Fiction's Embattled Infidel,' *New York Times Magazine*, January 29, 1989, 100.

8.4

'POSTCOLONIAL DIFFEREND: DIASPORIC NARRATIVES OF SALMAN RUSHDIE'

Vijay Mishra

RACE, IDENTITY, AND BRITISHNESS

The late 1960s saw the emergence of a new racism in Britain for which Enoch Powell was the best-known, but not the only, spokesperson. In what seemed like a remarkable reversal of old Eurocentric and imperialist readings of the black colonized as racially inferior, the new racists began to recast races on the model of linguistic difference. This 'difference,' however, had to be anchored somewhere, and the easiest means of doing this was by stipulating that nations were not imagined communities constructed historically but racial enclaves marked by high levels of homogeneity. Thus a race had a nation to which it belonged. The British had their nation and belonged to an island off the coast of Europe, and so on. In the name of racial respect and racial equality, this version in fact gave repatriation theorists such as Enoch Powell a high level of respectability in that, it was argued, what Powell stood for was not racism but a nationalism that the immigrants themselves upheld. What the argument simplified was the history of imperialism itself and the massive displacement of races that had taken place in the name of Empire. Nowhere was this more marked than in the Indian, African, and Chinese diasporas of the Empire. More importantly, however, the new racism was used to defend Britishness itself, to argue that multiculturalism was a travesty of the British way of life, which was now becoming extremely vulnerable. The only good immigrant was one that was totally assimilable, just as the only good gay or lesbian was someone who led a closet life. Writes Anna Marie Smith:

ARIEL, 26:3, July 1995, pp. 9–45. Extract: pp. 20–30.

> Only the thin veneer of deracializing euphemisms has shifted over this period, with blatantly racist discourse on immigration being recoded in discourse on criminality, inner-cities' decay and unrest, anti-Western terrorism, and multiculturalism. Indeed, the fundamentally *cultural* definition of race in the new racism allows for this mobile relocation of the racial-national borders to any number of sociopolitical sites. (62)

In *The Satanic Verses*, it is by way of the Sufyan family (Muhammad, the Bangladeshi schoolmaster with a weakness for European classics, his wife, Hind, and their daughters Mishal and Anahita) that we enter into changing demographic patterns and race relations in Britain, as well as see how homeland family norms negotiate the new gender politics of diasporas. The Sufyan family lives in Brickhall Street, the old Jewish enclave of tailors and small-time shopkeepers. Now it is the street of Bangladeshi migrants or Packies/Pakis ('brown Jews' [300]) who are least equipped for metropolitan life. Thus, in Brickhall, synagogues and kosher food have given way to mosques and halal restaurants. Yet nothing is as simple as it seems in this world of the diaspora. The space of the Shaandaar Cafe B&B becomes the space of new labour relations between husband and wife but also of new forms of sexuality. Mishal becomes pregnant by the second-generation diaspora Hanif Johnson, while Jumpy Joshi has sex with Pamela, even as her husband Saladin sleeps under the same roof. The diaspora here finally crumbles and falls apart because the pressures come not only from the newly acquired socio-sexual field of the participants in the diasporic drama but also because that drama has to contend with racist hooliganism as the diaspora becomes progressively an object of derision to be represented through the discourse of monsterism. It is through this brand of fascism that death finally comes to the diaspora and to those associated with it. Both the café and the community centre are burned down. Hind, Muhammad, as well as Pamela, die, and suddenly there is no room for nostalgia, no room for the discourse of mysticism (469) that had sustained the discourses of the homeland. Instead, the imperative is to transform one's memory into modes of political action because the world is far too Real (469). It is at this point in the narrative that diasporic identities become complicated by the presence in Britain of people who have already gone through the diasporic experience in other parts of the world. Having co-existed with Afro-West Indians, the Indian diaspora of the West Indies, for instance, is already a hybrid form. Thus Sewsunker Ram (Pinkwalla), the DJ, and John Maslama, the club proprietor, have political and cultural orientations that bring them close to the kinds of diasporic politics endorsed by a Dr Uhuru Simba. The alignments at work here—Bengali, Afro-Caribbean, East Indian Caribbean, East African Indian, Sikh, Indian, Pakistani, Bangladeshi, and so on—gesture towards new forms of diasporic awareness and coalitional politics. From the Africanist ideal of Dr Uhuru Simba to the multifaceted, decentred, simulative worlds of the Sufyan girls, Jumpy Joshi and Hanif Johnson, one now begins to see not one legitimation narrative of the diaspora but many.

'The trouble with the Engenglish is that their hiss hiss history happened overseas, so they dodo don't know what it means,' stutters S. S. Sisodia (343). When those who were instrumental in creating that history (as subject peoples on whose behest the Empire believed it was acting) are within the metropolitan centres of the Empire itself, the idea of Britishness is threatened. Both the challenge and the threat are summarized elegantly by Iain Chambers, who writes:

> It is the dispersal attendant on migrancy that disrupts and interrogates the overarching themes of modernity: the nation and its literature, language and sense of identity; the metropolis; the sense of centre; the sense of psychic and cultural homogeneity. In the recognition of the other, of radical alterity, lies the acknowledgement that we are no longer at the centre of the world. (*Migrancy, Culture, Identity* 23–24)

Chambers's 'we' here is British, but the definition that he gives of the British is very much an intermediate one. It is a definition in which the subjects of the centre—the British as an ethnic entity—also begin to find that subjectivity is 'interactively' constructed, on the move, so to speak. The cultural imperative that underlies Chambers's move is that the diaspora now invades the centre and makes prior, essentialist definitions of nation-states based on notions of racial purity (Enoch Powell), a historical relic of imperialism itself. It is the privileged site of that imperialist history and its constructions of Britishness that get replayed in the doctrines of purity in postcolonial Britain. Yet, as I say this I think what is implicit in the Chambers thesis—the need for a radical pedagogy about ethnic identities—is precisely what needs underlining. How does one make decisive interventions in the curriculum so that Britishness itself is opened up for debate? It is the agenda of the agents who would transform the apparatuses of control through which the idea of the self is constructed that requires further examination.

A 'post-diaspora community' in Britain, to use Rushdie's own phrase (*Imaginary Homelands* 40), now becomes a site from which a critique of Britishness itself (and the imperial relationship between the British and Indians that has a 300-year long history) is now being mounted. The migrant living here and elsewhere would find it difficult to fit into, say, Margaret Thatcher's imperious definition of a Briton during the Falklands War. As Chambers again has stressed, any attempt to decipher this appeal to 'Britishness' necessarily draws us to a complex, contradictory, and even treacherous terrain, in which the most varied elements 'entwine, coexist and contaminate one another' (*Border Dialogues* 15). For the Indian diaspora, this trope of 'Britishness' has multiple identities and can be expressed in a variety of ways. To be British in a post-diaspora Britain is to be conscious of multiple heritages and peoples' conflicting participation in the long history of Britain. For many, an easy, unproblematic re-insertion into a utopic or linear narrative of the British nation is impossible. In

The Satanic Verses, we get a strong affirmation of the undesirability of this version of linear history.

We are therefore faced with 'the possibility of two perspectives and two versions of Britishness' (Chambers, *Border Dialogues* 27). One is Anglocentric, frequently conservative, backward-looking, and increasingly located in a frozen and largely stereotyped idea of the national, that is, English, culture. The other is excentric, open-ended, and multi-ethnic. The first is based on a homogeneous 'unity' in which history, tradition, and individual biographies and roles, including ethnic and sexual ones, are fundamentally fixed and embalmed in the national epic, in the mere fact of being 'English.' The other perspective suggests an overlapping network of histories and traditions, a heterogeneous complexity in which positions and identities, including those relating to the idea of the 'citizen,' cannot be taken for granted and are not 'interminably fixed but tend towards flux' (Chambers, *Border Dialogues* 27).

The peculiar irony of Rushdie's own anti-racist rhetoric is that he has been used to fuel racism: the Muslim threat against Rushdie's life is used by the white majority to portray all Muslims as fundamentalists. As Rushdie himself has pointed out, '[t]he idea that the National Front could use my name as a way of taunting Asians is so horrifying and obscene to my mind that I wanted to make it clear: that's not my team, they're not my supporters, they're simply exploiting the situation to their own ends' (Interview with Blake Morrison 115). The uses made of Rushdie in defence of 'Britishness' imply a problematic incorporation of the name 'Rushdie' into British citizenry. The appropriation of Rushdie by British writers in the name of the autonomy of the aesthetic order again has a similar agenda. Rushdie, the politically correct defender of the diaspora, is now the equally correct 'British' citizen under the protection of Scotland Yard and defended by Harold Pinter.

THE DIASPORA, THE SACRED, AND SALMAN RUSHDIE

The Satanic Verses is one radical instance of diasporic recollection or rememoration. The questions that any such rememoration asks of the diasporic subject are: what is the status of its past, of its myths, of its own certainties? How has it constructed these certainties? Does anything or anybody have a hegemonic status within the diaspora itself? Or, do we read diasporas, as I have suggested, through the Gramscian definition of the subaltern? Do the Imams of Islam (in Bradford or in Tehran or in Bombay) constitute a ruling group within the subaltern?

Can one re-invigorate one's myths? One kind of reinvigoration was endorsed by Indian diaspora created in the wake of the British indenture system. In these nineteenth-century diasporas, loss was rewritten as a totality through the principle of a reverse millenarianism. There was a golden age back there that we have forfeited through our banishment. Let us imaginatively re-create this golden age, which would leap over the great chasm created in our history through indenture. One of the grand templates of Indian diasporic millenarianism was the myth of Rama and his banishment. The alternative to this millenarian ethos is a version of rememoration in which the continuum of imperial history is blasted through a radical mediation on the conditions of migrancy and displacement. The recapitulation of one's history (and not just the re-invigoration of myth) leads to a confrontation with the narratives of imperialism itself. Where the old diaspora's myths were, after all, commensurate with the imperial narratives of totality (insofar as these myths were considered to be equally forceful from the subject's point of view), the new diaspora attempts to penetrate the history of the centre through multiple secularisms. When, however, the interventions into secularity threaten an earlier memory, diasporas turn to versions of millenarian rememoration and retreat into an essentialist discourse, even though they know full well that the past can no longer redeem.

It is in this context that I would like to explore the intersection of the radical agenda of diasporas and the idea of the sacred. No reading of *The Satanic Verses* can be complete without considering the reception of the text in terms of the sacred. The sacred, in this instance, refuses to accept the aesthetic autonomy of the text and connects the narrator's voice unproblematically with that of the author. In his defence—and in the defence mounted on his behalf by the world literati—it is really the relative autonomy of art that has been emphasized. What this defence raises is a very serious question about whether a diasporic text that celebrates hybridity and rootlessness can be defended with reference purely to the privileged status of the aesthetic order. In the ensuing debates, the British South Asian diaspora has been read as a group that does not quite understand the values of a civic society and has the capacity to relapse into barbarism, precisely the condition that gave the Empire its humanist apology. If I return to the saturated discourses surrounding the Rushdie Affair, it is because the discourse reminds us of yet another kind of privilege, and one that questions the non-negotiable primacy of modernity itself.

Now here comes the difficult part of the presentation in the context of *The Satanic Verses* as a commodity with quite specific effects. The British Muslim response to *The Satanic Verses* has not been through the narratives of hybridity nor through an interventionist politics that would use Rushdie's book to point out the massive contradictions between the diaspora and the ideology of 'Britishness'; rather, it has been through a reappopriation of the myths of totality, or millenarianism, that was the survival mechanism of the old diaspora. In other words, the defence has been mounted not through a constantly revalidating and contingent subjectivity *in medias res* but through an unreal resistance based on the discourse of a prior diasporic mode of narrativization. *The Satanic Verses* as an intervention into the project of modernity now faces modernity itself as an unnecessary formation in diasporic culture. Clearly, the Bradford Imams cannot be both modern and anti-modern, but such indeed is the complex/contradictory narrative that is being articulated. Thus what we get is the second diaspora trying to cling to totalities, to the unreal completedness of the first, where, even for a Naipaul, there was never an unproblematic totality to aspire to in the first instance. The old diaspora, in spite of its ideologies of totality, could not have responded to *The Satanic Verses* with the same sense of unqualified rejection. The *fatwa* against Rushdie originated in the diaspora—in Bradford—and not in Iran.

From the borders, from the interstices of existence, from the liminal, the diasporic subject uses, in Rukmini Nair's and Rimli Bhattacharya's words,

> fragments of religious faith . . . [to] 'shore' up his existence, give him much needed stability in a hostile environment. When that stability is blown to bits by an author as well ensconced and integrated as Rushdie, panic results. The neurosis of *nemesis* replaces the certainties of *nostalgia*. (28–29)

One may disagree with Nair's and Bhattacharya's use of 'certainties,' but the point is valid. What is missing from diasporic theory is a theory of the sacred based not on the idea of the sacred as a pathological instance of the secular in itself defined along purely modernist lines but as a point from which interventions can take place. In short, as Al-e Ahmad pointed out, the sacred is a source of metaphors of empowerment easily available for ethnic mobilization. In all our debates about the diaspora, the sacred is missing. I return to *The Satanic Verses*, which, by its very title, foregrounds something highly contentious in Islam and in Islamic definitions of the sacred. Racialized politics meets its sacralized other here. To emphasize this, to find how Rushdie reads the sacred and how the unified discourse of the sacred is used by the diaspora to defend a lost purity from within the hybrid, the hyphen, is not to say that *The Satanic Verses* is best read along these lines. What I am doing is selectively using *The Satanic Verses* to underline the dual narrative of the diaspora: the hyphen and the total, the fracture and the whole. Clearly, both have different historical antecedents for the diaspora: the hyphen is the presencing of the boundary where the polities of epistemic violence and a self-conscious re-definition of the project of modernity are located firmly within the global politics of migrancy (which also affects the construction of the non-diasporic subject); the 'sacred' is a function of narratives that the almost self-contained diasporic communities constructed out of a finite set of memories. They gave permanence to mobility (the mothered space is always mobile—the child in the womb moves) by creating a fixed point of origin when none existed. The sacred refuses to be pushed to the liminal, to the boundary. It wants to totalize by centring all boundaries: the many and the one cease to be two dialectical poles. Since its narratives are transhistorical, the absurdity of the move for a disempowered diasporic community is overtaken completely by the illusory power of the act itself, from which the colonizer is excluded. This is true of all religious attitudes in the diaspora. As Ashis Nandy writes: 'Hinduism in the diaspora, for example, is much more exclusive and homogenic. Out of feelings of inferiority, many Hindus have tried to redefine Hinduism according to the dominant concept of religion' (104).

In *The Satanic Verses*, Rushdie, in fact, connects the moment of newness itself with the diasporic performance in the sense that the Prophet's intervention into the staid politics and religion of Jahilia is made possible only through people who are always on the margins of society, 'water-carrier immigrant slave' (104). The sacred is thus a means of radical self-empowerment, especially for those who work under the tyranny of the merchant classes of the Arab world. In that sacred discourse, the language, however, was not of the many, of the hybrid, but of the one. The radical, in other words, was not the idea of multiple narratives and contingency or coalitional politics, it was not the affirmation of the hyphen, but the starkness of the total, of the one:

> Why do I fear Mahound? [thinks the Grandee of Jahilia Abu Simbel]. For that: one one one, his terrifying singularity. Whereas I am always divided, always two or three or fifteen . . . This is the world into which Mahound has brought his message; one one one. Amid such multiplicity, it sounds like a dangerous word. (102–03)

The radical one, however, also carried a dangerous principle of female exclusion. Where the many had always found space for female goddesses, the Prophet, finally, excludes them from the position of divine intermediaries, though not before toying with the idea of their symbolic incorporation into the 'new':

> Messenger, what are you saying? Lat, Manat, Uzza—they're all *females*!
> For pity's sake! Are we to have goddesses now? Those old cranes, herons, hags?' (107)

In the deserts of Arabia and at a particular historical moment, the radical, the new, could be conceived of only as an austere unity around the mathematical one. In the version of radical alterity that defines the modern diaspora, it is the many that must now splinter the impregnable fortresses of the one. This is the monumental irony of the debates around the book. The trouble is that the nation-state has never acknowledged the diasporic contribution to modernity, always reading diasporas as the 'one,' always regarding them as a dangerous presence in the West. At the height of the controversy surrounding the burning of the book, the British Home Minister responsible for Race Relations, John Patten, issued a news release entitled 'On Being British' (18 July 1989), in which the ideology of the one is used to berate the excesses of another ideology of oneness. It can be seen that race relations in Britain itself produced a desire to return to the security of the past: both whites and Muslims in Britain return to their own essentialisms in moments of (perceived) crisis. Have the efforts of those who have struggled for a multiply centred nation-state therefore collapsed because the state itself created an environment in which a historical moment (that of the Prophet) would be de-historicized, reshaped, and used as a defence of the diaspora itself? Homi Bhabha confronts these questions in *The Location of Culture*:

> The conflict of cultures and community around *The Satanic Verses* has been mainly represented in spatial terms and binary geopolitical polarities—Islamic fundamentalists vs. Western literary modernists, the quarrel of the ancient (ascriptive) migrants and modern (ironic) metropolitans. This obscures the anxiety of the irresolvable, borderline culture of hybridity that articulates its problems of identification and its diasporic aesthetic in an uncanny, disjunctive temporality that is, at once, the *time* of cultural displacement, and the *space* of the 'untranslatable.' (225)

Bhabha's examination of the politics of *The Satanic Verses* very quickly becomes a kind of an aestheticization of the diaspora. The dominant semantics of this aesthetics may be stated through one of Bhabha's favourite metaphors, the metaphor of the 'trans-.' Applied to the diaspora, it means that a double timeframe, a double space, is always, everywhere, present. This is a good point, since the disjunctive temporality (both here and elsewhere; the space of present location and the rememoration of the past) is the diasporic condition. To ask the diaspora to function from one space, from one time, is to create what William Godwin in *Political Justice* (1793) called 'impostures.' Yet the decisive question remains: what political articulations indeed can be made from the position of a disjunctive temporality? And if this is also the condition of hybridity (the term goes back to the nineteenth-century botanists), then what hope is there for hybrids to become agents of change and not just positions that one may occupy for purposes of critique?

Clearly, Bhabha's reading of the diasporic subject within the European nation-state is more or less identical with the non-hegemonic or pre-hegemonic Gramscian subaltern whose histories are fragmented and episodic. In the context of the Rushdie Affair, the question that we may ask is, 'Does hegemony always suppress difference?' Or does it entertain and even encourage difference provided that it is a 'difference' that can be footnoted adequately in the grand history of Empire, which Sir Ernest Baker once referred to as a 'mission of culture—and of something higher than culture' (qtd. in Asad 250)? When the hegemonic power loses its clarity of vision in terms of its own definition of unity, then a crisis erupts – and both Salman Rushdie and Homi Bhabha believe that post-imperial British society is in crisis. Terms such as cultural minorities, ethnics, blacks, New Commonwealth immigrants, multiculturalism, are all used by a hysterical centre that no longer knows how to normalize the other in the nation within. It is then the celebration of difference by Rushdie that is endorsed by Bhabha:

> It has achieved this by suggesting that there is no such whole as the nation, the culture or even the self. Such holism is a version of reality that is most often used to assert cultural or political supremacy and seeks to obliterate the relations of difference that constitute the language of history and culture . . . Salman Rushdie sees the emergence of doubt, questioning and even confusion as being part of that cultural 'excess' that facilitates the

> formation of new social identities that do not appeal to a pure and settled past, or to a unicultural present, in order to authenticate themselves. The authority lies in the attempt to articulate emergent, hybrid forms of cultural identity. (qtd. in Asad 262–63)[1]

It goes without saying that social identities do need authenticating (Asad), but their authentication, according to both Rushdie and Bhabha, derives from our ability continuously to re-invent ourselves out of our hybrid cultural condition (Asad 263).[2] The sacred asks different questions. Hybridity for whom? Does the state apparatus always want homogeneity? Is it in its interest to pursue this? Or is difference (but difference within a panoptical power) the desired aim of the nation-state? At one level, how is postcolonial difference (as hybrid) to be re-theorized as postcolonial hybridity? Is hybridity the desirable aim or a fact of life? Does the sacred reject the aestheticization of culture? Is the sacred point of view homogeneous to begin with? The debates surrounding the aesthetic order, the diaspora, and the sacred reached a point of extreme dissonance once Khomeini invoked the *fatwa* against Rushdie. What the debates also underlined, in the general context of the relationship between diasporas and the nation-state, is that often the ground rules that govern the nation itself may not be applied uncritically to inhabitants who fashion themselves in ways that are not identical with those of the majority of the citizens of the state.

NOTES

1. Asad asks in footnote 21:

   > Does Bhabha mean (a) that it is not worth appealing to the past as a way of authenticating social identities because the act of articulating emergent identities authenticates itself or (b) that the past, albeit unsettled, is not worth contesting because it is merely an aesthetic resource for inventing new narratives of the self? (263)

2. Asad notes that to speak of cultural syncretism or cultural hybrids presupposes a conceptual distinction between pre-existing ('pure') cultures. Of course, all apparent cultural unities are the outcomes of diverse origins, and it is misleading to think of an identifiable cultural unity as having neutrally traceable boundaries. (262)

BIBLIOGRAPHY

Al-e Ahmad, Jalal. *Plagued by the West (Gharbzadegi)*. Trans. Paul Sprachman. New York: Caravan Books, 1982.

Anderson, Benedict. *Imagined Communities: Reflections on the Origin and Spread of Nationalism*. London: Verso, 1991.

Appignanesi, Lisa, and Sara Maitland, eds. *The Rushdie File*. London: Fourth Estate, 1989.

Asad, Talal. *Genealogies of Religion*. Baltimore: Johns Hopkins UP, 1993.

Bhabha, Homi. *The Location of Culture*. London: Routledge, 1994.

Carroll, David. 'Rephrasing the Political with Kant and Lyotard: From Aesthetic to Political Judgements.' *Diacritics* 14.3 (Fall 1984): 74–88.

Chambers, Iain. *Border Dialogues: Journeys in Postmodernity*. London: Routledge, 1990.

——————. *Migrancy, Culture, Identity*. London: Routledge, 1994.
Clifford, James. 'Diasporas.' *Cultural Anthropology* 9.3 (1994): 302–38.
Faruqi, M. H. 'Publishing Sacrilege is not Acceptable.' Appignanesi and Maitland 60–61.
Fischer, Michael M. J., and Mehdi Abedi, *Debating Muslims, Cultural Dialogues in Postmodernity and Tradition*. Madison: U of Wisconsin P, 1990.
Foot, Michael. 'Historical Rushdie.' Appignanesi and Maitland 242–44.
Fuentes, Carlos. 'Words Apart.' *The Guardian* 24 February 1989. Appignanesi and Maitland 245–49.
Gilroy, Paul. *The Black Atlantic: Modernity and Double Consciousness*. Cambridge, MA Harvard UP, 1993.
——————. 'Cultural Studies and Ethnic Absolutism.' *Cultural Studies*. Ed. Lawrence Grossberg, Cary Nelson, Paula A. Treichler. New York: Routledge, 1992. 187–98.
Lipstadt, Deborah. *Denying the Holocaust*. New York: The Free Press, 1993.
Lyotard, Jean-François. *The Differend: Phrases in Dispute*. Trans. Georges Van Den Abbeele. Manchester: Manchester UP, 1988.
Mahood, M. M. *The Colonial Encounter: A Reading of Six Novels*. London: Rex Collings, 1977.
Mishra, Vijay. 'The Diasporic Imaginary.' Paper presented at the Feminist Studies/Cultural Studies Colloquium Series, University of California, Santa Cruz, 2 February 1994.
Naipaul, V. S. *Among the Believers. An Islamic Journey*. London: André Deutsch, 1981.
Nair, Rukmini Bhaya, and Rimli Bhattacharya. 'Salman Rushdie: The Migrant in the Metropolis.' *Third Text* 11 (Summer 1990): 17–30.
Nandy, Ashis. 'Dialogue and the Diaspora: Conversation with Nikos Papastergiadis.' *Third Text* 11 (Summer 1990): 99–108.
Naqvi, Saeed. *Reflections of an Indian Muslim*. Delhi: Har-Anand Publications, 1993.
Rushdie, Salman. 'Crusoe.' *Granta* 31 (Spring 1991): 128.
——————. *East, West*. London: Jonathan Cape, 1994.
——————. *'Hobson-Jobson.' Imaginary Homelands: Essays and Criticism 1981–1991*. London: Granta/Viking, 1991. 81–83.
——————. *Imaginary Homelands: Essays and Criticism 1981–1991*. London: Granta/Viking, 1991.
——————. Interview with Blake Morrison. *Granta* 31 (Spring 1991): 113–25.
——————. Interview with Kerry O'Brien. 'Lateline.' Australian Broadcasting Corporation Television. 4 October 1994.
——————. *The Satanic Verses*. London: Viking, 1988.
Sen, Mala. *India's Bandit Queen: The True Story of Phoolan Devi*. Delhi: Indus/HarperCollins, 1993.
Smith, Anna Marie. 'The Imaginary Inclusion of the Assimilable "Good Homosexual": The British New Right's Representations of Sexuality and Race.' *Diacritics* 24.2–3 (Summer–Fall 1994): 58–70.
Shahabuddin, Syed. 'You Did This With Satanic Forethought, Mr. Rushdie.' *The Times of India* 13 October 1988. Appignanesi and Maitland 45–49.
Spivak, Gayatri Chakravorty. 'Reading *The Satanic Verses*.' *Third Text* 11 (Summer 1990): 41–60.
Tölölyan, Khachig. 'The Nation State and Its Others: In Lieu of a Preface.' *Diaspora* 1.1 (Spring 1991): 3–7.

COPYRIGHT ACKNOWLEDGEMENTS

For permission to reprint copyright material, I would like to thank: the Modern Humanities Research Association for Trevor R. Griffiths, '"This Island's Mine": Caliban and Colonialism', in G. K. Hunter and C. J. Rawson (eds), *The Yearbook of English Studies*, vol. 13, London: MHRA, 1983, pp. 159–80. © Modern Humanities Research Association. All rights reserved. Reproduced by permission of the editor and the Modern Humanities Research Association; The University of Chicago Press and the author for Rob Nixon, 'Caribbean and African Appropriations of *The Tempest*', *Critical Inquiry*, 13, Spring 1987, pp. 557–78. © 1987 by The University of Chicago; *Shakespeare Quarterly* for Meredith Anne Skura, 'Discourse and the Individual: The Case of Colonialism in *The Tempest*', *Shakespeare Quarterly*, 40:1, Spring 1989, pp. 42–69. Reprinted by permission of *Shakespeare Quarterly*; Africa World Press for Sylvia Wynter, 'Beyond Miranda's Meanings: Un/silencing the "Demonic Ground" of Caliban's "Woman"', in Carole Boyce Davies and Elaine Savory Fido (eds), *Out of the Kumbla*, Trenton, New Jersey: Africa World Press, 1990, pp. 355-65; the author for David Dabydeen, 'Daniel Defoe's *Robinson Crusoe* (1719)', in David Dabydeen and Nana Wilson-Tagoe, *A Reader's Guide to West Indian and Black British Literature*, London: Hansib, 1988, pp. 98–103. © David Dabydeen; the author for Peter Hulme, 'Robinson Crusoe and Friday', in *Colonial Encounters: Europe and the Native Caribbean, 1492–1797*, London: Methuen, 1986, pp. 184–9 and pp. 200–8; the author for Richard Phillips, 'The Geography of *Robinson Crusoe*', in *Mapping Men and Empire: A Geography of Adventure*, London: Routledge, 1997, pp. 29–35; the Johns Hopkins University Press for Roxann Wheeler, '"My Savage", "My Man": Racial Multiplicity in *Robinson Crusoe*', *English Literary History*, no. 62, 1995, pp. 821–61; Indiana University Press for Susan L. Meyer, 'Colonialism and the Figurative Strategy of *Jane Eyre*', *Victorian Studies*, 33:2, Winter 1990, pp. 247–68. © The Trustees of Indiana University. Reprinted with the permission of Indiana University Press; Duke University Press for Inderpal Grewal, 'Empire and the Movement for Women's Suffrage in Britain', *Home and Harem: Nation, Gender, Empire and the Cultures of Travel*, London: Leicester University Press, 1996, pp. 61–5. © 1996, Duke University Press. Reprinted with permission; The University of Chicago Press and the author for Joyce Zonana, 'The Sultan and the Slave: Feminist Orientalism and the Structure of *Jane Eyre*', *Signs*, 18:3, Spring 1993. © 1993 by The University of Chicago; Cornell University Press for Patrick Brantlinger, 'Kurtz's "Darkness" and *Heart of Darkness*', in *Rule of Darkness: British Literature and Imperialism, 1830–1914*, Ithaca: Cornell University Press, 1988, pp. 255–64. Copyright (©) 1988 by Cornell University. Used by permission of the publisher, Cornell University Press; the publisher and author for Robert Hampson, '*Heart of Darkness* and "The Speech that Cannot be Silenced"', *English*, 39:163, Spring 1990, pp. 15–32. © The English Association 1990; the author for Sally Ledger, 'In Darkest England: The Terror of Degeneration in Fin-de-Siècle Britain', *Literature and History*, Series 3, 4:2, 1995, pp. 71–86; the Institute for Race Relations for S. P. Mohanty, 'Kipling's Children and the Colour Line', *Race and Class*, 31, 1, 1989, pp. 21–40; The University of Chicago Press and the author for Sara Suleri, 'The Adolescence of Kim' in *The Rhetoric of English India*, University of Chicago Press, 1992, pp. 117–31. © 1992 by the University of Chicago; the Modern Humanities Research Association for Ian Adam, 'Oral/Literate/Transcendent: The Politics of Language Modes in *Kim*', in Andrew Gurr (ed.), *The Yearbook of English Studies*, vol. 27, London: MHRA, 1997, pp. 66–78. © Modern Humanities Research Association. All rights reserved. Reproduced by permission of the editor and the Modern Humanities Research Association; the Johns Hopkins University Press for Carol Schloss, 'Molly's Resistance to the Union: Marriage and Colonialism in Dublin, 1904', *Modern Fiction Studies*, 35:3, Autumn 1989, pp. 529–41; the Lilliput Press, 62–3 Sitric Road, Arbout Hill, Dublin, 7, Ireland for David Lloyd, *Anomalous States: Irish Writing and the Post-Colonial Moment*, Dublin: Lilliput, 1993, pp. 88–9 and pp. 100–15; the author and Cambridge University Press for Vincent Cheng, *Joyce, Race and Empire*, Cambridge: Cambridge University Press, 1995, pp. 191–8 and 211–18; the author and Jonathan Cape for Declan Kiberd, 'James Joyce and Mythic Realism', in *Inventing Ireland*, London: Jonathan Cape, 1995, pp. 338–55; Duke University Press for Teresa Hubel, 'Liberal Imperialism as a Passage to India', *Whose India? The Independence Struggle in British and Indian Fiction and History*, London: Leicester University Press, 1996, pp. 95–108. Copyright 1996, Duke University Press. Reprinted with permission; *NOVEL* for Brenda R. Silver, 'Periphrasis, Power and Rape in *A Passage to India*', *NOVEL: A FORUM ON FICTION*, 22.1, Fall 1988, pp. 86–105. Copyright *NOVEL*; Routledge for Zakia Pathak et al., 'The Prisonhouse of Orientalism', *Textual Practice*, 5:2, Summer 1991, pp. 195–218; Blackwell and the author for Homi Bhabha, 'Articulating the Archaic', in Peter Collier and Helga Geyer-Ryan (eds), *Literary Theory Today*, Ithaca: Cornell, 1990, pp. 203–18; *ARIEL, A Review of International English Literature* for Amin Malak, 'Reading the Crisis: The Polemics of Salman Rushdie's *The Satanic Verses*', *ARIEL*, 20:4, October 1989, pp. 176–86. Copyright © 1989, The Board of Governors, and the University of Calgary; the author for Timothy Brennan, 'Rebirth, Dissent and the Theory of Acquired Characteristics', in *Salman Rushdie and the Third World: Myths of the Nation*, London: Macmillan, 1989, pp. 152–66; The University of Chicago Press and the author for Michael Gorra, '"Burn the Books and Trust the Book": *The Satanic Verses*, February 1989', in *After Empire*, Chicago: Chicago University Press, 1997, pp. 149–56. © 1997 by The University of Chicago; *ARIEL, A Review of International English Literature* for Vijay Mishra, 'Postcolonial Differend: Diasporic Narratives of Salman Rushdie', *ARIEL*, 26:3, July 1995, pp. 9–45. Copyright © 1995, The Board of Governors, and the University of Calgary. We have been unable to trace the copyright holders for Wilson Harris, 'The Frontier on which *Heart of Darkness* Stands', *Research in African Literatures*, 12:1, 1981, pp. 86–93, and would be grateful to hear from them.

INDEX OF NAMES